# Talent Assessment

# THE SIOP PROFESSIONAL PRACTICE SERIES

*Series Editor*
Elaine D. Pulakos

**TITLES IN THE SERIES**

*Performance Management Transformation: Lessons Learned and Next Steps*
Edited by Elaine D. Pulakos and Mariangela Battista

*Employee Surveys and Sensing: Challenges and Opportunities*
Edited by William H. Macey and Alexis A. Fink

*Mastering Industrial-Organizational Psychology: Training Issues for Master's Level IO Psychologists*
Edited by Elizabeth L. Shoenfelt

*Mastering the Job Market: Career Issues for Master's Level Industrial-Organizational Psychologists*
Edited by Elizabeth L. Shoenfelt

*Overcoming Bad Leadership in Organizations*
Edited by Derek Lusk and Ted Hayes

*Talent Assessment: Embracing Innovation and Mitigating Risk in the Digital Age*
Edited by Tracy M. Kantrowitz, Douglas H. Reynolds, and John C. Scott

# Talent Assessment

*Embracing Innovation and Mitigating Risk in the Digital Age*

*Edited by*
TRACY M. KANTROWITZ,
DOUGLAS H. REYNOLDS, AND JOHN C. SCOTT

# OXFORD
UNIVERSITY PRESS

Oxford University Press is a department of the University of Oxford. It furthers the University's objective of excellence in research, scholarship, and education by publishing worldwide. Oxford is a registered trade mark of Oxford University Press in the UK and certain other countries.

Published in the United States of America by Oxford University Press
198 Madison Avenue, New York, NY 10016, United States of America.

© Society of Industrial Organizational Psychology 2023

All rights reserved. No part of this publication may be reproduced, stored in a retrieval system, or transmitted, in any form or by any means, without the prior permission in writing of Oxford University Press, or as expressly permitted by law, by license, or under terms agreed with the appropriate reproduction rights organization. Inquiries concerning reproduction outside the scope of the above should be sent to the Rights Department, Oxford University Press, at the address above.

You must not circulate this work in any other form
and you must impose this same condition on any acquirer.

Library of Congress Cataloging-in-Publication Data
Names: Kantrowitz, Tracy M., editor. | Reynolds, Douglas H., editor. | Scott, John C., editor.
Title: Talent assessment : embracing innovation and mitigating risk in the digital age / edited by Tracy M. Kantrowitz, Doug H. Reynolds, and John C. Scott.
Description: New York, NY : Oxford University Press, [2023] |
Includes bibliographical references and index.
Identifiers: LCCN 2023006164 (print) | LCCN 2023006165 (ebook) |
ISBN 9780197611050 (hardback) | ISBN 9780197611074 (epub) |
ISBN 9780197611081
Subjects: LCSH: Personnel management—Technological innovations. | Employee selection. | Psychological tests.
Classification: LCC HF5549.5.T33 T35 2023 (print) | LCC HF5549.5.T33 (ebook) |
DDC 658.3/125—dc23/eng/20230216
LC record available at https://lccn.loc.gov/2023006164
LC ebook record available at https://lccn.loc.gov/2023006165

DOI: 10.1093/oso/9780197611050.001.0001

Printed by Integrated Books International, United States of America

# Contents

*Contributors* ix
*Foreword* xiii

## SECTION 1: INTRODUCTION: THEMES, STRUCTURE, MAJOR TOPICS OF THIS VOLUME

1. Context and Overview 3
   *Tracy M. Kantrowitz, Douglas H. Reynolds, and John C. Scott*

## SECTION 2: ADVANCES IN THE FOUNDATIONAL SCIENCE OF ASSESSMENT AND SUPPORTING TECHNOLOGIES

2. When Worlds Collide: Using What We Know About Machine Learning to Inform Assessment Practices 13
   *Ann Marie Ryan, Anthony S. Boyce, and Christine E. Boyce*

3. Methodological Updates in Personality Assessment for High-Stakes Use 30
   *Adam W. Meade and Luke I. Priest*

4. Advances in Cognitive Ability Assessment in the Mitigation of Group Differences 47
   *Charles A. Scherbaum, Harold W. Goldstein, Kenneth P. Yusko, Elliott Larson, Annie Kato, Kajal Patel, and Yuliya Cheban*

5. Applying Natural Language Processing to Assessment 66
   *MQ Liu*

6. Personality Assessment: Past, Present, and Future 84
   *Ryne A. Sherman and Robert Hogan*

7. Reflections on Advancements in Assessment 97
   *Neal Schmitt*

## SECTION 3: INNOVATIONS AND TRENDS

8. Artificial Intelligence in Automated Scoring of Video
   Interviews   111
   *Nathan Mondragon*

9. Social Media Data in Assessments   128
   *Daly Vaughn and Marc Cubrich*

10. Transforming Leadership Assessment Using Natural
    Language Processing   149
    *Scott Tonidandel and Betsy H. Albritton*

11. Mobile-Enabled Assessment in the Modern Talent Landscape   169
    *Darrin M. Grelle and Sara L. Gutierrez*

12. Technology-Enabled Simulation in Selection: Opportunities
    and Cautions   183
    *Seymour Adler and Sarena Bhatia*

13. Fixing the Industrial-Organizational Psychology-Technology
    Interface (IOPTI): Avoiding Both IO/Tech and
    Tech/IO Conflict   202
    *Richard N. Landers*

## SECTION 4: REGULATIONS, PRINCIPLES, AND STANDARDS

14. Balancing Innovation and Professional Standards for
    Employment Tests   219
    *Nancy T. Tippins*

15. Data Privacy Implications of Assessment Technology   234
    *Katheryn A. Andresen*

16. Potential Impact of Disabilities and Neurodiversity on the
    Constructs Measured by Selection Procedures   250
    *Jone M. Papinchock, Angela L. Rosenbaum, and Eric M. Dunleavy*

17. Reflections on Legal and Standards Update: Opportunity
    Meets Reality   267
    *Kenneth M. Willner, Kathleen K. Lundquist,
    and Claire Saba Murphy*

## SECTION 5: ASSESSMENT FOR DEVELOPMENT

18. Coaching-Centric Assessments: Deep Data to Fuel Guided Growth — 281
    Evan F. Sinar

19. From Tried and True to Shiny and New: Current Best Practices in Assessment for Development and the New Technologies That Will Soon Replace Them — 297
    Matt Paese and Georgi Yankov

20. Maximizing the Effectiveness of Assessment-Rich Leadership Development Programs — 312
    Sarah Stawiski and Cynthia D. McCauley

21. Reflections on Assessment for Development — 328
    Lynn Collins and José David

## SECTION 6: CASE STUDIES

22. Connecting People and Opportunities With Artificial Intelligence — 349
    Robert E. Gibby and Adam J. Ducey

23. Applications of High-Stakes Rich-Media Simulations — 362
    Suzanne Tsacoumis

24. Psychoneurometric Assessments for High-Risk Jobs — 377
    Brennan D. Cox, Dan McHail, Kyle Pettijohn, and Tatana Olson

25. Gamified Assessments for Prehire Evaluation — 397
    Christina Norris-Watts, Kathleen E. Hall, and Nathan Mondragon

26. The Full (Assessment) Monty: Accelerating Individual and Organizational Development — 420
    Matt Dreyer, Vicki Walia, Sandra Hartog, and Lynn Collins

27. Driving Company Growth and Leader Development: Innovations from Asia — 433
    James D. Eyring

28. Assessment in a Large Multinational — 451
    Paul van Katwyk

## SECTION 7: CONCLUSIONS AND FUTURE DIRECTIONS

29. Putting the Pieces Together: Reflections on the Next Chapter of Assessment Progress 467
    *Paul R. Sackett*

30. Optimizing the Value of Assessments Through Myth Busting and Stakeholder Communications 480
    *Gina Seaton and Allan H. Church*

31. Venture Capital: Friend or Foe for Talent Assessment? 505
    *Darko Lovric*

32. Making Progress on Diversity: The Promise of Inclusive Leadership 515
    *Kathleen K. Lundquist and Robert E. Lewis*

33. Themes and Directions 526
    *Douglas H. Reynolds, Tracy M. Kantrowitz, and John C. Scott*

*Index* 543

# Contributors

**Seymour Adler**
Global Practice Leader
Leadership Assessment and Development
Kincentric
USA

**Betsy H. Albritton**
Organizational Science
The University of North Carolina
USA

**Katheryn A. Andresen**
Vice President and Shareholder
Nilan Johnson Lewis
USA

**Sarena Bhatia**
Director
Leadership Assessment and Development
Kincentric
USA

**Anthony S. Boyce**
Principal Research Scientist
Amazon
USA

**Christine E. Boyce**
Director
Global Assessment & Analytics Center
 of Excellence
ManpowerGroup
USA

**Yuliya Cheban**
Industrial-Organizational Psychology
 Research Associate
American Institutes for Research
USA

**Allan H. Church**
Managing Partner
Maestro Consulting, LLC
USA

**Lynn Collins**
Head of Talent Development Assessments
Chief Scientist
BTS
USA

**Brennan D. Cox**
Aerospace Experimental Psychologist
U.S. Navy
USA

**Marc Cubrich**
Analyst
Modern Hire
USA

**José David**
Executive Director
Learning and Development
Merck
USA

**Matt Dreyer**
Head of Talent Management
Prudential Financial
USA

**Adam J. Ducey**
People Research Scientist
Meta
USA

**Eric M. Dunleavy**
Vice President
Employment and Litigation Services Division
DCI Consulting Group, Inc.
USA

**James D. Eyring**
Chief Executive Officer
Organisation Solutions
SG

**Robert E. Gibby**
Director of People Analytics
Meta
USA

**Harold W. Goldstein**
Professor
Baruch College
USA

**Darrin M. Grelle**
Principal Research Scientist
SHL
USA

**Sara L. Gutierrez**
Chief Science Officer
SHL
USA

**Kathleen Hall**
HR Leader
Therapeutics Discovery for Janssen R&D
Johnson & Johnson
USA

**Sandra Hartog**
Partner
BTS
USA

**Robert Hogan**
President & Founder
Hogan Assessment Systems
USA

**Tracy M. Kantrowitz**
Chief Product Officer
Personnel Decisions Research Institute (PDRI)
USA

**Annie Kato**
Assistant Professor
Seattle Pacific University
USA

**Richard N. Landers**
John P. Campbell Distinguished Professor of Industrial and Organizational Psychology
University of Minnesota—Twin Cities
USA

**Elliott Larson**
Lecturer
Baruch College
USA

**Robert E. Lewis**
Chief Assessor
APT*Metrics*, Inc.
USA

**MQ Liu**
Senior Research Scientist
Amazon
USA

**Darko Lovric**
Managing Director
Studio Metis
USA

**Kathleen K. Lundquist**
President & CEO
APT*Metrics*, Inc.
USA

**Cynthia D. McCauley**
Honorary Senior Fellow
Center for Creative Leadership
USA

**Dan McHail**
Research Psychologist
Naval Medical Research Unit
USA

**Adam W. Meade**
Professor
North Carolina State University
USA

**Nathan Mondragon**
Chief I/O Psychologist
HireVue
USA

**Christina Norris-Watts**
Head of Assessment & People Practices
Johnson & Johnson
USA

**Tatana Olson**
Aerospace Experimental Psychologist
U.S. Navy
USA

**Matt Paese**
Senior Vice President
Executive Services
Development Dimensions
   International (DDI)
USA

**Jone M. Papinchock**
Director of Litigation Support Principal
   Consultant
DCI Consulting Group, Inc.
USA

**Kajal Patel**
Senior Analyst
PepsiCo
USA

**Kyle Pettijohn**
Research Psychologist
Naval Medical Research Unit
USA

**Luke I. Priest**
Doctoral Student
North Carolina State University
USA

**Douglas H. Reynolds**
Executive Vice President
Development Dimensions
   International (DDI)
USA

**Angela L. Rosenbaum**
Principal Consultant
Litigation Support
DCI Consulting Group, Inc.
USA

**Ann Marie Ryan**
Professor
Michigan State University
USA

**Claire Saba Murphy**
Associate Employment Law Department
Paul Hastings
USA

**Paul R. Sackett**
Beverly and Richard Fink Distinguished
   Professor of Psychology
University of Minnesota
USA

**Charles A. Scherbaum**
Professor
Baruch College
USA

**Neal Schmitt**
Professor Emeritus
Michigan State University
USA

**John C. Scott**
Chief Operating Officer
APT*Metrics*, Inc.
USA

**Gina Seaton**
Senior Director
Global Talent Management at PVH
PVH Corp.
USA

**Ryne A. Sherman**
Chief Science Officer
Hogan Assessment Systems
USA

**Evan F. Sinar**
Senior Research Scientist
Amazon
USA

**Sarah Stawiski**
Director
Insights and Impact
Center for Creative Leadership
USA

**Nancy T. Tippins**
Principal
The Nancy T. Tippins Group, LLC
USA

**Scott Tonidandel**
Professor of Management
The University of North Carolina
USA

**Suzanne Tsacoumis**
President & CEO
Human Resources Research
  Organization (HumRRO)
USA

**Paul van Katwyk**
Head of Executive Assessment &
  Coaching
Saudi Aramco
SA

**Daly Vaughn**
Account Director
Modern Hire
USA

**Vicki Walia**
Head of HR Business Partners
Prudential Financial
USA

**Kenneth M Willner**
Partner and Vice Chairman of Global
  Employment Law (Retired)
Paul Hastings
USA

**Georgi Yankov**
Senior Research Scientist
Development Dimensions
  International (DDI)
USA

**Kenneth P. Yusko**
Professor
University of Maryland
USA

# Foreword

For over 100 years, a key focal area for research and practice in the field of industrial and organizational psychology has been assessment. Work in this area has been prolific, yielding a large and robust body of evidence-based insights and implementation practices that have aimed to ensure that our assessments are fair, accurately measure the individual differences they are targeting, and are legally defensible. For most of this time, the basic practices for developing and evaluating assessments did not change. But starting about 20 years ago, we began seeing dramatic changes to assessment research and practice.

With significant advancements in technology, machine learning, and artificial intelligence, the development, delivery, and even look and feel of assessments have changed in striking ways. The vast majority of people who need to be assessed no longer drive to a company or testing center to take their assessments in proctored settings. They are no longer handed a paper-and-pencil testing booklet with a scannable answer sheet and instructed to fill in the circle for their answer with a #2 lead pencil.

Today, candidates are recruited online. Their resumes or social media profiles can be read automatically and screened instantaneously to determine if they meet the minimum qualifications for a job, sometimes without the person even knowing they have been targeted. Sophisticated assessment programs are launched globally and quickly to test thousands of candidates every day. These leverage online delivery platforms that enable testing almost any capability imaginable in any language.

Today's assessments are much more precise. They can quickly ascertain one's likelihood of succeeding on a job by customizing the questions that are delivered to quickly focus in on one's ability level, knowledge, or skill. Today's assessments are much more engaging. We have many more realistic measures that simulate work situations in a high-fidelity manner and present real job-relevant problems for candidates to solve. As technology continues to advance, assessments will almost certainly increase in their precision, efficiency, fairness, and cost effectiveness.

With so much change in recent years in the area of assessment and the potential for so many more changes to come, it was timely for the Professional Practice Series to devote a volume to the changing context of assessment—specifically focusing on new trends and innovations and the research evidence supporting their use. The editors of this volume, Tracy Kantrowitz, Doug Reynolds, and John Scott, are prominent assessment experts and thought leaders. All three have spent their careers providing assessment expertise and services globally and have collectively advised almost every organization imaginable on their hiring and employee development practices. They have brought their vast experience to bear in creating this volume, ensuring that the most promising avenues for future assessment innovations and pressing challenges facing assessments are covered here. They have gathered notable experts and curated the most relevant topic areas to yield an outstanding summary of the current state and future opportunities for assessment that will serve as an outstanding resource for years to come.

It takes a tremendous amount of work to create an edited volume like this one. I am grateful to Tracy, Doug, John, and all of the chapter authors for the time they have put into this volume and for all their contributions to the Society for Industrial and Organizational Psychology (SIOP) and the Professional Practice Series. I hope you—the reader—will find this volume a useful addition to your library and one you turn to often.

Elaine D. Pulakos, Series Editor
September 2022

# SECTION 1
# INTRODUCTION: THEMES, STRUCTURE, MAJOR TOPICS OF THIS VOLUME

# 1
# Context and Overview

*Tracy M. Kantrowitz, Douglas H. Reynolds, and John C. Scott*

Technology-enhanced assessments for selection and development have flourished over the past several decades. Sophisticated assessment programs that weren't possible even a few years ago can now be assembled and launched on a global scale to measure almost any attribute in any language with greater realism, efficiency, and precision than ever before. Large-scale assessment applications have emerged where candidates are recruited online; automatically screened, assessed, and prioritized; and presented with online interview questions based on the results of their assessments—all without any human contact. Many organizations have enthusiastically embraced these developments due to the obvious practical benefits and immediate payoff associated with increased efficiency and reduced costs to move candidates from recruitment through to selection.

The field of workplace assessment is at a critical stage in its evolution. The intersection of new technologies, globalization, and market shifts among assessment providers has created dramatic opportunities for the field along with some significant challenges. Artificial intelligence (AI) and other technological advances have completely altered what is possible in talent acquisition. As a new generation of technology-driven applications comes of age, a host of new issues and opportunities have emerged that require assessment professionals to respond with an informed perspective that balances return-on-investment priorities with appropriate professional and scientific rigor.

AI has also been touted by human resources (HR)-technology vendors and organizational users for effectively conquering a variety of intransigent talent acquisition issues such as "unconscious" bias and lack of diversity in the slating and hiring process. While these methods offer many promises for identifying previously unrecognized talent and reducing subjective decision-making, their use can be compromised by errors inherent in the data and the decisions that underlie the design of the algorithms themselves. Additionally, the variables being measured in AI-driven products are often

Tracy M. Kantrowitz, Douglas H. Reynolds, and John C. Scott, *Context and Overview* In: *Talent Assessment*.
Edited by: Tracy M. Kantrowitz, Douglas H. Reynolds, and John C. Scott, Oxford University Press.
© Society of Industrial Organizational Psychology 2023. DOI: 10.1093/oso/9780197611050.003.0001

considered proprietary and operate as a "black box"—the user must accept the output without understanding the specific bases on which the candidates are screened.

The well-understood rush to implement these latest technologies has empowered the commercialization of an increasing number of assessment tools that exist at the expense of sound professional practice and good science. Of course, the reason for the proliferation and successful marketing of these assessments is that organizations have a real need for efficient screening tools that will both engage potential candidates and evaluate their fit for the organization. However, the high-stakes nature of assessment and selection programs requires that decisions are based upon scientifically derived measurement criteria and professionally validated assessment tools. Organizations that use assessments must balance the attraction of "bright, shiny objects" with business needs, risk tolerance, and sound selection practices to ensure that critical talent acquisition and development decisions are made with efficiency, accuracy, and credibility.

It was with these issues in mind that we selected the topics for this volume. The origin of this book was the 2019 Society for Industrial and Organizational Psychology (SIOP) Leading Edge Consortium (LEC): *Advancing the Edge: Assessment for the 2020s*. The consortium brought together a diverse group of thought leaders to explore the evolving state of practice and related science. The goal was to frame practical solutions for managing the disruption in assessment and incorporate new insights and technologies into organizational assessment programs. The agenda allowed us to examine these disruptive forces from many sides, from consultants and technologists pushing the edges of what's possible with new tools, to practitioners putting them into practice and attorneys focusing on minimizing risk. We also heard from those closest to the research and others who have been instrumental to the latest professional standards and guidelines. The LEC audience was also treated to some unique assessment applications from professional sports, the military, and multinational organizations. This volume was intended to extend the thoughtful presentations to codify the research and practice advances presented at the LEC and bring them to a larger audience. With that in mind, many of the same presenters from the LEC were invited to contribute chapters to this volume.

In this chapter, we preview the changing context for talent assessment, the key issues that are challenging long-held assumptions and practices in assessment, the rise of a new class of empirically derived assessment techniques, and the business and societal landscape of assessment. The introduction also describes and discusses various stakeholders of assessments and the dynamics at play. We also preview the organization of the book, including the sections and topics, with the goal of providing an overview for how assessment researchers and practitioners are thinking about assessment for the second half of the 2020s.

## Organization of This Volume

Chapters are arranged by topical area and are intended to distill the trends and innovations, summarize the latest research evidence, and discuss the use cases for contemporary assessment techniques. The volume also includes several case studies from multiple organizations who have developed or are using innovative talent assessment concepts. The case study authors share their journey of exploring, implementing, and evaluating leading-edge assessment concepts.

This volume is intended to serve as the most contemporary view on talent assessment and is geared to industrial-organizational (IO) practitioners with a focus on closing the research-practice gap, sharing practices used in organizations vis-à-vis case studies, and making forward-looking projections regarding the future state of assessment. The book was designed to have a practical focus and includes a large number of short chapters, so that readers can gain an overview on topics most salient to their work. Next, we describe each section and preview the focus of the chapters in this volume.

## Section 2: Advances in the Science of Assessment

This series of chapters focuses on recent scientific advances in psychological measurement. Research findings are summarized regarding the efficacy of the new measurement approaches and issues related to their implementation within organizational contexts and assessment programs. Topics include research on the use of AI in assessment, advancements in forced-choice personality measurement, the use of response time as a measurement facet, innovations in cognitive ability assessment to mitigate long-standing group differences, and advances in natural language processing for psychological measurement.

The chapter by **Ann Marie Ryan** (Michigan State University), **Anthony S. Boyce** (Amazon), and **Christi E. Boyce** (Manpower Group) summarizes the latest multidisciplinary research on assessment. **Adam W. Meade** and **Luke I. Priest** (North Carolina State University) describe methodological updates in personality assessment for high-stakes use. Then, the chapter by **Charles A. Scherbaum** (Baruch College, City University of New York), **Harold W. Goldstein** (Baruch College, City University of New York), **Kenneth P. Yusko** (University of Maryland), **Elliott Larson** (Baruch College, City University of New York), **Annie Kato** (Seattle Pacific University), **Kajal Patel** (Baruch College, City University of New York), and **Yuliya Cheban** (Baruch College, City University of New York) discusses advances in cognitive ability assessment in the mitigation of group differences. **MQ Liu** (Amazon) provides an overview of the application of natural language processing to assessment. The chapter by **Ryne A. Sherman** and **Robert Hogan** (Hogan Assessment Systems) describes modern research and applications of personality assessment. Finally, the chapter by **Neal Schmitt** (Michigan State University) provides reflections on the science of assessment.

## Section 3: Innovations and Trends

Technological and methodological advances, including AI, gamification, machine learning, social media, mobile and virtual assessment technologies, automated interviews, and high-fidelity simulation, are contributing to a surge of new techniques for assessing talent. Chapters in this section focus on advances and trends in assessment techniques that incorporate these advancements. They summarize the use cases, benefits, challenges, state of the research, and adoption of these techniques into assessment processes. They focus on identifying key considerations when determining whether and how to apply new assessment methodologies to assessment programs and on describing the state of the research and adoption of these advanced assessment methods.

Specifically, the chapter by **Nathan Mondragon** (HireVue) describes the use of AI in interviews. **Daly Vaughn** and **Marc Cubrich** (Modern Hire) discuss the use of social media data in assessment. Then, the chapter by **Scott Tonidandel** and **Betsy H. Albritton** (University of North Carolina at Charlotte) summarizes leadership assessment using natural language processing. **Sara L. Gutierrez** and **Darrin M. Grelle** (SHL) describe assessment across devices and modalities. **Seymour Adler** and **Serena Bhatia** (Kincentric) describe technology-enabled assessment simulations. Finally, the chapter by **Richard N. Landers** (University of Minnesota) provides reflections on innovations and trends in assessment.

## Section 4: Updates on the Legal Implications and Standards for Assessment

The nature and future of selection and assessment are being influenced by the legal landscape, in updates to the SIOP *Principles for the Validation and Use of Personnel Selection Procedures* (5th ed., 2018), and by the implications for data privacy presented by technical advancements. Chapters in this section offer experiences, insights, and recommendations associated with recent key developments in the Equal Employment Opportunity Commission (EEOC) and other federal employment and workforce agencies and delve into the nature and implications of the major updates to the newest edition of the SIOP *Principles*. Data privacy issues in technology-based selection and assessment are also addressed, as are the risks and challenges associated with the rapid evolution of assessments for talent acquisition. Issues and opportunities related to diversity and the use of assessment are also addressed.

Specifically, the chapter by **Nancy T. Tippins** (Tippins Group) describes the balance between innovation and validation using updates on the SIOP *Principles*. The chapter by **Katheryn A. Andresen Nilan Johnson Lewis** (PA) discusses data privacy implications of assessment technology. **Jone M. Papinchock, Angela L. Rosenbaum,** and **Eric M. Dunleavy** (DCI Consulting) describe fairness, reasonable accommodations, neurodiversity, and updates for diversity considerations for assessment. The chapter by **Kenneth M. Willner** (Paul Hastings LLP), **Kathleen Lundquist** (APTMetrics), and **Claire Saba Murphy** (Paul Hastings LLP) summarizes risk management in a new era of assessments and reflections on legal implications of assessment technology.

## Section 5: Assessments for Development

Organizations are increasingly using assessments for development purposes. This series of chapters focuses on bridging the gap between assessment tools and how assessment data are utilized to help create results that drive growth. Chapters in this section address how assessments help individuals develop and organizations gain competitive advantage. They provide insight into how assessment data are used to drive individual and organizational growth and demonstrate how to leverage assessment data in making talent investment decisions. The focus of all chapters in this section is on the use of assessments for expediting development, measuring results of developmental interventions, and increasing the potency of developmental assessments for insight.

The chapter by **Evan F. Sinar** (Amazon) is focused on assessments as part of virtual coaching interventions. **Matt Paese** and **Georgi Yankov** (DDI) describe acceleration of leadership development through assessment. **Sarah Stawiski** and **Cynthia D. McCauley** (Center for Creative Leadership) discuss how to maximize the effectiveness of assessment-rich development programs. Finally, the chapter by **Lynn Collins** (BTS) and **José David** (Merck) provides reflections on assessment for development.

## Section 6: Case Studies

This section features case studies that highlight specific and timely applications of talent assessment innovations and trends in a wide range of industries. The introductory chapter in this section by **Robert E. Gibby** and **Adam J. Ducey** (Meta) reviews opportunities for advanced technology to enhance talent management processes across the span of an employee's engagement with an organization. **Suzanne Tsacoumis** (HumRRO) then describes applications of rich media simulations in assessment.

The case study by **Brennan D. Cox, Dan McHail, Kyle Pettijohn,** and **Tatana Olson** (all in U.S. military functions) describes psychoneurometric assessments for high-risk jobs. **Christina Norris-Watts, Kathleen Hall** (Johnson and Johnson), and **Nathan Mondragon** (HireVue) describe gamified assessments for prehire evaluation. **Matt Dreyer, Vicki Walia,** (Prudential) **Sandra Hartog,** and **Lynn Collins** (BTS) focus on assessments for accelerating development. The case study by **James D. Eyring** (Organisation Solutions) discusses assessment in Asia. Finally, **Paul van Katwyk** (Aramco) describes assessment in a large multinational company.

## Section 7: Critical Topics and Conclusions

This concluding section integrates the themes covered in this book and focuses on future directions, applications, and the business of assessment in this new era. **Paul R. Sackett** (University of Minnesota) describes predictions for the future of assessment. **Gina Seaton** (PVH) and **Allan H. Church** (Maestro Consulting) discuss how to communicate assessment to the organizations and the public. **Darko Lovric** (Studio Metis) discusses the role of venture capital in technical innovation in assessment and the business of assessment. The chapter by **Kathleen Lundquist** (APTMetrics) and **Robert Lewis** (APTMetrics) summarizes the role that assessment can play in realizing the promise of inclusive leadership. Finally, we provide a concluding chapter that summarizes the research, practice, themes, and future directions as we look toward the second half of the 2020s.

# SECTION 2
# ADVANCES IN THE FOUNDATIONAL SCIENCE OF ASSESSMENT AND SUPPORTING TECHNOLOGIES

# 2
# When Worlds Collide

Using What We Know About Machine Learning to Inform Assessment Practices

*Ann Marie Ryan, Anthony S. Boyce,[*] and Christine E. Boyce*

Over the past several years, there has been an explosion of interest in harnessing artificial intelligence (AI) and more specifically machine learning (ML)[1] techniques to improve assessment. Given the rate at which this work is occurring, both in the selection space and in areas outside industrial-organizational (I-O) psychology, we are at risk of duplicating efforts or drawing incorrect conclusions if we do not make a concerted effort to understand the research being done across disciplines. To help with this, we explore the work being done that is germane to the selection context (i.e., not learning or other environments) and provide a high-level overview of what research has shown and where there are gaps to fill, with an eye toward questions on the minds of hiring managers, human resources (HR) teams, and end users. We focus on three critical topics—measurement and prediction, bias detection and mitigation, and acceptability—and we include only those considerations that apply across different assessment methods. Readers are referred to other chapters in this volume for greater detail on specific technical tools (e.g., natural language processing [NLP]), application contexts (e.g., interviews, social media), and context considerations (e.g., the legal environment).

---

[*] This work is independent of Anthony S. Boyce's role at Amazon.
[1] AI is used here to refer broadly to computer-based decision processes and ML to the algorithms underlying those processes.

## Measurement and Prediction

Providing evidence of the psychometric quality of assessments is critical to supporting their use in hiring contexts, and this is no different for assessments that are based on AI methods (SIOP, 2018). That is, for the key issues of understanding and prediction, we would expect research to be conducted to identify the constructs measured using these approaches (construct validity) and to describe the use of these methodologies and their prediction of organizationally relevant criteria (criterion-related validity). We have organized our review of the relevant literature below around these two questions.

## Construct Validity

There is much criticism of the "black box" nature of ML implementation, and it is here where I-O psychologists can play a particularly valuable role in connecting ML applications to existing theories of work and individual differences, as well as in making contributions to theory building based on concepts emerging from ML applications. For example, I-O researchers have been examining what constructs are measured by automated resume screening, social media processing, and constructed response formats (including automatically scored interviews). Sajjadiani et al. (2019) used ML to connect work history information on applications to predict performance and turnover by finding and analyzing themes in work history that had a conceptual basis in the selection literature. Campion et al. (2016) supported the construct validity of computer-scored accomplishment records (generated from text mining) with human ratings of the same constructs. In addition, Hickman et al. (2021) evaluated how the Big Five personality traits (McCrae & Costa, 1987) can be assessed in automated video interviews (AVIs) using ML-based scoring.

While these studies provide evidence of the value I-O can add, there has yet to be sufficient work in the published literature to suggest its potential has been realized. To illustrate, there are many applications of ML using social media data that relate to measuring personality (D. Liu & Campbell, 2017; Park et al., 2015; Schwartz et al., 2013). However, these mostly showcase a different way of assessing the Big Five, rather than contributing knowledge that advances understanding of personality (Bleidorn & Hopwood, 2019). In addition, while Hickman et al. (2021) discussed how analyzing a model underlying AVI scoring might help with identifying behaviors that are more linked to one knowledge, skill, or ability (KSA) than another, in general, we have yet to see ML applications in selection contexts provide significant contributions in thinking about job-relevant psychological constructs or behavior.

In addition to examining what constructs are measured in ML applications, sources of construct-irrelevant variance that might arise from technology enhancement (e.g., irrelevant information in passive assessment; factors associated with media and platforms) should also be researched. Because ML draws upon a wide variety of features in creating algorithms, the need to consider systemic sources of irrelevant variance is a valuable research direction. Also, because these sources can introduce subgroup differences that might relate to bias and/or differential validity (e.g., cultural and demographic factors associated with facial and emotion recognition or with automatic speech recognition), investigating their existence and influence is of paramount importance to reduce adverse impact. One example of pursuing these types of questions is provided by Horn and Behrend (2017), who showed that viewing picture-in-picture windows during an interview increases cognitive load, potentially negatively impacting performance.

## Criterion-Related Validity

In terms of prediction and criterion-related evidence, while there has been an explosion of studies on ML in medical, psychological, and educational settings (e.g., predicting heart disease, Bharti et al., 2021; diagnosing autism spectrum disorder, Kumar & Das, 2022; predicting infidelity, Vowels et al., 2021), the proprietary nature of many assessment tools has led to less published information on validity in selection contexts. In cases where the research is publicly available, it is worth noting that most studies provide evidence of convergent validity with other measures of similar constructs, rather than evidence of the ability of the ML-based assessment scores to predict criteria of traditional interest to organizations (e.g., performance, turnover). For instance, Tay et al. (2020) conducted a meta-analysis of convergence of personality self-reports with social media text analyses. However, work is emerging in this space. Mondragon (2019) and Hickman et al. (2021), for example, described criterion validation studies of AVIs.

Looking across disciplinary fields, a consistent question has arisen regarding the incremental validity of ML approaches over simple regression analysis (e.g., for predicting responses to eating disorder treatment, Espel-Huynh et al., 2021). In the selection arena, Hickman et al. (2021) showed that an AVI provided relatively small increments over self-reported or interviewer-assessed personality traits in predicting grade point average (GPA) and standardized test scores. Vanegas et al. (2021) illustrated how different ML classification models can outperform logistic regression in predicting attrition based on personality and other data, but they also noted tradeoffs across models in the types of classification errors made as well as in interpretability. As one final example, Auer et al. (2021) demonstrated how trace data in a game-based assessment could be modeled to provide small increments (1% to 2% additional variance) over assessment performance in predicting a GPA criterion but had no value in predicting a conscientiousness criterion. There may be many reasons for a lack of evidence of substantial increments over traditional approaches; indeed, it may be that current assessments do an adequate job of tapping into true score variability in structured responses and there is little true score variance left over for ML approaches to add.

Another set of cross-disciplinary questions has to do with the importance of considering both how dynamic updating of algorithms impacts consistency in comparing candidates over time and how often one should be refreshing validation evidence (Tippins et al., 2021). These questions center on an idea known as "concept drift," which Babic et al. (2021) describe as the situation where the relationship between algorithm inputs and outputs is not stable over time, leading to misspecification. An example of this is when an algorithm, developed during a time when certain skills were seldom part of a formal degree program, is deployed at a time when those skills are ubiquitous and less predictive when hiring those with that degree. Goretzko and Finja Israel (2022) provide another example when they suggest that remote learning during the COVID-19 pandemic may change the relationship between grades and success in a training program or other criteria of interest.

A related but different issue is the idea of a "covariate shift." Covariate shifts occur when data used in training differs from data in use, even if the relationships are stable and there is no concept drift. For example, a training data set that has few individuals with advanced degrees may not capture their value for a position, and thus will make more errors when deployed. To address this, tools such as applicability domain analyses can be used to compare new data sets to training data in evaluating whether predictions from the trained model might be trusted (Goretzko & Finja Israel, 2022).

In response to both of these important considerations, Babic et al. (2021) discuss the decision to "lock or not" (i.e., let algorithms continuously evolve or introduce new versions at intervals and only after testing). While locking may be viewed as less risky to many in practice, Babic et al. (2021) note that unlocked versions may be more accurate and might capture environmental change, while locked versions can preserve biases. As Tippins et al. (2021) noted, validation strategies for unlocked systems may look quite different than for locked ones.

Thus, while validation evidence for ML-based assessments is required just as with other assessments, there are many questions about the nature of that evidence that are yet to be investigated. Beyond the well-established guidelines for validation (i.e., SIOP *Principles* (SIOP, 2018), American Psychological Association (APA) *Test Standards* (AERA, APA & NCME, 2014), best practice recommendations are emerging to help define how to approach validation with ML. For example, Short et al. (2010) illustrated how to gather construct validation evidence for computer-aided text analysis, and McKenny et al. (2018) offered best practices for assessing and minimizing measurement error in computer-aided text analysis. More detailed guidance is needed for validation in ML contexts, and we anticipate that professional associations will begin to provide that (see SIOP, 2023 for recent guidance).

Additional questions to be explored include those posed by Agrawal, Gans, et al. (2020). Their three basic questions for building a sustainable business in ML are also relevant to considering the viability of ML in assessment contexts. First, is sufficient training data available? In the selection assessment space this barrier to entry is high, as large-scale, quality data on people and success on the job is not that abundant and is often proprietary. There are also specific issues to consider in validation of ML approaches related to training data. For example, Hickman et al. (2021) illustrated that the psychometric properties of an automatically scored AVI were affected by development choices (e.g., choice of training data). Thus, we see a need for research and practice guidance on how to evaluate the sufficiency and appropriateness of training data in employment selection contexts. Agrawal, Gans, et al.'s (2020) second question, how fast are feedback loops, pertains to how quickly and how continuously data will be gathered on the accuracy of hiring predictions (i.e., validity evidence). Those of us in the selection space know that such feedback loops are nonexistent in too many cases, and available data will be plagued by many problems (small sample size, range restriction, criterion deficiency, etc.). However, the potential for creating systematic feedback loops is now greater than ever, and research and practical guidance as to how to ensure their existence and the quality of feedback data are also needed. Agrawal, Gans, et al. (2020) couch their third question—how good predictions are—in terms of both incremental validity and utility, or what one gets for the cost of ML. In terms of selection assessment, these questions are certainly paramount in considering the adoption of ML approaches; research to address incremental validity and utility is sorely needed.

## Bias Detection and Mitigation

A considerable amount of recent research across disciplines has focused on bias detection and mitigation related to the use of ML in assessments. While a review of all the work on this topic would be a volume on its own (see Favaretto et al., 2019, and Pessach & Shmueli, 2020, as examples), we note a few key findings and conclusions relevant to selection assessments. First, unclear and inconsistent definitions of what is meant by bias in a particular application or analysis have been noted as a challenge in the broader AI literature. In discussing bias with NLP systems, Blodgett et al. (2020) suggest that conceptualizations of bias should articulate "what kinds of system behaviors are harmful, in what ways, to whom, and why" (p. 1) to advance our ability to mitigate bias. Clarity on terminology use in assessment contexts is similarly important. Once again, the SIOP *Principles* and APA *Test Standards* provide information on adverse impact, bias, differential validity, and related concepts that apply equally well to ML uses, and new definitions need not be invented. However, more work on conceptualizing potential bias sources, forms, and mitigation strategies in the context of ML applications in assessment would ensure that research in this area does not become fragmented.

Second, the potential causes of bias discussed in the broader literature on AI (Hutchinson & Mitchell, 2018; Tolan, 2019) are relevant to its use in selection assessment: there can be bias in the training data used to develop an algorithm (e.g., historical bias, unrepresentative or incomplete data, reliance on proxy variables), bias in the way the algorithm development process was conducted (e.g., decisions regarding encoding, assumptions), and a lack of auditing to ensure absence of bias. All these factors necessitate consideration in evaluating bias in ML applications in assessment contexts. For example, automated speech recognition (ASR) is involved in many applications that assess audio and video responses, and the word error rate (WER) of these systems is influenced by gender, race, region, age, and other factors (e.g., Aksenova et al., 2021; Koenecke et al., 2020).

Third, many of the methods advocated for detecting and mitigating bias in the broader ML literature are applicable to assessment contexts. That is, assessment developers might take steps to address bias at preprocessing, in-processing, or postprocessing stages (Tolan, 2019; Turner Lee, 2018). For example, Geyik et al. (2019) described how LinkedIn ensures gender representation in ranked candidates presented to recruiters via a postprocessing step. Further, assessment developers can engage in bias impact assessments like using ML-based reverse-engineering approaches (Goretzko & Finja Israel, 2022), seeking stakeholder input, and engaging in auditing and other processes suggested in the broader ML literature to detect potential biases in assessment contexts (Turner Lee, 2018; Turner Lee et al., 2019). Landers and Behrend (2023) provide a useful framework for psychological audits of AI systems that may be well suited for employment situations.

Given that the broader literature on ML has paid considerable attention to bias, what is different about considering bias and adverse impact in ML applications in selection contexts from other uses? One difference is that this body of research was formulated outside of an understanding of the legal environment of employee selection, and therefore can focus on strategies (e.g., within-group norming, consideration of demographic attributes) that could be legally problematic in a selection decision application. Another is that mitigation is often focused on eliminating group differences without a direct consideration of job requirements (e.g., remove a feature that shows a gender difference, even if that feature might be linked to a key job requirement); that is, the legal standard that adverse impact may be permissible if there is evidence of the validity of the selection procedure is not considered. Finally, Morse et al. (2020) note there is some evidence that it is not uncommon for an algorithm to become biased over time as it learns with more data (e.g., differences between training data and applicant pool; changes in applicant pool). Hence, the nature of updating that can be an advantage with ML applications also requires careful monitoring in this regard. With decades of research on adverse impact in hiring contexts, I-O psychologists should be key players in research on understanding bias in ML applications in selection assessments.

We should also note that ML methods can have broader value in detecting potential discrimination in ways that may not be as easily examined with other methods. For example, Hangartner et al. (2021) were able to examine time spent by recruiters viewing immigrant and ethnic minority profiles on a recruitment platform relative to time spent on majority profiles. Thus, research and practice should be conducted not just with an eye toward finding and reducing bias in ML applications, but in using ML to find and reduce bias in selection contexts.

## Acceptability

One final area that has garnered a lot of research attention across disciplines in the past several years is explainability, often linked to the term XAI, or explainable AI (Turner Lee et al., 2019; Meske et al., 2020). This research has arisen because of the opacity of AI uses, due in some cases to the intrinsic nature of ML methods, in other cases to intentional lack of transparency to protect intellectual property, and in yet other cases to the lack of algorithmic literacy on the part of various stakeholder groups (Lepri et al., 2018; deLaat, 2018; see also Gonzalez et al., 2019, for the role of ML familiarity in reactions in a hiring context).

This area is one in which I-O psychologists seem to be more actively publishing, perhaps because of the field's history in examining the candidate experience or perhaps because of the ease of conducting such research with attitudinal measures. Research on reactions to use of AVI in selection settings has had mixed findings, with some studies finding AI scoring viewed no differently than human decision agents (Suen et al., 2019), and some finding that highly automated interviews are reacted to negatively (Acikgoz et al., 2020; Langer et al., 2019). Langer et al. (2021) demonstrated how the type of information provided to applicants might lead to more positive or negative reactions to AI use in interviews; they found that providing information on the process (e.g., what is scored) without justification for the usefulness of the process could potentially heighten privacy and fairness concerns. Note these mixed results are not limited to the use of AI with AVIs, although that has been the application of most focus. For example, Rigos and Nolan (2020) conducted a scenario study to demonstrate that procedures were seen as more job related when AI was used to evaluate qualifications in reviewing LinkedIn profiles as well as in reviewing AVIs than when human expert judgment was used.

In general, Lukacik et al. (2022) noted that there are multiple design choices made with AVIs (e.g., question times, re-recording of responses), each of which might impact reactions, with the use of AI to score the AVIs as only one of those. Hence, research needs to separate out the impact of specific design choices in ML applications on reactions rather than treating ML in selection assessments in a monolithic manner.

The broader literature on XAI provides guidance as to how to enhance the acceptability of ML in the selection assessment context. Based on the results of their research evaluating different styles of explanations, Ha et al. (2020) suggested that explanations provided should be designed to emphasize the stability of the system and the lack of controllability (i.e., nonmanipulatable), and that including visual and speech cues related to anthropomorphism (i.e., making the system more human-like) can increase trust in the system. Dodge et al. (2019) showed that judgments of algorithmic fairness are influenced not only by the type of explanation given (with a preference for process-oriented or "how" explanations) but also by individual differences; while they suggest using personalized and adaptive explanations because individuals differ in what they view as fair, this does not seem to be a viable approach in selection assessment contexts where consistency in information provided to applicants is likely viewed as important. In addition, Goretzko and Finja Israel (2022) discuss how interpretable ML tools (e.g., feature importance measures, global surrogate models, local interpretable model-agnostic explanations [LIMEs]) can be used to make a model more traceable and explainable. Finally, deLaat (2018) suggests we need to think about explainability as not necessarily requiring complete transparency as that can lead to things like gaming the system and loss of privacy.

Related research on "algorithm aversion" (Dietvorst et al., 2015) shows that people lose confidence in algorithms more quickly than in human forecasters after seeing them make the same mistake. Dietvorst et al. (2018) demonstrated that when people recognize an algorithm is imperfect in prediction, they would be willing to choose an algorithm over their own forecasts if they can modify it—even if the control they are given is a small amount. Similarly, Mirowska and Mesnet (2021) interviewed HR professionals regarding AI use in selection and noted that a preference for human evaluation over AI may be due to a desire for uncertainty reduction, even in cases where the objectivity of AI is acknowledged as superior to human biases. Indeed, research has long established the superior performance of mechanical-prediction techniques to clinical data combinations (see Kuncel et al., 2013, for meta-analysis specifically in selection contexts), but people tend to operate from the assumption that algorithms make decisions based on less accurate information and are therefore unfair (Newman et al., 2020). Thus, in addition to the focus on the candidate experience and enhancing acceptability of ML applications, attention must be paid to reactions of other key stakeholders (e.g., hiring managers) and ways to enhance acceptability for those individuals.

In their review of research on attitudes related to decision automation and augmentation, Langer and Landers (2021) found that the current consensus in the literature is that while people may sometimes question the ability of automated systems, they often believe they are less biased than humans. They also concluded there were mixed results regarding perceptions of fairness. Indeed, one of the key findings of their review was to point out the many potential moderators of attitudes toward AI use (e.g., characteristics of the decision-making process, characteristics of the system, characteristics of the individuals such as experience and personality, task characteristics and output characteristics). Thus, we should recognize that in selection assessment, it is naïve (irresponsible) to state that AI use is seen as fair/unfair or good/bad; the questions to be pursued should be around how the choices made in implementation impact perceptions of those affected by the system.

We should also note that perceptions of ML use in hiring may evolve as individuals gain greater exposure to AI uses in other aspects of their lives, as well as exposure to ML uses that are seen as beneficial to applicants (e.g., in job search engines, Maurer, 2017; in training interviewees, Agrawal, George, et al., 2020). That is, today's reactions might not be the same as tomorrow's, and monitoring of acceptability should be ongoing.

## Practical Implications

The list of unknowns regarding ML use in selection assessment contexts is still much longer than the list of knowns. Box 2.1 provides an example of how a typical set of questions for considering an assessment for use in practice might be expanded with an ML twist; note these are not the technical questions one might ask about the methodological choices made in algorithm development, but the practical and psychometric questions that any

## Box 2.1 Questions to Consider When Implementing ML-Based Selection Assessments

Measurement and Prediction
- What evidence exists regarding what constructs are measured (construct validity)?
- Does our ML approach provide new insights into measurement of specific KSAs?
- Are there any sources of construct-irrelevant variance that we might consider addressing?
- What evidence exists that the assessment provides prediction of organizationally relevant criteria?
- Is prediction enhanced over traditional approaches (i.e., is there incremental validity)?
- Will there be dynamic updating of the algorithm, or will it be locked? How likely is that choice to improve prediction?
- What changes to the environment can we foresee, and how will those be considered (i.e., concept and covariate drift)?
- Was the training data set sufficiently large and appropriate?
- What feedback loops exist, and what is the quality of that data? How can feedback loops be improved?
- What is the utility of ML over other approaches (i.e., gains in costs, efficiency, etc.)?

Bias Detection and Mitigation
- When reviewing evidence regarding bias and fairness, what definitions are being used?
- What training data was used, and how representative is it of the implementation population?
- What assumptions and approaches were used in algorithm development that might affect bias in use?
- What detection methods are being used to evaluate the presence of bias?
- What mitigation has been done to reduce or eliminate bias? How has the mitigation affected validity? Is the mitigation approach legally defensible?
- What are the processes for continual monitoring for bias?
- How can ML approaches help us gain knowledge of potential sources of bias?

Explainability
- What evidence is there regarding candidate reactions to the use of ML in assessment?
- How is the use of ML explained to job candidates? To hiring managers?
- How do specific assessment design choices impact reactions to ML use? What moderates perceptions of acceptability?

HR practitioner should be ready to ask when considering adopting an assessment that is an application of ML.

Agrawal, Gans, et al. (2020) noted that competitive advantages can be had in ML applications by early movers who have the data, have fast feedback loops, and can show good prediction. They also recommend ways to carve out new spaces in the market that have applicability to selection assessments, and we see these as likely directions for ML applications in assessment. One of their suggestions for competitive advantage is to secure alternative data sources. As a field, we should be asking: What other data might be used to predict who will be a success on the job? What are ways to streamline and speed up feedback loops (i.e., improve validation data collection)? A second suggestion is to tailor the product. In other words, we should address the question: For which groups might unique training data lead to better predictions? If we are to truly take advantage of ML in assessment, I-O psychologists must stand ready to partner with others to innovate.

## Conclusion

The challenges of covering evidence in what is inherently a multidisciplinary area in such a short chapter are many: There are numerous papers on ML applications that touch on issues of validity, bias, and acceptability, often with discipline-specific jargon that does not align conceptually across fields, and here we just scratch the surface. For those interested in ML use in selection contexts, awareness of this literature can prevent reinventing wheels. However, there are ample questions specific to ML in the hiring context that need to be addressed as evidence regarding validity, fairness, and acceptance in these settings is still nascent. In 2019, Cappelli argued that "data science can't fix hiring (yet)," noting that few employers collect large volumes of data of the type that is really needed for algorithms to make accurate predictions in a specific employment context, and the focus to date has been on data that is easy to gather. Our overview of the research also leaves us with a "not there yet" evaluation of the state of ML in selection assessments, but confident that our science and practice can contribute in significant ways to move ML applications in selection assessment forward.

# References

Acikgoz, Y., Davison, K. H., Compagnone, M., & Laske, M. (2020). Justice perceptions of artificial intelligence in selection. *International Journal of Selection and Assessment, 28*, 399–416.

Agrawal, A., Gans, J., & Goldfarb, A. (2020). How to win with machine learning. *Harvard Business Review, 98*, 126–133.

Agrawal, A., George, R. A., Ravi, S. S., Kamath, S., & Kumar, A. (2020). *Leveraging multimodal behavioral analytics for automated job interview performance assessment and feedback*. ArXiv. https://arxiv.org/abs/2006.07909v2

Aksenova, A., van Esch, D., Flynn, J., & Golik, P. (2021). How might we create better benchmarks for speech recognition? In *Proceedings of the 1st workshop on benchmarking: Past, present, and future*. Association for Computational Linguistics and the Asian Federation of Natural Language Processing. https://aclanthology.org/2021.bppf-1.pdf#page=32

American Educational Research Association, American Psychological Association, & National Council on Measurement in Education (Eds.). (2014). *Standards for educational and psychological testing*. American Educational Research Association.

Auer, E. M., Mersy, G., Marin, S., Blaik, J., & Landers, R. N. (2021). Using machine learning to model trace behavioral data from a game-based assessment. *International Journal of Selection and Assessment*. doi:http://dx.doi.org/10.1111/ijsa.12363

Babic, B., Cohen, I. G., Eugeniou, T., & Gerke, S. (2021). When machine learning goes off the rails. *Harvard Business Review, 99*(1), 76–84.

Bharti, R., Khamparia, A., Shabaz, M., Dhiman, G., Pande, S., & Singh, P. (2021). Prediction of heart disease using a combination of machine learning and deep learning. *Computational Intelligence and Neuroscience, 2021*, 11. http://dx.doi.org.proxy2.cl.msu.edu/10.1155/2021/8387680

Bleidorn, W., & Hopwood, C. J. (2019). Using machine learning to advance personality assessment and theory. *Personality and Social Psychology Review, 23*(2), 190–203.

Blodgett, S. L., Barocas, S., Daume, H., & Wallach, H. (2020). Language (technology) is power: A critical survey of "bias" in NLP. In *Proceedings of the 58th annual meeting of the Association for Computational Linguistics* (pp. 5454–5476).

Campion, M. C., Campion, M. A., Campion, E. D., & Reider, M. H. (2016). Initial investigation into computer scoring of candidate essays for personnel selection. *Journal of Applied Psychology, 101*(7), 958–975. http://dx.doi.org.proxy2.cl.msu.edu/10.1037/apl0000108

Cappelli, P. (2019). Data science can't fix hiring (yet). *Harvard Business Review*, May-June, 56–57.

deLaat, P. B. (2018). Algorithmic decision-making based on machine learning from big data: Can transparency restore accountability? *Philosophy and Technology, 31*, 525–541.

Dietvorst, B. J., Simmons, J. P., & Massey, C. (2015). Algorithm aversion: People erroneously avoid algorithms after seeing them err. *Journal of Experimental Psychology General, 144*, 114–126.

Dietvorst, B. J., Simmons, J. P., & Massey, C. (2018). Overcoming algorithm aversion: People will use imperfect algorithms if they can (even slightly) modify them. *Management Science, 64*, 1155–1170.

Dodge, J., Liao, Q. V., Zhang, Y., Bellamy, R. K. E., & Dugan, C. (2019). *Explaining models: An empirical study of how explanations impact fairness judgement*. ArXiv. 1901.07694v1

Espel-Huynh, H., Zhang, F., Thomas, J. G., Boswell, J. F., Thompson-Brenner, H., Juarascio, A. S., & Lowe, M. R. (2021). Prediction of eating disorder treatment response trajectories via machine learning does not improve performance versus a simpler regression approach. *International Journal of Eating Disorders, 54*(7), 1250–1259. http://dx.doi.org.proxy2.cl.msu.edu/10.1002/eat.23510

Favaretto, M., DeClercq, E., & Elger, B. S. (2019). Big data and discrimination: Perils, promises and solutions. A systematic review. *Journal of Big Data, 6*, 1–27.

Geyik, S. C., Ambler, S., & Kenthapadi, K. (2019). Fairness-aware ranking in search & recommendation systems with application to LinkedIn talent search. In *Proceedings of the 25th ACM SIGKDD International Conference on Knowledge Discovery & Data Mining (KDD '19*; pp. 2221–2231). Association for Computing Machinery. https://doi.org/10.1145/3292500.3330691

Gonzalez, M. F., Capman, J. F., Oswald, F. L., Theys, E. R., & Tomczak, D. L. (2019). "Where's the IO?" Artificial intelligence and machine learning in talent management systems. *Personnel Assessment and Decisions, 5*(3), 4–12. https://doi.org/10.25035/pad.2019.03.005

Goretzko, D., & Finja Israel, L. S. (2022). Pitfalls of machine learning-based personnel selection: Fairness, transparency, and data quality. *Journal of Personnel Psychology, 21*(1), 37–47. http://dx.doi.org/10.1027/1866-5888/a000287

Ha, T., Sah, Y. J., Park, Y., & Lee, S. (2020). Examining the effects of power status of an explainable artificial intelligence system on users' perceptions. *Behaviour & Information Technology, 41*(5), 946–958. doi:https://doi.org/10.1080/0144929X.2020.1846789

Hangartner, D., Kopp, D., & Siegenthaler, M. (2021). Monitoring hiring discrimination through online recruitment platforms. *Nature, 589*, 572–577.

Hickman, L., Bosch, N., Ng, V., Saef, R., Tay, L., & Woo, S. E. (2021). Automated video interview personality assessments: Reliability, validity, and generalizability investigations. *Journal of Applied Psychology, 107*(8), 1323–1351. doi:https://doi.org/10.1037/apl0000695

Horn, R. G., & Behrend, T. S. (2017). Video killed the interview star: Does picture-in-picture affect interview performance? *Personnel Assessment and Decisions, 3*(1), Article 5.

Hutchinson, B., & Mitchell, M. (2018). *50 years of test (un)fairness: Lessons for machine learning*. ArXiv. 1811.10104v2

Koenecke, A., Nam, A., Lake, E., Nudell, J., Quartey, M., Mengesha, Z., Roups, C., Rickford, J. R., Jurafsky, D., & Goel, S. (2020). Racial disparities in automated speech recognition. *PNAS Proceedings of the National Academy of Sciences of the United States of America, 117*(14), 7684–7689. doi:https://doi.org/10.1073/pnas.1915768117

Kumar, C. J., & Das, P. R. (2021). The diagnosis of ASD using multiple machine learning techniques. *International Journal of Developmental Disabilities, 68*(6), 973–983. doi:https://doi.org/10.1080/20473869.2021.1933730

Kuncel, N. R., Klieger, D. M., Connelly, B. S., & Ones, D. S. (2013). Mechanical versus clinical data combination in selection and admissions decisions: A meta-analysis. *Journal of Applied Psychology, 98*(6), 1060–1072. http://dx.doi.org/10.1037/a0034156

Landers, R. N., & Behrend, T. S. (2023). Auditing the AI auditors: A framework for evaluating fairness and bias in high stakes AI predictive models. *American Psychologist, 78*(1), 36–49. doi:https://doi.org/10.1037/amp0000972

Langer, M., Baum, K., Konig, C. J., Hahne, V., Oster, D., & Speith, T. (2021). Spare me the details: How the type of information about automated interviews influences applicant reactions. *International Journal of Selection and Assessment*. doi:https://doi.org/10.1111/ijsa.12325

Langer, M., Konig, C. J., & Papathanasiou, M. (2019). Highly automated job interviews: Acceptance under the influence of stakes. *International Journal of Selection and Assessment, 27*(3), 217–234. doi:https://doi.org/10.1111/ijsa.12246

Langer, M., & Landers, R. (2021). The future of artificial intelligence at work: A review of effects of decision automation and augmentation on workers targeted by algorithms and third-party observers. *Computers in Human Behavior, 123*, 106878. https://doi.org/10.1016/j.chb.2021.106878

Lepri, B., Oliver, N., Letouze, E., Pentland, A., & Vinck, P. (2018). Fair, transparent, and accountable algorithmic decision-making processes: The premise, the proposed solutions, and the open challenges. *Philosophy and Technology, 31*(4), 611–627.

Liu, D., & Campbell, W. K. (2017). The Big Five personality traits, Big Two meta traits and social media: A meta-analysis. *Journal of Research in Personality, 70*, 229–240. https://doi.org/10.1016/j.jrp.2017.08.004

Lukacik, E., Bourdage, J. S., & Roulin, N. (2022). Into the void: A conceptual model and research agenda for the design and use of asynchronous video interviews. *Human Resource Management Review, 32*(1), 15. doi:https://doi.org/10.1016/j.hrmr.2020.100789

Maurer, R. (2017). *Many job seekers are ready to work with AI, chatbots*. HRNews. http://ezproxy.msu.edu/login?url=https://www-proquest-com.proxy2.cl.msu.edu/trade-journals/many-job-seekers-are-ready-work-with-ai-chatbots/docview/2022194070/se-2?accountid=12598

McCrae, R. R., & Costa, P. T. (1987). Validation of the five-factor model of personality across instruments and observers. *Journal of Personality and Social Psychology, 52*(1), 82–90.

McKenny, A. F., Aguinis, H., Short, J. C., & Anglin, A. H. (2018). What doesn't get measured does exist: Improving the accuracy of computer-aided text analysis. *Journal of Management, 44*, 2909–2933.

Meske, C., Bunde, E., Schneider, J., & Gersch, M. (2020). Explainable artificial intelligence: Objectives, stakeholders, and future research opportunities. *Information Systems Management*.

Mirowska, A., & Mesnet, L. (2021). Preferring the devil you know: Potential applicant reactions to artificial intelligence evaluations of interviews. *Human Resources Management Journal, 32*(2), 364–383.

Mondragon, N. (2019). *Artificial intelligence (AI) as alternative methods of psychological measures* [Paper presentation]. Society for Industrial and Organizational Psychology Leading Edge Consortium, Atlanta, GA.

Morse, L., Teodorescu, M. H. M., Awwad, Y., & Kane, G. (2020). *A framework for fairer machine learning in organizations*. ArXiv. http://ezproxy.msu.edu/login?url=https://www-proquest-com.proxy2.cl.msu.edu/working-papers/framework-fairer-machine-learning-organizations/docview/2441676834/se-2?accountid=12598

Newman, D. T., Fast, N. J., & Harmon, D. J. (2020). When eliminating bias isn't fair: Algorithmic reductionism and procedural justice in human resource decisions. *Organizational Behavior and Human Decision Processes, 160*, 149–167. http://dx.doi.org/10.1016/j.obhdp.2020.03.008

Park, G., Schwartz, H. A., Eichstaedt, J. C., Kern, M. L., Kosinski, M., Stillwell, D. J., Ungar, L. H., & Seligman, M. E. P. (2015). Automatic personality assessment through social media language. *Journal of Personality and Social Psychology, 108*(6), 934–952. https://doi.org/10.1037/pspp0000020

Pessach, D., & Shmueli, E. (2020). *Algorithmic fairness.* Preprint ArXiv. 2001.09784

Rigos, J. C., & Nolan, K. P. (2020). *Fairness and respect: Applicant reactions to artificial intelligence in employee selection* [Poster presentation]. Society for Industrial and Organizational Psychology Conference, Virtual.

Sajjadiani, S., Sojourner, A. J., Kammeyer-Mueller, J. D., & Mykerezi, E. (2019). Using machine learning to translate applicant work history into predictors of performance and turnover. *Journal of Applied Psychology, 104*(10), 1207–1225. http://dx.doi.org/10.1037/apl0000405

Schwartz, H. A., Eichstaedt, J. C., Kern, M. L. Dziurzynski, L., Ramones, S. M., Agrawal, M., . . . Ungar, L. H. (2013). Personality, gender, and age in the language of social media: The open-vocabulary approach. *PLOS ONE, 8,* 1–16. https://doi.org/10.1371/journal.pone.0073791

Short, J. C., Broberg, J. C., Cogliser, C. C., & Brigham, K. H. (2010). Construct validation using computer-aided text analysis (CATA): An illustration using entrepreneurial orientation. *Organizational Research Methods, 13,* 320–347.

Society for Industrial and Organizational Psychology (SIOP). (2018). Principles for the Validation and Use of Personnel Selection Procedures. *Industrial and Organizational Psychology, 11*(1), 1–97. doi:10.1017/iop.2018.195

Society for Industrial and Organizational Psychology (SIOP). (2023). Considerations and Recommendations for the Validation and Use of AI-Based Assessments for Employee Selection. https://www.siop.org/Portals/84/SIOP%20Considerations%20and%20Recommendations%20for%20the%20Validation%20and%20Use%20of%20AI-Based%20Assessments%20for%20Employee%20Selection%20010323.pdf?ver=5w576kFXzxLZNDMoJqdIMw%3d%3d

Suen, H., Chen, M., & Lu, S. (2019). Does the use of synchrony and artificial intelligence in video interviews affect interview ratings and applicant attitudes? *Computers in Human Behavior, 98,* 93–101.

Tay, L., Woo, S. E., Hickman, L., & Saef, R. M. (2020). Psychometric and validity issues in machine learning approaches to personality assessment: A focus on social media text mining. *European Journal of Personality, 34,* 826–844.

Tippins, N. T., Oswald, F. L., & McPhail, S. M. (2021, January 28). *Scientific, legal, and ethical concerns about AI-based personnel selection tools: A call to action.* PsyArXiv. https://doi.org/10.31234/osf.io/6gczw

Tolan, S. (2019). *Fair and unbiased algorithmic decision making: Current state and future challenges.* ArXiv. 1901.04730

Turner Lee, N. (2018). Detecting racial bias in algorithms and machine learning. *Journal of Information, Communication and Ethics in Society, 16*(3), 252–260.

Turner Lee, N., Resnick, P., & Barton, G. (2019). *Algorithmic bias detection and mitigation: Best practices and polices to reduce consumer harms.* Center for Technology Innovation, Brookings Institute. https://www.brookings.edu/research/algorithmic-bias-detection-and-mitigation-best-practices-and-policies-to-reduce-consumer-harms/

Vanegas, J. M., Wine, W., & Drasgow, F. (2021). Predictions of attrition among US Marine Corps: Comparison of four predictive methods. *Military Psychology, 34*(2), 147–166. doi:https://doi.org/10.1080/08995605.2021.1978754

Vowels, L. M., Vowels, M. J., & Mark, K. P. (2021). Is infidelity predictable? Using explainable machine learning to identify the most important predictors of infidelity. *Journal of Sex Research, 59*(2), 224–237. doi:10.1080/00224499.2021.1967846

# 3
# Methodological Updates in Personality Assessment for High-Stakes Use

*Adam W. Meade and Luke I. Priest*

## Introduction

Personality has been one of the most often examined and used predictors of performance in organizations in the last two decades and for good reason: Personality traits have been shown to predict important individual and organizational outcomes such as job performance, job satisfaction, and turnover (Barrick et al., 2001; Barrick & Mount, 1991; Oswald & Hough, 2011; Tett & Christiansen, 2007). Additionally, personality assessments rarely show adverse impact across racial groups (Foldes et al., 2008) and demonstrate incremental validity over and above predictors such as cognitive ability tests (Ones et al., 1993). Because of these desirable characteristics, research and practice surrounding personality assessment has accelerated with respect to both information technology and psychometric theory. In this chapter, we will review some recent advances related to personality assessment in high-stakes contexts such as job applicant screening.

## Historical Role of Personality in High-Stakes Assessment

From the inception of industrial/organizational psychology, researchers have posited that some personal attributes are closely related to performance in the workplace. Despite the relatively intuitive notion that people who are more diligent or hardworking by nature may perform better than those who do not have these attributes, research on personality in the workplace suffered a number of limitations in the early years. Perhaps one of the most important limitations related to the lack of a coherent way to discuss personality. Early personality research has been described as a Tower of Babel in which a large

Adam W. Meade and Luke I. Priest, *Methodological Updates in Personality Assessment for High-Stakes Use* In: *Talent Assessment*. Edited by: Tracy M. Kantrowitz, Douglas H. Reynolds, and John C. Scott, Oxford University Press. © Society of Industrial Organizational Psychology 2023. DOI: 10.1093/oso/9780197611050.003.0003 number of relatively independent researchers each created their own personality framework complete with different ways of measuring these traits (see John & Srivastava, 1999, for a review). Early personality conceptualizations differed with respect to level of abstraction, theoretical perspectives, blended clinical and nonclinical personality traits, and method of measurement. The result was a research literature in which few generalizations could be made across the wide variety of personality traits and measures.

It was in this context that Dunnette (1962) called for a moratorium on the development of new personality measures until more was known about the wide variety of existing measures. Shortly thereafter, Guion and Gottier (1965) wrote a highly influential summary of the validity of personality assessments in the workplace that concluded, "In brief, it is difficult in the face of this summary to advocate, with a clear conscience, the use of personality measures in most situations as a basis for making employment decisions about people" (p. 160). The effect of this publication was quick and widespread as the use of personality assessments in the workplace was rare in the following years, that is, until the development of the Big Five model provided a common framework onto which measures could be mapped and evidence accumulated.

The Big Five model has deep roots in the lexical hypothesis, which states that important and relevant personality traits are likely to be encoded into language, often as a single word (Ashton & Lee, 2005), a concept that dates back to Sir Francis Galton (1884). Based on this hypothesis, Allport and Odbert (1936) created a list of nearly 18,000 adjectives that could be indicators of personality. Given the unwieldy size of this list, Cattell (1943) reduced the list to a mere 35 variables to provide for a representative but manageable list suitable for technological limitations of the day (e.g., conducting factor analyses by hand). The period between the late 1930s and the early 1960s saw many competing measures and models of personality with a wide range of approaches to the problem of creating a taxonomy of personality. Then in the 1960s, computers began to make factor analyses of larger data sets possible, and Tupes and Christal (1961/1992) utilized this technology to analyze personality data from eight samples using Cattell's (1943) 35 variables and found "five relatively strong and recurrent factors" (p. 14). These factors eventually came to be known as the Big Five (Goldberg, 1981), reflecting the broad nature of each factor.

The development of the Big Five was a hallmark of personality research as it provided a common framework for psychologists to discuss the otherwise large and unwieldy set of personality variables in use. Not only was the Big Five instrumental in providing a common understanding of personality but also, for the first time, meta-analysts could map a wide range of personality traits onto the Big Five and begin to draw conclusions regarding the efficacy of personality to predict outcomes in the workplace. In the years since the early 1990s, there have been several meta-analyses covering hundreds of studies that have established the utility of personality for predicting job performance, training performance, teamwork, job satisfaction, and employee turnover (Barrick et al., 2001; Barrick & Mount, 1991; Judge & Ilies, 2002; Oswald & Hough, 2011; Tett & Christiansen, 2007).

It is important to note that personality is of wide interest outside of workplace settings and is a topic prone to fads, internet "quizzes," and guruism from those ignorant of basic psychometric principles. As such, valid and reliable personality assessment in the workplace is prone to guilt by association by sharing similar response styles and item content from unvalidated assessments claiming to measure personality. In many ways, the development of easily administered internet-based assessments has exacerbated the problem as now anyone can put together a very attractive-looking internet-based assessment and market the assessment to organizations that are unaware of the lack of empirical evidence supporting the use of the assessment for the purpose of job applicant screening. Proper use of personality assessments starts with a firm rooting in a detailed job analysis to establish relevance of the assessment for the job in question. Similarly, modern valid personality assessments describe dimensions of nonclinical personality and carefully avoid assessment of personality disorders so as not to run afoul of laws and regulations concerning medical privacy. In this review, we focus on innovations in scientifically valid personality assessments that have been peer reviewed and appear in the scientific literature.

## Limitations of Likert-Type Personality Assessments in High-Stakes Situations

There is ample evidence that personality assessments are predictive of a host of important criteria when properly justified on the basis of job relevance for the given application (i.e., a detailed job analysis that indicates the importance of traits necessary for success on the job). Despite this, there are two concerns surrounding their use that have spurred innovation in the last decade: intentional response distortion (i.e., faking) and time required of job applicants.

**Faking.** The literature surrounding response distortion is both large and complex with no clear consensus regarding implications for the workplace in high-stakes settings. With respect to Likert scale–based measures of personality, there is clear evidence that such scales can be faked. These studies typically happen under laboratory conditions, often with convenience samples (e.g., students, crowdsourced samples), and under instructions to both respond honestly and "fake-good." The results of such studies indicate that when instructed, respondents can increase their scores on personality measures by as much as an entire standard deviation (Viswesvaran & Ones, 1999). Subsequent research has shown that faking to this extent changes the rank order of respondents in a way that would change the outcomes of hiring decisions (Ellingson et al., 1999).

Outside of the laboratory environment, research and opinions are more mixed. For instance, studies comparing applicants and incumbents (who are believed to have less motivation to fake) show significant but smaller differences ($d = .13$ to $.52$; Birkeland et al., 2006) in between-subjects designs and up to $d = .64$ (Griffith et al., 2007) with within-subjects designs. In a summary of a wide variety of papers, Griffith and Robie (2013) estimate that around 30% of all applicants engage in some type of faking. While it appears that faking can and does occur in high-stakes organizational settings, some researchers have downplayed the effect of faking on validity (Hogan et al., 2007; Ones et al., 1996), while others have argued that faking is both rampant (Birkeland et al., 2006; Oswald & Hough, 2011; Tett & Christiansen, 2007; Vecchione et al., 2014) and a threat to the validity of a selection system (Komar et al., 2008; Mueller Hanson et al., 2003; Rosse et al., 1998).

**Time for Assessment Completion.** A second limitation regarding the use of traditional Likert-type assessments of personality is their length. Big Five–based assessments often take up to 30 to 40 minutes to complete and contain as many as 300 items (Costa & McCrae, 2008). While longer assessments are generally more reliable, they pose pragmatic challenges in operational settings as longer surveys reduce respondent motivation (Ackerman & Kanfer, 2009; Ryan & Ployhart, 2000), impact perceptions of the hiring organization (Ryan & Delany, 2010), and can lead to more applicant attrition during the application process, which reduces the number of qualified applicants. In a large-scale review, Hardy et al. (2017) found that most applicants quit the process within the first 20 minutes.

## Recent Innovations

The past 10 years have seen many notable innovations in personality assessment. While a discussion of all innovations is beyond the scope of this chapter, we will discuss three major categories of innovation that have occurred in the last decade: big data and social media, forced-choice measures, and assorted novel technologies and models.

**Big Data and Social Media.** Social media has put a wealth of data at the disposal of personality researchers. Along with this increase in the amount of available data, machine learning has allowed for the automatic processing of large-scale data garnered via social media using both open- and closed-vocabulary algorithms (Tay et al., 2020). With an open-vocabulary approach, the algorithm used is not given any a priori words to consider and simply makes any connections that it finds. This approach is bottom-up and data driven. In contrast, with the closed-vocabulary approach, the analytical algorithms are given specific word banks to use in their analysis.

**Novel Assessment Technologies and Models.** New technologies have also given rise to new assessment approaches via wearable mobile sensors, including watches and smartphones, which have the ability to record biometric data. It has been proposed (Wiernik et al., 2020) that this data could be analyzed through machine learning in order to predict personality-based outcomes. Another trend in assessment is that of gamification (Ihsan & Furnham, 2018), which models assessments as games. While gamification has largely been used to assess aptitude and productivity, it has also been applied to personality with modest success (McCord et al., 2019). Lastly, ideal-point measurement models have been the focus of increased study in the past decade. These models question the assumption of dominance models that the probability of an individual's positive response to an item increases as their level of a corresponding trait increases. Instead, the assumption of ideal-point models is that individuals will give the responses that are closest to their trait level (Tay et al., 2009).

**Forced Choice.** While forced-choice measures have been around since the 1950s (Travers, 1951), this method of assessment has seen a recent renaissance due to concerns with the faking of Likert-type scales and innovations in psychometric models. Forced-choice measures differ from traditional, Likert-type questions in that they force an individual to choose between several positive alternatives. Thus, individuals cannot equally rate all socially desirable statements and must choose which statements are most applicable to them. There is evidence that forced-choice assessments are faking resistant (Cao & Drasgow, 2019; Trent et al., 2020), and meta-analysis suggests that they tend to have higher criterion-related validity than Likert-type scales (Salgado et al., 2015). However, a large limitation of traditional forced-choice measures is that they result in ipsative data, which is essentially normed within person rather than across persons. As such, the sum of the trait scores is equal for all respondents (Hicks, 1970; Meade, 2004). Limitations around ipsativity are removed, however, when advanced item response theory models are used to compute scores (see Brown & Maydeu-Olivares, 2012).

## Innovations Presented at Leading Edge Consortium 2019: Advances in Adaptive Personality Assessment

While the Tailored Adaptive Personality Assessment System (TAPAS) has been in existence since the mid-2000s and operational since 2009 (see Stark et al., 2014), recently there were a large number of studies published in a special issue of *Military Psychology*, some of which were presented by Drasgow (2019). This series of studies further investigated TAPAS for multiple aspects of performance in military settings. TAPAS combines multiple innovations into a single assessment including computer adaptivity, forced-choice format, and innovative item response theory (IRT)–based models. The special issue related to TAPAS in *Military Psychology* included a large number of findings, including the prediction of soldier in-unit performance over and above cognitive ability measures (Kirkendall et al., 2020; Nye, White, Horgen, et al., 2020), predictive of attrition (Hughes et al., 2020), and useful for placement (Nye, White, Drasgow, et al., 2020).

The benefits of forced-choice response formats were discussed previously and include, on average, somewhat higher validity and less faking than traditional Likert-type responses (Cao & Drasgow, 2019). While several personality assessments use such a format, TAPAS uses a multi-unidimensional pairwise preference model to present equally socially desirable statements in the same choice block. For instance, respondents are asked to choose between "I get along well with coworkers" and "I am known as a 'quick thinker,'" which are both appealing choices (Stark et al., 2014). Accordingly, the TAPAS has been shown to be resistant to faking (Trent et al., 2020).

Additionally, the TAPAS is an adaptive test. Computer adaptive tests have been prevalent with mental ability testing for quite some time, in which answering items correctly will result in more difficult items being administered. However, their application to the personality domain is relatively novel. Given the limitation of the length of static personality assessments, adaptive tests are very welcome to reduce testing length.

## Innovations Presented at Leading Edge Consortium 2019: Rapid Response Measurement

A novel attempt to address problems of lengthy assessments, respondent faking, and survey fatigue is Rapid Response Measurement (RRM; Meade et al., 2020). RRM is a general method of measurement in which stimuli (e.g., adjectives) are presented one at a time via either computer or mobile device and a dichotomous response is gathered (e.g., either "like me" or "not like me").

**Interface.** The mobile interface is extremely simple: A stimulus appears in the center of the screen just above two large buttons that record the dichotomous response. On a computer, there is an additional training session in which responses are associated with keys on the keyboard prior to presentation of the stimuli. While the interface for RRM is extremely simple, the method captures a large amount of information very quickly. In addition to the stimulus presented and the respondents' responses, the system also captures the response latency for each stimulus. While timed assessments are not new, RRM has the novel property of recording the response time for each stimulus, which then affords the use of response time in the scoring of the assessment. Another feature of RRM is that respondents are instructed to respond as quickly as possible and receive a warning message if their responses are too slow (e.g., > 2.5 seconds). The net effect of these characteristics is that respondents feel a sense of urgency and single-adjective stimuli take around 1 second each, on average, with responses rarely exceeding 2 seconds. A strength of RRM, then, is a very fast assessment in which 60 stimuli can be presented in around a minute, with a full 20-facet Big Five personality assessment with hundreds of stimuli taking around 5 to 7 minutes to complete.

**Scoring.** The scoring of the RRM is novel in that it incorporates the response latency associated with each stimulus. While commercial versions of the RRM include correction factors for individual overall response time, Meade et al. (2020) present results using a simple formula that is 2,500 ms minus the response latency (with a minimum weight of zero) as the scoring weight associated with each stimulus. Thus, if respondents take 2,500 ms or longer, the stimulus essentially carries no weight in the scoring of the trait, and faster responses carry more weight than longer responses. Response latency weighting is based on research suggesting that stimuli more closely related to a respondent's self-schema are associated with faster response latencies (Holden et al., 1991, 2001; Holden & Fekken, 1993; Holden & Hibbs, 1995; Holden & Kroner, 1992; Kuiper, 1981; Markus, 1977; Popham & Holden, 1990). As stated previously, RRM uses a dichotomous response, which, with traditional assessments, has a limitation of only allowing for two possible responses. In contrast, Likert-type response scales generally garner more information per item because they allow for multiple response options. By using response latency in the scoring, RRM essentially gains more information than traditional dichotomous items as participants are effectively indicating their strength of response using response latency. In other words, by using latency in the scoring, much more information is garnered per stimulus than would be the case if only the dichotomous response was used.

**Versions.** The first RRM was a Big Five version (B5-RRM) in which adjectives were pulled from a large-scale validation study of personality adjectives (Ashton et al., 2004). Validation evidence for the method was first introduced at the annual meeting for the Society for Industrial and Organizational Psychology (SIOP) in 2014 (Meade & Pappalardo, 2014), with additional results presented by Meade et al. in 2017 and published by Meade et al. in 2020. In addition to the B5-RRM presented in Meade et al. (2020), there is also a more comprehensive Big Five–based commercial version for leadership development (PerSight Assessments, 2019) and a workplace version (W-RRM) intended for employee selection (see Meade et al., 2020). More recently, Valone et al. (2020) presented validation results for a measure of "dark personality," and Wilgus and Meade (2020) presented the results of an RRM intended to assess job satisfaction.

**Reliability.** As the RRM uses response latency in the scoring, it is difficult to compute traditional coefficient alpha internal consistency estimates of reliability. Instead, a split-half reliability estimate with a Spearman-Brown correction is more appropriate as the scores of each half mirror the actual scoring of the RRM. Like any assessment, longer RRMs are more reliable. While each version of the RRM has demonstrated adequate reliability given the length tested by the authors, Meade et al. (2020) explored the question of how many stimuli were needed to achieve adequate reliability. They computed split-half reliability given only the first three adjectives per trait of the B5-RRM, then increased the number of adjectives in a computational loop, plotting RRM length by the estimated reliability. Meade et al. (2020) found that for the B5-RRM, a reliability of .70 was achieved with between six and 15 stimuli. Reliability of .80 was achieved with between six and 21 stimuli. Given response latencies of around 1 second per stimulus, reliable measurement can be achieved for the Big Five factors in around 15 to 20 seconds per factor on average.

**Validity.** The most comprehensive validity evidence for the RRM was presented in Meade et al. (2020), in which the B5-RRM was compared to different versions of the International Personality Item Pool (IPIP; Goldberg, 1999) across three samples. Uncorrected convergent validity correlations were generally in the moderate range (e.g., $r = .34$ for openness to $r = .75$ for extraversion). Similar convergent validity coefficients were reported for the W-RRM and the Workplace Big Five (Howard & Howard, 2009). Convergent validity for the job satisfaction RRM was very high ($r = .75$) with existing measures of job satisfaction (e.g., the Job Satisfaction Survey; Spector, 1994; see Wilgus & Meade, 2020). Valone et al. (2020) reported strong convergent validity as well as good criterion-related validity for the "dark personality" RRM.

Meade et al. (2020) reported comparisons of criterion-related validity coefficients between the W-RRM, the Workplace Big Five, and several multisource feedback criteria among managers undergoing leadership development. They found that the W-RRM tended to correlate as well with other-reported (supervisor, peer, direct report) criteria related to specific aspects of performance as self-reported performance. Zero-order correlations between single W-RRM scales and supervisor-rated performance criteria were as high as .39 for specific criteria (e.g., problems with interpersonal relationships) and .17 for general criteria (e.g., overall organizational effectiveness).

**Faking.** Meade et al. (2020) reported much lower correlations with measures of social desirability and impression management for the B5-RRM compared to the IPIP. Additionally, they asked respondents to complete both assessments under both "honest" and "fake good" instruction sets. The findings suggested that while the B5-RRM could be faked, the magnitude of faking ($d = .02$ for openness to $d = .54$, neuroticism) was much lower than on the IPIP ($d = .51$ for agreeableness to $d = 1.30$ for conscientiousness). Fisher et al. (2021) conducted a similar faking study using the B5-RRM and the IPIP. Fisher found nearly identical levels of faking on the RRM compared to Meade et al. (2020) but found much lower levels of faking on the IPIP ($d = .12$

for agreeableness to $d = .32$ for neuroticism). Meta-analytic estimates for Likert-type scale faking for within-subjects designs are approximately $d = .47$ to $d = .93$ (Viswesvaran & Ones, 1999).

## Other Recent Innovations in Personality Assessment

The past 2 years have seen notable innovations that can be broken down into two general categories: novel models and novel methods. One new model put forth was the item-response-tree model (Bryant-Lees et al., 2020). This model differs from a Likert-style assessment in that individuals do not simply indicate their degree of agreement or disagreement with a statement; they also indicate the degree to which that statement is applicable to them. Through this, not only the level of trait an individual possesses but also the degree to which that trait is relevant to their general behavior can be determined.

Another model considered for personality was the bifactor model, which is an older model but only recently applied to personality. In this model, traits are examined at a general factor level, as well as a group factor level. Giordano et al. (2020) modeled conscientiousness as a general factor and modeled group factors of prudent work orientation and conformity. They found that prudent work orientation was a better predictor of grade point average (GPA) than general conscientiousness.

Another interesting model from the past 2 years is the trait, reputation, identity model (Fang & Connelly, 2020). In this model, multiple sources of data are used to triangulate personality. The reputation level utilizes only informant reports, the identity level utilizes only self-reports, and the trait level utilizes overlap between reputation and identity. Initial evidence suggests that self-report information tended to be more predictive of job performance, while informant reports were more predictive of academic performance.

Related to the development of the trait, reputation, identity model is a general increase in the usage of interview reports for personality assessment. In their presentation, Pike et al. (2020) described a study where the honesty-humility of recorded interviewees was rated by participants. They found that participants were more accurate in their ratings when the questions that the interviewers asked were general, rather than specific to honesty-humility. The implication of this finding is that, in interviews, asking questions designed to probe for specific traits may serve as a cue for the desirability of those traits, leading interviewees to modify their behavior and responses.

Stachowski and Kulas (2020) assessed the impact of social desirability on participant responses by considering social desirability as a predictive factor for answers on self-report measures. This study found that a question's level of social desirability was significantly more predictive than its relationship to personality traits. In other words, if one question is high in social desirability and indicates high conscientiousness, and a second question is low in social desirability and indicates high conscientiousness, the social desirability factor of the question will be a better predictor of the participant's response than the conscientiousness level of the respondent.

## Limitations of Recent Advancements and Other Concerns

While recent work has introduced promising models and refined previous methods, they have also shown that participant deception and social desirability remain significant issues. And, while current developments are exciting, it would be somewhat disingenuous to argue that any of the methods presented represents a "silver bullet" that will completely address these issues. Instead, what we have is a growing toolbox, where each measure has unique benefits that must be weighed against their shortcomings. To that end, it is important to consider the potential weaknesses of each method.

Big data, while a valuable source of information, requires human judgments to serve as the final arbitrators of truth in the machine learning process (Tay et al., 2020). Because of this, machine learning algorithms are subject to the same fallacies and biases that restrain traditional human reasoning. Another important factor to consider is the context of social media. Rather than a straightforward expression of one's thoughts, social media involves unique desirability cues and social rules. Therefore, the findings of machine learning algorithms must be considered in light of this unique context.

A notable issue with both social media and wearable technology is that participants are likely to feel that their privacy is being encroached upon. Furthermore, as these assessments are refined, it may become tempting for organizations to use data from workers to assess them without their knowledge through data collected by company phones. Therefore, these measures must balance the collection of relevant data with respect for individual privacy. Further, any theoretical link between physiological measures and the behaviors that may lead to work performance are circuitous at best. With respect to gamification measures, current research suggests low to moderate validity (McCord et al., 2019). Thus, it is unlikely that these methods will, or should, replace traditional personality measures in research.

Concerning forced-choice measures, research has found somewhat mixed results. On one hand, forced-choice measures tend to show increases in validity compared to Likert-type scales (Salgado et al., 2015; Cao & Drasgow, 2019). However, there are also instances in which traditional scoring outperforms more theoretically appropriate item response theory–based methods (Fisher et al., 2019). Also, participants tend to have less positive feelings toward forced-choice measures than Likert-type scales (Converse et al., 2008; Dalal et al., 2021). The tradeoff of increased validity at the cost of a negative emotional response is a notable limitation, especially when recommending these measures to practitioners.

## Conclusion

In sum, the recent past has seen a large number of innovations surrounding assessments, especially with respect to personality assessment in the workplace. Recent technological advances associated with computer and mobile administration allows for novel selection and presentation of assessments as well as a host of additional options related to the capturing of responses. Ultimately time will tell how well these innovative personality assessments perform compared to more traditional measures.

## References

Ackerman, P. L., & Kanfer, R. (2009). Test length and cognitive fatigue: An empirical examination of effects on performance and test-taker reactions. *Journal of Experimental Psychology: Applied*, *15*(2), 163–181. https://doi.org/10.1037/a0015719

Allport, G. W., & Odbert, H. S. (1936). Trait-names: A psycho-lexical study. *Psychological Monographs*, *47*(1), i–171. https://doi.org/10.1037/h0093360

Ashton, M. C., & Lee, K. (2005). A defence of the lexical approach to the study of personality structure. *European Journal of Personality*, *19*(1), 5–24. https://doi.org/10.1002/per.541

Ashton, M. C., Lee, K., & Goldberg, L. R. (2004). A hierarchical analysis of 1,710 English personality-descriptive adjectives. *Journal of Personality and Social Psychology*, *87*(5), 707–721. APA PsycInfo. https://doi.org/10.1037/0022-3514.87.5.707

Barrick, M. R., & Mount, M. K. (1991). The Big Five personality dimensions and job performance: A meta-analysis. *Personnel Psychology*, *44*(1), 1–26.

Barrick, M. R., Mount, M. K., & Judge, T. A. (2001). Personality and performance at the beginning of the new millennium: What do we know and where do we go next? *International Journal of Selection and Assessment*, *9*(1–2), 9–30.

Birkeland, S. A., Manson, T. M., Kisamore, J. L., Brannick, M. T., & Smith, M. A. (2006). A meta-analytic investigation of job applicant faking on personality measures. *International Journal of Selection and Assessment*, *14*(4), 317–335. https://doi.org/10.1111/j.1468-2389.2006.00354.x

Brown, A., & Maydeu-Olivares, A. (2012). How IRT can solve problems of ipsative data in forced-choice questionnaires. *Psychological Methods*, *18*, 1135–1147. https://doi.org/10.1037/a0030641

Bryant-Lees, K. B., LaHuis, D. M., & Blackmore, C. E. (2020). *Clarifying personality measurement in I-O: The utility of item response tree models* ["Conference presentation"]. Society for Industrial and Organizational Psychology Conference, Virtual.

Cao, M., & Drasgow, F. (2019). Does forcing reduce faking? A meta-analytic review of forced-choice personality measures in high-stakes situations. *Journal of Applied Psychology*, *104*(11), 1347–1368. APA PsycInfo. https://doi.org/10.1037/apl0000414

Cattell, R. B. (1943). The description of personality: Basic traits resolved into clusters. *Journal of Abnormal and Social Psychology*, *38*(4), 476–506. https://doi.org/10.1037/h0054116

Converse, P. D., Oswald, F. L., Imus, A., Hedricks, C., Roy, R., & Butera, H. (2008). Comparing personality test formats and warnings: Effects on criterion-related validity and test-taker reactions. *International Journal of Selection and Assessment*, *16*(2), 155–169. https://doi.org/10.1111/j.1468-2389.2008.00420.x

Costa, P. T., Jr., & McCrae, R. R. (2008). The Revised NEO Personality Inventory (NEO-PI-R). In D. H. Saklofske (Ed.), *The SAGE handbook of personality theory and assessment, Vol 2: Personality measurement and testing* (pp. 179–198). Sage Publications. http://search.ebscohost.com/login.aspx?direct=true&db=psyh&AN=2008-14475-009&site=ehost-live&scope=site

Dalal, D. K., Zhu, X., Rangel, B., Boyce, A. S., & Lobene, E. (2021). Improving applicant reactions to forced-choice personality measurement: Interventions to reduce threats to test takers' self-concepts. *Journal of Business and Psychology*, *36*(1), 55–70. https://doi.org/10.1007/s10869-019-09655-6

Drasgow, F. (2019). *Fake resistant and efficient personality assessment*. Society for Industrial/Organizational Psychology Leading Edge Consortium, Atlanta, GA.

Dunnette, M. D. (1962). Personnel management. *Annual Review of Psychology*, *13*(1), 285–314. https://doi.org/10.1146/annurev.ps.13.020162.001441

Ellingson, J. E., Sackett, P. R., & Hough, L. M. (1999). Social desirability corrections in personality measurement: Issues of applicant comparison and construct validity. *Journal of Applied Psychology*, *84*(2), 155–166. https://doi.org/10.1037/0021-9010.84.2.155

Fang, R., & Connelly, B. S. (2020). *Multirater personality assessments: Sources of predictive power and group differences*. Society for Industrial and Organizational Psychology Conference, Virtual.

Fisher, P., Robie, C., Christiansen, N., Speer, A., & Schneider, L. (2019). Criterion-related validity of forced-choice personality measures: A cautionary note regarding Thurstonian IRT versus classical test theory scoring. *Personnel Assessment and Decisions*, *5*(1). https://doi.org/10.25035/pad.2019.01.003

Fisher, P. A., Robie, C., & Rock, L. (2021). *Does General Mental Ability Saturate Faking Behavior on the RRM?* Society for Industrial and Organizational Psychology Annual Conference, Virtual.

Foldes, H. J., Duehr, E. E., & Ones, D. S. (2008). Group differences in personality: Meta-analyses comparing five U.S. racial groups. *Personnel Psychology, 61*(3), 579–616. https://doi.org/10.1111/j.1744-6570.2008.00123.x

Galton, F. (1884). Measurement of character. *Fortnightly Review, May 1865–June 1934, 36*(212), 179–185.

Giordano, C., Ones, D. S., Waller, N. G., & Stanek, K. C. (2020). Exploratory bifactor measurement models in vocational behavior research. *Journal of Vocational Behavior, 120*, 103430. https://doi.org/10.1016/j.jvb.2020.103430

Goldberg, L. R. (1981). Language and individual differences: The search for universals in personality lexicons. In L. Wheeler (Ed.), *Review of Personality and Social Psychology* (pp. 141–165). Beverly Hills, CA: Sage Publication.

Goldberg, L. R. (1999). A broad-bandwidth, public domain, personality inventory measuring the lower-level facets of several five-factor models. In I. Mervielde, I. Deary, F. D. Fruyt, & F. Ostendorf (Eds.), *Personality psychology in Europe* (Vol. 7, pp. 7–28). Tilburg University Press.

Griffith, R. L., Chmielowski, T., & Yoshita, Y. (2007). Do applicants fake? An examination of the frequency of applicant faking behavior. *Personnel Review, 36*(3), 341–355. https://doi.org/10.1108/00483480710731310

Griffith, R. L., & Robie, C. (2013). Personality testing and the "F-word": Revisiting seven questions about faking. In N. D. Christiansen & R. P. Tett (Eds.), *Handbook of personality at work* (pp. 253–280). Taylor & Francis.

Guion, R. M., & Gottier, R. F. (1965). Validity of personality measures in personnel selection. *Personnel Psychology*, 135–164.

Hardy, J. H., III, Gibson, C., Sloan, M., & Carr, A. (2017). Are applicants more likely to quit longer assessments? Examining the effect of assessment length on applicant attrition behavior. *Journal of Applied Psychology, 102*(7), 1148–1158. https://doi.org/10.1037/apl0000213

Hicks, L. E. (1970). Some properties of ipsative, normative, and forced-choice normative measures. *Psychological Bulletin, 74*(3), 167–184. https://doi.org/10.1037/h0029780

Hogan, J., Barrett, P., & Hogan, R. (2007). Personality measurement, faking, and employment selection. *Journal of Applied Psychology, 92*(5), 1270–1285. https://doi.org/10.1037/0021-9010.92.5.1270

Holden, R. R., & Fekken, G. C. (1993). Can personality test item response latencies have construct validity? Issues of reliability and convergent and discriminant validity. *Personality and Individual Differences, 15*(3), 243–248. APA PsycInfo. https://doi.org/10.1016/0191-8869(93)90213-M

Holden, R. R., Fekken, G. C., & Cotton, D. H. (1991). Assessing psychopathology using structured test-item response latencies. *Psychological Assessment: A Journal of Consulting and Clinical Psychology, 3*(1), 111–118. APA PsycInfo. https://doi.org/10.1037/1040-3590.3.1.111

Holden, R. R., & Hibbs, N. (1995). Incremental validity of response latencies for detecting fakers on a personality test. *Journal of Research in Personality, 29*(3), 362–372. APA PsycInfo. https://doi.org/10.1006/jrpe.1995.1021

Holden, R. R., & Kroner, D. G. (1992). Relative efficacy of differential response latencies for detecting faking on a self-report measure of psychopathology. *Psychological Assessment, 4*(2), 170–173. APA PsycInfo. https://doi.org/10.1037/1040-3590.4.2.170

Holden, R. R., Wood, L. L., & Tomashewski, L. (2001). Do response time limitations counteract the effect of faking on personality inventory validity? *Journal of Personality and Social Psychology, 81*(1), 160–169. https://doi.org/10.1037/0022-3514.81.1.160

Howard, P. J., & Howard, J. M. (2009). *Professional manual for the workplace Big Five profile.* Center for Applied Cognitive Studies.

Hughes, M. G., O'Brien, E. L., Reeder, M. C., & Purl, J. (2020). Attrition and reenlistment in the Army: Using the Tailored Adaptive Personality Assessment System (TAPAS) to improve retention. *Military Psychology, 32*(1), 36–50. APA PsycInfo. https://doi.org/10.1080/08995605.2019.1652487

Ihsan, Z., & Furnham, A. (2018). The new technologies in personality assessment: A review. *Consulting Psychology Journal: Practice and Research, 70*(2), 147–166. https://doi.org/10.1037/cpb0000106

John, O. P., & Srivastava, S. (1999). The Big Five Trait taxonomy: History, measurement, and theoretical perspectives. In L. A. Pervin & O. P. John (Eds.), *Handbook of personality: Theory and research, 2nd ed* (pp. 102–138). Guilford Press.

Judge, T. A., & Ilies, R. (2002). Relationship of personality to performance motivation: A meta-analytic review. *Journal of Applied Psychology, 87*(4), 797–807.

Kirkendall, C., Bynum, B., Nesbitt, C., & Hughes, M. (2020). Validation of the TAPAS for predicting in-unit soldier outcomes. *Military Psychology, 32*(1), 24–35. APA PsycInfo. https://doi.org/10.1080/08995605.2019.1652484

Komar, S., Brown, D. J., Komar, J. A., & Robie, C. (2008). Faking and the validity of conscientiousness: A Monte Carlo investigation. *Journal of Applied Psychology, 93*(1), 140–154. https://doi.org/10.1037/0021-9010.93.1.140

Kuiper, N. A. (1981). Convergent evidence for the self as a prototype: The "inverted-U RT effect" for self and other judgments. *Personality and Social Psychology Bulletin, 7*(3), 438–443. APA PsycInfo. https://doi.org/10.1177/014616728173012

Markus, H. (1977). Self-schemata and processing information about the self. *Journal of Personality and Social Psychology, 35*(2), 63–78. APA PsycInfo. https://doi.org/10.1037/0022-3514.35.2.63

McCord, J.-L., Harman, J., & Purl, J. (2019). Game-like personality testing: An emerging mode of personality assessment. *Personality and Individual Differences, 143*, 95–102. https://doi.org/10.1016/j.paid.2019.02.017

Meade, A. W. (2004). Psychometric problems and issues involved with creating and using ipsative measures for selection. *Journal of Occupational and Organizational Psychology, 77*(4), 531–552.

Meade, A. W., & Pappalardo, G. (2014). *Development of an efficient and faking-resistant rapid response assessment method.* 29th annual meeting of the Society for Industrial and Organizational Psychology, Honolulu, HI.

Meade, A. W., Pappalardo, G., Braddy, P. W., & Fleenor, J. W. (2017, April). *Validation of a faking-resistant, rapid response method personality assessment.* 32nd annual meeting of the Society for Industrial and Organizational Psychologists, Orlando, FL.

Meade, A. W., Pappalardo, G., Braddy, P. W., & Fleenor, J. W. (2020). Rapid response measurement: Development of a faking-resistant assessment method for personality. *Organizational Research Methods, 23*(1), 181–207. https://doi.org/10.1177/1094428118795295

Mueller Hanson, R., Heggestad, E. D., & Thornton, G. C., III. (2003). Faking and selection: Considering the use of personality from select-in and select-out perspectives. *Journal of Applied Psychology, 88*(2), 348–355.

Nye, C. D., White, L. A., Drasgow, F., Prasad, J., Chernyshenko, O. S., & Stark, S. (2020). Examining personality for the selection and classification of soldiers: Validity and differential validity across jobs. *Military Psychology, 32*(1), 60–70. APA PsycInfo. https://doi.org/10.1080/08995605.2019.1652482

Nye, C. D., White, L. A., Horgen, K., Drasgow, F., Stark, S., & Chernyshenko, O. S. (2020). Predictors of attitudes and performance in US Army recruiters: Does personality matter? *Military Psychology, 32*(1), 81–90. APA PsycInfo. https://doi.org/10.1080/08995605.2019.1652486

Ones, D. S., Viswesvaran, C., & Reiss, A. D. (1996). Role of social desirability in personality testing for personnel selection: The red herring. *Journal of Applied Psychology, 81*(6), 660–679. https://doi.org/10.1037/0021-9010.81.6.660

Ones, D. S., Viswesvaran, C., & Schmidt, F. L. (1993). Comprehensive meta-analysis of integrity test validities: Findings and implications for personnel selection and theories of job performance. *Journal of Applied Psychology, 78*(4), 679–703. https://doi.org/10.1037/0021-9010.78.4.679

Oswald, F. L., & Hough, L. M. (2011). Personality and its assessment in organizations: Theoretical and empirical developments. In S. Zedeck (Ed.), *APA handbook of industrial and organizational psychology, Vol 2: Selecting and developing members for the organization* (pp. 153–184). American Psychological Association. https://doi.org/10.1037/12170-005

PerSight Assessments. (2019). *PerSight development theory and background tech report.*

Pike, M., Powell, D. M., & Bourdage, J. S. (2020). *Detecting honesty-humility in employment interviews.* Society for Industrial and Organizational Psychology Conference, Virtual.

Popham, S. M., & Holden, R. R. (1990). Assessing MMPI constructs through the measurement of response latencies. *Journal of Personality Assessment, 54*(3–4), 469–478. APA PsycInfo. https://doi.org/10.1207/s15327752jpa5403&4_4

Rosse, J. G., Stecher, M. D., Miller, J. L., & Levin, R. A. (1998). The impact of response distortion on pre-employment personality testing and hiring decisions. *Journal of Applied Psychology, 83*(4), 634–644.

Ryan, A. M., & Delany, T. (2010). Attracting job candidates to organizations. In J. L. Farr & N. T. Tippins (Eds.), *Handbook of employee selection* (pp. 127–150). Routledge.

Ryan, A. M., & Ployhart, R. E. (2000). Applicants' perceptions of selection procedures and decisions: A critical review and agenda for the future. *Journal of Management, 26*(3), 565–606. https://doi.org/10.1177/014920630002600308

Salgado, J. F., Anderson, N., & Tauriz, G. (2015). The validity of ipsative and quasi-ipsative forced-choice personality inventories for different occupational groups: A comprehensive meta-analysis. *Journal of Occupational and Organizational Psychology, 88*(4), 797–834. https://doi.org/10.1111/joop.12098

Spector, P. E. (1994). *Job satisfaction survey.* Tampa, FL: Department of Psychology, University of South Florida.

Stachowski, A., & Kulas, J. (2020). *A new approach to an old debate: Social desirability in personality assessment.* Society for Industrial and Organizational Psychology Conference, Virtual.

Stark, S., Chernyshenko, O. S., Drasgow, F., Nye, C. D., White, L. A., Heffner, T., & Farmer, W. L. (2014). From ABLE to TAPAS: A new generation of personality tests to support military selection and classification decisions. *Military Psychology, 26*(3), 153–164. https://doi.org/10.1037/mil0000044

Tay, L., Drasgow, F., Rounds, J., & Williams, B. A. (2009). Fitting measurement models to vocational interest data: Are dominance models ideal? *Journal of Applied Psychology, 94*(5), 1287–1304. https://doi.org/10.1037/a0015899

Tay, L., Woo, S. E., Hickman, L., & Saef, R. M. (2020). Psychometric and validity issues in machine learning approaches to personality assessment: A focus on social media text mining. *European Journal of Personality, 34*(5), 826–844. https://doi.org/10.1002/per.2290

Tett, R. P., & Christiansen, N. D. (2007). Personality tests at the crossroads: A response to Morgeson, Campion, Dipboye, Hollenbeck, Murphy, and Schmitt (2007). *Personnel Psychology, 60*(4), 967–993.

Travers, R. M. W. (1951). A critical review of the validity and rationale of the forced-choice technique. *Psychological Bulletin, 48*(1), 62–70. https://doi.org/10.1037/h0055263

Trent, J. D., Barron, L. G., Rose, M. R., & Carretta, T. R. (2020). Tailored Adaptive Personality Assessment System (TAPAS) as an indicator for counterproductive work behavior: Comparing validity in applicant, honest, and directed faking conditions. *Military Psychology, 32*(1), 51–59. https://doi.org/10.1080/08995605.2019.1652481

Tupes, E. C., & Christal, R. E. (1992). Recurrent personality factors based on trait ratings. *Journal of Personality, 60*(2), 225–251. https://doi.org/10.1111/j.1467-6494.1992.tb00973.x

Valone, A., Meade, A. W., Archibald, J., & Ahmad, U. (2020). *Development of a rapid response measure of dark personality.* 35th annual meeting of the Society for Industrial and Organizational Psychologists, Austin, TX.

Vecchione, M., Dentale, F., Alessandri, G., & Barbaranelli, C. (2014). Fakability of implicit and explicit measures of the Big Five: Research findings from organizational settings. *International Journal of Selection and Assessment, 22*(2), 211–218. https://doi.org/10.1111/ijsa.12070

Viswesvaran, C., & Ones, D. S. (1999). Meta-analyses of fakability estimates: Implications for personality measurement. *Educational and Psychological Measurement, 59*(2), 197–210. https://doi.org/10.1177/00131649921969802

Wiernik, B., Ones, D., Marlin, B., Giordano, C., Dilchert, S., Mercado, B., Stanek, K., Birkland, A., Wang, Y., Ellis, B., Yazar, Y., Kostal, J., Kumar, S., Hnat, T., Ertin, E., Sano, A., Ganesan, D., Choudhoury, T., & al'Absi, M. (2020). Using mobile sensors to study personality dynamics. *European Journal of Psychological Assessment, 36*, 1–13. https://doi.org/10.1027/1015-5759/a000576

Wilgus, S., & Meade, A. W. (2020). *Development and validation of a job satisfaction rapid response measure.* 35th annual meeting of the Society for Industrial and Organizational Psychologists, Austin, TX.

# 4
# Advances in Cognitive Ability Assessment in the Mitigation of Group Differences

*Charles A. Scherbaum, Harold W. Goldstein, Kenneth P. Yusko, Elliott Larson, Annie Kato, Kajal Patel, and Yuliya Cheban*

It is widely recognized that cognitive abilities are critical individual differences in industrial-organizational (IO) psychology. Their importance has only grown over time as the modern world of work has become increasingly complex and fluid. At the same time, individuals, organizations, and society are demanding that human capital systems, such as assessment and selection, operate in a manner that is equitable and inclusive, which can be challenging when it comes to typical cognitive tests that are often associated with group differences (Hough et al., 2001). Despite the increasing importance of cognitive abilities and increasing dissatisfaction with the status quo of cognitive ability assessment, the ways in which cognitive abilities are conceptualized and measured in IO psychology have changed very little over the past century (Scherbaum et al., 2012). Although there are many reasons for this stasis, including the belief that the predictive validity of cognitive assessments has already been established and we have learned all we need to know (cf. Murphy et al., 2003), the simple fact is that the field has generally failed to evolve its thinking about cognitive abilities.

However, many other fields (e.g., clinical and cognitive psychology, developmental and educational research, neuroscience) have taken a different approach and made considerable progress in understanding cognitive ability constructs, their role in the modern world, and how they can be measured (Goldstein et al., 2009; Scherbaum et al., 2015). IO psychology, for the most part, has not taken advantage of these developments. We continue to conceptualize intelligence using out-of-date theories (e.g., Spearman's theory) as well as develop and use cognitive ability tests that are difficult to distinguish from those developed and used 80 years ago. As a result, an opportunity to better understand, measure, and use cognitive abilities in human capital systems is being missed (Ployhart & Holtz, 2008). The goal of this chapter is to highlight modern and innovative theorizing about and measurement of cognitive abilities from other fields that have the potential to help move our field forward. Furthermore, we showcase the emerging work in IO that is demonstrating the value of adopting modern thinking and approaches for tackling the so-called validity/diversity dilemma, including a case example of the National Football League's (NFL's) predraft assessment.

## Rethinking the Measurement of Cognitive Abilities and the Assumed Inevitability of Group Differences

For most of its history, the field of IO psychology has embraced the classical psychometric approach to cognitive abilities (Goldstein et al., 2009). The classical psychometric approach is rooted in the work of Spearman, who posited the existence of a general factor of intelligence underlying all intellectual activity, called *g*. This unidimensional, *g*-centric approach has generally been embraced, in part, because of the success in establishing simple and generalizable relationships between cognitive ability and job performance (e.g., Schmidt & Hunter, 1998). This success, however, has come at a price. We have settled into a general complacency about the state of our knowledge that has discouraged further research into cognitive abilities (Goldstein et al., 2002; Murphy, 1996). The prevailing sense has been that "we know what we need to know" and "the case is closed" (Goldstein et al., 2009; Scherbaum et al., 2012). As a result, our field has implicitly or explicitly accepted many of the tenets of the classical psychometric approach to cognitive ability with little examination (Scherbaum et al., 2012).

However, individuals, organizations, and society in general are increasingly finding many of these tenets unacceptable or out of touch with reality. We highlight two prominent examples. First, the classical psychometric tenet of the Spearman hypothesis states that group differences on cognitive tests are inevitable and the more the test is "*g*-loaded," the larger the group differences (McDaniel & Kepes, 2014). In other words, this tenet states as a fact that White test takers have more cognitive ability (as measured by tests developed using the psychometric approach) than Black test takers and there is nothing that can be done about it. The practice of simply accepting this tenet serves to reinforce using assessments that maintain systemic inequality and the belief that nothing can be done about it. Many organizations and society in general find this tenet troubling and will no longer accept it. One could argue that even the regulatory framework for evaluating the fairness of selection procedures (i.e., *Uniform Guidelines for Employee Selection Procedures*) was designed to combat the acceptance of this tenant. Second, the classical psychometric tenet of indifference of the indicator states that the type of measure and the content of the measure are not important as long as there is a diverse set of measures that are $g$-loaded (Jensen, 1998). This tenet is often used to justify measuring a narrow set of abilities (e.g., reading comprehension, vocabulary, basic math) with little consideration of how cognitive abilities actually manifest on the job (Reeve et al., 2015). Organizations have been gravitating away from these narrow assessments and moving toward assessments that capture cognitive abilities closer to how they manifest at work (e.g., situational judgment tests, simulations).

Fortunately, we are witnessing the beginnings of a renaissance in IO research on cognitive abilities after decades of stagnation. This work is leading researchers to rethink many of the handed-down "truths" about cognitive ability, such as:

- cognitive ability is the best predictor of future job performance;
- measuring cognitive abilities must lead to group differences (i.e., Spearman hypothesis);
- the content of a cognitive ability measure is less important than its $g$-loading, meaning it does not really matter which measure you use (i.e., indifference of the indicator);
- identifying relevant specific cognitive abilities is less important than ensuring the general factor is assessed (i.e., "not much more than $g$");
- the positive correlation among different cognitive tests is proof that a $g$-factor exists (i.e., positive manifold).

For example, the recent meta-analysis by Sackett and colleagues leads to a complete re-evaluation of the primacy of cognitive ability tests in predicting job performance (Sackett et al., 2022). In the following sections, we highlight the modern thinking and measurement approach from other fields as well as from IO that have challenged these long-held beliefs and have the potential to simultaneously improve the measurement of cognitive abilities and reduce group differences.

## Insights from Modern Psychometric Theory and Research to Improve the Measurement of Cognitive Abilities and Reduce Group Differences

Modern psychometric approaches suggest that cognitive ability is much more than $g$ and, as a result, offer new insights for improving the measurement of cognitive abilities. The modern approaches often provide alternative assumptions about measuring cognitive ability that may offer ways for reducing group differences.

*Hierarchical Models.* Contemporary thinking on intelligence in other areas of psychology has long postulated that cognitive ability is a network of different cognitive constructs rather than a single entity (Horn & Blankson, 2012; Schneider & McGrew, 2012). Modern theories have focused on developing hierarchically arranged taxonomies of these abilities. The most supported, accepted, and influential of these models is the Cattell–Horn–Carroll (CHC) model (Schneider & McGrew, 2012). The CHC model represents the integration of Carroll's (1993) three-strata theory of intelligence with Horn and Cattell's (1966) theory of fluid and crystalized intelligence.

This model outlines cognitive abilities at three hierarchical levels of specificity (Schneider & McGrew, 2012; Schneider & Newman, 2015). At the highest and broadest level of this theory is a single general ability (stratum III; i.e., $g$). The next level (stratum II) includes broad cognitive abilities including fluid reasoning, short-term memory, long-term memory, processing speed, reaction and decision speed, psychomotor speed, comprehension/knowledge (i.e., crystalized intelligence), domain-specific knowledge, reading and writing, quantitative knowledge, visual processing, auditory processing, and three other abilities related to sensory functioning. Lastly, the lowest and narrowest level (stratum I) contains very specific cognitive abilities (e.g., inductive reasoning).

IO researchers are increasingly drawing on the CHC model and have begun advocating for the value of specific cognitive abilities in this model (e.g., ALMamari & Traynor, 2019, 2021; Chou, Omansky, et al., 2019; Hanges et al., 2015; Kell & Lang, 2017, 2018; Lang & Kell, 2020; Lang et al., 2010; Reeve et al., 2015; Schneider & Newman, 2015; Wee, 2018; Wee et al., 2014). These authors have argued that focusing on specific cognitive abilities may improve our understanding and prediction of intelligent behavior in the modern workplace while at the same time reducing group score differences. For example, several authors have found that the predictive validity of specific abilities increases relative to that of *g* when modern statistical techniques are applied (e.g., Hanges et al., 2015; Lang et al., 2010, Wee, 2018; Wee et al., 2014). Additionally, research by Wee and colleagues (2014, 2015) and Song and colleagues (2017) using Pareto optimization suggests that optimally weighting sets of job-relevant specific abilities can maximize predictive validity while minimizing group differences, offering superior outcomes in comparison to *g* (see Chapter 29 for a discussion of this methodology). These findings support the view that constellations of specific abilities may be useful predictors of job performance when matched to the specific requirements of the job—a more tailored and nuanced approach than focusing on *g* (Murphy, 2017; Wee, 2018). In other words, the use of specific abilities holds the potential to address both validity and diversity.

As has been argued elsewhere (Scherbaum et al., 2015; Thorndike, 1997), many cognitive ability tests used in employment contexts are not linked to any theory of cognitive ability, and the test content is not well aligned to the broad abilities that the tests seek to measure. Outside of IO, improved measurement and alignment of measures and constructs have been a focus. The cross-battery assessment approach (XBA) of Flanagan and colleagues (Flanagan & McGrew, 1997; Flanagan et al., 2007, 2018) is focused on creating theory-driven and comprehensive assessments of cognitive abilities. At the core of this approach is the alignment between the broad abilities (CHC's stratum II) that one wishes to measure and the abilities that are actually measured by the tests that one wishes to use. This alignment process can identify where there are deficiencies in measuring the desired broad abilities. Additional tests can then be incorporated to ensure that the abilities of interest are adequately measured. The benefit of this approach is that it requires the test user to clearly articulate the cognitive abilities that one needs to measure and then demonstrate that the tests actually measure those abilities. Such an approach could help the field move past cognitive ability tests that measure only a narrow range of abilities (e.g., math and reading), helping capture a fuller range of the criteria we wish to predict and potentially mitigate group score differences. This approach is also consistent with best practices in IO psychology for validating selection procedures. Typically, a key part of a validation effort is a job analysis in which the cognitive abilities that are critical for success on the job are identified and selection procedures measuring those abilities are either developed or identified.

*Non-g and Nonhierarchical Models.* Other modern psychometric research has reinterpreted the nature of *g* or excluded *g* altogether. For example, the dynamical model of intelligence by Van der Maas and colleagues (2006) proposes that $g$ is an emergent psychometric phenomenon rather than a psychological construct. The traditional explanation for the positive correlation between different cognitive ability tests (i.e., positive manifold) is a latent $g$ factor. In contrast, the dynamical model suggests that the positive manifold is the result of mutually beneficial interactions between cognitive processes that develop over time. As another example, nested factor theories conceptualize specific ability factors in parallel with $g$ rather than in subordination to it (Gustafsson & Balke, 1993; Lang & Bliese, 2012). According to these theories, correlations between $g$ and specific abilities could originate from $g$ causing specific abilities, specific abilities causing $g$, or a third factor such as common method variance. In other words, these theories call into question the practice of measuring a narrow set of abilities and justifying it by claiming that they collectively capture $g$. Practically, these models suggest that measures of specific cognitive abilities have the capacity to explain as much or more variance than $g$ as well as reduce score differences.

*Integrative Models and the Dynamic Interplay With Other Abilities.* Another advancement in psychometric research is the development of "meta-theories" that account for the dynamic interplay between individual differences and environmental factors in the development of adult intelligence. Ackerman's (1996) intelligence-as-process, personality, interests, and intelligence-as-knowledge (PPIK) theory is a prime example of such an approach. Ackerman proposes that abilities, personality, and interests jointly and dynamically influence the acquisition of knowledge and skills. Ability influences the probability of success in a particular task domain, personality and interests determine the motivation for attempting the task, and successful attempts at task performance increase knowledge and interest in the task domain (whereas unsuccessful attempts decrease interest and inhibit further knowledge acquisition). A key element of PPIK for measuring cognitive abilities is the distinction of intelligence as process and intelligence as knowledge. It is often the case that cognitive abilities are described or operationalized in terms of process, but they are measured in terms of acquired knowledge. A cursory review of traditional psychometric intelligence tests highlights this disconnect. This disconnect is particularly problematic in jobs where organizations are selecting candidates to attend formal job training (e.g., public safety personnel selected to start an academy). In these contexts, there is a desire to identify those that can learn the job. However, candidates are assessed on knowledge they have already acquired (e.g., reading comprehension, basic math).

PPIK provides a useful explanation for how a basic set of individual difference factors can produce myriad cognitive ability profiles, contextually influenced and yet individually distinct. Drawing on such theories will benefit how we conceptualize the interplay between cognitive and noncognitive predictors and lead to more effective strategies for combining them to better predict performance and minimize adverse impact. For example, selection models generally treat cognitive and noncognitive predictors as additive components in a linear model where more of an individual difference is generally better. It may be the case that there are interactions between abilities or more dynamic profiles (e.g., cluster analysis) that should be considered to understand how critical individual differences work in conjunction to achieve successful performance and that there can be multiple different profiles that achieve that success.

## Insights From Cognitive and Neuroscience Theory, Research, and Methods to Improve the Measurement of Cognitive Abilities and Reduce Group Difference

Researchers have posited that neuro- and cognitive sciences can be used to advance our understanding of psychological phenomena being measured. In their brain-as-predictor framework, Berkman and Falk (2013) argue that the brain mechanisms that have been linked to psychological processes can be used to predict real-world outcomes. Others have advocated for greater use of biologically based measures of cognitive processing (Becker et al., 2015). There are several streams of this research that merit consideration.

The first are the cognitive process approaches, such as Naglieri and colleagues' Planning, Attention-Arousal, Simultaneous, and Successive (PASS) theory (Naglieri et al., 2012; Naglieri & Das, 1997). PASS focuses on information processing and identifies three interrelated brain systems that support four cognitive processes. The planning process involves decision-making, evaluation, goal striving, and regulation of present and future behaviors. The attention process is responsible for maintaining general alertness to a task and resisting distraction. Simultaneous processing is responsible for organizing information into coherent patterns or recognizing information with shared characteristics. Successive processing is responsible for integrating information into a sequence. These processes represent capabilities that often appear in organizational competency models.

The Cognitive Assessment System (CAS; Naglieri & Otero, 2012) measures the four cognitive processes in the PASS model. This test involves a variety of tasks such as making decisions when facing novel tasks, closely examining the features of stimuli, performing tasks involving speech, and using memory when examining various geometric objects. Although this measure was originally designed for children and adolescents, CAS has shown lower race-based score differences than traditional psychometric cognitive ability tests (Naglieri et al., 2005). This suggests that it may be beneficial to adapt the CAS for use in the employment context as it measures critical cognitive processes and has the potential to reduce score differences.

A second stream of research is the use of neuropsychological tests to capture cognitive processes, such as executive functioning. Developed in clinical psychology, neuropsychological tests are tasks that have been found to capture differences in executive functioning in the brain (Miller & Maricle, 2012). The research in employment contexts finds that neuropsychological tests can be useful for predicting job performance and reducing score differences (e.g., Bosco et al., 2015; Higgins et al., 2007; Martin et al., 2020; Sabet et al., 2013).

Higgins and colleagues (2007) examined the relationship between job performance and a neuropsychological test battery made up of spatial conditional associative tasks, nonspatial conditional associative tasks, go/no-go tasks, word fluency tasks, stimulus ordering tasks, and stimulus discrimination tasks. They found uncorrected correlations between the scores on this neuropsychological test and supervisor ratings of job performance ranging from $r = .42$ (employees with at least a year of work experience) to $r = .57$ (employees with 3 or more years of work experience) on a set of moderate- to high-complexity jobs. However, they found a correlation of only $r = .12$ on a low-complexity job. Similarly, Bosco and colleagues (2015) reported three studies that found that a measure of executive attention, an underlying mechanism of neuropsychological cognitive ability related to resource allocation, was correlated with supervisory ratings of job performance (uncorrected $r$s = .21 to .25). They also found that executive attention was a relatively better predictor of job performance than traditional psychometric cognitive ability tests. Martin and colleagues (2020) developed an assessment of working memory, which is a core component of executive functioning. They found that their working memory assessment was correlated with other cognitive tests and with supervisor ratings for a variety of performance dimensions (uncorrected $rs = .11$ to $.27$). The initial results suggest that group differences on neuropsychological tests are smaller compared to what has been reported in the literature for traditional psychometric cognitive ability tests (e.g., Bosco et al., 2015; Martin et al., 2020; Sabet et al., 2013). Together, these studies indicate that neuropsychological tests may have the potential to capture important cognitive abilities, predict job performance, and result in smaller group differences.

A third stream of research is the use of neuroscience methods to understand cognitive processes in real time and incorporate these insights into test design. The value of these methods comes primarily from the opportunity to understand how cognitive processes are manifested in cognitive ability measures and in score differences. It is unlikely that these methods would be used in organizations because the technology and methods needed to study cognitive processes are considered too expensive and too difficult to implement and require too much specialized expertise to apply to complex workplace contexts (e.g., Becker et al., 2015; Becker & Menges, 2013), but they can inform best practices in the design of cognitive ability tests. An example of a neuroscience technology that has the potential to lead to insights for best practice is eye tracking. Eye tracking is a technology that can track natural movement of the eyes and pupils as an individual completes tasks, completes test items, or interacts with others (Beatty & Lucero-Wagoner, 2000; Sirois & Brisson, 2014). While individuals engage in these tasks/tests and interactions, eye trackers remotely capture visual fixation patterns and gaze duration (e.g., when, where, and how long an individual looks) and dynamic changes in pupil size (i.e., pupil dilations and constrictions) continuously in real time. Eye tracking can assess attention, arousal, cognitive load, and perceptual fluency (Meißner & Oll, 2017).

For example, cognitive pupillometry measures brief, minute fluctuations in pupil size that unveil real-time activation of neural systems, which underlie cognitive processes (Aston-Jones & Cohen, 2005; Gilzenrat et al., 2010). Thus, cognitive pupillometry is useful for investigating how dynamic mental activity levels correlate with individual differences in intelligent behaviors, cognitive performance, and cognitive ability. Chou, Scherbaum and Hanges (2019) measured cognitive pupillometry as individuals completed cognitive ability test items. They found that information processing measured using pupillometry covaried with the difficulty levels for some types of cognitive ability test items but not others. They also found that the race-based score differences on the test were considerably larger than the differences in information processing from the eye tracking. Additionally, this method can help understand how individuals attend to and process different aspects of test items. For instance, gaze patterns can be used to understand which aspects of an item are attended to by tests takers and if those patterns vary across groups. Differential attention could be the result of differential familiarity or cultural content. Items could then be revised so that all groups are processing items in similar ways.

## Leveraging Modern Test Design Principles to Improve the Measurement of Cognitive Abilities and Reduce Group Differences

There is a growing body of research focusing on how the design of cognitive ability tests leads to deficiency and contamination in measures of cognitive constructs and contributes to the score differences between groups. This work has offered a variety of modern design principles that can help address these limitations (e.g., Agnello et al., 2015; Flanagan & McDonough, 2018). We focus on three that we believe have the greatest potential to improve the measurement of cognitive abilities, improve validity, and minimize group score differences.

*Create Theory-Driven Cognitive Ability Tests.* Many cognitive ability tests lack a solid theoretical foundation that underlies their development (Kaufman, 2000). These tests were created by combining various verbal and quantitative items to generate a composite without much thought given to whether this leads to a comprehensive measure of the important cognitive abilities in a given context. In other fields, researchers have built tests that reflect modern theories of cognitive abilities (e.g., Kaufman & Kaufman, 1983) and revised existing tests to map them to modern theories (e.g., Stanford-Binet 5, Woodcock-Johnson III). Given that other areas have updated their tests to base them on modern theories of cognitive ability, it is clearly possible to build theoretically based tests that will be useful for making consequential decisions in IO psychology. Approaches that align the cognitive abilities of interest with the content of the test should help improve the theoretical rationale and construct validity of cognitive ability tests (e.g., XBA).

*Reduce Reliance on Non-Domain-Relevant and Cultural Content.* A variety of research points to the need to reduce non-domain-relevant and cultural-specific content that exists in many cognitive ability tests (e.g., Fagan & Holland, 2002, 2007; Helms-Lorenz et al., 2003; Malda et al., 2010; van de Vijver, 1997). These researchers have argued that requiring knowledge of non-domain-relevant and cultural-specific content in test items creates a source of contamination. Knowledge of and familiarity with this content may vary by background, country of origin, race, gender, culture, or economic standing and contributes to score differences on cognitive ability tests (Agnello et al., 2015; Goldstein et al., 2009). For example, Malda and colleagues (2010) experimentally manipulated the cultural content in measures of short-term memory, attention, working memory, and figural and verbal fluid reasoning to be consistent with White or Black South African culture. They found that when test content was consistent with the test taker's culture, test performance was higher, including Black test takers outperforming White test takers. Likewise, test items often include information that is nonrelevant to the ability measured, such as when a high reading level is required to understand math items.

It appears that the linguistic demands of a test can be confounded with the cultural content embedded in the test (Ortiz & Ochoa, 2005). Freedle and Kostin (1997) found that cultural differences in the use and interpretation of common words can lead to differential item functioning disadvantaging the cultural minority test taker. Helms-Lorenz and colleagues (2003) state that "differential mastery of the testing language by cultural groups creates a spurious correlation between $g$ and intergroup performance differences" (p. 13).

Other research has focused on confounds related to the use of items requiring previously acquired knowledge to measure information processing. Fagan and Holland (2002, 2007) found that race-based score differences on cognitive ability tests can be attributed to differences in the acquired knowledge that test items use, not information processing. Larson (2019) meta-analyzed measures of information processing and found that they are valid predictors of several outcomes and demonstrated smaller group differences. These findings are consistent with Ackerman's PPIK, which differentiates cognitive ability as knowledge versus cognitive ability as process, and XBA, which calls for an alignment between test content and constructs measured. This research points to the need to examine the use of previously acquired knowledge to measure cognitive processing and the need for items with nonrelevant information embedded.

*Use of Novel or Nonentrenched Tasks.* An alternative approach to removing non-domain-relevant and cultural-specific content is using nonentrenched tasks (e.g., Sternberg, 1981). Nonentrenched tasks use novel stimuli or concepts to solve problems. The core feature of nonentrenched items is that they do not represent the traditional state of stimuli in everyday life. Sternberg (1981) describes a number of nonentrenched tasks including one where individuals need to determine the physical state of an object (e.g., liquid or solid) and the object's fictional name (e.g., plin, kwef) as it moves from north to south or south to north on the fictional planet Kryon from a set of rules presented at the start of the task. Unentrenched items level the playing field for all test takers because they remove previously acquired knowledge as a potential source of contamination. Research has found that cognitive ability tests consisting of nonentrenched items correlate with existing ability tests, predict academic and job performance criteria, and show lower score differences between racial/ethnic groups (Yusko et al., 2012; Sternberg, 2006). Although data on applicant reactions on these types of items is very limited, it has been our experience that reactions are mixed. Some candidates find them interesting and enjoyable; other candidates find them challenging and surprising. Systematic research examining the perceived validity and fairness of these items is needed.

## Will Modern Cognitive Ability Tests Work? The Example of the NFL's Player Assessment Test

In 2008, Malcolm Gladwell published a *New Yorker* essay in which he raised the idea that for some jobs we are unable to predict future performance, coined as the "quarterback problem" given the difficulty of identifying which college quarterbacks will succeed in the NFL. Gladwell's point is supported by evidence that traditional psychometric cognitive ability tests do not predict performance in the NFL (Lyons et al., 2009). Given the high level of cognitive demands for many football positions (e.g., learning an opponent's plays and strategies in a week's time; making a series of quick if-then decisions at the line of scrimmage), the lack of prediction is surprising. This situation highlights many of the flaws of traditional cognitive ability tests that we have described in this chapter, such as the lack of alignment between what abilities need to be measured and what abilities are actually measured in the tests (e.g., using knowledge of vocabulary and basic math to predict complex information processing).

In 2012, the NFL adopted a league-wide testing process that focused on measuring very specific aspects of cognitive ability that matched the type of behavior on the field (Yusko et al., 2018). The assessment, called the NFL Player Assessment Test (PAT), was based on modern approaches to conceptualizing and measuring cognitive abilities. The process started with a job analysis involving executives, general managers, and former players from across the league to identify specific cognitive ability dimensions that were particularly relevant to football. Thus, instead of relying on a general test of cognitive ability to predict potentially widely divergent cognitive performance behaviors, as has been done historically in the NFL, the test development for the NFL-PAT identified specific cognitive abilities, including:

1. the ability to learn quickly to absorb new plays, improve one's understanding of the game, and, if necessary, master multiple positions quickly;
2. mental error resistance to minimize mental errors and breakdowns on the field, particularly when under pressure;
3. spatial visualization in order to better see the field and grasp the locations of players in relation to each other;
4. the ability to make rapid decisions in order to make good decisions under speeded game conditions;
5. direct thinking in order to execute set plays as flawlessly as possible;
6. ambiguous thinking to better deal with breakdowns in plays and perform under conditions of uncertainty.

To measure these cognitive abilities, the NFL-PAT drew on the test design principles described in this chapter (e.g., novel, unentrenched items; alignment of test content and test constructs).

The development of the NFL-PAT was followed by a 7-year validation study to examine its effectiveness at predicting player performance. Between 2013 and 2019, approximately 2,500 NFL prospects took the NFL-PAT at the NFL annual scouting combine. For many of those who were drafted, the teams provided detailed performance ratings on the cognitive performance dimensions the NFL-PAT was designed to predict (e.g., decision-making, learning ability) and overall performance. Additionally, objective on-the-field performance metrics (e.g., penalties) were gathered for these players at the end of each season.

Overall, uncorrected correlations of the scores on the NFL-PAT with a composite of the cognitive performance dimensions ($r = .26$) and with an overall performance rating ($r = .28$) were statistically significant and in range of what one would expect for a complex job. From the perspective of the teams and NFL, these correlations do not tell the whole story. In the NFL, a key determinant of success is physical capability. If one does not have the physical capability to be successful, cognitive abilities do not matter. When examining only the players that the teams evaluated as among the top 40% of physical capability, the correlations demonstrate the value of cognitive ability for differentiating those who are more successful from those who are less successful in the NFL using both team performance ratings (e.g., rating of performance on the cognitive dimensions of the job, $r = .38$; overall performance, $r = .46$) and objective on-the-field performance metrics (e.g., number of penalties, $r = -.25$; snaps, $r = .22$; approximate value, $r = .22$).

## Conclusion

Cognitive ability has been and will continue to be one of the more important individual difference variables in employment contexts. However, it has been our observation that IO psychology has failed to evolve while other fields have forged ahead. Our aim for this chapter is to highlight several advancements in psychometric theory, cognitive perspectives on intelligence, and techniques for improving the measurement of intelligence that we believe have potential to impact the measurement and use of cognitive abilities in the employment context as well as reduce group differences. While we believe these developments have promise, their implementation should be continued to accumulate evidence demonstrating the job-relatedness of the measures (Oswald & Hough, 2012). We encourage IO researchers and practitioners to engage in these efforts and modernize our field's perspectives on cognitive abilities.

## References

Ackerman, P. L. (1996). A theory of adult intellectual development: Process, personality, interests, and knowledge. *Intelligence*, 22(2), 227–257.

Agnello, P., Ryan, R., & Yusko, K. P. (2015). Implications of modern intelligence research for assessing intelligence in the workplace. *Human Resource Management Review*, 25(1), 47–55.

ALMamari, K., & Traynor, A. (2019). Multiple test batteries as predictors for pilot performance: A meta-analytic investigation. *International Journal of Selection and Assessment, 27*(4), 337–356.

ALMamari, K., & Traynor, A. (2021). The role of general and specific cognitive abilities in predicting performance of three occupations: Evidence from Bifactor Models. *Journal of Intelligence, 9*(3), 40.

Aston-Jones, G., & Cohen, J. D. (2005). An integrative theory of locus coeruleus-norepinephrine function: Adaptive gain and optimal performance. *Annual Review of Neuroscience, 28*, 403–450.

Beatty, J., & Lucero-Wagoner, B. (2000). The pupillary system. *Handbook of Psychophysiology, 2*, 142–162.

Becker, W. J., & Menges, J. I. (2013). Biological implicit measures in HRM and OB: A question of how not if. *Human Resource Management Review, 23*(3), 219–228.

Becker, W. J., Volk, S., & Ward, M. K. (2015). Leveraging neuroscience for smarter approaches to workplace intelligence. *Human Resource Management Review, 25*(1), 56–67.

Berkman, E. T., & Falk, E. B. (2013). Beyond brain mapping: Using neural measures to predict real-world outcomes. *Current Directions in Psychological Science, 22*(1), 45–50.

Bosco, F., Allen, D. G., & Singh, K. (2015). Executive attention: An alternative perspective on general mental ability, performance, and subgroup differences. *Personnel Psychology, 68*(4), 859–898.

Carroll, J. (1993). *Human cognitive abilities: A survey of factor analytic studies*. Cambridge University Press.

Chou, V. P., Omansky, R., Scherbaum, C. A., Yusko, K. P., & Goldstein, H. W. (2019). The use of specific cognitive abilities in the workplace. In D. McFarland (Ed.), *General and specific abilities* (pp. 436–471). Cambridge Scholars Publishing.

Chou, V. P., Scherbaum, C. A., & Hanges, P. J. (2019, April). *A neuroscience method to elucidate sources of score differences on ability tests* [Poster session]. 34th annual conference of the Society for Industrial and Organizational Psychology, Washington, DC.

Fagan, J. F., & Holland, C. R. (2002). Equal opportunity and racial differences in IQ. *Intelligence, 30*(4), 361–387.

Fagan, J. F., & Holland, C. R. (2007). Racial equality in intelligence: Predictions from a theory of intelligence as processing. *Intelligence, 35*(4), 319–334.

Flanagan, D. P., Costa, M., Palma, K., Leahy, M. A., Alfonso, V. C., & Ortiz, S. O. (2018). Cross-battery assessment, the cross-battery assessment software system, and the assessment–intervention connection. In D. P. Flanagan & E. M. McDonough (Eds.), *Contemporary intellectual assessment: Theories, tests, and issues* (pp. 731–776). Guilford Press.

Flanagan, D. P., & McDonough, E. M. (Eds.). (2018). *Contemporary intellectual assessment: Theories, tests, and issues*. Guilford Press.

Flanagan, D. P, & McGrew, K. (1997). A cross-battery approach to assessing and interpreting cognitive abilities: Narrowing the gap between practice and cognitive science. In D. Flanagan, J. Genshaft, and P. Harrison (Eds.), *Contemporary intellectual assessment: Theories, tests, and issues* (pp. 314–325). New York: Guilford.

Flanagan, D. P, Ortiz, S., & Alfonso, V. (2007). *Essentials of cross-battery assessment* (2nd ed.). Wiley.

Freedle, R., & Kostin, I. (1997). Predicting black and white differential item functioning in verbal analogy performance. *Intelligence, 24*, 417–444.

Gilzenrat, M. S., Nieuwenhuis, S., Jepma, M., & Cohen, J. D. (2010). Pupil diameter tracks changes in control state predicted by the adaptive gain theory of locus coeruleus function. *Cognitive, Affective, & Behavioral Neuroscience, 10*(2), 252–269.

Goldstein, H. W., Scherbaum, C. A., & Yusko, K. (2009). Adverse impact and measuring cognitive ability. In J. Outtz (Ed.), *Adverse impact: Implications for organizational staffing and high stakes testing* (pp. 95–134). Psychology Press.

Goldstein, H. W., Zedeck, S., & Goldstein, I. L. (2002). g: Is this your final answer? *Human Performance*, 15(1–2), 123–142.

Gustafsson, J. E., & Balke, G. (1993). General and specific abilities as predictors of school achievement. *Multivariate Behavioral Research*, 28(4), 407–434.

Hanges, P. J., Scherbaum, C. A., & Reeve, C. L. (2015). There are more things in heaven and earth, Horatio, than DGF. *Industrial and Organizational Psychology*, 8(3), 472–481.

Helms-Lorenz, M., Van de Vijver, F., & Poortinga, Y. (2003). Cross-cultural differences in cognitive performance and Spearman's hypothesis: g or c? *Intelligence*, 31, 9–29.

Higgins, D., Peterson, J., Pihl, R., & Lee, A. (2007). Prefrontal cognitive ability, intelligence, big five personality, and the prediction of advanced academic and workplace performance. *Journal of Personality and Social Psychology*, 93, 298–319.

Horn, J. L., & Blankson, A. N. (2012). Foundations for better understanding of cognitive abilities. In D. P. Flanagan & P. L. Harrison (Eds.), *Contemporary intellectual assessment: Theories, tests, and issues* (pp. 73–98). Guilford Press.

Horn, J., & Cattell, R. (1966). Refinement of the theory of fluid and crystalized general intelligences. *Journal of Educational Psychology*, 57, 253–270.

Hough, L., Oswald, F., & Ployhart, R. (2001). Determinants, detection and amelioration of adverse impact in personnel selection procedures: Issues, evidence and lessons learned. *International Journal of Selection and Assessment*, 9, 152–194.

Jensen, A. (1998). *The g factor: The science of mental ability*. Praeger.

Kaufman, A. (2000). Tests of intelligence. In R. J. Sternberg (Ed.), *Handbook of intelligence* (pp. 445–476). Cambridge University Press.

Kaufman, A. S., & Kaufman, N. L. (1983). *Kaufman Assessment Battery for Children*. American Guidance Service.

Kell, H. J., & Lang, J. W. (2017). Specific abilities in the workplace: More important than g? *Journal of Intelligence*, 5(2), 13.

Kell, H. J., & Lang, J. W. (2018). The great debate: General ability and specific abilities in the prediction of important outcomes. *Journal of Intelligence*, 6(3), 39.

Lang, J., & Bliese, P. (2012). I-O psychology and progressive research programs on intelligence. *Industrial and Organizational Psychology: Perspectives on Science and Practice*, 5, 161–168.

Lang, J. W., & Kell, H. J. (2020). General mental ability and specific abilities: Their relative importance for extrinsic career success. *Journal of Applied Psychology*, 105(9), 1047.

Lang, J., Kersting, M., Hülsheger, U., & Lang, J. (2010). General mental ability, narrower cognitive abilities, and job performance: The perspective of the nested-factors model of cognitive abilities. *Personnel Psychology*, 63, 595–640.

Larson, E. C. (2019). *A meta-analysis of information processing measures of intelligence, performance, and group score difference* [Doctoral dissertation, City University of New York].

Lyons, B. D., Hoffman, B. J., & Michel, J. W. (2009). Not much more than g? An examination of the impact of intelligence on NFL performance. *Human Performance*, 22(3), 225–245.

Malda, M., van de Vijver, F., & Temane, M. (2010). Rugby versus soccer in South Africa: Content familiarity explains most cross-cultural differences in cognitive test scores. *Intelligence*, 38, 582–595.

Martin, N., Capman, J., Boyce, A., Morgan, K., Gonzalez, M. F., & Adler, S. (2020). New frontiers in cognitive ability testing: Working memory. *Journal of Managerial Psychology, 35*(4), 193–208.

McDaniel, M. A., & Kepes, S. (2014). An evaluation of Spearman's Hypothesis by manipulating g saturation. *International Journal of Selection and Assessment, 22*(4), 333–342.

Meißner, M., & Oll, J. (2017). The promise of eye-tracking methodology in organizational research. *Organizational Research Methods, 22*(2), 590–617.

Miller, D., & Maricle, D. (2012). The emergence of neuropsychological constructs into tests of intelligence and cognitive abilities. In D. Flanagan & P. Harrison (Eds.), *Contemporary intellectual assessment: Theories, tests, and issues* (3rd ed., pp. 800–819). Guilford.

Murphy, K. R. (1996). Individual differences and behavior in organizations: Much more than g. In K. R. Murphy (Ed.), *Individual differences and behavior in organizations* (pp. 3–30). Jossey-Bass.

Murphy, K. (2017). What can we learn from "not much more than g"? *Journal of Intelligence, 5*(1), 8.

Murphy, K., Cronin, B., & Tam, A. (2003). Controversy and consensus regarding the use of cognitive ability testing in organizations. *Journal of Applied Psychology, 88*(4), 660–671.

Naglieri, J., & Das, J. (1997). Intelligence revised. In R. Dillon (Ed.), *Handbook on testing* (pp. 136–163). Greenwood Press.

Naglieri, J., Das, J., & Goldstein, S. (2012). Planning, Attention, Simultaneous, Successive: A cognitive-processing-based theory. In D. Flanagan & P. Harrison (Eds.), *Contemporary intellectual assessment: Theories, tests, and issues* (3rd ed., pp. 178–194). Guilford Press.

Naglieri, J. A., & Otero, T. (2012). The cognitive assessment system: From theory to practice. In D. P. Flanagan & P. L. Harrison (Eds.), *Contemporary intellectual assessment: Theories, tests, and issues* (3rd ed., pp. 376–399). Guilford Press.

Naglieri, J., Rojahn, J., Matto, H., & Aquilino, S. (2005). Black white differences in intelligence: A study of the PASS theory and cognitive assessment system. *Journal of Psychoeducational Assessment, 23*, 146–160.

Ortiz, S., & Ochoa, S. (2005). Advances in cognitive assessment of culturally and linguistically diverse individuals. In D. Flanagan & P. Harrison (Eds.), *Contemporary intellectual assessment: Theories, tests, and issues* (2nd ed., pp. 234–250). Guilford Press.

Oswald, F., & Hough, L. (2012). I–O 2.0 from intelligence 1.5: Staying (just) behind the cutting edge of intelligence theories. *Industrial and Organizational Psychology: Perspectives on Science and Practice, 5*, 174–177.

Ployhart, R. E., & Holtz, B. C. (2008). The diversity–validity dilemma: Strategies for reducing racioethnic and sex subgroup differences and adverse impact in selection. *Personnel Psychology, 61*(1), 153–172.

Reeve, C., Scherbaum, C., & Goldstein, H. (2015). Manifestations of intelligence: Expanding the measurement space to reconsider specific cognitive abilities. *Human Resource Management Review, 25*, 28–37.

Sabet, J., Scherbaum, C., & Goldstein, H. (2013). Examining the potential of neuropsychological intelligence tests for predicting academic performance and reducing racial/ethnic test scores differences. In F. Metzger (Ed.), *Neuropsychology: New research* (pp. 1–24). Nova Publishers.

Sackett, P. R., Zhang, C., Berry, C. M., & Lievens, F. (2022). Revisiting meta-analytic estimates of validity in personnel selection: Addressing systematic overcorrection for restriction of range. *Journal of Applied Psychology, 107*(11), 2040–2068. https://doi.org/10.1037/apl0000994.

Scherbaum, C., Goldstein, H., Ryan, R., Agnello, P., Yusko, K., & Hanges, P. (2015). New developments in intelligence theory and assessment: Implications for personnel selection. In J. Oostrom & I. Nikolaou (Eds.), *Employee recruitment, selection, and assessment. Contemporary issues for theory and practice* (pp. 99–116). Psychology Press-Taylor & Francis.

Scherbaum, C., Goldstein, H., Yusko, K., Ryan, R., & Hanges, P. (2012). Intelligence 2.0: Reestablishing a research program on g in I-O psychology. *Industrial and Organizational Psychology: Perspectives on Science and Practice, 5*, 128–148.

Schmidt, F. L., & Hunter, J. E. (1998). The validity and utility of selection methods in personnel psychology: Practical and theoretical implications of 85 years of research findings. *Psychological Bulletin, 124*(2), 262.

Schneider, W. J., & McGrew, K. (2012). The Cattell-Horn-Carroll model of intelligence. In D. Flanagan & P. Harrison (Eds.), *Contemporary intellectual assessment: Theories, tests, and issues* (3rd ed., pp. 99–144). Guilford Press.

Schneider, W. J., & Newman, D. A. (2015). Intelligence is multidimensional: Theoretical review and implications of specific cognitive abilities. *Human Resource Management Review, 25*(1), 12–27.

Sirois, S., & Brisson, J. (2014). Pupillometry. *Wiley Interdisciplinary Reviews: Cognitive Science, 5*(6), 679–692.

Song, Q., Wee, S., & Newman, D. A. (2017). Diversity shrinkage: Cross-validating pareto-optimal weights to enhance diversity via hiring practices. *Journal of Applied Psychology, 102*(12), 1636.

Sternberg, R. (1981). Intelligence and non-entrenchment. *Journal of Educational Psychology, 73*, 1–16.

Sternberg, R. (2006). The Rainbow Project: Enhancing the SAT through assessments of analytical, practical, and creative skills. *Intelligence, 34*, 321–350.

Thorndike, R. M. (1997). The early history of intelligence testing. In D. P. Flanagan, J. L. Genshaft, & P. L. Harrison (Eds.), *Contemporary intellectual assessment: Theories, tests, and issues* (pp. 3–16). Guilford Press.

van de Vijver, F. (1997). Meta-analysis of cross-cultural comparisons of cognitive test performance. *Journal of Cross-Cultural Psychology, 28*, 678–709.

van der Maas, H., Dolan, C., Grasman, R., Wicherts, J., Huizenga, H., & Raijmakers, M. (2006). A dynamical model of general intelligence: The positive manifold of intelligence by mutualism. *Psychological Bulletin, 113*, 842–861.

Yusko, K., Aiken, J., Goldstein, H., Scherbaum, C., & Larson, E. (2018). Solving the "quarterback problem": Using psychological assessment to improve selection decisions in professional sports. In R. Sims (Ed.), *Human resources management issues, challenges and trends: "Now and around the corner"* (pp. 213–227). Information Age Publishing.

Yusko, K., Goldstein, H., Scherbaum, C., & Hanges, P. (2012, April). *Siena reasoning test: Measuring intelligence with reduced adverse impact* [Invited M. Scott Myers Award talk]. 27th annual conference of the Society for Industrial and Organizational Psychology, San Diego, CA.

Wee, S. (2018). Aligning predictor-criterion bandwidths: Specific abilities as predictors of specific performance. *Journal of Intelligence, 6*(3), 40.

Wee, S., Newman, D. A., & Joseph, D. L. (2014). More than g: Selection quality and adverse impact implications of considering second-stratum cognitive abilities. *Journal of Applied Psychology, 99*(4), 547.

Wee, S., Newman, D. A., & Song, Q. C. (2015). More than g-factors: Second-stratum factors should not be ignored. *Industrial and Organizational Psychology, 8*(3), 482–488.

# 5
# Applying Natural Language Processing to Assessment

*MQ Liu*

Today, some of the most powerful software engines are fueled by machines that can process human language, such as search engines, smart-home devices, and dialogue systems. Over the past few years, the interest in using natural language processing (NLP) for assessment has grown exponentially. The goal of this chapter is to discuss how NLP can be applied to improve assessment in the selection context. I start by introducing what NLP is and how NLP techniques have evolved over time. I then dive into how various NLP methods can be applied in the assessment cycle, from assessment construction to analyzing assessment responses to predicting job-related outcomes. I end the chapter with a discussion of the key challenges and opportunities facing assessment researchers and practitioners when considering using NLP for assessment.

## Natural Language Processing

NLP is a subfield of artificial intelligence (AI) that aims to program computers that can automatically process and learn human natural language data (Manning & Schütze, 1999). Many NLP applications also leverage machine learning (ML) and deep learning (DL). ML is a subfield of computer science that aims to construct computer programs that can learn and improve with experience automatically (Mitchell, 1997). For instance, Putka et al. (2018) showed that ML methods such as elastic nets and support vector machines can improve biodata prediction compared to ordinary least squares regression. DL, a subfield of ML, consists of computational models based on artificial neural networks that use multiple processing layers to learn data representations with multiple levels of abstraction (LeCun et al., 2015). The key distinction between DL and other ML approaches is DL's layered structure (i.e., the network layers). One example application of DL is AlphaGo, a computer program that learns to play Go by processing data (e.g., description of Go, decisions made by human Go players, etc.) through neural network layers containing millions of connections.

The history of NLP dates back to the 1950s with early progress in machine translation. In 1954, the world saw the first public demonstration of an automatic machine translation system born out of a collaboration between Georgetown University and IBM (IBM, 1954). Despite high expectation, progress in NLP research remained slow for the next few decades; until the 1990s, most NLP applications were still running on rule-based systems. That is, the computer performs NLP tasks by following a collection of human crafted rules, step by step. Rule-based NLP systems are intuitive in concept but can quickly become unmanageable as the complexity of the rules increases.

From the 1990s to 2000s, significant progress was made on NLP thanks to the increase in computational power and the adoption of ML methods for NLP. These methods rely on statistical inference algorithms to learn language from data. Therefore, it is generally easier to improve the accuracy of an ML-based system (feeding it with more data) compared to that of a rule-based system (increasing the complexity of the rules). During this era, NLP relied mostly on feature-based ML algorithms, whereby a typical NLP pipeline would first extract features from documents using bag-of-words (BOW; a technique for counting words that appear in a document and transforming them into a mathematically useful matrix) to break down language by its words and phrases, followed by applying ML models to learn patterns from these features to classify or predict outcomes (e.g., sentiment), also referred to as labels.

A major shortcoming of statistical learning methods is their reliance on features and feature engineering (i.e., the process of selecting and transforming features from raw data). Aided by the advancement of graphics processing unit (GPU) technology, the field of NLP started using deep neural networks to train word embeddings (i.e., text representations that capture the meaning of words) and recurrent neural networks (RNNs; i.e., a type of neural architecture that uses sequential data, where computation at each step can use outputs from previous steps; Rumelhart et al., 1986). One popular type of RNN was long short-term memory (LSTM) that selectively carries important information and forgets unimportant information throughout the training process (Hochreiter & Schmidhuber, 1997). LSTM achieved state-of-the-art results in a number of NLP applications, such as speech recognition (Danko, 2015) and machine translation (Wu et al., 2016).

Starting from the late 2010s, we have witnessed a revolution with deep, pretrained language models substantially improving the state of the art. One of the most influential works has been Bidirectional Encoder Representations from Transformers (BERT; Devlin et al., 2019). BERT is a 340-million-hyperparameter Transformer model developed by Google to pretrain language representations based on a large corpus from Wikipedia and BooksCorpus. Language model pretraining refers to the process of feeding a large amount of unlabeled text data (i.e., text without the outcome/target variable), such as the entire Wikipedia, to a language model (i.e., a probability distribution over words or work sequences). This process helps the model "learn" the general language (the words as well as the context of each word based on surrounding words) before it is applied to a specific NLP task, such as translation. Once a model is pretrained, one can either apply it directly to an NLP task (i.e., zero-shot learning) or fine-tune the pretrained model on the task-specific dataset (usually much smaller compared to the pretraining corpus) before using it to predict outcomes. An oversimplified analogy would be asking a human being to read a history book before taking a history test (traditional ML-based NLP), versus first read an encyclopedia (pretraining) and then take a history test directly afterward (zero-shot learning), versus read both the encyclopedia and the history book (pretraining plus fine-tuning) before taking the history test. You can imagine the third scenario should lead to the highest score on the test, just as how BERT substantially improved upon the benchmarks on many NLP tasks (Devlin et al., 2019). With BERT, researchers no longer have to rely on their own limited data to train models from scratch. Instead, they can use pretrained BERT models that already capture a good understanding of the general language and then fine-tune it for their own NLP tasks.

Since BERT, many researchers have built Transformer-based models with improvements, such as the Robustly optimized BERT approach (RoBERTa; Y. Liu et al., 2019), T5 (Raffel et al., 2020), GPT/GPT-2/GPT-3/GPT-4 (Radford et al., 2018, 2019; Brown et al., 2020; OpenAI, 2023), Efficiently Learning an Encoder that Classifies Token Replacements Accurately (ELECTRA; Clark et al., 2020), and Decoding-enhanced BERT with Disentangled Attention (DeBERTa; He et al., 2021). The largest language model to date is the Megatron-Turing Natural Language Generation model

(MT-NLG), a language model codeveloped by Microsoft and NVIDIA, which has 530 billion parameters (Alvi & Kharya, 2021).

As NLP advances, we have seen human-level performances achieved in speech recognition, machine translation, and a range of natural language understanding (NLU) tasks. In 2017, Microsoft and IBM both achieved around human parity–level performance on speech recognition in the switchboard domain (Huang, 2017). In 2018, a Microsoft machine translation system achieved human-level quality and accuracy when translating news stories from Chinese to English (Linn, 2018). In addition, multiple models have surpassed human-level performance on the General Language Understanding Evaluation (GLUE; Wang et al., 2018) and SuperGLUE (Wang et al., 2019) benchmarks consisting of nine NLU tasks. Interested readers can review the GLUE and SuperGLUE sites for more information on the performance of specific models.

## Applying Natural Language Processing to Assessment

The latest NLP advances bring opportunities to talent assessment. The query "natural language processing talent assessment" on Google yields over 58 million results. There is a flurry of NLP applications in virtually every talent assessment scenario, such as resume screening, interviews, assessment centers, and simulations. While it can be difficult to evaluate the scientific merit of these commercial offerings due to intellectual property issues, we have started to see peer-reviewed, empirical articles in industrial-organizational (IO) psychology, organizational behavior (OB), and human resources management (HRM) journals where NLP techniques were applied to solve talent assessment problems, including scoring achievement record essays (e.g., Campion et al., 2016), assessing personality via automated video interviews (Hickman, Saef, et al., 2021; Hickman, Bosch, et al., 2022), and using applicant work history to predict performance and turnover (Sajjadiani et al., 2019). In 2021, *Personnel Psychology* had a special issue call for papers on applying ML and AI to personnel selection/staffing. The Society for Industrial and Organizational Psychology (SIOP) Annual Conference has also hosted multiple Machine Learning Competitions. In 2019, the competition focused on using unstructured text responses in five open-ended situational judgment items (SJIs) to predict self-report Big Five personality traits. In addition, methodological papers related to NLP also started to emerge (e.g., Banks et al., 2018; Kobayashi et al., 2018a, 2018b), offering best practice recommendations and tutorials that can be used in the talent assessment context.

Unbeknownst to many organizational researchers and practitioners, a lot of research using NLP for assessment has been published by computer scientists (e.g., Chen et al., 2016). For instance, the Association of Computing Machinery's (ACM's) Special Interest Group on Knowledge Discovery and Data Mining (KDD) has hosted workshops since 2018 focusing on talent and management computing, where data mining and NLP techniques were applied to solve challenges in talent assessment domains such as personality assessment and interviews (Xiong et al., 2018, 2019, 2020, 2021). Compared to research in the organizational literature, computer science papers tend to focus on cutting-edge techniques but often do not consider reliability, validity, and fairness evidence, thus limiting its direct applicability in the selection context.

Despite the increasing number of publications, organizational research still significantly lags behind practice, where the fast-paced implementation of NLP techniques in the industry outpaces the literature. Although a few methodological papers (Kobayashi et al., 2018a, 2018b) have been published to provide guidance on how to analyze text data, there is a lack of understanding on how to construct the end-to-end process for using NLP for personnel assessment. In this section, I will break down the key steps in this process and important considerations impacting the reliability, validity, and fairness of the assessment.

## Assessment Construction

The success of an NLP-based assessment starts with the construction of assessment stimuli. For assessment types such as constructed-response assessment (CRA) and interviews, crafting scenarios and prompts that precisely elicit the relevant knowledge, skills, abilities, and other characteristic (KSAOs) can be more important and technically challenging compared to selected-response assessment where the responses are predetermined. On one hand, an overly broad, vague, or construct-irrelevant assessment question will elicit highly variable or irrelevant responses that do not accurately reflect the target KSAOs. On the other hand, an assessment stimulus that is too narrow will result in limited variance in the responses and consequently impact the validity of the assessment. In addition to establishing a good understanding of the job and using best practices in assessment item/question development, it is also helpful to "test" versions of the assessment items/questions and examine the responses to further select or refine the stimuli.

Another emerging area where NLP can be used for assessment construction is automatic item generation (AIG), a process where computer programs are used to automatically generate assessment items. In computer science, relevant literature falls under the domain of natural language generation (NLG), defined as "the subfield of artificial intelligence and computational linguistics that is concerned with the construction of computer systems than can produce understandable texts in English or other human languages from some underlying non-linguistic representation of information" (Reiter & Dale, 1997, p. 1). AIG is not a new idea (Bormuth, 1970), but past efforts mainly focused on creating clones that replicate narrowly defined items or deriving item variations (e.g., difficulty) based on prespecified rules and constraints (Gierl & Haladyna, 2012; Gierl et al., 2021). It follows a two-step process: First, assessment developers create item templates and specify the item elements to be varied. Second, computer programs vary the specified elements to generate new items. However, recent advances in NLP show promise in using probabilistic language models to automatically generate assessment items. For instance, von Davier (2018) and Hommel et al. (2022) demonstrated success in using deep neural networks, specifically LSTM models (LSTM; Hochreiter & Schmidhuber, 1997; Jozefowicz et al., 2015) and Generative Pretrained Transformer-2 (GPT-2; Radford et al., 2018, 2019), respectively, to automatically generate personality items. Hommel et al. selected 1,715 validated personality items from the International Personality Item Pool (Goldberg, 1999; Goldberg et al., 2006) and used them to fine-tune the pretrained GPT-2 model, a process that teaches the model how to generate construct-specific personality items. Out of the model-generated personality items, 64% showed good psychometric properties (factor loadings > .40 when added to a confirmatory factor analysis model with human-generated items). Researchers have also experimented with cross-domain AIG, such as structured query language–to–question generation (e.g., Zhang et al., 2021), table-to-text generation (e.g., Su et al., 2021), and commonsense knowledge graph and equations-to-mathematical work problem generation (T. Liu et al., 2021). This growing research shows great promise in automating the creation of personality assessment, situational judgment tests, knowledge-based assessments, etc. Assessment expertise is still required to create/select the relevant input (e.g., seed items), review the item generation process, and evaluate the generated items.

## Voice-to-Text

Once open-ended responses are collected from an assessment, NLP can be used to analyze such responses. If the assessment response is in a voice format (e.g., interviews, audio-based CRAs), we need to first use automatic speech recognition (ASR) systems to transform the response into text. DL techniques have greatly improved the accuracy of ASR systems, pushing the word accuracy in common languages such as English and Chinese above 90% (Yu & Deng, 2016), but the accuracy can suffer in low-resource languages where the data are lacking (e.g., Anastasopoulos & Chiang, 2018) or when encountering speech variability (e.g., accents) and environmental distractions (e.g., background noise; Benzeghiba et al., 2007). It is recommended that assessment developers leverage one of the commercial offerings of ASR (Google Cloud, Microsoft Azure, Amazon Transcribe, etc.), instead of training one from scratch, and measure its accuracy in the specific assessment context both across all assessment takers and by subgroups of interest. Even a highly accurate ASR system like Azure reports varying word error rate (WER; i.e., number of incorrect words identified during recognition) for call centers (up to 30%) and videos (up to 50%; Microsoft, 2021). Assessment researchers who do not examine the accuracy of ASR for assessment are turning a blind eye to measurement errors that might disproportionally affect subgroups of the applicant population.

## Text Cleaning and Preprocessing

Once audio responses have been transcribed to text or if the responses are already in a text format, the next step is to apply text cleaning and preprocessing steps before the information can be fed into an ML or DL model. Standard text cleaning procedures include tokenization (i.e., splitting sentences into words and phrases), lowercase conversion (i.e., converting words to lowercase), removal of irrelevant characters (e.g., HTML tags, extra whitespace, and punctuation), and removal of stopwords (i.e., words that are commonly used but carry little meaning, such as "a," "an," "the," etc.). Word inflections can be dealt with using either stemming (i.e., directly reducing inflection in words to their root form, but it can lead to misspellings, e.g., "beautiful" to "beauti") or lemmatization (i.e., removing word inflections and mapping words to their meaningful root forms, e.g., "beautiful" to "beauty").

## Analyzing Text: Non-Neural Natural Language Processing Approaches

After proper text cleaning, we can choose a traditional, non-neural approach or an advanced, neural approach for representing text and building prediction models. In a non-neural approach, we can first represent text via the BOW model, a technique that breaks text into words and phrases and transforms them into a document-term matrix, where the columns represent the features (words and phrases) and the rows represent the "weights" of the features in each document (see Table 5.1 for an example). In an assessment context, a document is the body of text from a job candidate. The most straightforward way of computing the feature weights is to count the number of times each feature occurs in a document (i.e., term frequency). However, having a high raw count does not necessarily correspond to high feature importance because certain features can appear frequently across all documents and are not meaningful to help differentiate the documents. For instance, if 95% of the candidates describe themselves as "hardworking" in their interviews, this word will not differentiate candidates or predict job performance. A common technique to address this problem is normalizing term frequencies via term frequency-inverse document frequency (TF-IDF; Spärck Jones, 1972; Salton & Buckley, 1988). TF-IDF evaluates term importance by multiplying two statistics, term frequency (i.e., number of times a word appears in the document) and inverse document frequency (i.e.,

Table 5.1 BOW Example Using TF
Document 1: "This book is a follow-on to the 2019 SIOP LEC."
Document 2: "The topic of the 2019 SIOP LEC was Advancing the Edge: Assessment for the 2020s."

|    | book | siop | lec | assessment | follow | 2019 | edge | topic | advance | 2020 |
|----|------|------|-----|------------|--------|------|------|-------|---------|------|
| D1 | 1    | 1    | 1   | 0          | 1      | 1    | 0    | 0     | 0       | 0    |
| D2 | 0    | 1    | 1   | 1          | 0      | 1    | 1    | 1     | 1       | 1    |

inverse of the number of documents in the corpus that contain the term), to adjust for the fact that some terms appear more frequently in general.

After representing the text using BOW, dimension reduction is sometimes needed to transform the data from a high-dimensional space into a low-dimensional space to avoid the "curse of dimensionality" (i.e., the exponential difficulty experienced when designing algorithms and estimating parameters with data that has many features). Common dimension reduction techniques include feature selection and feature extraction (e.g., principal component analysis). After the data are reduced to a reasonable number of features, we can then build a feature-based ML model based on whether the criterion is a continuous variable (regression model) or a dichotomous variable (classification model). For instance, we can train a ridge regression (a multiple regression model suitable for handling highly correlated independent variables) to predict subject matter expert (SME)-rated KSAO ratings from interview responses, or a logistic regression model (a model that uses a logistic function to model the probability of a binary dependent variable) to predict turnover from CRA responses. Table 5.2 lists some of the commonly used, traditional ML models for NLP tasks.

In addition to predicting job-related outcomes, ML models can also be used to match jobs with candidates based on their assessment responses. Using a collaborative filtering system (i.e., a recommender system technique that makes interest predictions based on similarities between individuals), organizations with a large number of candidates and jobs can better recommend or route candidates to jobs that best fit their KSAOs and preferences.

## Analyzing Text: Neural Natural Language Processing Approaches

Since the 2010s, neural models have been increasingly used to solve NLP problems. Nowadays, it is rare to see computer scientists using non-neural techniques for NLP tasks, given the overwhelming advantage of neural methods across NLP benchmarks (see GLUE, 2021; SuperGLUE, 2021). Adoption of neural methods in the field of assessment has been lagging, especially in the published literature, due to the natural process of knowledge dissemination (from computer science to IO/OB), the learning curve associated with complex neural modeling, and the demand for computing resources.

Table 5.2 Descriptions of Common Feature-Based ML Models

|  | Description | Classification or Regression |
| --- | --- | --- |
| Linear Regression | Models a linear relationship between a continuous dependent variable and one or more independent variable(s) | Regression |
| Logistic Regression | Models the probability of a binary dependent variable using a logistic function | Classification |
| Ridge Regression | A multiple regression model with a penalty term equal to the squared magnitude of the coefficients to help shrink the coefficients and reduce model complexity and multicollinearity | Regression |
| K-Nearest Neighbors (K-NN) | A nonparametric pattern recognition method that makes predictions based on $k$ closest data points | Both |
| Decision Trees | A tree-like model that explicitly represents decision points going from observations to target values | Both |
| Random Forest | An ensemble learning method that combines a multitude of decision trees in parallel | Both |
| Support Vector Machine (SVM) | A nonprobabilistic model that constructs a hyperplane or set of hyperplanes in a high- or infinite-dimensional space to distinctly classify the data points | Both |
| Gradient Boosted Trees | An ensemble model that combines decision trees sequentially such that each tree addresses errors from the previous tree | Both |

That being said, we are starting to see organizational researchers use neural NLP approaches to solve workplace problems, such as using BERT to analyze public sentiment during COVID-19 (e.g., Min et al., 2021).

In a neural approach, BERT-like models can help represent text via word embeddings (i.e., text representations that capture the meaning of words) and perform downstream prediction tasks on KSAOs and job-related outcomes. Specifically, an assessment researcher can take a pretrained BERT model and fine-tune it on the task-specific dataset at hand (e.g., using interview responses to estimate customer orientation for a sales job). Because these models have been pretrained on a large corpus to gain a good understanding of word meaning and context, we can generally expect more accurate predictions from these approaches compared to the traditional, non-neural approaches relying on limited, task-specific data.

## Considerations and Future Directions

There are important considerations when applying NLP methods in an assessment context. First, NLP-based assessments need to be grounded in theory and job-relatedness (Tippins et al., 2021). Following a job analysis, assessment developers should consider the theoretical basis of the assessment stimuli and the elicited predictors, as well as how they relate to the KSAOs required for the job. Relatedly NLP models can be built to first predict KSAOs, where the predicted KSAO scores (output from the NLP model) are then used to predict job-related outcomes (direct correlation or via another model). Alternatively, NLP models can be designed to predict the job-related outcomes directly. The former approach brings more construct validity and explainability into the NLP system, whereas the latter approach is more likely to yield larger validity against job-related outcomes. If predicting KSAOs is the chosen approach, it is critical to obtain reliable, accurate, and unbiased KSAO scores (e.g., by training SMEs to rate the open-ended responses on target KSAOs) to help promote model accuracy and prevent model biases.

Second, rather than relying on a single NLP model, it is often beneficial to try several different methods that are suitable to the research question and data, evaluate their prediction accuracy, and select one that helps achieve the most optimal results. Ensemble methods that combine several models to make predictions can also be used as a way to overcome idiosyncratic variance and bias in individual models and to improve overall prediction accuracy.

Third, although neural NLP methods have shown superior results in common NLP tasks, there is no guarantee that more advanced and complex models will always give you better results for your assessment problem; it depends on the nature of the assessment, the prediction task, and the data. Therefore, it is recommended that you select the appropriate models based on the specific scenario. Meanwhile, more research is needed to compare the non-neural and neural NLP approaches in the assessment context to determine whether added model complexity translates to gains in model performance. Assessment practitioners also need to balance the tradeoff between maximizing prediction with other considerations, such as model explainability and resource constraints.

What will the future hold? It is almost certain that NLP techniques will continue to evolve, leading to methods that can further grasp the meaning of language and improve prediction accuracy across domains. As NLP models rapidly become more complex and diverse, we will also see multidisciplinary collaboration become the standard approach for designing and evaluating assessments using NLP, where knowledge and expertise are integrated across IO psychology, ML, NLP, and data science. Also, as we accumulate more sources of people data on the internet, organizations might start to extract online information (e.g., from LinkedIn) for job-relevant signals to assess candidates on their suitability for different jobs. Further, pretrained language models such as GPT series have shown promising results in natural language generation. In the next few years, we could see assessments that can interact with candidates and provide live feedback, taking assessment engagement to a whole new level.

## Challenges and Opportunities

NLP brings enormous excitement to the field of assessment. At the same time, assessment researchers and practitioners also face challenges when applying NLP to solve assessment problems. I discuss three main challenges (and opportunities) below, namely interpretability, resources, and legal and ethical considerations.

First, complex NLP systems are often seen as "black boxes" with limited interpretability. Users of NLP systems, and sometimes even the researchers themselves, have limited understanding on how and why the computer makes the decisions it does. NLP interpretability is important to assessment because it will help advance scientific understanding, detect and mitigate biases, facilitate stakeholder (e.g., candidates, recruiters) trust and adoption, and fulfill legal and regulatory requirements. A strength of IO-based approaches is the consideration of theory and job relatedness when designing selection tools. In NLP-based assessments, being able to demonstrate how the assessment stimuli and/or predictors relate to job-relevant KSAOs (e.g., speaking faster in an interview might indicate higher emotional stability; Feiler & Powell, 2016) is a key way of ensuring interpretability, even before any models are built. In the last few years, progress has been made in the computer science community toward explainable AI (Hoover et al., 2019; Nori et al., 2019; Rogers et al., 2020), where research and open-sourced tools are becoming available to provide both global interpretability (i.e., how a model makes its predictions in general) and local interpretability (i.e., how a specific prediction on a data point is derived) after a model has been trained. We as a field have an opportunity to develop consensus and provide guidance on the level of interpretability and the types of interpretability evidence required of NLP systems used for assessment.

The second challenge we face is a substantial increase in resource demand, namely data and machines. While most of the NLP models are open-sourced, large volumes of high-quality, labeled data are becoming key differentiators in producing meaningful and generalizable predictions. Organizations also need to invest in building robust data infrastructure and pipelines to support the proper storage and use of big data for NLP applications. Another key differentiator is computing power. The state-of-the-art language models have millions or billions of parameters, requiring advanced GPUs or tensor processing units (TPUs; Google Cloud, 2021) to just fine-tune on a data set. As this trend continues, NLP-based assessment research and practice will start to concentrate within companies and institutions with sufficient computing resources. To bridge this gap, we as a field should encourage industry-university collaboration, where organizations with data and computing resources can partner with researchers who have the scientific expertise and capacity to conduct NLP-based assessment research.

Third, we face uncertainty and challenges regarding legal and ethical considerations for using NLP in an assessment context. At a high level, we all know that assessments should have a conceptual and methodological basis, show evidence of validity, and lack systematic bias. But there is little guidance on what additional or different evidence we need when NLP is added to the mix. We have also started to see regulations requiring applicant consent and information sharing for algorithm-based assessments. For instance, the state of Illinois implemented the Artificial Intelligence Video Interview Act (2020), which requires informed consent, with explanations on how the algorithm works, when AI is used for analyzing video interviews. As companies continue to adopt ML and NLP into their assessment practices, we expect to see more regulations requiring consent and transparency. There is an opportunity for IO psychologists to influence lawmakers and regulators regarding what reliability, validity, and fairness evidence is required of NLP-based assessments.

## Conclusion

NLP advancements are far outpacing Moore's law and bring numerous opportunities to assessment. As a field, IO psychologists need to establish a basic understanding of the science behind NLP through education and translation of the relevant research and develop guidelines and best practices on how to apply NLP effectively and ethically to assessment. Better NLP-based assessment applications require IO psychologists to work with computer scientists, software engineers, and legal and compliance experts to further advance the research and practice.

## References

Alvi, A., & Kharya, P. (2021, October 11). *Using DeepSpeed and Megatron to train Megatron-Turing NLG 530B, the world's largest and most powerful generative language model.* https://www.microsoft.com/en-us/research/blog/using-deepspeed-and-megatron-to-train-megatron-turing-nlg-530b-the-worlds-largest-and-most-powerful-generative-language-model/

Anastasopoulos, A., & Chiang, D. (2018). Tied multitask learning for neural speech translation. *Proceedings of the 2018 Conference of the North American Chapter of the Association for Computational Linguistics: Human Language Technologies, 1*, 82–91. https://aclanthology.org/N18-1008

Artificial Intelligence Video Interview Act, 820 ILCS 42. (2020). https://www.ilga.gov/legislation/ilcs/ilcs3.asp?ActID=4015&ChapterID=68

Banks, G. C., Woznyj, H. M., Wesslen, R. S., & Ross, R. L. (2018). A review of best practice recommendations for text analysis in R (and a user-friendly app). *Journal of Business and Psychology, 33*(4), 445–459. https://doi.org/10.1007/s10869-017-9528-3

Benzeghiba, M., De Mori, R., Deroo, O., Dupont, S., Erbes, T., Jouvet, D., Fissore, P., Laface, A., Mertins, C., Ris, R., Tyagi, V., & Wellekens, C. (2007). Automatic speech recognition and speech variability: A review. *Speech Communication, 49*(10–11), 763–786. https://doi.org/10.1016/j.specom.2007.02.006

Bormuth, J. (1970). *On the theory of achievement test items.* University of Chicago Press.

Brown, T. B., Mann, B., Ryder, N., Subbiah, M., Kaplan, J., Dhariwal, P., Neelakantan, A., Shyam, P., Sastry, G., Askell, A., Agarwal, S., Herbert-Voss, A., Krueger, G., Henighan T., Child, R., Ramesh, A., Ziegler, D. M., Wu, J., Winter, C., . . . Amodei, D. (2020). Language models are few-shot learners. *Proceedings of Advances in Neural Information Processing Systems, 33*, 1877–1901. https://arxiv.org/pdf/2005.14165

Campion, M. C., Campion, M. A., Campion, E. D., & Reider, M. H. (2016). Initial investigation into computer scoring of candidate essays for personnel selection. *Journal of Applied Psychology, 101*(7), 958–975. https://doi.org/10.1037/apl0000108

Chen, L., Feng, G., Leong, C. W., Lehman, B., Martin-Raugh, M., Kell, H., Lee, C. M., & Yoon, S. Y. (2016). Automated scoring of interview videos using Doc2Vec multimodal feature extraction paradigm. *Proceedings of the 18th ACM International Conference on Multimodal Interaction*, 161–168. https://doi.org/10.1145/2993148.2993203

Clark, K., Luong, M. T., Le, Q. V., & Manning, C. D. (2020). ELECTRA: Pre-training text encoders as discriminators rather than generators. *Proceedings of the 8th International Conference on Learning Representations.* https://dblp.org/rec/conf/iclr/ClarkLLM20

Danko, Z. (2015). *Neon prescription . . . or rather, new transcription for Google Voice.* https://blog.google/products/google-voice/neon-prescription-or-rather-new/

Devlin, J., Chang, M., Lee, K., & Toutanova, K. (2019). BERT: Pre-training of deep bidirectional transformers for language understanding. *Proceedings of the 2019 Conference of the North American Chapter of the Association for Computational Linguistics: Human Language Technologies, 1,* 4171–4186. https://aclanthology.org/N19-1423

Feiler, A. R., & Powell, D. M. (2016). Behavioral expression of job interview anxiety. *Journal of Business and Psychology, 31*(1), 155–171. https://doi.org/10.1007/s10869-015-9403-z

Gierl, M. J., & Haladyna, T. M. (Eds.). (2012). *Automatic item generation: Theory and practice.* Routledge.

Gierl, M. J., Lai, H., & Tanygin, V. (2021). *Advanced methods in automatic item generation.* Routledge.

GLUE. (2021, October 10). https://gluebenchmark.com/

Goldberg, L. R. (1999). A broad-bandwidth, public domain, personality inventory measuring the lower-level facets of several five-factor models. *Personality Psychology in Europe, 7*(1), 7–28.

Goldberg, L. R., Johnson, J. A., Eber, H. W., Hogan, R., Ashton, M. C., Cloninger, C. R., & Gough, H. G. (2006). The international personality item pool and the future of public-domain personality measures. *Journal of Research in Personality, 40*(1), 84–96. https://doi.org/10.1016/j.jrp.2005.08.007

Google Cloud. (2021). *Cloud tensor processing units (TPUs).* https://cloud.google.com/tpu/docs/tpus

He, P., Liu, X., Gao, J., & Chen, W. (2021). *DeBERTa: Decoding-enhanced BERT with disentangled attention.* https://arxiv.org/pdf/2006.03654

Hickman, L., Bosch, N., Ng, V., Saef, R., Tay, L., & Woo, S. E. (2022). Automated video interview personality assessments: Reliability, validity, and generalizability investigations. *Journal of Applied Psychology, 107*(8), 1323–1351. https://doi.org/10.1037/apl0000695

Hickman, L., Saef, R., Ng, V., Woo, S. E., Tay, L., & Bosch, N. (2021). Developing and evaluating language-based machine learning algorithms for inferring applicant personality in video interviews. *Human Resource Management Journal.* Advance online publication. https://doi.org/10.1111/1748-8583.12356

Hochreiter, S., & Schmidhuber, J. (1997). Long short-term memory. *Neural Computation, 9*(8), 1735–1780. https://doi.org/10.1162/neco.1997.9.8.1735

Hommel, B. E., Wollang, F. J., Kotova, V., Zacher, H., & Schmukle, S. C. (2022). Transformer-based deep neural language modeling for construct-specific automatic item generation. *Psychometrika, 87,* 749–772. https://doi.org/10.1007/s11336-021-09823-9

Hoover, B., Strobelt, H., & Gehrmann, S. (2019). exBERT: A visual analysis tool to explore learned representations in transformers models. *Proceedings of the 58th Annual Meeting of the Association for Computational Linguistics,* 187–196. https://dblp.org/rec/journals/corr/abs-1910-05276

Huang, X. (2017). *Microsoft researchers achieve new conversational speech recognition milestone.* https://www.microsoft.com/en-us/research/blog/microsoft-researchers-achieve-new-conversational-speech-recognition-milestone/

IBM. (1954). *701 translator.* https://www.ibm.com/ibm/history/exhibits/701/701_translator.html

Jozefowicz, R., Zaremba, W., & Sutskever, I. (2015). An empirical exploration of recurrent network architectures. *Proceedings of the 32nd International Conference on International Conference on Machine Learning, 37,* 2342–2350. https://proceedings.mlr.press/v37/jozefowicz15.html

Kobayashi, V. B., Mol, S. T., Berkers, H. A., Kismihok, G., & Den Hartog, D. N. (2018a). Text classification for organizational researchers: A tutorial. *Organizational Research Methods, 21*(3), 766–799. https://doi.org/10.1177/1094428117719322

Kobayashi, V. B., Mol, S. T., Berkers, H. A., Kismihók, G., & Den Hartog, D. N. (2018b). Text mining in organizational research. *Organizational Research Methods, 21*(3), 733–765. https://doi.org/10.1177/1094428117722619

LeCun, Y., Bengio, Y., & Hinton, G. (2015). Deep learning. *Nature, 521,* 436–444. https://doi.org/10.1038/nature14539

Linn, A. (2018). *Microsoft reaches a historic milestone, using AI to match human performance in translating news from Chinese to English.* https://blogs.microsoft.com/ai/chinese-to-english-translator-milestone/

Liu, T., Fang, Q., Ding, W., & Liu, Z. (2021). Mathematical word problem generation from commonsense knowledge graph and equations. *Proceedings of the 2021 Conference on Empirical Methods in Natural Language Processing,* 4225–4240. https://aclanthology.org/2021.emnlp-main.348

Liu, Y., Ott, M., Goyal, N., Du, J., Joshi, M., Chen, D., Levy, O., Lewis, M., Zettlemoyer, L., & Stoyanov, V. (2019). RoBERTa: A robustly optimized BERT pretraining approach. *Proceedings of the 20th Chinese National Conference on Computational Linguistics,* 1218–1227. https://aclanthology.org/2021.ccl-1.108

Manning, C. D., & Schütze, H. (1999). *Foundations of statistical natural language processing.* MIT Press.

Microsoft. (2021, November 3). *Evaluate and improve Custom Speech accuracy.* https://docs.microsoft.com/en-us/azure/cognitive-services/speech-service/how-to-custom-speech-evaluate-data

Min, H., Peng, Y., Shoss, M., & Yang, B. (2021). Using machine learning to investigate the public's emotional responses to work from home during the COVID-19 pandemic. *Journal of Applied Psychology, 106*(2), 214–229. https://doi.org/10.1037/apl0000886

Mitchell, T. M. (1997). *Machine learning.* McGraw Hill.

Nori, H., Jenkins, S., Koch, P., & Caruana, R. (2019). *InterpretML: A unified framework for machine learning interpretability.* https://arxiv.org/abs/1909.09223

OpenAI. (2023). GPT-4 technical report. https://doi.org/10.48550/arXiv.2303.08774

Putka, D. J., Beatty, A. S., & Reeder, M. C. (2018). Modern prediction methods: New perspectives on a common problem. *Organizational Research Methods, 21*(3), 689–732. https://doi.org/10.1177/1094428117697041

Radford, A., Narasimhan, K., Salimans, T., & Sutskever, I. (2018). *Improving language understanding by generative pre-training.* https://www.cs.ubc.ca/~amuham01/LING530/papers/radford2018improving.pdf

Radford, A., Wu, J., Child, R., Luan, D., Amodei, D., & Sutskever, I. (2019). *Language models are unsupervised multitask learners.* http://www.persagen.com/files/misc/radford2019language.pdf

Raffel, C., Shazeer, N., Roberts, A., Lee, K., Narang, S., Matena, M., Zhou, Y., Li, W., & Liu, P. J. (2020). Exploring the limits of transfer learning with a unified text-to-text transformer. *Journal of Machine Learning Research, 21,* 1–67. https://arxiv.org/pdf/1910.10683

Reiter, E., & Dale, R. (1997). Building natural-language generation systems. *Natural Language Engineering, 3*(1), 57–87. https://doi.org/10.1017/S1351324997001502

Rogers, A., Kovaleva, O., & Rumshisky, A. (2020). A primer in BERTology: What we know about how BERT works. *Transactions of the Association for Computational Linguistics, 8,* 842–866. https://aclanthology.org/2020.tacl-1.54

Rumelhart, D. E., Hinton, G. E., & Williams, R. J. (1986). Learning representations by back-propagating errors. *Nature, 323,* 533–536. https://doi.org/10.1038/323533a0

Sajjadiani, S., Sojourner, A. J., Kammeyer-Mueller, J. D., & Mykerezi, E. (2019). Using machine learning to translate applicant work history into predictors of performance and turnover. *Journal of Applied Psychology, 104*(10), 1207–1225. https://doi.org/10.1037/apl0000405

Salton, G., & Buckley, C. (1988). Weighting approaches in automatic text retrieval. *Information Processing and Management, 24*(5), 513–523. https://doi.org/10.1016/0306-4573(88)90021-0

Spärck Jones, K. (1972). A statistical interpretation of term specificity and its application in retrieval. *Journal of Documentation, 28*(1), 11–21. https://doi.org/10.1108/eb026526

Su, Y., Meng, Z., Baker, S., & Collier, N. (2021). Few-shot table-to-text generation with prototype memory. *Findings of the Association for Computational Linguistics: EMNLP 2021, 77* (pp. 910–917). https://aclanthology.org/2021.findings-emnlp.77

SuperGLUE. (2021, October 10). https://super.gluebenchmark.com/

Tippins, N. T., Oswald, F. L., & McPhail, S. M. (2021). Scientific, legal, and ethical concerns about AI-based personnel selection tools: A call to action. *Personnel Assessment and Decisions, 7*(2), 1–22. https://doi.org/10.25035/pad.2021.02.001

von Davier, M. (2018). Automated item generation with recurrent neural networks. *Pychometrika, 83,* 847–857. https://doi.org/10.1007/s11336-018-9608-y

Wang, A., Pruksachatkun, Y., Nangia, N., Singh, A., Michael, J., Hill, F., Levy, O., & Bowman, S. R. (2019). SuperGLUE: A stickier benchmark for general-purpose language understanding systems. *Proceedings of the 32nd International Conference on Neural Information Processing Systems,* 3266–3280. https://arxiv.org/pdf/1905.00537

Wang, A., Singh, A., Michael, J., Hill, F., Levy, O., & Bowman, S. R. (2018). GLUE: A multitask benchmark and analysis platform for natural language understanding. *Proceedings of the 2018 Conference on Empirical Methods in Natural Language Processing Workshop BlackboxNLP: Analyzing and Interpreting Neural Networks for NLP,* 353–355. https://aclanthology.org/W18-5446

Wu, Y., Schuster, M., Chen, Z., Le, Q. V., Norouzi, M., Macherey, W., Krikun, M., Cao, Y., Gao, Q., Macherey, K., Kingner, J., Shah, A., Johnson, M., Liu, X., Kaiser, L., Gouws, S., Kato, Y., Kudo, T., Kazawa, H., . . . Dean, J. (2016). *Google's neural machine translation system: Bridging the gap between human and machine translation.* https://arxiv.org/pdf/1609.08144

Xiong, H., Zhu, H., & Xu, T. (2018). TMC 2018: 2018 International Workshop on Organizational Behavior and Talent Analytics. *Proceedings of the 24th ACM SIGKDD Conference on Knowledge Discovery & Data Mining.* http://bigdata.ustc.edu.cn/OBTA2018/

Xiong, H., Zhu, H., & Xu, T. (2019). TMC 2019: 2019 International Workshop on Talent and Management Computing. *Proceedings of the 25th ACM SIGKDD Conference on Knowledge Discovery & Data Mining.* http://bigdata.ustc.edu.cn/TMC2019/

Xiong, H., Zhu, H., Xu, T., Liu, J., Xue, Y., Rabenold, P., Henao, R., Xu, H., Ellis, J., & Zhang, K. (2020). TMC 2020: 2020 International Workshop on Talent and Management Computing. *Proceedings of the 26th ACM SIGKDD Conference on Knowledge Discovery & Data Mining*. http://bigdata.ustc.edu.cn/TMC2020/

Xiong, H., Zhu, H., Xu, T., & Zhang, X. (2021). TMC 2021: 2021 International Workshop on Talent and Management Computing. In *Proceedings of the 27th ACM SIGKDD Conference on Knowledge Discovery & Data Mining*. http://mine.ustc.edu.cn/TMC2021/

Yu, D., & Deng, L. (Eds.). (2016). *Automatic speech recognition*. Springer.

Zhang, A., Wu, K., Wang, L., Li, Z., Xiao, X., Wu, H., Zhang, M., & Wang, H. (2021). Data augmentation with hierarchical SQL-to-question generation for cross-domain text-to-SQL parsing. *Proceedings of the 2021 Conference on Empirical Methods in Natural Language Processing*, 8974–8983. https://aclanthology.org/2021.emnlp-main.707

# 6

# Personality Assessment

## Past, Present, and Future

*Ryne A. Sherman and Robert Hogan*

People feel, think, and act in different ways—they behave in unique ways even in the same circumstances. Social interaction crucially impacts our lives, and detecting patterns in the behavior of others to predict how they will act is quite useful. The observable patterns in others' behavior are commonly referred to as their personalities. If we know how others tend to think, act, or feel, we can predict how they might respond to our actions or to new situations. In everyday life, the judgments we make about others are practically useful.

But getting to know others can take a long time. During World War I the U.S. Army faced a practical problem. They needed to predict how new recruits would respond to the brutality of industrialized warfare. In particular, the Army wanted to identify soldiers who were at risk for "shell shock." Clinical interviews with recruits took too long. To make the evaluation process more efficient, Robert Woodworth created the Woodworth Personal Data Sheet; it contained 116 yes/no questions validated against diagnosed cases, to be used to identify persons who were poorly suited for combat. Although the test was developed too late to screen Army recruits, it was a milestone for personality psychology: it was the first self-report personality inventory (see Gibby & Zickar, 2008, for a detailed review) that solved a practical problem more accurately and more efficiently than human judgment.

Since then, thousands of self-report personality tests have been developed. Some widely used tests (e.g., the Minnesota Multiphasic Personality Inventory and the California Psychological Inventory) were developed using Woodworth's methodology: Identify a set of items that discriminate between two criterion groups, and then use those items to predict criterion group membership—or subsequent performance. But not all personality tests were designed for practical use. Based on trait theory (Allport, 1938)—which

Ryne A. Sherman and Robert Hogan, *Personality Assessment* In: *Talent Assessment*. Edited by: Tracy M. Kantrowitz, Douglas H. Reynolds, and John C. Scott, Oxford University Press. © Society of Industrial Organizational Psychology 2023.
DOI: 10.1093/oso/9780197611050.003.0006

argues that individual differences in behavior should be explained in terms of traits that exist somewhere inside actors—many personality inventories were developed to measure traits for their own sake, and for which predicting performance was an afterthought. This is a critical and often overlooked distinction concerning two very different uses for personality tests: (a) measuring traits or (b) predicting outcomes.

It is also useful to note a distinction concerning the meaning of "self-report" statements. Consider the item "I read at least 10 books per year." Answers to this item can be interpreted in two very different ways. On the one hand, trait theory takes the statement at face value—the item means what it says and people who endorse the item read a lot, because they have a trait for reading. In contrast, we interpret the item empirically by determining what it predicts (in terms of either career performance or the person's reputation). It turns out that people who endorse the item tend to be seen as smart and well informed—which is the message they are trying to send by endorsing the item. This distinction has important consequences for providing people feedback on their assessment results. Trait theory feedback tells people what they have said about themselves; our feedback tells people what others say about them. This distinction is important for the rest of our discussion.

Trait theory conflates the thing assumed to cause an action with the action itself. For example, trait theory leads to the conclusion that "Mike Tyson is aggressive because he has the trait for aggression" or "Volcanos erupt because they have the trait of eruptiveness." In addition, trait theory assumes that people have "true" selves (reflected in their traits), and true selves make faking (responding in ways that are inconsistent with one's true self) a major problem for personality assessment. We distinguish between what people do and why they do it (in more formal terms, we distinguish between prediction and explanation); we focus on behavior and ignore the causes of that behavior. More precisely, we focus on the consequences of people's behavior—their reputations—and ignore questions about authentic selves and other inner processes (as recommended by Occam's razor). We have outlined our concerns about trait theory elsewhere, so we shall not repeat them here (see Bredo, 2006; R. Hogan, 2005; R. Hogan & Sherman, 2020; Wittgenstein, 1958). But we would like to make two points. First, alternative (but less popular) theories of personality exist that are free from the logical incoherence of trait theory (e.g., R. Hogan, 1983; Wood et al., 2015). Second, despite its tautological nature, trait theory remains the theory most widely endorsed by modern personality psychologists and textbook authors. This is where problems with modern assessments begin.

## Trait Theory Meets Modern Technology

The term "machine learning" was coined by Arthur Samuel. An electrical engineer by training, Samuel originally worked on vacuum tubes and radar developments at Bell Labs. Later he moved to IBM and, using what is known as alpha-beta pruning with a minimax algorithm, he built a computer program to play checkers that could beat most amateurs. When this program was released, IBM's stock went up 15 points overnight.

Drawing on Samuel's work, further advances in so-called artificial intelligence (AI) followed. For example, Deep Mind's Alpha Zero won the top computer chess championship in 2016 with a record of 26 wins, 0 losses, and 74 draws. At the grandmaster level, such a record would be considered a complete demolishing of one's opponent. Deep Mind's Alpha Go crushed all human competitors at the ancient Chinese game Go. Beyond games, these developments in computing technology and AI inspired applications to many other arenas, including personality assessment.

In one of the first papers in this arena, Sumner and colleagues (2012) demonstrated that they could predict scores on a measure of dark triad personality traits using linguistic analyses of users' tweets on the social media application Twitter. A few years later, researchers demonstrated that a computer-based personality judgment algorithm—relying only on Facebook data—could predict gender, sexual orientation, substance use, parental separation, age, and even self-reported personality test scores (Kosinski et al., 2013). This last finding was extended to show that the computer algorithm could predict self-reported personality scores better than ratings by friends and family (Youyou et al., 2015). Further research has shown that static images of a person's face can predict, among other things, sexual orientation (Kosinski & Wang, 2018) and self-reported personality traits (Kachur et al., 2020).

These findings captured a huge amount of media attention, and, indeed, the notion that a computer could know you better than your friends or family sounds like big news. Even further, this research led to an explosion of commercial ventures aimed at automating personality assessment. For example, HireVue began using facial scans during recorded interviews to make hiring recommendations (Harwell, 2019), a practice they have since stopped (Maurer, 2021). Nonetheless, other companies (e.g., Phenometrix.ai) continue to offer personality assessment based on facial scans. Still others offer personality assessment based on social media usage or your LinkedIn profile pages. One (now defunct) company even offered to help people find the perfect babysitter by scanning potential sitters' Facebook, Twitter, and Instagram history (Merchant, 2018).

Whether scanning social media or faces, there are two big ideas behind these automated assessment techniques. The first is to make personality assessment more efficient. Because the scans work automatically, requiring only a link to a person's social media profile or an image, they operate as quickly as computer processors, or an internet connection, will let them go. An entire assessment can be done in fractions of a second. Such speed makes Woodworth's questionnaire look like a trivial improvement over interviews. The second idea behind these techniques is that they are less susceptible to faking. The logic here is that a person's face is hard to manipulate, and that a person's social media profile is a more authentic self—something that cannot be easily faked in order to create a job-specific impression. To summarize, AI promises to make personality assessment faster and more accurate. In the next section, we examine the degree to which AI has, and can, deliver on this promise.

## The Reality of Artificial Intelligence

The popular media often portrays automated personality assessment—processes such as those previously described—as rather scary, with authoritarian robot overlord themes. And it does seem a bit creepy to think that computers can know us better than our friends. However, media portrayals of research findings notoriously oversell reality, and that is the case here. Collectively, automated personality assessment research using social media and facial scans as inputs, and machine learning as the analytic tool, demonstrate that the things you do on social media are related to the things you say about yourself (the items you endorse) on personality tests. This is not to question the value of such findings, but simply to be clear about the facts. The way you talk about yourself on social media, or in a selfie, should reflect the way you talk about yourself on a personality assessment—because the underlying dynamics are the same.

It is important to be clear about the psychological dynamics of responding to items on a questionnaire (or in an interview). According to trait theory, self-reports—the things you say about yourself on a personality test (or in an interview)—reflect your authentic inner self; therefore, it seems a bit freaky that a computer would know these things about you. On the other hand, if we assume that the things you say about yourself on a personality test are self-presentations (statements about how you would like to be regarded by others), then finding that computer algorithms can predict them seems far less scary. In our view, "Liking" something on Facebook is the same as endorsing an item on a personality test. If one person Likes Starbucks and another person Likes Metallica, that reveals something about how they see the world—and how they would like the world to see them—which itself might predict outcomes of interest.

What outcomes of interest do social media endorsements predict? Unfortunately, we do not know. Virtually all the research so far has used social media data and facial scans to predict self-reported test results, which is as tautological as trait theory itself. No research (as far as we know) has asked whether these automated assessments predict practical outcomes. The research has focused on predicting predictors, not on predicting outcomes. From the perspective of trait theory these studies make sense; the various endorsements purport to capture inner traits. But from the perspective of theories focused on predicting important career outcomes, these studies do not offer much. As noted above, and at the risk of belaboring the point, there are two ways to interpret item responses. In our view, item responses are self-presentations whose meaning is determined by what they predict. For trait theory, item responses are caused by in-dwelling traits, they can be taken at face value, and they reflect a person's "true" self. We should note in this regard that trait theory is a serious violation of Occam's razor; it makes unverifiable claims about inner realities.

One of the best studies using automated assessments of social media (Youyou et al., 2015) concerned the degree to which people's Facebook "likes" predicted how their peers described them (i.e., their reputation), an important component of career success (i.e., other people's views of you are important). A key result from that study, shown in their supplemental Table 2, has been repurposed here in Table 6.1. As can be seen, the correspondence between self-reports and computer ratings of personality is quite high (average $r = .43$). This is to be expected because the self-reports and the

Table 6.1 Correlations Between Self-Reports, Peer Reports, and Computer Judgments From Youyou et al. (2015)

| Pair | O | C | E | A | N | r̄ |
|---|---|---|---|---|---|---|
| Bivariate | | | | | | |
|   Self-Computer | .51 | .42 | .45 | .38 | .40 | .43 |
|   Self-Peer | .30 | .26 | .37 | .29 | .29 | .30 |
|   Computer-Peer | .22 | .17 | .20 | .14 | .19 | .18 |
| Partial (controlling for third rater) | | | | | | |
|   Self-Computer | .48 | .40 | .42 | .36 | .36 | .40 |
|   Self-Peer | .22 | .21 | .32 | .26 | .24 | .25 |
|   Computer-Peer | .08 | .07 | .04$^{NS}$ | .03$^{NS}$ | .08 | .06 |

$N = 1,919$. $p < .001$ for all correlations except those indicated NS.
Adapted from Youyou et al. (2016) with permission.

computer inputs come from the same source (self-ratings) and (in our view) reflect self-presentational styles. The correspondence between self-reports and peer reports is also sizable (average $r = .30$), and consistent with the broader literature on self-other agreement (i.e., to what degree do we see ourselves as others see us?). In contrast, the correspondence between computer ratings and peer reports is significantly lower (average $r = .18$), and very low once information from self-reports is removed (average partial $r = .06$). This suggests that although computer judgments of a person's personality may correspond with that person's self-judgment, the correspondence with reputation is low. Combined with the fact that reputation ratings are the best predictors of applied outcomes (Connelly & Hülsheger, 2011; Connelly et al., 2021; Connelly & Ones, 2010; Oh et al., 2011), it is difficult to see how automated ratings of social media scans predict much in the way of consequential outcomes. Thus, the reality of AI for personality assessment falls far short of its perceived promise.

## The Ugly Reality of Artificial Intelligence

That AI applications of personality assessment have poor predictive validity is not the end of the bad news. Many commercially available AI-based assessments provide little to no evidence for their predictive validity, but they are largely harmless (i.e., like coin flips, they are fair even though they lack validity). However, there is a reality to AI-based assessments that can be harmful. For example, in 2018 Amazon dumped an AI-based recruiting tool that was biased against women (Dastin, 2018). More recently, investigative reporters have evaluated AI interview platforms that score candidates based on their facial expressions, voice prosody, and other features during a virtual (e.g., phone-recorded) interview. Among other things, these reports found candidates would receive high scores for English proficiency even though they were speaking in German (Wall & Schellmann, 2021) and that candidates' scores change depending on whether or not they are wearing eyeglasses, and other minor cosmetic features (e.g., lighting, head scarf; see Harlan & Schnuck, 2021).

Although it is tempting to blame the algorithms for these outcomes, the algorithms are typically trained to mimic human judgments; and we know that these judgments are biased (Gigerenzer, 2008; Kahneman, 2011; Kenrick & Griskevicius, 2013). Algorithms, such as those resulting from machine learning, are conceptually simple to understand. They try to match inputs to a set of outputs. And they are good at it. In fact, algorithms are so good at it that they will amplify small, previously unknown, and possibly undesired relationships. If an input has a biased relationship with an output, an algorithm will exploit this relationship to improve its "accuracy" (even though the outputs are biased). In a selection context, consider the practice of automatic resume screening wherein a computer reads the information on a resume and uses it to predict performance ratings in some job. If, for example, the job performance ratings are biased against minority candidates (e.g., White managers unfairly rate Black workers as performing worse) and there is information on the resume that might indicate the minority candidate's status (e.g., graduation from a historically Black university, name, etc.), algorithms designed to predict performance will learn these biased associations and replicate them in full force.[1] The problem here is not the algorithm, but the (undesired) association between the inputs (resume information), the outputs (job performance ratings), and minority status. It is worth noting that well-validated personality inventories do not have this problem because the inputs (personality test scores) are unrelated to minority status but still related to the outputs (job performance).

---

[1] The website www.survivalofthebestfit.com demonstrates this nicely.

## Beating the Machines

One purported advantage of AI-based personality assessments is the ability to reduce faking. Although a great deal of research has been done on faking, much of it using student samples, research in real-world employment settings shows that faking does not seriously impact the validity of assessments (J. Hogan et al., 2007). Moreover, we believe the topic of faking is conceptually nonsensical. For example, the existence of faking depends on assuming that authentic responses reflect the respondent's true inner reality; faked responses are inconsistent with (the unknowable) inner reality—and how can we ever know if they are inconsistent? In addition, consider that, during a job interview, reasonable candidates will try to present themselves favorably. No one questions the validity of job interviews on the grounds that candidates "fake."[2] Responding to items on a personality inventory is formally identical to responding to interview questions: Rational candidates try to portray themselves in a positive light. The problem for candidates is that they have no idea what the correct response to an item like "I read 10 books a year" might be—and the answer is, the correct response depends on the job. Nonetheless, when scales are properly aligned to performance criteria, properly validated personality assessments significantly predict job performance (Barrick & Mount, 1991; Hogan & Holland, 2003). But, for the sake of the argument, let us assume that faking is a problem. Do automated, AI-based personality assessments solve it? We believe the answer is no.

As mentioned previously, one company attempted to assess the personalities of potential babysitters using data from their social media accounts (i.e., Twitter, Instagram, Facebook). The available evidence suggests that this approach should generate scores that correlate ($r \approx .40$) with self-reports, provided that potential babysitters submit their real social media accounts for analysis. However, in practice, especially when the stakes are high, we suspect some candidates would submit fake or even professionally curated social media data. Most teenagers using social media today either have or have heard of "Finsta" (i.e., Fake Instagram) accounts. In other words, people regularly create multiple social media accounts, some of which are for public consumption and others that are only accessible to close friends.

---

[2] To be sure, job interviews—especially unstructured ones—have been criticized on other grounds, but that is not the point here.

Similarly, a well-known strategy for gaming automated resume readers (i.e., computers that search resumes for certain keywords to identify candidates for interviews) was to "stuff" resumes with keywords in white font. When printed on a white paper, the resumes looked normal, but computer algorithms that read the words in white font saw a very different resume. At that point, candidates who gamed the system had already advanced to the interview stage.

As another example, Kosinski and colleagues (2013) found that people who "Like" curly fries on Facebook scored higher on IQ tests. As the news broke, more people decided that they also "Liked" curly fries on social media and the relationship disappeared. Our point is that self-presentational processes govern social interaction even on social media, and there is no way to access some "true" or "authentic" personality; all that is ever available to us is self-presentational behavior—what you see is what you get. More broadly, although AI-based personality assessments claim to eliminate the faking problem, there is no evidence that faking is a problem with real job applicants and well-validated screening measures. Moreover, self-presentation is always at play, and when the stakes are high, people will find creative ways to present a self that will get them a job. Finally, the more talented the person, the more able they will be to self-present correctly and get the job—so in a real sense, faking" is valid variance.

## The Future of Personality Assessment

In this chapter, we have argued that, despite the excitement centered around AI-based personality assessment, the reality is that these assessments fall short of their promise. Although many automated assessments can generate scores instantly, and the scores are moderately correlated with scores from self-report inventories, there is little evidence that automated assessment scores predict outcomes that employers care about (e.g., job performance). Moreover, there is no evidence that these automated personality assessments are free from the effects of self-presentation. However, there is evidence that, without proper care, AI-based assessments can be substantially biased against members of protected groups. In fact, at the time of this writing, the Equal Employment Opportunity Commission (EEOC) is launching an investigation on AI and algorithm fairness (EEOC, 2021), and New York City is considering enacting a bill specifically targeted at automated screening tools. With these considerations in mind, it is worth reflecting on two lessons we have learned over the past decade and how personality assessment can be improved going forward.

The first lesson, and one that may come as a surprise to those of you who have read the preceding, is that machine learning algorithms have real utility in personality assessment. When machine learning algorithms are applied to social media or facial scan inputs, they yield results with questionable validity and sizable bias, but when these algorithms are applied to unbiased inputs (e.g., traditional personality test data), the validity of personality assessment increases substantially. In 2019 we updated our job family and competency-based scoring algorithms from a classic regression approach to one that involved machine learning (Hogan Assessment Systems, 2020a, 2020b). To do so, we capitalized on the Hogan personality-job performance archive, which has personality and job performance data on 81 different performance metrics for 47,175 individuals from 184 unique job titles, 156 organizations, and 19 different industries. To build job family algorithms, we aligned each job title to one of 12 job families (e.g., Customer Support, Sales, Managers, Professionals) and retained overall job performance as the performance metric. To build competency-based algorithms, we aligned performance metrics to one of 62 competencies in the Hogan competency library (e.g., Accountability, Detail Focus, Leading Others, Leveraging Diversity, Teamwork, etc.). To ensure generalizability, we created both training and testing datasets (building algorithms only on training data sets), using five-fold cross-validation on the training data sets. To create scoring algorithms, we regressed criterion scores onto Hogan Personality Inventory (Hogan & Hogan, 2007) subscales and Hogan Development Survey (Hogan & Hogan, 2009) scales simultaneously using lasso regression. Lasso regression penalizes regressions for complexity, increasing the likelihood that only the most essential predictors remain in the final scoring model (James et al., 2017). The average cross-validated predictive validity of the job family algorithms was $r = .35$. The average cross-validated predictive validity of the competency-based algorithms was $r = .26$. For comparison, the previous algorithms (on the same performance data sets) that were developed using classic unit-weighted regression had predictive validities of .12 and .13 respectively. In other words, these new algorithms predict performance with cross-validated correlation coefficients that are at least twice as large (on average) as those produced by the previous algorithms. Moreover, the results from these algorithms show no group differences. When applied properly, machine learning techniques can create scoring algorithms that improve predictive validity without creating bias.

The second lesson we have learned over the past decade of technological advances is that we should return to the fundamentals of personality assessment. Woodworth thought personality assessment could solve the practical problem of properly evaluating large numbers of people. Personality psychology is at its best when it is solving practical problems, and decades of research show that (well-validated) personality assessments are quite useful for solving practical problems. They are cheap to administer, they significantly predict workplace outcomes, and—perhaps most importantly—they do not discriminate against historically disadvantaged groups (i.e., non-Whites, nonmales). When used properly, personality assessments provide individuals, teams, and organizations with insights that help them make better decisions about careers and personnel. In this regard, personality assessment should not be about measuring hypothetical neuropsychic structures (traits) inside people; it should be about predicting outcomes (performance). Following trait theory and trying to measure traits, as opposed to predicting outcomes, is a self-defeating exercise. Going forward, we would like to see a personality science focused on solving practical problems.

# References

Allport, G. W. (1938). Personality: a problem for science or a problem for art? *Revista de Psihologie, 1*, 488–502.

Barrick, M., & Mount, M. K. (1991). The big five personality dimensions and job performance: A meta-analysis. *Personnel Psychology, 44*(1), 1–26.

Bredo, E. (2006). Conceptual confusion and educational psychology. In P. A. Alexander & P. H. Winne (Eds.), *Handbook of educational psychology* (2nd ed, pp. 43–57). Routledge.

Connelly, B. S., & Hülsheger, U. R. (2011). Sources of observers' advantages over self-reports for predicting performance. *Journal of Personality, 80*(3), 603–631.

Connelly, B. S., McAbee, S. T., Oh, I.-S., Jung, Y., & Jung, C.-W. (2021). A multirater perspective on personality and performance: An empirical examination of the trait-reputation-identity model. *Journal of Applied Psychology*, 1352–1368.

Connelly, B. S., & Ones, D. S. (2010). An other perspective on personality: Meta-analytic integration of observers' accuracy and predictive validity. *Psychological Bulletin, 136*(6), 1092–1122.

Dastin, J. (2018, October 10). *Amazon scraps secret AI recruiting tool that showed bias against women*. Reuters. https://www.reuters.com/article/us-amazon-com-jobs-automation-insight/amazon-scraps-secret-ai-recruiting-tool-that-showed-bias-against-women-idUSKCN1MK08G

Equal Employment Opportunity Commission. (2021, October 28). *EEOC launches initiative o artificial intelligence and algorithmic fairness* [Press release]. https://www.eeoc.gov/newsroom/eeoc-launches-initiative-artificial-intelligence-and-algorithmic-fairness

Gibby, R. E., & Zickar, M. J. (2008). A history of the early days of personality testing in American industry. *History of Psychology, 11*(3), 164–184.

Gigerenzer, G. (2008). *Gut feelings: The intelligence of the unconscious*. Penguin.

Harlan, E., & Schnuck, O. (2021, February 16). *Objective or biased? On the questionable use of Artificial Intelligence for job applications.* BR24. https://interaktiv.br.de/ki-bewerbung/en/

Harwell, D. (2019, October 22). A face-scanning algorithm increasingly decides whether you deserve the job. *Washington Post.* https://www.washingtonpost.com/technology/2019/10/22/ai-hiring-face-scanning-algorithm-increasingly-decides-whether-you-deserve-job/

Hogan Assessment Systems. (2020a). *Job family assessments technical manual.*

Hogan Assessment Systems. (2020b). *Competences technical manual.* Hogan Assessment Systems.

Hogan, J., & Holland, B. (2003). Using theory to evaluate personality job-performance relations. *Journal of Applied Psychology, 88*(1), 100–112.Hogan, J., Barrett, P., & Hogan, R. (2007). Personality measurement, faking, and employment selection. *Journal of Applied Psychology, 92*(5), 1270–1285.

Hogan, R. (1983). A socioanalytic theory of personality. In M. M. Page (Ed.), *Nebraska Symposium on Motivation, 1982* (Vol. 29, pp. 55–89). University of Nebraska Press.

Hogan, R. (2005). In defense of personality measurement: New wine for old whiners. *Human Performance, 18*(4), 331–341.

Hogan, R., & Hogan, J. (2007). *Hogan Personality Inventory Manual* (3rd ed.). Hogan Assessment Systems: Tulsa, OK.

Hogan, R., & Hogan, J. (2009). *Hogan Development Survey Manual* (2nd ed.). Hogan Assessment Systems: Tulsa, OK.

Hogan, R., & Sherman, R. A. (2020). Personality theory and the nature of human nature. *Personality and Individual Differences, 152*(1), 109561.

James, G., Witten, D., Hastie, T., & Tibshirani, R. (2017). *An introduction to statistical learning applications in R.* Springer.

Kachur, A., Osin, E., Davydov, D., Shutilov, K., & Novokshonov, A. (2020). Assessing the big five personality traits using real-life static facial images. *Scientific Reports, 10*, 8487.

Kahneman, D. (2011). *Thinking, fast and slow.* Farrar, Straus and Giroux.

Kenrick, D. T., & Griskevicius, V. (2013). *The rational animal: How evolution made us smarter than we think.* Basic Books.

Kosinski, M., Stillwell, D., & Graepel, T. (2013). Private traits and attributes are predictable from digital human records. *Proceedings of the National Academy of the Sciences of the United States of America, 110*(15), 5802–5805.

Kosinski, M., & Wang, Y. (2018). Deep neural networks are more accurate than humans at detecting sexual orientation from facial images. *Journal of Personality and Social Psychology, 114*(2), 246–257.

Maurer, R. (2021, February 3). *HireVue discontinues facial analysis screening.* SHRM. https://www.shrm.org/resourcesandtools/hr-topics/talent-acquisition/pages/hirevue-discontinues-facial-analysis-screening.aspx

Merchant, B. (2018, December 6). *Predictim claims its AI can flag "risky" babysitters. So I tried it on the people who watch my kids.* Gizmodo. https://gizmodo.com/predictim-claims-its-ai-can-flag-risky-babysitters-so-1830913997

Oh, I.-S., Wang, G., & Mount, M. K. (2011). Validity of observer ratings of the five-factor model of personality traits: A meta-analysis. *Journal of Applied Psychology, 96*(4), 762–773.

Sumner, C., Byers, A., Boochever, R., & Park, G. J. (2012). Predicting dark triad personality traits form Twitter usage and a linguistic analysis of tweets. *11th International Conference on Machine Learning and Applications,* 386–393.

Wall, S., & Schellmann, H. (2021, July 7). We tested AI interview tools. Here's what we found. *MIT Technology Review.* https://www.technologyreview.com/2021/07/07/1027916/we-tested-ai-interview-tools/

Wittgenstein, L. (1958). *Philosophical investigations.* Macmillan.

Wood, D., Gardner, M. H., & Harms, P. D. (2015). How functionalist and processes to behavior can explain trait covariation. *Psychological Review, 122*(1), 84–111.

Youyou, W., Kosinski, M., & Stillwell, D. (2015). Computer-based personality judgments are more accurate than those made by humans. *Proceedings of the National Academy of the Sciences of the United States of America, 112*(4), 1036–1040.

# 7
# Reflections on Advancements in Assessment

*Neal Schmitt*

This chapter includes my reflections on developments in assessment and quantitative data analysis over the last several decades including developments that are described in the preceding chapters. I begin with innovations in data analysis because they, along with technological advancements in computer software and hardware, have enabled the conceptual and practical developments in assessment. I will then provide commentary on various changes in personality and cognitive ability measurement outlined in the previous chapters. Finally, I will try to provide an assessment of the impact of these changes on everyday assessment.

## Data Analytic Advances

There are four advances in quantitative analyses that have had major impact on how we analyze data and the applications and conclusions we derive from those data. These four advances are item response theory (IRT) analytics, structural equation analyses and confirmatory factor analysis (CFA), multilevel modeling, and big data analytics. These quantitative techniques have enabled the evaluation and improvement of assessments directly, as is the case with IRT, CFA, and big data, and indirectly, through the quantitative evaluation of our measures and constructs to individual and organizational outcomes (multilevel analyses provide the capability to evaluate the role that constructs play at various levels of analysis. I will comment on some of these contributions in the sections that follow.

## Item Response Theory Analyses

Perhaps beginning with the Lord and Novick (1968) volume, measurement experts have begun to replace classical measurement theory and formulae with item response formulations. In IRT computations, item parameters and ability parameters are simultaneously estimated, which means these parameters are more stable. In fact, they are said to be invariant across samples. This formulation has allowed for major advances in measurement. In computer adaptive testing, the use of these stable parameter estimates allows us to estimate a person's ability with any set of items from a calibrated item pool. A person's ability is re-estimated after their response to each item along with the standard error of that ability estimate. This allows for accurate estimates of an examinee's standing on the construct of interest in far fewer items than with classical approaches to ability estimation. Computer adaptive tests are used by all major test publishers. IRT estimates are central to the Drasgow approach to the use of forced-choice measures of personality (Stark et al., 2006) in that their use circumvents the ipsative nature of the items. IRT is also central to the development and use of ideal point measures as described below (Cao et al., 2014).

## Structural Equation Modeling and Confirmatory Factor Analysis

Joreskog (1969; Joreskog & Sorbom, 1969) introduced the analysis of linear structural equation analyses, which allowed for the simultaneous estimation of multiple regression equations implied by complex sets of relationships among variables. It also provided tests of the fit of these models to existing data. These advancements allowed for confirmatory factor analyses of interrelated scales and measures. This analytic technique has been used routinely in the last several decades to better inform the degree to which our concepts of phenomena reflected the responses of our experimental participants. It allowed, for example, the evaluation of the Big Five constructs and the personality and cognitive models described in previous chapters. This led to data-based modifications of these measures that, in turn, could be evaluated by additional data collection and analysis.

## Multilevel Modeling

About three decades ago, human resource professionals began to recognize that their data often represented different levels of analysis (Klein & Kozlowski, 2000). While this was not accompanied by different methods of analysis, it definitely required novel uses of regression analyses that allowed inferences about these data at different levels (e.g., individual, team, organization, industry). In recent editions of our major journals, the majority of papers seem to include some form of multilevel analysis of the data. It is very likely that many of our measures explain meaningful variance at one level but are not helpful at other levels of analyses or the reverse. To date, there has been little attention to the quality or meaningfulness of measures, per se, at different levels of analysis (Chan, 1998).

## Big Data Analyses

The analysis and interpretation of large multidisciplinary data sets by organizational scientists has introduced whole new approaches to data analyses along with a new vocabulary (Harlow & Oswald, 2016). However, many big data analyses include data from other disciplines in which the measurement quality of the data is not evaluated or is not considered important. In addition, the search for relationships in a very large set of data means that even small effect sizes observed in a set of data in which measures are of poor quality are often significant. Big data analyses usually include efforts to develop models on multiple subsets of "training" data that are then cross-validated on "test" data. However, it remains the case that the measures in these analyses are not usually examined and their reliability and construct validity receive little, if any, attention.

Our field has advanced greatly in terms of the manner in which data are analyzed and interpreted. Of the techniques described above, IRT and CFA provide some direction as to how to evaluate the items or scales we use. IRT, however, is not very applicable with short scales. CFA is used to test various measurement models, but the meaningfulness of a good fit to data or better fit than some other model remains a question of concern. Some recent proposals to provide practical indices have been presented (Meade et al., 2008; Nye & Drasgow, 2011). Multilevel modeling affords the opportunity to evaluate the meaning of our assessments (and the constructs they represent) at individual, group, and organizational levels. Big data represents a challenge in that the "measures" are developed on the basis of empirical analyses rather than conceptual bases. Hence, the interpretation of these assessments is post hoc.

Finally, this discussion would be incomplete if we did not mention the seeming overreliance on alpha as a measure of unidimensionality or reliability (Cortina et al., 2020).

The use of many of these advancements (and perhaps some limitations) in analytic techniques is evident in the previous chapters in this book. In the remainder of this chapter, I will highlight these advancements in assessment and, in some cases, how analysis methods contributed to the advances.

## Advances in Personality Measurement

Everyone interested in personnel selection is aware of the resurrection of personality testing stimulated by the introduction of the Big Five as a framework (Digman, 1990; Goldberg, 1990) to organize the huge number of different names given to personality measures. Equally influential was the meta-analysis of personality studies of the relationship between personality measures and job performance (Barrick & Mount, 1991). That meta-analysis revealed that there were significant, though relatively small, and practically useful relationships between personality and job performance. This was especially true for conscientiousness measures.

The work in the previous chapters reflects the Big Five research but, in some respects, deviates quite significantly from this framework (e.g., darkside measures). It also represents several new ways of measuring personality (e.g., ideal point method, use of ipsative measures, and measures derived from social media). All of these developments go quite beyond the Big Five classification; one wonders if they have any further utility. An important question is whether these advancements add to our ability to understand work performance.

### Ideal Point Measures

The ideal point model, first proposed by Thurstone and resurrected by Stark and colleagues (2006), proposes that responses to items are often curvilinear in that there is some ideal point to which more (or better) of something is desirable and beyond that ideal point things are not so desirable. The usual assumption underlying the construction and use of personality items is that more is always superior or desirable (a dominance model). In comparing IRT models using dominance and ideal point models, Stark et al. (2006) found the ideal response models much better at identifying and using neutral items (i.e., these items were highly discriminating in ideal point models and often useless in classical or dominance models). Their analyses were based on items that were constructed with dominance models in mind. However, overall, these models are not likely to correlate much higher with external criteria since the two models are similar over the usual range of item responses; that is, extreme responders are infrequent.

Cao et al. (2014) demonstrated that it was possible to develop intermediately favorable items that better fit the ideal response model. They constructed personality scales that fit the ideal response model. Borman (2010) pointed out that the ideal response model was likely of use in performance appraisal scales since it was often difficult to write neutral anchors or items that proved useful when evaluated using classical test formulae. Ideal response models represent a significant change in how we view responses to scales, and their use should escalate though they are computationally complex and may be difficult to explain to typical users and clients. Further, Zhang et al. (2020) have demonstrated that ideal point models have some desirable characteristics, but they do not provide superior predictive validity to dominance models.

## Ipsative Scales and Item Response Theory

Ipsative scales require a respondent to endorse one of two equally desirable statements reflecting different constructs. A major problem in the use of personality scales is their susceptibility to faking. The use of ipsative scales was proposed as a solution to this problem (Edwards, 1957), but their use artificially distorts their relationships with external variables and with each other. As a solution to this distortion of correlations between scales and external criteria, Brown and Maydeu-Olivares (2013) and Stark et al. (2005) have proposed using IRT solutions to score these ipsative statements. This IRT-modified ipsative solution has significantly lessened the effect of socially desirable responding at little or no impact on validity (Lee et al., 2018).

## Rapid Response Measurement

Meade and Priest in this book and elsewhere (Chapter 3; Meade et al., 2020) present rapid response measurement (RRM), which purports to shorten radically the response time necessary to administer personality measures and to minimize the faking problem. Response time to very short items is part of the score, and quick response times are assumed to be indicative of unfaked responses. Reliabilities of the scales composed of these short items are excellent, but construct validity (as indicated by correlations with traditional measures) was not very good (Chapter 3). Responses between RRM and absenteeism and International Personality Item Pool measures and absenteeism were nearly identical, indicating similar criterion-related validity. Similar positive results were reported for correlations of RRM with reports of interpersonal problems and adaptation difficulties, but correlations with job performance were uniformly low. Much more research on RRM is needed, and given its practical advantages (low response times and low fakability), I suspect this research by Meade and others will be forthcoming.

## Advances in Conceptualizations of Personality

As stated above, the Big Five seems to be the accepted and favored taxonomy of personality constructs. However, Hough has argued repeatedly (e.g., Hough, 1992) that in the work context and in the prediction of job performance, the Big Five is inadequate in terms of both its completeness and the within-construct heterogeneity. Hough et al. (2005) compared four different taxonomies describing advantages and liabilities associated with each. Their conclusion and what seems to be true in practice is that going beyond the Big Five allows for better and more targeted predictions about work performance. The dark side of personality as presented by Sherman and Hogan in this volume (Chapter 6) represents a new set of 11 constructs and measures. More data are needed on these constructs as pertains to their criterion-related validity, their incremental validity over other personality variables, and the need for 11 such measures. Intercorrelations between these variables suggest that a more parsimonious set of variables would be sufficient to represent this domain. Indeed, research that originated in clinical areas suggests three (narcissism, Machiavellianism, and psychopathy) or four (sadism has been added by some) might be a representative set of dark traits. Coincidentally, there have also been attempts to measure three dark personality traits using linguistic analysis of tweets (Summer et al., 2012).

## Big Data

This is a perfect transition to a discussion of big data, which is the subject of three of the previous chapters in this volume (Chapters 2, 5, and 6). Perhaps no other topic has attracted more attention among assessment scholars across many disciplines than big data. Big data is a term that refers to the storing, retrieval, and analyses (mentioned above) of very large sets of data. These data can be interview data, archival data of various sorts and origins, physiological data, magnetic resonance imaging data, and social media data, obtained by "scraping" the web of Facebook, Twitter, Instagram, LinkedIn, and other methods used to communicate with others. Big data are often characterized by three Vs: volume, velocity, and variety. Volume refers to the number of cases and the number of pieces of information available on each case. Variety refers to the heterogeneity of the data: Data may relate to space, time, physiology, kinetics (e.g., touch, gesture), etc. Velocity refers to the number and speed of observations. Big data sets may refer to one or more of these Vs, so clearly we are talking of huge data sets.

Big data analytics refer to a "family" of procedures classified in a variety of ways (e.g., data mining, knowledge discovery, machine learning, and artificial intelligence). What they have in common is an attempt to discover patterns in the data that allow one to predict an outcome efficiently. Since assessments are usually oriented to making predictions about individuals' behavior, use of big data analyses to identify patterns of behavior or responses to assessments is a potentially valuable new tool for the human resource professional.

I cannot describe all the techniques used in the name of big data in this chapter, but there are several good sources of such descriptions. The December 2016 special issue of *Psychological Methods* contains 10 articles that describe a variety of methods used to analyze data from very different sources using a large number of different statistical procedures. A section in the December 2018 issue of *Organizational Research Methods* describes various opportunities and challenges afforded by big data.

Big data analyses afford many advantages. First, the data employed often do not require additional data collection from respondents. Second, since the purpose of the data collection very often is not selection per se, the respondent (and many times the object of research is not the participant or source of data) is unlikely to fake or present a socially desirable response. Third, data from various sources or disciplines can be used, which allows for a consideration of a broad array of information about subjects' backgrounds, interests, skills, and abilities. This should result in improved predictive capacity and the triangulation of sources referred to in many discussions of construct validity. Data sets that include velocity will allow for investigations of change that have never before been possible. Large-volume data sets may allow us to characterize entire populations and to engage in multiple cross-validations, which have now become standard practice in big data analyses.

These opportunities come with a large number of caveats or liabilities. First, many human resource specialists do not have the data analytic or computer skills to analyze big data. This will require that we work in multidisciplinary teams composed of data scientists, computer specialists, those expert in qualitative inquiry, and those who are familiar with the characteristics of data derived from different disciplinary foci. Second, a data set characterized by a large degree of variety may consist of data that are of varying degrees of quality; for example, not all disciplines have the same concern for measurement quality as do industrial-organizational (IO) psychologists. In addition, data across multiple sources are likely not the result of a single stimulus or set of stimulus conditions; such standardization is an elemental concern when we construct measures. Third, the algorithms derived from big data analyses and used to make predictions are often difficult to interpret; construct validity will almost always be a concern even when we have good criterion-related validity. Fourth, while large volumes of data may seem to describe a population, they may not be a representative sample and situations may change over time, producing overgeneralization and incorrect causal attributions. Finally, big data represents a variety of ethical issues that we have not previously faced. We have no way of collecting the usual informed consent from subjects who are the source of most big data sets. And, fifth, it may seem that data are anonymous when there are large numbers of cases, but patterns identified by an analysis of a large number of variables may be nearly uniquely representative of one or a small group of persons. Analyses of data patterns from historical archives may also simply reflect historical biases.

A relatively new (at least to human resource personnel) technique that is similar to and sometimes seen as one source of big data is referred to as natural language processing (see Chapter 5). Designed to retrieve and extract information from essays or other textual material, text mining involves the computerized extraction of meaningful information or knowledge structures from unstructured text data. Open-ended responses to essays, resumes, transcribed interview responses, and more can all be the target of text mining efforts. There are fifth different ways to mine text varying in the degree of computer and human involvement in the process. Validations of such efforts are only beginning to appear in professional journals (e.g., Campion et al., 2016; Sajjadiani et al., 2019). Text mining appears to produce meaningful and valid assessments of employee potential when carefully conducted and tied to work competencies, as was done in these two studies. Computer software designed to do these analyses is now widely available as part of R or Python and SPSS.

## Cognitive Ability Assessment

In this volume and elsewhere (Chapter 4; Scherbaum et al., 2012), Scherbaum argues that IO psychologists and those interested in human resource management need to rethink the measurement and use of cognitive ability in assessment. He asserts that some of the traditional specific cognitive abilities have been "reinvented" as competencies in the human resource literature. Competencies such as learning agility, decision-making, and strategic planning are cognitive in nature and have analogs in the literature on specific cognitive abilities. He and his colleagues (Reeve et al., 2015) assert that these specific abilities and recent literature on cognitive abilities in other areas of psychology such as neuroscience should be incorporated into the measurement and use of cognitive ability assessment. Their use would help in the interpretation of cognitive ability and may contribute to greater validity as well. Research and conceptualization of these competencies (specific abilities) will be needed as well as efforts to establish their incremental validity. However, efforts to establish such incremental validity for specific abilities has been noteworthy in the lack of success and has given rise to journal articles with titles that include "not much more than g" (e.g., Ree et al., 1994).

## Conclusions

This brief summary of my reflections leads to the following propositions. First, the past several decades have provided an array of new analytic tools that have the potential to add to the interpretative value of our data and make possible the evaluation of new conceptual advances. IRT solutions to the faking of personality measures and the evaluation of ideal point models are good examples. Second, the personality domain seems to have expanded beyond the Big Five to include more narrow work-oriented measures than those represented by the Big Five. It has also expanded to include the dark side of personality, whether that dark side is represented by three traits or a larger array of measures/constructs. Third, big data ideas and analytics provide many opportunities to expand the content and sophistication of our assessments, but there are a number of caveats as noted above. Perhaps the most important of these reservations is that we do not lose sight of the constructs we intend to measure. If we do not know what we are doing or how, advances are likely to be ephemeral. Fourth, the expansion or redevelopment of cognitive constructs must incorporate research on competencies and constructs suggested by other disciplines and areas of psychology and human resource management. In any event, there is no shortage of ideas, analytics, and changes in how work is defined and performed to keep academics busy and practitioners challenged as to how and what to evaluate in their efforts to enhance human performance and satisfaction. These advances will, and have, enhanced the assessment of human characteristics and their role in the modern workplace.

## References

Barrick, M. R., & Mount, M. K. (1991). The Big Five personality dimensions and job performance. *Journal of Applied Psychology, 78*, 1–26.

Borman, W. C. (2010). Cognitive processes related to forced-choice, ideal point responses: Drasgow, Chernyshenko, and Stark got it right! *Industrial and Organizational Psychology: Perspectives on Science and Practice, 3*(4), 504–506.

Brown, A., & Maydeu-Olivares, A. (2013). How IRT can solve problems of ipsative data in forced-choice questionnaires. *Psychological Methods, 18*, 15–35.

Campion, M. C., Campion, M. A., Campion, E. D., & Reider, M. H. (2016). Initial investigation into computer scoring of candidate essays for personnel selection. *Journal of Applied Psychology, 101*, 958–975.

Cao, M., Drasgow, F., & Cho, S. (2014). Developing ideal intermediate personality items for the ideal point model. *Organizational Research Methods, 18*, 252–275.

Chan, D. (1998). Functional relationships among constructs in the same content domain at different levels of analysis. *Journal of Applied Psychology, 83,* 234–246.

Cortina, J. M., Sheng, Z, Keener, S. K., Keeler, K. R. Grubb, L. K., Schmitt, N., Tonidandel, S., Summerville, K. M., Heggestad, E. D., & Banks, G. S. (2020). From alpha to omega and beyond! A look at the past, present, and (possible) future of psychometric soundness in the *Journal of Applied Psychology. Journal of Applied Psychology, 105,* 1351–1381.

Digman, J. M. (1990). Personality structure: Emergence of the five-factor model. *Annual Review of Psychology, 41,* 417–440.

Edwards, A. L. (1957). *The social desirability variable in personality assessment and research.* Dryden.

Goldberg, L. R. (1990). An alternative description of personality: The Big Five factor structure. *Journal of Personality and Social Psychology, 59,* 1216–1229.

Hough, L. M. (1992). The Big Five personality variables—construct confusion: Description vs. prediction. *Human Performance, 5,* 139–155.

Harlow, L. L., & Oswald, F. L. (2016). Big data in psychology: Introduction to the special issue. *Psychological Methods, 21,* 447–457.

Hough, L. M., Oswald, F. L., & Ock, J. (2015). Beyond Big Five: New directions for personality research and practice in organizations. *Annual Review of Organizational Psychology and Organizational Behavior, 2,* 183–209.

Joreskog, K. G. (1969). A general approach to confirmatory maximum likelihood factor analysis. *Psychometrika, 34,* 183–202.

Joreskog, K. G., & Sorbom, D. (1996). *LISREL 8: Structural equation modeling with the SIMPLIS command language.* Scientific Software International.

Klein, K. J., & Kozlowski, S. W. J. (Eds.). (2000). *Multilevel theory, research, and methods in organizations.* Jossey-Bass.

Lee, P., Lee, S., & Stark, S. (2018). Examining validity evidence for multi-dimensional forced-choice measures with different scoring approaches. *Personality and Individual Differences, 123,* 229–235.

Lord, F. M., & Novick, M. R. (1968). *Statistical theories of mental test scores.* Addison-Wesley.

Meade, A. W., Johnson, E. C., & Braddy, P. W. (2008). Power and sensitivity of alternate fit indices in tests of measurement invariance. *Journal of Applied Psychology, 93,* 568–592.

Meade, A. W., Pappalardo, G., Braddy, P. W., & Fleenor, J. W. (2020). Rapid response measurement: Development of a faking resistant assessment method for personality. *Organizational Research Methods, 23,* 181–207.

Nye, C. D., & Drasgow, F. (2011). Effect size indices for analyses of measurement equivalence: Understanding the practical importance of differences between groups. *Journal of Applied Psychology, 96,* 966–980.

Ree, M. J., Earles, J. A., & Teachout, M. S. (1994). Predicting job performance: Not much more than g. *Journal of Applied Psychology, 79,* 518–524.

Reeve, C. L., Scherbaum, C., & Goldstein, H. (2015). Manifestations of intelligence: Expanding the measurement space to reconsider specific cognitive abilities. *Human Resource Management Review, 25,* 28–37.

Sajjadiani, S., Sojurner, A. J., Kammeyer-Mueller, J., & Mykerezi, E. (2019). Using machine learning to translate applicant work history into predictors of performance and turnover. *Journal of Applied Psychology, 104,* 1207–1225.

Scherbaum, C. A., Goldstein, H. W., Yusko, K. P., Ryan, R., & Hanges, P. J. (2012). Intelligence 2.0: Reestablishing a research program on g in I-O psychology. *Industrial and Organizational Psychology, 5*, 128–148.

Stark, S., Chernyshenko, O. S., & Drasgow, F. (2005). An IRT approach to constructing and scoring pairwise preference items involving stimuli on different dimensions: The multi-unidimensional pairwise-preference model. *Applied Psychological Methods, 29*, 184–203.

Stark, S., Chernyshenko, O. S., Drasgow, F., & Williams, B. A. (2006). Examining assumptions about item responding in personality assessment: Should ideal point methods be considered for scale development and scoring? *Journal of Applied Psychology, 91*(1), 25–39.

Summer, C., Byers, A., Boochever, R., & Park, G. J. (2012). Predicting dark triad personality traits from Twitter usage and a linguistic analysis of tweets. *Proceedings of IEEE 11th International Conference on Machine Learning and Applications (ICMLA)*.

Zhang, B., Cao, M., Tay, L. Luo, J., & Drasgow, F. (2020). Examining the item response process to personality measures in high-stakes situations: Issues of measurement validity and predictive validity. *Personnel Psychology, 73*, 305–332.

# SECTION 3
# INNOVATIONS AND TRENDS

# 8
# Artificial Intelligence in Automated Scoring of Video Interviews

*Nathan Mondragon*

## The Promise of Artificial Intelligence–Based Assessments

Generally speaking, prehire assessments strive to achieve three pillars of success: validity, fairness, and a positive candidate experience. Achieving all three of these pillars in the design of a prehire assessment process has been difficult to achieve as tradeoffs are often involved. For example, achieving high levels of measurement accuracy typically require longer assessments, which can present a challenge for the candidate experience, or assessments with strong predictive validity such as general mental ability tests can have implications for adverse impact. In this chapter, I will describe how these pillars of success can be achieved with advanced analytic techniques and technologies all guided by the field of industrial-organizational (IO) psychology. The focus will be the design of autoscored asynchronous video interviews (AVIs; one-way recorded interviews) as a use case to creating an IO-guided advanced toolkit.

Big data, along with using new statistical procedures programmed by data scientists, has shown promise in achieving the three pillars of success. However, without the oversight of IO psychologists, statistical techniques imposed on big data in selection systems can result in impractical (e.g., a machine-directed 85 percentile cut score) or illegal practices (e.g., race norming in crafting feature sets or predictors). With the recent combination of both disciplines (data science and IO psychology), Alina von Davier coined the term "Computational psychometrics" to describe the fusion of psychometric theories and data-driven algorithms for improving the inferences made from technology-supported learning and assessment systems (Davier et al., 2021). The use of computational psychometrics is akin

Nathan Mondragon, *Artificial Intelligence in Automated Scoring of Video Interviews* In: *Talent Assessment*.
Edited by: Tracy M. Kantrowitz, Douglas H. Reynolds, and John C. Scott, Oxford University Press.
© Society of Industrial Organizational Psychology 2023. DOI: 10.1093/oso/9780197611050.003.0008

to using machine learning modeling techniques with large data sets to make data inferences (e.g., using natural language processing to score behavioral competencies from a recorded interview). In this chapter I will interchange the terms artificial intelligence (AI)-based assessments, machine learning, and computational psychometrics to essentially mean using advanced psychometrics with novel big data sets to predict outcomes.

Specifically, using computational psychometrics, I will describe in this chapter how big data sets from AVIs can enhance measurement accuracy, with minimal to no adverse impact, and provide an improved candidate experience with shorter evaluation times. Thus, with novel assessments drawing upon computational psychometrics, all three pillars are achievable within a single selection system.

Even a fourth pillar, process and cost efficiencies, can be realized with the deployment of these assessments; multiple steps in the hiring process can be combined into a single step with novel assessments. For example, many organizations use phone screens and multiple live interview rounds in the normal selection process. Twin goals of conducting a phone screen and one interview round can be achieved with a single asynchronous interview. Regardless of whether the scoring and evaluation are automated or manual, the process efficiency and cost savings can be significant. For example, organizations can save on a candidate's travel expenses by asking the candidate to conduct the AVI, at the day and time of their choosing (e.g., nonworking hours), without having to travel to the interviewer's location.

## Best Practices in Creating Artificial Intelligence–Based Assessments

While other chapters in this book deal with various forms of talent assessment innovations (e.g., Chapter 25 on Gamified Assessments for Prehire Evaluation), in this chapter I will mainly focus on test design and validation for innovative assessments. In general, the same psychometric, ethical, and legal guidelines govern AI-based selection assessments. That is, frameworks that have been used to guide traditional (non-AI-based) assessments should be used to develop AI-based assessment content. For instance, the assessment should be relevant for the job(s) in which it is intended to be used, demonstration of reliability and validity should be achieved, and indicators of fairness should be satisfied.

More specifically, when implementing AI-based assessments, it is still critical to follow job-relatedness best practices. Before any AI-based screening tool is implemented, the appropriateness or linkage between the job requirements and the assessment measurements must be established following job analytic procedures. These bedrock procedures of our field are paramount to establish job relatedness and the plan for how the assessment is used by the organization (e.g., cut scores or profiling). Unfortunately, many AI-based screening tool providers exist in the market that do not provide job analytic support to justify the use of the assessment (Tippins et al., 2021).

For example, when applied to AVIs, AI tools should follow IO best practice research by (a) following content validation methods to ensure the interview content matches the requirements of the job; (b) using standardized, behavior-based questions or situational scenarios; and (c) autoscoring the interview responses with AI and machine learning based on behaviorally anchored rating guides (see M. A. Campion et al., 1997, for a detailed review of standardized interview methods and research-based best practices). The real power of AI with AVIs is the autoscoring of the interview responses, but best practices from IO psychology still govern the development, validation, and scoring methods (Hickman et al., 2022; Leutner, Liff et al., 2021). Test design procedures and the computational psychometrics achieved with AI-based interviews will be discussed in the following sections.

## Machine Learning Scoring for Video Interviews

As previously discussed, the power of AVIs is driven by a combination of efficiencies, cost reductions, and candidate friendliness to complete on their time schedule. However, many organizations receive more completed AVIs than recruiters or hiring managers can feasibly review. In addition, training hiring managers in structured interviewing, which involves implementing and monitoring standardized rating systems, is costly and difficult in practice and a main limiting factor of structured interviews in application (Levashina et al., 2014). This challenge can be overcome using machine learning technologies to automatically score candidate responses using algorithms trained and validated on expert evaluator ratings. Thus, the decision rubrics of expert interview raters can be programmed into algorithms used to autoscore all candidate AVIs for a given job. However, as with any scoring rubric, the reliability and accuracy of the measurement must be shown, and this requirement does not change with AI-based technologies.

Advances in machine learning have opened new doors to extracting job-relevant information from novel data sets not previously available without tedious manual extraction by subject matter experts (Mischel, 1996). For example, language use on Twitter and personal blogs are claimed to be indicative of one's traits (Schwartz et al., 2013), and Facebook Likes have been studied as predictors of personality (Kosinski et al., 2013).

Generally, such approaches demonstrate good convergent validity with self-report measures of personality, and have even outperformed human judges when comparing the convergence of interjudge agreement for machine ($r = .62$, a good indicator of validity) versus human judgments ($r = .38$, lower indicator; Bleidorn & Hopwood, 2019). For example, machine learning algorithm predictions of the Big Five are more accurate ($r = .56$ versus $r = .49$; $z = 3.68$, $p < 0.001$) than average human or friends' judgments of Big Five traits (Youyou et al., 2015).

More specific to AVIs, research demonstrates the link between language use and personality (Kern et al., 2013; Pennebaker & King, 1999). The words we use are related to personal concerns and express the things we value (Chung et al., 2014). The lexical approach, the idea that underlying psychological characteristics are embedded in the structure of language, has been demonstrated in numerous studies (Gosling et al., 2007; Schwartz et al., 2013; Vazire & Gosling, 2004).

## Structure and Standardization

It stands to reason that if behavioral signals can be extracted from language, then the most accurate measurement of these signals may come from responses to structured prompts and then analyzed in standardized formats. The seminal meta-analysis by Schmidt and Hunter (1998), summarizing 85 years of selection validation research, found that structured interviews have among the highest validity in predicting job-relevant outcomes compared with other common selection methods. This effect can be further enhanced by applying machine learning–based scoring to the already standardized video interview process. In contrast, human raters make inferences that are not always job related, can bring idiosyncratic biases to the evaluation process, may struggle to recall job-related details of the interview, and are challenged to make criterion-related judgments and decisions that predict success on the job (M. A. Campion et al., 1997). By introducing automated scoring of candidates' text responses with machine learning, the fairness and standardization of human raters can be improved (M. C. Campion et al., 2016). This results in greater efficiency and significant time savings, allowing employers to collect unstructured data and analyze it in a structured and standardized manner.

During the development stages of the first machine-scored AVIs in the HireVue lab (starting in 2015), we found that following structured interview guidelines (M. A. Campion et al., 1997; Levashina et al., 2014) positively impacted the quality of the scoring algorithms as compared to using noncompetency or unstructured questions or no structured evaluation guidelines. As determined in previous research, structured and job-relevant interview questions designed to elicit behavioral competence signals provide the best predictor data set and subsequent criterion (M. A. Campion et al., 1997; Levashina et al., 2014; McDaniel et al., 1994) and construct validities (Hickman et al., 2022; Leutner, Codreanu et al., 2021; Wang et al., 2021).

## Predictor and Outcome Data

Extending the M. C. Campion et al. (2016) methodology for creating standardized autoscoring of essay text data, it is reasonable to assume that accurate competency and personality scores can be generated from open-ended structured interview responses via AVIs. However, this approach requires the additional technological step of transcribing the spoken words into a text file (speech-to-text) on which natural language processing (NLP) technology can be applied to conduct autoscoring. Various speech-to-text transcription services can be drawn upon (e.g., Apple, IBM, Google, Amazon, Microsoft) and should be evaluated for transcription accuracy and racial disparities (Koenecke et al., 2020). Researchers or practitioners must ensure the speech-to-text software they deploy is trained on diverse data sets to capture differences in local dialects of the respective language.

Once the AVI responses are transcribed, various NLP tools are available to draw upon, and many providers conducting text analytics are creating their own proprietary algorithms. Generally, the predictor data set is created from various language taxonomies such as the Linguistic Inquiry and Word Count (LIWC; Pennebaker et al., 2015), General Inquirer (Stone et al., 1966), the

Natural Language Toolkit (Loper & Bird, 2002), and the latest, called Robustly Optimized Bidirectional Encoder Representations from Transformers pretraining Approach (RoBERTa). RoBERTa or BERT data features decipher more nuance and context in speech and are robust to differences in word choice, focusing more on meaning and intention (Liu et al., 2019; Devlin et al., 2018). Advances in NLP are rapid, and other technologies based on large language models (e.g., Generative Pretrained Transformer [GPT-4] and Pathways Language Model [PaLM]) show additional promise in their use of language analytics.

In developing AVI scoring algorithms, after the predictor data set is obtained, the benchmark variables are then collected. As previously mentioned, the objective is to create competency measurements based on expert human evaluator ratings of the interview responses. These ratings are the benchmark data set; thus, the quality of these ratings is critical to the development of reliable and valid scores. Following structured interview best practices (M. A. Campion et al., 1997, Levashina et al., 2014), behavioral anchored rating scales (BARS) are generated for each interview question and/or competency to guide the expert evaluator ratings. Typical rater training, calibration discussions, and frequent quality checks of rating accuracy are minimal requirements to ensure high-quality outcome data.

Once the predictor and benchmark data sets are obtained, model building proceeds following normal psychometric procedures (i.e., conceptually related features are determined from a corpus of interview responses according to the nature of the interview questions), which can be enhanced with computational psychometrics. A range of techniques may be used, including linear and nonlinear modeling, along with cross-validation and regularization to control overfitting of the final model (i.e., the assessment scoring algorithm). Finally, adverse impact analyses are also undertaken on each model, and in some cases, mitigation is conducted to minimize protected group differences.

## Psychometric

To confirm that an assessment measures the job-related construct it is intended to measure, convergent validity is tested. Convergent validity evaluates the assessment's overlap with alternative measures of the trait or competency the assessment is purported to measure. These validities are affected not only by the true relationship between the constructs measured but also by variance resulting from the assessment method. Thus, the less similar the assessment formats are, the lower the expected correlation (e.g., the multitrait, multimethod matrix; Campbell & Fiske, 1959). Therefore, correlations observed between novel and traditional assessment scores are typically lower than correlations observed between two traditional questionnaires of the same trait. Two convergent validity tracks in the research will be discussed next: scoring AVI measures by modeling with either (a) self-report personality data or (b) expert rater evaluations, with the latter yielding the best results.

With four different student samples, Hickman et al. (2022) studied both of these relationships to determine the best method for scoring personality from AVI responses. This study found significant Big Five construct validities with an average correlation of $r = .40$ when linking AVI responses with interviewer evaluations of personality traits (extraversion was most accurately predicted at $r = .65$, and emotional stability was least accurately predicted at $r = .27$). However, a low average $r = .12$ was achieved when predicting self-reported personality (using the traditional 50-item International Personality Item Pool to measure the Big Five) with the AVI responses. Leutner, Codreanu et al. (2021) found a similar result using video interview data to predict a self-reported conscientiousness measure ($r = .21$). Wang et al. (2021) found an average construct validity ($r = .22$) between AVI data features and self-report Big Five measures confirming the Leutner, Codreanu et al. (2021) results. For more detailed information about expected convergent validities based on either self-report or evaluator classifications of personality with AVI responses, see Hickman et al. (2022, Table 2) for a review of various studies. This review suggests, in general, that evaluator reviews are more accurate than self-reports, with validities similar to the studies highlighted above. Nonetheless, these construct validities between novel data sets (AVIs) and traditional Big Five measures are lower than two traditional questionnaires of the same trait. Thus, more research is needed to tease out the measurements obtained with novel tools compared to traditional tools.

Possibly the most robust research using expert human ratings of structured and standardized interview responses to generate scoring algorithms for future AVI responses has been conducted by HireVue over several years. In numerous studies HireVue used expert human ratings of AVI responses to create scoring algorithms, then cross-validated these algorithms with subsequent AVI responses to the same or similar structured and standardized behavioral interview questions. With approximately 60,000 expert human ratings of approximately 30,000 AVI responses, an average construct validity of $r = .66$ was achieved (highest competency validity: compassion, $r = .74$; and lowest: team orientation, $r = .55$). These results indicate that scores resulting from algorithmically scored structured interview questions substantially overlap with expert human ratings of the same interview recordings for 15 different competencies (Hartwell et al., 2022; Liff et al., 2021). Thus, construct measurement of AVI responses can be achieved for personality and various behavioral competencies (e.g., team orientation), with the measurement accuracy of expert human ratings as found by other published research (see Hickman et al., 2022, and M. C. Campion et al., 2016). Further, average test-retest reliability across 181,610 interview scores over an average of 37 days (.72; Liff et al., 2021) is comparable to meta-analytic estimates of human rater interrater reliability from panel interviews (.74; Huffcutt et al., 2013).

## Predictors Removed

AVI responses provide more than language or text used in the answers. Audio data from the interview answer (e.g., voice intonations, length of pauses in the verbal answers, rates of speech, etc.) and video data (e.g., muscle movements in the face or facial action units like microexpressions) are also available and can provide rich data when analyzed with the various machine and deep learning technologies. Limited published research exists that looks at the audio and visual data sets garnered from AVI responses in prediction of personality. Hickman et al. (2022), Wang et al. (2021), and unpublished research by HireVue have analyzed language (transcription of the interview answer to text), audio, and video data sets to develop personality or competency-based measurements and consistently found that approximately 81%, 15%, and 4% of the prediction variance was from language, video, and audio, respectively. By far the most important feature category is the words spoken by a candidate in the interview. Additionally, criterion validity research conducted by HireVue originally found video and audio predictors to add incremental validity beyond language for predicting performance in high-service-oriented positions. However, the advances in NLP (e.g., BERT) have enhanced the predictive validity of the language predictor data such that incremental validity from audio and video has become insignificant in convergent and criterion validity studies.

## Adverse Impact

Given the dearth of research on the psychometric properties of AI-based assessment tools, more specifically AVIs, it is not surprising that there is no substantial published research on group difference or adverse impact analyses of AVI scores. Leutner, Codreanu et al. (2021) investigated a single AVI measure of conscientiousness and found no evidence of gender, ethnic, or age differences. However, the most robust analyses are from Hartwell et al. (2022), who studied subgroup differences in mean predicted scores across 15 competency-based AVI models. In this paper, gender, age, and ethnic subgroup differences for all 15 competency model scores were all below a Cohen's $d$ value of 0.20, indicating minimal subgroup differences. The robustness of the data set used for this study should be noted. For example, the subgroup differences on the communication model were based on an applicant sample ($n = 81,910$) consisting of applicants from over 300 different organizations across 16 distinct O*NET job families. The effect size range was $d = -0.05$ to $-0.01$ for gender, ethnicity, and age groups.

Additionally, the zero-to-small subgroup differences reported in Hartwell et al. (2022) were comparable or lower than the subgroup differences found in the human evaluator ratings that were used to generate the competency algorithms. This highlights one of the powers of using large predictor data sets (analyzed using NLP) such that subgroup differences can be mitigated during the model building process. These results align with adverse impact mitigation procedures reported by Rottman et al. (2023) in a paper describing the diversity-validity dilemma. Rottman et al. noted that advances in machine learning have identified two novel approaches to reducing adverse impact: iterative feature removal and bias penalization. Simply put, iterative feature removal is the zero-weighting of certain features during the algorithmic build process (e.g., creating the scoring key). Bias penalization is a new analytical technique that models the diversity-validity tradeoff by adding a bias penalization into the training objective function. In the Rottman et al. paper, both techniques were tested on three simulated AVI datasets with either low, medium, or high mean subgroup differences. Results demonstrate that while both techniques effectively decreased subgroup differences while maintaining validity, bias penalization outperformed iterative feature removal in all three simulations. During the design and with ongoing adverse impact studies, the improvements from the bias penalization method are bearing fruit. As documented in Hartwell et al. (2022), when subgroup differences can be minimized during the algorithmic build process, mitigation of adverse impact can be obtained before the algorithms are placed into production (i.e., launched as part of a selection system).

## Applicant Reactions

A global study of candidate experiences associated with video interviews, comprising approximately 645,000 candidates across 46 countries, found high satisfaction (measured with a postinterview survey asking applicants how effective the interview was in getting to know them and their overall satisfaction with the interview process) associated with both synchronous (live or panel over the internet) and AVIs. Candidates rated the live synchronous video interview slightly higher than the asynchronous interview (Griswold et al., 2021), a finding that is consistent with other applicant reactions research comparing AVIs to other selection tools (see Griswold et al., 2021, for a recent review of this literature). However, as noted in Griswold et al. (2021), the tradeoff of slightly lower applicant satisfaction with AVIs can be outweighed by the benefits in efficiency. In addition, the global and cultural differences found in this study were small, thus indicating that the applicant acceptance of AVIs was positive across all 46 countries and cultures, which indicates acceptability for global selection purposes.

On the other hand, recent articles have focused solely on negative applicant reactions to AVIs. One article, although the sample size was small (n = 20), made important recommendations to counter negative applicant impressions when using AVIs such as being transparent and providing feedback to the applicant when AI-based tools are deployed (Jaser et al., 2022). Being transparent about the use of AI in the evaluation of the interview responses, what is being measured by the AI, and the relationship of the AI measurement to the target job, and offering feedback to the candidate on how they performed are methods to improve the lower impressions applicants have concerning AVIs. These transparency and feedback methods are best practice recommendations most IO professionals would recommend when designing selection assessments. In addition, many of these methods are being required by the latest laws and proposed regulations (e.g., see New York City Counsel—Automated Employment Decision Tools, 2021, Algorithmic Accountability Act of 2022).

## Criterion-Related Validity

Predictive validity studies are rare to find in the published literature with new AI-based assessments. Given the dearth of this literature, I will summarize unpublished studies conducted at HireVue across a variety of industries. There are two general approaches to these criterion validity studies. The first is using already constructed competency-based algorithms that were used in the selection process and linked to ultimate job outcome measures. Off-the-shelf interview questions and autoscored algorithms of the verbal interview responses are used as the predictors. Across five studies (Hartwell et al., 2022; Liff et al., 2021), an average uncorrected criterion validity of .24 ($n$ = 1,687) was found using a variety of criterion measures (e.g., supervisory performance ratings, .20; quality assurance, .22; customer satisfaction, .26; and net revenue generated, .27).

In the second method, the same interview questions and applicant responses are used to create customized algorithms that directly predict the job performance criteria (instead of predicting the expert human evaluations at a competency level, then correlating with job performance). This approach has yielded larger validities since the predictor-criterion relationship is direct, whereas with the previous approach the predictor scores were modeled on human ratings of the interview responses and then correlated with the criteria. Liff et al. (2021) report validities ranging from .25 to .49 across a variety of industries, job roles, and criteria measures. These custom algorithms are particularly successful when many employees perform similar tasks and are evaluated consistently. In these studies, the custom algorithms directly predict a given job-related outcome, specific to the customer (e.g., uncorrected validities in call center service, .25; retail turnover, .29; technology sales, .42). These validities are comparable to the predictive validity of structured interviews in the employment context (McDaniel et al., 1994; Schmidt & Hunter, 1998), but without the resource-intensive requirements of interviewers and evaluators.

## Conclusion

Computational psychometrics has ushered in a whole new set of selection tools that are at our disposal and, as shown in this chapter, are showing promise in meeting the psychometric standards of our profession. The measurement accuracy of machine scoring structured interview responses to predict expert human evaluations and subsequent job performance metrics is well documented in this chapter. Early research results also show that the levels of adverse impact or subgroup differences in these new assessments methods are lower than, or the same as, traditional tools or tests. Additionally, the amount of data generated from these procedures (text transcriptions of interview responses) help facilitate new bias mitigation procedures (see Rottman et al., in press). These new methods for reducing adverse impact, in combination with little negative reduction in the validity of the measures, show promise in improving the diversity-validity dilemma of our assessment profession. There is a nascent amount of research on criterion validation and adverse impact mitigation with these new assessment methods, but early results are promising with similar predictive validities as traditional assessments.

A third pillar of success that is frequently de-weighted by our profession is the experience of the candidates who are taking our assessments. Most of the research on candidate acceptance of AVIs incorrectly compares the AVI with face-to-face live interviews. The reality of the hiring process is that AVIs aren't replacing live interviews; rather, they are replacing phone screens, resume screens, and maybe the first of multiple live interviews. More research is needed evaluating the acceptance levels of candidates being screened by the AVI compared to the candidates being screened by the selection steps in which the AVI is replacing (e.g., resume or phone screen). In a more realistic global comparison of applicant acceptance of asynchronous and synchronous video interviews, Griswold et al. (2021) found the differences were very similar, albeit in slight favor of synchronous interviews. A recent global study (8,343 applicants across 373 companies and 93 countries) evaluated how added stressors (COVID-19 rumination—constantly thinking or worrying about the pandemic) impact job interview anxiety during the AVI process. McCarthy et al. (2021) found a positive relationship between COVID-19 rumination and increased interview anxiety and decreased performance. This study highlights the importance of the best practices discussed earlier such as telling candidates what the AVI experience entails, giving practice time and the ability to redo responses, and explaining the competencies on which they are going to be measured.

Finally, process efficiencies and cost savings of using these novel assessments (e.g., AVIs) are significant. By combining the initial phone screen and first live interview into a single AVI experience, savings are realized in human reviewer time with automated scoring of the AVI, candidate experience is improved by combining multiple steps into one, and travel expenses are saved by eliminating the first live interview. One company documented $1 million in hard travel and expense savings with just replacing the first live interview and phone screen with a machine-scored AVI (HireVue unpublished case study).

Thus, the use of computational psychometrics to create novel methods to measure individual differences such as with AVIs, when compared to traditional tests or interview tools, appears to provide similar measurement accuracies, reduce or maintain subgroup differences, and have acceptable candidate reactions. These benefits, along with the significant process and cost savings, make novel assessments highly attractive in high-volume selection programs or when speed-to-hire without loss of quality of hire is desired.

Nevertheless, it should be clear that significant academic research is needed on these novel assessments to prove criterion validities and the improved levels of adverse impact. Some additional research needs are:

- compare human ratings (trained and untrained) of AVI responses with machine-scored results concerning overt and unconscious bias levels;
- compare reliability and consistency of human- and machine-scored AVI responses over time;
- determine if AVIs help prevent socially desirable or fakability as compared to traditional self-report assessment measures;
- evaluate the ability of AVIs to identify legitimate versus artificial voice responses to questions or the ability to fake good with previously constructed responses when a human evaluator isn't reviewing;
- determine if biometric data (e.g., pupil dilation) measured during the novel assessment has additive psychometric value (e.g., cognitive load during a live recorded interview).

## Future Directions

Modeling human decisions with novel assessment methods (e.g., AVIs, game-based assessment) is just the beginning of blending the sciences of AI and IO psychology. The promise of these multiple disciplines working together is already bearing fruit in academic research and applied settings. Logical extensions of this multidisciplined work are the use of machine learning to evaluate complex data sets garnered from more dynamic situations or interactions (versus static data collection with AVIs). For example, recordings of assessment center simulations or role-play scenarios, live structured interviews, and daily work interactions are all examples of how IO psychology and AI technology can interact to garner psychological measurements from unstructured day-in-the-life scenarios.

For computer scoring of these live scenarios to exist, even more advanced technologies must be used. For example, when combining video, audio, and language data sets together to analyze AVIs, as noted above, the prediction algorithm garners all its power from the language data set. Little to no incremental validity is added by video or audio data features. However, the power of video and audio data features lies in the slices of data (e.g., thin slicing) that are then mapped back on top of themselves to build a true understanding of the message and intent at that point in time. Just as humans analyze in real time the interaction between two people, and those judgments are fluid along with the interactive discussion, so must the computer be able to analyze in real time the interactive patterns. I believe the true power of video, audio, and text data features will be realized when the interoperability of these data sets can be identified by the AI machine to accurately mimic human judgments and measure personality traits, thinking styles, and abilities.

Early examples of this work are already underway in the health analysis arena (Winkler, 2021), whereby a variety of sensory data inputs (blood pressure, mobility, physical activity, sleep patterns, typing behavior, facial cues, and more) are analyzed in real time and potential health conditions (depression and cognitive decline) are flagged early with the hope of proactive, versus reactive, intervention improving the individual health status. This multidisciplinary project appears to involve work from data scientists, psychologists, medical professionals, technologists, and engineers (see www.viderahealth.com for an example).

I am not bringing up this new age work to elicit shock but rather to note that work in other disciplines can help expand or improve our traditional IO toolkits. It is naïve as a discipline to think IO psychology can achieve groundbreaking measurement techniques going solo. From an IO psychology perspective, the better we can mimic expert human judgments and traditional test scores with less biases, the more significant time and resource savings can be realized for the organizations in which we work. There appears to be evidence that these achievements are possible, but only with the assistance of data scientists and other disciplines working side by side with IO psychologists.

## References

Algorithmic Accountability Act of 2022. (2022, February 4). Congress.gov, H.R.6580 - 117th Congress (2021-2022). https://www.congress.gov/bill/117th-congress/house-bill/6580

Bleidorn, W., & Hopwood, C. J. (2019). Using machine learning to advance personality assessment and theory. *Personality and Social Psychology Review, 23*(2), 190-203.

Campbell, D. T., & Fiske, D. W. (1959). Convergent and discriminant validation by the multitrait-multimethod matrix. *Psychological Bulletin, 56*(2), 81-105.

Campion, M. A., Palmer, D. K., & Campion, J. E. (1997). A review of structure in the selection interview. *Personnel Psychology, 50*(3), 655-702. https://doi.org/10.1111/j.1744-6570.1997.tb00709.x

Campion, M. C., Campion, M. A., Campion, E. D., & Reider, M. H. (2016). Initial investigation into computer scoring of candidate essays for personnel selection. *Journal of Applied Psychology, 101*(7), 958-975. https://doi.org/10.1037/apl0000127

Chung, C. K., Rentfrow, P. J., & Pennebaker, J. W. (2014). Finding values in words: Using natural language to detect regional variations in personal concerns. In P. J. Rentfrow (Ed.), *Geographical psychology: Exploring the interaction of environment and behavior* (pp. 195-216). American Psychological Association. https://doi.org/10.1037/14272-011

Davier, A., Mislevy, R., & Hao, J. (2021). *Computational psychometrics: New methodologies for a new generation of digital learning and assessment.* Springer Nature Switzerland. https://doi.org/10.1007/978-3-030-74394-9

Devlin, J., Chang, M. W., Lee, K., & Toutanova, K. (2018). BERT: Pre-training of deep bidirectional transformers for language understanding. ArXiv preprint ArXiv:1810.04805.

Gosling, S. D., Gaddis, S., & Vazire, S. (2007). Personality impressions based on Facebook profiles. *ICWSM, 7*, 1-4.

Griswold, K., Phillips, J., Kim, M., Mondragon, N., Liff, J., & Gully, S. (2021). Global differences in applicant reactions to virtual interview synchronicity. *International Journal of Human Resource Management, 33*(15), 2991-3018. doi:10.1080/09585192.2021.1917641

Hartwell, C., Liff, J., Gardner, C., & Mondragon, N. (2022, April 28-30). Development and validation of asynchronous competency-based structured interview scoring algorithms. In J. Levashina & S. Baumgartner (Chairs), *New developments in structured interviews: From AI to technical interviews* [Symposium]. Society for Industrial and Organizational Psychology 2022 Convention, Seattle, WA.

Hickman, L., Bosch, N., Ng, V., Saef, R., Tay, L., & Woo, S. E. (2022). Automated video interview personality assessments: Reliability, validity, and generalizability investigations. *Journal of Applied Psychology, 107*(8), 1323-1351. https://doi.org/10.1037/apl0000695

Huffcutt, A. I., Culbertson, S. S., & Weyhrauch, W. S. (2013), Interview reliability. *International Journal of Selection and Assessment, 21*, 264-276. https://doi.org/10.1111/ijsa.12036

Jaser, Z., Petrakaki, D., Starr, R., & Oyarbide-Magana, E. (2022, January 27). Where automated job interviews fall short. *Harvard Business Review.* https://hbr.org/2022/01/where-automated-job-interviews-fall-short

Kern, M. L., Eichstaedt, J. C., Schwartz, H. A., Dziurzynski, L., Ungar, L. H., Stillwell, D. J., Kosinski, M., Ramones, S. M., & Seligman, M. E. (2013). The online social self: An open vocabulary approach to personality. *Assessment, 21,* 158–169.

Koenecke, A., Nam, A., Lake, E., Nudell, J., Quartey, M., Mengesha, Z., Toups, C., Rickford, J., Jurafsky, D., & Goel, S. (2020). Racial disparities in automated speech recognition. *Proceedings of the National Academy of Sciences, 117*(14), 7684–7689; doi:10.1073/pnas.1915768117

Kosinski, M., Stillwell, D., & Graepel, T. (2013). Private traits and attributes are predictable from digital records of human behavior. *Proceedings of the National Academy of Sciences, 110*(15), 5802–5805.

Leutner, F., Codreanu, S. C., Liff, J., & Mondragon, N. (2021). The potential of game- and video-based assessments for social attributes: Examples from practice. *Journal of Managerial Psychology, 36*(7), 533–547. https://doi.org/10.1108/JMP-01-2020-0023

Leutner, F., Liff, J., Zuloaga, L., & Mondragon, N. (2021). *HireVue's assessment science.* HireVue. https://webapi.hirevue.com/wp-content/uploads/2021/03/HireVue-Assessment-Science-whitepaper-2021.pdf?_ga=2.239366848.21559469.1628169017-383464143.1628169017

Levashina, J., Hartwell, C. J., Morgeson, F. P., & Campion, M. A. (2014). The structured employment interview: Narrative and quantitative review of the research literature. *Personnel Psychology, 67*(1), 241–293. https://doi.org/10.1111/peps.12052

Liff, J., Bradshaw, A., Shipp, R., Zuloaga, L., & Mondragon, N. (2021). *Interview- and game-based modular assessments technical validation report.* Unpublished technical report. HireVue.

Liu, Y., Ott, M., Goyal, N., Du, J., Joshi, M., Chen, D., Levy, O., Lewis, M., Zettlemoyer, L., & Stoyanov, V. (2019). RoBERTa: A Robustly Optimized BERT Pretraining Approach. ArXiv:1907.11692.

Loper, E., & Bird, S. (2002). NLTK: The Natural Language Toolkit. ArXiv preprint cs.CL/0205028.

McCarthy, J. M., Truxillo, D. M., Bauer, T. N., Erdogan, B., Shao, Y., Wang, M., Liff, J., & Gardner, C. (2021). Distressed and distracted by COVID-19 during high-stakes virtual interviews: The role of job interview anxiety on performance and reactions. *Journal of Applied Psychology, 106*(8), 1103–1117. https://doi.org/10.1037/apl0000943

McDaniel, M. A., Whetzel, D. L., Schmidt, F. L., & Maurer, S. D. (1994). The validity of employment interviews: A comprehensive review and meta-analysis. *Journal of Applied Psychology, 79*(4), 599–616.

Mischel, W. (1996). From good intentions to willpower. In P. M. Gollwitzer & J. A. Bargh (Eds.), *The psychology of action: Linking cognition and motivation to behavior* (pp. 197–218). Guilford.

New York City Counsel. (2021, December 11). Int 1894-2020 Version A (2020-2021): Automated Employment Decision Tools. https://legistar.council.nyc.gov/LegislationDetail.aspx?ID=4344524&GUID=B051915D-A9AC-451E-81F8-6596032FA3F9

Pennebaker, J. W., Boyd, R. L., Jordan, K., & Blackburn, K. (2015). *The development and psychometric properties of LIWC2015.* Austin, TX: University of Texas at Austin. https://doi.org/10.15781/T29G6Z

Pennebaker, J. W., & King, L. A. (1999). Linguistic styles: Language use as an individual difference. *Journal of Personality and Social Psychology, 77*(6), 1296–1312.
Rottman, C., Gardner, C., Liff, J., Mondragon, N., & Zuloaga, L. (2023). New strategies for addressing the diversity-validity dilemma with big data. *Journal of Applied Psychology.* https://doi.org/10.1037/apl0001084
Schmidt, F. L., & Hunter, J. E. (1998). The validity and utility of selection methods in personnel psychology: Practical and theoretical implications of 85 years of research findings. *Psychological Bulletin, 124*(2), 262.
Schwartz, H. A., Eichstaedt, J. C., Kern, M. L., Dziurzynski, L., Ramones, S. M., Agrawal, M., Shah, A., Kosinski, M., Stillwell, D., Seligman, M., & Ungar, L. H. (2013). Personality, gender, and age in the language of social media: The open-vocabulary approach. *PloS ONE, 8*(9), e73791. https://doi.org/10.1371/journal.pone.0073791
Stone, P. J., Dunphy, D. C., Smith, M. S., & Ogilvie, D. M. (1966). *The general inquirer: A computer approach to content analysis.* MIT Press.
Tippins, N. T., Oswald, F., & McPhail, S. M. (2021). Scientific, legal, and ethical concerns about AI-based personnel selection tools: A call to action. In *Personnel assessment and decisions.* PsyArXiv. doi:10.31234/osf.io/6gczw
Vazire, S., & Gosling, S. D. (2004). e-Perceptions: Personality impressions based on personal websites. *Journal of Personality and Social Psychology, 87*(1), 123–132.
Wang, J., Leutner, F., Brink, S., & Stillwell, D. (2021). How algorithms detect personality traces in video interviews: Explainable artificial intelligence as a psychometric test. Manuscript submitted for publication.
Winkler, R. (2021, September 21). Apple is working on iPhone features to help detect depression, cognitive decline. *Wall Street Journal.* https://www.wsj.com/articles/apple-wants-iphones-to-help-detect-depression-cognitive-decline-sources-say-11632216601?reflink=desktopwebshare_permalink
Youyou, W., Kosinski, M., & Stillwell, D. (2015). Computer-based personality judgments are more accurate than those made by humans. *Proceedings of the National Academy of Sciences, 112*(4), 1036–1040. https://doi.org/10.1073/pnas.1418680112

# 9
# Social Media Data in Assessments

*Daly Vaughn and Marc Cubrich*

## Social Media and Talent Assessment

The functionality and applications of social media platforms are ever-changing, and innovations and trends in talent assessment are reflected in the use of social media data in a staffing context. The ubiquity of social media is no longer limited to our personal lives but has become increasingly intertwined with recruitment and staffing processes over the past decade. Although debate continues surrounding the appropriateness of using social media data in this manner, the pervasiveness of social media is undeniable when considering its utilization by employers, hiring managers, and job seekers. In fact, 92% of employers report using social and professional networks to recruit talent, ranking above all other common hiring tactics (e.g., employee referrals, job boards, and advertisements) most used by employers today (CareerArc, 2021). Moreover, 86% of job seekers report using social media to search for potential jobs, apply directly to job postings using social sites, and engage with job-related content (CareerArc, 2021).

Trends in the utilization of social media in staffing contexts suggest it is not a passing fad, but rather an increasingly integral part of the hiring process. The potential applications of social media data in recruitment and staffing processes continue to evolve alongside the similarly dynamic talent landscape. To remain competitive, organizations and decision makers must be informed on the applications, benefits, and risks of social media platforms. The present chapter provides a research-informed overview of the use of social media data in hiring, delving specifically into the benefits, risks, and future opportunities resulting from its use, and ultimately informs a set of practical recommendations for practitioners in the current talent landscape.

## Foundational Principles for Social Media Assessment

A proper conceptualization of social media that is specific enough to reflect current use and application yet flexible enough to capture the rapidly changing functionality of these technologies is requisite to understanding its use in organizations. We rely on the conceptualization from Landers and Schmidt (2016) that defines social media as "a broad set of social technologies... including any Internet technology that enables the sharing of content created by users with other users" (Landers & Schmidt, 2016, p. 5). Among this growing list of social technologies, organizations can use several different social media platforms to gather information about candidates including Facebook, LinkedIn, Twitter, and Instagram, to name a few. To illustrate the rapidly changing nature of user preferences, even though it was only founded in 2016, TikTok now ranks in the top 10 most used social media platforms (Kemp, 2021) and has even introduced a functionality that allows users to create video resumes.

Regarding the specific application of social media data in an assessment context, the term "social media assessments" has been used to describe the evaluation of information from these social technologies for use in personnel decisions such as screening, selection, and promotion (Roth et al., 2016). Hiring managers often rely on diverse sources of information to inform personnel decisions, and the inclination to review social media information is a direct result of the rich information frequently contained on social media profiles. A common feature among these social technologies is the ability for users to share thoughts, opinions, or actions via images, via video, or in a text-based format. Also commonly present is a log of past images, videos, and text, as well as biographical information. Hiring managers may feel as though they can reduce uncertainty about a candidate and have a better understanding of whether a candidate is a good fit with the organization's culture by reviewing social media information (Carr, 2016).

Taking this a step further, some have argued that a failure to review a candidate's publicly available social media information can increase the risk of negligent hiring decisions (Berkelaar, 2014; Schmidt & O'Connor, 2016). However, research is sparse, and it is not evident today whether employers are using job seekers' social media data in a way that is aligned with science and best practices. Although structured methods for social media assessment exist (albeit with equivocal findings), the reality is that this information is often reviewed in an informal, unstructured way outside of the formal hiring process. To gain a better understanding of how social media assessments are being conducted today, the next section provides a review of applied survey data and employer-documented uses of social media.

## Social Media Assessments in Applied Settings

The use of social media in applied settings is evident in several domains within and outside organizations. In addition to being the most common recruitment method used by employers today (CareerArc, 2021), at least 70% of hiring managers report using social media to learn more about prospective talent, and 57% of those who do investigate candidates in this manner have found content that has led them not to hire candidates (CareerBuilder, 2018). Specific documented use cases involve practices such as cybervetting, in which an applicant's social media is evaluated by a hiring manager (Berkelaar, 2014). This practice is typically conducted to screen out candidates who engage in what is deemed as inappropriate behavior (e.g., profanity or substance use) and is often performed in an unstructured way (Becton et al., 2019; Berger & Zickar, 2016; Berkelaar, 2014). Formal practices involve structured ratings of social media for specific job-relevant characteristics, personality, and fit (Akhtar et al., 2018; Chiang & Suen, 2015; Liu & Campbell, 2017; Park et al., 2015; Van Iddekinge et al., 2016).

Although the present focus is primarily on the use of social media data in assessments, it should be noted that the use of social media in organizations extends well beyond recruitment, assessment, and selection alone. Organizations have increasingly recognized social media as a medium to engage with internal and external stakeholders, including customers, clients, employees, and job seekers. Public-facing social platforms can be used for external purposes such as promoting the organization and targeted recruitment, whereas internal-facing social platforms (e.g., enterprise social media) can be used to engage current employees and clients.

Social media tools within organizations, referred to as enterprise social media, can create online platforms to support onboarding and ongoing engagement for current employees, and can contribute to performance management, growth, and development, through activities such as sharing feedback, tips, and experiences (Leonardi et al., 2013; Willyerd, 2012). These internal use cases are supported by empirical evidence suggesting that work-related and social-related social media usage positively improves job satisfaction and reduces turnover intention through its effect on employees' engagement and organizational commitment (X. Zhang et al., 2019). What emerges from these findings is the undeniable pervasiveness of social media in several aspects of an organization's functioning. Looking beyond current applications and use cases of social media, the following sections delve further into the purported benefits of social media.

## Purported Benefits

The widespread utilization of social media is an ostensible testament to its utility in an organizational context. The specific benefits of the use of social media are framed through the lens of two key groups: job seekers and organizations (see Vaughn et al., 2019, for a more extensive review). The purported benefits described in existing literature coalesce around central themes for job seekers and organizations and are discussed more in depth hereafter.

### Benefits for Job Seekers

Social media has empowered job seekers to be even greater active agents in the hiring process, and as a result, social media can serve as a strategic resource for those seeking new employment opportunities. Strategically curated social media profiles allow job seekers a medium to elevate their self-reported skills, interests, and other job-relevant attributes. In this way, social media allows job seekers to build their "personal brand" and market their skills and abilities to organizations (Labrecque et al., 2011). Similarly, a well-curated social media presence on the part of the organization can be critical in the information-gathering stage as job seekers narrow their job search efforts. Professionally oriented social media platforms such as LinkedIn and Glassdoor not only allow prospective talent to search for jobs but also allow the opportunity to learn more about the role, company culture, interviewers, or hiring managers.

One of the primary benefits to job seekers of engaging in social media is the increased exposure to job opportunities. Both active and passive applicants are easily and instantly exposed to job opportunities through direct messages from recruiters, recommendations from friends or colleagues, and the appearance of listings in the user's social media feed (Vaughn et al., 2019). Prior to the digital era, professional networking often involved substantial effort, time investment, and even cost. Attending events hosted by professional or community organizations often meant travel, or membership dues were required to meet other professionals or connect with prospective employers. Users can easily connect with other professionals who have common interests at a much lower cost than previously required. In summary, social media allows a way for job seekers to market themselves, gain exposure to new career opportunities, and connect with likeminded professionals more efficiently and effectively than ever before.

## Benefits for Organizations

Organizations have been quick to recognize that the internet is not only a place to market their products or services but also a platform to continually engage with key external and internal parties. The continual engagement afforded by the use of social media creates several benefits for organizations. Among the most evident benefits, social media has enabled practitioners to engage in effective and efficient targeted recruitment strategies. More specifically, targeted recruitment strategies enable recruiters to seek out individuals they perceive as being a good fit for the company but who may not be actively looking for career opportunities (i.e., passive job seekers). The creation of communities of interest on social media outlets has made it easier for recruiters to target prospective talent with a specific set of shared values or skills, or even target underrepresented groups to increase diversity representation.

Social media has also increased access to the amount and type of candidate information that is available. Social media channels often contain rich information about an individual including their skills, experiences, interests, and other forms of biographical data. For example, LinkedIn allows users to display information about their education, professional experiences, past projects, extracurricular activities, and skills (Shields & Levashina, 2016). These platforms also offer informal sources of information not typically accessible through traditional assessment methods, and despite commonly accepted notions of impression management on social media, researchers have suggested that some forms of social media information are actually less susceptible to impression management compared to traditional sources of candidate information (Berkelaar, 2014; Brown & Vaughn, 2011; Carr, 2016).

Finally, all these benefits are associated with significantly diminished costs when compared to traditional methods. Research has indicated that e-recruitment methods reduce the cost of recruitment by up to 95% over traditional recruitment methods and can reduce time to hire by approximately 25% (Cober et al., 2000). The flexibility and diverse applications of social media platforms, coupled with time, cost, and effort savings, enable decisions makers to leverage social media for a variety of processes that benefit organizations and job seekers.

## Construct Validity Evidence: What Can Be Measured With Social Media Assessments

The mid-2000s witnessed the popularization of social technologies representative of our modern understanding of social media (e.g., Facebook; Boyd & Ellison, 2007). However, the personal nature of many social media platforms largely in the early years of adoption precluded them from serious consideration as part of the hiring processes. Although there was little evidence of the impact of social media use in the world of work at the time, precursory research contributed to our understanding of the psychological aspects of social media and the constructs that can be measured using them. A historical review indicates that the earliest social media research investigated topics such as determinants of social media use and the ability of social media profiles to accurately represent the owner (Brown et al., in press). Since that time, social media data has been linked to a disparate array of individual differences including personality, fit, intelligence, and other potentially job-relevant constructs.

If information derived from social media is to be used in a workplace context, especially for personnel decisions, it is important that research supports the notion that social media data accurately represent the user and that this information is meaningfully associated with job-relevant constructs. Given that social media platforms generally allow users the discretion to present themselves in any way they choose, the accuracy of social media as a representation of the owner is critical to consider. Using ratings of personal websites, research has indicated high levels of observer consensus and significant relationships with self-, ideal-, and informant ratings of Big Five personality traits (Vazire & Gosling, 2004), suggesting that digital representations of oneself convey valid information about the owner. Adding to these findings, close acquaintances of social media users report that the owners present themselves accurately (Gosling et al., 2007).

In terms of the constructs associated with social media data, a great deal of research has investigated the relationship between online behavior and personality and how these personality traits manifest in observable profile information. In addition to high levels of consensus for personality ratings across sources (Gosling et al., 2007; Vazire & Gosling, 2004), personality differences also manifest in the behaviors associated with social media. For example, extraversion is associated with the frequency and intensity of social media use such that extraverts show higher levels of activity compared to introverts (Gosling et al., 2011).

The observable profile information contained on social media sites has been described as "digital behavioral residue," suggesting that social media content is not only an indicator of past behavior but also ultimately indicative of something about the user (e.g., personality; Gosling et al., 2011). This stream of research has also been supported in the context of professional social networking platforms (e.g., LinkedIn). Roulin and Bangerter (2013) suggest that recruiters use LinkedIn profile information to make spontaneous personality inferences and specifically make judgments of a candidate's "fit" with the company culture. Adding to these findings, Caers and Castelyns (2011) indicate that recruiters believed they can determine the maturity, conscientiousness, and emotional stability of individuals using LinkedIn profiles. Finally, Chiang and Suen (2015) provide evidence that recruiters form perceptions of person–job, person–organization, and person–person fit based on LinkedIn profile information.

More recently, meta-analytic and technology-driven approaches to analyzing data have advanced our understanding of existing relationships. Meta-analytic results indicate modest but significant relationships between Big Five personality traits and social media behavior (Liu & Campbell, 2017). Rather than relying on human raters of social media profiles, researchers have increasingly advocated for automated approaches that capture "digital traces" derived from various aspects of a user's online activity (e.g., clicks, liked posts, time spent). Studies using this approach have found moderate relationships between digital traces and personality and between digital traces and intelligence, and these relationships are generally stronger when researchers use automated rather than manual procedures (Azucar et al., 2018; Settanni et al., 2018). In summary, existing construct validity evidence suggests that a diverse range of individual differences and behaviors can be reliably predicted from social media data and that automated approaches hold promise for improving the strength of these observed relationships.

## Criterion-Related Validity Evidence

If social media data are to be used in assessments, it is critical that the validity evidence of this information extends to job-relevant criteria. A growing body of research has investigated the criterion-related validity of the information contained on social media sites or associated with its use. With that said, a review of existing research indicates that findings have been equivocal and subject to some key limitations. It is important to distinguish between two streams of research in this area. The first is how personal and enterprise social media use for current employees can affect job performance and other key outcomes by increasing personal resources such as social capital. For example, Chen and colleagues (2019) demonstrate that affordances gained from social media use affect social network ties, which in turn positively influence the employees' job performance. The latter stream of research, and focus of the chapter, investigates the predictive utility of this information in a prehiring or assessment context.

Existing peer-reviewed research has been mixed in assessing the potential utility of social media assessments and the likelihood of these assessments to result in adverse impact. Although they have greatly contributed to our understanding of the validity of social media assessments, many studies have examined personal, rather than professional, social networking sites (e.g., Facebook). Using a student sample of Facebook profiles, Kluemper et al. (2012) demonstrated that profile ratings were significantly related to student job performance and perceptions of hireability, and these ratings accounted for incremental variance in job performance above and beyond cognitive ability. Counter to these findings, Van Iddekinge et al. (2016) found that ratings derived from Facebook information were unrelated to supervisor ratings of job performance, turnover intentions, and observed turnover. Further, these social media ratings did not contribute incremental validity above and beyond more traditional predictors (Van Iddekinge et al., 2016). Similarly, a recent study by L. Zhang et al. (2020) found that both unstructured and structured ratings of Facebook profiles were unrelated to key criteria. Further, there were no observed improvements in the prediction of future job performance or withdrawal intention by structuring these social media assessments (L. Zhang et al., 2020).

Within this vein of research, scholars have advocated for an examination of professional rather than personal social media to increase job relevance, legal defensibility, and ultimately the prediction of key criteria. In addition to demonstrating reliability and temporal stability of LinkedIn-based assessments, Roulin and Levashina (2019) found that hiring recommendations based on LinkedIn were positively associated with several career success indicators. Adding to these findings, Aguado et al. (2019) found a significant and positive relationship between four underlying LinkedIn profiles factors and productivity, absenteeism, and potential for professional development. Finally, a study by Cubrich et al. (2021) examined the relationships between LinkedIn profile elements and objective sales performance and tested the potential for subgroup differences in the presence of profile elements. With few exceptions, the results suggest that LinkedIn profile elements are not strongly correlated with sales performance metrics. Although there were some small-to-medium effects observed for group differences that favored majority groups, these characteristics were either unrelated to objective sales performance or unlikely to be relevant in a hiring context (Cubrich et al., 2021).

Taken together, it appears that professionally oriented social technologies such as LinkedIn may offer promise in terms of increasing predictive validity, job relevance, and legal defensibility. However, considering the equivocal findings across this body of research, coupled with challenges in terms of cost, scalability, and practicality, there remains continued cause for concern when it comes to social media assessments. If organizations and decision makers elect to use this information, they should strive to continually educate themselves on the evolving risks and concerns associated with social media use, particularly in an organizational context.

## Risks and Concerns

Although we acknowledge the myriad benefits of social media, a balanced treatment of the use of social media data in assessments must acknowledge the inherent risks resulting from its use. The specific benefits of social media are clear, and empirical research has demonstrated that social media information can be linked to a wide array of individual differences (e.g., personality, intelligence, and fit), and even job performance in some instances. Despite these promising areas of continued research, organizations and decision makers should remain informed about the potential risks and related concerns. As evidenced by our review of extant validity evidence, and while acknowledging promising reliability and temporal stability results (e.g., Roulin & Levashina, 2019), the criterion-validity evidence remains equivocal. Although some have advocated for structured ratings of social media content to mitigate validity and reliability concerns, the reality in practice is that these evaluations are often conducted in a spontaneous, unstructured manner. In addition to a lack of standardized content generated by users, the use of this data introduces the potential for bias and legal risks. For example, platforms like Facebook often contain protected class information (L. Zhang et al., 2020), and using such information increases the risk of bias, adverse impact, and illegal hiring practices. Next, job seekers may feel the use of social media information in hiring is invasive and may ultimately negatively impact the candidate experience. Finally, although researchers have begun to offer promising conceptual frameworks (e.g., McFarland & Ployhart, 2015; Roth et al., 2016), the lack of theoretical clarity surrounding the use of this information to inform personnel decisions remains. To weigh these competing concerns with the benefits, Table 9.1 presents a matrix of the benefits and risks associated with social media for both job seekers and organizations.

## Future State: Opportunities and Ongoing Risks

We anticipate several trends emerging as practitioners and researchers continue to explore possibilities of how social media data can be used in recruitment and assessment contexts. As of the time of this writing, within the United States and across large swaths of the global economy, we are amid a labor shortage crisis (Elkin et al., 2021) coupled with increased virtual workspaces for many roles bringing decision makers out of traditional hiring settings. These market conditions and societal changes have placed increased pressure on talent acquisition professionals to challenge and question the utility of traditional hiring approaches, such as lengthy multistage in-person prehire interviews and assessments and expensive on-site recruitment and hiring visits. Organizations have increasingly sought new and innovative ways to leverage available technologies that can allow them to quickly

Table 9.1 Benefit and Risk Matrix of Social Media Use by Group

|  | Benefits | Risks and Concerns |
|---|---|---|
| Job Seekers | • Medium to promote skills and attributes<br>• Easy exposure to more job opportunities<br>• Reduced effort and investment to network widely | • Disqualification for social media or web presence (or lack thereof)<br>• Ethical and privacy concerns (e.g., invasion of privacy)<br>• Reduced perceptions of fairness or poor candidate experience |
| Organizations | • Enables targeted recruitment<br>• Increased access to prospective talent<br>• Access to more or new candidate information<br>• Low cost<br>• Feeling of reduced uncertainty for decision makers<br>• Reduced impression management | • Limited reliability and validity evidence<br>• Lack of standardized content or procedural consistency in use<br>• Lack of theoretical clarity or existing frameworks<br>• Legal risks (e.g., risk of adverse impact or use of non-job-relevant information)<br>• Rapid pace of change in features, functionality, and availability of data |

recruit, qualify, and make an offer to secure talent in a virtual environment. In the current market conditions, organizations are placing a premium on speed-to-hire and reducing candidate friction in the application process. Organizations are seeking to leverage available technology to streamline their hiring processes and seek more passive and candidate-centric ways to find good-fit candidates deemed a strong match to roles within an organization. This environment leads to several potential trends we anticipate continuing to emerge in the marketplace in the coming years.

## Applications of Machine Learning Models to Social Media Data

One of the challenges that has plagued social media data as a potential source of assessment data is that it is a noisy signal. However, newer analytical methods are better at handling noisy signal data. Advanced computer-mediated approaches can be leveraged to point toward relevant knowledge, skills, ability, and other characteristics, and are superior to human raters at distilling the noise given the quantity of data available to process (Settanni et al., 2018). With the emergence of data science–driven paradigms, social media data can be leveraged more effectively than ever before. Traditional supervised approaches to train machine learning (ML) models requires subject matter experts to hand-label large amounts of data, which can be both time-consuming and expensive. With distant supervision or weak supervision approaches, the labels from unstructured data sources (e.g., social media data) can be inferred (in the case of distant supervision) or noisy labels can be utilized (in the case of weak supervision) to train an ML model. Compared to traditional supervised models, distant and weak supervision are methods of obtaining training data that require much fewer hand-labeled samples, by using either lower-quality labels in the case of weak supervision or training on unlabeled data sources in the case of distant supervision. These ML approaches have the advantage to supervised approaches in that they increase the amount of data that can be utilized in a model while drastically reducing the time and cost requirements of training the models using manually hand-labeled samples (Sabeti, 2019).

Despite advances in these approaches to handling unstructured data, as of the time of this writing, no peer-reviewed literature has provided evidence that these approaches yield more valid or reliable assessments within selection contexts. Further, advances in these approaches will continue to struggle to address some of the more intractable challenges associated with the use of social media data for selection purposes such as privacy and ethical concerns, as well as the general lack of standardization and missing data challenges. Nonetheless, we anticipate that more attempts will be made in research and practice to deploy ML model–based approaches to evaluate opportunity to increase the efficiency, scalability, and utility of using social media data within hiring contexts.

## Blockchain-Based and/or Job Seeker–Specific Transferrable Profile

Though perhaps a more speculative prediction, we anticipate the emergence of a job seeker–centric paradigm to supplement existing practices such that measurable traits, characteristics, certifications, skills, and abilities can be maintained pertaining to a person's unique digital identifier as may be enabled through blockchain and social technologies. IBM (2018) defines blockchain technology as "a shared, immutable ledger that facilitates the process of recording transactions and tracking assets in a business network." Assets might be tangible items or intangible items. Under a blockchain paradigm, it might be possible for an applicant to have a universal profile when applying for a job, which can be shared with a prospective employer or recruitment agency. Doing so may create opportunities for job seekers to share their unique and transferrable (from company to company or intracompany) profile and qualification information and create a more streamlined process that reduces redundancies when applying within and across organizations. A related but distinct concept that has received significant coverage in popular press is China's social credit system (Wong & Dobson, 2019). While a shareable profile for employment purposes would take shape differently in Westernized democracies, some of the concepts are similar in that one could build a profile that remains with the individual along one's career journey.

## Continued Caution and Emerging Guidance

An unanswered question is how these newer models and job-matching technologies will hold up to legal scrutiny. Specifically, will they be convincing enough in evidencing construct validity, clear job relevance, criterion-related validity evidence, and low risk of adverse impact relative to available alternatives to warrant exploration and use? There is also continued progress in creation of regulations to protect the privacy of individuals and create more transparency and awareness of how one's data are being used (e.g., California Consumer Privacy Act [CCPA], California Privacy Rights Act [CPRA], General Data Protection Regulation [GDPR]). The public's acceptance of these approaches in hiring from an ethics and fairness perspective is still unclear and will be evidenced in coming years as more automated matching and qualification approaches are explored by organizations.

Entrepreneurs and human capital management technology firms seeking to create service offerings deploying automated methods are also likely to continue to encounter resistance from the social media companies no longer willingly allowing their users' data to be scraped by third-party providers for potential commercial gain. Scraping user data for commercial gain is often against social media companies' terms of use, and social media companies may act to prevent access if more definitive forthcoming legal precedent allows. Using bots to scrape social media site data may be viewed as competitive to social media sites' own current or future offerings, or may pose concerns to the parent social media company in maintaining user trust. Alternatively, not allowing bots to scrape the publicly available data may create precedent that could limit some forms of research and innovation or may be perceived as overstepping antitrust laws.

The definitive case to follow in this ongoing area will be *LinkedIn Corporation v HiQ Labs, Inc.* The crux of this case is whether HiQ, a talent management company, can scrape publicly available LinkedIn members' profiles for use in their predictive algorithms. LinkedIn previously sent a cease-and-desist letter and implemented deterrents for their data to be accessed in this manner. HiQ then sued LinkedIn, seeking injunctive relief and a declaratory judgment that LinkedIn could not lawfully prevent HiQ from accessing this publicly available information. After a preliminary victory for HiQ in 2019 with the Ninth District Court of Appeals, which upheld HiQ's right to access this publicly available information, the U.S. Supreme Court has more recently granted a writ of certiorari vacating the Ninth District Court's decision and opening it up for reconsideration in the lower courts (*LinkedIn Corporation v HiQ Labs, Inc.*, 2021). At the time of this writing, the case has been remanded and is undergoing further review by the Ninth District Court. A more definitive decision as to whether the Ninth District Court will reaffirm the previous position carries significant impact to the landscape of data scraping. All the above poses significant risk to organizations looking to explore these more automated and scalable approaches.

## Practical Recommendations for Practitioners Now

Given social media's pervasiveness, it is important that organizational practitioners have strong guidance in navigating the appropriate use of data from these technologies in hiring and sourcing contexts. Building upon several resources that provide practitioners with recommendations (e.g., Chambers & Winter, 2017; SHRM, 2016; Vaughn et al., 2019), we take an updated look and offer the following recommendations (see Box 9.1 for a summary).

For recruiter or hiring managers performing manual reviews of applicant social media data, we suggest employers have organizational policy and ongoing training regarding best practices in consultation with one's own legal counsel. If information is being collected or ratings are being made based on social media data in an assessment context, it should be evaluated for job

> **Box 9.1 Summary of Practice Recommendations**
>
> 1. Avoid use of social media–based assessment (manually rated or automated) without criterion-related validity evidence.
> 2. Explore viability with extreme caution.
> 3. Stay current and apply known best practices.
> 4. Apply strategies to reduce legal risk—for example, create social media and hiring policy; deference to existing hiring guidelines such as the *Principles* (Tippins et al., 2018) and *Standards* (American Educational Research Association [AERA], American Psychological Association [APA], & National Council on Measurement in Education [NCME], 2014); systematic approach to data classification process.
> 5. Monitor and evaluate group differences.
> 6. Monitor candidate perceptions of privacy and ethical concerns.
> 7. Consider social media as part of targeted recruitment strategy.
> 8. Provide ongoing training on common potential biases, as well as the rapidly evolving privacy regulations; use modern case study examples in training.
> 9. Communicate how social media data is reviewed to job seekers and offer option to opt in or out from having job-relevant social media data reviewed.
> 10. Capture what information is collected and how data is documented at different stages of the hiring process.
> 11. Avoid automated approaches without strong evidence of utility, fairness, legal compliance, and positive candidate experience.
> 12. Work with diverse cross-functional teams if exploring viability of automated approaches.

relevance, connection to posthire outcomes, and potential for unintended biases or adverse impact. Further, not all prospective candidates will have a comparable social media presence, and organizations should have a clear rule in place to handle candidates with missing or incomplete social media profiles. A CareerBuilder (2018) survey indicated that 47% of employers would be less likely to call a candidate for an interview if they were unable to find that job candidate online. To counteract these risks for biases, measures should be taken to prevent the penalization of candidates without a social media presence, or there should be a method to obtain the same information through alternative channels. Ongoing training sessions should be provided by subject matter experts to present updated legal and regulatory guidance with modern examples for decision makers to help reduce risk of improper use.

In addition, organizational policies should be consistent with the spirit of emerging data privacy regulations. For example, if decision makers in an organization choose to allow online searches or reviews as part of the screening process, they should also consider informing job seekers about these practices in advance. If social media is used in the hiring process for assessment purposes, employers are encouraged to share information on whether and how publicly available information from social media may be examined. Employers should consider allowing job seekers the opportunity to proactively opt in or self-select out of having work-related social media data reviewed in the screening process. If employers do not feel comfortable with disclosing information about their social media data evaluation process, this may signal that these practices should be strongly reconsidered or modified.

Given the adoption rates, ubiquity, and conveniences offered, it may not be realistic (or even preferred) to enforce policies that recommend outright bans to access all forms of social media data across the job seeker–employer life cycle. However, it may be possible to offer strong guidance and structure on when and how data should be accessed across the various steps of the recruitment, and what information needs to be communicated to the applicant and documented by the decision maker in line with updated regulations. Ongoing and modernized recruiter and hiring manager training could include guidance on applicable privacy law and hiring practice guidelines. Training could include information regarding unconscious biases such as presenting research regarding "similar to me" biases and tying those back to how they could stymie organizational efforts toward diversity, equity, and inclusion initiatives. If utilized strategically, social media may allow for targeted recruitment within historically underrepresented communities of interest. Candidate fairness, privacy, and ethical considerations should be considered alongside investigations of business utility.

Currently, we do not believe there is sufficient evidence of utility to warrant the risk of employers deploying more automated methods of social media assessment in practice. However, if an employer is exploring the potential of deploying automated approaches that incorporate social media assessments or digital traces generated through job seekers' use of social media data, we advise an extremely conservative and rigorous approach to exploring the potential application. We believe this is important for both applications of job-matching technologies and more traditional qualification or screening assessment approaches deployed after candidate application using social media data. Both early-stage use cases create an opportunity to unintentionally introduce bias into a staffing process if not carefully designed and monitored. Applied at scale early in the life cycle, even small biases driven by automated algorithmic decisions could have sizable impact on the composition of qualified applicant pools and subsequent hires for a given role.

If implementing these automated approaches, cross-functional expertise would be essential. At minimum, the composition of a research team exploring these methods in practice might include members with strong data analytics proficiency; legal, compliance, and privacy expertise; engineering and computer science capabilities; and industrial-organizational psychology domain area knowledge.

## Conclusion

With emerging trends such as virtual reality, augmented reality, workplace virtual conferencing, and a host of other forms of immersive and engaging company-branded experiences on the horizon for social media users, the talent assessment community may only be scratching the surface of what is possible at the intersection of workplace hiring and social media use. Many interesting and exciting opportunities remain unexplored in this burgeoning space. To proceed with more confidence in practice, the talent assessment community will need to continue to develop a more refined understanding of whether and what types of additional information gleaned from social media digital traces offer value within the context of job seeker assessment versus simply introducing more noise and potential for bias to the hiring process. Presently, based on the available peer-reviewed research, Human Capital Management professionals are encouraged to use extreme caution if contemplating deploying these methods. With increasing conveniences, considerable risks are introduced to the hiring process. Nonetheless, this remains an area worthy of continued monitoring within the talent assessment community as research and practice continues to develop in this area.

## References

Akhtar, R., Winsborough, D., Ort, U., Johnson, A., & Chamorro-Premuzic, T. (2018). Detecting the dark side of personality using social media status updates. *Personality and Individual Differences, 132*, 90–97.

American Educational Research Association, American Psychological Association, & National Council on Measurement in Education. (2014). *Standards for Educational and Psychological Testing*. American Educational Research Association.

Aguado, D., Andrés, J. C., García-Izquierdo, A. L., & Rodríguez, J. (2019). LinkedIn "Big Four": Job Performance Validation in the ICT Sector. *Journal of Work and Organizational Psychology, 35*(2), 53–64.

Azucar, D., Marengo, D., & Settanni, M. (2018). Predicting the Big 5 personality traits from digital footprints on social media: A meta-analysis. *Personality and Individual Differences, 124*, 150–159.

Becton, J. B., Walker, H. J., Schwager, P., & Gilstrap, J. B. (2019). Is what you see what you get? Investigating the relationship between social media content and counterproductive work behaviors, alcohol consumption, and episodic heavy drinking. *International Journal of Human Resource Management, 30*(15), 2251–2272.

Berger, J. L., & Zickar, M. J. (2016). Theoretical propositions about cybervetting: A common antecedents model. In R. N. Landers & G. B. Schmidt (Eds.), *Social media in employee selection and recruitment: Theory, practice, and current challenges* (pp. 43–58). Springer.

Berkelaar, B. L. (2014). Cybervetting, online information, and personnel selection: New transparency expectations and the emergence of a digital social contract. *Management Communication Quarterly, 28*(4), 479–506.

Boyd, D. M., & Ellison, N. B. (2007). Social network sites: Definition, history and scholarship. *Journal of Computer Mediated Education, 13*(1), Article 11.

Brown, V. R., Cubrich, M., & Vaughn, E. D. (in press). Social media in the workplace. In Z. Yan (Ed.), *Cambridge handbook of cyber behavior*. Cambridge University Press.

Brown, V. R., & Vaughn, E. D. (2011). The writing on the (Facebook) wall: The use of social networking sites in hiring decisions. *Journal of Business and Psychology, 26*(2), 219.

Caers, R., & Castelyns, V. (2011). LinkedIn and Facebook in Belgium: The influences and biases of social network sites in recruitment and selection procedures. *Social Science Computer Review, 29*, 437–448. https://doi.org/10.1177/0894439310386567

CareerArc. (2021). *2021 future of recruiting study*. https://explore.careerarc.com/future-of-recruiting

CareerBuilder. (2018, August 9). *More than half of employers have found content on social media that caused them NOT to hire a candidate, according to recent CareerBuilder survey*. http://press.careerbuilder.com/2018-08-09-More-Than-Half-of-Employers-Have-Found-Content-on-Social-Media-That-Caused-Them-NOT-to-Hire-a-Candidate-According-to-Recent-CareerBuilder-Survey

Carr, C. T. (2016). An uncertainty reduction approach to applicant information-seeking in social media: Effects on attributions and hiring. In R. N. Landers & B. G. Schmidt (Eds.), *Social media in employee selection and recruitment: Theory, practice, and current challenges* (pp. 157–174). Springer International Publishing.

Chambers, R., & Winter, J. (2017, August 9). *Social media and selection: A brief history and practical recommendations*. https://www.siop.org/Research-Publications/Items-of-Interest/ArtMID/19366/ArticleID/1716/Social-Media-and-Selection-A-Brief-History-and-Practical-Recommendations

Chen, X., Wei, S., Davison, R. M., & Rice, R. E. (2019). How do enterprise social media affordances affect social network ties and job performance? *Information Technology & People, 33*(1), 361–388.

Chiang, J. K. H., & Suen, H. Y. (2015). Self-presentation and hiring recommendations in online communities: Lessons from LinkedIn. *Computers in Human Behavior, 48*, 516–524.

Cober, R. T., Brown, D. J., Blumental, A. J., Doverspike, D., & Levy, P. (2000). The quest for the qualified job surfer: It's time the public sector catches the wave. *Public Personnel Management, 29*(4), 479–496.

Cubrich, M., King, R. T., Mracek, D. L., Strong, J. M., Hassenkamp, K., Vaughn, D., & Dudley, N. M. (2021). Examining the criterion-related validity evidence of LinkedIn profile elements in an applied sample. *Computers in Human Behavior, 120*, 106742. https://doi.org/10.1016/j.chb.2021.106742

Elkin, E., Chau, M. N., & de Sousa, A. (2021, September 2). *Your food prices are at risk as the world runs short of workers*. Bloomberg. https://www.bloomberg.com/news/features/2021-09-02/food-prices-driven-up-by-global-worker-shortage-brexit

Gosling, S. D., Augustine, A. A., Vazire, S., Holtzman, N., & Gaddis, S. (2011). Manifestations of personality in online social networks: Self-reported Facebook-related behaviors and observable profile information. *Cyberpsychology, Behavior, and Social Networking, 14*(9), 483–488.

Gosling, S. D., Gaddis, S., & Vazire, S. (2007, March). *Personality impressions based on Facebook profiles* [Paper presentation]. International Conference on Weblogs and Social Media, Boulder, CO.

IBM. (2018, July 31). *What is blockchain technology?* https://www.ibm.com/blogs/blockchain/2018/07/what-is-blockchain-technology/

Kemp, S. (2021, July 21). *Digital 2021: July global Statshot report*. DataReportal. https://datareportal.com/reports/digital-2021-july-global-statshot

Kluemper, D. H., Rosen, P. A., & Mossholder, K. (2012). Social networking websites, personality ratings, and the organizational context: More than meets the eye. *Journal of Applied Social Psychology, 42*(5), 1143–1172.

Labrecque, L. I., Markos, E., & Milne, G. R. (2011). Online personal branding: Processes, challenges, and implications. *Journal of Interactive Marketing, 25*(1), 37–50.

Landers, R. N., & Schmidt, G. B. (2016). Social media in employee selection and recruitment: An overview. In R. N. Landers & G. B. Schmidt (Eds.), *Social media in employee selection and recruitment: Theory, practice, and current challenges* (pp. 3–14). Springer International Publishing.

Leonardi, P. M., Huysman, M., & Steinfield, C. (2013). Enterprise social media: Definition, history, and prospects for the study of social technologies in organizations. *Journal of Computer-Mediated Communication, 19*(1), 1–19.

LinkedIn Corporation v. HiQ Labs, Inc. 593 U.S. (2021). https://www.supremecourt.gov/orders/courtorders/061421zor_6j36.pdf

Liu, D., & Campbell, W. K. (2017). The Big Five personality traits, Big Two metatraits and social media: A meta-analysis. *Journal of Research in Personality, 70*, 229–240.

McFarland, L. A., & Ployhart, R. E. (2015). Social media in organizations: A theoretical framework to guide research and practice. *Journal of Applied Psychology, 100*(6), 1653–1677.

Park, G., Schwartz, H. A., Eichstaedt, J. C., Kern, M. L., Kosinski, M., Stillwell, D. J., & Seligman, M. E. (2015). Automatic personality assessment through social media language. *Journal of Personality and Social Psychology, 108*(6), 934–952.

Roth, P. L., Bobko, P., Van Iddekinge, C. H., & Thatcher, J. B. (2016). Social media in employee-selection-related decisions: A research agenda for uncharted territory. *Journal of Management, 42*(1), 269–298.

Roulin, N., & Bangerter, A. (2013). Social networking websites in personnel selection: A signaling perspective on recruiters' and applicants' perceptions. *Journal of Personnel Psychology, 12*(3), 143–151.

Roulin, N., & Levashina, J. (2019). LinkedIn as a new selection method: Psychometric properties and assessment approach. *Personnel Psychology, 72*(2), 187–211.

Sabeti, B. (2019, June 8). *Various types of supervision in machine learning.* Medium. https://medium.com/@behnamsabeti/various-types-of-supervision-in-machine-learning-c7f32c190fbe

Schmidt, G. B., & O'Connor, K. W. (2016). Legal concerns when considering social media data in selection. In R. N. Landers & G. B. Schmidt (Eds.), *Social media in employee selection and recruitment: Theory, practice, and current challenges* (pp. 265–288). Springer International Publishing.

Settanni, M., Azucar, D., & Marengo, D. (2018). Predicting individual characteristics from digital traces on social media: A meta-analysis. *Cyberpsychology, Behavior, and Social Networking, 21*(4), 217–228.

Shields, B., & Levashina, J. (2016). Comparing the social media in the United States and BRIC nations, and the challenges faced in international selection. In R. N. Landers & B. G. Schmidt (Eds.), *Social media in employee selection and recruitment: Theory, practice, and current challenges* (pp. 157–174). Springer International Publishing.

SHRM (2016, January 7). *Using social media for talent acquisition–recruitment and screening.* https://www.shrm.org/hr-today/trends-and-forecasting/research-and-surveys/documents/shrm-social-media-recruiting-screening-2015.pdf

Tippins, N., Sackett, P., & Oswald, F. (2018). Principles for the validation and use of personnel selection procedures. *Industrial and Organizational Psychology, 11*, 1–97. 10.1017/iop.2018.195.

Van Iddekinge, C. H., Lanivich, S. E., Roth, P. L., & Junco, E. (2016). Social media for selection? Validity and adverse impact potential of a Facebook-based assessment. *Journal of Management, 42*(7), 1811–1835.

Vaughn, D., Petersen, N., & Gibson, C. (2019). The use of social media in staffing. In R. Landers (Ed.), *The Cambridge handbook of technology and employee behavior* (pp. 232–268). Cambridge University Press.

Vazire, S., & Gosling, S. D. (2004). e-Perceptions: Personality impressions based on personal websites. *Journal of Personality and Social Psychology, 87*(1), 123–132.

Willyerd, K. (2012). Social tools can improve employee onboarding. *Harvard Business Review*. https://hbr.org/2012/12/social-tools-can-improve-e.

Wong, K. L. X., & Dobson, A. S. (2019). We're just data: Exploring China's social credit system in relation to digital platform ratings cultures in Westernised democracies. *Global Media and China*, 4(2), 220–232. https://doi.org/10.1177/2059436419856090

Zhang, L., Van Iddekinge, C. H., Arnold, J. D., Roth, P. L., Lievens, F., Lanivich, S. E., & Jordan, S. L. (2020). What's on job seekers' social media sites? A content analysis and effects of structure on recruiter judgments and predictive validity. *Journal of Applied Psychology*, 105(12), 1530–1546. https://doi.org/10.1037/apl0000490

Zhang, X., Ma, L., Xu, B., & Xu, F. (2019). How social media usage affects employees' job satisfaction and turnover intention: An empirical study in China. *Information & Management*, 56(6), 103136. https://doi.org/10.1016/j.im.2018.12.004

# 10
# Transforming Leadership Assessment Using Natural Language Processing

*Scott Tonidandel and Betsy H. Albritton*

The science and practice of leadership assessment is primed for a transformation. With advances in computer science, artificial intelligence (AI), machine learning, and natural language processing (NLP), the organizational sciences are in a unique position to leverage big data sources and methods to vastly improve our understanding of phenomena of interest in organizational science (Tonidandel et al., 2018). Nowhere is this truer than in the area of leadership assessment. The purpose of this chapter is to explore the ways in which NLP can transform leadership assessment by extracting meaning from text data. First, we will introduce a variety of NLP techniques that can be leveraged to assess leaders. Then, we will discuss the advantages of using such an approach over more conventional approaches. We will also review some of the most recent applications of these techniques to evaluate leadership and offer recommendations for implementing these approaches in future work.

## What Is Natural Language Processing?

NLP is not a single tool but instead describes a host of different methodological approaches to understanding textual data. Figure 10.1 illustrates the positioning of NLP with respect to AI, machine learning, and deep learning methods. AI simply describes any computational solution to a human task. Within AI is a subset of methods, machine learning methods, where the computer "learns" from its "experience" to improve upon its prediction of some outcome. These machine learning models can be either supervised

150   TALENT ASSESSMENT

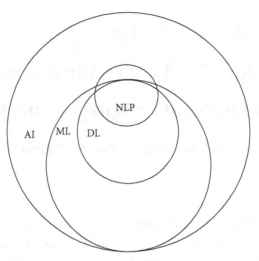

**Figure 10.1.** Positioning of natural language processing (NLP) with respect to artificial intelligence (AI), machine learning (ML), and deep learning (DL) methods

or unsupervised. Supervised methods involve providing the algorithm labeled data from which to learn. Labeled data simply means that the criterion is known to the training algorithm, whereas unsupervised machine learning methods work to identify patterns in the data without the need for a priori human intervention. Familiar examples of supervised machine learning are linear and logistic regression, and examples of unsupervised machine learning include techniques such as cluster analysis and principal components analysis. A specific form of machine learning is deep learning. Deep learning utilizes a model based on the structure of connected neurons called an artificial neural network (ANN). These neuron-like structures can be layered on top of one another to create "deep" networks that are able to achieve incredible predictive accuracy across a range of tasks. As can be seen from the Venn diagram in Figure 10.1, NLP intersects with each of these approaches.

## Non–Machine Learning Natural Language Processing

Readers are probably most familiar with NLP methods that are not machine learning methods. These non–machine learning methods are what have historically been labeled as computer-assisted text analysis (CATA). These approaches usually begin by representing text in matrix form using a term-document matrix where each column is a word (i.e., term) and each row is a document. So, the number of rows matches the total number of documents, the number of columns corresponds to the total number of unique words found in the entire set of documents, and each cell represents the number of times a particular word appears in each individual document. The approach of creating a term-document matrix is sometimes referred to as a bag-of-words (BOW) model. This BOW can then be subject to a variety of queries to generate meaning from the text. The word cloud is a simple example of creating a visual illustration of the frequency of words across the various documents. Other approaches for text mining involve applying dictionaries or lexicons, a collection of words belonging to a particular category, to the term-document matrix. A familiar application of this might be sentiment analysis, where one attempts to assign a numerical score to text based on the quantity of positive or negative sentiments expressed. To do this, one simply counts the frequency of positive and negative words found in text by cross-referencing the term-document matrix with a sentiment dictionary and assigning an overall sentiment score based on the number of positive and negative sentiment words that are present in each document. An example of a binary classification of sentiment words is the Bing lexicon (Hu & Liu, 2004) that contains nearly 7,000 words. This same strategy can be expanded upon to use more refined sentiment dictionaries, such as the NRC lexicon (Mohammad & Turney, 2013), which goes beyond simple polarity to catalog specific emotion words (e.g., fear, disgust, joy). Though frequently applied to sentiments, the same approach can be used to catalog other features of text that might be of interest, such as parts of speech or an individually customized word list.

Looking up the frequencies of words in a BOW or assigning scores to individual words is a relatively straightforward task. However, these BOWs are quite limited for several reasons. First, analyzing these term-document matrices can be quite challenging. These matrices have a column to represent every word that appears anywhere in your corpus. Thus, there are often many, many columns of data, and the number of columns typically far exceeds the number of rows (i.e., the number of documents). In addition, most documents will likely only contain a small subset of all of the available words in your corpus, meaning that most of the cells in the matrix will be zero. Thus, a term-document matrix composed of mostly zeros is what is known as a sparse matrix. This high-dimensional sparse matrix poses a number of analytical challenges that make leveraging the information contained within quite difficult as it suffers from the "curse of dimensionality" (Bellman, 1961), where the computer resources required increase exponentially and prediction accuracy decreases. A second major limitation with the BOW models is that the mere presence of a word does not help elucidate the meaning of what was actually said. For example, a word such as "happy" would be scored as a positive sentiment even if it appears in a sentence such as "I am not happy." In a similar way, an identical word can take on very different meanings depending on the context, called polysemy. For example, the word "mole" could refer to a spy, a skin blemish, or a small animal depending on the context (McCaughren, 2009).

## Machine Learning Natural Language Processing

Machine learning and specifically deep learning techniques provide a solution to both of these problems via word embeddings. Word embeddings are simply a way of assigning numbers to words that capture the meaning of words. ANNs typically make use of one of two different strategies for creating word embeddings. These strategies are known as prediction-based word embeddings. One type of prediction-based embedding predicts the probability of a given word appearing given the context of words around it. This is known as a *continuous bag of words* model. Alternatively, one can attempt to do the converse and predict the context given a particular word, known as a *skip-gram* model. Both of these approaches essentially create a numeric score, an embedding, for each word that captures the usage context of the word and thus the inherent meaning of that word. In this way, embeddings can identify other words that have a similar meaning because they have similar usage contexts and thus similar embedding scores. Word embeddings also solve the sparse matrix problem by mapping the high-dimensional matrix into a simpler lower dimensional space. In simple terms, what this means is that instead of having each word independently represented in the data set, words can now be grouped together based on the semantic similarity of the words.

The list of NLP approaches and algorithms is nearly endless and constantly evolving. Nevertheless, the categories above provide a general way for thinking about different approaches to gaining insight from unstructured text. It is important to note that these categories are not mutually exclusive. For example, although a BOW can be used for simple non–machine learning methods like a word cloud, these same BOWs can be used as input for complex ANNs. Similarly, though embeddings are frequently used in supervised deep learning applications, they can also be used in unsupervised models such as topic models.

## Why Use Natural Language Processing for Leadership Assessment

Leadership assessment quite often relies on follower evaluations of the leader via questionnaires. These questionnaires are often employed in scientific research or in industry in the form of performance evaluation batteries such as 360 assessments. While questionnaires certainly have their purpose, they are known to suffer from a variety of issues such as retrospective bias and social desirability (Fischer et al., 2020). These evaluations are also deficient because they fail to account for actual leader behaviors. That is, most questionnaires do not seem to relate to what leaders are actually doing but instead represent an overall subjective assessment of "goodness" or "liking of one's boss" (Yammarino et al., 2020). Some items contained in 360 assessments are structured to target specific leader behaviors, but these still conflate evaluations of behaviors by peers, supervisors, and direct reports with the behaviors themselves. Alternatively, leaders may be assessed via assessment center methods. While this approach is an improvement over simpler follower evaluations, in-person assessment centers are quite costly and difficult to scale to lots of individuals. NLP provides a mechanism of leadership assessment that can overcome some of these shortcomings.

One advantage of text data is that it shifts the focus of assessment back to the behaviors of a leader. While at first glance text may not seem like a behavior, it does capture what a leader is saying or signaling to followers and thus aligns with signaling theory. Signaling theory has been identified as a useful explanatory framework to understand whether and how a sender might choose to signal information to a receiver (Connelly et al., 2011). Like behaviors, signals possess many characteristics such as observability, frequency, and consistency to name a few. Leadership by definition is a social influence process and textual data serves as a form of signal in this leadership process (Bastardoz & Van Vugt, 2019). For example, leaders attempt to influence followers via signals in text data to communicate shared values, goals, or a vision.

Another advantage of relying on text data for assessing leaders is the sheer abundance of text that is available. For example, over 300 billion emails are sent every single day. In addition, there are myriad other data sources that can easily be transformed into text such as audio files from Zoom meetings. Not only is there more of it, but also textual data are much richer and more nuanced than our conventional numerical surveys. Along with increased richness come continuous streams of data. Rather than one-shot surveys, text data can be passively collected throughout the day as it is being produced in various forms by a leader. For example, one could collect emails sent by leaders to their direct reports or subordinates, messages sent via the chat function in virtual meetings, or transcriptions of virtual meetings on platforms such as Zoom.

By focusing on text data, one can have greater insight into a leader through access to continuous streams of richer data that represent what leaders are actually saying and doing (signaling) on a daily basis as they interact with their followers and other constituents. NLP methods provide a mechanism for analyzing this text data at scale without the need for subject matter experts (SMEs) to manually rate or content code all of the text.

## Natural Language Processing Applied to Leadership

The many decisions involved in running NLP methods can be overwhelming. Fortunately, industrial-organizational psychologists have already begun to apply NLP to study various aspects of leadership. These exemplar studies offer insight into which NLP methods were shown to be helpful in measuring and assessing different leader behaviors and experiences. In what follows, we present some of the most recent NLP research as it relates to leadership assessment using the typology from Figure 10.1. Additional summaries of NLP techniques and helpful resources for getting started are provided in Table 10.1.

### Non–Machine Learning: Computer-Assisted Text Analysis

One recent example of the use of CATA in studying leadership is Sergent and Stajkovic's (2020) investigation of gender differences in political figures

Table 10.1  A Summary of NLP Techniques and Relevant Resources

| NLP Technique | Definition and Considerations | Resources to Get Started |
| --- | --- | --- |
| Text Preprocessing | Any steps taken to prepare text data for analysis. Some examples include stemming, lemmatizing, and the removal of stopwords. Not all NLP methods require text preprocessing and special consideration should be given to the decisions made about text preprocessing as it can impact the results of the analysis. | • Banks et al. (2018)<br>• Hickman et al. (2022)<br>• Singh and Gupta (2017) |
| Labeling | The process of generating ground-truth data to be used in supervised machine learning methods. | • Snorkel (Ratner et al., 2017)<br>• Prodigy (https://prodi.gy/) |
| CATA | A BOW approach involving the comparison of word frequencies from term-document matrices to preset or customized dictionaries (lists of words representative of a specific topic, sentiment, or construct). This is an ideal technique for a beginner of NLP. | • LIWC (Pennebaker et al., 2001)<br>• SEANCE (Crossley et al., 2017)<br>• CAT Scanner (McKenny et al., 2012, http://www.catscanner.net/dictionaries/) |
| Unsupervised machine learning (i.e., topic modeling) | NLP techniques that do not contain ground-truth or criterion data. These methods attempt to identify clusters or patterns in the data. Ultimately, the analyst of the data must assign conceptual meaning to the clusters or topics identified by unsupervised machine learning techniques. LDA topic modeling is an ideal entry point to novices of unsupervised machine learning methods. | • quanteda (Benoit et al., 2018)<br>• BERTopic (Grootendorst, 2020) |
| Deep Learning | A supervised machine learning technique used for prediction and classification tasks. Devised to mimic neural pathways of the brain, deep learning techniques (i.e., neural networks) contain multiple layers of weights that attempt to model more abstract concepts than can be represented in other NLP methods. Although it is possible to run deep learning algorithms in R, more sophisticated packages and libraries are available in Python. | • spaCy (https://spacy.io/)<br>• Keras in R (https://cran.r-project.org/web/packages/keras/vignettes/index.html)<br>• Transformers (BERT, Devlin et al., 2019; RoBERTa, Liu et al., 2019; huggingface, https://huggingface.co/models)<br>• Urban and Gates (2021) |

using a dictionary-based approach, specifically Linguistic Inquiry and Word Count (LIWC). They identified LIWC dictionaries of four constructs (feelings, death, money, and work) and evaluated what percentage of the total words used by individual U.S. governors during COVID fell into the four respective construct categories. These frequency values were then used as criterion measures in an analysis of covariance (ANCOVA) model with gender as a predictor. Results of the ANCOVA model were interpreted to identify gender differences in leader rhetoric and style during the COVID crisis. For example, they found that female governors more frequently used words constituting feelings or empathy. Sergent and Stajkovic (2020) illustrate how one can use NLP methods, specifically CATA, to measure constructs of interest and use those measures to test differences in behaviors between leaders.

## Supervised Machine Learning

An example of NLP that builds upon the dictionary-based approaches was conducted by Marshall et al. (2021). Marshall and colleagues proposed the combination of multiple NLP tools to alleviate the time-consuming classification of leaders as charismatic, ideological, or pragmatic leader types. Past methods involved teams of researchers to read biographical texts of leaders, assign labels from the Charismatic-Ideological-Pragmatic (CIP) leadership style model, and assess interrater reliability between raters (Marshall et al., 2021). However, labeling for any classification task is a costly endeavor. To reduce the costs and leverage modern advancements in web scraping and NLP, Marshall et al. (2021) combined dictionary approaches and supervised machine learning to classify U.S. governors according to the CIP model. LIWC was used to measure CIP leader types and was aggregated with human-assigned labels to create a sample of labeled text to train the supervised machine learning model. Using this sample of labeled text, the authors trained eight different kinds of supervised machine learning models (e.g., multinomial logistic regression, logistic model trees, neural networks) to classify unseen text data as charismatic, ideological, or pragmatic. By utilizing both CATA and supervised machine learning techniques, Marshall et al. (2021) were able to build a prediction model that could efficiently classify leaders according to the CIP model using actual leader speech. Their method increased the speed of measurement as compared to past methods, while also demonstrating evidence of traditional validity inferences.

## Unsupervised Machine Learning

There have also been several recent examples of an unsupervised machine learning method, topic modeling, applied to the leadership domain. Topic models are a family of tools that can impose structure on text by taking unstructured text documents and identifying the "topics" being discussed in those documents. One particular approach, structural topic models, allows one to gain additional insight by leveraging document metadata when evaluating the solution. Document metadata includes information that might be known about the document itself such as who created it, what kind of document it is (e.g., tweet vs. Facebook post), when it was created, or any other number of qualitative or quantitative variables about the document itself. Importantly, topic models do not require any a priori dictionary of words or topics. Rather, the algorithm inductively generates the topics based on patterns in the data. In many ways, topic modeling is like exploratory factor analysis (EFA). While EFA takes quantitative scores and uses those to figure out how many latent constructs might be measured by a set of items and which items correspond to which topics, topic modeling uses words in a corpus to identify the latent topics being discussed and to assign words to topics.

Doldor and colleagues (2019) used latent Dirichlet allocation (LDA) topic modeling to investigate the presence of gender biases in developmental feedback given to UK politicians to identify themes (i.e., topics). Then, they reviewed the most frequent words from each topic to assign topic names, including Balance, Decision Making, and Public Speaking. A linear regression was run on the topic proportions to determine if certain topics occurred more or less frequently in feedback given to male or female UK politicians. The examination of developmental feedback topics from the structural topic model by Doldor and colleagues (2019) showed an absence of gender differences in topics present. Nevertheless, they took additional steps to qualitatively compare documents within each topic and identify any differences in how these developmental topics were communicated to male versus female politicians. This qualitative analysis resulted in a theoretical framework for understanding gendered messaging of leader developmental feedback. Although the final theoretical framework was not identified directly from the original structural topic model, the inductive, unsupervised learning method provided a foundational model from which to explore more nuanced, gendered language in the text.

More recently, we (Tonidandel et al., 2022) used LDA structural topic modeling to examine a corpus of text from over 8,000 leaders who reported on their most significant challenges as a leader or manager. This corpus of text was generated by over 8,000 managers who took a 360 assessment from an international leadership development firm. Using this approach, we were able to identify nine main challenges that these leaders experienced. In addition to identifying the topics, we were able to use structural topic modeling to investigate if the types of challenges experienced by leaders differed as a function of the leader's attributes. These attributes included basic demographic information provided by the leader in the 360 assessment including their gender, organization level, race, and citizenship status in the United States along with performance ratings provided by their boss. For example, we were able to identify the most frequent, Executive Presence and Change Management, and least frequent, Leading Teams, challenges along with which challenges tended to co-occur in leaders in our sample (e.g., Executive Presence and Communication). We also explored whether different challenges were more frequent for some leaders versus others. As but one illustration of this, we found that female leaders were significantly more likely to identify challenges related to Executive Presence, Communication, and Leading Others, whereas male leaders reported challenges related to Daily Management Activities, Business Unit Issues, and Change Management. Importantly, this topic model solution can now be deployed to instantly score new text produced by participants in a leadership development program (e.g., future 360 assessments) to automatically determine the challenges most likely faced by this leader and to provide instant feedback and instruction for combating that challenge.

## Deep Learning

As noted above, a potential advantage of NLP applied to leadership assessment is that it changes the focus of leadership assessment from subjective evaluations to instead what leaders are actually doing behaviorally in terms of the signals that they send via their words. Several recent examples have emerged in the leadership literature using these techniques. The first is a set of articles by Antonakis and colleagues, where they leverage deep learning to assess charismatic leadership. Antonakis et al. (2021) developed a supervised machine learning–based algorithm called Deep Charisma that can take any textual data (a letter, an email, a transcribed speech) and evaluate the extent to which that leader is employing Charismatic Leadership Tactics (CLTs). Jensen and colleagues (2021) have since deployed this deep learning algorithm to U.S. governor speeches during COVID and coded each sentence of the speech for CLTs. Each speech was given an overall score of charisma, which was then used to predict the likelihood of public adherence to physical distancing guidelines. They wanted to assess the effectiveness of CLTs in eliciting the desired follower outcome of abiding by public safety suggestions. The utilization of Deep Charisma as a measure of behaviors demonstrative of charismatic leadership allowed Jensen and colleagues (2021) to include actual leader behaviors in their models, rather than relying on traditional self-report measures that merely capture follower perceptions of the leader's charisma.

In a similar vein, along with several colleagues (Banks et al., 2022), we have employed a parallel strategy to study ethical leadership behaviors. First, we developed a typology of ethical leader signals in text. Next, we experimentally demonstrated that those verbal signals cause followers to perceive leaders who employ those signals as more ethical and causally impact follower behaviors by increasing follower organizational citizenship behavior and decreasing follower counterproductive behavior. Given this evidence, being able to identify these signals in leaders becomes critical, and NLP, specifically deep learning, provides the mechanism to do this. We were able to train a deep learning algorithm to accurately score these signals in textual data, either written or transcribed audio. Although this algorithm has not been deployed for use in practice yet, you can imagine multiple scenarios where a leader may consider using such a tool to assess their behavior. For instance, one can consent to have their email communications scored for the presence of ethical leader signals. Those scores can be used to evaluate their current behaviors and then identify opportunities to increase their ethical signaling to followers, peers, and upper-level leadership. Additionally, a CEO may need to release a company-wide statement to address a crisis or critical incident and wants to ensure that they are signaling ethical leader behaviors to the company. In these scenarios and more, we now have a method that enables us to quickly and at scale evaluate the ethical signals leaders are sending and provide them with developmental feedback on how they might improve in terms of their ethical leadership behaviors.

Overall, the majority of leadership assessment research leveraging NLP focuses on the measure of leader behaviors and leadership styles. Many of the articles presented above (i.e., Marshall et al., 2021, Antonakis et al., 2021, Banks et al., 2021) directly respond to calls for more efficient, behaviorally focused ways to measure leader behaviors and leader types. The ability to include algorithmic measures of actual leader behaviors in models predicting leader performance or leader impact on follower behavior can fundamentally change how we assess the efficacy of specific leader actions. For example, one could coach the governors to engage in specific CLTs in their speech, which were shown by Jensen et al. (2021) to influence constituent behaviors. Notably, these developmental or coaching conversations with leaders require understanding of broader, thematic experiences by leaders. The work by Doldor et al. (2019) and Tonidandel et al. (2022) are a reminder of the more exploratory questions in NLP research surrounding leadership and leadership assessment or development that are also crucial to guide and support leaders. The investigation of challenges experienced by male versus female leaders by Tonidandel and colleagues (2022) found that women struggle with executive presence and communication more than men; therefore, female governors may desire more guidance and coaching on various tactics or behaviors to include in their speeches since they report being most challenged in that area. Regardless of the specific use, NLP methods certainly have considerable impact on how we assess and develop leaders moving forward.

## Considerations When Using Natural Language Processing to Assess Leaders

### Data Sources

As mentioned previously, traditional leadership assessments already involve the collection of text data from leaders. Assessment centers, interviews, and 360 assessments are frequently employed in both selection and development contexts. An organization's engagement surveys may also include open-ended questions asking an employee to describe the abilities of their leader or manager. Lastly, there are numerous informal sources of text data like emails, Slack chats, virtual meeting transcripts, and public communications by leaders. Consider your own work. Where is your company already collecting text data from current or future leaders with their consent? Do you have access to publicly available text data that can inform your understanding of leader phenomena? When exploring the use of NLP in leadership assessment, begin with data that is already provided to you by your leaders with a clear understanding of how that data will be used (e.g., selection or developmental purposes). More informal sources are trickier to scrape or collect and carry a host of ethical considerations (see Bauer et al., 2020; Paxton, 2020; and Tippins et al., 2021, for more information on data privacy and ethics).

## Text Preprocessing

Any NLP project often begins with some type of text preprocessing. Text preprocessing involves any steps taken to prepare the data for future analyses. At its most basic level, this usually involves transforming all of the text to lowercase. One might then tokenize the text; segment the text into words, punctuation, etc.; and further clean the text by removing punctuation, numbers, and symbols and correcting common spelling mistakes. Then there are several decision points that must be considered for any individual project. One of those is whether you should remove stop words from your text. Stop words are common words that do not really contribute to the meaning of a sentence such as "a," "the," and "so." Because these words are frequent yet unnecessary for understanding the meaning of the text, some algorithms (e.g., topic models) perform better when they are removed. There are many freely available stop word dictionaries such as the one in the quanteda package in R (Benoit et al., 2018).

Another decision point is the unit of analysis. Some algorithms can analyze single-word units, called grams, but they can also analyze two-word (bi-gram), three-word (tri-gram), and n-word grams. At times, the inclusion of n-grams can improve the performance of certain NLP approaches. One should also consider whether it is appropriate to stem words, that is, reduce words to identical root forms based on their patterns. An example of stemming would be to transform the words "manager," "manages," "managed," and "management" to "manage." Similarly, lemmatization is another technique to extract roots of words that relies on morphological analysis of words (Singh

& Gupta, 2017). In this case, very dissimilar words such as "is," "am," and "are" would all be transformed to their root form "be." Other considerations are how you might handle text in different languages or what tools you might use to create your text corpus (e.g., transcribe audio into text).

There is no single list of steps that must always be taken for every project. Different NLP approaches typically have different text cleaning requirements. For example, in LDA topic modeling, it is recommended that stop words be removed. However, for deep learning, stop words are usually retained. Banks et al. (2018) provides a useful review of many of these steps. Although most NLP applications in the literature tend to gloss over these initial preprocessing steps, they are crucial and your choices can dramatically impact the quality of your results.

## CATA Dictionaries

If you are interested in getting started with NLP, a good entry point might be CATA. Once your text data are in the correct format, all that is needed is to apply a dictionary or lexicon. One popular dictionary that has been used extensively in psychology and the organizational sciences is LIWC (Pennebaker et al., 2001). LIWC contains nearly 100 dictionaries that can catalog parts of speech as well as a variety of psychological constructs (e.g., achievement orientation). Another popular CATA tool is Diction (Hart, 2000). Diction contains 40 dictionaries as well as the unique ability to compare your results to thousands of previously analyzed text data sets. CAT Scanner (McKenny et al., 2012) is a free open-source compendium of over 100 dictionaries used across a variety of fields. For sentiment analysis, SEANCE is a comprehensive tool that contains 254 sentiment indices (Crossley et al., 2017). Finally, one can find a large number of other dictionaries and lexicons in various packages in both R and Python.

## Labeling Data for Supervised Machine Learning

More advanced approaches to NLP have a higher bar to entry. To get familiar with the more state-of-the-art approaches to NLP, we would recommend spaCy (https://spacy.io/), a free open-source NLP ecosystem for Python. When applying any of the supervised machine learning NLP approaches, one of the challenges is the need for large amounts of labeled text. Several of the aforementioned examples used supervised learning to develop the algorithm that scores leaders' signaling in text. That is, we took a large amount of leader text, over 10,000 individual sentences, and had trained coders indicate whether a particular signal was present. We then used this labeled data to train the algorithm to accurately score new text. Obviously, this was a time-consuming process and may be perceived as a barrier to entry for those wishing to employ one of these techniques.

Fortunately, there are promising new advances that may reduce the burden of labeling large quantities of data. One recent solution is the use of weak supervision (Ratner et al., 2017), a labeling tool that reduces the burden on SMEs by programmatically generating training data from weak signals. Instead of manually rating individual examples, SMEs' knowledge about the process of labeling is used to generate programmatic labeling functions (Mracek & Thompson, 2021). Thus, much of the initial labeling can happen without the need for direct human intervention. Another alternative is active machine learning that reduces the burden placed on SMEs by having raters label only those examples that would be most informative for the predictive model (Zhao et al., 2006). Active machine learning uses a small initial training data set to build a base model. A search strategy is then employed to identify the most informative examples, which are then presented to SMEs for labeling (Mracek & Thompson, 2021). Another helpful advancement is transformer-based models. Transformer-based models such as Bidirectional Encoder Representations from Transformers (BERT) (Devlin et al., 2019) and RoBERTa (Liu et al., 2019) have made it possible to accurately train deep learning models to score text with sample sizes much smaller than ever thought possible (e.g., $N \approx 200$; Thompson et al., 2023). Despite the challenges posed by the need for labeled data, as discussed earlier, there exists a whole host of techniques—unsupervised machine learning methods—that permit one to gain valuable insights in unlabeled data.

## Algorithmic Bias

The quality of any of the aforementioned solutions is only as good as the data that the algorithm is trained on. A critical concern whenever one is employing algorithmic solutions is algorithmic bias. If bias is present in the training data, then the algorithm can learn that bias and reproduce it in any predictions produced by the model. Several steps are necessary to mitigate such bias. First, care must be taken to ensure that the training data has sufficient representation among subgroups. This is particularly true when considering applications to leadership as females and racial and ethnic minorities are extremely underrepresented in the leadership ranks. Second, efforts should be made to reduce the presence of bias in the training data. This can be done by leveraging measurement principles in both the elicitation of text and the labeling process. For example, utilizing rater training, removing context cues (e.g., names) from the labeling process that could bias the labels, and using a construct-based approach to both generate and label text can all help reduce bias. Making sure that the SMEs who will perform any labeling are also diverse can help. Finally, an audit of algorithmic bias is always recommended as best practice.

## Natural Language Processing and the Future of Leadership Assessment

The exemplar articles presented in this chapter varied in the specific NLP method used and the central focus of their investigation, but almost all of the articles acknowledged and justified the value of NLP methods in their specific study and leadership assessment broadly. Marshall and colleagues (2021) specifically noted the limitations of traditional methods and stated that CATA "provides rich insights into individual cognitions, values, and identities" (p. 4). Given these acknowledgments and the efficacy of the NLP methods in measuring leader behaviors, the leadership assessment and NLP scientific literature has already begun to expand work to measure other types of leader signals beyond just charismatic leadership and ethical leadership such as transformational leadership and destructive leadership behaviors. The next natural step would be to look at other types of signaling evidenced in leaders' textual data, such as emotional signaling. We (Banks et al., 2022) have done some exploratory work showing that different ethical leadership behaviors correspond to several discrete emotions being displayed simultaneously. Using NLP to assess a leader's behavioral signaling in text, one can envision a new paradigm where leaders can receive instantaneous automatic feedback on their behaviors by analyzing their emails, social media posts, and meeting transcripts. As the field of NLP applied to leadership assessment advances, we would encourage scientist-practitioners to continue to view text as meaningful sources of behavioral data and leader signals that impact followers.

The exemplar articles also acknowledged the public availability of large leader text data sets that scientist-practitioners can access and analyze in their research. Many of the existing publications that use NLP to study leadership are applying these methods to publicly available data sets. Doldor et al. (2019) did not use a publicly available data set but still called for increased use of methods like topic modeling in leadership assessment, especially in qualitative feedback data that is often evaluated as a costly dataset to analyze using human coders. Scientist-practitioners should be creative in identifying sources of leader text data within organizations (e.g., email, meeting transcriptions, shareholder letters) and consider the use of large, publicly available data sets (i.e., leader speeches, tweets) to train NLP models.

The recent applications of NLP discussed above provide a roadmap for what we see as some future applications of NLP in leadership assessment. There is a long history of NLP methods applied to text using CATA approaches in the organizational sciences. As we have seen, though, our science has begun to move beyond dictionary-based, context-free approaches to more advanced unsupervised and supervised machine learning methods for analyzing textual data from leaders. We hope to see continued precision in the performance of these models and increased use of them in leadership assessment in order to provide leaders with efficient, low-cost, and targeted behavioral feedback as well as the continued understanding of leader experiences and challenges. And although the exemplars in this chapter centered on leader development, it is easy to transfer these ideas to the context of selection (see Campion & Campion, 2020, for a review of CATA applications in personnel selection). Envision an applicant for a leadership or managerial position going through an assessment center. To the extent that any text is produced in that assessment center, these methods can be used to score and evaluate that text. The same advantages, challenges, and considerations listed above for the use of NLP in leadership assessment and development translate to selection.

In the future, we envision NLP as but one piece of an overall evaluative model of leader behaviors. Deep learning models can be employed to evaluate not only what is being said (a leader's text) but also how it is being said (pitch, vocal tone, emotional displays, etc.). This obviously moves beyond NLP to also include visual analytics, which is beyond the scope of this chapter, but it hints at possible future directions. Until then, it would behoove leadership researchers and practitioners to take note of exemplars presented in this chapter and consider how to start leveraging NLP methods to go above and beyond traditional methodological tools to better measure, describe, and explain leader text and leadership phenomena.

## References

Antonakis, J., d'Adda, G., Weber, R. A., & Zehnder, C. (2021). "Just words? Just speeches?" On the economic value of charismatic leadership. *Management Science, 68*(9), 6355–6381.

Banks, G. C., Ross, R., Toth, A. A., Tonidandel, S., Goloujeh, A. M., Dou, W., & Wesslen, R. (2022). The triangulation of ethical leader signals using qualitative, experimental, and data science methods. *Leadership Quarterly*, 101658. https://doi.org/10.1016/j.leaqua.2022.101658

Banks, G., Woznjy, H., & Mansfield, C. (2021). Where is "behavior" in organizational behavior? A call for a revolution in leadership research and beyond. *Leadership Quarterly*, 101581. https://doi.org/10.1016/j.leaqua.2021.101581

Banks, G. C., Woznyj, H. M., Wesslen, R., & Ross, R. (2018). A review of best practice recommendations for text-analysis in R (and a user friendly app). *Journal of Business and Psychology, 33*(4), 445–459. https://doi.org/10.1007/s10869-017-9528-3

Bastardoz, N., & Van Vugt, M. (2019). The nature of followership: Evolutionary analysis and review. *Leadership Quarterly, 35*(1), 81–95. https://doi.org/10.1016/j.leaqua.2018.09.004

Bauer, T. N., Truxillo, D. M., Jones, M. P., & Brady, G. (2020). Privacy and cybersecurity challenges, opportunities, and recommendations: Personnel selection in an era of online application systems and big data. In S. E. Woo, L. Tay, & R. W. Proctor (Eds.), *Big data in psychological research* (pp. 393–410). American Psychological Association. http://www.jstor.org/stable/j.ctv1chs5jz.21

Bellman, R. E. (1961). *Adaptive Control Processes*. Princeton University Press.

Benoit, K., Watanabe, K., Wang, H., Nulty, P., Obeng, A., Müller, S., & Matsuo, A. (2018). Quanteda: An R package for the quantitative analysis of textual data. *Journal of Open Source Software, 3*(30), 1–4. https://joss.theoj.org/papers/10.21105/joss.00774.pdf

Campion, E. D., & Campion, M. A. (2020). Using Computer-assisted Text Analysis (CATA) to Inform Employment Decisions: Approaches, Software, and Findings. *Research in Personnel and Human Resources Management, 38*, 285–325.https://doi.org/10.1108/S0742-730120200000038010

Connelly, B. L., Certo, S. T., Ireland, R. D., & Reutzel, C. R. (2011). Signaling theory: A review and assessment. *Journal of Management, 37*(1), 39–67.

Crossley, S. A., Kyle, K., & McNamara, D. S. (2017). Sentiment Analysis and Social Cognition Engine (SEANCE): An automatic tool for sentiment, social cognition, and social-order analysis. *Behavior Research Methods, 49*(3), 803–821. https://doi.org/10.3758/s13428-016-0743-z

Devlin, J., Chang, M. W., Lee, K., & Toutanova, K. (2019). BERT: Pre-training of bidirectional transformers for language understanding. In *Proceedings of the 2019 Conference of the North American Chapter of the Association for Computational Linguistics* (pp. 4171–4186). Human Language Technologies.

Doldor, E., Wyatt, M., & Silvester, J. (2019). Statesmen or cheerleaders? Using topic modeling to examine gendered messages in narrative developmental feedback for leaders. *Leadership Quarterly, 30*(5), 101308. https://doi.org/10.1016/j.leaqua.2019.101308

Fischer, T., Hambrick, D. C., Sajons, G. B., & Van Quaquebeke, N. (2020). Beyond the ritualized use of questionnaires: Toward a science of actual behaviors and psychological states. *Leadership Quarterly, 31*(4), 101449. https://doi.org/10.1016/S1048-9843(20)30076-X

Grootendorst, M. (2020). *BERTopic: Leveraging BERT and c-TF-IDF to create easily interpretable topics* (v0.70) [Computer software]. https://doi.org/10.5281/zenodo.4381785

Hart, R. P. (2000). *DICTION 5.0: The text-analysis program.* Scolari/Sage Publications.

Hickman, L., Thapa, S., Tay, L., Cao, M., & Srinivasan, P. (2022). Text preprocessing for text mining in organizational research: Review and recommendations. *Organizational Research Methods, 25*(1), 114–146. https://doi.org/10.1177/1094428120971683

Hu, M., & Liu, B. (2004). Mining and summarizing customer reviews. In *Proceedings of the 10th ACM SIGKDD International Conference on Knowledge Discovery and Data Mining* (pp. 168–177). https://doi.org/10.1145/1014052.1014073

Jensen, U., Rohner, D., Bornet, O., Carron, D., Garner, P., Loupi, D., & Antonakis, J. (2021). *Combating COVID-19 with charisma: Evidence on governor speeches and physical distancing in the United States.* PsyArXiv. https://doi.org/10.31234/osf.io/ypqmk

Liu, Y., Ott, M., Goyal, N., Du, J., Joshi, M., Chen, D., Levy, O., Lewis, M., Zettlemoyer, L., & Stoyanov, V. (2019). RoBERTa: A robustly optimized BERT pretraining approach. ArXiv. https://arxiv.org/pdf/1907.11692.pdf

Marshall, J., Yammarino, F. J., Parameswaran, S., & Cheong, M. (2021). *Using CATA and machine learning to operationalize old constructs in new ways: An illustration using US Governors' COVID-19 press briefings.* PsyArXiv. https://doi.org/10.31234/osf.io/84ux5

McCaughren, A. (2009). Polysemy and homonymy and their importance for the study of word meaning. *Institute of Technology Blanchardstown, 10*(1), 107–115. https://d1wqtxts1xzle7.cloudfront.net/6205827/issue-18.pdf

McKenny, A. F., Short, J. C., & Newman, S. M. (2012). *CAT Scanner (Version 1.0)* [Software]. http://www.catscanner.net/

Mohammad, S. M., & Turney, P. D. (2013). Crowdsourcing a word–emotion association lexicon. *Computational Intelligence, 29*(3), 436–465. https://doi.org/10.1111/j.1467-8640.2012.00460.x

Mracek, D., & Thompson, I. (2021) *The state of the art and science of rating unstructured data* [Symposium]. Annual conference of the Society for Industrial and Organizational Psychology, New Orleans, LA.

Paxton, A. (2020). The Belmont report in the age of big data: Ethics at the intersection of psychological science and data science. In S. E. Woo, L. Tay, & R. W. Proctor (Eds.), *Big data in psychological research* (pp. 347–372). American Psychological Association. http://www.jstor.org/stable/j.ctv1chs5jz.19

Pennebaker, J. W., Francis, M. E., & Booth, R. J. (2001). *Linguistic inquiry and word count: LIWC 2001.* Lawrence Erlbaum Associates.

Ratner, A., Bach, S. H., Ehrenberg, H., Fries, J., Wu, S., & Ré, C. (2017). Snorkel: Rapid training data creation with weak supervision. *Proceedings of the VLDB Endowment, 11*(3), 269–282. https://doi.org/10.14778/3157794.3157797

Sergent, K., & Stajkovic, A. D. (2020). Women's leadership is associated with fewer deaths during the COVID-19 crisis: Quantitative and qualitative analyses of United States governors. *Journal of Applied Psychology, 105*(8), 771–783. https://doi.org/10.1037/apl0000577

Singh, J., & Gupta, V. (2017). A systematic review of text stemming techniques. *Artificial Intelligence Review, 48*(2), 157–217. https://doi.org/10.1007/s10462-016-9498-2

Thompson, I., Koenig, N., Mracek, D., & Tonidandel, S. (2023). Deep learning in employee selection: Evaluation of algorithms to automate the scoring of open-ended assessments. *Journal of Business and Psychology.* https://doi.org/10.1007/s10869-023-09874-y

Tippins, N. T., Oswald, F. L., & McPhail, S. M. (2021). Scientific, legal, and ethical concerns about AI-based personnel selection tools: A call to action. *Personnel Assessment and Decisions, 7*(2), 1–22. https://doi.org/10.25035/pad.2021.02.001

Tonidandel, S., King, E. B., & Cortina, J. M. (2018). Big data methods: Leveraging modern data analytic techniques to build organizational science. *Organizational Research Methods, 21*(3), 525–547. https://doi.org/10.1177/1094428116677299

Tonidandel, S., Summerville, K. M., Gentry, W. A., & Young, S. F. (2022). Using structural topic modeling to gain insight into challenges faced by leaders. *Leadership Quarterly, 33*(5), 101576. https://doi.org/10.1016/j.leaqua.2021.101576

Urban, C. J., & Gates, K. M. (2021). Deep learning: A primer for psychologists. *Psychological Methods, 26*(6), 743–773. https://doi.org/10.1037/met0000374

Yammarino, F. J., Cheong, M., Kim, J., & Tsai, C.-Y. (2020). Is leadership more than "I like my boss"? In *Research in personnel and human resources management* (Vol. 38, pp. 1–55). Emerald Publishing Limited. https://doi.org/10.1108/S0742-730120200000038003

Zhao, Y., Xu, C., & Cao, Y. (2006). Research on query-by-committee method of active learning and application. In *Advanced Data Mining and Applications: Second International Conference, ADMA 2006, Xi'an, China, August 14–16, 2006 Proceedings 2* (pp. 985–991). Springer Berlin Heidelberg.

# 11
# Mobile-Enabled Assessment in the Modern Talent Landscape

*Darrin M. Grelle and Sara L. Gutierrez*

Talent assessments are used by organizations to help them make the best possible decision regarding who to hire, how to develop current talent, and which employees have the potential for upward mobility. By utilizing data-driven, empirical measures to make better people decisions, organizations can improve their business performance.

Although talent assessment has been an established practice for more than 100 years, it did not always look the way we know it today. Prior to the internet, the use of such tools was mainly limited to the largest organizations such as the military and large industrials. There was essentially one modality for all assessment: paper based and delivered as proctored administrations in offices or training rooms on location with the hiring organization. Even as talent assessment progressed to the early days of computer-based assessment, the administration was limited to on-site testing, and assessments were primarily text based with a set of response options from which the candidate selected a single response. This limited the data generated by assessments to closed-ended responses and provided limited feedback to test developers. As a result, little was known about the effectiveness of the tools across organizations, and commercially available tests were rarely updated or improved once initially released. During this period, talent assessment existed mainly as paper-based or computer-administered copies of the paper-based tests, and evolution of the practice of talent assessment was very slow.

With the internet and the move toward unproctored internet testing, the landscape for talent assessment has changed dramatically (Fallaw et al., 2009; Pearlman, 2009), and the science of talent assessment has been able to scale and evolve. While some organizations began developing selection

Darrin M. Grelle and Sara L. Gutierrez, *Mobile-Enabled Assessment in the Modern Talent Landscape* In: *Talent Assessment*. Edited by: Tracy M. Kantrowitz, Douglas H. Reynolds, and John C. Scott, Oxford University Press.
© Society of Industrial Organizational Psychology 2023. DOI: 10.1093/oso/9780197611050.003.0011

assessments to hire candidates for their specific organization, other organizations and assessment vendors emerged that designed assessments and online platforms from which this content could be administered to candidates for any organization paying for the content. These assessment platforms collect test data as well as client and candidate information (within the parameters of General Data Protection Regulation [GDPR] and other data privacy regulations). These data paved the way for massive leaps forward in assessment development, customization, and iteration.

The last two decades have seen talent assessment evolve away from static multiple-choice assessments to those that use advances in psychometrics, increased computing power, and enhanced user experience/user interface (UX/UI) design to create shorter and more precise tests, multimedia simulations, gamified assessment, situational judgment tests that offer richer and more face-valid experiences, and constructed response measures that utilize machine learning and natural language processing for unbiased measurement tailored to specific competencies. The evolution of talent assessments, once only delivered on paper, then on large personal computer or laptop screens, continues, now driving the application of assessment on mobile devices.

Multiple disciplines including industrial-organizational (IO) psychology, data science, user experience, psychometrics, and software development came together to advance assessment delivery to where it is today. Within this chapter, we will cover some of the factors driving the demand for mobile-enabled assessment and discuss why making assessment available on mobile devices is so critical from a fairness perspective. We will then cover how psychometric theory and assessment design principles guided the evolution of selection assessment from unproctored internet delivery to mobile device administration. We will conclude with a discussion of examples of successful deployment of mobile-enabled assessment.

## What Has Changed Recently?

The COVID-19 pandemic has had such a profound impact on all aspects of working life that IO psychologists will be studying and writing about it for generations to come. The pandemic is not the only recent driver of change in how assessments are delivered, however. This section addresses key areas that are driving the evolution of mobile-enabled assessment design and delivery. One area, the Great Resignation, has been accelerated by the pandemic (Tessema et al., 2022), while others, including concern for diversity, equity, and inclusion (DEI) and accessibility (Society of Industrial and Organizational Psychology [SIOP], 2021), have been driven by societal shifts that have necessitated the need to rethink how assessments are delivered.

## The Great Resignation

The Great Resignation refers to the substantial increase in workers leaving the workforce in 2021. Paired with the Great Resignation is a general reluctance to join or return to the workforce, especially in roles that deal with the public. Businesses are facing acute talent shortages in this postpandemic era; shortages are at a 15-year high with 69% of employers reporting challenges in filling open roles (ManpowerGroup, 2021). With candidate scarcity on the rise, it is more important than ever to meet the candidate where they are and to ensure the selection procedure provides a positive candidate experience while remaining effective and efficient for the hiring organization. It is also critical to make it as easy as possible for candidates to apply to open positions. Mobile-enabled assessment can assist in both improving the candidate experience and increasing access.

There are multiple factors that positively impact the candidate experience. Candidates are looking for an interesting and engaging experience that allows them to demonstrate their skills. Much of what impacts a candidate's assessment experience is how the information is presented (Arthur et al., 2017; Is there too much information displayed on screen at once? Is the text easy to read?) and how the candidate responds to it (How many taps/clicks are required to submit a response? Is the response format intuitive?). Even if an assessment is not delivered on a mobile device, mobile-enabled assessments can improve the candidate experience. Prior to the introduction of mobile phones, not much thought went into website design. This included how assessments were delivered online. When people began accessing content on their phones, it quickly became apparent that many websites needed to be redesigned to make it easier to read and navigate. Responsive web design (Marcotte, 2010), mobile-first design (Wroblewski, 2011), and other similar concepts emerged that incorporated user experience expertise and information processing theories to design internet content that could be easily consumed and navigated regardless of which device someone utilized to access it. These design principles can and have been applied to assessment, and we have included an example of how these principles improved the candidate experience of an existing personality test later in this chapter.

In addition to improving the candidate experience through mobile-first design principles, mobile-enabled tests make assessments easier to access, which can increase the number of candidates in the pipeline and also itself improves the candidate experience. That is, the easier it is for a candidate to engage in the assessment process, such as the use of social sign-on (the use of existing login credentials from social media to register for an assessment) and unproctored and short tests (that minimize the burden of the assessment), the better the experience will be for the candidate (SHL, 2017). Mobile-enabled assessments increase access in two ways. First, the ability to complete assessments on a mobile device creates access for candidates whose only or primary access to the internet is through their phones. We will discuss how this relates to creating a more diverse workforce later in the chapter. Second, most people with a mobile device have it within reach most of the day (Rainie & Zickuhr, 2015), so even if they do have access to a computer, having a mobile device within reach at all times allows candidates to apply at any time. Interest may wane if they need to wait for a convenient time to complete assessments on a computer. Intelligently designed mobile-enabled assessments can help maximize the number of candidates applying for a given job opportunity, allowing organizations to find qualified candidates even during times when there are fewer candidates applying.

## Concerns for Diversity, Equity, and Inclusion

Diversity, equity, inclusion, and belongingness (DEI&B) ranked as the third trend in SIOP's eighth annual Top 10 Workplace Trends in 2021 (SIOP, 2021), highlighting its importance in the field of IO psychology. Although fairness in testing has always been a concern for psychometricians in designing assessments, a welcomed global focus on DEI has paved the way for assessment developers to further elevate its importance to all stakeholders in the talent assessment field and to drive substantial positive change in this area. This section will discuss how mobile-enabled assessments, the focus of this chapter, can also help DEI initiatives.

Data collected by Pew Research Center shows that there are demographic differences in mobile internet dependence. Women and minorities are much more likely to be dependent on their mobile devices for the internet (McClure-Johnson & Boyce, 2015). Individuals who primarily access the internet through their mobile device may have access to laptop or tablet devices but depend on public spaces like libraries or coffee shops for internet access. This access was likely eliminated or severely limited during the height of pandemic shutdowns. Mobile-enabled assessment is also particularly important in certain geographies. SHL data show that there is considerable variance from country to country in the percentage of candidates that use mobile devices to complete their assessments. Low- and middle-income countries (LMICs) showed significantly more mobile usage than high-income countries. For example, SHL data show that 23% of candidates in Kenya completed assessments using a mobile device versus 5% of candidates in the United States in 2020. Given that women, minorities, and those in LMICs are disproportionately reliant on mobile devices to access the internet, mobile-enabled assessment increases access to a more diverse group of candidates, which is a critical step in DEI initiatives.

While many DEI initiatives tend to focus on gender, race, ethnicity, and age, increased attention has been given to other groups recently, such as individuals with disabilities. Individuals with disabilities are a diverse group (considering the number and types of disabilities), and accommodation requests are unique to each individual. As such, current best practice recommends providing reasonable adjustments and accommodations based on the individual's unique requirements. In some cases, accommodations best suited to a disability are well known, such as the use of a screen reader for those with vision impairment or closed captioning to supplement audio for those with hearing impairment. However, despite the growing interest in hiring neurodiverse talent, there is a lack of empirical research on the use of hiring assessments for the neurodiverse talent pool, leading to a gap in evidence-based best practices on which accommodations, if any, are needed to ensure fair testing procedures. Traditional assessment can be reconfigured to be suitable for neurodiverse candidates as reliance on traditional forms of assessment may perpetuate bias and exclusion of this population.

Increased litigation in accessibility issues as they relate to mobile-enabled web pages (Liebler & Cunningham, 2018) highlights the importance of making sure assessments can be made accessible regardless of which type of device is used to complete them. Mobile-first design principles can aid in developing assessments that are accessible to a broad range of candidates following internationally accepted standards for accessibility like 508 compliance. Mobile-first design strategies feature some goals like reduced screen clutter (the number of objects on the screen during the assessment), limited text, multiple response inputs (e.g., tap/click/voice command), and simplified instructions that improve the assessment experience for all candidates but also have the added benefit of making assessments more accessible. Similarly, mobile-enabled assessment has the potential to increase assessment access to candidates with mobility issues. For example, the use of mobile-enabled video interviewing as an option in the hiring process may open doors for candidates who otherwise would not be able to attend an in-person interview.

A truly inclusive selection process should start with eliminating all barriers to entering the selection process in the first place. Mobile-enabled assessment allows for a much larger group of candidates to demonstrate their skills and abilities to potential employers. Research on enhancements to mobile-enabled assessments (e.g., delivery mechanisms such as video, animation/avatars, streamlined candidate workflows, better design to reduce screen clutter) should be conducted and results implemented to build assessments aimed to effectively measure across all populations, ensuring a fair experience for all candidates.

## Mobile-First Assessment Design

To this point in the chapter, we have focused on why mobile-enabled assessment is so important for candidate engagement, accessibility, and opening access to a more diverse pool of candidates. The rest of this chapter will propose a framework from which to evaluate mobile-first design strategies, discuss the importance of ensuring equivalence across devices, and provide some examples of successful mobile-enabled assessments.

### Effectiveness, Efficiency, Experience Paradigm

The intersection between testing and technology has driven users of talent assessment to demand more from their tools. Today's talent assessments must blend assessment science with technology to meet the evolving needs of assessment consumers. Whereas traditional test development would focus on the psychometric characteristics of the measures to be developed (e.g., reliability, validity), market requirements are pushing IO psychologists to consider the candidate experience and utilize innovations in assessment design to make the assessment experience more engaging (Sullivan, 2014).

Achieving positive candidate experiences when enabling assessments on mobile devices has been a moving target over the past 10 years. As mobile device familiarity, usage, and reliance continually increase, so do the expectations of candidates. In the early days of mobile-enabled assessment administration, candidates strongly noted their preference for completing talent assessments on laptops or PCs rather than mobile devices (Fursman & Tuzinski, 2015). Just 2 years later, SHL's candidate preference research (2017) found 58% of candidates preferred to complete assessments on a mobile device. Research has shown that candidate reactions to mobile delivery of assessments are less favorable when an assessment has not been designed specifically for administration on the smaller screen (Gutierrez & Meyer, 2013), but that when proper design principles are considered, reactions will be similar regardless of device type utilized (Kinney et al, 2014). Below, we present a framework of current market demands and consumer considerations for use of talent assessments that we will use to evaluate the transition to mobile-enabled assessment.

**Effectiveness:** This market demand relates to the ultimate economic value that organizations experience from the use of a talent assessment. Typically, this is demonstrated through the traditional psychometric soundness of an assessment. The tool needs to be valid, reliable, secure, and legally defensible. Users of the tool should be able to demonstrate some degree of utility from the assessment, providing evidence of what business issues are solved and/or what important metrics are positively impacted (i.e., high scorers on the assessment sell three times as much as low scorers). An important piece of effectiveness is fairness. Assessments should accurately measure the construct of interest without introducing unintended bias.

**Efficiency:** Another piece of market demand is the expectation for shorter administration times for assessment tools. Although research has indicated candidates are not looking for a sub-10-minute assessment (Speer et al., 2016), there is a point at which a tool is too long to retain candidate engagement. Additionally, efficiency refers to the ease of implementation and integration across existing technology and processes within the organization. For example, assessments can be combined with applicant tracking systems for a seamless candidate experience and easier access to candidate information for administrators. Automated, near-instantaneous scoring and report generation can facilitate quick decision-making.

**Experience** : As mentioned above, talent assessment users are increasingly focused on the impact these tools can have on their pool of candidates. Users are looking for leading-edge user experiences and accessible solutions. When talent pools are limited, the candidate experience can have a large impact on candidate dropout, which can further limit the pipeline of potential candidates for open roles (Zhao, 2019). Candidate experience can also impact how candidates view an organization as customers/clients. If a candidate has a negative experience when applying to an organization, that candidate's willingness to use that organization's goods or services can be negatively impacted (TalentBoard, 2021).

Assessment developers must jointly consider effectiveness, efficiency, and experience when developing new assessments or updating existing ones. Computer adaptive tests, for example, can reach much higher accuracy (effectiveness) in a shorter amount of time (efficiency), but some evidence suggests that because questions are targeted at a candidate's ability level, candidates perceive computer adaptive tests as more difficult (experience) (Tonidandel et al., 2002). Numerous factors must be considered to create an engaging candidate experience that maintains the established effectiveness and efficiency of the assessment. In many cases, this is not possible, and the entire assessment needs to be rebuilt from the ground up.

## Consumer Internet Access

Whereas access to the early internet was largely stationary, requiring individuals to be tied to a single location through broadband cables, the last decade has seen a shift where digital information is increasingly accessed "on the go" using mobile devices (Pew Research Center, 2021). Mobile ownership of smartphones continues to increase, with 85% of Americans owning a smartphone, whereas fewer than 77% own a desktop or laptop computer. Research shows that 15% are "smartphone dependent"; these are individuals who own smartphones and do not have home broadband. Additionally, 28% of 18- to 29-year-olds are smartphone dependent and cannot apply for jobs or take assessments unless the process is 100% mobile (Pew Research Center, 2021).

## Mobile Equivalence

The look and feel of assessments have changed greatly over the years depending on modality and technology. Psychometricians are very aware that even slight changes to how test questions are presented can have an impact on how a construct is measured. For example, changes to assessment instructions might cause candidates to consider response options differently, notifying a candidate when time is about to run out on a timed test might increase careless errors due to stress, or changes to a font might make an assessment more or less accessible. These changes can affect how candidates respond to items. When assessments started to move from paper and pencil to computer based, dozens of studies (e.g., Meade et al., 2007; Wang et al., 2008) were conducted to ensure measurement equivalence. The conclusion was that the shift for most assessments moving to computer based had no impact on how constructs were being measured. When mobile devices became an option and the first studies on measurement equivalence between computer (desktop/laptop) and mobile (phone/tablet) based were conducted, the results were much more mixed. Early in the movement to mobile-enabled assessment, the practice was to simply make the PC-optimized content available on mobile devices. For some constructs and certain types of assessment, no differences were found between scores on the same assessment completed on a mobile device versus a PC (e.g., Arthur et al., 2014; Illingworth et al., 2015; Lawrence et al., 2013; Morelli et al., 2014). For other constructs, namely cognitive ability, large differences were found across modalities (e.g., Arthur et al., 2014; Impelman, 2013; King et al., 2014; LaPort et al., 2016).

It turns out that simply rebuilding an assessment "as is" onto a mobile device introduces a great deal of non-construct-related variance. Similarly, assessments created for mobile devices that utilize touch screen functionality do not always function the same when moved to larger devices. If a candidate can see all the information needed to answer a question on their screen on any device selected, score differences across devices indicate that there is likely more at play in device equivalence than simply screen size. Arthur et al. (2017) evaluated device-related factors like screen size that may impact how assessments are completed and how candidates respond. They developed a model called the structural characteristics/information processing (SCIP) framework that describes these factors and elaborates on considerations to make when developing content intended for use across all devices. The four factors they describe are screen size, screen clutter, response interface, and permissibility.

Screen size can impact how a candidate completes an assessment. If scrolling is required, working memory is introduced into how the candidate responds. This can make cognitive ability questions more difficult, but it can also impact responses to other types of assessment. Screen clutter deals with how many objects are on the screen within the assessment. This can be blocks of text, graphs, images, buttons, or response options. The response interface covers how the candidate interacts with the assessment. This could be clicking on a multiple-choice option or dragging something from one side of the screen to another. This also involves whether the assessment uses touch screen functionality. The final factor, permissibility, deals with how freely a device could be used in various locations. Devices with low permissibility like desktop computers require the user to be in a specific spot, whereas someone using a mobile device (high permissibility) could complete an assessment virtually anywhere if they have an internet connection.

## Examples of Successful Implementation

Research shows that when cognitive ability assessments are developed following the SCIP framework, device-type differences can be eliminated (Grelle & Gutierrez, 2019). Traditional multiple-choice cognitive ability questions require candidates completing the assessment on a mobile device to scroll up and down to see all the response options and the question. Because the candidate cannot see all the information needed to respond to the question at once, the working memory burden is increased. If candidates completing the assessment on a PC do not need to scroll but candidates completing the assessment on a mobile device do need to scroll, then the working memory demands will generate score differences between the two groups. When the formats of the questions are changed such that the candidate is using drag-and-drop features in addition to tapping/clicking to manipulate charts, graphs, and other objects to input their responses, rather than selecting multiple-choice options, question text is limited and scrolling is either eliminated entirely or greatly reduced and made equivalent across devices, thus removing score differences (Grelle & Gutierrez, 2019).

Though research has shown that, generally, personality assessments maintain measurement equivalence across devices without using mobile-first design principles, these principles can be implemented to improve the candidate experience. Take, for example, the redesign of an existing, traditional forced-choice personality assessment that was updated using mobile-first design principles to improve the response mechanism. Advances in technology allowed the items in this test to shift from static triplets to dynamic presentation. Although forced-choice personality assessments are known to reduce impression management distortion or "faking" (Cao & Drasgow, 2019), they often require candidates to consider themselves across polarities in the same interaction (e.g., select which statement most describes you and which statement least describes you). This multidimensional forced-choice format can be cognitively challenging for candidates. In this example, to optimize the design process and reduce the cognitive load for the participant, the redesigned assessment focused on one task at a time. The participant is asked one question: "Select the statement that describes you best." Once they make their selection, the statement selected as "most" descriptive disappears and the participant is asked to choose the next-best option out of the remaining two statements. The highest ranked statement is no longer shown, allowing the participant to focus only on the task at hand and not get distracted by decisions already made. The cognitive load is further reduced by asking the participants to think in one direction, to select those statements that best describe them out of the options presented and not have to think in extremes of "most like me" and "least like me." In addition to enhancing the candidate experience through the reduction of cognitive load, this redesign also increased the efficiency of the assessment, driving overall testing time down by 30% (SHL, 2019).

## Conclusion

Over the past few decades, the design and administration of talent assessment have evolved alongside the advancements made in technology. We should expect this evolution to continue to move at a fast pace, as computer and mobile device capabilities continue to grow and transform, and new devices may even emerge that completely upend how we access internet content. Throughout the next phase of technological advancement, psychometricians must continue to partner with experts across multiple fields (e.g., computer engineering, user interface/experience) to ensure sound research guides proper assessment design so that the fundamental requirements of reliability, validity, and equivalence across device types are retained. Talent assessment developers should continue to maintain a strong focus on increasing assessment access to as many candidates as possible.

## References

Arthur, W., Jr., Doverspike, D., Muñoz, G. J., Taylor, J. E., & Carr, A. E. (2014). The use of mobile devices in high-stakes remotely delivered assessments and testing. *International Journal of Selection and Assessment, 22*, 113–123.

Arthur, W., Jr., Keiser, N. L., & Doverspike, D. (2017). An information-processing-based conceptual framework of the effects of unproctored internet-based testing devices on scores on employment-related assessments and tests. *Human Performance, 31*, 1–32.

Cao, M., & Drasgow, F. (2019). Does forcing reduce faking? A meta-analytic review of forced-choice personality measures in high-stakes testing. *Journal of Applied Psychology, 104*(11), 1347–1368.

Fallaw, S. S., Solomonson, A. L., & McClelland, L. (2009). Current trends in assessment use: A multi-organizational survey [Poster presentation]. 24th annual conference of the Society for Industrial and Organizational Psychology, New Orleans, LA.

Fursman, P. M., & Tuzinski, K. A. (2015). *Reactions to mobile testing from the perspective of job applicants* [Paper presentation]. 30th annual conference of the Society of Industrial and Organizational Psychology, Philadelphia, PA.

Grelle, D. M., & Gutierrez, S. L. (2019). Developing device-equivalent and effective measures of complex thinking with an information processing framework and mobile first design principles. *Personnel Assessment and Decisions, 5*(3), 21–32.

Gutierrez, S. L., & Meyer, J. M. (2013). Assessments on the go: Applicant reactions to mobile testing. In N. A. Morelli (Chair), *Mobile devices in talent assessment: Where are we now?* [Symposium]. 28th annual conference of the Society of Industrial and Organizational Psychology, Houston, TX.

Illingworth, A. J., Morelli, N. A., Scott, J. C., & Boyd, S. L. (2015). Internet-based, unproctored assessments on mobile and non-mobile devices: Usage, measurement equivalence, and outcomes. *Journal of Business and Psychology, 30*, 325–343.

Impelman, K. (2013, April). Mobile assessment: Who's doing it and how it impacts selection. In N. A. Morelli (Chair), *Mobile devices in talent assessment: Where are we now?* [Symposium]. 28th annual conference of the Society for Industrial and Organizational Psychology, Houston, TX

King, D. D., Ryan, A. M., Kantrowitz, T., & Grelle, D. (2014). MIT versus PCIT: Assessing equivalence, individual differences, and reactions. In T. Kantrowitz & C. M. Reddock (Chairs), *Shaping the future of mobile assessment: Research and practice update* [Symposium]. 29th annual conference of the Society for Industrial and Organizational Psychology, Honolulu, HI.

Kinney, T. B., Lawrence, A. D., & Chang, L. (2014). Understanding the mobile candidate experience: reactions across device and industry. In T. Kantrowitz & C. M. Reddock (Chairs), *Shaping the future of mobile assessment: Research and practice update* [Symposium]. 29th annual conference of the Society for Industrial and Organizational Psychology, Honolulu, HI.

LaPort, K., Huynh, C. T., Stemer, A., Ryer, J. A., & Moretti, D. M. (2016). Mobile assessment: Comparing traditional cognitive, cognitive-reasoning, and non-cognitive Performance. In T. D. McGlochlin (Chair), *Mobile equivalence: Expanding research across assessment methods, levels, and devices* [Symposium]. 31st annual conference of the Society for Industrial and Organizational Psychology, Anaheim, CA.

Lawrence, A. D., Wasko, L., Delgado, K., Kinney, T. B., & Wolf, D. (2013, April). *Understanding the mobile experience: Data across device and industry* [Paper presentation]. 28th annual conference of the Society for Industrial and Organizational Psychology, Houston, TX

Liebler, R., & Cunningham, G. (2018). Can accessibility liberate the lost ark of scholarly work: University library institutional repositories are places of public accommodation. *University of Illinois Chicago Law Review, 52*, 327.

ManpowerGroup. (2021). *ManpowerGroup employment outlook survey Q3 2021: Global results*. MPG_2021_Outlook_Survey-Global.pdf (manpowergroup.com)

Marcotte, E. (2010). *Responsive web design*. A List Apart. http://alistapart.com/article/responsive-web-design/.

McClure-Johnson, T. K., & Boyce, A. S. (2015). Selection testing: An updated look at trends in mobile device usage. In N. Morelli (Chair), *Mobile devices in talent assessment: The next chapter* [Symposium]. 30th annual conference of the Society for Industrial and Organizational Psychology, Philadelphia, PA.

Meade, A. W., Michels, L. C., & Lautenschlager, G. J. (2007). Are internet and paper-and-pencil personality tests truly comparable?: An experimental design measurement invariance study. *Organizational Research Methods, 10*(2), 322–345.

Morelli, N. A., Mahan, R. P., & Illingworth, A. J. (2014). Establishing the measurement equivalence of online selection assessments delivered on mobile versus nonmobile devices. *International Journal of Selection and Assessment, 22*, 124–138.

Pearlman, K. (2009). Unproctored Internet testing: Practical, legal, and ethical concerns. *Industrial and Organizational Psychology: Perspective on Science and Practice, 2*, 14–19.

Pew Research Center. (2021). *Mobile fact sheet*. https://www.pewinternet.org/fact-sheet/mobile/

Rainie, L., & Zickuhr, K. (2015, August). *Americans' views on mobile etiquette*. Pew Research Center. http://www.pewinternet.org/2015/08/26/americans-views-on-mobile-etiquette/

TalentBoard. (2021). *North American candidate experience research report*. http://www.thetalentboard.org

Tessema, M. T., Tesfom, G., Faircloth, M. A., Tesfagiorgis, M., & Teckle, P. (2022). The "Great Resignation": Causes, consequences, and creative HR management strategies. *Journal of Human Resource and Sustainability Studies, 10*, 1.

Tonidandel, S., Quiñones, M. A., & Adams, A. A. (2002). Computer-adaptive testing: The impact of test characteristics on perceived performance and test takers' reactions. *Journal of Applied Psychology, 87*(2), 320–332.

SHL. (2017). *SHL candidate preferences survey*.

SHL. (2019). *OPQ32r™ reimagined technical manual supplement*.

Society of Industrial and Organizational Psychology (SIOP). (2021). *Top 10 workplace trends for 2020*. https://www.siop.org/Research-Publications/Items-of-Interest/ArtMID/19366/ArticleID/3361/Top-10-Workplace-Trends-for-2020

Speer, A. B., King, B. S., & Grossenbacher, M. (2016). Applicant reactions as a function of test length: Is there reason to fret over using longer tests? *Journal of Personnel Psychology, 15*(1), 15–24.

Sullivan, J. (2014). *The power has shifted to the candidate, so current recruiting practices will stop working.* The Power Has Shifted to the Candidate, So Current Recruiting Practices Will Stop Working – ERE.
Wang, S., Jiao, H., Young, M. J., Brooks, T., & Olson, J. (2008). Comparability of computer-based and paper-and-pencil testing in K-12 reading assessments: A meta-analysis of testing mode effects. *Educational and Psychological Measurement, 68*, 5–24.
Wrolebsky, L. (2011). *Mobile first.* A book apart. https://mobile-first.abookapart.com/
Zhao, D. (2019). *The rise of mobile devices in job search: Challenges and Opportunities for Employers.* Glassdoor Economic Research. The Rise of Mobile Devices in Job Search: Challenges and Opportunities for Employers - Glassdoor.

# 12
# Technology-Enabled Simulation in Selection
## Opportunities and Cautions

*Seymour Adler and Sarena Bhatia*

Simulation-based assessments enjoy a long and distinguished role as selection tools, with roots dating back to the OSS and AT&T Management Progress Study work in the 1940s and 1950s, respectively. Meta-analytic reviews over the decades have demonstrated significant and meaningful validities for simulation methods in selection contexts across a wide range of target positions, from entry level to senior executive (e.g., Hoffman et al., 2015; Schmidt & Hunter, 1998; Thornton et al., 2014).

Arguably more than any other testing method, the design and administration of simulation tools for assessment have been very much impacted by recent and accelerating technology advances. In this chapter, we would like to share our perspective on the exciting opportunities created by the advances in technological enablement and some of the cautions that need to be considered as we embrace increasingly sophisticated technology-enhanced simulation methods in high-stakes talent assessment.

## The Value of Simulations

Let's begin with a reminder of why simulations add value in the selection process.

***Signs Versus Samples.*** Simulations immerse participants in situations that (ideally) mimic those likely to occur in "real life." During the simulation, participants have opportunities to react behaviorally in the moment to situational cues and challenges embedded in the simulation's design. Underlying capabilities, knowledge, and traits are then assessed based on the behaviors that candidates demonstrate. The expectation is that behaviors demonstrated in the simulation are more likely to be demonstrated in future, similar situations when they occur on the job. In their classical behavioral consistency formulation, Wernimont and Campbell (1968) characterized simulations as capturing performance-relevant behavioral *samples* rather than—as in the case of traditional psychometric testing approaches—attempting to measure more indirect *signs* that might predict effective future performance.

*Credibility.* Over the past 30 years, selection science has become increasingly sensitive to the need for assessments not only to *be* valid and fair but also to *appear* to candidates as valid and fair (Bauer et al., 2011). Simulations as a whole, almost by definition, tend to have greater real-world "face validity" than other selection tools (O'Leary et al., 2017). A respectful and credible simulation experience can promote a favorable employment brand, especially important in competitive labor markets. To the degree that a simulation appears to candidates like a taste of their future roles, they are more likely to accept the outcome of the assessment process, seeing assessment feedback as more relevant to their likely future performance. One benefit of that perceived credibility might be new hires having more realistic expectations when onboarding. In this regard, simulations serve as realistic job previews. Moreover, in industries where the applicant pool and the customer base have material overlap (e.g., retail), a credible pre-employment assessment experience can more generally promote the company's product or service branding.

*Application of Multitrait/Multimethod Measurement.* Simulations are typically designed to assess a range of attributes (most often defined as competencies) across a series of situations and contexts that unfold over some period of time, even if only over a 10- or 15-minute span. The simulation thus allows for each target attribute to be measured repeatedly across shifting situational conditions, and several target attributes to be assessed across a series of situations. In addition, different assessment methodologies can be applied in a simulation to measure the same target competency. For example, in assessing a competency like decision-making, the quality of a decision made during the simulation can be scaled (say, using subject matter expert input) and included in a composite with a timestamp measure of speed of decision-making from the point that new information was provided to the participant to when the participant responded with a decision. The use of multiple methodologies allows for triangulation on a capability "true score" by minimizing common method variance.

## Technology-Mediated Simulations: The Opportunities

These valuable attributes mentioned above have made simulations an integral part of the selection testing toolkit for decades. Today, technology has opened exciting opportunities to materially expand the value of simulations in operational settings. What are some of the key ways that technology has impacted simulation design and delivery?

*Expanded Behavioral Sampling.* Technology allows for the potential measurement of hundreds of data points that were not accessible in more traditional simulations. Sound and visual recordings can capture features of speech such as frequency and length of pauses, variation in tone or volume, use of verbal "tics," smiles, frowns, and microexpressions not noticeable under ordinary real-world conditions. Sensing technologies attached to participants can track underlying physiological measures (e.g., heart rate, changes in blood pressure, signs of anxiety) as the participants encounter simulation challenges. Contemporary technology can use natural language processing to assess verbal content for sentiment, complexity of language use, and aspects of personality. Indeed, as these tools have been refined in the last decade, they have been deployed to assess the Big Five, general mental ability, attitudes, emotions—a range of individual trait and state attributes that until now were typically measured through self-report surveys or assessor observation. These technologies, then, allow for the mitigation of reactivity and self-conscious response bias. Importantly, relative to attempts at web scraping and other ways of tapping into naturally occurring behaviors to infer individual difference attributes, in the context of a simulation, conditions are more standardized across participants and the stimuli in the simulation setting more purposefully intended to elicit attribute-relevant behavior.

Technology also allows for the measurement of candidate activity over time, in addition to evaluating the outcome of that activity. In the past, assessors attempted to retrieve those activities after the fact, asking candidates during debrief interviews to describe how they had arrived at a particular decision or solved a particular problem. Technology allows real-time tracking as the simulation unfolds. For example, during a simulation, the resources participants retrieve to address a challenge, the time spent perusing each resource, the lag between a text message from the participant's boss, and the participant's response to that text message can all be measured with great precision and can be used as possible data sources for simulation scoring. Indeed, eye-tracking technology can indicate precisely where and for how long the participant examined a particular item of information. In addition, tracking processes in real time can provide insight into how candidates learn and the number and types of mistakes they make on the road to reaching a solution. More importantly, assuming the data are intentionally captured to reflect an underlying attribute, technology can instantaneously aggregate the data into a composite score with weightings that maximize reliability.

*Algorithmic Scoring.* One of the most robust findings in all of psychology is the superiority of "mechanical" scoring over clinical judgment in the predictive validity of the composite outcomes produced (e.g., Kuncel et al., 2013). Historically, however, overall assessment outcomes based on simulations were often arrived at through assessor roundtable discussion of individual assessor judgment, looking across the multiple competencies rated on the simulation. This is still the case when simulation exercises are embedded in high-stakes individual executive assessments.

Algorithms based on natural language processing and machine learning can score open-field text more consistently and hence more reliably than human assessors (Park et al., 2015), for example, analyzing a participant's email or text message responses that are part of a managerial simulation. Technology allows for the quick and efficient use of algorithmic scoring to generate aggregate results. Components can be weighted to generate composite scores, with technology smoothly standardizing individual scores that may vary in scale characteristics (e.g., combining minutes, 5-point scale ratings, and stanine scoring of a SWOT [strengths, weaknesses, opportunities, and threats] analysis). Technology allows for the seamless and consistent application of different weighting schemes for aggregating individual scores to arrive at composites. As criterion information is fed into the database, machine learning can automatically refine scoring algorithms to enhance predictive power if they can be cross-validated. In that sense, technology allows for self-correction with repeated administrations of the simulation, leveraging real-time information on criterion measures (e.g., candidate performance or turnover) to reduce over time the probability of false-positive and false-negative assessment outcomes.

*A Richer, More Natural Candidate Experience.* Simulations—in the form of video games—are ubiquitous in our culture. As assessment simulations begin to incorporate the media-rich capabilities that are already routine elements of video games, designers have the opportunity to create assessment environments that are much more engaging to the participant than, say, the in-basket exercises of yesteryear. Discussions of simulation fidelity often differentiate between the fidelity of stimuli (the simulation's hypothetical scenario with its context and challenges) and the fidelity of the available response modality (through selection of multiple-choice response alternatives on the one hand and natural real-world communication and interaction on the other; Boyce et al., 2013). Technology can allow for high fidelity on both dimensions (stimulus *and* response), providing a far richer and more authentic experience for participants more likely to elicit behaviors more indicative of a participant's underlying attributes. We can envision simulations in which the participant is in the metaverse, a multichannel virtual and augmented reality environment, interacting with avatars around a conference table, or delivering a presentation to an "audience" of 75 executives, with the wide range of natural participant responses—verbal and nonverbal—captured, recorded, and automatically scored.

We credit technology with enabling the delivery of traditional face-to-face simulation exercises in the context of the constraints of the pandemic. In many organizations, existing live leadership simulations were initially abruptly suspended in hopes that the pandemic-mandated shutdown would be short-lived. As pandemic restrictions dragged on for months and the need for objective assessment results to guide high-stakes leadership talent decisions became acute, many organizations—in some cases, reluctantly—adopted virtual approaches to administering the simulations, much in the spirit of the adjustments made to virtual work more generally. As virtual technology rapidly improved in 2020 and 2021, organizations were able to enhance the simulation experience. Of course, many organizations had already transitioned traditional simulation-based leadership assessment to all-virtual delivery well before the pandemic (Grubb, 2011). In the view of some organizations, virtual delivery was forced by the exigencies of transient pandemic conditions and compromises the rigor and credibility of well-established processes for assessing leaders, especially when applied at more senior executive levels. This, despite the lack of clear findings that virtual assessment differs significantly in outcome or validity from in-person delivery. Many of those organizations fully intend to return at the earliest feasible opportunity to the embedded and trusted simulation delivery processes that historically served them well. However, others—and especially those larger and more geographically dispersed—have embraced virtual assessment as a welcome and permanent advance in assessment practice.

More generally, the work we perform day to day is increasingly mediated by technological tools. Hence, technology-mediated simulations are likely to be more representative of target on-the-job situations, often incorporating the very same technologies (e.g., Zoom, email, multidimensional visual displays) as those used to perform in the real world. The use of technology as the channel for organizational interaction was certainly accelerated by the global COVID pandemic. So in addition to enhancing a candidate's sense of familiarity and engagement during the simulation experience, performance in these high-fidelity simulated challenges is likely to be even more predictive of performance (O'Leary et al., 2017). From the perspective of a typical corporate leader who operated virtually for much of 2020 and 2021, the experience of a simulation that involves video meetings, emails and text, online chats and breakout rooms, collaborative whiteboards, and the other technology tools is likely to feel very natural and authentic, reflecting strong face validity and likely to enhance the perceived procedural fairness and credibility of the assessment (Bauer et al., 2011). This comfort may extend to the smartphone environment, given that time spent on smartphones (PwC, 2021) dramatically increased during the pandemic. Completing a simulation on a smartphone may more closely mirror the increasingly reality of everyday working, especially for responding to quickly answered questions and pressing short-term demands. Certainly, though future research should empirically test the psychometric equivalence of simulations delivered across varying technology platforms (Arthur & Traylor, 2019), much has been done for establishing measurement equivalence for traditional assessment methods (e.g., Brown & Grossenbacher, 2017; Illingworth et al., 2015; King et al., 2015).

## Technology-Mediated Simulations: Cautions

Simulations offer great advantages, especially with the incorporation of technological elements. Here we discuss cautions and limitations when using these tools.

## Psychometric Foundations

*Construct Validity.* Industrial-organizational (IO) psychologists are trained to maintain standards in assessments (Society for Industrial and Organizational Psychology [*Principles*], 2018; Equal Employment Opportunity Commission et al. [*Uniform Guidelines*], 1978). The measured constructs have not changed hugely since the early days of personnel selection (cognitive ability, personality, etc.), but through technology-enhanced simulations there is an opportunity to measure differently than we did in the past (Ryan & Derous, 2019). We may be measuring more dynamic skills like creativity and learning agility in new ways through high-fidelity behavior-based simulations that fundamentally assess differently than traditionally formatted static measures. When we then go to evaluate construct validity through convergence with existing measures of the same constructs, this presents a challenge because the technology-enhanced assessments may show limited overlap with traditional measures. In one example, when attempting to validate a gamified learning tool, the construct validity of reasoning scores captured within the game did not correlate with a well-established static reasoning assessment (Wang et al., 2015). The explanation was that the game assessed reasoning over several levels of complexity as one progressed on the game, where players had to use knowledge from previous levels to solve challenges in the later levels. The static reasoning assessment only assessed one's ability to use information provided directly and in the moment to solve a problem. The game was arguably assessing a more meaningful type of reasoning, but the traditional approach to construct validation was unable to demonstrate convergence. Ultimately, a criterion-oriented study comparing the predictive accuracy of alternate ways of defining and operationalizing the target constructs against measures of performance would help clarify the nomological network. Construct validation approaches need to accommodate when constructs are measured over time, in different parts of the assessment, or when constructs are assessed wholly differently than they have been in the past. As another illustration, think of an emotional intelligence measure where the candidate is working with lifelike avatars and interpreting their facial expressions and voice tone rather than with pictures of faces or a self-report.

An additional challenge is *how* outcomes of interest are being predicted. We are using artificial intelligence and machine learning to create predictive algorithms, but there is little documentation or transparency into how these algorithms are being trained. This is often referred to as the "black box problem," where there are inputs and outputs but little insight to the process in between. Besides the much-talked-about challenge of these algorithms replicating the biases we find in human raters (Totty, 2020), IO psychologists and organizational decision makers often do not fully understand precisely how artificial intelligence (AI) and machine learning are predicting outcomes and what the implications are for validity, reliability, and adverse impact. In part this gap reflects a lack of familiarity with such data science skillsets as working with big data; programming in R, Python, Java, or C++; and algorithm development (Sheets et al., 2019). Nor are those building self-correcting AI algorithms always sensitive to the need for cross-validation to test the robustness of the algorithm when applied to future populations. This leaves the creators of newer assessments with free reign and potential for dustbowl empiricism and puts organizational decision makers in the difficult position of choosing between assessments that integrate cutting-edge technology and those less exciting but statistically sound, robust, tightly defined, job-relevant predictors.

*Incremental Validity.* There is also a research gap in our understanding of the incremental criterion validity of using technology-enabled simulations over traditional approaches. This calls into question whether the initial investment in designing a technology-enabled simulation is worth the added cost and time of development; it is possible that organizations that use these approaches get a boost in applicants' reactions to them, being seen as more sophisticated or engaging (Landers et al., 2020), but is there actually better prediction of job performance? We are still missing a body of research that indicates whether there is incremental validity in using technology-enhanced simulations over traditional approaches for selection, or whether the validity is about the same but the other benefits such as efficiency, cost, and participant experience make it worth the while (Woods et al., 2020).

*Nonlinear Scoring.* One benefit of a more technologically infused experience is the opportunity to individualize the assessment experience while retaining the automated scoring; a primary way to do this is through branching, where a candidate's previous answer determines what they see next in the assessment (Reddock et al., 2020). A candidate who is having a simulated conversation with a direct-report avatar and who is using an authoritarian style may get a more defensive reaction from the avatar than another using a coaching approach. This creates a life-like experience for the candidate but introduces issues in comparing their behaviors and scoring to another candidate who had a different approach in an automated assessment. Branching has several positive implications, but this level of dynamism means it is very difficult to measure the reliability and validity of these tools in traditional ways (Reddock et al., 2020).

## Standardization

***Accessibility and Conditions.*** Organizations and employees are the most equipped in history to hire and be hired virtually as an outgrowth of pandemic-era conditions, but the increasingly high incorporation of technology into simulations still requires access that is not a given for all candidates. Higher fidelity experiences require extensive internet bandwidth, and without it, candidates can experience a lag or delay in the simulation that can affect both their experience and performance. A simulation that is using time as a proxy for decisive decision-making can put a candidate with a slower connection at a disadvantage. Immersive assessments may require the candidate to have a quiet and uninterrupted environment, though initial research shows that if the stakes are high enough, candidates may perform similarly despite distractions (Traylor et al., 2021). Regardless, not all home environments can offer uninterrupted time with the mix of children, pets, or ambient noise. Immersive assessments may also need more complex equipment than just a mobile computer device (e.g., virtual reality headsets), and lack of access to a desktop or large screen can put mobile testers at a disadvantage on more cognitively loaded tasks (Arthur & Traylor, 2019). Lastly, administration of technologically enabled simulations—for example, with heavy media elements like videos, or that require dexterous hand movements—can affect performance and the candidate experience. Organizations using these kinds of tools should examine whether the assessment is unintentionally measuring or even differentially screening on an ability that is nonessential to the job.

***Comparability.*** As discussed earlier, branching can create a more tailored and positive candidate experience. In simulations that use branching, the candidate's decisions have consequences for what transpires next, and this generally increases the face validity of the simulation. However, it also means that candidates come into contact with different stimuli at different times, which can influence perceptions of justice, validity, and attractiveness of the hiring organization (Bruk-Lee et al., 2016). Branching also means that all constructs of interest may not be measured for each candidate, especially if the simulation is limited in length. This leaves gaps in the scoring algorithm and uneven amounts of information across target constructs to make decisions. There are options like using convergence where different storylines come back to a limited number of branches so that all constructs can be measured, looping where candidates can visit previous parts of the simulation, or even using item-response theory (Reddock et al., 2020), but there is a lot more work to be done to understand how these approaches can result in equivalent candidate experiences and measurement.

## The Glister of Gamification

Many technology-enhanced simulations incorporate game elements like storylines, avatars, feedback, and problem-solving to make them more immersive. Here we explore some of the limitations of gamifying.

*Feedback.* Providing participants real-time feedback during the assessment can change their motivation and candidate perceptions, either positively or negatively (Bryant & Malsey, 2012; Bruk-Lee et al., 2016). Real-time feedback can provide or deny a participant access to new information or tools and have positive or negative effects on a participant's feelings of competence, and on ascribed meaningfulness of the assessment (Sailer et al., 2017; Jahn et al., 2021). Feedback is a powerful game element, but the negative can outweigh the positive when applied to the high-stakes measurement context.

*Realism.* Gamification typically aims at high levels of realism, maximizing through technology the extent to which the assessment metaverse feels like a real-world environment. Assuming that realistic environment mirrors the target on-the-job environment, high-fidelity simulation may, as noted earlier, provide a realistic job preview experience and higher predictive validities, although the fidelity-validity issue is still unresolved (Boyce et al., 2013). Augmented and virtual reality simulations are especially useful when real-life scenarios are difficult or impractical to incorporate into an assessment (such as testing pilot, police, or firefighter capacity to respond in emergencies). Note, though, that the augmented and virtual reality gamification experience is far from perfect; dizziness, nausea, and disorientation are common side effects when using headsets and can be especially pronounced for women (Kim, 2019). However, given concerns with the lack of authentic, "high-touch" human connection during and in the hybrid aftermath of the pandemic, organizations may need to be more intentional about the role that gamified high-fidelity simulations play in the selection process to mitigate the risk of alienating candidates.

## Ethics

*Informed Consent.* Organizations are able to collect vast amounts of data while candidates are in these immersive assessment environments. Eye-tracking, facial expressions, heart rate spikes, and reaction times can be easily measured, and this will only expand as the assessments become more sophisticated (Wood et al., 2020). Many of these behaviors are not in the candidates' own conscious awareness or under their discretionary control and yet can be consequential in affecting the simulation's outcome (Lefkowitz & Lowman, 2017). With some of the technology, data are collected incidentally and without a direct measurement purpose (Tippins et al., 2021), and without candidates' consent or awareness. Candidates have to be informed of what kind, how, and where their data are being stored. Organizations have more and more regulations to be mindful of as government and regulatory bodies try to keep up with the ever-changing standards of protecting individuals' privacy around both the capturing and communication of personal information (see Guzzo et al., 2015, for a more detailed discussion of these topics).

*Accommodation.* Many advanced simulations make use of immersive elements to create the engagement, enjoyment, and fidelity that are marketed as the biggest benefits. By virtue of this immersion, accommodation for different disabilities is hard without removing or fully reimagining parts of the assessment. A candidate may be using a mouse to navigate a virtual landscape through an avatar while a guide voices over instructions on what the candidate needs to do next. Accommodations for sight, sound, or tactile manipulation would all fundamentally change the experience. Simply put, the greater the range of sensory, psychomotor, and cognitive abilities required by the simulation, the more challenging the task of accommodating disabilities in the assessment context.

*Sampling Life Though Stealth Assessment.* Stealth assessments are those that are embedded in a form of interaction (often a game) and measure the constructs of interest in a way that is unobtrusive and dynamic (Shute & Ventura, 2013). This has the benefit of reducing candidate anxiety, distortion, and reactivity (Chiang et al., 2011). These are most often used in the educational learning field presently, but imagine being able to use data gathered in a candidate's everyday life as a form of assessment. Going beyond scraping their social media for meaningful data, hiring teams may be able to watch a candidate's interactions in a controlled but public setting with the candidate's permission, to measure emotional intelligence, extraversion, or conscientiousness. Organizations may be able to access data from wearables that give data on exercise, sleep, and even health metrics. At some point in the future, candidates may not even formally enter into an application process but rather, once they signal interest in a role or even just in a company, the organization can gather the huge amount of latent data on the individual, analyze the data for patterns and insights, and recommend or build a role that would be a good fit. This is exciting but requires consideration of topics discussed earlier on validity, reliability, consent, and accommodation as well as adverse impact.

## Investment

*Maintaining Credibility.* Simulations that use advanced elements like augmented/virtual reality, digital avatars, and interactive graphics require a lot of up-front investment in design. Some of the priciest parts of creating a lifelike simulation are the computer-generated imagery that make the virtual environment feel real and that allow a candidate to maneuver freely in the environment. Because of the unprecedented pace of change, highly interactive assessments will likely need to be updated frequently. If a simulation designed even 5 years ago showed a laptop without a touch screen, it would quickly feel dated, especially to younger candidates. Vendors need to weigh the decisions of how much to invest in the development of a given iteration of a technology-enhanced simulation, and whether a more "up-to-date" but pricy simulation will fetch an appropriate financial return in a market crowded with options. Designers also need to remember that small changes in the simulation environment, the order of interactions, or the tasks incorporated can upset the stability of established simulation reliability and validity measures. Without shortcuts for re-establishing these psychometrics, designers are at risk of needing to reassess the psychometric properties after each relatively small change (Bhatia & Ryan, 2018). The market for rolling out innovative simulations is not likely to slow down, so without a faster approach to measuring the underlying psychometrics, IO psychologists risk being unable to influence the narrative toward solutions that are more valid and fair.

*Business Model.* Most organizations that use technology-enabled simulations in their selection process are purchasing usage rights from third-party vendors, indicating that this space will continue to be crowded, by one research firm's measure, reaching more than US$11 billion globally by 2027 (Emergen Research, 2021). This then raises the question of the business model for designing technology-enabled simulations. Do vendors invest heavily up front to create a few of these simulations, and then continuously update them? Or are they set up to expect that every few years a totally fresh offer will be needed? Vendors will need to justify the size and frequency of their investment and balance this with the market's spending appetite.

## Candidate-Based Contaminants

*Experience.* Organizations using technology-enhanced simulations often worry about the contaminating effect of previous exposure to similar types of tools, and whether experience with these tools reduces the learning curve and gives experienced candidates a performance edge. Some work has shown that technology experience does not change candidates' reactions to the assessment (Langer et al., 2018), but that still leaves the issue of performance differences. This can be partially mitigated by giving candidates the opportunity to get familiar and comfortable in the simulation environment before the official assessment session begins.

*Demographics.* Research suggests that women and older applicants may be less engaged in environments that make heavy use of the gamified elements, many of which are incorporated into technology-based simulations. Jent and Janneck (2016), in designing an online coaching intervention intended to train people on how to optimize the design of their jobs, found that women responded less positively to typical gamified feedback elements like points and badges. Melchers and Basch (2021), in a rare examination of demographic differences in simulation performance, found that men and younger participants performed better. While the difference was small, it was significant, indicating that stereotype threat, lack of experience, or other variables may lead to reduced performance, and a more negative experience for minority participants. In a hiring environment that is increasingly sensitive to capturing diverse applicant pools, technology-enhanced simulations could be more of a barrier than a benefit without proper messaging and context setting to help applicants feel prepared.

## Technology-Mediated Simulations: Lingering Research Questions and Opportunities

Thanks to the advances in technology, the simulation experience is becoming increasingly sophisticated. Research is needed to address a number of questions—many of which have been explored for decades in less technology-rich contexts—on the impact of simulation design on assessment outcomes. Below we raise four initial questions related to elements of simulation design that could benefit from (re)examination in future research.

a) **Fidelity.** As noted, fidelity reflects the degree to which the simulation experience mirrors the target real-world experience. Prior research, summarized by Boyce et al. (2013, pp. 21–23), suggests that a high degree of fidelity is *not* a necessary condition for effective simulation design. But the level of fidelity achievable with today's technology (let alone tomorrow's)—with the ability to create immersive environments with virtual reality, wearables, and natural voice interaction (e.g., Amazon's Alexa technology)—was almost unimaginable to simulation designers a decade or more ago when most of the fidelity research was done. We suggest that the fidelity question needs to be re-examined under conditions where almost complete replication of on-the-job experiences—-sight and sound—in a rigorous simulation-based assessment tool is within reach.

b) **Situational strength.** Relatedly, a lingering question on simulation design relates to the degree of structure provided to channel the participant's responses. To the degree that the simulation restricts responses to defined alternatives, the simulation begins resembling what Mischel (1977) long ago described as a *strong* situation, an environment that minimizes individual differences. To the degree that tech-enabled simulation stimuli are so overwhelmingly vivid, and the demand characteristics so clear as to focus the participant on a narrow set of response options, will situational strength limit individual variation in responding? In contrast, to the degree that the simulation allows for a full range of naturally emerging responses, where the elements of the situation are ambiguous, subject to different perspectives and interpretations, are the responses demonstrated by a particular candidate likely to be more reflective of underlying individual differences? Will simulations designed to reflect weak situations be more likely to uncover the meaningful individual differences most relevant in the assessment context? The rich simulations of the future will allow for exploration of these questions.

c) **Incremental validity.** As noted above, incorporating sophisticated technology into simulation design can be costly. Is there a corresponding return on investment in enhanced test validity? Advanced simulations provide a broader range of variables measured and a greater number of observations captured to assess each competency which—all other factors held constant—increases scale reliability. Moreover, they provide a more natural experience by using an immersive media-rich assessment. Do these sufficiently increment validity to justify the cost and effort? If indeed technological sophistication does meaningfully raise validity coefficients, which of the design elements most account for that increment?

d) **Descriptive framework.** Arthur and his colleagues (e.g., Arthur & Traylor, 2019) proposed a taxonomy to reflect structural dimensions that represent variations in traditionally designed psychometric assessments delivered across different computer screens. Their model identifies four facets—screen size, screen clutter, response interface, and permissibility—as key dimensions that are hypothesized to determine cognitive load and consequent participant performance. Arthur and his colleagues have used this taxonomy effectively to test the equivalence of different computer testing environments. These four dimensions, however, represent *just a fraction* of the set of facets on which technology-mediated, media-rich, immersive simulations can potentially differ. Understanding the impact of these and other structural variations of technology-mediated simulations on participant perceptions (e.g., of perceived fairness or difficulty), behavior, and performance, as well as on the measurement of target attributes (Morelli et al., 2017), will require a more complex and granular taxonomy. The taxonomy in turn would guide systematic research where these characteristics can be experimentally varied and their effects measured. Facets such as screen resolution, sound quality and directionality, color and brightness, and responsiveness of controller devices are just a few of the facets that may need to be considered in the construction of a taxonomy useful for describing variation in simulation environments. Systematic research would help us understand performance equivalence, user experience, and measurement reliability and validity when simulations are administered across an ever-widening range of device types and configurations and are performed by candidates in any and all human surroundings.

*Opportunities.* Technology may (re)raise some interesting research questions, but technology also equips us with opportunities to explore those questions in new ways. Design characteristics can be programmed to experimentally vary across random samples in pilot phases and hypothesized effects studied using the A/B testing methodology so popular in e-commerce marketing (Kohavi et al., 2020). Technology provides simulation designers with a virtual global reach to potential research samples. Advances in big data mean that validation research can potentially incorporate a broader array of criteria beyond measures of performance or turnover. Career mobility, measures of engagement, sentiment analysis drawn from a sample of emails, and social network mapping are just some of the potential criteria that can extend understanding of relationships between simulation-based assessments and real-world outcomes of interest.

## Conclusion

We can envision an assessment in which, anywhere on the globe, participants enters a virtual office building, "walk" down a virtual corridor, step into a virtual but well-appointed conference room, greet the avatar members of the executive committee around the table, and present their analysis of a potential new venture, fielding questions from the audience specifically addressed to challenge some of the key points in their presentation in lively give-and-take exchanges. In fact, simulations with levels of immersion similar to this already exist in training and entertainment contexts. Soon we will see this level of real-world look-and-feel in simulations explicitly designed to evaluate job-related capabilities in high-stakes employment or promotion settings. With the accelerating development of technology, the future of technology-mediated simulations will undoubtedly create exciting opportunities to materially advance assessment practice, if we can successfully address the associated challenges.

## References

Arthur, W., Jr., & Traylor, Z. (2019). Mobile assessment in personnel testing: Theoretical and practical implications. In R. N. Landers (Ed.), *The Cambridge handbook of technology and employee behavior* (pp. 179–207). Cambridge University Press. https://doi.org/10.1017/9781108649636.009

Bauer, T. N., Truxillo, D. M., Mack, K., & Costa, A. B. (2011). Applicant reactions to technology-based selection: What we know so far. In N. T. Tippins & S. Adler (Eds.), *Technology-enhanced assessment of talent* (pp. 190–223). John Wiley.

Bhatia, S., & Ryan, A. M. (2018). Hiring for the win: Game-based assessment in employee selection. In D. Stone & J. Dubebohn (Eds.), *The brave new world of eHRM 2.0* (pp. 81–110). Information Age Publishing.

Boyce, A. S., Corbet, C. E., & Adler, S. (2013). Simulations in the selection context: considerations, challenges, and opportunities. In M. Fetzer & K. Tuzinski (Eds.), *Simulations for personnel selection* (pp. 17–41). Springer.

Brown, M. I., & Grossenbacher, M. A. (2017). Can you test me now? Equivalence of GMA tests on mobile and non-mobile devices. *International Journal of Selection and Assessment, 25*(1), 61–71.

Bruk-Lee, V., Lanz, J., Drew, E. N., Coughlin, C., Levine, P., Tuzinski, K., & Wrenn, K. (2016). Examining applicant reactions to different media types in character-based simulations for employee selection. *International Journal of Selection and Assessment, 24*(1), 77–91.

Bryant, S. E., & Malsey, S. (2012, April). *21st century assessment centers: Technology's increasing role and impact* [Paper presentation]. Annual meeting of the Society for Industrial and Organizational Psychology, San Diego, CA.

Chiang, Y. T., Lin, S. S. J., Cheng, C. Y., & Liu, E. Z. F. (2011). Exploring online game players' flow experiences and positive affect. *Turkish Online Journal of Educational Technology, 10*(1), 106–114.

Emergen Research. (2021, May 10). *Assessment services market size to reach USD 11.47 billion in 2027*. GlobeNewswire Newsroom. https://www.globenewswire.com/en/news-release/2021/05/10/2226531/0/en/Assessment-Services-Market-Size-to-Reach-USD-11-47-Billion-In-2027-Growing-Demand-for-Evaluation-of-Skills-for-Better-Employability-is-Key-Factor-Boosting-Industry-Growth-says-Emer.html

Equal Employment Opportunity Commission, Civil Service Commission, Department of Labor, & Department of Justice. (1978). Uniform guidelines on employee selection procedures. *Federal Register, 43*, 38290–38315.

Grubb, A. D. (2011). Promotional assessment at the FBI: How the search for a high-tech solution led to a high-fidelity low-tech simulation. In N. T. Tippins & S. Adler (Eds.), *Technology-enhanced Assessment of Talent* (pp. 293–306). San Francisco: Jossey-Bass.

Guzzo, R. A., Fink, A. A., King, E., Tonidandel, S., & Landis, R. S. (2015). Big data recommendations for industrial–organizational psychology. *Industrial and Organizational Psychology, 8*(4), 491–508.

Hoffman, B. J., Kennedy, C. L., LoPilato, A. C., Monahan, E. L., & Lance, C. E. (2015). A review of the content, criterion-related, and construct-related validity of assessment center exercises. *Journal of Applied Psychology, 100*, 1143. www.ncbi.nlm.nih.gov/pubmed/25798555.

Illingworth, A. J., Morelli, N. A., Scott, J. C., & Boyd, S. L. (2015). Internet-based, unproctored assessments on mobile and non-mobile devices: Usage, measurement equivalence, and outcomes. *Journal of Business and Psychology, 30*(2), 325–343.

Jahn, K., Kordyaka, B., Machulska, A., Eiler, T. J., Gruenewald, A., Klucken, T., . . . Niehaves, B. (2021). Individualized gamification elements: The impact of avatar and feedback design on reuse intention. *Computers in Human Behavior, 119*, 106702.

Jent, S., & Janneck, M. (2016). Using gamification to enhance user motivation in an online-coaching application for flexible workers. In *Proceedings of the 12th International Conference on Web Information Systems and Technologies (WEBIST), 2016*(2), 35–41.

Kim, M. (2019, August 25). *Why you feel motion sickness during virtual reality.* ABC News. https://abcnews.go.com/Technology/feel-motion-sickness-virtual-reality/story?id=65153805

King, D. D., Ryan, A. M., Kantrowitz, T., Grelle, D., & Dainis, A. (2015). Mobile internet testing: An analysis of equivalence, individual differences, and reactions. *International Journal of Selection and Assessment, 23*(4), 382–394.

Kohavi, R., Tang, D., & Xu, Y. (2020). *Trustworthy online controlled experiments: A practical guide to A/B testing.* Cambridge University Press.

Kuncel, N. R., Klieger, D. M., Connelly, B. S., & Ones, D. S. (2013). Mechanical versus clinical data combination in selection and admissions decisions: A meta-analysis. *Journal of Applied Psychology, 98*(6), 1060–1072.

Landers, R. N., Auer, E. M., & Abraham, J. D. (2020). Gamifying a situational judgment test with immersion and control game elements: Effects on applicant reactions and construct validity. *Journal of Managerial Psychology, 35*(4), 255–270. https://doi.org/10.1108/JMP-10-2018-0434

Langer, M., König, C. J., & Fitili, A. (2018). Information as a double-edged sword: The role of computer experience and information on applicant reactions towards novel technologies for personnel selection. *Computers in Human Behavior, 81*, 19–30.

Lefkowitz, J., & Lowman, R. L. (2017). Ethics of employee selection. In J. L. Farr & N. T. Tippins (Eds.), *Handbook of employee selection* (2nd ed., pp. 575–598). Taylor & Francis.

Melchers, K. G., & Basch, J. M. (2021). Fair play? Sex-, age-, and job-related correlates of performance in a computer-based simulation game. *International Journal of Selection and Assessment, 30*(1), 48–61.

Mischel, W. (1977). The interaction of person and situation. In D. Magnusson & N. Endler (Eds.), *Personality at the crossroads: Current issues in interactional psychology.* (pp. 333–352). Hillsdale, NJ: Erlbaum.

Morelli, N., Arthur, W., Potosky, D., & Tippins, N. (2017). A call for conceptual models of technology in I-O psychology: An example from technology-based talent assessment. *Industrial and Organizational Psychology, 10*(4), 634–653. doi:10.1017/iop.2017.70

O'Leary, R. S., Forsman, J. W., & Isaacson, J. A. (2017). The role of simulation exercises in selection. In H. W. Goldstein, J. P. Pulakos, & C. Semedo (Eds.), *The Wiley Blackwell handbook of the psychology of recruitment, selection, and employee retention* (pp. 247–270). John Wiley & Sons.

Park, G., Schwartz, H. A., Eichstaedt, J. C., Kern, M. L., Kosinski, M., Stillwell, D. J., & Seligman, M. E. (2015). Automatic personality assessment through social media language. *Journal of Personality and Social Psychology, 108*(6), 934.

PwC. (2021). *2021 Outlook segment findings*. https://www.pwc.com/gx/en/industries/tmt/media/outlook/segment-findings.html?WT.mc_id=CT1-PL52-DM2-TR2-LS4-ND30-TTA9-CN_GEMO-2021-segments-two

Reddock, C. M., Auer, E. M., & Landers, R. N. (2020). A theory of branched situational judgment tests and their applicant reactions. *Journal of Managerial Psychology, 35*, 255–270.

Ryan, A. M., & Derous, E. (2019). The unrealized potential of technology in selection assessment. *Revista de Psicología del Trabajo y de las Organizaciones, 35*(2), 85–92.

Sailer, M., Hense, J. U., Mayr, S. K., & Mandl, H. (2017). How gamification motivates: An experimental study of the effects of specific game design elements on psychological need satisfaction. *Computers in Human Behavior, 69*, 371–380.

Schmidt, F. L., & Hunter, J. E. (1998). The validity and utility of selection methods in personnel psychology: Practical and theoretical implications of 85 years of research findings. *Psychological Bulletin, 124*, 262–274. http://citeseerx.ist.psu.edu/viewdoc/download?doi=10.1.1.172.1733&rep=rep1&type=pdf

Sheets, T. L., Belwalkar, B. B., Toaddy, S. R., & McClure, T. K. (2019). Filling the IO/technology void: Technology and training in I-O psychology. In R. N. Landers (Ed.), *Cambridge handbook of technology and employee behavior* (pp. 22–37). Cambridge University Press.

Shute, V., & Ventura, M. (2013). *Measuring and supporting learning in video games: Stealth assessment*. MIT Press.

Society for Industrial and Organizational Psychology. (2018). *Principles for the validation and use of personnel selection procedures* (5th ed.). https://www.apa.org/ed/accreditation/about/policies/personnel-selection-procedures.pdf

Thornton, G. C., III, Rupp, D. E., & Hoffman, B. J. (2014). *Assessment center perspectives for talent management strategies*. Routledge.

Tippins, N. T., Oswald, F. L., & McPhail, S. M. (2021, January 28). *Scientific, legal, and ethical concerns about AI-based personnel selection tools: A call to action*. https://doi.org/10.31234/osf.io/6gczw

Totty, M. (2020, November 3). How to make artificial intelligence less biased. *Wall Street Journal*. https://www.wsj.com/articles/how-to-make-artificial-intelligence-less-biased-11604415654

Traylor, Z., Hagen, E., Williams, A., & Arthur, W., Jr. (2021). The testing environment as an explanation for unproctored internet-based testing device-type effects. *International Journal of Selection and Assessment, 29*(1), 65–80.

Wang, L., Shute, V., & Moore, G. R. (2015). Lessons learned and best practices of stealth assessment. *International Journal of Gaming and Computer-Mediated Simulations (IJGCMS), 7*(4), 66–87.

Wernimont, P. F., & Campbell, J. P. (1968). Signs, samples, and criteria. *Journal of Applied Psychology, 52*, 372–376. http://psycnet.apa.org/record/1968-19528-001

Woods, S. A., Ahmed, S., Nikolaou, I., Costa, A. C., & Anderson, N. R. (2020). Personnel selection in the digital age: A review of validity and applicant reactions, and future research challenges. *European Journal of Work and Organizational Psychology, 29*(1), 64–77.

# 13
# Fixing the Industrial-Organizational Psychology-Technology Interface (IOPTI)

Avoiding Both IO/Tech and Tech/IO Conflict

*Richard N. Landers*

Historically, industrial-organizational (IO) psychologists focusing on assessment development did not need to rely substantially on advanced technology. For a century of psychology, assessments were almost universally spoken aloud or written down. Even the most cutting-edge and experimental assessment types, like assessment centers, ultimately only substituted other-ratings for self-ratings in terms of their technological sophistication. Most IO assessments were designed and developed on paper, or more recently in Microsoft Word, with the drafting of items and scenarios done at a conference table, or more recently in a Zoom call. Once development was complete, the assessment would still most frequently be administered verbally or on paper well into the early 2000s, an era when the first website URL printed on a billboard in San Francisco made national news. Within IO psychology, the rise of internet-administered assessments initially created a bit of a firestorm (see Tippins, 2009), only to fizzle out with practitioners throwing their hands in the air to exclaim, "I guess we're doing this anyway," in response to inescapable candidate and executive demand. Over the past 20 years, the assessment development and administration process has become increasingly automated and algorithmic. It is a trend that is likely to accelerate in the decades to come, especially as innovative assessment technologies, like immersive simulation, natural language processing, and alternative scoring methods with machine learning, continue to evolve.

As such, understanding why IO assessment experts, both practitioner and academic, are generally so bad at understanding and working with

Richard N. Landers, *Fixing the Industrial-Organizational Psychology-Technology Interface (IOPTI)* In: *Talent Assessment*. Edited by: Tracy M. Kantrowitz, Douglas H. Reynolds, and John C. Scott, Oxford University Press.
© Society of Industrial Organizational Psychology 2023. DOI: 10.1093/oso/9780197611050.003.0013

technology and technologists, including people like programmers, machine learning engineers, and web designers, has become a pressing concern for IO psychologists (Hu et al., 2021; Landers, 2021), or at least those who want to remain employed across the coming decades. Without significant understanding, conflict between IO psychologists and technologists has become common. Many IO psychologists have experienced the frustration of asking a technologist for a change to their systems only to be told a seemingly simple change would be too expensive, too complex, or too risky without much clarity as to why. But similarly, many technologists are frustrated at the kinds of requests they get from the IO perspective, seemingly divorced from the realities of the technical systems that the IO psychologists nevertheless rely upon. These disagreements at best cause friction between IO and technologist teams and at worst threaten IO psychology's core value in these organizations. As more Silicon Valley firms appear in the business of "disrupting" hiring, it has never been more critical that IO psycholoigists actively work to build shared mental models with their technologist colleagues, to overcome long-standing differences in mindset, priorities, strategy, and even language. Without a shared understanding between IO psychologists and technologists, it is the IO psychologists who are more likely to be sidelined, and thus it falls largely on their shoulders to build related competencies.

Fortunately, building true interdisciplinary understanding is an achievable goal (Klein, 1990), and together, IO psychologists and technologists can use that understanding to create something better than either could create alone. To help you do this, in this chapter, I will present the foundations of these conflicts so that each side can better appreciate, and perhaps develop greater empathy for, the perspective of the other. I refer to this general topic as the *IO psychology-technology interface* (IOPTI), to draw parallels to the IO-familiar concept of the *work-family interface* (Frone et al., 1997). Similar to how both work demands can create familial challenges (i.e., work-family conflict) and family demands can create work stress (i.e., family-work conflict), so can IOPTI conflict run in both directions. Sometimes the IO psychologist creates the problem, by bringing their IO-flavored assumptions to decisions about technology, and sometimes the technologist does, by bringing their own assumptions to decisions about people. In both cases, failing to look beyond one's own assumptions is the major cause of these conflicts, which is amplified when decisions must be made about both people and technology, simultaneously. Thus, to build your interdisciplinary competency, so that you can continue to effectively create and manage assessments as the assessment marketplace continues to evolve, I will focus here on helping you to understand the assumptions you bring and appreciate the assumptions being brought to you.

## Philosophy of Science in Psychology Versus Computing

In modern graduate training, the philosophy of a discipline is rarely explicitly taught (Grüne-Yanoff, 2014), yet most people cannot graduate with an advanced degree in any field without having absorbed one (Proctor & Capaldi, 2012). Disciplinary philosophies are embedded in academic cultures, guiding how we approach and understand the subjects of the fields we are trained in. Most likely, you never had a course explicitly laying out the philosophy of science underlying everything you learned; nevertheless, that philosophy serves as the bedrock of your knowledge. Since fully explicating the philosophy of science is beyond the scope of this chapter, I will give you a few shortcuts to help give shape to the assumptions you have already absorbed, to better contrast them with the assumptions others bring, and to use your new understanding to help avoid IOPTI conflicts.

The first of these is understanding both the similarities and differences between the scientific philosophies in which IO psychologists are generally trained and the philosophies in which technologists are generally trained. Fortunately, we do have many similarities. The greatest similarities are in *ontology*, which refers to the assumptions that we make about the nature of reality itself. Ontologies, broadly speaking and simplifying greatly, exist on a spectrum between realist and relativistic perspectives (Manicas & Secord, 1983). Whereas realists believe a true and objective reality exists, relativists do not. Both IO psychologists and technologists are usually trained to be realists. In IO psychology, this philosophy is evident in our treatment of organizational and interpersonal phenomena, in that we assume groups' "true scores" to exist, whether in terms of means, correlations, or whatever else, and set our measurement goals at measuring those true scores as accurately as we can. In technology-related fields, it is more blatant: The technologies that technologists manage and develop exist in an obvious, immediate, and physical sense. There are both realist and relativist engineers, scientists, psychologists, and computing professionals, but most are realists. So, we at least all have this mostly in common, as shown in Table 13.1.

Table 13.1 Prototypical Commonalities and Differences in Approach Between Science and Engineering

|  | IO Psychologist | Technologist |
| --- | --- | --- |
| Ontology | Realism: I believe a shared, objective reality exists. | |
| Historical Paradigm | Empiricism: I believe the world can be understood through data collected under carefully defined and optimized rules to minimize confounding interpretations. | |
| Epistemology | Mixed Objectivism and Subjectivism: I can understand this world by observing it through the lens of my own biases. | Objectivism: I can understand this world by observing it. |
| Typical Modern Paradigm | Postpositivism: I can test specific rules about reality by carefully manipulating causes I'm interested in and isolating the effects of those causes. If causes cannot be manipulated directly, I may assume them to exist through their effects. But in either case, I must actively work to minimize the effects of my own biases in interpretation. | Logical Positivism: I can test specific rules about reality by carefully manipulating causes and isolating the effects of those causes, observing those effects directly. |
| Broader Discipline | Science: I can find the best solution to a problem by consulting past scientific research and adopting the "best practices" that have been previously validated. | Engineering: I can develop the best product for a given use case by using scientific research as a starting point and then optimizing my product development process to local conditions using iteration. |
| Project Management Approach | Waterfall: I want to carefully document goals, use that to create specific plans, implement those plans, test that the implementation worked, and then maintain what we created until no longer needed. This maximizes project alignment with long-term goals. | Agile: Because project requirements can change at any time mid-project, I am ready to change my approach whenever needed. I freely revisit assumptions and past decisions. This maximizes immediate customer satisfaction at minimum cost. |
| Example Starting Question | "How do best practices suggest we might use machine learning? What has been done before?" | "How can we develop a machine learning system so that it is useful to us? How can we innovate to maximize value to each customer?" |

*Note.* This is a significant simplification of the complexities surrounding all these concepts and presents general rules for entire groups that likely apply to only a majority. It was *engineered* to be useful to you at the expense of precision and comprehensiveness. This will annoy scientific readers and philosophers alike.

Where things begin to diverge is in our *epistemologies*, which refer to the assumptions that we make about how humans can learn about this reality that we realists assume we all share (Diesing, 1966). In technology, most professionals lean toward *objectivism*, which describes the assumption that we, as humans, can observe the world objectively. This perspective makes a lot of sense when you consider the world technologists live in: They write code, develop algorithms, or create tech products, and the code, algorithms, and products do exactly what the technologists wrote, designed, and developed them to do. If an end-product doesn't meet the technologist's goals, it's because the code, algorithm, or product was not developed correctly. There is always a one-to-one relationship between what the professional does and how reality appears to be affected. In contrast, psychologists tend to be trained with more *subjectivism*, which describes the assumption that the world as we see it is blurred through the lens of human interpretation. This perspective also makes a lot of sense when you consider the world of psychology: Nothing is surface level. Everything psychologists want to know about is a construct or a process or something else lurking beneath the surface of the observable. We live in a world of inference about people rather than a world of direct observation about technology.

Ontologies and epistemologies together inform specific practical approaches to creating and understanding knowledge called *paradigms* (Kuhn, 1962), and it is through the lens of the paradigm we were trained in that we tend to view the world. An older paradigm at the foundation of science, engineering, psychology, and computing alike is *empiricism*, the idea that through sensory experience, we can collect data about phenomena to understand those phenomena (Toulmin & Leary, 1985). To make empiricism more practical, a paradigm called *logical positivism* imposes constraints on empiricism via its *verification principle*, which states that it is only through directly observed and verified empirical data that new knowledge can be created. Yet logical positivism is also practically limited, because it limits knowledge to what can be observed. Because the idea of a psychological construct cannot be directly observed, the idea of constructs is considered *tautological* to a logical positivist, which is to say constructs only exist because you say they exist, not because of any connection to our shared objective reality. Tautological claims are a waste of time to a logical positivist, because they can never be supported via empirical observation, making much of psychology seem like magical thinking. With the notable exception of diehard supporters of B. F. Skinner's behaviorism, *postpositivism* gradually replaced logical positivism in psychology, and this change reflected the addition of a subjectivistic lens over logical positivism (Popper, 1963). A postpositivist is likely to say that all human observation is through the lens of human interpretation, past experience, cognition, and bias. We may try to reduce these biases through good research design or careful planning, but the postpositivist understands that they are always present.

Differences in paradigm go to the very core of how researchers tend to understand how the world works and often shape their priorities. For example, for the assessment IO psychologist, it is only with postpositivistic assumptions that psychometrics makes any sense at all. In both classical and modern test theories, constructs are reflected by imperfect indicators, and it is only through observation of shared variance across multiple indicators of a construct, caused by carefully refined instruments, that psychologists are willing to claim constructs are in fact being measured (American Educational Research Association et al., 2014). But this is only possible if one assumes constructs exist in the first place and furthermore that empirical observation of indicators can help describe them. To the logical positivist, which includes most technologists,[1] trying to measure something that is "unobservable" can just sound like a fiction that psychologists have invented to make themselves appear useful. To the logical positivist, the only things that are "real" are the things they can observe themselves. Thus, disagreements in paradigm often sit at the foundation for much bigger disagreements. For example, when IO psychologists find themselves arguing with the machine learning engineers about "better measurement," yet the tech folks just want to "use the ground truth we have," it is this paradigmatic conflict that is ultimately to blame.

## Problem Solving in Science Versus Engineering

Another major challenge in working at the IOPTI are differences between scientific and engineering approaches to problem-solving. IO psychologists are almost exclusively trained as scientists, typically in the tradition of mostly quantitative social science. This makes us, mostly, realists with mixed epistemologies trained in a postpositivistic paradigm. We generally believe

---

[1] There is likely greater variability in paradigm among those trained in technology fields than among those trained in psychology (see Eden, 2007), but in my experience, this view is modal among technologists, broadly speaking.

that the world is real and objectively exists, that we can understand this world by testing it through the lens of our own biases, and that we can test specific rules about reality by carefully controlling the features we are interested in. We are taught that the basic purposes of our field are to describe, understand, and predict reality, and we organize our behaviors around these purposes, in both academia and practice. For example, imagine that you are about delve into a new subdomain of IO psychology that you have never dealt with before, like the use of natural language processing (NLP) to score candidate essays (e.g., Campion et al., 2016). Your instinct in this situation is likely to consult existing research literature for "best practices on NLP" and "best practices on scoring essays" according to the most trustworthy research you can identify, whether industry or academic, and then follow the recommendations you find as best you can, within the constraints applied to you. Yet this approach does not describe at all what an engineer will do if asked to develop an NLP system. Understanding why is a key step to navigating the IOPTI to successful product creation.

## Thinking Like an Engineer

Engineers initially approach problems with a similar lens as scientists do, by consulting past research; both engineering and scientific disciplines are rooted in empiricism and therefore value evidence. The differences emerge after this point. First, rather than viewing conclusions from past evidence as a blueprint for future behavior, they consider it a starting point for further iteration and improvement. For example, an IO psychologist working on an assessment development team interested in implementing a new cheating prevention strategy in their online testing platform is likely to first consult "past evidence," probably in the form of scientific research, presentations at major IO psychology conferences, white papers from industry colleagues, and word-of-mouth recommendations from colleagues who have previously tried something similar; use all of that to make a decision about what to do; and then articulate that vision to the web engineering team. The web engineering team, however, is unlikely to view that vision as definitive and final. Instead, they will treat that vision as a game plan subject to change, nothing more than a general idea of what the new system's capabilities should be, one that can be modified when newly discovered challenges or changes along the development process emerge. To understand why engineers approach problems this way, we will next explore the three ways of thinking where the conceptual approach taken by IO psychologists and technology engineers tends to be the most dissimilar.

## Mindset 1: Algorithmic Thinking

Engineers default to thinking in terms of algorithms (Lamagna, 2015), whereas the average IO psychologist most likely doesn't know what an algorithm is, despite hearing the term an awful lot these days. The good news is that the term "algorithm" is very easy to understand; it refers to any step-by-step process defined in terms of inputs, procedures applied with and without consulting those inputs, and outputs. Algorithms are not necessarily digital. For example, if I were to describe an algorithm for adding three numbers together with mental math, I might put it as follows:

> Three numbers are used as input. First, I add together the first and second number in the set to get a subtotal. Second, I add the subtotal to the third number. The output of this algorithm is this new sum.

This block of text might also be considered a type of *pseudocode*, a technique for making an algorithm concrete, but in human terms, to make it easier for a programmer to convert it into actual code. Next, let's try to increase the complexity of our algorithm—now we want to add an arbitrary number of integers together with mental math:

> Any count of numbers is used as input. First, I add together the first two numbers in the list to create a subtotal. Second, I remove the first two numbers from the list. Third, I add the subtotal to the first number remaining on the list. Fourth, I remove the top number from the list. Fifth, I return to the second step until there are no numbers remaining in the list. The final subtotal is the output of this algorithm.

As can be seen, even for a relatively simple task, algorithmic thinking requires you to be specific, precise, and exhaustive in terms of how you approach a problem. Even this algorithm is not sufficiently complex given its purpose and will fail under certain conditions; see if you can determine them for yourself before consulting the footnote for the answer.[2] With that mastered, try to solve the algorithmic problems supplied by Burton (2010).

## Mindset 2: Systems Thinking

Although thinking in terms of algorithms is arguably the most fundamental approach to think more like an engineer (Frank, 2000), algorithms rarely stand alone; more frequently, collections of algorithms are used that are dependent on one another, creating a *system*. Systems thinking thus refers to viewing problems through the lens of highly interconnected algorithms, with many dependencies and interactive complexity. Any change to any algorithm—and remember, literally everything in a digital product is algorithmic input, output, or both—is going to affect all the other algorithms it is connected to. No change can occur in isolation. Instead, it is always a question of degree. To what extent will the inputs, processes, and outputs of all the other algorithms in this system be affected by the proposed change?

My favorite example of systems thinking comes from my own experience while working at an employee engagement consultancy on their questionnaire delivery software. One of our customers wanted their organizational logo to be displayed about a half-inch lower on their engagement questionnaire to be compliant with the logo's brand guidelines, which required a certain minimum amount of whitespace in all directions around the logo. The engineering team balked, saying this was not a reasonable request. On the surface, this seems like a simple issue; surely moving an image on a webpage a half-inch from its current location is not a complex problem, so this perception caused some tension between the sales staff and the engineering team. It was only some years later that I fully understood what had happened. You see, the engineers understood the algorithms that drove logo placement, and more specifically, they knew that logo placement was a single set value. It was not an input to an algorithm anywhere. It was set in the code

---

[2] Engineers reading this will immediately notice that the input was "any number of numbers," which means it's possible that the input is zero, one, or two. In all three of these cases, the algorithm will fail but at different points in its execution. The zero- and one-number conditions will fail at the first step, since there are not two numbers to add together, whereas the two-number condition will fail at the third step, since the third number needs to be added to the subtotal before the algorithm checks if it has run out of numbers but cannot do this if the third number does not exist. This is the kind of reasoning the typical engineer will immediately apply any time you ask for a change in a system they oversee. As a challenge, try to redesign this pseudocode block to handle all three of these input types.

and therefore the same for all customers. To allow the logo to be in a different position, there were four undesirable potential solutions: (a) the logo's placement could be moved for all customers, (b) this customer's request could be ignored, (c) an exception could be programmed into the system to detect when this particular customer's questionnaire was being delivered and alter the algorithm's process whenever that happened, or (d) the entire display system would need to be redeveloped: Logo placement information would need to be added as an input value for that algorithm; the team would need to agree on what inputs were reasonable (e.g., right now, a customer just wants "lower," but what if another customer wants "further to the right" later?); the change might affect *other* algorithms' inputs, which would need to be analyzed and tested; and so on. In short, the engineers immediately thought of logo placement as one small but deeply embedded aspect of numerous systems of algorithms that in concert create what people see on the webpage. The sales team did not see it the same way.

## Mindset 3: Design Thinking

Given that algorithms involve specifying inputs, processes, and output to an intensely specific degree; that individual systems can be made up of dozens or hundreds of algorithms; and that dozens or hundreds of systems may compose a particular piece of software or website or other product, you might wonder: How does anything get created successfully? How can a successful product be created if doing so relies on so many tens of thousands of decisions all being made correctly, perhaps with little or no prior research to serve as a foundation?

Historically, this was accomplished with a process called *waterfall development*, a rigidly structured, step-by-step design and development procedure that flows linearly through six stages: requirements analysis, design, implementation, testing, deployment, and maintenance (Highsmith, 2002). When a stage is completed, its results are finalized and become the foundation of the next stage. Although waterfall results in the creation of products that closely align with their initial visions, it is less suitable for projects where information changes mid-development, which occurs in essentially all large-scale software engineering projects today (Clear, 2003). To address such limitations and related challenges, the philosophy of *agile development* was created to refocus the goals of software development on the people working on and

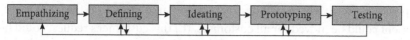

**Figure 13.1.** Iterative steps in design thinking

affected by the software, on fulfilling the software's core purpose rather than comprehensively building extras and add-ons, on actively collaborating with customers, and on being able to respond well to any needed change, even if contrary to the initial plan. These ideas were documented in the Agile Manifesto (https://agilemanifesto.org/), a webpage drafted in 2001 by a team of 17 software developers who were frustrated with both the increasingly poor outcomes resulting from waterfall and inefficiencies associated with the corporatization of computer programming. Over the years, agile development came to refer to the use of small, cross-functional teams working collaboratively and iteratively on components of larger challenges (Dikert et al., 2016) and is now the dominant philosophical orientation toward software development industry-wide. Agile is associated with many specific methods for implementation, perhaps most famously the scrum framework (Schwaber & Sutherland, 2020).

Whereas being "agile" reflects a philosophy of software development, *design thinking* is a practical toolkit for being agile of significant value for IO psychology. Design thinking is a design and development process theory[3] (Plattner et al., 2011) popularized by the Stanford Design School (Bjogvinsson et al., 2012). As shown in Figure 13.1, design thinking comprises five key stages in the development of modern complex technical products, like the kinds of software platforms that IO psychologists increasingly find themselves managing or helping to create. The first stage, empathizing, asks developers to collect data concerning their design goals, often in the form of end-user focus groups and/or subject matter expert consultation. The second stage, definition, asks developers to use the information they obtained from empathizing to imagine the major sorts of challenges they are likely to face in the future when designing systems to address those goals. The third stage, ideating, asks developers to brainstorm and then refine ideas about how to address the defined challenges. The fourth stage,

---

[3] Design and development process theories are uncommon in IO psychology. For a more complete explanation of such theories and how they apply in the IO assessment context, see Landers et al. (2022).

prototyping, asks developers to create increasingly complete versions of the final product for testing purposes, such as without final audio, graphics, or more major components. The fifth stage, testing, involves evaluation of whether goals were met, challenges were addressed, and targeted end-user outcomes were achieved.

Most importantly, design thinking is both iterative and flexible. There is no expectation that the development process will occur linearly, from step 1 to 5. Instead, earlier steps are revisited or repeated as needed. The product itself is never truly finished; it is instead continuously improved until you no longer wish to spend resources to improve it. For example, in development of the game-based assessment described by Landers et al. (2022), the engineering team often created a few alternative designs of the assessment, presenting different options for a particular design decision in the morning, asking people in the organization to play each version for a few minutes and provide feedback, then repeating this prototyping and testing cycle throughout each workday. This resulted in the creation of thousands of prototypes over each year of development for each of the seven mini-games in their assessment battery, in addition to prototypes for games that were eventually eliminated from the battery after they could not be revised to meet defined goals. Even after the formal "release" of the assessment, the developer continued creating, testing, and deploying new prototypes as new bugs arose, as new requirements for accessibility became values, and as clients suggested additional features.

IO psychologists often default to work strategies akin to waterfall development, although there are some exceptions. For example, basing decision-making only on comprehensive and complete job analytic data or on the results of an exhaustive needs assessment mimics waterfall in its focus on making "final" decisions as early in the project as possible. Much as with software development, when organizational realities shift mid-project, this can make course correction difficult. Fortunately, IO psychologists do already engage in a condensed version of design thinking in assessment development, although they rarely think of this in terms of a formal design and development process. A typical psychometric measure development process likely involves specifying a construct (defining) for a particular applied purpose and existing constraints (empathizing), discussing the item universe (ideating), drafting items (prototyping), collecting data (testing), revising or dropping items (prototyping again), collecting more data (testing), and so on. In this sense, design thinking simply formalizes this kind of development strategy and applies it to the creation of any technical product, even ones for which science-derived "best practices" have not yet been created. Expanding this type of thinking throughout your assessment projects, focusing a bit more on agility and a bit less on technical precision, will help improve your ability to respond effectively in a rapidly changing world.

## Initial Steps to Bridge the Gap

By learning about and internalizing these three approaches to problem-solving, the average IO psychologist can dramatically improve their interactions at the IOPTI and, as a result, the quality of the technical products created with both IO and technologist expertise. Another way to think about the risk from not doing so is that in technical product development, the IO psychologist is functionally the subject matter expert, whereas the technologist is the creator. Ultimately, it is the technologists who have control of the product, because they are the people literally building it; the IO psychologist only provides advice and direction. Even a single instance of a technologist deciding, "That IO psychologist is not going to understand why we had to make the decision this way, so I'm not even going to tell them we did it," is a problematic IOPTI failure of team communication and trust that will weaken the final product. The IO psychologist's expert judgment cannot make its way into the product except through the technologist as an intermediary.

The term "affordances" refers to the capabilities that a technology provides to a human that the human did not have without them, and provision of meaningful affordances is the primary driver of technology success. Put another way, well-designed and effectively developed technology affords humans with new capabilities. It provides new potential for human behavior. It does not, however, inherently create change. Failing to recognize the importance of affordances is a common mistake both technologists and IO psychologists make when assuming that simply by buying, acquiring, or building a new technology, problems will suddenly be solved and improved performance will suddenly be unleashed. Yet believing this is essentially believing in magic. Technology only improves outcomes when it successfully provides new capabilities that someone wants or otherwise benefits from, and it only benefits the organizational bottom line when someone is further willing to pay for those affordances.

Developing products to provide meaningful affordances is where the need for successful collaboration between IO psychologists and technologists emerges as most critical. IO psychologists generally better understand humans than technologists do. They are primed, by virtue of their ontology, epistemology, and trained paradigms, to grasp what is important about humans. Similarly, technologists, by virtual of their ontology, epistemology, and trained paradigms, generally better understand what technology can realistically achieve and what investments are necessary to achieve it. It is only by combining these two perspectives and skills that meaningful affordances, and therefore value, can be created at the IOPTI. But to reach that point, of effective, efficient, interdisciplinary, cross-functional collaboration, we must understand each other first, and this will require olive branches in both directions.

# References

American Educational Research Association, American Psychological Association, & National Council on Measurement in Education. (2014). *Standards for Educational and Psychological Testing*. American Educational Research Association.

Bjogvinsson, E., Ehn, P., & Hillgren, P.-A. (2012). Design things and design thinking: Contemporary participatory design challenges. *DesignIssues, 28*, 101–116.

Burton, B. A. (2010). Encouraging algorithmic thinking without a computer. *Olympiads in Informatics, 4*, 3–14.

Clear, T. (2003). The waterfall is dead: Long live the waterfall!! *ACM SIGCSE Bulletin, 35*, 13–14.

Campion, M. C., Campion, M. A., Campion, E. D., & Reider, M. H. (2016). Initial investigation into computer scoring of candidate essays for personnel selection. *Journal of Applied Psychology, 101*(7), 958.

Diesing, P. (1966). Objectivism vs. subjectivism in the social sciences. *Philosophy of Science, 33*(1/2), 124–133.

Dikert, K., Paasivaara, M., & Lassenius, C. (2016). Challenges and success factors for large-scale agile transformations: A systematic literature review. *Journal of Systems and Software, 119*, 87–108.

Eden, A. H. (2007). Three paradigms of computer science. *Minds and Machines, 17*(2), 135–167. https://doi.org/10.1007/s11023-007-9060-8

Frank, M. (2000). Engineering systems thinking and systems thinking. *Systems Engineering, 3*(3), 163–168.

Frone, M. R., Yardley, J. K., & Markel, K. S. (1997). Developing and testing an integrative model of the work–family interface. *Journal of Vocational Behavior, 50*(2), 145–167.

Grüne-Yanoff, T. (2014). Teaching philosophy of science to scientists: Why, what and how. *European Journal for Philosophy of Science, 4*(1), 115–134.

Highsmith, J. (2002). What is agile software development? *CrossTalk: The Journal of Defense Software Engineering, 15*(10), 4–9.

Hu, X., Barber, L., Park, Y., & Day, A. (2021). Defrag and reboot? Consolidating information and communication technology research in I-O psychology. *Industrial and Organizational Psychology: Perspectives on Science and Practice, 14*(3), 371–396.

Klein, J. T. (1990). *Interdisciplinarity: History, theory, and practice.* Wayne State University Press.

Kuhn, T. (1962). *The structure of scientific revolutions.* University of Chicago Press.

Lamagna, E. A. (2015). Algorithmic thinking unplugged. *Journal of Computing Sciences in Colleges, 30*(6), 45–52.

Landers, R. N. (2021). Practical theory about workplace technology requires integrating design perspectives. *Industrial and Organizational Psychology, 14,* 444–447.

Landers, R. N., Armstrong, M. B., Collmus, A. B., Mujcic, S., & Blaik, J. (2022). Theory-driven game-based assessment of general cognitive ability: Design theory, measurement, prediction of performance, and test fairness. *Journal of Applied Psychology, 107*(10), 1655–1677.

Manicas, P. T., & Secord, P. F. (1983). Implications for psychology of the new philosophy of science. *American Psychologist, 38*(4), 399–413.

Plattner, H., Meinel, C., & Leifer, L. (2011). *Design thinking: Understand, improve, apply.* Springer-Verlag.

Popper, K. (1963). *Conjectures and refutations: The growth of scientific knowledge.* Routledge.

Proctor, R. W., & Capaldi, E. J. (Eds.). (2012). *Psychology of science: Implicit and explicit processes.* Oxford University Press.

Schwaber, K., & Sutherland, J. (2020). *The scrum guide: The definitive guide to scrum: The rules of the game.* https://billlewistraining.com/wp-content/uploads/2017/02/PMP-Agile-Study-Materials.pdf

Tippins, N. T. (2009). Internet alternatives to traditional proctored testing: Where are we now? *Industrial and Organizational Psychology, 2*(1), 2–10. https://doi.org/10.1111/j.1754-9434.2008.01097.x

Toulmin, S., & Leary, D. E. (1985). The cult of empiricism in psychology, and beyond. In S. Koch & D. E. Leary (Eds.), *A century of psychology as science* (pp. 594–617). American Psychological Association. https://doi.org/10.1037/10117-041

# SECTION 4
# REGULATIONS, PRINCIPLES, AND STANDARDS

# 14
# Balancing Innovation and Professional Standards for Employment Tests

*Nancy T. Tippins*

## Introduction

There are two primary sets of professional standards for employment tests:[1] the *Principles for the Validation and Use of Personnel Selection Procedures* (*Principles; Principles*, 2018) and the *Standards for Educational and Psychological Testing* (*Standards*; American Educational Research Association, et al., 2014). The *Standards* was revised in 2014. The *Principles* was updated in 2018 to align the *Principles* with the *Standards*, add new material where there have been new developments, and reinforce ideas that are often problematic, for example, the treatment of missing data and outliers, consideration of the conditional standard error in the vicinity of the cutoff score, and the feasibility of validity studies when the population size is small or the job does not exist. The purpose of this chapter is to discuss innovative assessments relative to the expectations set forth in the *Principles*.

An innovative assessment broadly refers to new types of assessments such as those that are based on games, video interviews, facial characteristics, voice quality, and "big data," and that frequently use artificial intelligence to evaluate the information collected. Often, these assessments are based on thousands of data points that are collected from various sources, including social media, resumes and applications, and the assessment itself. For example, games and video interviews may produce data ranging from the correct response and the number of response changes to response times and cursor location throughout the assessment. Video interviews may

---

[1] The terms "test," "assessment," "selection tool," "assessment tool," and "selection procedure" are used interchangeably throughout this chapter. All refer to "a measure or procedure in which a sample of an examinee's behavior in a specified domain is obtained, evaluated, and scored using a standardized process" (*Principles*, p. 95).

Nancy T. Tippins, *Balancing Innovation and Professional Standards for Employment Tests* In: *Talent Assessment*. Edited by: Tracy M. Kantrowitz, Douglas H. Reynolds, and John C. Scott, Oxford University Press.
© Society of Industrial Organizational Psychology 2023. DOI: 10.1093/oso/9780197611050.003.0014

generate data related to multiple aspects of facial features and voice quality. Algorithms are trained on these many variables to predict a criterion or to separate cases into groups that are either like a defined successful group or unlike that group.

The *Principles* acknowledges a variety of new forms of testing:

> In addition, unproctored Internet-based tests, "big data" and machine learning methods (e.g., harvesting information about candidates from social media sites, resumes, or other sources of text or information), gamification, and computer-based simulations of varying levels of technological sophistication are examples of contemporary testing and assessment approaches. (p. 4)

The *Principles* applies to all kinds of tests and assessments used in employment settings for employee selection. Any claim of validity made for a selection procedure should be documented with appropriate research evidence built on the principles discussed in the *Principles* (p. 9).

This chapter is not an exhaustive review of all the revisions in the latest edition of the *Principles*; instead, it is focused on parts of the *Principles* that are particularly relevant to innovative assessment tools and for which there are open questions regarding how the guidance in the *Principles* applies to innovative selection techniques. This chapter will briefly review six topics in the context of innovative assessment procedures: (a) work (or job) analysis, (b) validity, (c) predictors, (d) fairness and bias, (e) operational issues, and (f) Americans with Disabilities Act (ADA) accommodations.

## Work Analysis

Work analysis (or job analysis) that defines job requirements has traditionally been an early step in test development and validation. In the United States, work analysis is especially important because of the legal requirement for job relevancy of predictors when adverse impact exists. The *Principles* (p. 12) makes clear that there are two major purposes for analyzing work—the development and the identification of appropriate selection procedures and criterion measures—and it acknowledges that there is no single method of work analyses that must be followed. Questions regarding work analysis that guides employee selection have long existed on topics ranging from the level of detail required to the appropriate methodology when future jobs do not yet exist or when the work environment is rapidly changing. Although silent on the job analytic approach that should be taken, the *Principles* recommends documentation of work behaviors, tasks, activities, KSAOs (knowledge, skills, abilities, and other characteristics), and competencies that are derived from a current or past analysis of work.

The increase in the use of innovative assessments has called attention to work analysis issues such as the need for formal work analysis, the level of detail required, and the appropriate methods for obtaining relevant and reliable information about job and worker requirements. The *Principles* emphasizes that "the level of detail required of an analysis of work is directly related to its intended use and the availability of information about the work" (p. 14). When there is existing information about a job, a less detailed analysis of work may be needed; however, the testing professional is still expected to compile evidence regarding work behaviors and required KSAOs. Although the *Principles* does not advocate a preferred method for the analysis of work, it makes clear that the chosen methods should be based on the nature of the work and workers and the organizational setting as well as on the relevant literature, and the analysis of work should identify reliable and relevant job information related to work behaviors, activities, KSAOs, or competencies.

As with developers of traditional forms of assessment, some developers of innovative selection procedures do not incorporate work analysis into their development processes at all. There is no specification of work behaviors, activities, tasks, KSAOs, or competencies. Some big data applications take the "dust bowl empiricism" approach and simply determine which variables among many are statistically related to a criterion measure. Often, they argue that the existence of a predictor-criterion relationship is indicative of job relevancy. However, the rationale behind that relationship may not be apparent, and these developers ignore the spurious correlations that sometimes result.

Some developers have created selection tools that measure a set of skills related to an occupation or a job (e.g., supervisory skills, sales skills). They make the assumptions that these jobs have similar requirements regardless of the organization and that organizations buy tests measuring the skills they need for a particular job. However, sales jobs in different organizations may or may not involve the same set of tasks and the same set of KSAOs. Other developers use a fixed set of KSAOs or competencies that are measured by their instrument and ask subject matter experts (SMEs) to select the ones relevant to the job in question; however, this set may not be comprehensive and measure all the important KSAOs for a specific job. There may also be concerns about how well the person identifying the important KSAOs knows the job and its requirements. The comprehensiveness of the predictors and the criteria and ultimately the accuracy of predictions that are made may be affected if the specification of the job requirements is deficient. In addition, asking SMEs to choose KSAOs may not result in reliable job information unless those choices are grounded in task requirements.

The lack of a systematic analysis of work can create other problems related to determining the job relevancy of predictors. If the job requirements are not well understood, it will be difficult to determine if the measures used are job relevant. Selection procedures based on big data typically include many variables whose relevancy is difficult to establish even when the job requirements are known. Similarly, many games produce variables related to speed of responding; however, in many cases, the requirement for speed on the job is not demonstrated.

## Validity

Validity is the fundamental requirement of employee selection procedures. The *Principles* uses the *Standards*' definition of validity: "the degree to which evidence and theory support the interpretations of test scores for proposed uses of tests" (American Educational Research Association et al., 2014, p. 11) and emphasizes that validity must be evaluated relative to the inferences made from the test score. Test vendors of all types, including those who market innovative forms of testing, make many claims about what their test actually does. Yet, claims such as identifying the top salespeople, increasing diversity, reducing turnover, and enhancing organizational effectiveness require different types of supporting evidence.

Innovative forms of testing based on algorithms often raise questions regarding the evidence for the inferences made. For example, the claim that a test predicts job performance may not be warranted if the selection process is based on a model that differentiates good performers from other people in the developer's database. Without the evidence that the test score predicts job performance, the test vendor is only inferring that people who are similar to those believed to be successful will also be successful. Another common inference made by vendors of innovative selection tools is an increase in diversity through the use of algorithms that eliminate group differences. However, diversity of the workforce and the absence of group differences among applicants are not necessarily the same thing. Although some vendors use algorithms to eliminate group mean differences, it is not uncommon to find adverse impact in qualification rates on the test.

Many of the innovative selection procedures rely on machine learning algorithms that result in nonlinear models, which make interpretation of scores very difficult. A measure of overall model fit is often used to infer a predictor-criterion relationship. Thus, the importance of a job analysis that identifies relevant predictors and a criterion to include in the model training process grows.

The *Principles* advises that existing evidence of validity should be considered when determining if new validity evidence is needed. An important question for many employers regardless of the type of test used is whether or not a local validation study is needed when the employer uses off-the-shelf tests with validity evidence based on jobs with unknown requirements in other organizations. Professional judgment is needed to assess the adequacy of the test vendor's validity evidence for the inferences the employer wants to make, determine the relevance of that evidence to the employer's job and applicant population, and evaluate the risks associated with relying on data collected elsewhere.

As in the past, the *Principles* reviews different sources of validity such as evidence based on relationships with other variables and on test content. The *Principles* clarifies that negative consequences do not in and of themselves detract from the validity of intended test interpretations but should prompt examination of their causes. The causes of negative consequences such as small percentages of qualified women and racial/ethnic minorities relative to men and Whites can be difficult to uncover when some innovative forms of testing are used. The variables that contribute to differences in qualification rates and the weighting placed on them by the algorithm are often unknown to the user. Regardless of whether the causes of negative consequences can be identified, the consequences may affect decisions about test use.

The *Principles* also emphasizes the importance of documentation of validity evidence:

> In cases where scores from such algorithms are used as part of the selection process, the conceptual and methodological basis for that use should be sufficiently documented to establish a clear rationale for linking the resulting scores to the criterion constructs of interest. (p. 22)

Often, evidence of validity for inferences made from innovative tools is not documented with enough detail for the user to evaluate the validity evidence presented. Consequently, the clear link between scores and criteria is not apparent, and assessment of the existing validity evidence is impossible.

## Predictors

The current version of the *Principles* describes selection procedures in terms of both the constructs that are measured and the methods by which they are measured. The *Principles* (pp. 21–22) points out that newer techniques for selection (e.g., big data, games, computer simulations) are selection procedures and should meet the requirements of the *Principles* and that there are no exceptions because of the nature of the predictor. The *Principles* emphasizes the need to validate scores produced by algorithms, but it does not discuss what methodologies are acceptable in this evolving area of research. Nor does the *Principles* discuss what alternatives to traditional forms of correlation (e.g., area under the curve, precision, recall) are acceptable. Cross-validation is necessary to ensure that predictive relationships are not sample specific, and again, the innovative nature of a selection procedure does not exempt it from the requirement to cross-validate in an independent sample.

Users should take steps to avoid systematic bias against relevant subgroups in the predictors they use. Systematic bias may be a critical but undetected issue for some innovative forms of selection procedures because the relationships of some variables to other variables that define protected classes are not always clear. For example, if men have more leadership experiences than women and if the number of leadership experiences held is a predictor, women may be at a disadvantage although they possess leadership skills.

It merits noting that human judgments are predictors (e.g., combination of tests, reference checks, and interview information), may be biased, and should be validated. Except in some emerging approaches to automating assessment centers, human judgments are often not a component of predictors in innovative selection procedures, but the caution regarding the need for validation would apply if they were used.

## Predictor Deficiency

The *Principles* discusses two kinds of predictor deficiency: deficiency in measuring a construct (e.g., measuring only orderliness when intending to measure the broader construct conscientiousness) and deficiency in measuring all possible job-relevant determinants of a criterion. Both forms of predictor deficiency can be problematic when algorithms based on artificial intelligence are applied to large sets of data. These forms of prediction are often atheoretical; the constructs being measured may not be discernible; and the reasons that there should be a relationship between the predictor and the criterion are often abstruse. When what is being measured is not apparent, there can be no evaluation of either form of predictor deficiency.

The *Principles* acknowledges that professional judgment is required to determine if measuring only a subset of the determinants of performance is problematic. There are certainly many selection programs that evaluate only a subset of the relevant KSAOs or use a multiple-hurdle approach that eliminates candidates based on measures of a subset of critical KSAOs at each stage. The testing professional is expected to document the relevance of the content of the test to the job requirements and the rationale for tests used in the validation effort. Often, this documentation takes the form of a KSAO-×-test matrix (p. 47). Although not stated in the *Principles* specifically, there is an underlying assumption that there are some data on which to base that professional judgment. Again, when documentation regarding the relationship of innovative selection procedures and their components to relevant criteria is lacking, evaluating the existence or the extent of either kind of predictor deficiency is difficult if not impossible.

## Predictor Contamination

Predictor contamination occurs when the measure incorporates something that is not job relevant (e.g., a game that evaluates speed when speed is not a component of job performance, a facial feature or voice characteristic that is not required by the job). Predictor contamination has the potential for being acute and undetected when large data sets are used and the construct being measured is not apparent. If what is being measured is not known, there can be no determination of job relevance. If job relevance cannot be evaluated, the test user cannot comply with professional standards.

In summary, many innovative selection tools appear to incorporate variables that are not obviously related to a KSAO, use variables for which the relevancy to the job is not apparent, and do not measure all the KSAOs required by the job. Thus, evaluation of predictor deficiency and contamination can be particularly problematic in innovative selection tools, especially when the construct being measured is not clear and when the job requirements have not been defined.

## Fairness and Bias

The *Principles* offers multiple perspectives on fairness, which apply to all forms of tests, innovative or not. Equitable treatment means treating all test takers the same with respect to factors such as testing conditions, access to preparation and practice materials, performance feedback, and retest opportunities. Equitable treatment also includes reasonable accommodations for people with disabilities. Fairness in terms of bias refers to both predictive bias and measurement bias. Equal access relates to providing all examinees the opportunity to demonstrate the construct of interest that is measured by the selection procedure without being advantaged or disadvantaged by personal characteristics such as age, race, ethnicity, gender, socioeconomic status, cultural background, disability, and language proficiency. The *Principles* points out that the test user may need to consider whether personal characteristics affect the measurement of the construct of interest, which is particularly important when new technology is used in the selection procedure. An equal outcome alludes to equal passing rates for subgroups of interest. There is agreement among testing professionals who work in employment settings that equitable treatment, absence of bias, and equal access are important goals related to fairness. There is also agreement that equal outcomes should be rejected as a component of fairness although different passing rates may prompt evaluation of the test for other sources of bias. Innovative forms of testing raise concerns related to each of these other conceptualizations of fairness.

### Equitable Treatment

Some forms of innovative assessment such as games or video interviews are highly standardized and treat all candidates in identical ways. For example, each person sees the same game or is asked the same question in a video interview, and performance on the game or interview is scored in the same way without human intervention. (Despite standardized machine scoring, the mechanical scoring process for some video-based interviews is derived from scores generated by humans who themselves may be biased.) Other types of innovative selection tools raise questions about equitable treatment. The use of facial features or voice characteristics may violate the principle of equitable treatment when the candidate cannot control either and accommodations cannot be made to one's face or voice. Another inhibitor to consistent treatment of test takers is machine learning techniques that continuously optimize the algorithms. When this occurs, the scoring procedures change each time new data are evaluated and are inconsistent over time and across candidates.

## Equal Access

Several forms of innovative selection procedures pose potential concerns regarding equal access. For example, people with certain disabilities and those with darker skin may not fare well on video interviews that take into account facial features. Whether they possess the underlying KSAO being measured is hard to determine because the constructs being measured are not clear. Equal access may also be questioned when the data for predictive models are based on data scraped from social media and other sources. An applicant who lacks a presence on social media, including those from cultural backgrounds whose members do not regularly engage in social media activities, may be disadvantaged on such a test despite having the KSAOs necessary to perform the job. Although much of the evidence is anecdotal, there are concerns about the effect of familiarity with games on game-based test performance.

## Bias

**Measurement Bias**
Measurement bias occurs when there is systematic error in test scores that affects the performance of subgroups of test takers differentially. Two individuals drawn from two different subgroups with equal standing on the construct of interest have different scores on the test measuring the construct. For example, a man and woman have equal levels of reading ability; however, the woman scores higher on a test of reading ability.

Differential item functioning analysis (DIF) is sometimes used to evaluate measurement bias. The *Principles* highlights the problems of using DIF to determine measurement bias in employment tests (e.g., sufficient sample sizes are difficult to obtain; results are rarely replicable, and results that do hold up are typically small and hard to explain; roughly equal numbers of differentially functioning items favoring each subgroup, indicating no systematic bias at the test level, are often found for cognitive tests). Because of these problems, DIF is not a routine step in the development of tests used for employment decisions. Nevertheless, the test user may find DIF useful in some situations (e.g., cross-cultural settings). DIF analyses may be particularly difficult to execute when machine learning models are developed on a relatively small sample.

As an alternative approach to DIF, the *Principles* suggests item sensitivity reviews to identify items that result in measurement bias. Although sensitivity reviews are used frequently in the development of traditional forms of tests with a limited number of items, sensitivity reviews are practically impossible when massive data sets are used. It is simply not feasible to review thousands of variables pulled from social media, resumes, applications, or other sources. Some vendors do embed routines to compare subgroups on variables in their modeling process and eliminate those for which significant differences are found. However, this process does not evaluate the bias of items or variables for each group, and it runs the risk of eliminating items that accurately predict the criterion despite subgroup differences.

**Predictive Bias**

Predictive bias occurs when irrelevant sources of variance affect the predictor-criterion relationships for subgroups of test takers differentially, resulting in systematic errors against subgroups of interest. Predictive bias is typically evaluated using moderated multiple regression and comparing slopes and intercepts of regression lines for the majority group and the minority group. Although slope and intercept differences indicate predictive bias, consideration is usually given to whether or not the subgroup of interest is over- or underpredicted. For many, underprediction for the minority group is the major cause for concern. Others argue that underprediction for the majority group would be equally troubling from the standpoint of legal defensibility.

Machine learning models applied to massive numbers of data points do not necessarily use any form of regression to produce an algorithm. To date, there is no agreement on procedures for evaluating bias when regression is not used to determine the predictor-criterion relationship. As noted above, an open question is whether users of selection procedures based on such algorithms should conduct regression analyses that establish a predictor-criterion relationship in addition to the modeling techniques they already employ. Appropriate alternative methodologies for evaluating predictive bias are not discussed in the *Principles* as the use of big data and artificial intelligence-based algorithms is an emerging field with significant methodological questions that need to be answered.

The *Principles* lists technical concerns about assessing predictive bias, such as analyzing predictive bias on predictors as they are used in practice, using an unbiased criterion, basing analyses on a sample of adequate power, assuming homogeneity of error variance, and using an unbiased estimate of intercept difference and operational validity parameters instead of observed parameters. Finding a large enough sample with statistical power to detect slope and intercept differences can be a challenge with some innovative selection procedures. Many innovative selection procedures rely on hundreds if not thousands of predictors and relatively few observations. However, if predictive bias is only assessed through traditional methods such as moderated multiple regression, the test user may end up in a situation where there is insufficient statistical power to evaluate bias.

Some of the modeling techniques include methods for avoiding group mean differences. However, the *Principles* notes that subgroup differences and predictive bias are independent and advises evaluation of predictive bias when there are reasons to question the predictor-criterion relationship among subgroups and when it is feasible. In the United States, a compelling reason to assess predictive bias is the legal requirement to do so.

The use of an unbiased criterion can be a problem when machine learning is used with innovative assessment procedures. When small groups of "successful" performers are used to train the model, bias in the criterion should be questioned. Specifically, the process for defining "successful" should be considered carefully.

## Operational Issues

The *Principles* covers a number of operational issues that arise, including issues such as the appropriate role of costs in the decision-making process, equivalency of scores from tests delivered by different media, mechanisms to detect careless responding, raters' knowledge and opportunity to observe, and the pros and cons of unproctored internet testing (UIT). While some operational concerns apply only to some testing formats, many apply to all forms of testing, including more innovative forms of assessment. Some issues like equivalency of scores on tests delivered by different media are important only when there are multiple devices used. Other issues like a rater's opportunity to observe may not be related to an innovative form of assessment, but it remains an important consideration in the development of criteria that rely on raters' judgments. Two operational issues that are relevant to many forms of innovative assessments are those related to UIT, including (a) candidate identification, cheating, and test security and (b) data privacy and integrity.

## Unproctored Internet Testing, Candidate Identification, Cheating, and Test Security

Almost all innovative selection techniques involve UIT. Thus, some of the most salient operational issues related to innovative forms of tests involve candidate identification, protection of test materials, and cheating. When a test is administered in an unproctored setting, the identity of the person taking the test is difficult to discern unless some extraordinary form of remote proctoring is used. An exception to the problem of candidate identification is video interviews that are recorded. Presumably, the recording could be compared to the person who shows up for subsequent steps of the hiring process or the job.

UIT can also make cheating and compromising test security easier. Evidence of compromised test materials can be found on the internet for many selection procedures. In addition, coaching for ways to achieve high scores on measures ranging from games to video-based interviews exists on the internet. Other sites advise applicants on embedding keywords into resumes, applications, letters, etc., to heighten the chance of passing an initial screen based on an algorithm that uses such data.

Although there are many concerns related to the use of data pulled from social media, one of the advantages is its relative imperviousness to the issues associated with UIT. Unless someone is assuming a completely new identify, the data on social media about an applicant are not usually distorted because of the testing event, although they may be incomplete or inaccurate or present an unrealistic picture of the individual. In fact, some applicants may not even know they are being evaluated and not know to embellish their social media presence. Except for detailed knowledge of the algorithm used, which is usually not available, test security seems not to be an issue for such applications.

Because the problems of UIT are not unique to innovative assessments, many of the existing solutions (e.g., warnings) used for traditional forms of testing can be more broadly applied. The *Principles* advises that users of UIT be familiar with its advantages and disadvantages and monitor the emerging research related to UIT and malfeasant behaviors.

## Data Privacy and Integrity

A significant issue with several forms of innovative assessments is data privacy and integrity. A central question frequently addressed in the popular press is the right of an employer to use data from social media and the right of the applicant to withhold negative information. In addition, the accuracy of data pulled from social media is often not known. Archival data pose special problems related to currency of information as well as consistent use of variable names and ranges of acceptable values. Concerns regarding data privacy are growing around the world and may impose limits on what data can be used, what the owner of the data must be told about their use, what the limits on data retention are, and what rights the owner of the data has related to deletion and modification of the data collected. While acknowledging these challenges, the *Principles* advises caution in the use of archival data and counsels the user to take steps to ensure data privacy and protection that are consistent with legislation.

## Americans with Disabilities Act Accommodations

The ADA requires accommodating people with disabilities in employment testing. The *Principles* differentiates accommodation, which is a change in test content or administration that does not alter the construct being measured, and modification, which is a change in test content or administration that alters the construct. Accommodations do not affect direct comparisons of scores, but modifications do. When an individual has a qualifying disability, accommodation and/or modification must be made regardless of the nature of the test.

In some situations, appropriate accommodations and modifications are clear. For example, some games provide accommodations or modifications such as changing the colors used for test takers who are color blind or increasing the time allowed for those with motor impairments. Appropriate accommodations and modifications are less clear for other innovative forms of testing. For example, there may not be an appropriate accommodation or modification in a video-based interview for people who have a physical disability that distorts their facial features, voice characteristics, or speech patterns. The impact of disabilities on social media is largely unknown. Does a mental health disability or a physical ability limit certain kinds of activities that might be posted on social media and predict job performance? Operationally, a question about accommodation under the ADA when big data are used is particularly difficult to answer because the variables used in the algorithm and their weights are not usually known to the test taker. Additionally, machine learning models that differentiate successful performers from others may inadvertently disadvantage applicants with disabilities if none or few of the successful performers possess disabilities themselves.

## Conclusion

The *Principles* is clear that the guidance it provides pertains to all forms of selection procedures while noting that all standards are not required to be met and may not be feasible to meet. Further, the *Principles* emphasizes the role of professional judgment in determining what is important in terms of evidence of validity for the inference to be made from a test score. The current version of the *Principles* acknowledges the growing interest in innovative forms of testing; however, because scientific research in this area is still emerging, the *Principles* does not always explain how professional standards and expectations should be met. Test users interested in innovative forms must monitor the evolving research for acceptable procedures.

# References

American Educational Research Association, American Psychological Association, & National Council on Measurement in Education (Eds.). (2014). *Standards for Educational and Psychological Testing*. American Educational Research Association.

Principles for the Validation and Use of Personnel Selection Procedures. (2018). *Industrial and Organizational Psychology: Perspectives on Science and Practice, 11*(Suppl 1), 2–97. https://doi.org/10.1017/iop.2018.195

# 15

# Data Privacy Implications of Assessment Technology

*Katheryn A. Andresen*[*]

## Introduction

While data may be a key source of revenue for companies, it may also be the greatest source of legal and business risk. When systems and software became prevalent in the 1980s and early 1990s there were no regulations, federal or otherwise, regarding data privacy considerations. While data security was already an issue, it was primarily focused on securing the company's ownership interests in the software. The subsequent development of regulations, at the state, federal, and international levels, often distinguishes between privacy obligations (use and disclosure rights) and security of protected data and obligations in the event of a security incident or breach.

From a legal perspective, "data" is not a simple concept, even when defined in a contract. It is even more complex when the media used to store or transmit data may also be used to create data. Companies must understand the type of data collected and used in order to assess the legal and business risks associated with their obligations to protect and secure such data under applicable data privacy and data security regulations. For example, a decision to have data processed outside of the country of origin can trigger a compliance obligation with additional laws and regulations.

For employers and those managing data related to employment, there are additional data considerations under employment laws. Employment-related

---

[*] Katheryn A. Andresen is a vice president and shareholder with Nilan Johnson Lewis and former chair of the Corporate and Complex Transactions practice group. She has been practicing law for over 25 years, assisting clients with complex transactional, intellectual property, and corporate matters. She is the author and editor of *The Law and Business of Computer Software* (2nd ed., Thomson West, 2007–2019).

Katheryn A. Andresen, *Data Privacy Implications of Assessment Technology* In: *Talent Assessment*. Edited by: Tracy M. Kantrowitz, Douglas H. Reynolds, and John C. Scott, Oxford University Press.
© Society of Industrial Organizational Psychology 2023. DOI: 10.1093/oso/9780197611050.003.0015

technologies for assessment and screening of candidates often include data that is inputted by the candidate, collected from third-party sources, or even created through the assessment technology. Automated decisions related to such technology are subject to compliance with data privacy and security regulations but also must comply with applicable employment laws. This chapter will focus on the obligations and implications of using assessment tools and the related data in compliance with data privacy and security laws and regulations.

## Data Categorization

What should also be abundantly clear as we are entering the third decade of the 21st century is that data comes in all shapes, flavors, and colors; it's as versatile as we are. While "customer data" may often be presumptively owned by the customer and may be generally defined as "any data that is entered into or processed through the software system," this is not a rational way to approach the complexity of data. Simplistic data models are insufficient for today's complex digital world. A brief look at categories of data addressed in a typical privacy policy might include:

- Personal information[1] (or PII)—data that is tied to an identifiable individual. Note: A subcategory of PII would include sensitive data such as financial, protected health information, etc.
- Public information—data that is publicly available and that may or may not be tied to an identifiable individual. For example, a public address might be to a specific apartment (i.e., identifiable), but the address of the building generally or just the town and state would not be identifiable.
- System information—data that is autogenerated and collected from system usage. This might include the version of the software, the last date updated, and even the license number.
- Usage data—data that is collected from a user as they interact with a website (e.g., what is clicked on, how long the user stays on a page, what pages are viewed).

---

[1] The California Consumer Protection Act uses "personal information" as the defined term, the General Data Protection Regulation uses "personal data" as the defined term, and other regulations use "identifiable to an individual" or "personally identifiable information" as the key defined terms. The reference in this chapter to PII is not intended to refer to a specific regulation.

- User data—data collected about a specific user of a website. This may include data about the user's device type, browser version, privacy settings, IP address, etc.
- Location data—both the data about the device location (IP address indicating city and state) and the specific device location using GPS technology if permitted and active; this data may or may not be identifiable. For example, geo-fencing technology can target all devices in a specific room of a conference center, without ever knowing the identity of the individual who owns the device. If location data, however, was tied to other data such as an IMEI number or phone number, the identity of the individual may be identifiable based on tying location data with other data.

In the workforce industry, data related to assessment technology may be either identifiable to an individual or not. For example, it may be relevant to know that all applicants for a position met certain objective standards (proximity to position's location, educational level, language, or other characteristics). Conversely, it may also be relevant to know that the individual applicant achieved particular scores on assessments of specific skills, psychological characteristics, or other factors. Separate from the output of the assessment technology, the underlying data used to develop the assessment may also be ultimately critical to either prove or disprove a claim of bias in the actual assessment (e.g., the wording of the questions, scoring factors based on improper characteristics such as race and gender).

Before a company can accurately assess its obligations with regard to data privacy and data security, it needs to fully understand the type of data involved, the source of the data, and which party owns or has responsibility for such data. Once a company has the involved data mapped out to type, source, and responsible party, it will be in a position to assess if it is regulated, what the legal obligations are, and how such obligations are documented in the applicable agreement (e.g., whether the responsibility lies with the company or its vendors, suppliers, contractors, and/or affiliates).

## Data Privacy Regulatory Development

In the mid-1990s, both the United States and the European Union concluded that certain types of data had to be protected from exploitation. In that first wave of data protection regulation, including the Gramm-Leach-Bliley Act (GLBA) for financial information, the Health Insurance Portability and Accountability Act[2] (HIPAA) for health information, and the European Union's 1995 directive telling all member states to enact data privacy regulations, the regulations were focused on certain types of sensitive information that could be tied to an identifiable individual.

The regulatory realm related to data privacy and data security continues to build on those early regulatory models, including the European Union's General Data Protection Regulation[3] (GDPR) and various U.S. state-level regulations[4] such as the California Consumer Protection Act (CCPA) as amended by the Consumer Privacy Regulation Act (CPRA). These new regulations are still focused on personal information related to an identifiable individual, but what constitutes "identifiable" has changed. For example, under the CCPA, an IP address is deemed "identifiable" even though commentators pointed out that VPN software artificially creates an IP address, which would make it not an identifiable factor.

While the specifics of the various international, federal, and state regulations on data privacy vary, there are certain commonalities. Namely, all of the regulations have a definition of "personal information" (whether the term is "personal data," "personally identifiable information," "identifiable to an individual," etc.). In addition, most have a general category of identifiable information, as well as a subcategory for special or sensitive data, when tied to the individual. Sensitive data is defined in the applicable regulations and may include data related to race, ethnicity, religion, biometric data, criminal convictions, or certain categories of health information. For employee selection or assessment purposes, sensitive data may be focused on race, ethnicity, or background check information such as criminal convictions.

Finally, almost all of these regulations clarify the obligations regarding data privacy and usually include only general standards for data security (i.e., "appropriate administrative, physical and technical controls to secure the PII from unauthorized use or disclosure"). While the regulations do not mandate

---

[2] HIPAA's final rule was enacted in March 2013 and may be found on the U.S. Health and Human Service's website at https://www.hhs.gov/sites/default/files/hipaa-simplification-201303.pdf.

[3] It is interesting to note that the European Union's original 1995 directive was simply a mandate that each member state enact its own regulation, whereas the GDPR was an actual regulation that set the floor of protections with each member state permitted to increase protections in their implementing regulations.

[4] In addition to California, Virginia has a regulation equivalent to CCPA effective as of the beginning of 2023 and Colorado, Connecticut, and Utah will have equivalents in effect later in 2023.

a checklist of security standards, there are definitely industry standards that have developed over time, including the National Institute of Science and Technology (NIST) special publications (e.g., *Security and Privacy Controls for Information Systems and Organizations*, NIST, 2022) and the Center for Internet Security's Critical Security Controls.

Both the CCPA and GDPR also codified five basic individual rights:

- Right to review personal information/personal data
- Right to request corrections
- Right to request that personal information be transmitted in electronic form either to the individual or a third party as requested by the individual
- Right to limit use rights to solely those necessary for services (i.e., no ancillary uses such as marketing, newsletters, etc.)
- Right to be forgotten or have PII deleted (note that this right supersedes the company's right to retain data it requires to provide its services or to fulfill its legal obligations)

Another right in many of these regulations is the right to direct notice of any breach of the security and privacy obligations related to PII. The breach terms vary; for example, HIPAA requires notice within 60 days of the breach, but the GDPR requires notice within 72 hours of a security incident. There may not be express timing requirements for responses to individual requests in all of the regulations, but the CCPA grants a company 45 days from the request to respond to the individual, with an allowance for an additional 45-day period if necessary to investigate the legitimacy of the request and the individual requesting. In the event of a security incident that results in a breach of PII, some regulations require notification to either the regulator, the affected individual, or both. Many of the state-level privacy regulations leave the enforcement to the state's attorney general. In addition to some regulations requiring regulator notice, some also require publication notice (such as HIPAA), which is in addition to the direct notice to the affected individual. Some state regulations also require notice to the state's attorney general when the breach affects a certain number of individuals in that state.

It is also important to note that the timing is generally based on when the breach is discovered. For example, if a client noticed a system slowdown and during the investigation into the system issue it was determined that an unauthorized Bitcoin mining application had been installed that was using all of the system bandwidth, it might require further forensic review to determine if there had actually been a breach of any PII. From a timing perspective, there could be days' (or even weeks') difference between when the slowdown was noted and a final conclusion as to whether any private data had been breached. Whether this delay is reasonable or not could end up being another fact issue if the breach is litigated.

The data collected through employment assessment technology will likely be treated as part of the candidate data and/or employee data once hired. This means this data is also subject to compliance with employment law, separate from the requirements of data privacy regulations. For example, the federal government has a 1-year data retention requirement, while states have various requirements, including up to 2 years of data retention. The data privacy regulations, however, may have a data retention maximum requirement, such as the Illinois Biometric Information Privacy Act, which mandates deletion within 3 years of collection. Compliance with employment laws may also affect some of the individual rights noted above, regarding what data must be maintained in the employment records. This may impact an individual's right to request correction (if the employer is simply documenting information from another source) or the right to be forgotten (since the employer will have an obligation to maintain).

## Data Privacy Technology Considerations

Tracking technologies may also create or store data that is subject to data privacy obligations. There are various types of tracking technologies that can be used in websites or in software applications: spiders, various types of cookies, pixels,[5] web beacons, bots, etc. In addition, there are numerous software applications that may be added to websites for tracking, analytics, customer surveys, and other means to assess user experience and data analytics to improve the website, software, or mobile application. In particular, tracking technologies such as cookies enhance a user's experience in retaining user viewing and other preferences, as well as automating the login for the user account.

---

[5] Tracking pixels are transparent graphic images (also called web beacons or tracking beacons) placed on website pages. The pixel collects data from the user such as IP address, browser type, location, etc., which may then be fed to an advertising platform or used to analyze website interaction. A spider is basically coding that tracks movement within a website or from one website to another.

In the area of employment candidate screening or assessment, companies performing these services may use tracking technologies both for user convenience and better experience in using the company's website and to track where a user came from (e.g., a customer link or a search engine link) and where they connect to when they leave the company's website. This can allow the company to ascertain the ways in which users and potential candidates can more easily connect with the company. It also allows a company to assess possible benefits of interaction with other sites based on commonality of users' follow-on site access.

Although most users of any website or mobile application have encountered "cookie" notices requiring either acceptance or a click to acknowledge the use of cookies, there are actually various types of cookies. The initial "cookie" concept was simple code that stored certain data points to make it easier for a user to interact with the website and/or application (i.e., user name, password, or simple viewing preferences). In this way, the cookie could be used for session management (remembering the user and recalling preferences), personalization, or tracking (e.g., remembering which items we viewed or added to our shopping cart). In the assessment industry, tracking may be used to ensure a candidate user has completed all of the assessment, or to take a user back to the location of the assessment if a user leaves the website or page for any reason. As with all online technology, the use of cookies or other tracking tools may help improve the user experience.

Session cookies are used for that particular access time period and deleted once the session ends. Persistent cookies are maintained for a period of time or even indefinitely and are usually used for authentication or tracking. Websites may categorize the cookies as "necessary" to be able to access private areas of a website (such as a user account), "performance" to help with analytics and user interface analysis, "functional" to personalize your preferences (language, region, etc.), or "tracking" to follow where you came from or went to in the website or upon leaving the website. The privacy policy typically specifies the types of cookies used and may indicate that not allowing cookies may mean that some functionality is not accessible. Some websites have cookie policies that allow you to vary your allowance for some or all of the categories of the cookies used.

There can be first-party cookies (i.e., owned by the company that owns the website or the application), but there can also be third-party cookies, which are owned and managed by third parties such as advertisers, affiliates, and analytic companies. Third-party cookies are concerning because they are often unknown and the user does not have a direct relationship with the third party, so understanding and managing these cookies may be difficult. Finally, there may be "zombie" cookies, which are third-party cookies permanently installed on computers (without regard to a user's election to opt out of cookies), and they may be stored in atypical locations, making deletion difficult.

While most websites use secure socket layer technology (SSL) to transmit data from and to a user's device, this encryption technology is often limited to transmission. Using HTTPS for transmission is considered the standard for secure transmission. This is denoted with the closed lock symbol on the browser address line. Whether or not the data is also encrypted when at rest (i.e., once transmitted and now just stored or hosted on a website) should also be considered. Note, however, that there can be functional issues with encryption at rest (it may slow down response times), but these issues need to be assessed in terms of risk for not encrypting at rest. If encryption is considered necessary to mitigate risk, the terms of use (for website uses) or the contract (between the company and its customers or vendors) should specify that encryption requirement and clarify if encryption is required for data in transit, at rest, or both.

There are different types of user controls that should also be used to further protect private data and to mitigate against risks of security incidents or breaches. For example, an administrative user account usually means the user has the right to add, delete, modify, and read all files. Limiting this type of user account to only those persons with a true need for this level of access would be a way to both verify unauthorized access attempts and mitigate against data breach risks. Other user accounts might be read only, add and read only, or add, read, and delete only for those files added by that specific user. Additional user controls might include limiting which drives, applications, files, or folders may be accessed. In addition, user controls can include requiring strong user credentials (ID and password) and that the passwords change often. In addition, user actions can be tracked and monitored based on the user credentials and logins.

As noted above, there are industry standards that have developed over time as to what constitutes appropriate security measures to protect PII such as NIST's (2022) *Security and Privacy Controls for Information Systems and Organizations*. Generally these include having written security policies, for which employees are trained, and which are enforced and monitored. These policies include physical and technical controls to limit access and transmission of protected data. They also include the administrative controls to ensure policies are written, reviewed, trained upon, and enforced.

There are certain types of technology that can result in a greater risk of violating applicable law in the employment context. For example, while an employer may have an obligation to screen applicants to avoid a claim of "negligent hiring" (e.g., hiring someone who poses a threat of injury to others), certain screening actions may be deemed in violation of employment laws. Some states have also implemented "ban the box" rules, which preclude the assessment of criminal convictions in hiring decisions, but this could directly conflict with a "negligent hiring" claim of failing to conduct a background check, especially in certain industries (such as health care). Automated background check processes may also increase risk if the process does not comply with applicable law related to notice, consent, and a good-faith analysis that the factors considered are reasonable based on the nature of the position. The nature of the data collected or analyzed in background checks may also make employers subject to compliance with various federal laws such as the Fair Credit Reporting Act (15 U.S.C. § 1681, et seq.) and state background check laws.

Using video or voice recordings as part of the assessment technology also has to be reviewed to ensure the convenience of the methodology does not increase business and legal risks. Video recordings could be the basis of a bias claim (on the basis that it was used to identify an applicant as a minority, even if that data point was not asked), so the controls to ensure no bias might be an additional security requirement in order to comply with discrimination laws. It is also unclear if a recording alone would be deemed biometric data subject to compliance with a specific law governing the same.

For example, the Illinois Biometric Information Privacy Act (BIPA, 2008) defines voiceprint (such as that collected in an online structured interview) as a type of biometric data, and then biometric data that is identifiable to an individual is defined as biometric information. The BIPA regulations, however, do not define voiceprint (presumably something more specific than a voice recording), so it is unclear what additional steps would need to be taken to make this biometric data subject to BIPA. For example, if the recording was analyzed and coded to reflect cadence and tone and other identifiable factors, then it would logically be more like a voiceprint and more likely meet a biometric data definition. If the recording in and of itself is not further assessed or coded for such factors, does that mean it is not a voiceprint? The same would be true of a video recording that theoretically could be further processed to capture identifiable features from a recording (eye space, facial dimensions, nose length, etc.).

There have been cases in the EU member states in which the protections under the GDPR for biometric data were analyzed to determine when a video recording became biometric data, and the holding was that videos were not automatically biometric data unless this additional processing for identifiable features was conducted; this was then confirmed by the European Union Data Protection Committee in their guideline dated March 2019.[6] Identifiable features include analyzing a facial image and identifying certain data points (e.g., distance between eyes, length of nose, facial width and length) to determine if one baseline image matches a new image. However, the ability to collect and use the videos or camera images in the first place for identification requires a legal basis. This is best exemplified by the controversy with Clearview AI, a U.S.-based company, that uses facial recognition algorithms in its technology, when it was discovered that multiple EU member states used the technology for law enforcement purposes. The European Union investigated and then elected to publish its findings in *Decision of the Executive Committee of the Commission Nationale de l'Informatique et des Libertés* n°MEDP-2021-002 of December 6, 2021, to make public the order n°MED-2021-134 of November 26, 2021, issued to Clearview AI.[7] The order held Clearview AI liable for not having a legal basis for the processing of the biometric data.

## Data Privacy Contractual Terms

With the risks associated with the type of data collected and created through assessment technology and candidate screening, it is critical that contracts for such technology licensing or usage include express terms related to data privacy, data security, and how such sensitive data may be used in order for both contracting parties to be compliant with applicable data privacy laws. Some data protection laws require specific contract terms (e.g., the GDPR and the standard contractual clauses), while others simply specify the

---

[6] See https://edpb.europa.eu/sites/edpb/files/files/file1/edpb_guidelines_201903_video_devices.pdf.
[7] Found online at https://www.cnil.fr/sites/default/files/atoms/files/decision_ndeg_medp-2021-002.pdf.

obligations for those parties that own or control the data versus those that process the data on behalf of the owner or controller.

There is a fine line, however, between wanting a very comprehensive contractual obligation on the part of any vendor, supplier, contractor, etc., to protect the privacy of all PII and the company inadvertently creating a higher standard than the regulations require with regard to such privacy obligations. For example, if a company has as part of its standard contractual terms that all confidential information, including PII, is maintained by the other party (e.g., the vendor, supplier, or contractor) for a minimum of 10 years, then the HIPAA standard of keeping the data for 6 years has been lengthened, which increases both parties' (the covered entity's and the business associate's) data protection obligations and risks of possible noncompliance. This may also directly conflict with a law that precludes retention for longer than a specific period (i.e., the Illinois Biometric Information Privacy Act requiring deletion within 3 years from collection).

While a confidentiality obligation may address the other party's obligation to protect the confidentiality of data, it may not include a separate-notice obligation for a data security incident or breach. In addition, these should now add standard carved-out language for "unsuccessful security incidents" such as normal pings. Also, while the confidentiality obligation may or may not address limiting access to persons with a need to know, it is almost certain that it will not limit the disclosure to the "minimum necessary."

A confidentiality obligation needs to clarify what type of data is being protected and what, specifically, is required to limit use and to secure the data. Depending on the applicable law, the form of this obligation may be handled by way of a data processing agreement (DPA; i.e., under the GDPR the DPA has certain mandatory and optional elements). The European Union recently created new standard DPA versions for standard processing for exporting data to a country not deemed secure and therefore requiring standard clauses.[8] These new standards were developed in response to a case, *Data Protection Commission v. Facebook Ireland and Maximillian Schrems* (C-311/18, Court of Justice of the European Union [CJEU], July 16, 2020; "Schrems II"),[9] under which the CJEU issued its decision invalidating the

---

[8] The standard DPA can be found online at https://eur-lex.europa.eu/legal-content/EN/TXT/PDF/?uri=CELEX:32021D0915&from=EN. The standard contractual clauses can be found online at https://eur-lex.europa.eu/legal-content/EN/TXT/PDF/?uri=CELEX:32021D0914&from=EN.

[9] COMMISSION DECISION of 5 February 2010 on Standard Contractual Clauses for the Transfer of Personal Data to Processors Established in Third Countries under Directive 95/46/EC of the European Parliament and of the Council (2010).

Privacy Shield Framework under which the United States was previously deemed a secure country for the export of EU data under the GDPR, but retained the use of EU standard contractual clauses as an alternative.

A limitation of liability provision should be assessed both from the risk mitigation perspective and from the carved-out exceptions to ensure that any willful violations of applicable law do not result in one contracting party putting the other party in significantly greater risk of violating the law. For example, if an employer used a third-party assessment technology vendor that limited liability (no secondary or indirect damages and a low cap on direct damages) but the vendor did not comply with applicable law either on a negligent or willful basis, then the employer would still be liable for the damages from those negligent acts or willful misconduct; however, the employer's ability to recover the same from the vendor would be limited.

Likewise, while indemnification clauses allow the shifting of liability to the contractual party that has the ability to control or mitigate the risk associated with the liability, it may not be sufficient if the indemnifying party creates significant liability but does not have the means to address the same. For example, if a vendor agreed to maintain employment records and provide copies as necessary or requested but the vendor provides the same service to hundreds of employers and does not appropriately secure the data (or segregate between clients), then it is possible a data breach incident could occur for which the vendor would not have sufficient assets (or insurance) to cover, even subject to an indemnification clause, but the employer entity would still be liable for the individual breach obligations and claims.

## Data Privacy Risk Mitigation

It is important that a company collecting, storing, or processing PII understand the relevant definition of PII (whether called "personal information," "personal data," etc.). In addition, if the PII has the additional level of "sensitive" data collected, stored, or processed, this should also be documented. Some of the ways to protect against data privacy risks include limiting access, using encryption, de-identifying PII, and retaining PII only as long as required for legal and business purposes. For companies using assessment and selection technology, PII would include a candidate's name, address, and email address, and sensitive data would include race or ethnicity if this data was collected.

A company holding PII should limit access to the PII to those persons with a need to know[10] in order to provide the relevant services. "Persons" in this context include employees, contractors, vendors, suppliers, etc. It is reasonable to adopt the practice of limiting the data shared, both the amount and the "with whom" components, to protect all regulated data such as PII, even if not expressly required in the regulation, as it ensures that the risks of a breach or security incident are further limited.

Data privacy obligations generally require three main things: (a) an obligation to protect the PII so that it is only used or disclosed for authorized purposes, (b) an obligation to track who accesses/discloses PII, and (c) an obligation to maintain PII in a specific record. In order to comply with the first of these obligations, a company must have a clear understanding of required uses (i.e., necessary to provide the services) versus incidental or ancillary uses. While all data protection regulations grant a company the right to use PII in order to provide the required services, the regulations may limit, or allow the individual to limit, the ancillary uses. The second obligation requires administrative controls over who has the right to access PII and a way to track such access. The third obligation does two things: compiles all individually relevant data into one record set and for regulatory purposes clarifies what constitutes the designated record set. This last obligation is especially relevant as almost every regulation allows an individual to review their data record.

Deidentification or pseudonymization are both methods of removing the identifiable part of the data from the rest of the data. The GDPR references pseudonymization as a means of reducing risk for "personal data." The difference from a technical perspective is that de-identification means that the identifiable portion is permanently removed from the rest of the data, but in pseudonymization the identifiable portion could be reinserted to make the data identifiable again.[11] Data that has been de-identified, whether aggregated or not, could be used without obligations under data privacy

---

[10] HIPAA takes this one step further in that the use of PII must also include only the "minimum necessary" for the business purpose.

[11] Imagine a spreadsheet where the first column consists of row numbers, the second column is the identifiable information, and the remaining columns are the other data. If the row numbers column is left in the original spreadsheet but the row numbers column and the identifiable information column are copied into another spreadsheet before the identifiable information column is removed from the original spreadsheet, then the original spreadsheet has been pseudonymized (since the row numbers column would allow the reinsertion of the identifiable information back to the correct row of the other data). Conversely, if the identifiable information column was simply deleted (and not retained), then the data would be de-identified. NIST has a standard for de-identification (NIST IR 8053).

regulations as such data would not be PII. So if a company created a "data lake" to aggregate employee data for research purposes and such underlying data was fully de-identified, such aggregated data is also not subject to data privacy regulations. Conversely, if the data in the "data lake" is merely pseudonymized and reidentification remains possible, then the aggregated data may also be deemed to still be subject to data privacy regulations.

Risk mitigation may also be handled by cyber liability coverage requirements. For cyber liability concerns, the potential for insurance coverage gaps should be analyzed to ensure this mandated coverage is actually protecting the risk assessed. For example, if a client has coverage under commercial general liability (CGL), errors and omissions (E&O), and cyber liability/data privacy and an issue arises that an employee may have wrongfully acquired and disclosed sensitive personal information of a customer, more than one policy may apply. The E&O policy would typically cover risk for an employee's bad act (i.e., wrongfully acquiring PII and using or disclosing to a third party without authorization); however, this policy may also have an express exclusion for any claim related to personal information. If both policies are held, however, it is more likely that the combination will provide coverage. Cyber liability policies were just developed in the last 20 years and are named various things but generally include:

- Professional and technology services errors and omissions liability
- Media activities liability
- Network security and privacy liability
- Privacy breach
- Data assets breach
- Cyber extortion threat[12]
- Electronic business interruption

Another way to mitigate risk is to ensure that data is appropriately backed up and that appropriate disaster recovery protocols are in place. Backups can be scheduled in various timeframes (i.e., monthly, weekly, daily, every 15 minutes) and there can be full and partial backups. For example, a full backup is completed weekly, with incremental backups every 15 minutes the rest of the time. This means that in the event of a data loss event, the

---

[12] Note that many of these policies cover the damage but not any ransom that may be paid under a ransomware attack.

weekly backup would be restored and then the incremental backups would be added in. The effect on business operations, the costs, and the risk for data loss are all factors used in deciding on a data backup schedule. In addition, the disaster recovery protocol (how the backups are reinstated) is also important. The business continuity disaster recovery (BCDR) provisions will specify if the backup restoration is ever tested, or how often it is live tested, and whether the backups are stored offline and/or in a separate location.

## Data Privacy Anticipated Changes

It is undisputed that the prevalence of new data privacy regulations is increasing at the state, federal, and even international levels. In addition, there are specific variations of data privacy regulations such as biometric information that have been enacted. It is highly likely that in the next couple of years there will be artificial intelligence regulations that will deal with both data privacy considerations and liability assessment for improper or negligent coding of the artificial technology. While there may still be legal recourse for improper artificial intelligence coding (i.e., based on a tort or other regulatory violation), as the use of artificial intelligence grows, the possible risks associated with such use increase.

For example, using artificial intelligence to scan a candidate video and assess for gender, race, or other factors may be acceptable, but if the technology then uses the factors in violation of employment laws by not selecting women or persons of color, the artificial intelligence will have caused both direct legal issues (such as a claim for employment law violations) and business risk because the trial over the same would potentially necessitate disclosure of proprietary algorithms or simply be a deterrent for prospective customers. At a minimum there needs to be a clear understanding of whether there is a regulatory or government authority with the right to audit and/or oversee use of such technology.

It is likely the standards for security will continue to be developed away from generic industry standards to minimum regulatory standard expectations. This is in part because the technology has advanced to a point that a technology provider would no longer be able to claim that encryption was not feasible, for example, so mandating encryption as a baseline obligation could be spelled out in regulations. In addition, common practices such as strong user credentials, utilizing current antivirus software, and having a reasonable backup and BCDR process in place are all additional elements that are likely to be expressly included in regulations in the future. The GDPR/CCPA model of individual rights will likely become the standard, along with some obligation regarding notification of breaches.

## Conclusion

The protection of data is almost universal at this point, applying to both the discloser and the recipient. While data privacy and data security obligations are often regulated, the confirmation of such obligations should be documented in relevant agreements. Any obligations at a company level should also be documented and passed downstream to any affiliates and/or vendors acquiring access to PII subject to data privacy and data security regulations. For example, an assessment technology company would have limited data use rights from its customers (to process and/or select the candidates for further review), but an affiliate not providing any additional services for the customer would likely not have a valid purpose in having or using such data. Conversely, if an affiliate or a vendor provided services on behalf of the company (i.e., as a subcontractor), then that affiliate or vendor would have a legitimate right to access and use the data, but all of the company's data privacy and data security obligations to its customers should be passed on to the affiliate or vendor by way of a contractual obligation to comply with data privacy regulations.

Understanding what the specific provisions mean in trying to address such regulatory obligations is critical to making sure that the data is protected as a commercial asset, secure from misappropriation or unauthorized disclosure, and that the company has taken all appropriate measures to reduce, mitigate, or eliminate risk of noncompliance with the data privacy regulations.

## References

Illinois Biometric Information Privacy Act (BIPA), 740 ILCS 14/1 et seq. (2008). ilga.gov/legislation/publicacts/fulltext.asp?Name=095-0994

National Institute of Science and Technology. (2022, January). *Security and Privacy Controls for Information Systems and Organizations* (File No. NIST SP 800-53).

# 16
# Potential Impact of Disabilities and Neurodiversity on the Constructs Measured by Selection Procedures

*Jone M. Papinchock, Angela L. Rosenbaum, and Eric M. Dunleavy*

In our experience many traditional and technology-enhanced selection procedures use a variety of methods intended to measure knowledge, skills, abilities, and other characteristics (e.g., personality characteristics, attitudes, and related constructs). This chapter is relevant to these methods. We will consider frequently overlooked and potentially hidden impacts of neurodiversity and disabilities on the outcomes of selection procedures. It is highly recommended, and in some situations, a necessary methodological step in test development, to conduct sensitivity reviews of test items to identify content that may be affected by neurodiversity or disabilities covered under the Americans with Disabilities Act (ADA). Sensitivity reviews can identify potential consequences of item writing related to disabilities that cannot be measured through traditional means such as psychometric or adverse impact analyses.

## A Primer on the Americans with Disabilities Act

What is a disability under the ADA? According to the Appendix to Part 1630—Interpretive Guidance on Title I of the ADA:

> Physical or mental impairment means — (1) Any physiological disorder or condition, cosmetic disfigurement, or anatomical loss affecting one or more body systems, such as neurological, musculoskeletal, special sense

organs, respiratory (including speech organs), cardiovascular, reproductive, digestive, genitourinary, immune, circulatory, hemic, lymphatic, skin, and endocrine; or (2) Any mental or psychological disorder, such as an intellectual disability (formerly termed "mental retardation"), organic brain syndrome, emotional or mental illness, and specific learning disabilities.

Also:

*Disabilities include, but are not limited to*: autism; autoimmune disorder, for example, lupus, fibromyalgia, rheumatoid arthritis, or HIV/AIDS; blind or low vision; cancer; cardiovascular or heart disease; celiac disease; cerebral palsy; deaf or hard of hearing; depression or anxiety; diabetes; epilepsy; gastrointestinal disorders, for example, Crohn's disease or irritable bowel syndrome; intellectual disability; missing limbs or partially missing limbs; nervous system conditions, for example, migraine headaches, Parkinson's disease, or multiple sclerosis (MA); psychiatric condition, for example, bipolar disorder, schizophrenia, PTSD, or major depression.(https://www.dol.gov/sites/dolgov/files/OFCCP/regs/compliance/sec503/Self_ID_Forms/503Self-IDForm.pdf)

In addition to the ADA, federal agencies and federal contractors are required to follow the stipulations of Section 503 of the Rehabilitation Act of 1973. The Rehabilitation Act provides protection in employment settings for individuals with disabilities much like the ADA does. "The two statutes are generally interpreted and applied consistently with one another" (Hensel, 2017, p. 80). Therefore, this chapter relies on the ADA perspective.

ADA is a particular concern when using tests that might be defined as medical. The Equal Employment Opportunity Commission (EEOC) has developed guidance on when medical examinations can be conducted in the employment process:

Title I of the Americans with Disabilities Act of 1990 (the "ADA") (1) limits an employer's ability to make disability-related inquiries or require medical examinations at three stages: pre-offer, post-offer, and during employment. In its guidance on preemployment disability-related inquiries and medical examinations, the Commission addressed the ADA's restrictions on disability-related inquiries and medical examinations at the pre- and post-offer stages. (https://www.eeoc.gov/laws/guidance/enforcement-guidance-disability-related-inquiries-and-medical-examinations-employees)

Disability statistics help us gain perspective on the prevalence of individuals with disabilities in the general population. In 2018, the Centers for Disease Control and Prevention (CDC) indicated that one in four, or 61 million, Americans have a disability that affects a major part of their lives. "At some point in their lives, most people will either have a disability or know someone who has one," according to Coleen Boyle, PhD, director of the CDC's National Center on Birth Defects and Developmental Disabilities. CDC researchers analyzed a national database and categorized six types of disability: (1) mobility (i.e., serious difficulty walking or climbing stairs), (2) cognition (i.e., serious difficulty concentrating, remembering, or making decisions), (3) hearing (i.e., serious difficulty hearing), (4) vision (i.e., serious difficulty seeing), (5) independent living (i.e., difficulty doing errands alone), and (6) self-care (i.e., difficulty dressing or bathing). When ordered by frequency of occurrence, after mobility disability, the next most common disability types were cognition, independent living, hearing, vision, and self-care.

According to the Court of Appeals in *Karraker v. Rent-A-Center, Inc.*:

> Congress enacted three provisions in Title I which explicitly limit the ability of employers to use "medical examinations and inquiries" (42 U.S.C. § 12112 (d) (1)) as a condition of employment; a prohibition against using pre-employment medical tests; a prohibition against the use of medical tests that lack job-relatedness and business necessity; and a prohibition against the use of tests which screen out (or tend to screen out) people with disabilities. (p. 3)

Further, the EEOC indicates that a "'disability-related inquiry' is **a question (or series of questions) that is likely to elicit information about a disability**" (EEOC, 2000). As a result, personality tests that ask such questions may be viewed by the EEOC as medical in nature. The guidance on Preemployment Questions and Medical Examinations from the EEOC lists the following factors to determine whether a test (or procedure) is a medical examination:

1. whether the test is administered by a health care professional;
2. whether the test is interpreted by a health care professional;

3. whether the test is designed to reveal an impairment or physical or mental health;
4. whether the employer is trying to determine the applicant's physical or mental health;
5. whether the test is invasive;
6. whether the test measures an employee's performance of a task or measures his/her physiological responses to performing the task;
7. whether the test normally is given in a medical setting; and
8. whether medical equipment is used (EEOC, 2000).

## Current Focus on Personality Tests and the Americans with Disabilities Act

A focal article in *Industrial and Organization Psychology* in 2019 on personality tests and the ADA (Melson-Silimon et al., 2019) stimulated many thoughtful responses. The focal article's concern was that personality tests might be deemed to be medical tests if personality traits are considered to be on a single continuum. A major concern was the perceived increase in overlap between *Diagnostic and Statistical Manual of Mental Disorders*, fifth edition (DSM-V) designations of personality traits and traditional workplace personality traits. The authors who responded to the article made practical and insightful points about the lack of litigation tying workplace personality tests to medical tests (Christiansen et al., 2019; Saxena & Morris, 2019; Winterberg et al., 2019).

To date there is only one published judicial opinion at the Seventh Circuit Court of Appeals level, *Karraker v. Rent-A-Center*, that addresses personality tests used for employment and the possibility that they measure psychological or psychiatric disabilities under the ADA. In addition to lower court cases, there are a handful of recent federal agency conciliation agreements and consent decrees related to the use of personality tests in employment and potential discrimination on the basis of disability. It is generally accepted that theory within industrial-organizational (IO) psychology should be separate from legal precedents regarding testing. However, understanding legal precedent provides insight into actions IO psychologists can take now to be able to establish either nondiscrimination or job-relatedness and the business necessity of psychological tests. It is important to note that the battery of tests used by Rent-A-Center may be of limited applicability in discussion of more familiar personality tests developed by IO psychologists strictly for employment purposes, because the personality test was the Minnesota Multiphasic Personality Inventory (MMPI), which the court found to be a medical test. Many IO psychologists would agree that the MMPI was developed for the purpose of diagnosing psychological and psychiatric disorders and therefore would be deemed a medical test when used in employment settings.

Cognitive ability tests may also be scrutinized under the ADA, with particular attention to items that might impact individuals with cognitive or neurological disabilities. Along with personality measurement under an ADA lens, an associated emerging area is the nascent empirical review of neurodiversity. Judy Singer in her 1998 honors thesis coined the term "neurodiversity." Although there are many perspectives on neurodiversity, from a social movement to a paradigm (Milton, 2019), finding a definition that is agreed upon across groups is very difficult. We use the following definition:

> Neurodiversity refers to the idea that neurological differences . . . reflect normal variations in brain development. The term originally referred most commonly to autism but has since come to include ADHD, dyslexia, Tourette's, synesthesia, as well as other learning and developmental differences.
> (https://www.psychologytoday.com/us/basics/neurodiversity)

Test performance differences associated with neurodiversity, or more generally cognitive ability, mirror the concerns of the impact of psychological or psychiatric disorders on personality tests. Cognitive and personality tests may be responded to differently by test takers with some form of neurodiversity. As a result, there may be unintentional outcomes (e.g., construct-irrelevant variance) that occur because a test taker's neurodiversity interferes with standard interpretation of the test items. Beyond neurodiversity, items on cognitive and noncognitive tests may not be interpreted in the same way by individuals with physical disabilities.

For the purposes of this chapter, the four fundamental inquiries regarding the impact of disabilities on test performance are:

1. Are there types of tests or test items that disadvantage individuals with disabilities (i.e., cognitive, psychological or psychiatric, or physical disabilities)?

2. What impacts are there on the construct validity of five factor model personality employment tests that may inadvertently be measuring an individual's disability by their response to a personality test item (e.g., avoiding eating spicy food due to gastrointestinal disease versus not liking spicy food)?
3. What challenges exist for measuring the adverse impact of test scores and item-level responses on individuals with disabilities?
4. Are the psychometric properties of items changed when the test taker's response is based on a limitation resulting from a disability or neurodiversity, rather than personality?

These fundamental questions apply to the appropriateness of test items and of the job-relatedness of the selection procedures themselves. Test developers and publishers should be aware of and take reasonable precautions to ensure that other elements of an individual's makeup (e.g., neurodiversity, psychological or psychiatric disorders, physical disabilities) do not impact the responses to items that appear neutral and that may even be quite common in current assessment batteries. Professionals who might be helpful in these determinations are IO psychologists with specialization in testing who can interpret the psychometrics and are aware of item-writing fundamentals; however, other fields that study psychometrics and/or have content expertise may also be valuable resources (e.g., clinical psychologists, educational measurement). The developer needs to ensure that the test is measuring the same constructs across test takers of varying abilities. Importantly, these precautions are likely to be dependent on the process of test development and review of items instead of after-the-fact use of psychometric or adverse impact analyses.

Test developers should focus attention on the evaluation of potential items for all types of tests (e.g., personality tests, cognitive ability tests) that could be problematic for test takers with disabilities. This evaluation typically includes an attempt to determine whether there is adverse impact against individuals from a protected group. However, for a variety of reasons these standard approaches to the calculation of adverse impact statistics are not likely to work from an ADA perspective. This is in part because all calculations of adverse impact are affected by the groupings of individuals applying for jobs, such as more traditional decisions about groupings by race and national origin, sex identification, and intersectionality. Meaningful groupings are even more complex for individuals with disabilities. Using data for analysis of possible impacts of assessments of individuals with disabilities relying on dichotomous membership (i.e., an individual with a disability or without a disability) is likely an extreme oversimplification of the nature of disabilities. These concerns are exacerbated by the fact that there are likely interactions between types of disabilities and types of tests (e.g., disabilities that affect cognitive processing and tests that are heavily cognitive in nature). The EEOC has noted, "Each disability is unique. An individual may fare poorly on an assessment because of a disability, and be screened out as a result, regardless of how well other individuals with disabilities fare on the assessment. Therefore, to avoid screen out, employers may need to take different steps beyond the steps taken to address other forms of discrimination" (https://www.eeoc.gov/laws/guidance/americans-disabilities-act-and-use-software-algorithms-and-artificial-intelligence).

This simple fact related to the nature of disability status leads to complex questions. For example, how would multiple disabilities be categorized and handled in a calculation of adverse impact? Can individuals who share the same category of disability even be grouped together given variations in the symptomology of disabilities? How does one determine the extent of a disability? Diagnoses of autism spectrum and myriad disabilities can vary widely in functional differences and severity; so, how would this be reflected in self-disclosure? Without such details, a category for a disability might include individuals who do not have the most common features of the disorder that might impact performance on a personality test mixed with individuals who do.

Additional challenges in analysis of adverse impact exist because the EEOC and Office of Federal Contract Compliance Programs (OFCCP) do not share a common method regarding the collection of disability information. The OFCCP requires federal contractors to collect disability information from applicants; in contrast, the EEOC forbids employers from collecting disability information under the ADA. Further, methods must be determined for handling missing data versus nonresponse. Since the Department of Labor's OFCCP introduced the "Voluntary Self-Identification of Disability" form (OMB Control Number 1250-0005), federal contractors have had access to data that they could potentially use for statistical purposes in calculating the adverse impact of tests against individuals with disabilities. However, there are problems that can arise from the self-report required for such a form (e.g., misattribution of a condition that would not be qualified as a disability for the individual, misattribution by individuals with a qualifying disability who do not define themselves as having a disability, and hesitancy to self-identify for fear of being excluded from selection).

One recommendation for addressing the lack of data due to government prohibition against collection of data regarding disabilities in employment settings is to have test vendors collect data voluntarily from individuals with disabilities in their criterion studies (Timmons, 2021). Specifically, Timmons (2021) recommends that "personality test vendors should research whether and to what extent their products tend to screen out applicants with disabilities" (p. 389). This may be particularly important for tests scored through algorithms, which is very common. It is unlikely that the existing top performers in organizations, upon whom some scoring algorithms are based, represent a cross section of individuals with personality and psychiatric disorders. According to the Bureau of Labor Statistics, in 2019, there were only 30.9% of individuals with disabilities in the workforce (Bureau of Labor Statistics, 2020). The bottom line is that there are myriad disabilities with myriad potential cognitive/emotional/physical impacts on selection procedure outcomes, and this scenario would produce a matrix so complex that it cannot be meaningfully analyzed using traditional approaches to adverse impact measurement. The field, and in particular test vendors, should strive for meaningful research in the face of this complexity.

Because the problem with obtaining an adequate sample for subgroups of individuals with differing disabilities is nearly intractable, a more comprehensive approach is required. A more viable approach to addressing this research dilemma is a call to action for IO academic and practice research.

## A Fresh Look at Item Sensitivity Reviews

Notwithstanding the need for more robust research on adverse impact for disability subgroups, it may be valuable to develop item sensitivity review methods that focus on disability-related outcomes. The IO psychology academic literature describes item sensitivity reviews as being "undertaken to remove any content that could conceivably distract test takers or otherwise prevent them from appropriately demonstrating their true standing on the construct the test is designed to assess" (Golubovich et al., 2014, p.1). Grand et al. (2010) state that "sensitivity reviews are distinct from efforts that target test performance issues. Specifically, whereas performance examinations are post hoc statistical procedures, the sensitivity review process is an expert judgment exercise that occurs prior to test administration with little to no association to psychometric data for reference (Ramsey, 1993)" (p. 1). Importantly, item sensitivity reviews are intended to identify test content that "may activate emotional states that distract test takers' attention from the constructs intended to be measured" (McPhail, 2010, p. 2). Indeed, the EEOC recommends employing psychologists throughout the test development process to identify test elements that may impact individuals with disabilities (https://www.eeoc.gov/laws/guidance/americans-disabilities-act-and-use-software-algorithms-and-artificial-intelligence).

In the authors' recent work, we have seen recommendations for item sensitivity reviews as a response to challenges of alleged disability discrimination. On its surface it might seem that a quick review of items that might elicit emotional state would be the primary concern, but a thorough exploration of the subject identifies the need for a far more complex review and analysis. Questions of interest in the equal employment opportunity context require more than just attention to emotional state or the potential for measuring psychological disorders, so the review must be broader.

Cognitive differences in processing information can heavily impact all tests, not just cognitive ability tests. Such concerns are often addressed through reference to good item-writing principles; however, actions such as reading level analyses and grammar checks alone are insufficient for ameliorating potential problems arising for individuals with disabilities. Problematic wording of items (e.g., unnecessarily complex sentence structure, confusing sentence structure, unnecessary use of idioms, difficult vocabulary) will make an item more difficult for an individual with a learning disability than it would be for other test takers. Thus, an increase in the item difficulty for the individual with a learning disability will arise from irrelevant sources of difficulty that are not shared by individuals who do not have learning disabilities. Similar to limitations related to traditional adverse impact measurement in this context, the simple solution of identifying item-writing problems through traditional item analyses is unlikely to uncover such problems.

Item structure such as that found in personality tests, where more casual language and idioms are used, may also impose a hardship on individuals with cognitive disabilities. Personality tests and measurement of related constructs are often written with a more casual or idiomatic tone or require understanding of a nuanced situation that may be more difficult for a person with a learning disability to interpret. As a result, the reading and comprehension ability (e.g., interpreting idioms, understanding complex sentence structure) of the individual may be assessed instead of a preference-based response to these types of items.

More generally, the way items are written to assess personality can introduce varied concerns for individuals with disabilities. Typical items usually target what people are drawn to, what their preferences are, and what they do or do not feel comfortable doing. But what happens when, for some individuals, the selection procedure is actually measuring the impact of a disability instead of a preference? It is well understood that items like those on the MMPI should be avoided in personality tests used for most employment purposes because they can diagnose "abnormal" psychological or psychiatric conditions. It is more common on workplace personality tests to collect information such as a preference for being alone/social or the amount of worrying a test taker does (presumably at a subclinical level). Yet for some test takers, responses to these items may be driven by psychological or psychiatric disorders.[1] It is important to step back to think about whether the item is operating in the same way and collecting the same information from an individual who is a "little shy" versus an individual who has a clinical social anxiety disorder. The test developer should define the purpose of the item and whether the item is collecting the same information from all test takers and measuring the same construct. Is error introduced when some test takers respond based on preference and others respond based on their current level of psychological disorder? The answer is undeniably "yes." Would the reliability of the responses be the same for the two groups? The answer is indisputably "no."

Similarly, assessments of personality and other constructs often collect information about likes and dislikes regarding food, travel, and other life experiences. The basis for the answer from an individual with a gastric disorder would be very different to an item purportedly measuring openness to experimenting with different types of foods than for an individual without a gastric disorder. That is, a gastric disorder may require an individual to have

---

[1] "Note, however, that even if a request for health-related information does not violate the ADA's restrictions on disability-related inquiries and medical examinations, it still might violate other parts of the ADA. For example, if a personality test asks questions about optimism, and if someone with Major Depressive Disorder ('MDD') answers those questions negatively and loses an employment opportunity as a result, the test may 'screen out' the applicant because of MDD. As explained in Questions 8–11 above, such screen out may be unlawful if the individual who is screened out can perform the essential functions of the job, with or without reasonable accommodation" (https://www.eeoc.gov/laws/guidance/americans-disabilities-act-and-use-software-algorithms-and-artificial-intelligence).

a restricted diet regardless of preference (i.e., openness to experiment with different types of foods).

An item sensitivity review may also be needed to address the impact of physical disabilities on responses. An item about enjoyment of paintings and other visual arts for an individual with a visual impairment is less likely to be based on a preference. Further, in alignment with McPhail (2010), an individual with a visual impairment may perform differently on the remainder of a selection procedure following such an item due to feelings that they would not fit in the organization or because their disability may be measured through responses to items. In another example, personality test items about travel can be impacted by many physical, psychological, and cognitive difficulties rather than preference. The problems faced in traveling by individuals with disabilities are so well established that the Department of Transportation enforces the Air Carrier Access Act (Title 14 CFR Part 382) to ensure that airlines do not discriminate against individuals with disabilities on flights within the United States. In 2019, roughly 29 wheelchairs and scooters were lost, damaged, delayed, or stolen each day during airline travel in the United States. These types of issues likely impact the desire to travel for people who require mobility assistance in daily life. Along these same lines, situational judgment test items can also introduce inconsistencies in the basis for a response. For example, a scenario item that attempts to measure conscientiousness by asking about working extended hours may illicit preference from one individual but be based on a physical condition for another (e.g., person with diabetes who needs to test sugar level at a particular time and eat accordingly).

## Item Sensitivity Review Panel Training and Ratings

The identification of offensive material through procedures such as sensitivity review relies upon judgment (Waters, 2010). Consequently, the establishment of guidelines for item review panel members is extremely important to ensure consistency in the criteria that are used to identify objectionable content for revision or removal. As mentioned previously, IO psychologists are well suited to make item sensitivity review judgments and provide item sensitivity review ratings given their experience in test development, knowledge of the testing authorities (i.e., *Uniform Guidelines on Employee Selection Procedures*, Society for Industrial and Organizational Psychology *Principles for the Validation and Use of Selection Procedures*, and American

Psychological Association *Standards for Educational and Psychological Testing*) and employment laws and regulations (e.g., ADA), and specialized knowledge of calculating and interpreting adverse impact. Depending on the type of test (e.g., cognitive ability, personality), consideration should be given to the expertise required on the review panel.

Prior to evaluating items, regardless of their expertise, item sensitivity review panel members should receive training focused on the development of a common frame of reference as to what type of content might be perceived by test takers as measuring a disability or as having a chilling effect and on establishing a method to be followed in identifying such content to ensure that items do not unlawfully discriminate against individuals with disabilities.

The focus of the item sensitivity review concentrates on whether each test item would create a negative perception for individuals with disabilities. Effective training includes a presentation and discussion of item sensitivity research, a primer on the ADA for thorough understanding of the nuances of the statute, and definition of what is deemed a disability under the ADA. When appropriate, training should also include the primary categories of disabilities listed in the ADA and the typical manifestations of disorders. This is essential because reviewers need to be aware of symptomology that might be indirectly referenced in a question. Similarly, reviewers should share a common understanding of major psychological and psychiatric disorders as referenced in the DSM-V. It is valuable for training to include an in-depth discussion of the characteristics demonstrated by individuals who have psychological and psychiatric disorders based on the descriptions in the DSM-V.

The rating scales must be explained, and the trainer should consider the inclusion of mock ratings by trainees for a set of test items. These data should be reviewed for interrater reliability. The independent ratings should be discussed in meetings that are held until all reviewers achieve consensus. This allows for a structured discussion and redirection, if necessary, of any idiosyncratic understandings of the impact of disabilities on responding to test items and the use of the rating scales.

An example of a set of rating scales follows:

1. *Could the content of this test item distract an individual with a disability or interfere with his/her performance on the assessment?*
    a. It is not likely that the test item would interfere with performance on the test for an individual with a related disability.

b. It is somewhat likely that the test item would interfere with performance on the test for an individual with a related disability.
  c. It is very likely that the test item would interfere with performance on the test for individuals with disabilities.
2. *Would a test taker's answer provide as much or more information about his/her disability than the construct being measured?*
  a. It is not likely that the test item would provide more information about an individual's disability than the construct being measured.
  b. It is somewhat likely that the test item would provide more information about an individual's disability than the construct being measured.
  c. It is very likely that the test item would provide more information about an individual's disability than the construct being measured.
3. *Can the item be easily revised or should it be deleted?*
  a. The item can be revised.
  b. The item should be deleted.

In making the ratings, a useful method for evaluating the items is use of specialized questions such as:

- Is a test item exclusionary in terms of assumptions about life experiences and ways of physically doing things that are irrelevant to the construct being measured? Is there content, context, or a situation presented in a test item that might cause an individual with a mobility disability to be uncomfortable, upset, or distracted, or otherwise interfere with test performance? Are directly or subtly pejorative terms (e.g., "slow," "shaky," "weak") that could be related to decrements in physical ability contained in the item? For example:
  o I have been *running so fast* at work but do not feel I can catch up.
  o To present myself well, I always *stand up straight*.
  o *Walking around* the office is the best way to manage.
  o I am a little *shaky* about learning new things.
  o I am *slow* when making friends.
- Will the content, context, or a situation presented in a test item cause an individual with a sensory disability to be uncomfortable, upset, or distracted, or otherwise interfere with test performance? Does a test item incorrectly include reference to sensory disabilities (e.g., visual, touch, speaking, hearing, tasting)? For example:

## IMPACT OF DISABILITIES AND NEURODIVERSITY

- o I *see* myself as a helpful person.
- o I *see* rules as flexible.
- o I enjoy *looking at paintings*.
- o Sometimes I feel *dumb* compared to my co-workers.
* Will the content, context, or a situation presented in a test item cause an individual with a psychiatric or personality disorder to be uncomfortable, upset, or distracted, or otherwise interfere with test performance? Item sensitivity reviewers should understand the following psychological or psychiatric disabilities. The primary psychological or psychiatric disabilities as described in the DSM V are neurodevelopmental disorders; schizophrenia; bipolar disorders; depressive disorders; anxiety disorders; borderline personality disorder; panic disorder; agoraphobia disorders; obsessive compulsive disorder; trauma and stressor-related disorders (e.g., posttraumatic stress disorder [PTSD]); dissociative disorders; feeding and eating disorders; disruptive, impulse-control, and conduct disorders (e.g., antisocial personality disorder); substance-related and addictive disorders; neurocognitive disorders (major or mild); and personality disorders. For example:
  - o Sometimes I get *depressed* when I can't finish a project.
  - o I am always *stressed*.
  - o Sometimes I feel like I could go *crazy*.
  - o When looking at my schedule, I sometimes become somewhat *hysterical*.
  - o It's *insane* to work as hard as I do.
* Will the content, context, or a situation presented in a test item cause an individual with a physical disability to be uncomfortable, upset, or distracted, or otherwise interfere with test performance? Does a personality test item elicit an answer that may be the result of a physical disability (e.g., gastric disorders, mobility) rather than preference (e.g., openness to experience)? For example:
  - o I *enjoy trying new foods*.
  - o I *prefer to travel* instead of staying at home.
  - o Sometimes I feel *dumb* compared to my co-workers.
* Will the content, context, or a situation presented in a test item cause an individual with a cognitive disability to be uncomfortable, upset, or distracted, or otherwise interfere with test performance? (It should be noted that cognitive disabilities are also tapped when a noncognitive item includes difficult vocabulary, complex sentence structure, or

unnecessary use of idioms. These introduce irrelevant sources of difficulty and interfere with measuring the intended construct.) For example:
- People say I *learn quickly*.
- I get *confused easily* by things other people think are simple.
- My *memory is better than others*.

The above examples demonstrate that just because items are common on personality tests does not mean they will pass legal or regulatory scrutiny.

## Recommendations for Handling Item-Writing Problems

A set of general recommendations/considerations for avoiding problematic test items includes:

- Item writers may require training to increase their awareness of the potential for particular items that may be problematic for test takers with disabilities.
- Consider describing the work outcomes that might occur because of emotional responses instead of describing the emotions themselves. Items should avoid describing behavior, thoughts, or conditions in terms of abnormal psychology. Words such as "stress," "stressor," "mood," and "anxiety" should be used with extreme caution. For example, consider that "I rarely finish projects on time" is less offensive than "I become so stressed I cannot finish my work on time."
- Test developers should be aware of any term that may cause a negative response in an individual with disabilities such as PTSD, anxiety, or bipolar disorder. References to physical conflict, bombs, fear, vigilance, weapons, being monitored/watched, etc., should not be used unnecessarily.
- It is generally recognized that even in cognitive ability tests, care should be taken in the choice of vocabulary, sentence structure, and the use of idioms unless the construct being measured is language skills. Misuse of language is more problematic in personality tests.

There are many approaches to reviewing item sensitivity; however, this topic has generally not been discussed in depth from the perspective of individuals with disabilities. The recommendations here are offered as a start for the discussion of testing content and the reactions by and potential negative outcomes for individuals with disabilities. Obviously, many of the items identified as problematic in this chapter may have a place and purpose in tests. As with all test item development, the item writer must use professional judgment when creating concepts for testing. This chapter is intended to be a reminder of the importance of considering the potential for unintended discrimination against individuals with disabilities; we must consider the reaction to test items and outcomes for this group of test takers. Given the complexity described earlier, we may not have current methods to reliably assess adverse impact or differential psychometric characteristics on the basis of disability, but we can take steps to even the playing field for individuals with disabilities.

# References

Air Carrier Access Act (Title 14 CFR Part 382). 2008.
Bureau of Labor Statistics. (2020). *Persons with a disability: Labor force characteristics – 2019*. Retrieved October 16, 2021, from https://www.bls.gov/news.release/archives/disabl_02262020.pdf
Centers for Disease Control and Prevention. (2018, August 16). *CDC: 1 in 4 US adults live with a disability*. Retrieved October 16, 2021, from https://www.cdc.gov/media/releases/2018/p0816-disability.html
Christiansen, N. D., Fisher, P. A., Robie, C., & Quirk, A. (2019). Tilting at windmills and improving personality assessment practices. *Industrial and Organizational Psychology, 12*(2), 177–183.
Equal Employment Opportunity Commission. (2000, July 26). *Enforcement guidance on disability-related inquiries and medical examinations of employees under the ADA*. Retrieved October 16, 2021, from https://www.eeoc.gov/es/node/130104
Golubovich, J., Grand, J. A., Ryan, A. M., & Schmitt, N. (2014). An examination of common sensitivity review practices in test development. *International Journal of Selection and Assessment, 22*, 1–11.
Grand, J. A., Golubovich, J., Ryan, A. M., & Schmitt, N. (2010). The detection and influence of problematic item content in ability tests: An examination of sensitivity review practices for personnel selection test development. *Organizational Behavior and Human Decision Processes, 121*, 158–173.
Hensel, W. F. (2017). People with autism spectrum disorder in the workplace: An expanding legal front. *Harvard Civil Rights-Civil Liberties Law Review, 52*, 73–102.
Karraker vs. Rent-A-Center, Inc. (411 F.3d 831, 837 (7th Cir. 2005)).
McPhail, S. M. (2010). *Rationales for conducting item sensitivity reviews* [Symposium presentation]. Meeting of the Society for Industrial and Organizational Psychology, Atlanta, GA.
Melson-Silimon, A., Harris, A. M., Shoenfelt, E. L., Miller, J. D., & Carter, N. T. (2019). Personality testing and the Americans with Disabilities Act: Cause for concern as

normal and abnormal personality models are integrated. *Industrial and Organizational Psychology, 12*(2), 119–132.

Milton, D. E. M. (2019, November). Disagreeing over neurodiversity. *The Psychologist, 32*, 8.

Saxena, M., & Morris, S. B. (2019). Adverse impact as disability discrimination: Illustrating the perils through self-control at work. *Industrial and Organizational Psychology, 12*(2), 138–142.

Timmons, K. C. (2021). Pre-employment personality tests, algorithmic bias, and the Americans with Disabilities Act. *Penn State Law Review, 125*(2), 389–452.

Waters, S. (2010). *Practical considerations in developing sensitivity reviews* [Symposium presentation]. Meeting of the Society for Industrial and Organizational Psychology, Atlanta, GA.

Winterberg, C. A., Tapia, M. A., Nei, K. S., & Brummel, B. (2019). A clarification of ADA jurisprudence for personality-based selection. *Industrial and Organizational Psychology, 12*(2), 172–176.

# 17
# Reflections on Legal and Standards Update
## Opportunity Meets Reality

*Kenneth M. Willner, Kathleen K. Lundquist, and Claire Saba Murphy*[*]

Leveraging new assessment technology presents the opportunity to make selection decisions that are accurate, fair, and job related using methods that promise greater flexibility and efficiency. This opportunity, however, must be realized within the context of legal, policy, and technical considerations that may constrain the use of these advances.

## Artificial Intelligence in Applicant Screening or Employment Testing

Artificial intelligence (AI) in the employment context typically means that the selection decision relies in whole or in part "on the computer's own analysis of data to determine which criteria to use when making the employment decision" (Equal Employment Opportunity Commission [EEOC], 2022b, p. 4). AI enables employers to recruit potential applicants, assess eligible candidates in the applicant pool, and predict the likelihood of success at a job in a flexible way using varying criteria that are learned by the AI. As many as 83% of employers and 90% of Fortune 500 companies use some form of automated tools to screen or rank candidates for hiring (Mulvaney, 2021). For example, video interview systems use AI to analyze facial movements, word choice, and speaking voice to rank candidates based on an "employability" score (Harwell, 2019). Employers are increasingly using such AI-based

---

[*] Dr. Lundquist is the president and CEO of APTMetrics, Inc. Mr. Willner is a partner, and Ms. Saba Murphy is an associate, with Paul Hastings, LLP. The authors acknowledge and thank Daniel S. Richards, an associate with Paul Hastings, LLP, for his assistance with this chapter.

assessments as resume scanning software, chatbots, video interviewing, and gaming software.

AI advocates say AI helps make decisions that are data driven and not influenced by the possibility of bias in subjective decision-making. However, AI is dependent on the data from which it learns, and care is warranted to "look under the hood" of the algorithm to eliminate potentially discriminatory inputs. For example, if a hypothetical algorithm identified shoe size as strongly correlated with job success, that facially neutral characteristic could have a discriminatory impact on women, who typically have smaller shoe sizes. A hypothetical example with a more obvious bias would be a resume screening AI that identifies the word "Korea" on a resume as negatively correlated with selection and assigns it a negative coefficient. An employer would be well advised to avoid algorithms with such potentially biased elements.

## Managing the Risks

Managing the legal risks associated with new assessment technology requires an understanding and a balancing of legal, policy, and technical considerations.

From a legal perspective, the same laws that apply to traditional assessments also apply to assessments based on AI. Title VII of the Civil Rights Act of 1964 ("Title VII"), the Age Discrimination in Employment Act of 1967 (ADEA), and the Americans with Disabilities Act of 1990 (ADA) all provide a basis for challenging assessments. In addition to current federal anti-discrimination laws, some states have already enacted, and Congress is currently considering, legislation specifically addressing the fairness of AI in testing. Privacy laws relating to the collection and use of biometric identifiers (e.g., retina scans, voiceprints) impose additional constraints on the use of such information in assessments.

From a policy perspective, the same considerations of adverse impact, validation, and less adverse alternatives articulated in the *Uniform Guidelines on Employee Selection Procedures ("Uniform Guidelines"*; 29 C.F.R. § 1607, *et seq.*, 1978) also apply to these new assessment technologies. So, despite the promise that algorithms based on machine learning will be more objective and "unbiased," such assessments may present continued risks for adverse impact based on race, age, and gender when variables in the algorithm are unintentional correlates of these protected characteristics. Moreover, increasing emphasis on the potential for discrimination on the basis of disability has recently led to technical guidance from the EEOC and the Department of Justice (EEOC, 2022a, 2022b) concerning access to technology platforms and the potential for such assessments to be deemed pre-employment medical evaluations.

Finally, from a technical perspective, these new assessment devices often fail to define a theoretical rationale for what is being measured, may lack adequate psychometric characteristics (e.g., incomplete data, inadequate representation in training samples), and require professional judgment in evaluating the sufficiency of any validity evidence produced for the assessment.

To realize the potential of new assessment technologies, employers must take care to implement and evaluate these technologies within the contours of evolving notions of nondiscrimination and privacy based on new and existing laws.

## The Legal Framework

*Federal Laws.* Federal anti-discrimination laws apply broadly to workplace assessments. This includes Title VII, the ADEA, and the ADA. State and local anti-discrimination laws also apply, and in some cases may exceed the requirements of the federal requirements. Further, some states and localities have begun to develop state or local laws that specifically address AI and biometrics, and Congress is currently considering similar legislation.

Each of the federal and state anti-discrimination laws prohibits both intentional discrimination (disparate treatment) and unintentional discrimination (disparate impact). Disparate impact discrimination is the usual allegation in litigation about assessments. Disparate impact discrimination cases target practices that are facially neutral but result in a disproportionate impact on a protected group.

Under Title VII, if a plaintiff shows that a practice has a disparate or adverse impact, the employer can defend the practice by demonstrating that it is "job related for the position in question and consistent with business necessity" (42 U.S.C. § 2000e et seq., as amended). However, even if the employer meets that burden, a plaintiff may still prevail by showing that the employer refuses to adopt an available alternative employment practice that has less adverse impact and serves the employer's legitimate needs. Federal case law and the *Uniform Guidelines* (1978) further detail the concepts of adverse impact, validation, and less adverse alternatives.

The ADEA (29 U.S.C. § 623, et seq.) prohibits discrimination based on age against a person aged 40 years or older. While Title VII permits practices that are a "business necessity," the ADEA permits any "otherwise prohibited" practice "where the differentiation is based on reasonable factors other than age" (29 U.S.C. § 623(f)(1)). As a result of this difference, disparate impact claims are more easily defensible under the ADEA than under Title VII, because an employer need prove only that the practice is "reasonable," not that it is a business necessity and the least adverse alternative.

The ADA (42 U.S.C. § 12101, et seq.) prohibits discrimination against qualified individuals with disabilities.[1] The ADA specifically bans hiring "using . . . employment tests . . . [that] tend to screen out an individual with a disability or a class of individuals with disabilities unless the . . . test . . . is shown to be job-related for the position in question and is consistent with business necessity" (42 U.S.C. § 12112(b)(6); see also id. § 12113(a)). The ADA also makes it unlawful to fail to make selections and administer employment tests "in the most effective manner" to ensure that the test results "accurately reflect the skills, aptitude, or whatever other factor of such applicant or employee that such test purports to measure, rather than reflecting the impaired sensory, manual, or speaking skills of such employee or applicant (except where such skills are the factors that the test purports to measure)" (42 U.S.C. § 12112(b)(7)). In addition to the prohibition on discrimination, the ADA requires employers to provide reasonable accommodations to qualified individuals with disabilities and imposes restrictions on the use of medical examinations, including a general prohibition on medical examinations and inquiries before an offer is extended to a job candidate (42 U.S.C. §12112(d)(2)(A)).

Federal law does not currently contain any anti-discrimination law unique to AI assessments. Therefore, AI assessments are considered under the same standards as other assessments. However, Congress has repeatedly introduced legislation aimed at the use of algorithms in the workplace, and eventually one may become law. Most recently, the proposed Algorithmic

---

[1] The definition of a protected "disability" was expanded in the Americans with Disabilities Act Amendments Act of 2008. A protected disability now includes "a physical or mental impairment that substantially limits one or more major life activities of such individual . . . a record of such impairment; or . . . being regarded as having such an impairment" (42 U.S.C. § 12102(1)).

Justice and Online Platform Transparency Act of 2021 would impose notice requirements and make it "unlawful for an online platform to employ any proprietary online platform design features, including an algorithmic process, or otherwise process the personal information of an individual for the purpose of... contracting for... employment... in a manner that discriminates against or otherwise makes the opportunity unavailable on the basis" of a protected class or biometric information (S. 1896, 117th Cong. (1st Sess. 2021) § 6(b)). This proposed law would impose liability on a disparate impact-like model, with a defense available where a "disparate outcome is justified by a non-discriminatory, compelling interest, and such interest cannot be satisfied by less discriminatory means" (S. 1896, 117th Cong. (1st Sess. 2021) § 6(e)(2)(B)). Interestingly, this proposed law would vest enforcement authority with the Federal Trade Commission, not the EEOC.

*State and Local Laws.* State and local legislatures have taken the lead with legislation that specifically addresses AI. AI-specific state and local laws fall into two categories: (a) notice/consent laws and (b) bias audit laws.

Illinois enacted a notice/consent law, the Artificial Intelligence Video Interview Act (AIVIA), in 2019, effective starting in 2020. With respect to hiring for Illinois-based positions, the AIVIA requires employers using video-recorded applicant interviews and using AI to analyze the videos to (a) notify each applicant that AI may be used, (b) provide applicants with information explaining how the AI works and the general types of characteristics it uses to evaluate applicants, and (c) obtain consent from each applicant to be evaluated by the AI program (820 ILCS 42, et seq.). The employer may only share the video with persons whose expertise or technology is necessary to evaluate the applicant's fitness for the position. Finally, upon request from the applicant, the employer must delete the video interview and instruct others who receive copies of the video to do the same within 30 days.

Similarly, Maryland prohibits an employer from using facial recognition technology during pre-employment job interviews unless the applicant consents by signing a specified waiver (Md. Code, Lab. & Empl. § 3-717).

New York City enacted the first, and presently the only, bias audit law (New York City Code Title 20, Sec. 1, Ch. 5, subchapter 25). Effective January 2, 2023, the law bars the use of automated hiring and promotion tools unless those tools have been subject to a bias audit. The law also requires employers to notify employees or candidates if the tool was used to make job decisions. The law defines an "automated employment decision tool" as "any computational process, derived from machine learning, statistical modeling, data analytics, or artificial intelligence," that provides a simplified output, "including a score, classification, or recommendation, that is used to substantially assist or replace discretionary decision making" for screening candidates for employment or promotions. Notably, New York City's law covers only race, ethnicity, and sex discrimination and does not currently apply to disability and age discrimination.

Other jurisdictions are considering similar laws. For example, on December 9, 2021, Washington, DC announced proposed legislation, the Stop Discrimination by Algorithms Act, to address "algorithmic discrimination" and require companies to submit to annual audits about their technology (District of Columbia Office of Attorney General, 2021). On February 20, 2020, California proposed a similar new law, the Talent Equity for Competitive Hiring (TECH) Act (SB 1241), which would apply to all AI technology in selection procedures. In March 2022, the California Fair Employment and Housing Council published draft modifications to its current anti-discrimination laws to explicitly include "automated-decision systems" as tests covered by the same requirements for validation as other types of tests, that is, shown to be job related and consistent with business necessity (Lazzarotti & Yang, 2022).

Compliance with the notice/consent type of laws should be relatively straightforward for employers that recruit for positions only in one jurisdiction and can manage the notice requirements; however, for employers in multiple jurisdictions, with differing notice requirements in various locations, compliance will become increasingly complex as additional laws are added. Additionally, test vendors may be reluctant to disclose in notices the contents of their algorithms, which they may view as proprietary.

The bias audit laws are poised to create a new industry for experts, as employers using AI assessments will have to hire auditors to assess the "fairness" of the algorithms in the assessments. Thus far, the laws provide little explicit guidance as to what constitutes a "bias audit" and what credentials may be required to conduct one, nor whether the adequacy of an audit approving of an assessment is an absolute bar to suit or can be challenged in litigation. Additionally, test vendors may be reluctant to permit potential competitors filling the role of auditors to review the contents and impact of their proprietary algorithms.

Thus far, there has been little litigation specifically targeting AI elements of assessments. In 2019, the Electronic Privacy Information Center (EPIC) filed a Federal Trade Commission complaint against HireVue challenging the company's AI-driven assessments that assess job candidates based on facial analysis. In response, HireVue announced it would stop relying on facial analysis to assess job candidates but will continue to analyze some biometric data (such as speech and intonation) from job applicants (EPIC, 2021). However, litigation targeting AI is bound to increase as AI assessments proliferate and the applicable law gains clarity.

Automated assessments pose some additional challenges with respect to the application of traditional validation principles, such as those expressed in the *Uniform Guidelines*. For example, some automated assessments are designed to select follow-up questions of varying difficulty based on an applicant's ability to answer prior questions correctly. This results in each applicant taking a test with different questions of differing difficulty levels. Similarly, where the AI underlying an assessment continues to learn and evolve after an assessment is first established, the assessment in use may differ over time. Such moving targets present a challenge for the validation of the assessment. Thus far, courts have not been called upon to determine whether validation methods require any modification in these contexts. This too is an area of future development in the courts.

## Disability Discrimination and Assessments

Government regulatory agencies have targeted their concerns about AI-based assessments on the potential for discrimination against disabled job applicants and employees, both as to the accessibility of the technology used for disabled candidates and as to the concern that such tests may actually be preoffer medical inquiries, which are prohibited by the ADA.

*Reasonable Accommodation.* Under the ADA, employers must reasonably accommodate qualified employees or applicants with disabilities unless the accommodation would impose an undue hardship. Accordingly, employers must provide reasonable accommodations to qualified individuals with disabilities when using assessment technology. One way to meet or exceed this requirement is to ensure that web-based assessments conform to generally adopted accessibility standards. The Web Content Accessibility Guidelines (WCAG) are an international web content standard created by the World Wide Web Consortium. The WCAG "explain[s] how to make web content more accessible to people with disabilities" (World Accessibility Iniative, 2021). Similarly, the U.S. Government's Electronic and Information

Technology Accessibility Standards provide a standard to enable federal employees with disabilities to access and use information technology (36 C.F.R. § 1194; see also section508.gov/manage/laws-and-policies).

*Assessments as Preoffer Medical Examinations.* The ADA's prohibition against preoffer medical examinations has posed problems for a personality test with origins in medical diagnostics and could cause similar problems for neuroscience "games" or other assessments with diagnostic origins. In 1995 and 2000, the EEOC published enforcement guidance on pre-employment disability-related questions and medical examinations (EEOC, 1995, 2000). The EEOC identified eight factors that assist in determining whether a test constitutes a medical exam:

1. whether the test is administered by a health care professional or someone trained by a health care professional;
2. whether the results are interpreted by a health care professional or someone trained by a health care professional;
3. whether the test is designed to reveal an impairment of physical or mental health;
4. whether the employer is trying to determine the applicant's physical or mental health or impairments;
5. whether the test is invasive (e.g., does it require the drawing of blood, urine, or breath);
6. whether the test measures an applicant's performance of a task or the applicant's physiological responses to performing the task;
7. whether the test is normally given in a medical setting; and
8. whether medical equipment is used.

One circuit court and two district courts have considered whether a personality test is a prohibited preoffer medical examinations under this standard. In *Karraker v. Rent-A-Center* (411 F.3d 831 (7th Cir. 2005)), the U.S. Court of Appeals for the Seventh Circuit considered an employer's use of the Minnesota Multiphasic Personality Inventory (MMPI) with an employment-related scoring protocol for preoffer selections. The court found that it violated the ADA even though the employer did not use it for diagnostic purposes, because it had diagnostic origins and it would tend to screen out disabled individuals.

Two district court decisions pre-dating *Karraker* (see *Thompson v. Borg-Warner Prot. Serv.*, No. C-94-4015 MHP, 1996 WL 162990 (N.D. Cal. Mar.

11, 1996), and *Barnes v. Cochran*, 944 F. Supp. 897 (S.D. Fla. 1996)), on the other hand, focused on whether the employer used a psychological test for diagnostic purposes, rather than on the possible impact of the test, and found no ADA violation where the purpose was employment selection, not diagnosis. The district courts considered whether the test's origin is in medicine or is used for medical diagnosis, whether the test relies on medical use or validation in its scientific or marketing material, whether the test's impact on people with disabilities has been measured, and whether the test will screen out persons with medical conditions such as depression, anxiety, or attention deficit hyperactivity disorder.

In our professional opinion, the Seventh Circuit's decision in *Karraker* was wrongly decided, because it improperly conflated the ADA's antidiscrimination provision with the ADA's preoffer medical examination/disability inquiry prohibition and imported an adverse impact analysis into the preoffer medical examination question (Willner et al., 2016). Neither the text of the ADA nor EEOC guidance supports using an adverse impact analysis in considering preoffer medical examinations. Furthermore, applying a disparate impact analysis to the preoffer medical examination ban is contrary to the purpose of the statute and is generally impractical. Although *Karraker* was incorrectly decided, and courts have good reason to follow *Thompson* and *Barnes* instead, *Karraker* remains good law and employers, especially in the Seventh Circuit, should be mindful of it when choosing assessments with medical diagnostic origins or that may have the effect of excluding some individuals with disabilities, such as results from some personality tests and neuroscience "games."

## Privacy and the Use of Biometrics

Employers utilizing assessment technology must also be mindful that the use of biometrics is subject to additional legal requirements under state law. In Illinois, the Biometric Information Privacy Act (BIPA) "regulate[s] the collection, use, safeguarding, handling, storage, retention, and destruction of biometric identifiers and information" (740 ILCS 14/5(g)). BIPA defines biometric identifiers as a retina or iris scan, fingerprint, voiceprint, or scan of the hand or face geometry. Under BIPA, a private entity that processes biometric identifiers or information must develop and make public a written policy "establishing a retention schedule and guidelines for permanently destroying biometric identifiers and biometric information when the initial purpose for collecting or obtaining such identifiers or information has been satisfied or within 3 years of the individual's last interaction with the private entity, whichever occurs first (740 ILCS 14/5(a)). The private entity in possession of the biometric identifiers must comply with its retention and destruction guidelines. BIPA has led to extensive litigation challenging biometric practices in Illinois.

Arkansas, Texas, and Washington passed similar biometric privacy laws that employers should be aware of before using biometric information (see Ark. Code § 4-110-104; Tex. Bus. & Com. Code § 503.001; Wash. Rev. Code § 19.375.020). California adopted a comprehensive privacy statute, the California Consumer Privacy Act, that requires employers to issue notices to applicants and employees that describe the categories of information being collected, as well as how the information is collected, used, shared, and disposed of (Cal. Civ. Code § 1798.100). California is also considering a similar biometric privacy law, Biometric Information (SB 1189), that mirrors the Illinois BIPA.

## Conclusion

In summary, technology-based assessments certainly may promote fairness and efficiencies in the workplace. However, employers should be aware that nondiscrimination and validation requirements apply to them in the same way as to other assessments, and further that some states and localities have enacted notice and bias audit laws that specifically target algorithm-based assessments. Additionally, assessments with medical diagnostic origins such as personality tests and neuroscience games should be vetted for preoffer medical examination status.

## References

District of Columbia Office of Attorney General. (2021, December 9). *AG Racine introduces legislation to stop discrimination in automated decision-making tools that impact individuals' daily lives* [Press release]. https://oag.dc.gov/release/ag-racine-introduces-legislation-stop

Electronic Privacy Information Center. (2021, January 12). *HireVue, facing FTC complaint from EPIC, halts use of facial recognition* [Press release]. https://epic.org/hirevue-facing-ftc-complaint-from-epic-halts-use-of-facial-recognition

Equal Employment Opportunity Commission. (1995, October 10). *Enforcement guidance: Preemployment disability-related questions and medical examinations* (EEOC No. 915.002). https://www.eeoc.gov/laws/guidance/enforcement-guidance-preemployment-disability-related-questions-and-medical

Equal Employment Opportunity Commission. (2000, July 27). *Enforcement guidance on disability-related inquiries and medical examinations of employees under the Americans with Disabilities Act (ADA)* (EEOC No. 915.002). https://www.eeoc.gov/laws/guidance/questions-and-answers-enforcement-guidance-disability-related-inquiries-and-medical

Equal Employment Opportunity Commission. (2022a, May 12). *U.S. EEOC and U.S. Department of Justice warn against disability discrimination* [Press release]. https://www.eeoc.gov/newsroom/us-eeoc-and-us-department-of-justice-warn-against-disability-discrimination

Equal Employment Opportunity Commission. (2022b). *The Americans with Disabilities Act and the use of software, algorithms, and artificial intelligence to assess job applicants and employees.* https://www.eeoc.gov/laws/guidance/americans-disabilities-act-and-use-software-algorithms-and-artificial-intelligence

Harwell, D. (2019, November 6). A face-scanning algorithm increasingly decides whether you deserve the job. *Washington Post.* https://www.washingtonpost.com/technology/2019/10/22/ai-hiring-face-scanning-algorithm-increasingly-decides-whether-you-deserve-job

Lazzarotti, J. J., & Yang, R. (2022, April 25). *California draft regulations would curb employer use of artificial intelligence.* SHRM. https://www.shrm.org/resourcesandtools/legal-and-compliance/state-and-local-updates/pages/cal-draft-regulations-employer-use-of-artificial-intelligence.aspx

Mulvaney, E. (2021, December 29). *Artificial intelligence hiring bias spurs scrutiny and new regs.* Bloomberg Law. https://news.bloomberglaw.com/daily-labor-report/artificial-intelligence-hiring-bias-spurs-scrutiny-and-new-regs

Web Accessibility Initiative, Web Content Accessibility Guidelines (WCG Overview), https://www.w3.org/WAI/standards-guidelines/wcag/ (last updated Dec. 6, 2021).

Willner, K. M., Sonnenberg, S. P., Wemmer, T. H., & Kochuba, M. (2016). Workplace personality testing: Towards a better way of determining whether personality tests are prohibited pre-offer medical exams under the Americans with Disabilities Act. *Employee Relations Law Journal, 42*(3), 4+. https://link.gale.com/apps/doc/A471000388/AONE?u=anon~fa4baa47&sid=googleScholar&xid=aad31487

# SECTION 5
# ASSESSMENT FOR DEVELOPMENT

# 18
# Coaching-Centric Assessments
## Deep Data to Fuel Guided Growth

*Evan F. Sinar*

## Introduction

In this chapter, I focus on assessment applied to a development-centric coaching program and platform. As a form of talent assessment innovation, this application diverges from the use of assessment for hiring and promotion purposes in its use to exclusively guide development action rather than decision-making. I also will review important distinctions in the nature and breadth of the resulting assessment data and through the intricacies of the "coach in the loop" model such that an experienced, long-duration coach is in many ways an equal assessment stakeholder to organizations and participants. As organizations invest in data-driven talent analytics across the full breadth of talent management, developmental assessments can be both integral and incremental to other data sources, while also involving a unique set of deployment considerations and potential risks (Diaz & Young, 2021).

**Clarifying Terms and Definitions.** For the meaning of coaching, I use Jones et al.'s (2016) coaching definition: "a one-to-one learning and development intervention that uses a collaborative, reflective, goal-focused relationship to achieve professional outcomes that are valued by the coachee." I focus on external coaching (coach outside the organization), which is thought to be more effective because of the safe and trusting relationships it enables (Jones et al., 2018). I focus on virtual coaching (e.g., remote via phone or video), which can produce accessibility, convenience, and scalability advantages compared to in-person coaching (Ghods et al., 2019). As a subset of all such interventions, workplace coaching informed by psychological principles—such as the model discussed here—has accumulated consistent evidence for its positive impact on a range of work-related outcomes, including self-efficacy and goal attainment (Wang et al., 2022). Additionally, coaching appears to have restorative and preventative benefits on employee well-being in environments of high change and challenge (e.g., David et al.; 2016; Schermuly et al., 2020; Weinberg, 2016).

## Foundational Principles for Developmental Assessment

A primary goal for developmental assessments is to inform precision development, through configurability, modularity, versatility, and dynamism, with coaching a primary intersection point of psychometrics and individualized development planning (e.g., Passmore, 2012). Assessments are configurable to the degree that they can adapt, through either content or reporting, to a member's needs at any one point in time. Modularity allows for accumulation of data across a core set of measures, while enabling combinations to match differentiated experiences and choice paths across a broad swath of potential focus areas. Versatility over time and across purposes allows developmental assessment data to be revisited and reinterpreted through new lenses, informed though not governed by the needs of the organization, oriented instead toward the growth needs of the individual—that is, about where they can start and about where they go next. Dynamic assessments capture and account for changes in members' environment, circumstances, and goals—what are key changes, in work or life, that individuals are experiencing or anticipating? These assessments are created and sequenced to align to those changes and the accompanying needs they represent, paired with offerings and interventions to deliver timely and relevant behavioral interventions to members. These interventions are designed and researched to drive progression toward both long-term aspirations and short-term goals.

To serve as a sustained-impact growth engine, the model is heavily dependent on the data generated by assessments. For this data to function and be seen as credible, it needs to take into account the authentic space within which information is gathered—about skill standing, aspirations, and perceived barriers to growth. Securing this space, and the benefits it accords, is a particular strength for external coaching, with these coaches better able to create confidential, trusted, and psychologically safe relationships (Jones et al., 2018). Assessments are seen as a tool not just to inform how someone should be using the platform, but also to track and course-correct their progress along the way. The assessment experiences themselves serve as inducements to platform engagement by fulfilling members' ongoing

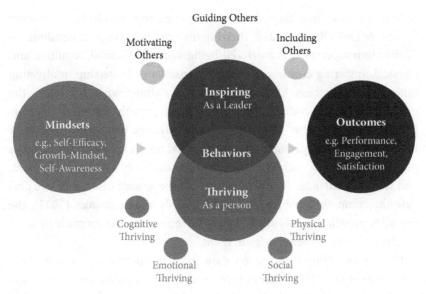

Figure 18.1. Whole Person Model used as the basis for coaching and assessment

expectations for receiving value and insight commensurate with their engagement with the program. Assessment data modeling is essential to the analytical foundations of the platform and coaching model, as key inputs to resource recommendations and to build a common mental model for personal and professional growth, incorporating both quantitative and qualitative data sources to surface information back to members, coaches, and, at the aggregate level, the organization (Graßmann & Schermuly, 2021).

## Content Model for a Whole-Person Assessment

BetterUp's Whole Person Model (WPM) serves as the content foundation for the assessment as well as the approach to personal growth described in this chapter. At its core, the WPM (Figure 18.1) is centered on the themes of thriving as individuals and inspiring as a leader. The WPM has four core components: mindsets, behaviors that promote thriving, behaviors that promote inspiring, and key personal and professional outcomes. Mindsets include key psychological resources and states (e.g., growth mindset, psychological capital) that can either propel members toward or via their absence hold them back from their development goals and aspirational outcomes (Fontes & Dello Russo, 2021). Thriving includes behavioral dimensions reflecting four aspects of personal well-being: social, emotional, cognitive, and physical. Inspiring consists of three dimensions of leadership: motivating others, guiding others, and including others—dimensions that reflect the extent to which individuals foster professional growth and greater performance in others, either formally or informally. The outcomes component includes a variety of personal and professional results impacted by the other model components, such as engagement, productivity, stress management, and work-life balance. Though the specific assessments discussed here predate the comprehensive review by Wijngaards and colleagues (2022), the overall approach is tightly aligned with the recommendations made by these researchers for well-being measurement.

In a recent study drawing on data from the platform discussed here (Jeannotte et al., 2021), these components show consistent and statistically significant elevation, with some variance in trajectories, alongside virtual coaching. More specifically, this research found the largest overall growth within the first 3 months of coaching for thriving components such as strategic planning, emotional regulation, and social connection; mindsets such as self-awareness and self-efficacy; and outcomes such as stress management. As the coaching relationship extends into the second 3 months, the WPM outcomes resilience, life satisfaction, and purpose and meaning show significant increases. As an alternative view of a representative set of results associated with use of this virtual coaching platform, for members who onboard to the platform at a relatively low standing on WPM components, respectively, aggregate results for mindsets, thriving behaviors, and inspiring behaviors indicate a 172% increase for self-awareness, 90% increase for social connection, 92% increase for emotional regulation, 77% increase for cognitive agility, 104% increase for coaching skills, and 54% increase for relationship building. For indexed outcomes, aggregate results for those starting low show a 35% decrease in burnout, an 83% increase in life satisfaction, a 149% increase in resilience, and a 114% increase in productivity.

As this approach is inherently development centric, the assessments focus on understanding and providing data about developable constructs. Information about these content components comes from the members themselves, based on their own perceptions of where they stand at onboarding (using scales capturing consistency and frequency of mindsets, skills, and outcomes) and at periodic reflection points utilizing an identical assessment with matched items. The model also incorporates a 360 assessment component, allowing others—peers, managers, and direct reports—to be observers and feedback providers. We include 360s alongside coaching to draw on the advantages conveyed by high-quality coaching to contextualize and generate action plans based on feedback received (e.g., Bozer & Jones, 2018; Luthans & Peterson, 2003). Developability is also reinforced by the coaching and platform, which pair assessment-derived data on strengths and growth areas with opportunities to practice, gain deeper awareness of, and pursue multimodal learning and development resources on these topics. We feel this degree of integration across both human and digital components of coaching is critical and comparatively distinctive in scale, while capturing via the assessments data representing a broad content model spanning member-provided and observer-rated inputs.

**Relationship to Common Leadership Models.** In many of our partner deployments, an initial phase involves a mapping between the WPM and existing competency models in the partner organization. This stage helps us confirm the relevance of the WPM and the associated assessments to an existing framework—in many cases, organizations are seeking to provide as much cohesiveness as possible, in both content and data, between existing competency models as the basis for other talent management tools and new frameworks, such as the one described here, for broad-scale workforce coaching. We've found the collective learnings from these mappings informative as a signal for the complementary and supplementary nature of the WPM and the assessment data it produces within the model. The relationship between these models is important because these patterns of overlap and incremental coverage demonstrate the innovative nature of the approach in terms of what's covered in the assessment and what outcomes in turn are potentially more strongly predicted through its use.

Summarizing our findings to date on the convergence and divergence between these models (also depicted in Figure 18.2), we've found that nearly all competency models (often created with a leadership population) included leader-related constructs such as encouraging participation, building relationships, and alignment, as well as execution-oriented constructs such as cognitive agility, strategic planning, and problem-solving. One tier down in prevalence, appearing in many or most models, are the constructs of coaching, authenticity, empathy, and focus. Rarely included in competency models—and the areas where the WPM assessment data is most incremental accordingly—are constructs relating to emotional well-being

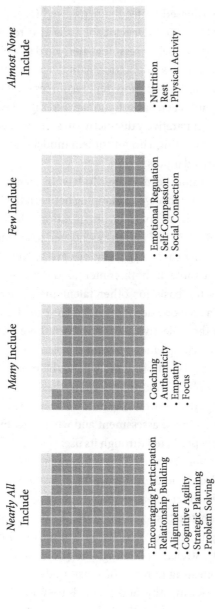

**Figure 18.2.** Whole Person Model components by frequency of inclusion in competency models

(e.g., emotional regulation, self compassion), physical well-being (e.g., nutrition, rest), and social connection. By including these otherwise unmeasured constructs in the assessment model, they generate additional prediction and outcome coverage for outcomes such as belonging, productivity, stress management, and purpose and meaning. Combined with information about key behavioral drivers of these outcomes, more actionability and ultimately more progression and advancement are produced for individual and organizational outcomes, by expanding the assessment (and coaching) apertures through approaches such as the WPM.

## Assessments Within a Coaching-Digital Resources Ecosystem

Assessments are used across the coaching and platform ecosystem, placed at various points and for various purposes within this model, to steer and shape two types of developmental interventions.

**Assessments and Human (Coach) Developmental Interventions.** Assessments inform coaches on key information about where a member starts as they onboard to the program—based on their scores on the whole-person assessment described above—and about how and to what extent they are progressing. Effective coaches are able to quickly establish a trusted relationship with members. The assessment gives coaches an initial grounding and common mental model for how to think and talk with members about growth and change and development. Self-report assessments such as that used at onboarding can also drive self-reflection (Duckworth, 2019) for members, giving them language and clarity they would have otherwise lacked, hindering awareness of and progression against growth needs. The assessments provide members with data in a framework that the coaches are well trained on and that they can in turn map to developmental guidance—the resources they suggest, and the actions they recommend. The assessment serves to catalyze and crystallize the initial relationship of a member with their coach (e.g., Passmore, 2012).

**Assessments and Digital (Platform) Developmental Interventions.** Assessments inform resource recommendations for members as they progress through the duration of their coaching engagement. Digital resources are automatically curated for them based on assessment data, and they can further explore a full resource library using the tagged association between the WPM and each piece of content. The platform also includes a nudging function to send more targeted and periodic assessments about platform satisfaction. Additional assessments either administered through coach assignment or selected by the member allow for resource recommendations to be refreshed, expanded, and refined. Assessment data is also available to members at any point they wish to access it to view their standing on constructs of interest to them.

A general usage pattern is for members to heavily emphasize in their coaching sessions the areas they're weaker on in their assessment profile: That is, those areas tend to be where they focus their resource engagement and where they focus their coaching sessions. As three representative examples of this pattern, members who begin low in coaching skills are 4.6 times more likely to pursue coaching as a topic with their coach, those who begin low in strategic planning are 4.8 times more likely to pursue strategic planning with their coach, and those who begin low in purpose and meaning are 14.0 times more likely to discuss finding purpose and passion with their coach, compared to those who begin high in those WPM components.

## Purposes of Assessment Within a Coaching and Developmental Application

**Measuring Change—Behavioral and Contextual.** The primary purpose of assessment in this model is to track change, growth, and impact. The data to do so initiates at the time a member onboards to the platform, with repeated measures of the same core assessment approximately every 3 or 4 months as a reflection point in the experience. The reflection point is triggered alongside a conversation with the member's coach, based on when it's most relevant and appropriate within a target range. The resulting information about change—typically growth though in some cases certain outcomes show declines if impacted by a personal change or circumstance, such as a shift to or from a remote working arrangement—generates an individualized report for the member; reflection individually and with one's coach on this report can be highly beneficial (Brockbank & McGill, 2012). This information is also reported to partners for their overall program, and it can be split by other parameters they use to define the population.

In addition to the average degree of change, we also research and report on growth for individuals who start particularly low relative to others on specific behaviors or outcomes. When that information is paired with a consistent finding (described above) that members seek out resources and coaching advice for growth needs rather than strengths, this view can provide a more representative perspective on expected growth through the program. Assessments after the member is onboarded to the platform—for example, at the 1-month point or following individual coaching sessions—also capture information about notable changes the member has experienced. The observed associations between member behavior change and intervening experiences fuel ongoing research into key moderators and mediators of key outcomes and are instructive for updating resource and learning recommendations drawing on these observed patterns.

**Gathering Manager Input on Growth Needs and Progress.** Supplementary to the assessments the member completes directly, additional assessments are completed by managers at the outset and approximately 2 months into the program. It's important to note that the manager component is optional and at the discretion of the member, to preserve the member's agency in whether and how they incorporate manager input into their coaching plan. Manager input into the plan is also available to members if they opt in to it. Managers can identify areas that they would like to see the member focus on to optimize their professional growth. Manager-specified growth areas include creating an inclusive work environment, aligning others around a clear strategy, and the ability to adapt to change. This information can then be used by members, if they so choose, in decisions and discussions with their coach on where to orient time and focus, in coaching conversations and on the virtual coaching platform. After the member has been using the platform for 2 months, the manager has the opportunity to provide quantitative feedback on these same areas, as well as qualitative input on what they've observed from the member as an outcome of the program.

**Gathering Peer and Direct-Report Feedback.** We have an initial emphasis on how the member is perceiving their own standing and growth to recognize the personal roots of behavior change. However, beyond self-provided data, other inputs can also be valuable to gauge when and how growth is occurring (Kochanowski et al., 2010). The platform includes a 360 assessment as an optional component to the assessment, as a purely developmental tool and focused on the components of the model that are observable. The 360 assessment collects quantitative and quantitative feedback about the WPM described above from peers, direct reports, and a member's manager. As a source of structured input beyond oneself, 360s are particularly valuable for coaching engagements in that they identify "blind spots," areas of self–other alignment, and underrecognized strengths (Bozer & Jones, 2018; Smither et al., 2003).

**Comparing to External Reference Points.** Though the primary metric for tracked change is within an individual member and over time, their assessment scores need to be placed into context. We do so by enabling assessment benchmarking comparisons with a broader working population to provide representative samples across industry, function, level, and other factors. These and other "like me" factors can make assessment information more relevant for members. The broader set of factors used within the platform includes target populations like new managers, underrepresented group members, and working parents, as well as those experiencing similar contexts—work pressures, life changes, promotions, and important transitions. This information in turn advances the underlying artificial intelligence modeling for the virtual coaching platform (e.g., Graßmann & Schermuly, 2021).

**Identifying Top Drivers for Key Personal and Professional Outcomes.** Assessment data is used in aggregate to identify the behaviors most strongly linked to key outcomes, such as productivity, belonging, and work-life balance. Assessment data—separated when assessments are administered, at the outset or during the coaching program—is the core of these models. This information is used as an interpretative lens on assessment data, drawing focus to the areas with the highest relevance to the outcomes targeted by the program. We use the link between assessments and outcomes to identify key behaviors and interventions that can drive someone toward a particular set of outcomes. At the individual level, this could be the link between the initial onboarding behaviors (where they start), how those in turn improve over time, and what are the key drivers of certain outcomes such as belonging, productivity, or resilience. Each outcome has a distinct combination of contributing behaviors; one such example is displayed in Figure 18.3 for the links between WPM and the outcome of resilience. For our partners, this information allows them to target the behaviors and skills that are most relevant, either through the virtual coaching program or through other talent systems.

**Assessment Impact on Group Coaching Experiences.** At the core of our model is assessment at the individual level. However, we think of the broader development space as including group interventions as well, either for intact teams or for those that share a common interest. Those common interests can

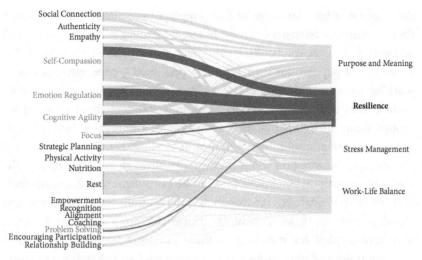

**Figure 18.3.** Whole Person Model components shaded/sized by relative influence on resilience

be surfaced and identified through use of the assessment—the assessment can be used to identify and potentially form groups and communities of interest around certain topics, generating a collective form of self-awareness and shared identity (e.g., Sutton & Crobach, 2022). Data from the assessment can also feed into the group discussions themselves. Across a group of members completing an identical assessment, when reported back to them this information can initiate discussion using the common language of the assessment, which can help members learn from and identify with others. Assessment data can also be valuable to a member in selecting the group coaching topic areas, based on development areas to remedy or strengths to leverage.

## Assessments to Drive Partner (Organizational) Value

Developmental assessments can add distinct forms of value to an organization's talent management strategy, with each form of value rooted in actionability and contingent on quality of the data surfaced to stakeholders.

**Diagnose the Needs of and Align With Key Employee Populations.** For many organizations, their adoption of a coaching and development platform is driven in part by the expectation of new layers of workforce assessment data—across a broader range of their employee population and providing more expansive construct coverage to target learning and growth-oriented action (e.g., Diaz & Young, 2021). This data can be particularly valuable for high-interest populations such as underrepresented groups, new managers, working parents, and remote or hybrid workers. Drawing on this information, they can gain a deeper level of understanding about where these groups stand on well-being, as one example of a domain receiving much stronger recent attention (e.g., Wijngaards et al., 2022). Though they may already have information about these groups through existing talent tools, the challenges these employees face can be both distinct and salient, such that more personalized development interventions may be necessary. Development-centric assessment data can enable programs to be designed and implemented for members of these groups, often guiding creation of communities of interest on relevant topics such as belonging and stress management.

**Bolster Group-Level Learning and Ownership/Accountability.** Developmental assessments can aid organizations in bolstering group- and cohort-level learning, as well as ownership and accountability surrounding the learning program itself. Examples include the degree of commonality of growth areas across an organizational function or target population and the correspondence between patterns in the assessment data and organization or group-level contextual factors such as coaching culture or perceived organizational support. By surfacing and learning from these relationships, organizations can be more precise in their time and resource investments in workforce support, reprioritizing allocations and reinforcing accountability systems as warranted.

**High-Authenticity Employee Sensing.** Information authenticity and veracity are hallmarks of well-designed systems for workforce data gathering (e.g., Macey & Fink, 2020). As noted above, communication to all parties about data use and sharing, primacy of member agency, and firm policies for privacy and security is critical. The model using individual coaches allows for data use for developmental purposes, while preserving a firewall for performance management or decision-making purposes. This information can provide an additional layering of annotation or understanding to other aggregated information about an organization's workforce from an employee engagement survey, as an example, or synchronized in time to other events occurring within the company.

## Assessments to Drive Coach Value

Developmental assessments provide value to coaches by strengthening, deepening, and elevating their role (e.g., Steele, 2021). In the case of the virtual coaching platform described here, members joining the platform expect and seek to confidently and rapidly progress into a deep, trusted relationship with their coach. One of their first conversations with their coach is to review their assessment data. As expert observers and interpreters of human behavior, coaches often surface new understanding about data patterns and their intersection with the individual's context, goals, and support systems. Assessments provide insights into where members stand on the mindsets and behaviors that are especially predictive of beneficial outcomes.

Assessments also stimulate ideas about areas to target throughout the coaching engagement and provide a cohesive framework to discuss behavior change and progress with members. Assessments are the mechanism by which coaches track member growth and progression. Assessments provide this regular reporting to show how a member is progressing or, in some cases, stalling in certain areas of growth or perhaps even stepping back. With that common over-time metric in mind, a coach will probe into why positive changes have occurred or why other forms of change have stalled. The common ground provided by the assessment data and framework removes noise and adds clarity to these conversations. This in turn allows the coach to emphasize the whys and hows underlying the data patterns and to recommend resonant and relevant next step actions.

## Risks and Recommendations for Assessment-Guided Coaching

In this final section, I discuss risks to and corresponding recommendations for the effectiveness of assessments in development and coaching-centric settings.

**Breaching Trust and Assessment Veracity via Data Misuse/Ulterior Purposes.** Threats to the trust and veracity of assessment data, due to poor communication, data misuse, or ulterior purposes, can rapidly degrade resulting value and utility. For members, a psychological contract for data use is in place not only implicitly about the context within which the information is gathered but also explicitly in messaging and expectation setting for how data will be used and shared. Lapsed or lacking attentiveness to this contract would compromise trust for those using the platform as a member or interpreting data from the assessments as a coach or organizational stakeholder. Clear and accurate communication about assessment data use both upfront and on an ongoing basis preserves the data "safe space" deeply underlying many of the benefits and differentiators for this information.

**Coach Not Considered an Equal Partner/Stakeholder.** In a scenario where assessment data is shared with and interpreted by a professional coach, this represents a distinct and critical stakeholder group, and one that is often absent from many prevailing assessment models prioritizing decisions over development. The role of the coach—to be committed to the assessment approach, to be thoroughly informed on its content framework, and to have a channel for feedback about these topics back to the assessment design and researcher teams—is extremely critical to this model. Importantly, this form of involvement extends not only to the coach role itself but also to any type of digital coaching provided through the platform supplementary to the direct human coaching. In our experience, coaches—expert observers of human behavior—can be key curators of assessment information as they have a deep understanding of the approach and draw on data to guide the recommendations they provide to members. Coaches are also often the first line of support and questions for members, through whom confidence in the assessment approach can be conveyed.

## Conclusion

By integrating assessment data with coaching relationships and a digital learning platform, organizations can draw on the complementary advantages of each to drive individual growth and organizational value. Assessment-infused coaching uniquely blends standardization with personalization, and scalability/workforce reach with participant engagement.

## References

Bozer, G., & Jones, R. J. (2018). Understanding the factors that determine workplace coaching effectiveness: A systematic literature review. *European Journal of Work and Organizational Psychology, 27*(3), 342–361.

Brockbank, A., & McGill, I. (2012). *Facilitating reflective learning: Coaching, mentoring and supervision.* Kogan Page Publishers.

David, O. A., Ionicioiu, I., Imbăruș, A. C., & Sava, F. A. (2016). Coaching banking managers through the financial crisis: Effects on stress, resilience, and performance. *Journal of Rational-Emotive & Cognitive-Behavior Therapy, 34*(4), 267–281.

Diaz, J. B., & Young, S. F. (2021). The future is here: A benchmark study of digitally enabled assessment and development tools. *Consulting Psychology Journal: Practice and Research, 74*(1), 40–79.

Duckworth, A. (2019). Self-reports spur self-reflection. *MIT Sloan Management Review, 60*(3), 14–16.

Fontes, A., & Dello Russo, S. (2021). What changes with coaching? Investigating within-person changes in reflection, the predicting role of implicit person theory and the effects on perceived utility of coaching. *International Journal of Training and Development, 25*(3), 316-340.

Ghods, N., Barney, M., & Kirschner, J. (2019). Professional coaching: The impact of virtual coaching on practice and research. In R. Landers (Ed.), *The Cambridge handbook of technology and employee behavior* (Cambridge Handbooks in Psychology, pp. 315–346). Cambridge University Press. doi:10.1017/9781108649636.014

Graßmann, C., & Schermuly, C. C. (2021). Coaching with artificial intelligence: Concepts and capabilities. *Human Resource Development Review, 20*(1), 106–126.

Jeannotte, A. M., Hutchinson, D. M., & Kellerman, G. R. (2021). Time to change for mental health and well-being via virtual professional coaching: Longitudinal observational study. *Journal of Medical Internet Research, 23*(7), e27774.

Jones, R. J., Woods, S. A., & Guillaume, Y. R. (2016). The effectiveness of workplace coaching: A meta-analysis of learning and performance outcomes from coaching. *Journal of Occupational and Organizational Psychology, 89*(2), 249–277.

Jones, R. J., Woods, S. A., & Zhou, Y. (2018). Boundary conditions of workplace coaching outcomes. *Journal of Managerial Psychology, 33*(7/8), 475–496.

Kochanowski, S., Seifert, C. F., & Yukl, G. (2010). Using coaching to enhance the effects of behavioral feedback to managers. *Journal of Leadership & Organizational Studies, 17*(4), 363–369.

Luthans, F., & Peterson, S. J. (2003). 360-degree feedback with systematic coaching: Empirical analysis suggests a winning combination. *Human Resource Management, 42*(3), 243–256.

Macey, W. H., & Fink, A. A. (Eds.). (2020). *Employee surveys and sensing: Challenges and opportunities.* Oxford University Press.

Passmore, J. (Ed.). (2012). *Psychometrics in coaching: Using psychological and psychometric tools for development* (2nd ed.). Kogan Page.

Schermuly, C. C., Wach, D., Kirschbaum, C., & Wegge, J. (2020). Coaching of insolvent entrepreneurs and the change in coping resources, health, and cognitive performance. *Applied Psychology, 70,* 1–19.

Smither, J. W., London, M., Flautt, R., Vargas, Y., & Kucine, I. (2003). Can working with an executive coach improve multisource feedback ratings over time? A quasi-experimental field study. *Personnel Psychology, 56*(1), 23–44.

Steele, C. (2021). Assessment in coaching psychology. In S. O'Riordan & S. Palmer (Eds)., *Introduction to coaching psychology* (pp. 66–77). Routledge.

Sutton, A., & Crobach, C. (2022). Improving self-awareness and engagement through group coaching. *International Journal of Evidence Based Coaching and Mentoring, 20*(1), 35–49.

Wang, Q., Lai, Y. L., Xu, X., & McDowall, A. (2022). The effectiveness of workplace coaching: a meta-analysis of contemporary psychologically informed coaching approaches. *Journal of Work-Applied Management, 14*(1), 77–101.

Weinberg, A. (2016). The preventative impact of management coaching on psychological strain. *International Coaching Psychology Review, 11*(1), 93–105.

Wijngaards, I., King, O. C., Burger, M. J., & van Exel, J. (2022). Worker well-being: What it is, and how it should be measured. *Applied Research in Quality of Life, 17,* 795–832.

# 19
# From Tried and True to Shiny and New

## Current Best Practices in Assessment for Development and the New Technologies That Will Soon Replace Them

*Matt Paese and Georgi Yankov*

Being a leader in today's world means facing continuous change. Being an *effective* leader means making oneself a part of that change and, more particularly, making changes to one's leadership approach as role requirements shift. Those changes are development—the personal and professional adjustments that leaders adopt as assignments become more varied, complex, and frequent over the course of one's career. The key question is, "Which changes (development) will yield the greatest benefit?"

Sadly, when left to their own judgment, many leaders make suboptimal choices. Witness the strikingly high failure rates among executives (Saporito & Winum, 2012), slow and unsuccessful transitions into new leadership roles (McGill et al., 2019), and steadily declining organizational bench strength (as rated by management) over the last decade (Gartner, 2019; Neal et al., 2021). As the velocity of change heaps unanticipated challenges on leaders at unprecedented speeds, the ability to maintain effectiveness becomes more elusive. Operating on their own, most leaders choose either no development or the wrong development as they progress. As one CEO put it to us, "No leader can succeed in every situation. If you do this long enough, eventually you'll learn what it means to fail."

On the plus side, however, there is evidence suggesting that high-quality assessment plays an important role in mitigating the risk of leadership failure by accelerating the speed and success of transitions into new roles, heightening self-reported energy for work, and increasing resilience (Devine & Nieuwstraten, 2021; Neal et al., 2021). Because human judgment (of self and others) is fraught with error, assessment is essential to enhance evaluation accuracy, calibrate language, sharpen self-insight, and guide change in the right direction. But not all assessment tools and methods are equal in this regard, and further, the design and application of assessments that support development are changing rapidly.

An important preview to the remainder of this chapter is that we outline two very different versions of how assessment enables development: the one in place today, and the one that is rapidly moving to supplant it. In the first part "Guiding Development: The Essential Roles of Different Assessment Methods," we outline the current state of assessment as it is applied to development. Many of these methods and approaches have been in place for decades, yet in practice they are far from ubiquitous. As more advanced assessment methods make their way onto the scene, these traditional methods remain important for research and practice.

In the second part, "How Technology Is Changing the Way Assessment Fuels Development," we look to a future whose contours are visible enough today that we can see dramatic transformation on the horizon. New developments in a series of technology arenas (e.g., artificial intelligence [AI]-powered systems, wearables, virtual reality) are creating exciting new pathways relevant to assessment, some of which are in use already and others which remain nascent and require more experimentation and research.

Our assertions, both in the summary of current practices and in our predictions for the future, are drawn from both research (as cited) and more than two decades of applied work across hundreds of organizations and many thousands of leaders across levels from front line to the C-suite. Assessment designers and participants alike will see shifts in the coming decade (or less, probably) that will render today's approaches antiquated. We briefly summarize the principal methods and uses of assessment for development in contemporary applications, after which we discuss emerging trends, technologies, and research that together will have sweeping impact on leadership assessment and how it is applied to enable and accelerate the growth of leaders.

## Guiding Development: The Essential Roles of Different Assessment Methods

**Simulations—for Developing Complex Skills.** Leadership simulations enable precise self-insight into complex skill sets because they allow for reflection and debrief on the specific, observed actions that participants take in response to one or more leadership challenges. As such, simulations are most useful for development when they are future oriented (i.e., when they sample leadership challenges with which the participant has little or no experience). Examples include:

- Challenging an individual contributor with the supervisory task of providing feedback to a direct report whose performance has begun to slip
- Asking a mid-level leader to construct a long-range business plan for a regional business unit (an executive-level responsibility)
- Tasking a senior executive with the CEO-level challenge of influencing several board members to gain alignment around a high-risk strategic investment

By placing participants into realistic yet novel leadership situations and reliably evaluating their responses (leveraging trained and certified assessors with consistent evaluation criteria), simulations produce rich insight into individual leadership behaviors and tendencies. Using well-defined behavioral competencies, participant responses are evaluated against "best practice" approaches, and via one-to-one feedback sessions, participants gain insight into how to navigate more complex leadership challenges.

Either as stand-alone exercises to target specific skills or combined to create a holistic experience to simulate an entire role (e.g., a full- or multiday executive experience with many different integrated scenarios), simulations allow leaders to "step into the future" and receive structured feedback as to how their leadership behaviors compare to the standards and expectations to which higher level leaders are held. This then enables thoughtful construction of development plans that target critical skill gaps and areas in which leaders can enhance skills before being placed into the role (Paese et al., 2016).

**Interviews—for Targeting the Right Experiences.** Unlike simulations, which are designed to reflect a leader's future, interviews seek to summarize a leader's past in ways that are relevant to the future. But like simulations, interviews also typically target behaviors, seeking to identify leadership patterns against behavioral competencies (such as decision-making, influence, and leading change).

By their nature, interviews anchor on prior leadership experiences, such as leading a significant organizational change, navigating a conflict with an internal partner, coaching a direct report through a performance challenge, re-engaging a demoralized team, or launching a new business unit. Skilled interviewers probe into these experiences to uncover patterns of behavior and areas of common emphasis (or de-emphasis). In this manner, interviews provide critical insight into both skills/competencies and key areas of experience that leaders may need to emphasize as they reach toward higher level roles and assignments.

Interviews are also essential in assessing leadership motivations and aspirations. While it is useful to add one or more inventories to achieve the best assessment of motivation (see below), interviews are a critical ingredient to understanding the values and aspirations of individual leaders and how development should be directed to capitalize on them.

Taken together, interviews enable the assessment of both past experiences and motivation that guides leaders toward essential new (i.e., untried) assignments that capitalize on their aspirations while enabling them to focus on skills (competencies) that they may need to enhance as they progress. In this manner, interviews offer a broad focus on competencies, experiences, and motivations in the development of leaders.

**Personality Assessment—for Shaping Mindsets and Self-Awareness.** While leaders can change their behaviors, cultivate new skills, and shape their experiences, personality will remain largely unchanged. And because these stable individual dispositions have direct influence on our behavior patterns and how we respond to new situations, understanding one's personality is crucial to development. More specifically, personality can be thought of as the moderator of behavior change, with some behavior patterns being more (or less) malleable based on one's personality. This moderating effect might be more pronounced at director and executive levels where leaders are more autonomous and less constrained by the work situations to express their personality characteristics (G. L. Stewart & Barrick, 2004).

Take, for example, a highly passionate, expressive leader. She is talkative, extroverted, and tenacious in pursuing her goals. She has succeeded with high energy, by motivating her teams, and with a tireless passion for getting results. As she progresses, she may find it relatively easy to grow into roles with responsibility for broader operational execution. However, she may struggle to master the more strategic, long-range planning that comes with wider scope of responsibility. Because her personality (ambition, achievement motivation, dependability) drives her toward speed, concrete action, and tangible evidence of progress, she may find it difficult to construct more forward-looking plans that will result in success beyond the current horizon.

This example highlights the integral connection between individual personality and leadership development. Because personality is complex and highly individualized, self-awareness is typically only partial at best, and the evaluation of others' personalities is fraught with even more error. As such, measurement of personality with the use of well-researched measures is invaluable. This includes both the enabling aspects of personality, such as calmness, openness to new experiences, and interpersonal sensitivity, and the aspects of one's personality that disrupt or "derail" leadership success, such as emotional volatility, arrogance, or extreme risk aversion.

Without an accurate understanding of personality, development can often be misdirected, or may take place without the essential enablers to facilitate growth (Day et al., 2014; McCormick & Burch, 2008). Our expressive leader mentioned above may find it challenging to develop strategic planning skill, but with a bit of formal learning about the structure of strategy and/or some one-on-one coaching through the construction of her first few strategic plans, we may find that she can be sufficiently adept to sustain effectiveness in larger roles (i.e., she may never be a "natural strategist," but she may be able to achieve the level of proficiency that her future roles require).

We note here that there are other trait-based measures of individual differences that can lend useful insight into the development of leaders. Among other psychological constructs, common measures assess emotional intelligence, cognitive or thinking styles, learning preferences, career aspirations, and/or work-related motivations and preferences. In our experience, however, well-researched personality inventories are the essential starting place for the understanding of stable individual traits and how they must be factored into leadership development.

**Multirater (360) Assessments—for Broadening Perspectives.** Multiperspective assessments rely on coworker input to gather feedback and can take the form of online surveys or direct interviews with colleagues of a target leader. For lower level leadership roles, survey-based methods are most common, while at senior executive levels, multiple coworkers may be interviewed by a professional assessor or coach who creates a report summarizing results. Either of these may be combined with other measures such as personality inventories to add insight and developmental value to the feedback.

Multiperspective feedback exposes variation between one's self-perception and those of other individuals or groups. Often, a leader's direct reports have very different observations than peers and managers, and these differences inform development. Direct reports may provide feedback on how a leader coaches, provides direction, or shares responsibility, while peers may call out opportunities for the leader to communicate more frequently to partners, and managers encourage the leader to spend less energy on short-term operations and more on long-range strategy. While unique, each perspective offers the leader meaningful ways to enhance performance moving forward.

## The Essential Role of Coaching in Building Self-Awareness for Leadership Development

To achieve the most accurate, in-depth understanding of leaders and to guide their development in the most beneficial ways, some use of all previously discussed methods is valuable. This is not to say that every development process must include each method. Rather, multiple methods will yield deeper insight, which in turn will fuel more well-informed, nuanced development action plans. This multimethod approach is particularly important to consider as leaders advance and roles become more complex (Paese et al., 2016). Front-line leader development may do well with one or another of the more scalable methods (e.g., brief online simulations, learning style inventories, competency self-evaluations), while executive development is most effective when all methods are leveraged to some degree.

This means that as leaders move upward into more advanced management and executive roles, the value and necessity of individualized coaching become essential to help translate assessment results, sharpen self-insight, anticipate new challenges, and construct actionable development plans. More complex role responsibilities combine with more complex assessment inputs, making it challenging for individual leaders to (a) glean the most important messages from assessment and (b) craft the right plans that will help them grow and develop in the most high-impact ways.

Coaches, who may be managers, peers, internal human resources experts, or external professional coaches, are crucial players in translating assessment into action. Skilled coaches, with experience in the performance space toward which the leader is developing, can help leaders to proactively evaluate their own leadership tendencies against the demands of new scenarios. And because past approaches are often insufficient for new challenges, this preemptive approach to development is crucial in preventing leaders from derailing.

Ultimately, leaders who make the best use of both assessment and coaching stand a far better chance of maintaining success as their leadership contexts evolve (Hunt & Weintraub, 2006). Combining self-insight with structured anticipation of future leadership challenges allows leaders to proactively practice and apply more effective behaviors and mindsets to the most complex leadership tasks. Over time, the practice of continuous self-reinvention enables leaders to become (and remain) part of the change in which they are engaged or are trying to lead.

And as change progresses, so too do the foundational assessment methods that are part of it. As foreshadowed earlier, our discussion so far represents only those "best practices" that characterize where the field has come to date. The field of assessment as it is applied to development is shifting rapidly and dramatically in ways that signal exciting new horizons for leaders and the professionals who seek to support them in their journeys of growth.

## How Technology Is Changing the Way Assessment Fuels Development

In the near future, we expect leadership assessment for development to avail and blend deeply with technological innovation. The process has already begun and can be observed in the rapid adoption of technologies targeted at improving our physical and mental health as well as workplace productivity. The global shipments of wearable health and wellness devices such as smart watches, wristbands, clothing, and glasses are expected to reach 320 million in 2022 and 440 million by 2024 (D. Stewart et al., 2021). Exoskeletons are now actively used to augment workers' strength in lifting objects in sorting and shipping jobs. Head-mounted virtual reality (VR) sets are being adopted for skills training outside of the military and medical fields. Futurists and software designers have introduced paradigm-shifting concepts and movements such *transhumanism, cognitive enhancement, intelligence amplification, quantified self* (Lupton, 2016), and *the internet of us* (Lynch, 2017). The most recent addition is the *metaverse,* which goes beyond the immersive physical rendering of VR and augmented reality (AR) and allows its users to interact and generate social meaning for themselves (Wang et al., 2022). Furthermore, our body can become the centerpiece of a cluster of technologies called the *internet of bodies* (IoB; Lee et al., 2020). In the IoB, smart wearable devices are implanted in our bodies (e.g., ingestible products, brain stimulation devices, microchip implants); they collect biometric data, send it over via the internet for analysis, and can potentially alter our body functions. Two major IoB applications could be to monitor health diseases and understand naturally occurring behavior.

We believe that in the best possible future scenario, technology has the potential to usher a humanistic agenda into the workplace. Human-centered technology is now equipped to provide workers with various career paths and options such as remote work arrangements, which have proliferated in the post-COVID-19 world. The pandemic has amplified this process and now many talented professionals are leaving jobs in search of remote work, work-life balance, and, in general, the personal actualization they seek. In other words, far fewer workers will be satisfied to adapt to the options provided by their employers. More likely, workers of the future will choose jobs that they deem to provide the resources for them to become the best versions of themselves, not simply to be the best employees or to make companies more profitable.

Technology has the potential to empower workers to create more happiness and productivity for themselves and, in this way, balance the bargaining power of employers. For the purposes of individual leadership assessment and development, technological offerings might evolve from the currently health-oriented tracking devices to intelligent AI-powered assistants. These will continuously track leaders' behavior in context and provide them with metrics and recommendations on how to improve their behavior to master a particular leadership skill. Also, a service can be provided to leaders where assistants connect them to the questions and needs of other leaders, especially leaders having the same current challenges. Such connectivity might spur the person-centric model of leadership development to evolve toward what has been called *team* or *swarm leadership*—a technological infrastructure of leaders learning from the intersection of ideas generated from networks of other leaders and machines (Kelly, 2019). With this form of leadership, instead of feeling alone at the top, new executive leaders will be able to gain insight from experienced executives in vastly more efficient ways. This interactive process might create a social facilitation effect for new leaders where constant contact with experienced leaders might stimulate faster learning and greater effort.

In the wake of these exciting technological advances, today's leadership assessment and development might appear to be nonautomatable, and the multimethod approaches discussed in the first part of this chapter may seem laborious and slow. Leadership assessment outside of high-volume preemployment testing (e.g., personality and cognitive instruments, biodata checklists) requires complex thinking and ample practical expertise to understand the specific skills and developmental challenges of each leader. In particular, leadership simulations require expert assessors, feedback providers, and coaches. This is especially true at higher level leadership where the leader operates in a distinct company context, faces unique dilemmas, and needs highly personalized development. However, the emerging technological infrastructure that will connect, track, and recommend behaviors may soon emerge as an accessible and efficient new way of assessing and developing nonexecutive leaders. It may be costly and take the usual adoption curve, but once set up, it could provide tremendous economy of scale when compared with the current human labor–driven approaches of assessment and development for more common skill deficiencies.

## Technology for Developing New Leadership Habits

Leadership development is facilitated by self-awareness, and self-awareness is also the basis for emotional intelligence (Hall, 2004). Self-awareness refers to fully knowing one's moods, emotions, and drives, as well as their effect on others. Presuming that leaders' self-awareness will improve simply by assessing their current self-awareness is, however, not optimal. Serving leaders with an assessment report stating that they need to develop their self-awareness does not guarantee that leaders will know how, or will do it at all. Thus, using current approaches, assessment (whether from a single measure or the multimethod approach described above) might yield a recommendation for a leader to monitor the emotional impact of their behavior on others—a challenging assignment to do successfully on one's own. In this scenario, actual developmental progress (i.e., change) would likely occur only with some form of one-on-one coaching.

Could technology automate basic development for self-awareness and other leadership skills by providing more direct, in-the-moment guidance? What if it were possible to capture voice and body positions during common leadership tasks that require social skills and understanding of people such as coaching, building partnerships, influencing, negotiating, and delegating? The emerging promise of technological assessment is to actively, on an ongoing, day-to-day basis, help leaders self-evaluate, change, adapt, and maintain their skills (Ruderman & Clerkin, 2020).

Currently, Microsoft Outlook users enjoy AI-powered insights and recommendations based on social networks, message history, or calendar appointments. These recommendations aim at improving basic leadership skills such as planning and organizing or delegating. However, automated, bespoke, and scalable training for psychological and leadership skills is still unavailable. Pioneering companies such as STRIVR and Talespin are developing this market through the promise of VR. We do not believe that we are yet at the stage of mass VR-ization, especially with a professional workforce spanning four generations. We also anticipate that the road to VR will go through a more widespread adoption of AI-powered supporting technologies. In fact, AI-powered skills coaching through mobile phones and push notifications has already arrived (Barney, 2018).

We believe that wearable and implanted devices will accelerate the current coaching revolution. For example, assume that a leader wants to develop their skills at coaching an angry employee. The leader's wearable device reports that their blood pressure, cortisol levels, and voice tone quickly rise at the beginning of the conversation (this is what we generally understand by assessment nowadays—episodically registering data and reporting it back to the leader). However, now imagine that the device turns on its "trainer mode" and suggests helpful in-the-moment strategies to help the leader navigate the scenario more effectively (e.g., take a breath, speak slowly, ask questions to allow the person to vent frustration). All the while, the leader's device compares how coaching is executed to a predefined set of psychophysical indicators and behavioral principles and reports back discrepancies to the leader.

Moreover, if the wearable device is paired with a VR infrastructure, coaching can then be practiced in a safe-learning environment where stimuli can be replayed and physiological responses carefully observed and reflected upon. For example, with VR, variables such as ethnicity, age, and body language of the coachee can be easily changed, enabling variations that could simulate a wide variety of challenges far more easily than currently available methods. Regardless of the delivery method, the key notion here is the immediate feedback loop from assessment to development, modification of behavior, and then back to assessment. This constant, personalized, and relevant feedback stands to increase leaders' self-efficacy and eventually boost intrinsic motivation (Burgers et al., 2015). This process is further facilitated by the fact that the device continuously assembles snapshot-like data from the leader while the leader continuously interprets and reflects upon newly received data and recommendations and reinterprets the old ones.

As Ruderman and Clerkin (2020) point out, technology can help leaders to understand psychophysical aspects of their leadership styles and skills that observers might not be able to observe or articulate. In this sense, leaders form a personalized feedback loop with technology and can oversee their own training and development. As devices become more sophisticated and "learn" leaders' patterns, they will be able to nudge and recommend context-relevant behaviors and help leaders set and persevere in their behavioral goals. Of course, device algorithms will need to encapsulate the tenets of our best known and most actionable models and theories (e.g., goal-setting theory, theory of planned behavior, self-efficacy theory, cognitive dissonance theory; cf. Oinas-Kukkonen, 2013), and adoption will be driven by cost, user experience, and, most notably, how specific their recommendations can be to the contexts in which leaders need development.

Imagine further that teams of animation artists, user experience designers, behavioral scientists, and software engineers blend their expertise and create leadership assistants that operate as smart training environments, delivered in a VR format. This reality may be close at hand. VR has been found effective for accelerating training and decision-making capabilities among health care, education, and industry workers (Alcañiz et al., 2018). Many leadership skills involve interacting with people, and VR could, through the application of instantaneous feedback loops, provide leaders with a safe environment to practice, fail, repeat, and learn.

This environment will be highly responsive and likely very engaging for leaders because VR devices (which are currently headsets) have the potential to collect behavioral and neurophysiological data. These data can be used as indicators of state- and trait-based psychological constructs. For example, cortisol levels have been used as indicators for stress, skin conductance for affective arousal, heart variability for emotional intelligence, eye tracking for decision-making and problem-solving, etc. (Alcañiz et al., 2018).

VR also promises increased immersiveness with human-like avatars whose facial expressions are in tune with their speech. VR avatars can be especially useful for leadership development in multicultural contexts because avatars can be easily customized to mimic the diversity in the workplace. The goal is to use VR for training and development by putting leaders in situations with which they have had very little exposure and in which they might make (and learn from) errors. Furthermore, avatars can be used to pose situations with increasing difficulty to the leader such as coaching an angry employee, resolving conflict between two avatars, or even delivering a speech to a disengaged workforce.

Eventually, we anticipate that VR will evolve beyond 2D rendering, and toward highly realistic 3D holograms. Steps in this direction are already being taken in the medical, education, and military fields. The wide adoption of a 6G network (with speeds 10 to 100 times greater than 5G) will enable use of extended reality (XR)—the combination of VR, AR, and mixed reality. The combination of these technologies creates the likelihood that avatar holograms will at some point become nearly indistinguishable from real humans. XR merges the physical and virtual worlds by allowing the user to manipulate objects and interact with avatars, just as if they were real. Interacting with these virtual humans may prove to be as engaging as interacting with real humans (Hill, 2014). We find it thrilling to imagine what assessment and development might be like when a real-life avatar assistant works with leaders to practice skills, evaluate progress, suggest changes, and enable leaders to relive what other leaders have experienced. It is at this point, we believe, that assessment and development will converge.

## Old Meets New: The Convergence of Assessment, Development, and Work

As technology enables more real-time diagnostics, feedback, and guidance surrounding individual leader behavior, the gap between assessment, learning, and performance will continue to close, inevitably leading to an environment in which devices strengthen leadership behavior as a matter of daily habit. This stands in stark contrast to traditional practices in which assessment, development, and workplace behavior are largely separate endeavors to which tools, technology, and people are continually applied to attempt to close the gap, with only limited progress—so far.

Does this foreshadow the end of direct human involvement in leadership assessment and development? We expect not. Rather, like so many aspects of progress in the modern era, augmented human functioning seems the more proximal and likely next phase. The trajectory of augmented leadership development and coaching seems likely to follow the pattern of other emerging technologies. Take, for example, self-driving vehicles. Many were surprised at the speed with which their viability was initially demonstrated. And this led to outsized expectations such as Elon Musk's now-discredited 2015 prediction that self-driving vehicles would be driving "anywhere" within 3 years. Clearly, the gap between viability and ubiquity remains large, and some now estimate that we may be decades away from the omnipresence of fully automated driving.

In the same way, technology-augmented leadership development will face challenges that stretch the current capacities of human ingenuity and limit the speed of widespread adoption. After all, someone will need to write the code that accurately interprets real-time human inputs and instantly recommends behavioral alternatives that are (or are perceived to be) superior to what leaders might have chosen on their own. In this sense, we speculate that the efficacy of leadership development technologies will be limited by the utility of the models and theories upon which they are developed. How will "correct" or "better" approaches be determined? From what criteria will algorithms derive their interpretations and recommendations, and how will we ensure the absence of unwanted bias or the reinforcement of behaviors that an organization may be working to change or eliminate? It may happen that leadership development technology will evolve through the application of neural networks (Satinover, 2002) in which the best leadership behaviors are "learned" by devices over time as opposed to being preprogrammed with the knowledge we believe leaders need.

The field has yet to solve for many challenges, and we have primarily been discussing the development of behavior. It seems likely, if not inevitable, that new technologies will follow the multimethod foundations discussed above and automate learning as it pertains to mindsets, dispositions, motivations, and the perspectives of others in guiding leaders to their ideal behavior patterns. We anticipate substantial change in these directions in the coming years and look forward to a world in which technology leaps from our longstanding practices into a realm of faster, better, more immediate guidance for leaders, and more progress and fulfillment among the people and organizations they lead.

## References

Alcañiz, M., Parra, E., & Chicchi Giglioli, I. A. (2018). Virtual reality as an emerging methodology for leadership assessment and training. *Frontiers in Psychology, 9,* 1658. https://doi.org/10.3389/fpsyg.2018.01658

Barney, M. (2018). *Artificially intelligent coaching has arrived.* Training Industry. https://trainingindustry.com/magazine/may-jun-2018/artificially-intelligent-coaching-has-arrived/#:~:text=When%20combined%20with%20a%20real,deep%20learning%20%E2%80%9Cflight%20simulators.%E2%80%9D

Burgers, C., Eden, A., van Engelenburg, M. D., & Buningh, S. (2015). How feedback boosts motivation and play in a brain-training game. *Computers in Human Behavior, 48*, 94–103. https://doi.org/10.1016/j.chb.2015.01.038

Day, D. V., Fleenor, J. W, Atwater, L. E., Sturm, R. E., & McKee, R. A. (2014). Advances in leader and leadership development: A review of 25 years of research and theory. *Leadership Quarterly, 25*(1), 63–82.

Devine, M., & Nieuwstraten, I. (2021). *Leadership transition coaching.* McGraw Hill.

Gartner. (2019). *How to build leadership bench strength.* https://www.gartner.com/smarterwithgartner/how-to-build-leadership-bench-strength

Hall, D. T. (2004). Self-awareness, identity, and leader development. In D. Day, S. Zaccaro, & S. Halpin (Eds.), *Leader development for transforming organizations* (pp. 173–196). Psychology Press.

Hill, R. W. (2014). Virtual reality and leadership development. In C. D. McCauley & M. W. McCall (Eds.), *Using experience to develop leadership talent: How organizations leverage on-the-job development* (pp. 278–304). Jossey-Bass.

Hunt, J. M., & Weintraub, J. R. (2006). *The coaching organization: A strategy for developing leaders.* Sage Publications.

Kelly, R. (2019). *Constructing leadership 4.0. Swarm leadership and the fourth industrial revolution.* Palgrave Macmillan.

Lee, M., Boudreaux, B., Chaturvedi, R., Romanosky, S., & Downing, B. (2020). *The Internet of Bodies: Opportunities, risks, and governance.* RAND Corporation. https://www.rand.org/pubs/research_reports/RR3226.html

Lupton, D. (2016). *The quantified self.* Wiley.

Lynch, M. (2017). *Internet of us: Knowing more and understanding less in the age of big data.* Norton.

McCormick, I., & Burch, G. S. J. (2008). Personality-focused coaching for leadership development. *Consulting Psychology Journal: Practice and Research, 60*(3), 267–278. https://psycnet.apa.org/doi/10.1037/1065-9293.60.3.267

McGill, P., Clarke, P., & Sheffield, D. (2019). From "blind elation" to "oh my goodness, what have I gotten into" . . . Exploring the experience of executive coaching during leadership transitions into C-suite roles. *International Journal of Evidence Based Coaching & Mentoring, 17*(1). https://doi.org/10.24384/atmb-dw81

Neal, S., Boatman, J., & Watt, B. (2021). *Global leadership forecast 2021.* Development Dimensions International. 10–11.

Neal, S., Rhyne, R., & Paese, M (2021). *CEO leadership report 2021: Global leadership forecast series.* Development Dimensions International.

Oinas-Kukkonen, H. (2013). A foundation for the study of behavior change support systems. *Personal and Ubiquitous Computing, 17*, 1223–1235. https://doi.org/10.1007/s00779-012-0591-5

Paese, M., Smith, A., & Byham, W. (2016). *Leaders ready now: Accelerating growth in a faster world.* DDI Press.

Ruderman, M. N., & Clerkin, C. (2020). Is the future of leadership development wearable? Exploring self-tracking in leadership programs. *Industrial and Organizational Psychology, 13*(1), 103–116. https://doi.org/10.1017/iop.2020.18

Satinover, J. (2002). *The quantum brain: The search for freedom and the next generation of man*. Wiley.

Saporito, T. J., & Winum, P. (2012). *Inside CEO succession: The essential guide to leadership transition*. Wiley.

Stewart, D., Lee, P., Bucaille, A., & Crossan, G. (2021). *Deloitte insights TMT predictions 2022*. Deloitte. https://www2.deloitte.com/content/dam/insights/articles/GLOB164 581_TMT-Predictions-2022/DI_TMT-predictions-2022.pdf?icid=learn_more_co ntent_click

Stewart, G. L., & Barrick, M. R. (2004). Four lessons learned from the person-situation debate: A review and research agenda. In B. Schneider & D. B. Smith (Eds.), *Personality and organizations* (pp. 61–85). Lawrence Erlbaum Associates Publishers.

Wang, F. Y., Qin, R., Wang, X., & Hu, B. (2022). MetaSocieties in Metaverse: MetaEconomics and MetaManagement for MetaEnterprises and MetaCities. *IEEE Transactions on Computational Social Systems, 9*(1), 2–7.

# 20
# Maximizing the Effectiveness of Assessment-Rich Leadership Development Programs

*Sarah Stawiski and Cynthia D. McCauley*

As organizations navigate increasingly complex and turbulent times, leaders at all levels are being stretched to think in new ways, to be flexible and resilient in the face of uncertainty, and to collaborate across the organization (and beyond) to create needed change. An important component of a leadership strategy for dealing with these challenges is leadership development interventions that engage leaders in a deeper understanding of their strengths and weaknesses in this new context and that motivate and equip them to grow beyond current capabilities. One such intervention is an assessment-rich development program.

An assessment-rich leadership development program embeds an in-depth assessment and feedback experience within traditional elements of leadership development programs: content on effective leadership, a cohort of fellow learners, facilitators who support active inquiry, and short-term coaching. Sometimes called feedback-intensive programs, these interventions create a challenging yet safe environment for individuals to closely examine themselves as leaders and identify important next steps in their development (Conger, 1992; King & Santana, 2010). The broad goals of these programs are to deepen self-awareness, motivate self-improvement efforts, and launch action plans for enhanced effectiveness in leadership roles.

Assessment-rich development programs are grounded in a diverse body of research that documents the positive relationship between self-awareness and both performance in organizations (e.g., creativity, leader effectiveness, and career progression) and helpful behaviors and attitudes (e.g., feedback

Table 20.1 Types of Self-Awareness and Corresponding Assessments

| Type[a] | Examples | Relevant Assessments |
| --- | --- | --- |
| *Inner Self:* aspects of self not directly visible to others | Beliefs, traits, emotions, physical sensations | Personality, values, complexity of thinking, physiological indicators |
| *Visible Self:* physical or behavioral manifestation of self | Physical appearance, behavior | Observations of own behavior, artificial intelligence–aided assessment of communication, sociometric badges |
| *Social Self:* how aspects of self are seen or interpreted by others | Others' observations of behaviors, others' perceptions of skills and abilities | 360 feedback, real-time feedback from fellow participants, assessments by trained observers |

[a] See Chon & Sitkin (2021).

seeking, goal setting, and citizenship behavior; Chon & Sitkin, 2021). The "assessment richness" of these programs is achieved first by including a variety of assessment methods aimed at increasing three key dimensions of self-awareness: the beliefs, emotions, and physical states of the inner self; the visible behavior of the external self; and the social self as seen through the eyes of others (Chon & Sitkin, 2021). These programs are also designed to foster a deeper understanding of how these three aspects of the self are interrelated and how they impact one's effectiveness in leadership roles. Given that assessment-rich development programs are well established and have been implemented for a wide range of leader populations, there is a considerable knowledge base about what makes them effective.

## Assessment-Rich Development Programs in Practice

Although many leadership development programs make use of personality measures and 360 feedback surveys, assessment-rich development programs use multiple assessment methods to increase awareness of the inner self, the visible self, and the social self (see Table 20.1). These programs are also designed to help participants integrate and make sense of these assessments as a whole, reflect on their implications for continued development as a leader, and plan and implement a focused development plan.

## Inner Self

Self-report personality assessments are regularly used to help leaders understand their typical patterns of thinking, feeling, and acting. These assessments of the inner self are used to help leaders better understand how their natural tendencies and ingrained preferences may differ from and impact others with whom they work. For example, extraverted leaders may better understand how their tendency to be assertive and talkative can help them gain exposure for their ideas yet may cause more introverted colleagues to be increasingly reserved, thus reducing feedback and access to diverse thinking. In this way, personality assessments can help leaders understand how to both make use of their natural tendencies and adjust their behaviors to the needs of others.

Because leaders face increasingly complex environments as they move up management hierarchies and as they deal with turbulent environments, assessments of an individual's ability to think in complex and systemic ways are making their way into leadership development programs (Heaton, 2021; Petrie, 2015). These assessments help participants to understand how their habitual ways of thinking are being challenged and to recognize the growing edge of their mental models. With access to the data from these assessments, facilitators are also better equipped to customize the kind of developmental support each participant needs.

The increasing complexity and turbulence of leadership work is also stimulating growth in assessments focused on the leader's physical and psychological well-being. Such assessments range from self-reports of physical symptoms related to health to a full professional health and fitness evaluation. Digital technology in particular is making it possible for individual leaders to monitor physiological signals associated with stress, thus increasing their awareness of what triggers stress reactions and their ability to modify reactions (Ruderman & Clerkin, 2020).

## Visible Self

Developing greater awareness of the visible self has typically been achieved in leadership development programs by watching or listening to recordings of oneself in action. The recording may be of a role play (e.g., delivering negative feedback, influencing a colleague) or a group exercise (e.g., solving a problem, generating new ideas). Often a behavioral checklist or framework directs attention to the presence or absence of positive or negative actions. Individuals can also engage in self-assessments in real time, for example, noting the number of times they interrupted others during a group discussion or checked in with their direct reports during the day. In comparing the visible self with standards of effective behavior, participants are motivated to reduce the discrepancy by engaging more regularly in effective behaviors (Higgins, 1987).

As with the internal self, technology is expanding opportunities to assess the visible self. Technology now facilitates the assessment of written and verbal communication skills, for example, providing feedback on writing tone, persuasive impact, and inclusiveness of communication (Diaz & Young, 2022). Sociometric badges can assess patterns of interaction by tracking proximity to others, conversational time, and vocal features (Kim et al., 2012).

## Social Self

One of the most widely used assessments of the social self in leadership development is 360 feedback, which provides an assessment of an individual's leadership competencies from bosses, peers, and direct reports. We have found that this feedback is one of the most anticipated features of a development program. In one internal study of a program for front-line leaders, 85% of the participants noted that the 360 assessment data contributed positively to the impact they experienced from the program to a great or very great extent.

In addition to 360 assessments, development programs use trained observers to assess leadership skills and behaviors displayed in role plays, group exercises, and simulations. These programs may also include structured processes for participants to give feedback to one another on behaviors they observe and the impact of those behaviors. Since leadership is a social process, awareness of how one is viewed and experienced by others is particularly important for identifying ways to become more effective and in motivating efforts to improve. Feedback from others also encourages the perspective taking needed to see the world from another's point of view.

## Case Example: Leading for Organizational Impact Program

One of the Center for Creative Leadership's (CCL's) long-standing assessment-rich development programs is *Leading for Organizational Impact (LOI)*, a 5-day program designed for senior managers who lead organizational functions or divisions. Any leader at the appropriate organizational level can enroll, and therefore, program cohorts are composed of participants from a wide range of organizations and industries. The development goals of the program include improving self-awareness, strategic thinking and acting, working across boundaries, and influencing across the system.

### Assessment Practices in Leading for Organizational Impact

On the first day of the program, participants receive the results of a Big Five personality measure. They have time to reflect independently on their personality profile and share their reflections with another participant. The intention is to help leaders understand their underlying traits and how those traits can impact their behavior and effectiveness in leadership roles. Participants are also encouraged to pay attention to how their personality traits are playing out throughout the upcoming simulation.

The centerpiece of the program is an intense behavioral simulation called Looking Glass—so named because the simulated setting is a glass manufacturing company and because the simulation's ultimate purpose is to enable participants to better see themselves in action. While the simulation occurs on Day 2 of the program, the participants are preparing for (Day 1), debriefing (Day 3), and reflecting (Days 4 and 5) on the simulation throughout the week. The simulation places participants in roles ranging from president to plant manager in the Looking Glass Company, which is organized into three divisions. The participants enter their roles by reading company reports, job descriptions, and a role-specific set of emails they have recently written or received. Within these interrelated "in-baskets" are more than 150 problems, varying in strategic importance and often requiring collaborative action. The next day, participants are instructed to run the company for 6 hours. Working in an office-like setting, they hold meetings, drop in on each other, write emails, read, and plan, "as the spirit moves them and the other participants allow them" (Drath & Kaplan, 1984). Much of the interaction in the simulation occurs within the three divisional groups. A program facilitator is assigned to each of these groups to observe and record what they see happening, with particular attention to each participant's consistent patterns of behaviors and demonstration of personality traits.

A postsimulation questionnaire allows participants to assess their internal motivation (i.e., energy and engagement) and emotions (i.e., times they were disappointed or proud) during the simulation. The questionnaire also asks participants about the specific visible actions they took related to the various problems embedded in the simulation and to evaluate the performance of their division as a whole and of each divisional member. A summary of the questionnaire data serves as a starting point for debriefing the simulation experience with their facilitator in divisional groups.

The debriefs start by examining the division as a team—its results and the individual and collective actions that impacted those results. In a second debrief, the focus is on the behaviors of individual team members. Using a structured process, each individual summarizes how they performed in the simulation, giving attention to both strong and weak points. The individual then hears how each of the other team members viewed their performance. The facilitator manages the process and adds their own observations. Prior to beginning this session, norms are established and participants are given time to prepare valuable feedback.

The final piece of assessment data that participants receive is a 360 feedback report based on ratings from their manager, peers, and direct reports. The feedback focuses on 13 competencies particularly relevant for leaders at their organizational level, including executive communication, strategic perspective, and self-awareness. The participants are encouraged to look for connections between the simulation-based feedback and the feedback from at-work colleagues. The 360 feedback is not reviewed until Day 4 of the program so that fellow participants are not influenced by this feedback, allowing for the simulation-based feedback to be independent from the at-work feedback.

The participants are given time to reflect on and consolidate what they have learned about themselves as leaders during the program. They are then guided through a process for setting specific goals and action plans for changing behaviors and enhancing leadership capabilities, supported by the program facilitators and fellow participants.

From time to time, a CCL program will experiment with emerging assessments to both collect research data and evaluate their benefits for

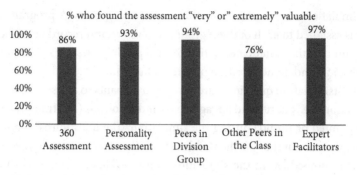

**Figure 20.1.** Participant Ratings of Each Type of Assessment in LOI

program participants. For example, VoiceVibes, an artificial intelligence–based assessment of an individual's vocal characteristics and delivery, was recently used in LOI to assess the speeches given by participants who were interested in being chosen (by election) for one of the top two leadership positions in Looking Glass. Those who were assessed as more likely to make a good first impression through their vocal delivery were more likely to be elected (Truninger et al., 2021), which demonstrated the potential value of this type of real-time assessment and feedback for leaders.

## Evidence of Program Effectiveness

As with all of our leadership development programs, in evaluating LOI programs, we examine multiple data points to determine their impact on the individuals and the groups they lead (Stawiski et al., 2020). First, as seen in Figure 20.1, all types of assessments are rated favorably by LOI participants, with the vast majority rating each type as very or extremely valuable. Further, the quality of feedback from both peers and expert facilitators is very high, with more than 90% agreeing or strongly agreeing that they respected the opinions of the observers, the feedback was useful, and the observers were considerate of the leaders' feelings.

Second, using a dataset of 1,200 participants collected 3 months after they completed LOI, we found that, on average, leaders reported modest improvement in all impact areas assessed. The three outcomes with the highest percentage of leaders (80% or higher) reporting improvement were awareness of the impact of their behavior on others, ability to use feedback to make changes, and readiness for leadership responsibilities. Additionally, 83% reported they had made at least some progress on goals and 14% reported they had made significant improvement following the development program. The leaders also commonly report impact extending to the teams they lead, with more than 70% of program participants reporting improvement in the teams' openness to diverse perspectives, overall management capabilities, and cross-boundary collaboration.

Finally, and potentially most compelling, participants' colleagues also notice postprogram improvements. Using data from more than 10,000 raters, we see results that are very consistent with the leaders' reports. Some of the commonly reported areas of improvement by leaders' managers are confidence in leadership, managing performance, and managing a team.

## Programmatic Design Elements That Maximize Effectiveness

Of course, not all assessment-rich development programs are going to be equally effective. Based on research and experience, this section highlights some of the design elements that can improve the impact of an assessment-rich development experience.

### Embedding Assessment Within Challenge and Support

Assessment works best when surrounded by two other key elements to development: challenge and support (McCauley et al., 2010). Challenge refers to placing people in situations that require new skills or approaches to navigate. Support refers to helping people handle the struggle and pain of developing and helping them maintain a positive self-view even though they may feel like they are failing at times.

During a development experience, this may entail receiving assessment data and then taking on a leadership role in a high-pressure simulation while being encouraged by a facilitator, other leaders in a program, or a professional coach. Designing programs around "table groups" (i.e., small groups of participants who interact in person or virtually throughout the program) challenges leaders to practice new behaviors with one another and receive feedback and support from peers and a trained table group facilitator. The rapport and trust needed in a learning group quickly develop. One possible downside of gaining self-awareness is rumination about weaknesses, which points to another reason that support is so critical (Chon & Sitkin, 2021).

## Establishing Psychological Safety and Trust Among Participants

Similar to providing support, leaders who are receiving feedback via assessments should do so in an environment that is psychologically safe (Fleenor et al., 2020). This typically involves ensuring that someone who has expertise in the assessments is present to help leaders interpret the feedback they are receiving and answer questions without judgment. Trust can affect how open a leader stays to the feedback, how credible they find it, and how much they are willing to curiously reflect and consider what they can do differently in their leadership practices. For this reason, allowing leaders total control over who they share their assessment data with, as well as not mixing leaders in groups with their direct reports or managers, can be particularly helpful.

## Triangulating and Integrating Insights From Multiple Sources of Data

Triangulation from multiple sources such as expert coaches, workplace colleagues, and peers in the program helps to reinforce feedback messages. As one participant in the LOI program commented, "In the beginning, I was seeking feedback from the facilitator but by the end the feedback from peers was most impactful." Feedback about a particular behavior from a difficult boss may sink in differently if the same thing is heard from a trusted peer.

Another way to increase the effectiveness of assessment-rich development programs is to build in time for leaders to reflect on and integrate what they are learning—for example, after a leader receives assessment feedback from colleagues, allowing some time for the individual to step back and think about what is most surprising or most consistent with their own perceptions. Then, as new assessment data is received, leaders should be encouraged to "connect the dots" and think about how the new information aligns or does not align with the previous data.

## Incorporating Goal Setting and Development Planning Into the Experience

Insights from the assessments are valuable for increasing leaders' self-awareness, but whether those insights translate into taking action or actual change is determined in part by whether the leader sets specific development goals. One strategy commonly used during an assessment-rich program is to have participants bring a Key Leadership Challenge, that is, an existing project or challenge that requires new approaches to be successful (Young et al., 2016). They can practice applying insights from their assessments to this challenge and can work toward setting specific postprogram goals for addressing the challenge. Facilitators and coaches can guide leaders to set goals that are Specific, Measurable, Achievable, Relevant, and Timely (SMART). In addition to just setting a goal, there is evidence that writing the goal down, sharing it with others, and having an accountability partner can each add to the likelihood of achieving the goal (Locke & Latham, 1984).

## Postprogram Support and Accountability

Accountability is a critical element of any feedback process (Bracken et al., 2016). Accountability and support go hand in hand; thus, many of the strategies that are useful for providing support can be useful for providing accountability, and vice versa.

Coaching is one way to support leaders' development and hold them accountable after an assessment-rich development program. We analyzed data from 685 leaders who completed a development program that included multiple assessments (360, live, and personality). Of those, 91% participated in an optional postprogram coaching session. Those who participated were rated higher by their managers on every item that measured program impact (Raper, 2020).

Other examples include formally identifying at-work learning partners (Reinhold et al., 2015), follow-up sessions to discuss goals with a manager, and technology-enabled tools. For example, CCL has recently developed the Everyday Leader Learning Assistant (ELLA), a personalized leadership development tool that provides leaders with advice, short developmental experiences, and other resources. The tool is designed to help leaders translate the insights from their assessment experience into concrete action steps back in the workplace. Early data suggest that when made available, leaders do leverage this tool to seek advice, and user feedback suggests that on-demand availability is the most helpful aspect of the tool. More research is needed to better understand the impact that tools like this can have on leaders.

Finally, measuring a leader's progress after an assessment-rich development program can also help with accountability. One tool we routinely use is the Reflections Assessment. This assessment is designed to be administered 3 to 6 months after completing a development experience and measures behavior change and individual- and group-level outcomes. It provides leaders with quantitative feedback and written comments by their designated raters about how they have or have not improved in their leadership. User-driven feedback tools can also provide leaders with real-time feedback from others about their leadership behaviors. These tools are typically much shorter and more targeted than 360s and give leaders control around the type of feedback that would be most helpful for them.

## Individual Leader Factors That Maximize Effectiveness

### Individual Readiness for Feedback

Research suggests that individuals high on leader developmental readiness experience the largest gains in leadership development outcomes (Reichard & Beck, 2017). One aspect of leaders' readiness is how well prepared they are for a development experience. This includes basic things such as what they know about the program and the assessments being used, whether they understand the purpose of the program and are clear on logistics, and how seriously they take the assessments they are completing. Further, participants should be encouraged to start thinking about and engaging in conversations about their development goals prior to the development experience officially beginning (Reinhold et al., 2015).

Another aspect of leaders' readiness for the feedback is whether they are open and motivated to learn more about themselves as leaders, even if the feedback may be difficult to hear. Van Velsor and Musselwhite (1986) outline four situations in which managers are better able to listen to feedback from others and learn. One situation, career transitions, refers to whether a leader has recently taken on a new job such as becoming a new manager.

The authors caution, though, that leaders may not be fully ready in the early months of their new role since they are inundated with new learning. A second situation is a midlife crisis. This is a time where people often experience self-doubt and are particularly open to personal re-examination. They may be eager to learn something new about themselves that will help them navigate this phase of their lives. The third and fourth situations are when a leader is experiencing decreased satisfaction or organizational stress. These leaders may be open to identifying opportunities to lead differently in the hopes of decreasing stress and dissatisfaction.

## Commitment to New Behaviors and Goal Achievement

One factor in how committed a leader is to integrating feedback, setting goals, and trying new leadership behaviors is their level of self-efficacy. Leader developmental efficacy is one's belief in their ability to develop leadership knowledge or skills and is associated with an increase in leader efficacy following a leader development program (Reichard et al., 2016). Recently, we have begun analyzing data from a sample of 509 leaders who attended various leadership development programs in 2021. In this sample, 81% report feeling confident in their ability to achieve their goals 8 weeks postprogram to a great or very great extent. Among these highly confident leaders, 90% reported improvement in leadership effectiveness. In contrast, among the leaders who were only somewhat confident, only 63% reported improvement in leadership effectiveness.

In addition to self-efficacy, taking action is also an important aspect of commitment. Using the same data set described previously with 1,200 leaders who completed LOI, we found that leaders who experienced the most postprogram progress are more likely to have proactively applied insights from their learning experience compared to leaders who experienced less progress. More specifically, 70% of leaders who were very successful in goal achievement took every opportunity to integrate what they learned, compared to 53% of leaders who were somewhat successful in goal achievement.

## Organizational Factors That Maximize Effectiveness

Development program goals are more achievable in organizations where there is a strong climate for development, that is, where opportunities for development are readily available and employees are encouraged and expected to learn and grow. This belief in the value of employee development is reflected in the priorities of senior management, in what gets tracked and rewarded, and in human resources practices (McCauley et al., 2010).

The elements of a developmental climate that are particularly important for maximizing the effectiveness of assessment-rich development programs include:

- Managers who have the skills and motivation to develop their employees. These managers ensure that employees use their program experience to articulate development goals, gain access to stretch experiences and ongoing feedback for enhancing targeted skills, and are tracking their progress (Young et al., 2017).
- Easy access to learning and development resources that support goal achievement. Advances in technology are making available a wide range of tools that help employees keep their development intentions front of mind, seek immediate feedback on their efforts to practice new behaviors, and get access to advice and support when they encounter unexpected challenges (Diaz & Young, 2022).
- Performance management systems that emphasize development. Such systems do not just focus on performance goals but require the setting and tracking of development goals and reward employees for achieving those goals.
- Regular conversation in the organization about learning and development. In a strong development climate, teams regularly reflect on what they are learning and how they can improve. Senior managers openly communicate about their own development goals and progress. This focus on and openness about development make it a normal and expected part of organizational life.

## Future Directions

Assessment-rich development experiences that consider best practices in program design, leader selection and preparation, and organizational factors are well positioned to be effective. Innovation in assessment is also critical, as is the need to continue to explore what works best. Emerging issues that will continue to shape research and innovations include virtual development experiences, emerging technologies for assessment, and the changing world of work and expectations of leaders.

The COVID-19 pandemic sparked a sharp turn toward more virtual leadership development experiences. A meta-analysis of leadership training (Lacerenza et al., 2017) had reported that face-to-face training tended to outperform virtual training. However, the pandemic necessitated significant investment in the training industry to improve the quality of virtual learning experiences. Reviewing our own data from thousands of leaders in 2021 and 2022, we have early indications that participants can still have a positive and impactful assessment-rich development experience in a virtual setting. However, more work is needed to better understand how these experiences compare to face-to-face experiences and how to best create the conditions for success for assessment-rich development in a virtual environment.

The technology available to assess leaders is also evolving every day. For example, wearable assessments can measure more aspects of the inner self, such as emotions and mood, while providing real-time coaching (Diaz & Young, 2022). Facial expression software is being used to track emotions and arousal, and eye-tracking technology is being used to assess task- and relationship-oriented leadership skills (Parra et al., 2021), just to name a few examples. With all of the potential for improving assessment-rich development for leaders, a lot is still unknown about challenges that we will face in trying to maximize the effectiveness of these emerging technologies.

Finally, the contexts in which leaders are operating are constantly evolving, being shaped by numerous factors, including technological, demographic, sociopolitical shifts, and other major world events. Much has been written about the impact of the global pandemic and how it has required leaders to demonstrate agility, resilience, and crisis management in the face of constantly changing conditions. This, along with other changes in the way we work, may necessitate new ways of using assessment-rich development to help leaders grow in new ways.

There are numerous avenues to explore with assessment-rich development, far more than the few outlined above. Assessment-rich development experiences have the potential to be highly impactful for leaders, but consistent, ongoing measurement of effectiveness is critical. Doing so allows us to differentiate which of the "cutting-edge" approaches are truly helping leaders gain new insights about their inner, visible, and social selves, and what this means for how they lead.

# References

Bracken, D. W., Rose, D. S., & Church, A. H. (2016). The evolution and devolution of 360° feedback. *Industrial and Organizational Psychology: Perspectives on Science and Practice, 9*(4), 761–794. https://doi.org/10.1017/iop.2016.93

Chon, D., & Sitkin, S. B. (2021). Disentangling the process and content of self-awareness: A review, critical assessment, and synthesis. *Academy of Management Annals, 15*(2), 607–651. https://doi.org/10.5465/annals.2018.0079

Conger, J. A. (1992). *Learning to lead: The art of transforming managers into leaders*. Jossey-Bass.

Diaz, J. B. B., & Young, S. F. (2022). The future is here: A benchmark study of digitally enabled assessment and development tools. *Consulting Psychology Journal, 74*(1), 40–79. Advance online publication. https://doi.org/10.1037/cpb0000201

Drath, W. H., & Kaplan, R. E. (1984). *The Looking Glass experience: A story of learning through action and reflection*. Center for Creative Leadership.

Fleenor, J., Taylor, S., & Chappelow, C. (2020). *Leveraging the impact of 360-degree feedback* (2nd ed.). Berrett-Koehler.

Heaton, L. (2021). Sense-making in a VUCA world: Applying vertical development to enhance learning agility. In V. S. Harvey & K. P. De Meuse (Eds.), *The age of agility: Building learning agile leaders and organizations* (pp. 401–423). Oxford University Press.

Higgins, E. T. (1987). Self-discrepancy: A theory relating self and affect. *Psychological Review, 94*(3), 319–340.

Kim, T., McFee, E., Olguin, D. O., Waber, B., & Pentland, A. (2012). Sociometric badges: Using sensor technology to capture new forms of collaboration. *Journal of Organizational Behavior, 33*(3), 412–427. https://doi.org/10.1002/job.1776

King, S. N., & Santana, L. C. (2010). Feedback-intensive programs. In E. Van Velsor, C. D. McCauley, & M. N. Ruderman (Eds.), *The Center for Creative Leadership handbook of leadership development* (3rd ed., pp. 97–124). Jossey-Bass.

Lacerenza, C. N., Reyes, D. L., Marlow, S. L., Joseph, D. L., & Salas, E. (2017). Leadership training design, delivery, and implementation: A meta-analysis. *Journal of Applied Psychology, 102*(12), 1680–1718. https://psycnet.apa.org/doi/10.1037/apl0000241

Locke, E. A., & Latham, G. P. (1984). *Goal setting: A motivational technique that works*. Prentice-Hall.

McCauley, C. D., Kanaga, K., & Lafferty, K. (2010). Leader development systems. In E. Van Velsor, C. D. McCauley, & M. N. Ruderman (Eds.), *The Center for Creative Leadership handbook of leadership development* (3rd ed., pp. 29–62). Jossey-Bass.

Parra, E., Chicchi Giglioli, I. A., Philip, J., Carrasco-Ribelles, L. A., Marín-Morales, J., & Alcañiz Raya, M. (2021). Combining virtual reality and organizational neuroscience for leadership assessment. *Applied Sciences, 11*(13), 5956. https://doi.org/10.3390/app11135956

Petrie, N. (2015). *The how-to of vertical leadership development*. Center for Creative Leadership. https://www.nicholaspetrie.com/_files/ugd/a8b141_7243e9c83c01457eac15f6cd69073de2.pdf

Raper, M. (2020). *Discovering the impact of leadership coaching*. Center for Creative Leadership. https://cclinnovation.org/news-posts/discovering-the-impact-of-leadership-coaching/

Reichard, R. J., & Beck, J. E. (2017). Leader developmental readiness: Deconstructed and reconstructed. In M. G. Clark & C. W. Gruber (Eds.), *Leader development deconstructed* (pp. 115–140). Springer International Publishing. https://doi.org/10.1007/978-3-319-64740-1_6

Reichard, R. J., Walker, D. O., Putter, S. E., Middleton, E., & Johnson, S. K. (2016). Believing is becoming: The role of leader developmental efficacy in leader self-development. *Journal of Leadership and Organizational Studies, 24*(2), 137–156. https://doi.org/10.1177/1548051816657981

Reinhold, D., Patterson, T., & Hegel, P. (2015). *Make learning stick: Best practices to get the most out of leadership development.* Center for Creative Leadership. http://cclinnovation.org/wp-content/uploads/2015/06/makelearningstick.pdf

Ruderman, M. N., & Clerkin, C. (2020). Is the future of leadership development wearable? Exploring self-tracking in leadership programs. *Industrial and Organizational Psychology, 13*, 103–116. https://doi.org/10.1017/iop.2020.18

Stawiski, S., Jeong, S., & Champion, H. (2020). *Leadership development impact (LDI) framework.* Center for Creative Leadership. https://doi.org/10.35613/ccl.2020.2040

Truninger, M., Ruderman, M. N., Clerkin, C., Fernandez, K. C., & Cancro, D. (2021). Sounds like a leader: An ascription-actuality approach to examining leader emergence and effectiveness. *Leadership Quarterly, 32*(5), 101420. https://doi.org/10.1016/j.leaqua.2020.101420

Van Velsor, E., & Musselwhite, W. C. (1986). The timing of training, learning, and transfer. *Training & Development Journal, 40*(8), 58–59.

Young, S., Champion, H., Raper, M., & Braddy, P. (2017). *How bosses can make or break leadership development programs.* Center for Creative Leadership. https://doi.org/10.35613/ccl.2017.1072

Young, S. F., Gentry, W. A., & Braddy, P. W. (2016). Holding leaders accountable during the 360 feedback process. *Industrial and Organizational Psychology, 9*(4), 811–813. https://doi.org/10.1017/iop.2016.90

# 21
# Reflections on Assessment for Development

*Lynn Collins and José David*

This chapter includes reflections on the trends and innovations in assessments for development. As we review the chapters in this section, we begin by exploring the current business environment. For development to deliver on business goals, it must respond to the rapidly evolving imperatives confronting companies. Much has changed in a few short years. We are facing a new era of work. Key changes include new and different skill demands and associated talent gaps, an escalating need for talent recruitment and retention, exponential growth in virtual work, a focus on inclusion as a strategic necessity, and an accelerating evolution in how people work in the gig economy. As the velocity of change heaps unprecedented challenges on leaders, the ability to maintain effectiveness becomes more elusive (Paese & Yankov)—elevating the importance of assessment and development. With this context in mind, we reflect on the work done by the authors in this section and share perspectives on (a) the constructs and content domain that is measured and developed (the what), (b) the methodology deployed in both assessment and development (the how), and (c) the targets of these efforts (the who); and we conclude with (d) a critical look at the degree of innovation we see at present.

## Workforce Upheavals and the Context of Development Today

The global corporate training market hit a record $370.3 billion in 2019 (Taylor, 2020) and is estimated to surpass the $414 billion mark by 2026 (IndustryARC, 2019). This growth reflects companies' concerns about their leaders' ability to lead their organization into the future (GP Strategies

Lynn Collins and José David, *Reflections on Assessment for Development* In: *Talent Assessment*.
Edited by: Tracy M. Kantrowitz, Douglas H. Reynolds, and John C. Scott, Oxford University Press.
© Society of Industrial Organizational Psychology 2023. DOI: 10.1093/oso/9780197611050.003.0021

Corporations & Future Workplace, 2021). Leaders will need to deepen and expand their capabilities in business acumen along with their interpersonal people skills for organizations to build a high-quality pipeline of next-level talent to deliver on their strategy.

This need has become even more urgent due to the COVID-19 pandemic and ensuing "Great Resignation" (Ready & Conger, 2007). In 2021, over three-quarters of employers (77%) in the United States reported having problems finding and keeping employees (Willis Towers Watson, 2021). Amid this fierce competition, companies are investing in development as a key strategy for attracting and retaining top talent.

Also, a heightened awareness of diversity, equity, and inclusion has spotlighted the need for leaders with high levels of emotional intelligence and empathy and the ability to create psychological safety for all within the workplace. As organizations look to build new leadership muscles within their majority groups, they also are seeking to enhance diversity at senior levels by accelerating and expanding the development of early talent. Leadership assessments and development need to be accessible to the many, not the few.

In addition, employers forced by the pandemic to embrace remote work are rethinking what can be done virtually in assessment and development. Online, mobile, always-on, social, and gamification elements are being used to drive motivation and application and enhance the participant experience.

Finally, the rise of the gig economy—with the majority of the workforce predicted to be freelancers by 2027 (Freelancers Union & Upwork, 2017)—is causing a major shift. We expect that models will emerge to develop capabilities in how people create value for organizations, replacing the traditional focus on targeted capabilities for a specific job or role.

## Reflections on the Constructs and Content Domain That Are Measured and Developed (the What)

Amid the changes, an industrial-era approach to assessment remains prevalent. As scientist-practitioners of industrial-organizational (IO) psychology, we are well versed in the due diligence behind using any scientifically grounded assessment process: understanding the business need behind conducting an assessment, targeting the audience in question, engaging in an analysis of the job or work involved in the population, and then building a reliable and valid measurement approach that allows us to gather insights and make valid and practical inferences about future development needs (based on outcomes gathered inside the organization).

There is a role with a set of tasks and responsibilities, capabilities that contribute to job performance, and measures that tell whether people are thriving in their role. Stawiski and McCauley highlight such an approach in their description of the Leading for Organizational Impact program. In this program, the work-relatedness of the constructs and the assessment approach is very explicit, and great measures are taken to approximate the look, feel, and challenges of the role (Collins & Hartog, 2021). In parallel, all the authors in this section also discuss other constructs and predictors that have recently been incorporated into traditional IO-centric assessments for development. We are labeling them whole-person predictors (Covey, 2004), constructs that contribute to overall personal effectiveness and that, although somewhat distal from their relevance to the job itself, have either a direct or a moderating effect on traditional measures of an individual's success in an organization. Finally, we highlight two areas that receive much less emphasis: the measurement of relevant criteria of individual success and the measurement of contextual factors that contribute to the success of developmental assessment efforts.

## Work-Related Predictors

The authors in the preceding sections have referenced the traditional notion of KSAOs (knowledge, skills, abilities, other characteristics) in the context of developing toward success in an organization. Several predictors that have significant volumes of validity evidence come into the picture: conscientiousness, motivation, self-efficacy, ambition, emotional stability, agreeableness, collaboration, strategic thinking, problem-solving, and executive communication, among others. The measurement of these constructs has predictive benefits: gains in self-awareness, face validity, and positive participant experience.

Because this volume is focused on innovations in assessment, we turn our attention to constructs that have arisen recently in developmental assessment practices. Although these constructs are at different stages of empirical evidence in relation to their unique variance explained and incremental validity in relation to more established constructs, their relevance to current organizational reality makes them worthy of continued academic and applied research.

**Learning Agility.** In the face of rapid change, employees and their leaders must be able to learn from experience (Lombardo & Eichinger, 2000) and to use what they have learned to scan, understand, and react appropriately to their surroundings. Learning agility has been referenced in other work as a construct present in many developmental assessments as an indicator of leadership potential (Church et al., 2015).

While the definition of learning agility has evolved (DeMeuse, 2017; Harvey & DeMeuse, 2021; Hoff & Burke, 2017), one notion remains constant: Learning agility is composed of speed and flexibility, along with a series of enabling behaviors, such as seeking feedback, experimenting, and reflecting.

Evidence supporting the use of learning agility as a tool during developmental assessment interventions is solid and growing. DeMeuse (2017) cites several studies that empirically link measures of learning agility to leadership performance and potential. Research conducted by Hoff and Burke (2017) also points to construct- and criterion-related validity evidence linking dimensions of learning agility to different facets of leader performance.

**Resilience.** While agility refers to the ability to adapt, resilience represents how we respond to stress. Once again, the vortex and speed of change inside organizations is testing people's long-term sustainment of drive and performance. Resilience is a construct that adds to developmental efforts by having people focus on adapting in times of disruption and accelerated change.

Notwithstanding the debates on whether resilience needs to be coupled with either an experience of adversity or evidence of growth (Britt et al., 2016), resilience provides a set of mindsets, skills, and attributes that allows the replenishment of energy, drive, and focus.

Resilience has empirically demonstrated correlations with measures of well-being (DeSimone et al., 2017), and organizationally based programs designed to develop resilience demonstrate a modest effect size (Vanhove et al., 2016). It is also worth mentioning that resilience outside of organizational contexts is highly related to those personal effectiveness predictors we will discuss in the next section.

**Inclusivity.** Ken Frazier, formerly of Merck & Co, *Chief Executive Magazine*'s 2021 CEO of the Year, was asked to make the business case for diversity. He replied: "First, I want you to make the case for homogeneity" (Schuyler, 2018). With demographic shifts in employee populations encompassing gender, race, ethnicity, nationality, gender identity, sexual orientation, religion, and disability status, individuals inside an organization more and more often find themselves working with, leading, or reporting to people who are very much unlike them on the "outside." Couple that with ideological, educational, political, and socioeconomic differences, and the business case for learning how to leverage the power of inclusion has never been more real. The skill and ability to harness the power of these differences becomes a differentiator to successful performance inside organizations. Pat Wadors, a chief talent officer from Procore, said, "When we listen and celebrate what is both common and different, we become a wiser, more inclusive, and better organization" (Reilly, 2017). Organizations today need to create an inclusive culture that celebrates diversity and to be careful that their practices do not flatten diversity by assimilating talent to a single standard.

There are correlates of inclusivity from more established constructs, such as openness to experience within the five-factor model of personality and social awareness within models of emotional intelligence. Recent work has built on some of these correlates of inclusivity to construct instruments specifically designed to measure inclusivity. For example, research by practitioner organizations (Bourke et al., 2017; ETU, 2022) has provided initial empirical evidence linking assessment results to 360-degree ratings of the leader's inclusivity, team effectiveness and decision-making, and cognizance of bias.

**Business Acumen.** With volatility, uncertainty, ambiguity, and the rate of disruption increasing, today's leaders need business acumen more than ever (BTS, 2015). Business acumen—defined as an intuitive and applicable understanding of how a company makes money—includes strategic thinking, financial acumen, market orientation, innovation, collaboration, and influencing skills (D. Parisi, 2016). There are multiple indicators that business acumen will continue to evolve as a critical leadership skill (Adl, 2021). At the Society for Industrial and Organizational Psychology (SIOP) Annual Conference in 2019, a panel of chief human resource officers (CHROs) indicated that helping to maximize the performance of employees to better achieve an organization's overall strategy was one of their top priorities (Collins & Morris, 2019). There was overwhelming agreement among hundreds of respondents that insufficient business skills often limit an organization's ability to achieve its strategic priorities. In an Economist Intelligence survey, 65% of respondents said that a lack of business acumen limits an organization's ability to execute its strategy (Reddy, 2017). However, while most corporations recognize business acumen as necessary, companies typically struggle with how to measure and develop it across the organization. Developing these capabilities creates strategic alignment, improves business decision-making, focuses leaders on customers and markets, and teaches leaders how to manage risk and embrace innovation (D. Parisi, 2016).

**Digital Readiness.** The final construct discussed in this section references a pervasive buzzword in today's organizations: digital. Digital transformation is unique to each company, therefore making it a highly variable construct. Definitions encompass elements of attitudes, behaviors, and skills in relation to the most current technological changes, including the use of mobile computing, the application of analytics to harness large bodies of data, the shift from physical to cloud computing, and the use of automation and artificial intelligence. The adoption of and intent behind the use of all these technologies varies by organization, but organizations that plan to incorporate any of these technologies require leaders and individual contributors who are advocates, learners, and adopters of these technological shifts. Because of the degree of technology change, organizations are willing to invest in the development of their employees to accelerate the speed of change.

Assessment for digital readiness is relatively nascent. Although a few tools and approaches are currently in the market, more research is needed before they can be considered consistent predictors of individual success in organizations. However, given the technological transformation taking place across all industries, we are flagging this construct for inclusion and additional research in developmental assessment practices.

## Whole-Person Predictors

One of the big innovations and trends in the overall practice of developmental assessments is the inclusion of what we earlier referred to as whole-person predictors: constructs that contribute to overall effectiveness across multiple arenas. In a few human resources practices, we have observed that compensation and benefits practices prepare benefits that go beyond employees' health. They extend into a greater notion of wellness that includes physical, emotional, social (dependents and beyond), and financial arenas. The reasoning is that employees can thrive and contribute much more fully to the organization if they have the focus that comes from stability outside of work.

Sinar brings this approach to life by including physical measures in the Whole Person Model and looking at their impact on outcomes such as work-life balance and stress management. Lovelace et al. (2007) summarize the literature pointing to the benefits of physical fitness to leader effectiveness, not only in the prevention of disease and stress, but also in increased stamina and enhanced mood. Sinar's measurement of physical attributes recognizes their importance and contributes to the whole-person view of effectiveness.

Just as physical health has been brought into greater focus, measures of emotional states and mood have been incorporated into developmental leadership assessments to introduce greater self-awareness and reflection. Additionally, mindfulness is a construct that has been introduced to focus attention on the experience at hand, in addition to accepting and valuing the experience for what it is (Bishop et al., 2004). The benefits of mindfulness to human functioning include improvements to attention, cognition, emotion, behavior, and physiology (Good et al., 2015). Therefore, the degree to which mindful behaviors are present in leader performance is making its way into both stand-alone and multitrait, multimethod developmental assessment approaches.

## The Matter of Criteria

The preceding chapters have focused mostly on the predictor variables measured in the methods that participants course through as part of their development programs. Of equal interest is the matter of the criteria variables these predictors are validated against.

The selection of criteria variables is significant to allow for meaningful and more powerful inferences to be drawn from the results of developmentally focused assessments. Sinar points to the outcome measures during coaching-centric assessment approaches, including productivity, engagement, work-life balance, and stress management. Likewise, Stawiski and McCauley identify self-reporting and coworker feedback of different behaviors and constructs, including self-awareness, leadership readiness, leader confidence, and managing individual and team performance.

We are interested in seeing greater innovation in the criteria space along the lines of Table 21.1.

Table 21.1 Opportunities for Future Innovation to Criterion Measurement

| From... | To... |
| --- | --- |
| Using individual performance measures as sole criteria | Gathering criteria beyond the individual (e.g., financial measures, measures of organization-level engagement, changes in team effectiveness or organizational networks) |
| Snapshots about the participants' outcomes | Continuous gathering of participants' outcomes on constructs developed during the development program |
| Feedback from self and others to measure developmental improvements | Multimedia observations of constructs through technology (e.g., text analysis, voice inflection [Stawiski & McCauley], metadata from PC application usage) |
| Use of standardized instruments to gather criterion data | Ensuring criterion relevance between developmental program constructs and outcome measures |

## Measurement of Contextual Factors

A welcome innovation built from much of IO psychology's scientific research has been the measurement of contextual factors present during developmental assessment programs. Lehman (2017) reports:

> Harvard researchers Groysberg, McLean, and Nohria analyzed the performance of twenty former executives from GE who became either the Chairman, CEO, or CEO designate. They examined the individuals' experience at GE (e.g., growing a business, cutting costs, etc.) and found those that went into environments where they were able to capitalize upon their experiences yielded 14.1% annualized abnormal returns (i.e., actual returns compared to expected returns). Those who went to organizations that did not fit with their skill set saw -39.8% annualized abnormal returns. Context matters.

Sinar, as well as Stawiski and McCauley, discusses the importance of an environment supportive of the development the participants go through. Measures of perceived organizational and manager support (Stawiski & McCauley) can enhance and prolong the developmental impact of a program on participants.

Stawiski and McCauley also look at other constructs that could impact the effectiveness of a developmental assessment, such as "challenge and support" and psychological safety. Having a lens toward the circumstances in which participants can apply skills developed and receive reinforcement and recognition can make the difference between participants taking their development to new heights or struggling to find meaningful outlets to practice new capabilities.

These contextual factors often take a secondary priority to the individual-level insights and measures gathered from the participants going through programs. We encourage practitioners to continue gathering and measuring these factors to accelerate the degree of innovation in programs. The continued measurement and publication of contextual factors provide an opportunity to aggregate contextual factors across multiple organizational contexts (e.g., country, industry, business scenarios) and gain insight on how to elevate leaders.

## Reflections on the Measurement Approaches and Feedback Methods (the How)

In this section, we review the trends and innovations in measurement approaches used to evaluate development opportunities and the feedback methods used to inform and plan for behavior change.

### Trends: Multimethod, 360 Feedback, Simulations, and Self-Report

A trend that each of the authors in this section addresses is the benefit of multimethod input. Stawiski and McCauley discussed multiple methods to evaluate the inner self, visible self, and social self; Sinar described multiple methods to evaluate a Whole Person Model composed of mindsets, behaviors that promote thriving and inspiring, and key personal and professional outcomes; and Paese and Yankov highlight how multiple methods yield deeper insight, which fuels more well-informed, nuanced, development action plans. The multiple-method approach provides holistic insights for leaders regarding how they are seen, what they do, and who they are. Multiple assessment tools are combined and interpreted by a professional to support personalized and targeted development. Based on our experiences and input from the authors in this section, the tried-and-true methods of 360, personality, interviews, and simulations appear here to stay. Yet, digital advances discussed later in this section are opening a new world of possibilities.

Long recognized as a tool to promote self-awareness, 360 feedback provides important insight into how participants show up at work. These 360s focus on observable behavior, collecting data, and accumulating observations of a participant's performance from multiple perspectives (managers, colleagues, direct reports) to build participant insight that reinforces skills and exposes blind spots. In 2016, *Forbes* magazine reported that 85% of all Fortune 500 companies used the 360 feedback process as a cornerstone of their overall leadership development process (Zenger, 2016). Multiperspective feedback provides awareness of how aspects of the leader are seen and interpreted by others (Stawiski & McCauley); exposes variation between one's self-perception and those of other individuals or groups (Paese & Yankov); and is particularly insightful for members to the degree it surfaces blind spots, unrecognized growth needs, or unseen strengths (Sinar).

Simulations are discussed in two of the chapters and are strongly rooted in development practices, as they provide an opportunity to observe participant capabilities in a future or more demanding role. Simulations are carefully constructed to mirror on-the-job situations and provide participants the opportunity to experience critical leadership challenges and receive feedback on their observed behavior. Simulations range from experiences like Looking Glass, with more than 150 problems ranging in strategic importance (Stawiski & McCauley); to simulations where participants take a role inside the leadership team of a company, running the business and making strategy and investment decisions (Dreyer, Hartog, Collins); to something as simple as a participant developing and delivering a presentation. These assessments provide candidates with a highly realistic, interactive experience of challenges in the life of a leader. Trained observers provide behavioral feedback about a participant's strengths and development needs. Participants also learn by reflecting on their intents, actions, and outcomes. Along with the typical people-leadership examples described by Paese and Yankov (e.g., challenging an individual contributor with the supervisory task of providing feedback; asking a mid-level leader to construct a long-range business plan; tasking a senior executive with the CEO-level challenge of influencing several board members to gain alignment), the authors have seen a surge in strategy and business acumen assessments.

Self-report measures are also a popular tool. These measures are used to help leaders reflect on and gain insight into their own patterns of thinking, feeling, and acting (Stawiski & McCauley). The most well-known and frequently used self-report instruments are personality assessments. Other self-report measures include surveys gauging mindsets that impact attitudes and beliefs and surveys that relate to "thriving," which ask respondents to reflect on areas such as emotional, physical, and financial health. Finally, interviews are yet another self-report measure, providing insights on competencies, experiences, and motivations, which are then used to guide the development of leaders (Paese & Yankov). This information helps the assessor/coach responsible for feedback more effectively guide and coach each participant by placing observations of behavior in context for leaders (Collins & Hartog, 2021).

### Emerging Methods: Bio Measures, Artificial Intelligence, Virtual Reality, and Assessment in the Flow of Work

This section looks at some of the newer methods that demonstrate promise. Each takes advantage of quickly evolving technologies. While some of the concepts have been used, they are in their infancy in their application to development assessments. They offer an exciting future for our fields as we explore them with rigor and disciplined experimentation.

Digital wearable technologies offer a nonintrusive observational method. While capturing data in a method akin to the field-based research of the past, they have elevated and expanded the type of insights available. These technologies capture data and make it possible to monitor physiological signals, such as those associated with stress or other emotions, thus increasing leader awareness of what triggers stress reactions and their ability to modify reactions (Stawiski & McCauley; Ruderman & Clerkin, 2020). Paese and Yankov envision a time when these will continuously track leaders' behavior and provide them with metrics and recommendations for how to improve their behavior to master a particular leadership skill. "As with other forms of assessment, the data itself is a starting point" (Ruderman & Clerkin, 2020). The key to how effective these tools are for leader development is how the data are used to drive development.

The rise of artificial intelligence (AI) and machine learning (ML) was the number one workplace trend in both 2019 and 2020 (SIOP, 2020). AI is not new, but it has advanced over the last few years. For example, AI audio, video, and written analytics engines are being used to provide insights on how people speak and how they are perceived by others. The technology can be used to provide feedback on writing tone, persuasive impact, and inclusiveness of communication. Stawiski and McCauley also reference sociometric badges, wearable devices that can track proximity to others, conversational time, and vocal features (Kim et al., 2012; Kozlowski & Chao, 2018). We too have seen the rapid growth of the use of AI, including a 360 that uses digital collaboration patterns to determine who should be included in a 360 and AI platforms that sync to emails and chat. We at BTS have applied natural language processing (NLP) to measure and develop strategic understanding and sentiment analysis of feedback insights to facilitate leader development.

Virtual reality (VR) immersive assessments and experiences are also on the rise. According to O'Brien (2019), the VR market is expected to grow from $7.9 billion in 2018 to $44.7 billion by 2024. These experiences transport the participant into a new reality that feels, looks, and sounds like real life. The experiences are being used for both assessment and learning, as they provide insight into how participants would behave in real-life scenarios. The goal is to use VR for training and development by putting leaders in situations that they have had little exposure to and in which they might make and learn from errors (Paese & Yankov). In the early 2000s, there were multiple technological advances in development assessment centers, including virtual individual assessment centers with an interactive in-basket, live role plays, multiple exercises, and assessor tools for standardization and calibration. We imagine the new virtual development assessment center having endless possibilities with VR, such as the Accenture Nth Floor created by teams across Microsoft and AltspaceVR that enables people to meet, interact, and collaborate in virtual offices.

We also now have tools that can be considered assessments in the flow of work. Microsoft Viva provides daily briefings and monthly digests. Sharing a personal example, one of this chapter's authors recently received a personalized "insight of the month" stating, "It looks like you read and respond to email quickly outside your working hours." This insight took the author to a recommendation to turn off email notifications during the evening and schedule a single after-hours block of time to address them instead. This type of insight based on tasks performed in our daily work offer yet another source of information that can be used to support development. The emerging promise of technological assessment is to actively, on an ongoing, day-to-day basis, help leaders self-evaluate, change, adapt, and maintain their skills (Paese & Yankov; Ruderman & Clerkin, 2020).

## Feedback Methods

"Assessment without development is like a diagnosis without treatment" (Busine, 2019), leaving the connection to learning undone (Collins & Hartog, 2021). The outcomes of an assessment typically include high-touch, personalized feedback based on the assessment results and some type of report that outlines strengths and development needs, suggests development activities for the participant's development planning, and identifies coaching opportunities (Collins & Hartog, 2021).

Technology has expanded feedback opportunities by enabling individuals to review recordings of themselves in action, and for assessors to use those recordings to provide feedback on communication tone and impact (Stawiski & McCauley). With video technology, we can record and score any range of behaviors and capabilities and then return annotated feedback linked to specific behaviors (Collins & Hartog, 2021). Video clips can be selected, and notes can be added to the video to enhance the learning. For example, imagine evaluating how a person communicates, engages, and inspires others, and remains calm under pressure, and then sharing with the participant an annotated video that provides examples of and insights on that person's actions (Collins & Hartog, 2021), helping leaders understand their behavior and its impact.

Quality feedback should lead to development, then additional assessment and further development. Development is a lifelong journey. We are missing deep insight opportunities because assessment today is not set up that way. Today, we take more of a "snapshot" approach—assessing participants at fixed points in time. However, today's digital assets enable a "streaming video" view of oneself or a participant engaged in development. Sinar explains an approach where change, growth, and impact are measured over time. Repeated measures are used every 3 or 4 months as a reflection point in the experience. The resulting information about change is reported back to the team member. Now imagine the use of data over a career, similar to the world of ongoing data insights our field has created in the organizational survey research discipline. We get smarter about where we are and understand the history trends and where we are today. Many leaders have plenty of data available for personal aggregation. Why not use big data analytics in the context of the individual to provide deeper, more personalized insights and recommendations, with an extensive understanding of where people have been, where they are, and where they want to be?

Feedback goes beyond the insights about an individual. Organizations can learn from the strengths and gaps identified. Providing aggregate-level insights on strengths and development gaps, as well as development themes, aids in planning and helps the business prioritize and support talent today and accelerate future role development.

## The Targets of These Efforts (the Who)

Sinar spoke about the personalization of development (precision development); the select few chosen for developmental assessment programs are the beneficiaries of technologies that automate content curation based on needs and preferences, or executive coaches who provide firsthand insights into the custom developmental needs of those they coach. Talent management practitioners (Church & Silzer, 2014) have emphasized the need to differentiate investments in those employees who are considered to have the highest potential to exhibit growth into greater and broader responsibilities. Pragmatically, organizations also have fixed resources to make those higher cost investments in developmental assessment programs. This leads to a double-barreled focus on exclusive populations; only the critical few get invitations to participate.

However, the movement in organizations toward greater diversity, equity, and inclusion (DEI) runs counter to that focus on the few. In assessment practitioner circles, there is less conversation about the democratization and equitable access to development (and developmental assessments). Concerns are evolving around fairness of how people are selected for programming in the first place.

An opportunity for greater innovation in the field of developmentally focused assessments is increasing access. Among the quotes we have heard along these lines are "hugging our diverse talent" and "investing in the top 100% of our talent." The struggles that diverse constituencies (women, racial and ethnic minorities, people with disabilities, LGBTQ+ employees) experience to grow and thrive inside of organizations beg for access to developmental assessments as a solution to increase DEI (Burns et al., 2021).

A noteworthy example of expanded access to the benefits of assessment inside an organization is PepsiCo's LEAD program and its assessment of potential leaders deepest in the organization (Silzer et al., 2016). This approach allows thousands of people inside the organization to go through the initial assessment battery in the LEAD program and benefit from the insights gained and follow-up coaching by their managers. The overall LEAD program is also able to benefit from this "assessment of many" by then identifying those highest potential employees and investing further in them through future leadership development offerings (Silzer et al., 2016).

Any discussion about expanding access has to acknowledge that most often the targets of developmental assessment programs are leaders or aspiring leaders. Audiences outside of the leadership realm have less visibility. With high-pros (as opposed to "hipos," the term used to describe high-potential employees) constituting the sheer majority inside organizations, there is an opportunity to innovate in ways that expand and offer the benefits of assessments for the development of talented individual contributors. Among the individual contributor populations the authors have been able to work with are internal auditors, key account managers, and project managers. Given the opportunity, these less considered audiences can engage in development programs that allow them to build capabilities that can further accelerate their career.

The matter of choice also becomes important in selecting the targets for assessments and development. Although assessment practitioners and providers normally build in disclosures, notices, and data collection to ensure there is consent in participating in developmental assessments, those normally come at a point where the decision for the investment has already been made. Silzer et al. (2016) discuss the notion of opting in as a greater indicator of choice, far beyond consent. The decision to engage in leadership development is often one that might even be outside of the realm of consideration for participants in these kinds of programs. The absence of career conversations or a focused development plan may catch recipients of invitations to these programs completely unaware, unprepared, and even unwilling. Church and Silzer (2014) note career ambition as one of the factors of the growth dimension of potential; without an inherent desire to advance their career and step into higher degrees of leadership responsibility, participants of developmental assessment programs may not have the full drive and commitment to build new skills and expose themselves to significant growth opportunities. Innovations in program design that allow for systematic opting-in of participants can not only ensure participants have the right frame of mind but also create a more inclusive option that can reach a more diverse constituency.

## Incremental Versus Transformative Innovation

As we discussed in the beginning of this chapter, we are living in times of rapid change and high demand to keep up with accelerating trends: digital transformation; virtual and highly personalized development; diversity, inclusion, and social justice as a top priority; and the changing workforce due to a gig economy. In 2019, a panel of CHROs (Collins & Morris, 2019) convened to discuss how IO psychologists can better serve organizations. They identified what is not working: They cited a need to reinvent our profession—to succeed fast and stay relevant. Considering today's organizational environment and the challenges ahead, what got us this far won't be enough to get us where we need to go. The future of development requires that we begin to create what might be referred to as new "thought roads"—based on how our environment is changing—and move with speed and rigor.

We are at a tipping point, at risk of not keeping pace with changing needs. We can all ask ourselves whether we have missed opportunities because of biases that make it hard to imagine things that haven't happened before. At a consortium in 2019, Jessica Parisi shared an example of accelerated growth, comparing the microchip and the Volkswagen Beetle. The microchip's computing power has doubled every 2 years. Compared to its inception, it has 3,500 times the performance, is 90,000 times more energy efficient, and is 60,000 times less expensive. If the Volkswagen Beetle had followed the same trajectory, it could go 300,000 mph, get 2,000,000 miles per gallon of gas, and cost 4 cents; assuming fuel efficiency had also improved, you would be able to drive it your entire life on one tank of gas. What would a similar comparison look like for development assessments? Can we imagine a world in which:

- We are assessing and supporting the whole person?
- Individuals and their leaders co-create their choices about development?
- We have the skills and methods we need to provide precise and personalized development?
- We deeply understand the contexts that impact the effectiveness of development?

- The use of promising and emerging digital methods provides real-time assessments, feedback, and development?
- Assessment data does not provide a one-off snapshot but a deep and continuous understanding of the participant?
- All who are interested have access?

We can imagine just that and look forward to accelerating the change in our field with our esteemed colleagues.

## References

Adl, R. (2021). *Cracking the code: The secret to successful execution & lessons for the C-suite.* https://bts.com/app/uploads/2021/05/cracking-the-code-research-report.pdf

Bishop, S. R., Lau, M., Shapiro, S., Carlson, L., Anderson, N. D., Carmody, J., Segal, Z. V., Abbey, S., Speca, M., Velting, D., & Devins, G. (2004). Mindfulness: A proposed operational definition. *Clinical Psychology: Science and Practice, 11*(3), 230–241. https://doi.org/10.1093/clipsy.bph077

Bourke, J., Dillon, B., Gindidis, A., Nicholson, T., Fowler, S., Karvelas, G., & Espedido, A. (2017). *Inclusive leadership assessment technical report.* Deloitte Touche Tohmatsu.

Britt, T., Shen, W., Sinclair, R., Grossman, M., & Klieger, D. (2016). How much do we really know about employee resilience? *Industrial and Organizational Psychology, 9*(2), 378–404.

BTS. (2015). *Skills mismatch: Business acumen and strategy execution.* https://www.bts.company/docs/white-papers/skills-mismatch-business-acumen-and-strategy-execution-researchC276E653B841.pdf

Burns, T., Huang, J., Krivkovich, A., Yee, L., Rambachan, I., & Trkulja, T. (2021, September 27). *Women in the workplace.* McKinsey. https://www.mckinsey.com/featured-insights/diversity-and-inclusion/women-in-the-workplace

Busine, M. (2019, November). *The dynamic duo: Assessment and development* [Paper presentation]. 42nd International Congress on Assessment Center Methods, Shanghai, China.

Center for Creative Leadership. (2016). *Driving performance: How leadership development powers success.* https://www.ccl.org/articles/white-papers/driving-performance-development-success/

CGS. (2021). *Enterprise learning 2021 annual report* [Review]. Retrieved January 24, 2022, from https://www.cgsinc.com/sites/default/files/media/resources/pdf/CGS_2021LearningReport_Final_030321.pdf

Church, A. H., & Silzer, R. F. (2014). Going behind the corporate curtain with a blueprint for leadership potential: An integrated framework for identifying high-potential talent. *People + Strategy, 36*, 50–58.

Church, A. H., Rotolo, C. T., Ginther, N. M., & Levine, R. (2015). How are Top Companies Designing and Managing Their High-Potential Programs? A Follow-up Talent Management Benchmark Study. *Consulting Psychology Journal: Practice and Research, 67*, 17–47.

Collins, L. G., & Hartog, S. B. (2021). Assessment centers: A blended adult development strategy. In M. London (Ed.), *The Oxford handbook of lifelong learning* (2nd ed., pp. 299–330). New York, NY: Oxford University Press.

Collins, L., & Morris, M. (2019). How can we as I-Os better serve organizations? *The Industrial-Organizational Psychologist, 57*(1). Retrieved electronically on April 4, 2023 from, https://www.siop.org/Research-Publications/Items-of-Interest/ArtMID/19366/ArticleID/3019/preview/true

Covey, S. R. (2004). *The 8th habit: From effectiveness to greatness*. Free Press.

DeMeuse, K. P. (2017). Learning agility: Its evolution as a psychological construct and its empirical relationship to leader success. *Consulting Psychology Journal: Practice and Research, 69*, 267–295.

DeSimone, J. A., Harms, P. D., Vanhove, A. J., & Herian, M. N. (2017). Development and validation of the five-by-five resilience scale. *Assessment, 24*(6), 778–797. https://doi.org/10.1177/1073191115625803

ETU. (2022). DEI training: diversity, equity, & inclusion simulations with impact. Retrieved April 4, 2023 from, https://www.etu.co/expertise/diversity-equity-and-inclusion?hsCtaTracking=b7b52e25-e7e3-4797-b25a-306b3a642d9a%7C3b1e2453-ba29-4d10-863f-7c0e2f79f934

Freelancers Union & Upwork. (2017). *Freelancing in America: 2017*. https://assets.freelancersunion.org/media/documents/FreelancingInAmericaReport-2017.pdf

GP Strategies Corporations & Future Workplace. (2021, December). *The evolving role of learning in workforce transformation*. https://www.gpstrategies.com/wp-content/uploads/2021/11/ResRpt-Evolving-Role-Workforce-Transformation-Fall-2021-OLopt-1.pdf

Good, D. J., Lyddy, C. J., Glomb, T. M., Bono, J. E., Brown, K. W., Duffy, M. K., Baer, R. A., Brewer, J. A., & Lazar, S. W. (2015). Contemplating mindfulness at work. *Journal of Management, 42*(1), 114–142. https://doi.org/10.1177/0149206315617003

Guidelines and Ethical Considerations for Assessment Center Operations. (2015). *Journal of Management, 41*(4), 1244–1273. doi:10.1177/0149206314567780

Harvey, V. S., & DeMeuse, K. P. (2021). Learning agility: What we know, what we need to know, and where do we go from here? In V. S. Harvey & K. P. DeMeuse (Eds.), *The age of agility: Building learning agile leaders and organizations* (pp. 445–478). Oxford University Press; Society for Industrial and Organizational Psychology. https://doi.org/10.1093/oso/9780190085353.003.0019

Hoff, D. F., & Burke, W. W. (2017). *Learning agility: The key to leader potential*. Hogan Press.

IndustryARC. (2019). *Corporate training market share, size and industry growth analysis 2021-2026*. https://www.industryarc.com/Report/18696/corporate-training-market.html

Kim, T., McFee, E., Olguin, D., Waber, B., & Pentland, A. (2012). Sociometric badges: Using sensor technology to capture new forms of collaboration. *Journal of Organizational Behavior, 33*, 412–427. https://doi.org/10.1002/job.1776

Kozlowski, S. W. J., & Chao, G. T. (2018). Unpacking team process dynamics and emergent phenomena: Challenges, conceptual advances, and innovative methods. *American Psychologist, 73*(4), 576–592. https://doi.org/10.1037/amp0000245

Lehman, M. (2017). Leadership is relentlessly contextual and here is why. Retrieved on April 4, 2023 from, https://bts.com/2017/06/01/leadership-is-relentlessly-contextual-and-here-is-why/

Lombardo, M., & Eichinger, R. (2000). High potentials as high learners. *Human Resource Management, 39*, 321–329.

Lovelace, K., Manz, C., & Alves, J. (2007). Work stress and leadership development: The role of self-leadership, shared leadership, physical fitness and flow in managing demands and increasing job control. *Human Resource Management Review, 17*, 374–387. https://doi.org/10.1016/j.hrmr.2007.08.001

O'Brien, J. (2019). *Virtual and augmented reality market volatile but promising*. https://techbuzzireland.com/2019/12/03/virtual-and-augmented-reality-market-volatile-but-promising-vr-ar/

Parisi, D. (2016). *Business acumen for the 21st century*. https://bts.com/2016/04/01/business-acumen-for-the-21st-century

Parisi, J. (2019). *Can assessments help us grow?*[Conference presentation] Society for Industrial and Organization Psychology Leading Edge Consortium, Atlanta, GA.

Ready, D. A., & Conger, J. A. (2007). Make your company a talent factory. *Harvard Business Review, 85*(6), 68.

Reddy, M. (2021, May 19). *3 essential components of business acumen for middle managers*. BTS. Retrieved April 4, 2023, from https://bts.com/2017/08/01/3-essential-components-of-business-acumen-for-middle-managers/

Reilly, K. (2017). *How LinkedIn's HR chief is changing the diversity conversation with "belonging."* https://www.linkedin.com/business/talent/blog/talent-acquisition/how-linkedins-hr-chief-is-changing-diversity-conversation-with-belonging

Ruderman, M. N., & Clerkin, C. (2020). Is the future of leadership development wearable? Exploring self-tracking in leadership programs. *Industrial and Organizational Psychology, 13*(1), 103–116.

Schuyler, S. (2018, March 16). *The one thing we cannot do . . . is nothing*. U.S. Chamber of Commerce Foundation. Retrieved March 23, 2022, from https://www.uschamberfoundation.org/blog/post/one-thing-we-cannot-do-nothing

Silzer, R., Church, A., Rotolo, C., & Scott, J. (2016). I-O practice in action: Solving the leadership potential identification challenge in organizations. *Industrial and Organizational Psychology, 9*, 814–830. https://doi.org/10.1017/iop.2016.75

Society for Industrial and Organization Psychology (SIOP). (2020). *Top 10 workplace trends for 2020* . Retrieved January 24, 2022, from https://www.siop.org/Research-Publications/Items-of-Interest/ArtMID/19366/ArticleID/3361/Top-10-Workplace-Trends-for-

Taylor, K. (2020, August 6). *The business of corporate training landscape*. Training Industry. https://trainingindustry.com/articles/outsourcing/the-business-of-corporate-training-landscape-a-guide-to-the-training-market/

Vanhove, A. J., Herian, M. N., Perez, A. L. U., Harms, P. D., & Lester, P. B. (2016). Can resilience be developed at work? A meta-analytic review of resilience-building programme effectiveness. *Journal of Occupational and Organizational Psychology, 89*, 278–307. https://doi.org/10.1111/joop.12123

Willis Towers Watson. (2021, November 10). *Three quarters of employers are struggling to recruit and retain staff in the Great Resignation*. [Press release]. https://www.wtwco.com/en-GB/News/2021/11/three-quarters-of-employers-are-struggling-to-recruit-and-retain-staff-in-the-great-resignation

Zenger, J. (2016, March 10). *How effective are your 360-degree feedback assessments?* Forbes. Retrieved January 24, 2022, from https://www.forbes.com/sites/jackzenger/2016/03/10/how-effective-are-your-360-degree-feedback-assessments/?sh=99f13d4a6908

# SECTION 6
# CASE STUDIES

# 22
# Connecting People and Opportunities With Artificial Intelligence

*Robert E. Gibby and Adam J. Ducey*

Consider a moment in a person's career journey when data is used by your organization to support someone in making a decision. Given that this journey spans from being a candidate hired into the job onward through onboarding, performance, development, mobility, and—at some point—exit, there are many moments where data can be used to support decisions enabling a person's success. Next, consider the data that is leveraged to support the decision at this moment in the career journey. What does that data look like? Is it a single metric, a table of numbers, a nicely visualized dashboard, a hologram, or simply text?

Depending on the maturity of the talent management practices at your organization, it is likely that text and other qualitative data play a large role in supporting decisions on people. Given that all organizations need to hire people at some point in their existence, let's take the first moment in the career journey—becoming a candidate for a job—as an example. When initiated by the candidate, this process often starts with them providing a profile describing their experiences, education, skills, and other aspects of what makes them a fit for the role and organization. When initiated by the organization, this process starts with a search of potential candidates' profiles from an increasing range of sources that include prior applications to the organization, profiles from online professional networks like LinkedIn, profiles posted to job search sites like Indeed, or even profiles that are scraped and curated from across multiple sources on the internet.

With a diverse array of profiles in hand, it is now typically the task of the recruiter, hiring manager, or human resources (HR) partner to review the profiles to determine who to move forward in the hiring process to

Robert E. Gibby and Adam J. Ducey, *Connecting People and Opportunities With Artificial Intelligence* In: *Talent Assessment*. Edited by: Tracy M. Kantrowitz, Douglas H. Reynolds, and John C. Scott, Oxford University Press. © Society of Industrial Organizational Psychology 2023. DOI: 10.1093/oso/9780197611050.003.0022 an assessment, often in the form of a screening interview. When there are a few profiles to review, this task is relatively straightforward. When there are thousands of profiles to review, however, this task can be daunting, with not all candidates able to be reviewed for the job. Over the last decade, existing companies providing solutions in the hiring space, along with a host of startups, have turned to artificial intelligence (AI) solutions to address this hiring pain point of having too many applicants. While addressing this need, these companies have also worked to enable effective and inclusive hiring decisions through AI.

## Leveraging Artificial Intelligence to Screen Applicants

The concept of AI was originated by Turing (1950) many decades ago when he posited, "Can machines think?" This question sparked a wide range of work (e.g., computer vision, learning, natural language processing [NLP], reasoning, robotics) that Russell and Norvig (2021) integrate when describing AI as a branch of computer science focused on designing and building intelligent agents that receive percepts from the environment and take actions that affect that environment. In our screening example, the "percept" is the text from the candidate's profile. The "intelligent agent" is an existing algorithm that is fed this text and then "takes an action" to classify the content from the text in a meaningful way. This classified content can then "affect the environment" as decision support—either as direct output or as input to additional algorithms—in considering the person for a job with the organization.

Machine learning is a subfield of AI where computers are able to do just this—learn from data inputs to classify features or predict outcomes. In many applications with people data, the machine learns by being fed a training set of inputs with clearly defined features along with the correct outputs expected to be returned by the machine, which is called supervised learning. Algorithms based on these classifiers can then be used with new data inputs to identify, extract, and organize the content into meaningful outputs that can be leveraged as decision support. In our example, a machine learning algorithm would be trained with a set of job profiles that contain the elements we want to classify, such as skills, education, and prior employment experience, along with the expected output for each of these elements for each training profile. Depending on the nature and quality of the classifications or predictions required from the machine learning algorithm, many training runs using modified features to help adjust, or tune, the algorithm may be required to reliably achieve the desired result.

Considering the importance of classifying people data, much of the work with machine learning has been performed through supervised training methods. In cases where classification of data elements is of interest but training data sets are either unavailable or not desirable because the focus is on generating new understanding and classification of the data elements or relationships, it is possible to use an unsupervised machine learning approach and see what the machine returns. It is also possible to blend supervised and unsupervised approaches if only some elements of the data set are well understood. As you may expect, there exists a wide range of machine learning techniques that vary based on the data inputs submitted, the nature of classifications being made, and other aspects.

Given the prevalence of spoken and written data that can be amassed to understand and engage people in an organization, an important application of machine learning techniques is the understanding and processing of natural language by machines. NLP tasks can range across assigning categories to text (e.g., sentiment analysis), extracting concepts from text, translation of text from one language to another, and even generating language (e.g., automated answers to questions). In our candidate profile example, NLP would be deployed to consistently extract the concepts we are most interested in (e.g., skills, experiences, education) to support a decision on whether the candidate should continue in the hiring process. Moving beyond this initial moment in the career journey, let's consider some examples for the range of possibilities that exist with applying AI to help support people across their careers.

As depicted in Figure 22.1, there are a number of key milestones that exist within a person's career journey in an organization. Also displayed is the nonlinear nature of the journey as people gain new experiences and progress in their career, and some steps may co-occur, as shown in the overlap between onboarding and team assignment. In viewing the career journey through a data lens, each of these milestones can be seen as both using and generating data that helps to support deciding on the next step a person should take in their career. At some point, this decision could be to leave the organization, with some people even "boomeranging" back to the company after leaving. For the rest of this chapter, let's explore how AI could help support these decisions.

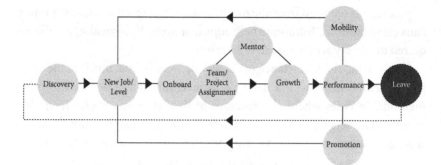

Figure 22.1. Moments in a person's career journey where key decisions are made

## Leveraging Artificial Intelligence Across the Career Journey

### Discovery and Hiring

Let's pick up with our introductory example of supporting hiring decisions. Over the last decade, existing companies playing in the hiring space—along with many startups—have realized that AI solutions provide a unique opportunity for identifying prospective candidates to move forward in the hiring process based on profile data. Fueled by the proliferation of and ready access to huge amounts of position and candidate data, NLP and machine learning have been implemented to go one step further in solving our sourcing need by examining prospective candidates' match with the job to identify and recommend those best matching the job requirements.

The matching algorithm works by first leveraging NLP to parse structured or unstructured prospective candidate profiles (e.g., resumes, social media profiles) and extract relevant concepts (e.g., skills, job titles, years of experience, previous employers, education level, degree type, location). Similar to the process for extracting concepts from the candidate profile, concepts can be parsed and extracted from the content of the job posting, including the job description, job responsibilities, qualifications, and other elements. Algorithms can then be trained to identify the concept overlap that exists, including weighting elements of the job that are more critical such as basic or required qualifications.

Given the wide range of companies adopting AI approaches to enable sourcing and recruiting efforts, there is no shortage of outcomes that have been leveraged to train matching algorithms. While all of these algorithms focus on providing matches between the prospective candidate and job, they differ in the target outcome, the data elements they use, and the decision maker, or persona, they support.

As an example, algorithms have been developed to match prospective candidates against an ideal candidate profile instead of the requirements of a job profile. In this scenario, the most common approach is to leverage profiles from candidates who were successful in previous hiring for the position in the organization. A potential improvement to this approach is to use profiles from candidates who were both successful and unsuccessful in prior hiring for the role. In this way, the matching algorithm can be trained to match and recommend prospects and candidates based on data elements influencing the full spectrum of candidate quality in the hiring process.

A key drawback to this method is that many small to midsize organizations may not have enough examples from prior hiring or the role may be new with no prior candidates. To help close this gap, vendors have developed solutions that pull forward resumes likely to fit or not fit the target job profile and then have recruiters and/or hiring managers from the organization review and rate sample resumes. Evaluation results are then fed into the matching algorithm to specify the ideal profile the company is looking for and help prioritize candidates as they apply for the position. Guo et al. (2019) describe how the LinkedIn Recruiter algorithm for their candidate-to-job matching solution works: The product provides a ranked list of candidates corresponding to a search request in the form of a query, a job posting, or a recommended candidate. Given a search request, candidates that match the request are selected and then ranked based on a variety of factors (such as the similarity of their work experience/skills with the search criteria, job posting location, and the likelihood of a response from an interested candidate) using machine-learned models in multiple passes.

For each of these candidate-job matching methods, the breadth of profiles in terms of content and candidate demographics is critical to ensure algorithms are focused on features that are relevant and inclusive in predicting the match. Care should be taken to understand and evaluate the data elements that will become the classified elements, or features, used to predict the desired outcome through training of the algorithm. For example, candidate-job matching algorithms trained based on the elements of

(a) previously working for a specific set of competitors, (b) graduation from a certain set of universities, and (c) proximity of the candidate to the office where they will work could result in a very homogenous matched set of prospective candidates if these three sources have limited availability of diverse talent.

Similarly, consideration of data elements is also critical on the outcome side when training and deploying a machine learning algorithm for sourcing and recruiting purposes. To help support development of job postings that not only attract prospective candidates but also enable the effectiveness of matching algorithms, companies like Textio have developed augmented writing AI solutions that review job posting content to identify biased phrases and recommend more inclusive alternatives.

In addition to focusing on the data elements that will be classified by the job matching algorithm, a trend in focusing on the candidate and employee experience has led to a more balanced focus of designing and delivering AI solutions that support multiple decision makers, or personas, in the sourcing process. Given the hiring decision is a function of the employer and candidate, matching algorithms that may have been initially developed to help recruiters and hiring managers have been repurposed to directly support prospective candidates in finding a job that matches their skills, experience, and interests.

As prospective candidates apply and move forward in the hiring process, profile information can be supplemented by application forms to collect more uniform and structured information about the candidate's knowledge, skills, abilities, and other (KSAO) job-related elements. This data collection overcomes the challenge of missing or inconsistent data that could occur from using only a candidate's profile. Available products on the market use this data in machine learning algorithms much the same way that traditional weighted application blanks and biographical data solutions have been deployed for decades. Other available products incorporate AI to more fully engage the candidate by leveraging text, audio, and video to collect information that can be used to generate job matches.

Beyond the application, many organizations move candidates forward to interviews without incorporating results from one or more of a wide range of assessments validated to accurately and fairly predict desired posthire outcomes. A critical reason cited by hiring managers and recruiting organizations for not using assessments is the poor experience and face validity provided to candidates who are eager to speak to a person and demonstrate their capability to the employer. As noted previously, some employers receive millions of applications a year for a limited number of jobs, necessitating that only a small percentage of these candidates receive an interview with someone from the organization.

To help improve the candidate experience while also delivering on the proven, unbiased predictive power of assessments, companies have incorporated AI into assessment design and delivery. One approach for increasing engagement and candidate reactions has been to develop game-based assessments measuring cognitive ability and/or personality constructs. Another approach has been the video interview, with candidates recording video responses to structured interview questions. With AI techniques, candidate responses to questions can be used by converting speech to text and then classifying the content of the response. Algorithms can then be trained to focus on elements of the response that coincide with receiving a higher rating on the interview and/or achieving more desirable posthire outcomes.

Traditional, structured interviews have also integrated AI to improve consistency, reduce bias, and increase the accuracy of prediction of interviewers' evaluations of the candidate. Let's consider a structured interview focused on evaluating a candidate's relational (e.g., collaboration, communication) and technical (e.g., programming, analysis) skills required for a specific job. To most effectively deliver and conduct this interview, the organization needs to ensure that the interviewer is (a) trained on interviewing best practices, (b) uses questions that best elicit relevant information on these skills from the candidate, and (c) evaluates the candidate's responses using standard rating guidance.

While many organizations develop robust interview training programs to share best practices for conducting and evaluating the interview, these programs tend to be delivered at a single point of time that may or may not be refreshed prior to each recruiting cycle. Given challenges for retaining information from learning, organizations have moved to delivering interviewers nudges to remind them of best practices. Leveraging AI techniques, these nudges could be tailored to the interviewer based on their judgments and behavior in the interview. Consider, for example, an AI system trained to monitor full use of the rating scale to evaluate a diverse candidate pool.

Short training modules could also be developed and delivered to interviewers based on their alignment with best practices. Interviewers rating every candidate at the midpoint of the rating scales could be delivered an exercise reminding them to review the rating scales as they make their evaluations and use the behavioral anchors to determine where the candidate best fits in the skill range. In addition, interviewers consistently rating a specific group (e.g., gender, graduation from a specific university, prior work at a competitor) of candidates higher than candidates outside of this group could be delivered training modules focused on awareness and inclusion.

Similar to leveraging AI to more effectively deliver training tailored to the interviewer, machine learning algorithms could be trained to identify features of interview questions that (a) are inclusive across groups (e.g., remove gender-specific language or colloquialisms not understood cross-culturally), (b) are predictive of the hiring decision, or (c) adjust difficulty based on the distribution of candidate evaluations on the rating scale. As interviewers develop and submit questions to use in the interview, these algorithms could evaluate and provide feedback on their appropriateness and effectiveness for inclusion in the interview.

Machine learning algorithms could also be trained to evaluate how calibrated and predictive an interviewer's evaluations are within and across skills. Within skills, algorithms would evaluate whether an interviewer is biased in their evaluation based on a specific skill or similar set of skills. For example, an interviewer consistently rating collaboration much harder than problem-solving may weigh the importance of collaboration for the roles higher than is intended for delivering candidates with a balanced skillset.

In evaluating across skills, a key outcome of structured interview programs is to ensure consistency between interviewers in evaluating candidates. For interview programs where interviewers overlap on evaluated skills, AI systems could be developed to identify the level of calibration between interviewers, taking into account the questions asked and the responses of the candidate, among other elements. In this system, interviews would need to be recorded with AI used to identify the person speaking, convert the speech to text, and then convert the text into meaningful concepts that could be used to classify and score candidate responses. While considered futuristic a decade ago, the increased use of video interviews during the COVID pandemic has made the recording of "live" videos—along with asynchronous video assessments described above—a reality.

Note, however, that video recording, along with broader concerns for how AI could be used in hiring decisions, has also raised data privacy concerns and led to new laws and regulatory guidance globally. As an example in the United States, Illinois passed the Artificial Intelligence Video Interview Act (Illinois General Assembly, 2020), which requires organizations to ensure transparency, consent, and data destruction when leveraging AI to evaluate applicants to positions located in the state. Similarly, New York City passed a bill requiring bias audits of AI-based hiring technology (Kays, 2021).

While these concerns need to be addressed, a natural progression of AI for interviewing would be development of an interview agent able to independently conduct and evaluate the interview in real time. Challenges of reacting to nonverbal cues, determining probe questions, gaining a complete response (situation, action, result) from the candidate, and other aspects of the interview experience would need to be addressed in the development of the solution. As a first step, and with the help of industrial-organizational (IO) practitioners, each of these elements could be designed and incorporated in augmented interview experiences with human interviewers to enable more consistent and accurate interviews.

While adoption of AI-based solutions has increased over the last decade in the hiring space, there are few criterion-related validation results in the research literature, with Chen et al. (2017) and Hickman et al. (2021) as notable examples. In addition, while many companies provide evidence of improved candidate reactions, hiring process efficiency, and improved yield of diverse candidates, few provide evidence that these new assessments deliver unbiased prediction of posthire outcomes for underrepresented people. These gaps surface a need that IO practitioners are perfectly suited to help address, especially for startup organizations relying heavily on recruiters, hiring managers, and HR professionals to identify data sources and relevant outcomes for algorithm development without formal training in validation and bias methodology. Without retaining the proven rigor of traditional assessment design, development, and validation, it will be challenging to convince many organizations, regulatory agencies, and governments to trust AI solutions—especially if transparency doesn't exist for the employed algorithms.

## Onboarding and Growth

While much attention for incorporating AI into the career journey has focused on discovering and hiring talent, there is no shortage of opportunities for leveraging data and analytics to create insights and solutions that support people after they join the organization. Given the potential for learning a great deal about the new hire across the hiring process, algorithms could be developed to match new hires to learning solutions based on their strengths and opportunities and enable hiring managers to develop an effective onboarding plan, promoting faster ramp. Similarly, algorithms could be developed based on the ability to match strengths and opportunities of new hires with those of the team they will join—or to people more broadly in the organization—to identify mentors or pair people to learn from each other while performing the job.

As employees become more tenured, these same algorithms could be enhanced with additional data collected as they make connections within the organization, engage in learning, and deliver their work. The wide range of data captured in people programs and products makes it possible to use AI in creating a wide range of solutions to help connect people to opportunities and opportunities to people as they grow across their career. For example, AI could help accelerate employees' development by recommending learning goals, curricula, stretch projects, or potential career paths based on their current role, KSAOs, and preferences. These recommendation engines would allow employees to spend more time on the most impactful reskilling and upskilling opportunities for them and the organization, rather than asking employees to navigate these difficult decisions primarily on their own.

From the manager's perspective, an AI-based approach to development could provide them with insights about their team's development goals and enable opportunities to better support their team's development by providing personalized career conversation guides and coaching materials for each team member to help prepare them for the next step in their career journey. This gap analysis for the skills and capabilities required to deliver the work could also be leveraged to create AI bench and workforce planning systems to guide more effective movement of talent to deliver value for the organization while also developing people across their career.

## Mobility and Retention

A critical manager responsibility is to help their team members identify the next assignment or project that will allow them to broaden their skillset, expand the domain in which they operate, or gain experience for promotion. As with the hiring solutions provided above, algorithms could be developed to identify people ready for a next assignment and even push the opportunities to them to review and consider. As ways of working continue to evolve, these algorithms could go beyond formal assignments to incorporate gig opportunities and projects that fit the employee's profile.

Similarly, people who are challenged in being able to deliver impact, grow, or progress in their careers and who may be considering leaving the organization could be identified—and flagged—using machine learning algorithms. These algorithms could then be expanded to create proactive retention programs that connect these people to opportunities and retain them. Given the cost and disruption of losing talented people (especially to competitors), such retention systems would be a valuable tool for organizations. Learnings from exit prediction and proactive retention algorithms could also be built into more macro-focused strategic and workforce planning capabilities to identify teams and organizations that need support to promote organizational health and enable their people.

Another challenge faced by many organizations at the moment of exit is the loss of skills and institutional knowledge when an employee retires. In certain markets, industries, and organizations where a significant portion of the workforce is at or nearing retirement eligibility, the loss of capability could be crippling. Similar to designing algorithms that connect new hires to mentors or teams in the organization, algorithms could be designed to match new hires and tenured employees with employees about to retire or even retirees interested in sharing their knowledge. By leveraging the experience of this segment of the workforce to upskill and develop people in the organization, learning can be transferred while reducing mistakes or failures already realized.

## Artificial Intelligence People-Opportunity Ecosystem

While focusing on a specific moment in the career journey to identify, design, and train AI algorithms to connect people to opportunities—or other people—can add tremendous value for an organization and its people, the potential of horizontally integrated AI-driven capabilities to create an ecosystem of support is becoming a reality through advances in technology and access to data. As specific AI use cases in the career journey are developed, implemented, and evaluated, it will become clearer which data elements are important to consider and leverage in AI solutions across the career journey.

One common thread we've found that connects most, if not all, moments in the career journey is the interplay of jobs and skills. Leveraging a standardized job architecture, along with a clear understanding of the skills required to deliver the work and responsibilities of the job, provides a common connector through which to understand how the needs and strengths of the individual align with the needs and deliverables required by the organization. As Bersin (2021) has described, there has been a proliferation of work over the last few years by vendors and organizations to develop skill databases and then elevate these into taxonomies and ontologies using AI capabilities. The end goal is to enable skill concepts to be brought together from disparate programs, products, or systems to enable a common understanding of skills across the career journey.

Looking across the touchpoints in the career journey where skills are a key data element, predictor, or outcome in helping to connect people to opportunities, we would concur that more effort and attention should be paid to creating a solid skills foundation for people processes, programs, and products. Linked with jobs, this common thread allows for a mutual understanding of how the needs of the individual and the organization influence AI matching and decision support solutions.

Through a shared understanding, an organization can then start its AI journey based on where data exists to initially define and train algorithms, even if this space isn't where the biggest pain points will be resolved by connecting people and opportunities. As mentioned previously, a lot of organizations have focused on training matching algorithms in the sourcing space, given the amount of data available on the potential candidate and the job. If a pain point exists in connecting people with learning opportunities to upskill, the features predicting job success for skills and other common data elements could serve as a starting point to train algorithms in the learning space. In addition to expediting training, this iterative process of developing AI solutions to address needs across the career journey would shed light on those elements common in supporting decisions and enabling people's success. Over time, these solutions could be integrated through the common elements to create AI as a service that could be called by products that people interact with to match them to opportunities or other people within and potentially even beyond the organization.

# References

Bersin, J. (2021, June 28). *Building a skills system of record: EdCast releases Skills Studio.* https://joshbersin.com/2020/01/workday-skills-cloud-a-big-idea-with-much-more-to-come/

Chen, L., Zhao, R., Leong, C. W., Lehman, B., Feng, G., & Hoque, M. E. (2017). Automated video interview judgment on a large-sized corpus collected online.

[Paper Presentation]. *International Conference on Affective Computing and Intelligent Interaction*, San Antonio, TX.

Guo, Q., Geyik, S. C., Ozcaglar, C., Thakkar, K., Anjum, N., & Kenthapadi, K. (2019, April 22). *The AI behind LinkedIn Recruiter search and recommendation systems*. LinkedIn Engineering. https://engineering.linkedin.com/blog/2019/04/ai-behind-linkedin-recruiter-search-and-recommendation-systems

Hickman, L., Bosch, N., Ng, V., Saef, R., Tay, L., & Woo, S. E. (2021). Automated video interview personality assessments: Reliability, validity, and generalizability investigations. *Journal of Applied Psychology, 107*(8), 1323–1351.

Illinois General Assembly. (2020, January 1). *Public Act 101-0260*. https://www.ilga.gov/legislation/publicacts/fulltext.asp?Name=101-0260

Kays, K. (2021, November 12). *New York City passed a bill requiring "bias audits" of AI hiring tech*. Protocol. https://www.protocol.com/bulletins/nyc-ai-hiring-tools?utm_campaign=hrb&utm_medium=newsletter&utm_source=morning_brew

Russell, S. J., & Norvig, P. (2021). *Artificial intelligence: A modern approach*. Pearson.

Turing, A. M. (1950). Computing machinery and intelligence. *Mind, 49*, 433–460.

# 23
# Applications of High-Stakes Rich-Media Simulations

*Suzanne Tsacoumis*

Organizations have long relied on job simulations to provide valuable insight into one's knowledge, skills, abilities, and other characteristics (KSAOs). Simulations are high-fidelity assessments that require the individual to participate in activities that reflect relevant job tasks and, in turn, provide a vehicle for assessing both declarative and procedural knowledge (Thornton & Mueller-Hanson, 2004), as well as numerous skills, abilities, and competencies linked to those job tasks. They often offer an opportunity to assess difficult-to-measure constructs, such as judgment and problem-solving, conflict management, planning and organizing, adaptability and resilience, decisiveness, oral communication, relating with others, teamwork, and persuasiveness (Goldstein et al., 1992; Schmitt & Ostroff, 1986). Some of the most common examples of these types of high-fidelity assessments include live simulations such as role plays, in-basket exercises, and oral presentations.

For over half a century, simulations have proven to be powerful tools for both selection/promotion and developmental purposes, and their validity is well documented (e.g., Arthur et al., 2003; Bray & Grant, 1966; Gaugler et al., 1987; Klimoski & Brickner, 1987; Moses, 1977; Schmidt & Hunter, 1998; Thornton & Byham, 1982; Tsacoumis, 2007). They are well accepted by candidates (Rynes & Connerley, 1993; Thornton, 1992), they have a high degree of face validity (Cascio & Phillips, 1979; Schmidt et al., 1977; Tsacoumis, 2007; Wernimont & Campbell, 1968), and they are harder to fake (Thornton & Mueller-Hanson, 2004).

Although the value of high-fidelity simulations is clear, their high-touch nature is often a deterrent to their use due to the cost and time required to

Suzanne Tsacoumis, *Applications of High-Stakes Rich-Media Simulations* In: *Talent Assessment.*
Edited by: Tracy M. Kantrowitz, Douglas H. Reynolds, and John C. Scott, Oxford University Press.
© Society of Industrial Organizational Psychology 2023. DOI: 10.1093/oso/9780197611050.003.0023

develop and implement them. In addition, their viability has become more tenuous given the increased reliance on automation to screen and evaluate job candidates or to develop job incumbents. As such, organizations are continuing to search for more efficient ways to gather the information they need about one's capabilities. There is no doubt that the technological tools are available that can enhance the assessment process. The challenge is to use the benefits offered by technology to help master the complexities associated with effectively measuring one's competencies with enough precision and confidence to make high-stakes personnel decisions, such as those associated with hiring and promoting employees.

Some of the initial mechanisms to reduce costs and increase efficiencies involved reliance on very basic tools such as the telephone or video. For example, one alternative to a live role play is to conduct the candidate-assessor interactions using the phone or videoconferencing. Another approach to increasing efficiency is to record the candidates' responses to a scenario presented in an assessment and then send those recordings to assessors to score from their separate locations. This eliminates the need to have assessors meet in person to score and discuss each candidate. A now-common approach to in-baskets is to have the test taker type their responses to each item into a response box, which are then scored remotely by assessors. Although effective and routinely used, there isn't much that is particularly innovative about these methods anymore.

Organizations are pressing for engaging, interactive online assessments that are efficient and valid and include an automated scoring process, particularly for their selection and promotion efforts. That is, rather than the high-touch, live job simulations, there is a demand for tools that portray an innovative and cutting-edge culture, while also offering meaningful results. In response, the testing industry has embraced the use of rich media as a substitute for the traditional high-fidelity components of live simulations. For purposes of this chapter, "rich media" refers to video or animation, and a "simulation" is an assessment that closely mirrors the job where the candidate proceeds through a scenario based on their responses to various stimuli. One can think of them as a slice of a day in the life of the target position. Therefore, a rich-media simulation (RMS) is "an assessment that uses animation or live video along with branching technology to present the test material in a manner that simulates how the scenario may unfold in real life by allowing the test taker to dictate how the assessment proceeds or unfolds" (Tsacoumis, 2015).

There is a rich history of using media-enriched tools for training and development purposes, such as those used to train pilots and law enforcement officers. In fact, organizations have embraced the use of rich media as one component of their employee development programs for a wide range of jobs (e.g., sales, customer service representative, law enforcement officer, supervisory positions), as well as for recruitment efforts including realistic job previews and self-assessments of organizational fit. However, of particular interest in this chapter are those assessments used in high-stakes situations that involve personnel decisions such as in entry-level and promotion programs since those applications set a higher bar in terms of measurement and validity.

## Common Stimuli Formats

Similar to a traditional job simulation, an RMS presents typical job situations that elicit behaviors associated with the targeted KSAOs. In some cases, an RMS may be based on a particular character or role, such as a call center or customer service representative (Hawkes, 2013). In this case, the context is agnostic. In other instances, the assessment may replicate a software application that the incumbent uses to evaluate one's ability to navigate and effectively use the tool. An even more immersive approach is to create a virtual environment where the candidate "enters" the scene and interacts with other characters and manipulates objects. As an example, the assessment may involve navigating around a warehouse floor to address various situations (Hawkes, 2013). A fourth approach reflects a more customized solution, likely developed for a specific position within an organization that requires the candidate to address unique circumstances that mandate organizational knowledge.

Tsacoumis (2015) provided a detailed description of how to develop an RMS by implementing a content-oriented development process so that validity is built in from the outset. The stimuli in an RMS may be video using actors, 2D animation, or 3D animation. Among the three mediums, video with live actors rather than animated characters offers the most realistic experience for candidates. However, 2D animation is faster than showing the full motion of 3D or live action. In a study directly comparing the three options, Bruk-Lee et al. (2016) found that test takers rated a video-based version of a situational judgment test (SJT) to be more engaging than that same assessment using 2D and 3D animation. The comparison between 2D and 3D animation is less obvious. Hawkes (2012) pointed out that many perceive 3D animation to be uncanny, often eliciting a reaction that the stimuli are creepy. However, test takers rated the 3D version of the SJT as being more realistic and giving a better impression of the organization than the 2D version (Bruk-Lee et al., 2016). It is also very likely that continued technological advances may be able to address the unsettling aspects of 3D animation so that it would evoke a less negative reaction. That said, another perspective suggests that we have learned to accept, and even embrace, 2D images given their prevalence in our entertainment (e.g., *The Simpsons*) as well as in countless commercials, marketing campaigns, and infographics. In fact, Bruk-Lee and colleagues (2016) found that candidates overcame the limitations of 2D animation even though the characters are not able to express realistic emotions.

Ultimately, organizations and test developers should consider the following four factors when determining which of the three options to use in their assessments (Bruk-Lee et al., 2016):

- Production costs and time: Live action is quite costly, with some providing estimates in terms of cost per minute (e.g., $2,000/minute). Granted, those costs can be somewhat reduced if the shoot is not complex and is done in one location. The production cost of 3D animation is significantly more than 2D animation.
- Practicality: There are some scenarios that may be difficult to create with live action (e.g., a burning building, a large crowd).
- Flexibility: Given the nature of the test development process, it is imperative to consider the likelihood that the scenarios will need to be modified to suit different organizational contexts. This is much easier to accomplish with 2D animation; it can be quite costly with 3D animation and video, which involves re-engaging the actors.
- Aesthetics and brand: How important are the look and feel of the assessment to the organization's image? For higher level positions (e.g., C-suite and executives) or for assessments that are very visible externally, an organization may want to invest in live action. However, in other instances it may opt for a 3D or 2D solution.

## Common Response Formats

In the simplest form, an assessment can incorporate media by using a video to present a scenario to which a candidate provides a written response. This response could be scored either by a trained assessor/evaluator or by using a computer-based application designed to score written text. A very basic and common modification to this approach is to require the candidate to respond to closed-ended questions, such as "Which is the best response?" or "Rate the effectiveness of each response." This type of assessment is akin to an SJT where there is a discrete set of short scenarios followed by a query(ies) specific to each situation. The scenarios are not related to, or dependent on, one another. Given this, for the purposes of this chapter, an SJT is not considered an RMS since subsequent scenarios in an RMS are related to earlier ones.

The RMSs are those that progress based on the test taker's responses, similar to how a live simulation (e.g., role play) would proceed. After viewing the stimulus, the candidate is then asked questions to collect competency-based information, as well as a way to move the simulation forward. Although the questions are typically close-ended, often there is no correct answer. They are designed to evaluate the test taker's thought processes and decisions and, in some places, may dictate the next scene (e.g., an answer to the test taker's question, a person the test taker wanted to interact with). Responses to questions may be (a) on a Likert scale (e.g., rate the effectiveness of each action), (b) a discrete rating (e.g., this action should not be taken; this is a top priority, do it immediately), (c) a rank ordering, or (d) a dichotomous response (e.g., approve or not approve). At various points, candidates are asked what action they would like to take (e.g., call someone, ask questions, read materials) and then the simulation proceeds accordingly. They may also receive emails, phone or video calls, or visits from a character.

Some RMSs may give an appearance of branching based on the participant's choices of what action to take when, in fact, the simulation is proceeding in an identical manner for all test takers. This is similar to how live simulations proceed. In contrast, other RMSs, or portions of the assessment, use intelligent branching to incorporate true branching capabilities that allow users to determine who they meet with, what they do next, and what type of information to review. Intelligent branching increases realism and the test taker's engagement while simultaneously allowing the focal competencies to be assessed with increased fidelity. Test developers need to be prepared to address the measurement issues and increased scoring complexities associated with incorporating branching since, by definition, not all test takers will proceed in an identical manner, and therefore, they may not have the same interactions, obtain the same information, or be posed the same sets of questions.

## Applications

One basic augmentation to a traditional computer-based assessment is to deliver some of the test content via audio. For example, some operational contact center assessments for entry-level selection require the test taker to click on an audio icon to hear the concerns of customers. After hearing the issue, the individual can gather information by clicking on tabs on the screen. Then, they select how they would address the customer's complaint. Other organizations have added still images to accompany the audio. Targeted competencies for these types of assessments include accurate typing, attentiveness, issue resolution, navigation, and service orientation.

Several organizations add realism and interactivity by simulating one's email inbox. The test content is delivered via email messages, voicemails that are accessed via a link in an email, and, in some cases, a recorded video message delivered during the assessment. In these instances, participants often type their response into a box that is then scored by human assessors. Of course, close-ended responses, such as multiple-choice questions, are also used in some assessments. One variation on this theme is to add short interactions with live assessors by having them "call" the candidate during the test to discuss a situation. This increases the fidelity of the assessment and more closely replicates the engagement offered by live role plays.

Although these example applications are interesting and offer a more engaging assessment than a traditional text-based measure, similar to video-based SJTs, they do not fall into the definition used in this chapter of a high-stakes RMS designed to provide a rich, interactive experience that simulates the day in the life of the incumbent. And, as noted, by "high stakes," we are referring to those that generate a score that serves as the basis for a personnel decision.

Nevertheless, there are a few good illustrations of operational RMSs. Several organizations employ very similar types of custom RMSs for either entry-level selection or promotion to supervisory and managerial positions. In all cases, these RMSs use 2D animation to portray various job-related situations that simulate conditions and issues an incumbent may face on the job (see Figure 23.1). In contrast to an SJT, these RMSs focus on one larger, multifaceted situation that mandates gathering additional information, making multiple interim decisions, and ultimately addressing all aspects of the issue at hand. These scenarios are akin to a live simulation such as a role play given their complexity and that they require the test taker to thoroughly

Figure 23.1. Example of a 2D Animated Stimulus

review the details to address the issues presented. For one RMS, candidates for an executive position are informed they need to stand up a new division and within a few hours make recommendations regarding several critical factors to a senior official. In another assessment for executive selection, the test taker is informed that they are going to lead an organization that is being created by merging two different companies. By the end of the assessment, they provide input to be used at a meeting with the press on how the organization will address several contentious issues. And, as a completely different example, candidates for a supervisory law enforcement position are presented with an active case that poses a serious safety concern and requires immediate action. This particular RMS also incorporates emails, phone calls, and drop-by visits from staff throughout the assessment that are not related to the case but reflect the types of inquiries the job incumbent may receive on any given day.

Prior to taking the assessment, the test taker is given background information about their role and to establish the context of the fictitious office or organization. Then, the RMS begins with a character appearing on the screen as if they are entering the test taker's office. This character explains the circumstances, which, of course, need to be addressed immediately. In some places, the assessment unfolds based on the test taker's responses, whereas at other points everyone receives the same stimuli (e.g., an unannounced visitor, an email). At any point, the test taker can click on a tab with relevant written materials or they can request to talk with another individual, which will bring up another animated clip. The test taker can "talk" with characters by selecting from a list of actions/questions to which the character will respond. At various points throughout the assessment, the test taker must respond to different close-ended questions such as: How effective is each response? How soon would they take this action, if ever? What would they do next? There are some options for branching throughout the assessments; however, all test takers interact with the same core set of individuals and respond to the same core set of questions. That is, regardless of the paths taken due to different lines of inquiries and requested meetings, all test takers are brought back to the same core interactions.

Typically, test takers are given up to 90 minutes to complete the RMS, although there are a few assessments that are much more involved, so their time limits are 4 to 5 hours. These longer simulations are those that provide a more comprehensive day-in-the-life experience that require the test taker to address a variety of issues while also attending to the "crisis" initially introduced at the onset of the assessment.

As previously noted, some organizations prefer to use live action given the importance of the corporate brand, particularly when searching for the most senior leaders of the organization. As an example, these organizations use high-quality film segments, along with simulated emails, reports, and spreadsheets, to create a highly realistic and immersive work environment for executive-level candidates (see Figure 23.2). Similar to the RMSs described above, the scenario evolves as the test taker responds to various stimuli and respond to questions that provide options for proceeding, which then, in turn, dictates how they navigate through the complex scenario.

Traditional live simulations are scored by having assessors observe participants' performance and make ratings by comparing observed behaviors to behaviorally anchored scales. Most RMSs pose numerous close-ended questions as a means to understand the test takers' thoughts and to capture how they would respond. Although it is feasible that the questions have a correct answer, commonly the queries are more nuanced to try to capture degrees of effectiveness of various potential responses and to allow for multiple actions. This is done in an effort to mirror reality, where actions aren't necessarily right or wrong but may be more or less effective, and where individuals may take more than one course of action. There also may be questions that are not scored but are presented as a means to continue the simulation. In many instances, responses to all scored queries are

**Figure 23.2.** Example of a Video-Based Stimulus

compiled to compute competency scores (which reflect the response options retranslated into discreet competencies) along with an overall assessment score. Tsacoumis (2015) provides a more detailed explanation of how RMSs may be scored.

## The Value and the Evidence

RMSs offer a viable, more efficient alternative to live simulations. Their interactive nature makes them appealing and engaging, and organizations are starting to demonstrate the value they have to their business and operations. For example, the cost to develop and administer a supervisory promotion process was reduced by $1 million by switching from a live assessment center to an RMS (McBeth & Tsacoumis, 2014). Another organization found that their customer service RMS reduced administration costs by 50% and saved the organization $5 million in turnover costs (A. Boyce, personal communication, March 30, 2016). In addition, the top scorers were three times more likely to be rated as having high advancement potential. Consolidated feedback from participants across four different rich-media experiences (senior manager level to C-suite executives) revealed that 90% felt their participation afforded them the opportunity to improve their leadership skills (J. Scott, personal communication, September 21, 2021). Interestingly, the reactions were uniformly positive regardless of one's overall assessment score, which has a direct impact on promotion decisions. A large technology organization with several different modular simulations found that those with higher scores were more satisfied and engaged in their roles, and they stayed with the company longer (J. Geimer, personal communication, September 29, 2021).

When surveyed 12 to 18 months after completing an RMS, participants displayed an average of 88% improvement in the targeted competencies (J. Scott, personal communication, September 21, 2021). In addition, early- to mid-level executive participants who scored in the highest band of the assessment program were promoted at 1.5 to 2.5 times the speed of those who scored in the lowest band (J. Scott, personal communication, September 21, 2021). Consistent with the finding by Bruk-Lee and colleagues (2016), there is evidence that candidates who complete an RMS that relies on 2D animation have no problem accepting that type of stimuli; they remain engaged and take the assessment seriously (McBeth & Tsacoumis, 2014).

Although there are few published studies documenting the validity of RMS as defined in this chapter, available evidence is promising. For example, internal criterion-related validity studies performed by one of the big five American information technology companies suggested that their high-fidelity simulations are related to job performance as measured by managerial ratings of job competencies or objective metrics (J. Geimer, personal communication, September 29, 2021). In addition, they found that the lowest test performers were disproportionately affecting productivity, quality, and attrition. When looking across several media-rich assessments for service providers (e.g., collection agent, bank teller, customer service provider, and retail sales associate), LaTorre and Bucklan (2013) found overall criterion-related validity coefficients that ranged from .41 to .48, corrected for unreliability of the criterion. Using supervisor ratings as the criterion measure, McBeth and Tsacoumis (2014) found an uncorrected validity coefficient of .45 for an RMS used to assess candidates for promotion to a first-line supervisory position. This simulation used branching technology and relied entirely on scoring responses to close-ended questions posed throughout the assessment (e.g., How effective is each response? How much of a problem are each of the following issues?).

## Challenges

Cost is one of the greatest barriers to the use of RMSs. This is no surprise; historically, simulations for high-stakes processes have been expensive to develop. Adding rich media to the equation significantly amplifies those costs.

That said, technological advances associated with the production of all three mediums—live action, 3D animation, and 2D animation—are driving the costs down, making their use more accessible. Organizations are also finding ways to develop the software platforms for housing and delivering RMSs so they are more generalizable across situations. This helps minimize costs and greatly facilitates scalability. Additionally, organizations that were at the forefront with early applications of media-rich assessments learned quickly that insufficient bandwidth rendered the assessments essentially inoperable. Of course, that is easily solvable with advanced planning and clear implementation guidelines.

Technological advances, coupled with increased efficiencies and reduced costs associated with creating rich media, have opened countless options for delivering engaging online high-stakes job simulations. At the same time, these enhancements to traditional simulations introduce several unique measurement challenges. At the most basic level, test developers must determine the best way to collect information associated with the targeted KSAOs and competencies. Given the situation posed, is there a definitive correct answer? Assuming they are proceeding with close-ended responses, how do they handle the situation if the course of action a test taker would choose is not an option? How do they capture those instances when someone would take more than one action in real life? And in the simplest forms, what specific questions should be included?

In many instances, test developers are opting to include a variety of different item types to better understand one's thoughts and thought processes, to more accurately assess one's competencies, and to try to simulate a real situation more closely. In doing this, however, they are then faced with the issue of determining how best to combine data collected from responses to these different types of items. Consider the following potential types of items:

- Effectiveness ratings on a Likert scale
- Rank ordering of options
- Checklist and hot-spot forms (click on section of form that contains an error)
- Multiple choice (e.g., yes, no, not sure)
- Categorization of options by level of priority

Measurement experts understand that simply combining scores across different item types may lead to unintended weighting of items (Oswald et al.,

2014). To address this, test developers can convert the different item types to a common metric, for example, by using a linear transformation to put responses on a common 7-point scale.

Given the nature of effective job simulations, it is likely that many of the scenarios in an RMS do not have clear-cut answers. That is one of the beauties of simulations, but also a curse, particularly if the goal is to administer a low-touch assessment that relies entirely on close-ended responses. Test developers often address this by asking questions that are scored using a distance scoring method, which involves comparing the test taker's answer to the keyed response as determined by subject matter experts (e.g., how effective is each response?). Unfortunately, this type of scoring is susceptible to coaching (Cullen et al., 2006) and increases the potential for subgroup differences (McDaniel et al., 2011). However, McDaniel and colleagues (2011) point out that this can be addressed by using a variant of the simple distance-based metric that involves standardizing test taker responses (within persons, across item responses) and keyed responses prior to calculating the distance score.

Branching capabilities introduce a unique set of measurement challenges since respondents may complete a slightly different set of items. Of course, branching also contributes to the realism of the assessment, making it more engaging and interactive, and, in turn, more consistent with the spirit of a job simulation. One way of handling the use of branching is during the development process. For example, the assessments could be built so that they offer realistic options but, in fact, there is no new information presented in those interactions not experienced by all test takers. Alternatively, test developers can ensure that all participants see a core set of scenarios and questions so that anything outside of that core set either is not scored or is treated as supplemental information. If the latter option is pursued, then, when computing the reliability of the overall assessment score, developers need to deal with an ill-structured measurement design where items are not fully nested within or fully crossed with test takers. This situation can be addressed by computing a $G(q,k)$ coefficient, which is an estimate of the internal consistency among items composing the overall assessment score that is similar to coefficient alpha yet accounts for the fact that not all test takers completed all items due to branching (Putka et al., 2008).

One final, yet critical, challenge rests with the novelty of RMSs and the lack of published research that documents the validity of these measures. Consistent with the process to create live simulations, test developers tend to follow a content-oriented development approach when creating simulations that incorporate rich media. This provides some validity evidence, although given the response format, particularly if the assessment relies on scoring answers to specific close-ended questions, one could argue that content validity evidence may not be sufficient. Therefore, it is encouraging that the available criterion-related validity evidence, as described above, is promising, although additional study is warranted.

## Future Directions

The success and sustainability of RMSs are dependent on additional research regarding the measurement properties of these assessments. In addition to collecting further criterion-related validity evidence, we need to demonstrate their construct validity to better understand the meaning of resulting scores, particularly those reported at the competency level. Researchers should continue to evaluate the scales used in the questions, the methods of combining scores, the relationship among the different scale scores, and the reliability of the scales. At this point, we may be in a situation where practice is ahead of the literature and scientific support.

Given the rate of technological advances, future augmentations to RMSs are likely to reflect these evolving capabilities as well as developments in our measurement expertise. For example, it seems logical that these types of simulations will more readily take advantage of automated scoring of open-ended responses and use text-to-speech features to eliminate the need for voice-over actors. It may become commonplace to build in features that allow participants to provide video responses to the situations that are then scored using artificial intelligence even to rate some of the characteristics of one's speech (e.g., friendliness, hostility). Also, synthetic media techniques (aka deepfakes) will likely soon be able to produce automated video that is nearly indistinguishable from live person while still offering the flexibility and speed of change provided by animation. This will put the discussion around 2D versus 3D versus live video to rest. Granted, any of the above-mentioned modifications are likely to introduce new measurement challenges; however, we can expect organizations to demand such embellishments and efficiencies. We must, in turn, rise to the occasion and determine how to conquer them.

## Conclusions

RMSs are an engaging and efficient approach to capturing multiple indicators of one's competencies and capabilities. They offer a sense of realism for test takers that come as close to a live simulation as feasible via an online delivery platform, while still adhering to professional standards, principles, and guidelines for developing high-stakes assessments. Although the nature of RMSs has manifested in different ways across organizations, it is clear they are well-received, powerful tools. And they have opened the window to what may be possible when marrying software engineering capabilities with measurement expertise.

## References

Arthur, W., Day, E. A., McNelly, T. L., & Edens, P. S. (2003). A meta-analysis of the criterion-related validity of assessment center dimensions. *Personnel Psychology, 56*, 125–153.

Bray, D. W., & Grant, D. L. (1966). The assessment center in the measurement of potential for business development. *Psychological Monographs, 80*, 1–27.

Bruk-Lee, V., Lanz, J., Drew, E. N., Coughlin, C., Levine, P., Tuzinski, K., & Wreen, K. (2016). Examining applicant reactions to different media types in character-based simulations for employee selection. *International Journal of Selection and Assessment, 24*(1), 77.

Cascio, W. F., & Phillips, N. F. (1979). Performance testing: A rose among thorns? *Personnel Psychology, 32*, 751–766.

Cullen, M. J., Sackett, P. R., & Lievens, F. (2006). Threats to the operational use of situational judgment tests in the college admission process. *International Journal of Selection and Assessment, 14*, 142–155.

Gaugler, B. B., Rosenthal, D. B., Thornton, G. C., III, & Bentson, C. (1987). Meta-analysis of assessment center validity. *Journal of Applied Psychology, 72*, 493–511.

Goldstein, I. L., Zedeck, S., & Schneider, B. (1992). An exploration of the job analysis-content validity process. In N. Schmitt & W. C. Borman (Eds.), *Personnel selection* (pp. 3–34). Jossey-Bass.

Hawkes, B. J. (2012, April). *Test-takers' empathy for animated humans in SJTs* [Paper presentation]. Annual meeting of the Society for Industrial and Organizational Psychology, San Diego, CA.

Hawkes, B. J. (2013). Simulation technologies. In M. S. Fetzer & K. A. Tuzinski (Eds.), *Simulations for personnel selection* (pp. 63–82). Springer.

Klimoski, R., & Brickner, M. (1987). Why do assessment centers work? The puzzle of assessment center validity. *Personnel Psychology, 40*, 243–260.

LaTorre, J., & Bucklan, M. A. (2013). Simulations for service roles. In M. S. Fetzer & K. A. Tuzinski (Eds.), *Simulations for personnel selection* (pp. 187–214). Springer.

McBeth, R., & Tsacoumis, S. (2014, October). *Going fully automated: A case study* [Paper presentation]. 38th International Congress on Assessment Center Methods, Alexandria, VA.

McDaniel, M. A., Psotka, J., Legree, P. J., Yost, A. P., & Weekley, J. A. (2011). Toward an understanding of situational judgment item validity and group differences. *Journal of Applied Psychology, 96*, 327–336.

Moses, J. L. (1977). The assessment center method. In J. L. Moses & W. C. Byham (Eds.), *Applying the assessment center method* (pp. 3–11). Pergamon Press.

Oswald, F. L., Putka, D. J., & Ock, J. (2014). Weight a minute, what you see in a weighted composite is probably not what you get. In C. E. Lance & R. J. Vandenberg (Eds.), *More statistical and methodological myths and urban legends* (pp. 187–205). Taylor & Francis.

Putka, D. J., Le, H., McCloy, R. A., & Diaz, T. (2008). Ill-structured measurement designs in organizational research: Implications for estimating interrater reliability. *Journal of Applied Psychology, 93*, 959–981.

Rynes, S. L., & Connerley, M. L. (1993). Applicant reactions to alternative selection procedures. *Journal of Business and Psychology, 7*, 251–277.

Schmidt, F. L., Greenthal, A. L., Hunter, J. E., Berner, J. G., & Seaton, F. W. (1977). Job sample versus paper-and-pencil trades and technical tests: Adverse impact and examinee attitudes. *Personnel Psychology, 30*, 187–197.

Schmidt, F. L., & Hunter, J. E. (1998). The validity and utility of selection methods in personnel psychology: Practical and theoretical implications of 85 years of research findings. *Psychological Bulletin, 124*, 262–274.

Schmitt, N., & Ostroff, C. (1986). Operationalizing the "behavioral consistency" approach: Selection test development based on a content-oriented approach. *Personnel Psychology, 39*, 91–108.

Thornton, G. C., III. (1992). *Assessment centers in human resource management*. Addison Wesley.

Thornton, G. C., III, & Byham, W. C. (1982). *Assessment centers and managerial performance*. Academic Press.

Thornton, G. C., III, & Mueller-Hanson, R. A. (2004). *Developing organizational simulations: A guide for practitioners and students*. Lawrence Erlbaum Associates.

Tsacoumis, S. (2007). Assessment centers. In D. L. Whetzel & G. R. Wheaton (Eds.), *Applied measurement: Industrial psychology in human resources management* (pp. 259–292). Lawrence Erlbaum.

Tsacoumis, S. (2015). Rich-media interactive simulations: Lessons learned. In Y. Rosen, S. Ferrara, & M. Mosharraf (Eds.), *Handbook of research on technology tools for real-world skill development* (pp. 261–283). IGI Global.

Wernimont, P. F., & Campbell, J. P. (1968). Signs, samples, and criteria. *Journal of Applied Psychology, 52*, 372–376.

# 24
# Psychoneurometric Assessments for High-Risk Jobs

*Brennan D. Cox, Dan McHail, Kyle Pettijohn, and Tatana Olson*[*]

## Introduction

A variety of occupational classifications can be characterized as "high risk" based on personnel exposure to environmental stressors, as well as their overall risk of injury, illness, or fatality. For these jobs, traditional assessment tools (e.g., self-report, paper-and-pencil measures) may be insufficient for evaluating a person's potential or performance in meaningful ways. Technological advancements have produced alternative assessments that reliably capture human capabilities and aptitudes in novel, objective ways to help inform our overall understanding of one's fitness for high-risk employment. Advanced technologies also provide a means to simulate the unique stressors found within these jobs under realistic, repeatable, and highly controlled conditions as needed to assess personnel in extremis. The information derived from these alternative assessments may be combined with traditional measures to revise existing construct knowledge or even provide a mechanism to develop new constructs. In this chapter, we describe how innovations in neurophysiological assessments, biotechnologies, and simulation can improve our understanding of human performance and our ability to make predictions for those employed in high-risk jobs.

---

[*]Disclaimer. We are military Service members or employees of the U.S. Government. This work was prepared as part of our official duties. Title 17, U.S.C., § 105 provides that copyright protection under this title is not available for any work of the U.S. Government. Title 17, U.S.C., § 101 defines a U.S. Government work as a work prepared by a military Service member or employee of the U.S. Government as part of that person's official duties.

Brennan D. Cox, Dan McHail, Kyle Pettijohn, and Tatana Olson, *Psychoneurometric Assessments for High-Risk Jobs*
In: *Talent Assessment*. Edited by: Tracy M. Kantrowitz, Douglas H. Reynolds, and John C. Scott, Oxford University Press.
© Society of Industrial Organizational Psychology 2023. DOI: 10.1093/oso/9780197611050.003.0024

## Characterizing "High-Risk" Jobs

High-risk jobs differ from other lines of work based on their inherent danger. That is, for high-risk jobs, the nature of the work itself carries with it the potential for threat or harm to the incumbent and/or those with whom this person interacts. Of course, the source, nature, frequency, and severity of these threats depend largely upon the job in question.

In general, high-risk jobs present some combination of physical stressors (e.g., chemical, biological, environmental hazards), psychological stressors (e.g., isolation; exposure to violence, trauma, or death; ethical or moral judgments), or other extreme demands (e.g., high workload, complicated machinery, irregular hours, small margin for error). Indicators of these characteristics are present across a variety of high-risk jobs, including emergency responders, construction crews, health care workers, and positions throughout the military, agriculture, forestry, and fishing industries (American Psychological Association, 2011).

The specific knowledge, skills, and abilities associated with successful performance in high-risk jobs understandably vary by position, though some competencies are commonplace across these occupations. These largely align within the global construct of stress management, but also rule abidance, adaptability, and decision-making autonomy. For example, the Occupational Information Network (National Center for O*NET Development, 2021) lists the following work styles as characteristic among skilled laborers, firefighters, logging equipment operators, nurses, pilots, and security guards: stress tolerance, self-control, persistence, integrity, dependability, flexibility, initiative, and independence.

Taken together, high-risk jobs expose personnel to extreme environmental conditions and physical and psychological demands, which, if not appropriately mitigated, can lead to injury, illness, or death. These job characteristics, in turn, necessitate certain personal attributes to sufficiently protect personnel from these threats, both in the short term (to achieve ongoing task objectives) and in the long term (to sustain a career). From an assessment standpoint, the challenge is determining how to measure these attributes in reliable, valid, and meaningful ways.

## Military Applications

For perspective, consider the range of stressors placed upon military personnel, who historically have conducted operations on the open battlefield (on land, sea, or air), but more recently find themselves engaged in dense, urban, and politically sensitive environments. Despite these evolving requirements, many of the tests and measures used to select and classify military personnel have remained largely unchanged since World War II. Indeed, the most common military screening tools are self-report measures validated against early career training performance. Although beneficial for large-scale administrations focused on entry-level screening, these traditional batteries offer limited insights into the wide array of psychological characteristics that enable modern warfighters to endure and thrive in prevailing conditions.

The Naval Aviation Selection Test Battery (ASTB), the primary tool for selecting student pilots and flight officers for the U.S. Navy, Marine Corps, and Coast Guard, provides context for this argument. For decades, the ASTB comprised paper-and-pencil tests of general cognitive abilities and job-specific knowledge; however, since its initial release in 1941, there have been numerous groundbreaking advancements in aircraft technologies and flight performance standards, in addition to developments in personnel assessment practices, which prompted an overhaul of the battery. As part of this revision, the ASTB adopted a computer-based format using hands-on stick and throttle devices, which allowed for performance-based testing of several psychomotor abilities, including multilimb coordination, spatial orientation, perceptual speed, reaction time, dexterity, and control precision.

The "hands-on" portion of the ASTB more accurately reflects the requirements for piloting high-performance aircraft and introduced a means to evaluate candidates' potential for real-time decision-making and maneuvering capability under duress. These tests are face valid, in that candidates use realistic flight controls to chase enemy aircraft in a computer simulation. But, more importantly, they are construct and criterion valid. Prior to the ASTB revision, factors associated with stress tolerance were assessed with self-report items that were highly susceptible to impression management and more likely to assess candidates' perceptions rather than skill or ability. Introducing performance-based measures overcame these hurdles, while also yielding a 16% improvement in the prediction of flight training grades and savings of several million dollars annually in training costs (Operational Psychology, 2019). Indeed, in less than 2 years, the updated ASTB delivered a full return on investment in transitioning from a traditional static test battery to a more modern computer-adaptive, performance-based assessment.

Testing, human performance assessment, and simulation technologies have undergone tremendous advancements in recent years, providing opportunity for more complex measurement of the knowledge, skills, and abilities associated with success in high-risk jobs. Realizing the full benefit of these technologies will require a calculated approach that:

1. identifies the relevant operational stressors of high-risk jobs;
2. identifies job-relevant cognitive, behavioral, and emotional constructs;
3. develops controlled environments to elicit stressors; and
4. leverages alternative assessments (e.g., physiological, neuroimaging, biochemical measures) to quantify performance and potential in novel ways.

The outcomes of this approach will include an improved understanding of whether and to what degree various competencies are impaired or enhanced when exposed to specific operational stressors, and how individual differences in these factors serve to protect an individual (or not) during stressor exposure. This will allow assessment professionals to enhance existing selection and training tools as well as develop more targeted, operationally relevant measures to maximize performance prediction in extreme environments.

Our aim here is not to completely replace traditional assessments. In many cases, traditional methods of testing are the most efficient and cost-effective means to screen candidates and/or capture human performance data. Rather, we propose that assessments for high-risk jobs can be improved by integrating traditional measures of performance with physiological and behavioral metrics made accessible by recent technological advances.

## Psychoneurometric Assessment Model

A useful guide to this process is the psychoneurometric model (as described by Patrick in National Research Council, 2013). This model provides a mechanism to revise existing and develop new constructs by combining insights from neurobiology with research on individual differences to bridge multiple domains, including physiology, self-report, and behavioral studies, to form composite measures with both psychological and physiological meaning. For example, constructs that have clear psychometric referents (e.g., readiness, hardiness) can be enhanced by incorporating physiological data (e.g., brain activity, neuroendocrine function). This framework helps refine the operationalization of these constructs and clarifies the relationships across measurement domains.

The psychoneurometric model offers a number of key benefits for the assessment community. First, traditional assessments such as questionnaires are prone to response bias, whereby respondents tailor their responses to match the test administrator's perceived expectations. Incorporating physiological measures into these assessments helps eliminate response bias. Additionally, physiological activity that underlies performance provides important mechanistic information as to how people respond to a given challenge. This physiologic component to performance may be a source of individual differences and could further explain variability found in traditional assessment outcomes. Multidomain constructs developed with the psychoneurometric model can also be used outside of the selection context to optimize the design of training tools.

Limitations of this model also merit consideration as neurobiological activity is complex and driven by a number of factors. As such, it can be challenging to separate the reliable person variance of a physiological marker from sources of variability other than the capability being measured. Further, to effectively bridge the domains of physiology and performance, neurobehavioral constructs must have clear referents in both neurobiology and behavior.

To apply the psychoneurometric model to the study of individual differences, Patrick (National Research Council, 2013) recommends three steps:

1. Identify validated neurophysiological markers for the psychometric measures of a construct of interest.
2. Determine the extent to which these neurophysiological factors covary.
3. Modify psychometric measures to improve coherence with the underlying neurophysiology.

To illustrate, Patrick referenced the construct of inhibitory control, defined as the "ability to restrain or modulate impulses." Neural correlates of inhibitory control include the P300 event-related potential (ERP) and the error-related negativity ERP, which are two types of brain responses that can be detected and recorded using electroencephalography (EEG), a measure of the brain's electrical activity from the scalp surface. Following the psychoneurometric model, Patrick combined neural markers of inhibitory control with self-report measures of inhibition (e.g., impulsiveness, risk taking) to inform a new, composite construct with psychological and physiological significance.

Using a similar approach, there is considerable opportunity to enhance the predictive ability of assessment tools for high-risk jobs. This will require first identifying risk factors and constructs associated with a given job and determining what psychometric measures and physiological indicators have been validated for these constructs. Then, relevant neurobehavioral constructs can be used to incorporate different domains into a composite construct that more fully describes the performance capability of interest.

## Case Studies in Military Aviation

The military aviator must maintain performance under a combination of extreme stressors and task demands. The primary preconditions to aviation mishaps include fatigue, spatial disorientation, visual illusions, and hypoxia (Federal Aviation Administration, 2016). In the sections that follow, we describe several of these leading risk factors for aviator performance and review how impacts of these stressors on performance are traditionally assessed. We also discuss how emerging technologies can leverage the psychoneurometric approach to better understand the neurobiological constructs underlying performance and to maximize the criterion, construct, and content validity of aviator assessments.

### Hypoxia

At high altitudes, aviators may be exposed to low-oxygen environments and subsequently experience decreased oxygen in the blood supply, termed hypoxia. While aircraft life support systems mitigate exposure to low-oxygen environments, hypoxia remains a significant concern in aviation. Effects of hypoxia on the nervous system include impairments in sensory processing (e.g., reduced color vision) and cognition (McMorris et al., 2017). In the cockpit, hypoxia may lead to decrements in flight performance and can interfere with the ability of aviators to execute emergency procedures. Following reports of impairment and even fatalities due to hypoxia early in the history of aviation, techniques were developed to model hypoxic exposure in a ground-based environment. This included the use of hypobaric chambers, which continue to be used when training aviation personnel today.

In a typical hypobaric chamber exposure for U.S. Air Force aviator training, an instructor will accompany students in the chamber as they "ascend" to progressively higher simulated altitudes and note changes in their sensory perception (e.g., color vision), cognitive performance (e.g., completing simple puzzles), and communication ability. While effective in training students to recognize and respond to hypoxic symptoms, the high cost of these chambers led researchers to develop the Reduced Oxygen Breathing Device (ROBD), which delivers a normobaric hypoxic exposure via an oronasal mask. The ROBD was found to deliver effective hypoxia training at a comparatively lower cost (Artino et al., 2006; Vacchiano et al., 2004) and is the current standard for hypoxia training of naval aviators.

The aeromedical research community has also used these training tools to assess the impacts of hypoxia on cognition. Behavioral studies have found that hypoxia impairs reaction time, working memory, attentional control, and decision-making (Asmaro et al., 2013; McMorris et al., 2017; Petrassi et al., 2012). This work addressed a major limitation of traditional, self-report measures of hypoxia: asking people to self-assess while their ability to do so was compromised. Using alternative measures to assess vulnerability to hypoxia exposure is therefore a leap in the positive direction.

Furthering the aim to bridge self-report and psychological data, neurobiological effects of hypoxia exposure have been identified. In particular, research using a noninvasive technique to record brain activity, EEG, has shown that well-established ERPs that index sensory processing integrity recorded over the frontal cortex are sensitive to hypoxia. ERPs represent a specific pattern of electrical activity produced in the brain in response to cognitive stimuli. One such experiment identified effects of hypoxia in the visual domain using the visual mismatch negativity, an ERP paradigm in which intermittent changes in a series of visual stimuli (e.g., differences in color) elicit a negative deflection in the EEG signal that is maximal over the frontal cortex (Blacker et al., 2021; see Figure 24.1). Hypoxia effects have also been shown in the auditory domain using the auditory mismatch negativity, an ERP paradigm where infrequently presented "oddball" tones interspersed with more familiar "standard" tones elicit a negative deflection maximal over the frontal cortex (Seech et al., 2020). Both the visual and auditory mismatch negativities are evoked passively by unattended differences in background sensory input.

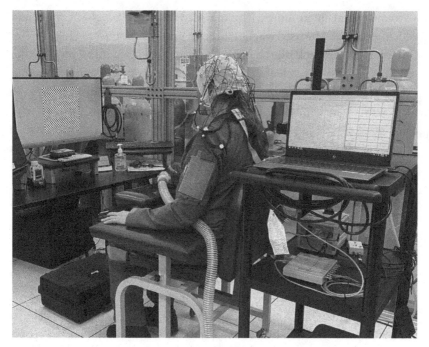

**Figure 24.1.** A research subject's brain activity is assessed via electroencephalography while performing a visual mismatch negativity task under simulated hypoxic conditions in the reduced oxygen breathing environment.

Photo courtesy of Naval Medical Research Unit Dayton.

As in-flight hypoxia symptoms are currently measured via self-report, adding objectively assessed symptoms and sensor data will enable better understanding of the relationship between self-report/perceptions and objective experiences. Furthermore, neurobiological effects of hypoxia identified using EEG can be integrated with self-report and behavioral data to form a composite construct of hypoxia susceptibility with psychological and physiological meaning. This new construct may then be used to inform aviator selection, classification, training, and policy decisions.

## Spatial Disorientation

Spatial disorientation (SD) occurs when pilots incorrectly perceive the attitude of their aircraft with respect to the earth, gravitational vertical, or other aircraft (Stott & Benson, 2016). Many aspects of the flight environment can give rise to SD. For example, degraded visual environments may require the pilot to transition to instrument-only flying, which they may not trust over their "seat of the pants" gut feeling. The acceleration forces experienced during flight can cause the pilot to experience gravity through the floor of the aircraft, even though this may not truly represent vertical. Other forces may be so subtle or prolonged that the pilot does not perceive changes in the aircraft's attitude or heading (Stott & Benson, 2016).

Whatever the causes of SD, the effects can be devastating, leading to controlled flight into terrain, loss of control of the aircraft, or other inappropriate control inputs. One study implicated SD in up to 33% of aviation mishaps, with a fatality rate close to 100% (Gibb et al., 2011). In military aviation, SD continues to pose a major threat. The Naval Safety Center (2019) regards SD as the leading cause of Class A mishaps (defined as an incident that results in more than $2,500,000 in damages and/or loss of aircraft, loss of life, or permanent disability). Additionally, SD is involved in 12% to 25% of Class A or Class B mishaps by the U.S. Air Force and Army (Edens & Higginbotham, 2014; Poisson & Miller, 2014). Given its potentially fatal consequences, understanding SD is critical to the aviation community.

Because there are multiple causes of SD, a variety of measurements exist to capture and quantify this experience. Much of the laboratory research on SD involves recreating situations in a simulator that are likely to cause SD and then measuring behavioral outcomes. Self-reports of disorientation can provide some insight into the degree of SD experienced, and pilot behavior can be used to measure its effects.

For example, control reversal errors (CREs) occur when a pilot makes a stick input in the wrong direction, such as the direction that would steepen the aircraft's angle of bank rather than return it to level (Williams et al., 2018). The amount of time a pilot spends in unusual attitudes (e.g., extreme angles of bank) is also a good indicator they have become disoriented. These behaviors may serve as a proxy for SD because it is unlikely that a pilot would maneuver into these positions under normal circumstances.

In addition to behavioral measures of SD, there are some potential neurological correlates. One preliminary study found that changes in alpha activity, an EEG oscillation from 8 to 13 Hz that varies in power inversely with cortical activation, were associated with stronger subjective reports of vection (Palmisano et al., 2016). Vection is an illusory sense of motion that often disorients helicopter pilots when hovering (Ungs, 1989). Functional magnetic resonance imaging (fMRI) studies have found that vection activates a variety of brain regions, including areas associated with motion perception and visual processing (Kovács et al., 2008). Refining the neurological responses to SD would allow the psychometric response to potentially disorienting situations to be measured before it poses a threat. Of course, in order to measure SD, it must first be induced in a safe and reliable way.

Flight simulators used to recreate SD events may be fixed or motion based. While it may seem counterintuitive that fixed-base simulators could reliably induce SD, given the importance of vestibular input to orientation, this is not necessarily the case. Visual input accounts for approximately 80% of a pilot's orientation cues (Newman, 2007), thereby allowing fixed-base simulators to recreate visually related SD scenarios. However, fixed-base simulators can also induce some vestibular-related illusions, such as the leans (when a pilot feels a sensation of tilt during level flight; Eriksson, 2010; Moore et al., 2008). Motion-based simulators are also used to simulate SD, particularly forms of SD that require vestibular sensory input. Such simulations allow pilots to experience situations in which they cannot trust vestibular cues and must rely on their instruments (Tropper et al., 2009). While costly centrifuge-based simulators can add to the realism of disorienting scenarios using acceleration, virtual reality (VR) headsets are also being adopted as a cost-effective and portable means of replicating SD. However, there remain some technological limitations that must be overcome for VR devices to accurately recreate the cockpit (and resulting pilot behavior; F. E. Robinson & Biggs, 2019).

Individual differences with respect to SD are not particularly well studied, but there are indications that some people may be more prone to disorientation than others. For instance, individual differences have been observed in the strength and duration of vection when people are exposed to apparent motion through an optokinetic drum (Kennedy et al., 1996). These findings suggest some people are more prone than others to the disorienting effects of vection. Neurological differences have also been found in which people who performed better in a spatial learning and orienting task showed more activity in several brain regions (Arnold et al., 2014). While this study did not address SD directly, it suggests that the differences in orienting ability have a counterpart in propensity to become disoriented. Identifying these individual differences will allow application of the psychoneurometric model to inform novel assessments.

## Workload

Despite decades of research, and its intuitive appeal, the concept of workload (or cognitive workload) remains difficult to define. Workload can be fundamentally conceptualized as a combination of the task demands imposed on a person and that person's limited resources to deal with those demands (Young et al., 2015). Examples of task demands include time pressure or task complexity, while resources can include a person's attentional resources or level of training. When task demands exceed available resources, people often respond by changing the strategies they employ to perform the task (Young et al., 2015). Another possible outcome has the overloaded individual focusing on one task element for longer than is necessary, often at the expense of other responsibilities (Wickens & Alexander, 2009). In aviation, many of these behaviors would degrade a pilot's ability to control their aircraft, resulting in departure from prescribed flight parameters (e.g., altitude, heading; Braithwaite et al., 1998) and increased potential for an accident or mishap event.

Numerous subjective reports are available to capture a person's workload experience. Among these are the NASA Task Load Index (Hart, 2006), the Subjective Workload Assessment Technique (Reid & Nygren, 1988), and the Pilot Workload Rating Scale (Roscoe & Ellis, 1990). Objective assessments include physiological measures, such as heart rate variability, galvanic skin response, and pupillometry (Charles & Nixon, 2019). However, the adequacy of these measures may vary based on task-specific characteristics. Studies of neurophysiological changes due to workload have found increases in theta band (an EEG oscillation from 4 to 7 Hz) power and decreases in alpha band power during conditions with higher workload (Borghini et al., 2013; Dussault et al., 2004, 2005). Additionally, the theta/alpha power ratio increases in conditions with increased cognitive load (Holm et al., 2009). Thus, while there are a variety of measures of workload available, the appropriate measurement strategy will depend on the nature of the tasks and the assessment objectives.

Researchers have devised methods for manipulating pilot workload. One is to increase the difficulty of flight conditions by varying the complexity of the flight plan or creating more demanding meteorological conditions. Another is to add a secondary task to the flight itself. For instance, Williams et al. (2018, 2021) had pilots fly a simulation while either performing a working memory task or repeatedly adjusting their following distance from a lead aircraft; in both cases, the induced workload condition led to more CREs than in the control condition.

There is some evidence that people vary in their ability to handle increased workload. Yu et al. (2014) measured workload capacity, which assesses information processing efficiency, and compared it to working memory capacity. They found that people who were higher in working memory capacity also had higher workload capacity, but only when the information was presented through different modalities (e.g., auditory and visual signals). When the information was presented in the same modality (e.g., visual only), the difference in performance between high and low working memory capacity conditions was not significant. This suggests that there may be instances in which people differ in their ability to handle varying levels of workload; however, these differences might only apply when different aspects of working memory are tapped by the task. In other words, individual differences rely on ensuring that no single component of working memory is overloaded.

The psychoneurometric approach provides a method to refine how to measure the workload construct. However, workload also reveals one of the limitations of this approach—specifically, the complexity of biological measures. For example, heart rate variability can be used as a proxy for workload, but care must be taken when interpreting this measure. Research using heart rate variability indicates it is sensitive to increased task demand but unaffected by increased task complexity (Charles & Nixon, 2019). This nuance highlights the need to combine physiological and self-report/behavioral data to ensure the target construct is being measured properly.

## Decision-Making Under Stress

A variety of physical, psychological, and environmental stressors can combine to impact an aviator's decision-making ability. Despite the important role of stress in performance, traditional assessments often fail to capture how an individual's decision-making ability is impacted by stress. However, advances in the ability to simulate stressful events and measure psychological and physiological responses may enable the development of an integrated, multidomain assessment of decision-making under stress. Understanding individual differences in this capability will aid efforts to identify stress-resilient personnel for high-risk jobs, including military aviation.

Research efforts over the past century have developed techniques to induce stress in the laboratory and evaluate its impact on behavior and physiology. Methods to induce stress are varied and include exposure to aversive sensory stimuli (e.g., loud noise, bright lights, hot or cold temperature), sleep deprivation, physical exercise, time pressure, or social pressure (e.g., public speaking; for a review, see Bali & Jaggi, 2015). In aviation research, ecologically valid stressful stimuli have also been applied, including helicopter underwater evacuation training (S. J. Robinson et al., 2008); Survival, Evasion, Resistance, and Escape training (Lieberman et al., 2016); and flight simulator training (Wickens et al., 2015; for a review, see Dismukes et al., 2015). Of note, findings from a study using one stressor may not generalize to studies using a different type of stressor, and individuals may respond differently to different types of stressors.

Psychological referents for the impacts of stress on cognition are well understood. Well-practiced or automatic behaviors (e.g., manual control skills) are relatively spared by stress, while attention and working memory are especially vulnerable to stress. Both attention and working memory underlie decision-making. Thus, despite training to automatically execute emergency procedures, impaired working memory and attention due to stress can inhibit a pilot's ability to make decisions, thereby leading to mishap conditions (Dismukes et al., 2015). In addition to measuring behavioral performance in response to stress, self-report measures of stress have also been validated (e.g., the Dundee Stress State Questionnaire; Matthews et al., 1999).

Following the psychoneurometric model, neurobiological responses to stress can be measured to bridge the self-report and psychological domains. In general, stress activates two body systems, the hypothalamic-pituitary-adrenal (HPA) axis and the autonomic nervous system (ANS). Circulating levels of hormones associated with both systems can be measured peripherally in the saliva, including cortisol and alpha-amylase, respectively. While moderate stress may improve cognition, too little or too much stress tends to degrade performance (e.g., the inverted-U model of arousal; Yerkes & Dodson, 1908). Similarly, levels of stress hormones, in particular glucocorticoids, also follow an inverted-U relationship with performance (Lupien et al., 2007). However, researchers using salivary biomarkers should carefully account for potential confounding factors, including diurnal cycles and gender differences (Strahler et al., 2017). The choice to use salivary cortisol, salivary alpha-amylase, or different stress hormone markers found in the saliva, blood, or urine depends on experimental considerations and may provide differing information about HPA or ANS activity.

Other physiological measures of stress include heart rate and heart rate variability, breathing rate, pupillometry, and galvanic skin conductance. Additionally, neuroimaging and neuroendocrine studies suggest that stress increases dopaminergic activity via cortisol in brain regions involved in decision-making, including the limbic system, basal ganglia, and prefrontal cortex. This elevated dopamine response is associated with heightened reward sensitivity and diminished punishment sensitivity and may lead to incomplete and rushed decision-making (Starcke & Brand, 2016). Indeed, functional neuroimaging evidence suggests stress impairs executive control networks supported by the frontoparietal cortex that are vital for decision-making (Hermans et al., 2014). On the genomic level, individual differences in decision-making under stress are related to single-nucleotide polymorphisms in dopaminergic/noradrenergic genes expressed in prefrontal cortex (Parasuraman & Jiang, 2012).

While traditional assessments lack a measure of stress vulnerability, a composite measure of individual susceptibility of decision-making ability to stress could be obtained from a combination of self-report, behavioral, physiological, and genomic data. Further investigation of the effects of stress across these domains can help clarify how they interact in relation to performance. Novel assessments could leverage emerging technologies, including VR integrated with physiological monitoring, to induce stress using realistic simulations while collecting concurrent subjective, performance, and physiology data to help refine this construct. This combined approach could improve the predictive ability of assessments for decision-making under specific stressors encountered in military aviation and other high-risk jobs.

## Implementation Considerations

Practical considerations for implementing the psychoneurometric model include equipment cost and availability as well as privacy and ethical concerns. More expensive and less portable technologies may be more useful for assessing small or highly specialized groups at later levels of screening or for addressing basic research questions relating physiology to behavioral and psychological measures.

Technologies that noninvasively measure brain activity can provide valuable physiological data to integrate with psychological or behavioral data. These tools exist along a continuum of tradeoffs in cost, portability, and spatial/temporal resolution. More costly and less portable tools include fMRI, which permits indirect observation of brain activity in deep as well as surface brain structures. Magnetoencephalography (MEG) is also costly and nonportable but has an advantage of measuring deep and surface brain signals directly with millisecond as well as millimeter precision. Access to fMRI and MEG facilities can be difficult to obtain and would be impractical for routine use; nonetheless, they provide valuable data to guide researchers to develop more cost-effective means of capturing relevant brain activity.

EEG and functional near-infrared spectroscopy (fNIRS) systems are relatively inexpensive and portable but have the drawback of only reliably measuring activity near the surface of the brain. EEG and fNIRS both have poor spatial resolution, while EEG has excellent temporal resolution compared to the slower fNIRS signal. Fortunately, brain structures critical for higher cognitive and perceptual functions are located near the surface of the brain in the cerebral cortex, and cortical activity can be reliably measured by both EEG and fNIRS. Brain imaging capabilities continue to rapidly expand, but even current neurotechnology holds much untapped potential for building psychoneurometric models.

Many of the alternative assessments discussed in this chapter produce data that carry increased exposure risk, and strict privacy measures must be in place to safeguard individual data and manage the disclosure of any incidental findings. This is especially relevant for any data that qualify as protected health information (PHI). The size of the data files produced by these tools exacerbates this challenge. In many cases, large data files collected over a series of time points (e.g., EEG) preclude the use of local hard drive storage, leading to cloud-based services for data management. While cloud storage solutions exist that are compliant with the Health Insurance Portability and Accountability Act of 1996, assessment specialists must first verify that these services meet their organization's security requirements for uploading, storing, sharing, and retrieving PHI, and take the associated costs into account when developing their data management plans.

Psychoneurometric constructs developed for personnel assessment and selection have additional value for training purposes. It would be informative, for instance, to administer a given assessment periodically throughout training to determine whether an individual's resilience to a stressor improves with repeated exposure to the stressor or with coping strategies gained in training. This can be used to better understand individual growth responses to training as well as to evaluate the efficacy of novel training tools.

High-risk jobs can involve exposure to a combination of stressors simultaneously. For instance, a pilot may experience SD differently while fatigued, hypoxic, stressed, or under high workload. Performance assessments may benefit from considering individual differences in job-related constructs in isolation as well as together. Facilities that can deliver a combination of extreme conditions are best equipped to assess these interactions. One such facility is the Naval Aerospace Medical Research Laboratory at Naval Medical Research Unit Dayton (NAMRU-D). NAMRU-D's laboratory spaces include the Disorientation Research Device, a six-axis motion-based simulator compatible with pilot-in-the-loop flight scenarios that approximate forces encountered in flight, alongside fixed-base and VR flight simulators. A neighboring fatigue laboratory contains overnight spaces for sleep deprivation research in conjunction with a cognitive and physiological testing suite. To simulate breathing conditions such as hypoxia, researchers use a variety of devices including the ROBD, on-demand hypoxia trainer and, for simultaneous exposure of multiple individuals, the Reduced Oxygen Breathing Environment. While this is not an exhaustive list of NAMRU-D capabilities, it serves to illustrate how close proximity of these different resources enables the evaluation of multistressor interactions. For example, a participant could undergo a fatigue or hypoxia exposure and then perform a flight simulator evaluation.

## Conclusion

In this chapter, we have explored how recent technological innovations provide new opportunities to advance the predictive potential of assessments for high-risk jobs, referencing the psychoneurometric model as one approach for improving construct knowledge and using case studies from military aviation. Traditional measures used to assess personnel for high-risk jobs often fail to assess individual differences in response to extreme environment exposure. This gap can be met by developing tools that accurately model these threats and assess individual responses using constructs informed by psychological and physiological data. Developing these constructs will also increase our understanding of how complex neurobiological systems that enable performance operate. Beyond preliminary training, focused assessments can also be established to predict performance for specialized jobs. Such improvements can potentially help maximize performance, improve retention, and reduce mishaps.

Technological advances including neuroimaging and simulation will continue to produce new, increasingly accessible tools that can be incorporated into assessment processes. By broadening existing assessments to include physiological data and simulation capabilities offered by current and emerging technologies, a foundation may be laid to keep pace with future technological growth and further increase the predictive validity of assessments for high-risk jobs.

## References

American Psychological Association. (2011). *High-risk jobs and high-risk populations.* https://www.apa.org/wsh/past/2011/high-risk-jobs

Arnold, A. E. G. F., Protzner, A. B., Bray, S., Levy, R. M., & Iaria, G. (2014). Neural network configuration and efficiency underlies individual differences in spatial orientation ability. *Journal of Cognitive Neuroscience, 26*(2), 380–394.

Artino, A. R., Folga, R. V., & Swan B.D. (2006). Mask-on hypoxia training for tactical jet aviators: Evaluation of an alternate instructional paradigm. *Aviation, Space, and Environmental Medicine, 77*(8), 857–863.

Asmaro, D., Mayall, J., & Ferguson, S. (2013). Cognition at altitude: Impairment in executive and memory processes under hypoxic conditions. *Aviation, Space, and Environmental Medicine, 84*(11), 1159–1165.

Bali, A., & Jaggi, A. S. (2015). Clinical experimental stress studies: Methods and assessment. *Reviews in the Neurosciences, 26*(5), 555–579.

Blacker, K. J., Seech, T. R., Funke, M. E., & Kinney, M. J. (2021). Deficits in visual processing during hypoxia as evidenced by visual mismatch negativity. *Aerospace Medicine and Human Performance, 92*, 326–332.

Borghini, G., Aricò, P., Astolfi, L., Toppi, J., Cincotti, F., Mattia, D., Cherubino, P., Vecchiato, G., Maglione, A. G., Graziani, I., & Babiloni, F. (2013, July). *Frontal EEG theta changes assess the training improvements of novices in flight simulation tasks* [Conference Presentation]. Annual international conference of the IEEE Engineering in Medicine and Biology Society, Osaka, Japan.

Braithwaite, M. G., Durnford, S. J, Groh, S. L., Jones, H. D., Higdon, A. A., Estrada, A., & Alvarez, E. A. (1998). Flight simulator evaluation of a novel flight instrument display to minimize the risks of spatial disorientation. *Aviation, Space, and Environmental Medicine, 69*(8), 733–742.

Charles, R. L., & Nixon, J. (2019). Measuring mental workload using physiological measures: A systematic review. *Applied Ergonomics, 74*, 221–232.

Dismukes, R. K., Goldsmith, T. E., & Kochan, J. A. (2015). *Effects of acute stress on aircrew performance: Literature review and analysis of operational aspects.* NASA/TM—2015-218930.

Dussault, C., Jouanin, J-C., & Guezennec, C-Y. (2004). EEG and EEC changes during selected flight sequences. *Aviation, Space, and Environmental Medicine, 75*(10), 889–897.

Dussault, C., Jouanin, J-C., Phillipe, M., & Guezennec, C-Y. (2005). EEG and EEC changes during simulator operation reflect mental workload and vigilance. *Aviation, Space, and Environmental Medicine, 76*(4), 344–351.

Edens, T. J., & Higginbotham, M. D. (2014, March). Degraded visual environments: A leading factor in aviation accidents. *Army Aviation Magazine, 31,* 22–23.

Eriksson, L. (2010). Toward a visual flow integrated display format to combat pilot spatial disorientation. *International Journal of Aviation Psychology, 20,* 1–24.

Federal Aviation Administration. (2016). *Pilot's handbook of aeronautical knowledge.* U.S. Department of Transportation. https://www.faa.gov/regulations_policies/handbooks_manuals/aviation/phak/media/pilot_handbook.pdf

Gibb, R., Ercoline, B., & Scharff, L. (2011). Spatial disorientation: Decades of pilot fatalities. *Aviation, Space, and Environmental Medicine, 82*(7), 717–724.

Hart, S. G. (2006, October). NASA-task load index (NASA-TLX); 20 years later. *Proceedings of the Human Factors and Ergonomics Society Annual Meeting, 50*(9), 904–908.

Hermans, E. J., Henckens, M. J. A. G., Joëls, M., & Fernández, G. (2014). Dynamic adaptation of large-scale brain networks in response to acute stressors. *Trends in Neurosciences, 37,* 304–314.

Holm, A., Lukander, K., Korpela, J., Sallinen, M., & Muller, K. M. I. (2009). Estimating brain load from the EEG. *Scientific World Journal, 9,* 638–651.

Kennedy, R. S., Hettinger, L. J., Harm, D. L., Ordy, J. M., & Dunlap, W. P. (1996). Psychophysical scaling of circular vection (CV) produced by optokinetic motion (OKN): Individual differences and effects of practice. *Journal of Vestibular Research, 6*(5), 331–341.

Kovács, G., Raabe, M., & Greenless, M. W. (2008). Neural correlates of visually induced self-motion illusion in depth. *Cerebral Cortex, 18*(8), 1779–1787.

Lieberman, H. R., Farina, E. K., Caldwell, J., Williams, K. W., Thompson, L. A., Niro, P. J., Grohmann, K. A., & McClung, J. P. (2016). Cognitive function, stress hormones, heartrate and nutritional status during simulated captivity in military survival training. *Physiology & Behavior, 165,* 86–97.

Lupien, S. J., Maheu, F., Tu, M., Fiocco, A., & Schramek, T. E. (2007). The effects of stress and stress hormones on human cognition: Implications for the field of brain and cognition. *Brain and Cognition, 65*(3), 209–237.

Matthews, G., Joyner, L., Gilliland, K., Campbell, S. E., Huggins, J., & Falconer, S. (1999). Validation of a comprehensive stress state questionnaire: Towards a state "Big Three"? In I. Mervielde, I. J. Deary, F. De Fruyt, & F. Ostendorf (Eds.), *Personality psychology in Europe* (Vol. 7, pp. 236–251). Tilburg University Press.

McMorris, T., Hale, B. J., Barwood, M., Costello, J., & Corbett, J. (2017). Effect of acute hypoxia on cognition: A systematic review and meta-regression analysis. *Neuroscience & Biobehavioral Reviews, 74,* 225–232.

Moore, S., MacDougall, H., Lesceu, X., Speyer, J., Wuyts, F., & Clark, J. (2008). Head-eye coordination during simulated orbiter landing. *Aviation, Space, and Environmental Medicine, 79,* 888–898.

National Center for O*NET Development. *O*NET OnLine.* Retrieved August 2, 2021, from https://www.onetonline.org/

National Research Council. (2013). *New directions in assessing performance potential of individuals and groups: Workshop summary.* National Academies Press.

Naval Safety Center. (2019). *Current mishap definitions and reporting criteria.* https://navalsafetycenter.navy.mil/Resources/Current-Mishap-Definitions

Newman, D. G. (2007). *An overview of spatial disorientation as a factor in aviation accidents and incidents* (Research and Analysis Report B2007/0063). Australian Transport Safety Bureau.

Operational Psychology. (2019, September 23). *Aviation selection test battery: Presentation to the chief of naval air training.* Navy Medicine Operational Training Detachment, Naval Aerospace Medical Institute.

Palmisano, S., Barry, R. J., DeBlasio, F. M., & Fogarty, J. S. (2016). Identifying objective EEG based markers of vection in depth. *Frontiers in Psychology, 7*, 1–11.

Parasuraman, R., & Jiang, Y. (2012). Individual differences in cognition, affect, and performance: Behavioral, neuroimaging, and molecular genetic approaches. *NeuroImage, 59*(1), 70–82.

Petrassi, F. A., Hodkinson, P. D., Walters, P. L., & Gaydos, S. J. (2012). Hypoxic hypoxia at moderate altitudes: Review of the state of the science. *Aviation, Space, and Environmental Medicine, 83*(10), 975–984.

Poisson, R. J., & Miller, M. E. (2014). Spatial disorientation mishap trends in the U.S. Air Force 1993–2013. *Aviation, Space, and Environmental Medicine, 85*, 919–924.

Reid, G. B., & Nygren, T. E. (1988). The Subjective Workload Assessment Technique: A scaling procedure for measuring mental workload. In P. A. Hancock & N. Meshkati (Eds.), Human mental workload (pp. 185–218). North-Holland. https://doi.org/10.1016/S0166-4115(08)62387-0.

Robinson, F. E., & Biggs, A. T. (2019). *The use of virtual and augmented reality technologies in spatial disorientation training: Current uses and future opportunities* (Publication No. NAMRU-D-19-13). Naval Aeromedical Research Unit–Dayton.

Robinson, S. J., Sünram-Lea, S. I., Leach, J., & Owen Lynch, P.J. (2008). The effects of exposure to an acute naturalistic stressor on working memory, state anxiety and salivary cortisol concentrations. *Stress, 11(2)*,115–24. doi: 10.1080/10253890701559970. PMID: 18311600.

Roscoe, A. H., & Ellis, G. A. (1990). *A subjective rating scale for assessing pilot workload in flight: A decade of practical use* (Royal Aerospace Establishment Report No. 90019). Royal Aerospace Establishment.

Seech, T. R., Funke, M. E., Sharp, R. F., Light, G. A., & Blacker, K. J. (2020). Impaired sensory processing during low-oxygen exposure: A noninvasive approach to detecting changes in cognitive states. *Frontiers in Psychiatry, Vol (11)*, 1–8.

Starcke, K., & Brand, M. (2016). Effects of stress on decisions under uncertainty: A meta-analysis. *Physiological Bulletin, 142*(9), 909–933.

Stott, J. R. R., & Benson, A. J. (2016). Spatial orientation and disorientation in flight. In D. P. Gradwell & D. J. Rainford (Eds.), *Ernsting's aviation and space medicine* (5th ed., pp. 281–319). CRC Press.

Strahler, J., Skoluda, N., Kappert, M. B., & Nater, U. M. (2017). Simultaneous measurement of salivary cortisol and alpha-amylase: Application and recommendations. *Neuroscience & Biobehavioral Reviews, 83*, 657–677.

Tropper, K., Kallus, K. W., & Boucsein, W. (2009). Psychophysiological evaluation of an antidisorientation training for visual flight rules pilots in a moving base simulator. *International Journal of Aviation Psychology, 19*, 270–286.

Ungs, T. J. (1989). The occurrence of the vection illusion among helicopter pilots while flying over water. *Aviation, Space, and Environmental Medicine, 60*(11), 1099–1101.

Vacchiano, C. A., Vagedes, K., & Gonzales, D. (2004). Comparison of the physiological, cognitive, and subjective effects of sea level and altitude-induced hypoxia. *Aviation, Space, and Environmental Medicine, 75*(4), B56.

Wickens, C. D., & Alexander, A. L. (2009). Attentional tunneling and task management in synthetic visual displays. *International Journal of Aviation Psychology, 19*(2), 182–199.

Wickens, C. D., Stokes, A., Barnett, B., & Hyman, F. (2015). The effects of stress on pilot judgment in a MIDIS simulator. In D. Harris & L. Wen-Chin (Eds.), *Decision making in aviation* (1st ed., pp. 387–408). Routledge.

Williams, H. P., Horning, D. S., Etgen, C., & Powell, C. R. (2021). *Effects of cockpit workload and motion on incidence spatial disorientation in simulated flight* (Publication No. NAMRU-D-21-034). Naval Aeromedical Research Unit–Dayton.

Williams, H. P., Horning, D. S., Lawson, B. D., Powell, C. R., & Patterson, F. R. (2018). *Effects of various types of cockpit workload on spatial disorientation in simulated flight* (Publication No. NAMRU-D-19-06). Naval Aeromedical Research Unit–Dayton.

Yerkes, R. M., & Dodson, J. D. (1908). The relation of strength of stimulus to rapidity of habit formation. *Journal of Comparative Neurology and Psychology, 18*, 459–482.

Young, M. S., Brookhuis, K. A., Wickens, C. D., & Hancock, P. A. (2015). State of science: Mental workload in ergonomics. *Ergonomics, 58*(1), 1–17.

Yu, J-C., Chang, T-Y., & Yang, C-T. (2014). Individual differences in working memory capacity and workload capacity. *Frontiers in Psychology, 5*(1465), 1–15.

# 25
# Gamified Assessments for Prehire Evaluation

*Christina Norris-Watts, Kathleen E. Hall, and Nathan Mondragon*

Over the past decade the use of gamified assessment in the workplace has expanded quickly, at a pace faster at times than academic research can keep up with, resulting in a wide variety of gamified vendors in the marketplace and unclear guidelines on how to use and evaluate these assessments (Povah et al., 2017). At the same time, the emergence of gamification has left many applied industrial-organizational (IO) practitioners and human resources (HR) professionals questioning their preparedness to appropriately evaluate, validate, and recommend these offerings within their organizations. The current chapter aims to address common questions, providing a practical lens framing what gamified assessments are, and are not, to organizations.

In this chapter, we will review common uses and applications of gamified assessments, potential misuses, barriers, and other considerations which IO scientist-practitioners and HR professionals should be aware when evaluating gamified assessments. In addition, our hope is that through the discussion of concrete examples currently available to organizations, this chapter will also provide a useful resource to researchers, academics, and students of assessment and selection. We aim to uncover future research and growth opportunities within the field of selection and advance the appropriate use of gamified assessment in industry, thereby informing the field's understanding of best practices in this area, by sharing knowledge on the current state of practice and research.

## What Are Gamified Assessments?

There are many terms used interchangeably to describe gamified assessments, including gamification (e.g., Deterding et al., 2011), game-like (e.g.,

Armstrong et al., 2016), game thinking (e.g., Bhatia & Ryan, 2018), and many more iterations of a similar turn of phrase. The current chapter will exclusively use the terms "gamified" and "game-based" when describing assessments that incorporate game-based assessment (GBA) elements (Deterding et al., 2011; Gkorezis et al., 2021) for clarity. The extent to which an assessment is gamified can best be represented on a spectrum (see Figure 25.1). Since the emergence of gamified assessments, examples of these offerings have varied by their incremental level of GBA attributes (e.g., Armstrong et al., 2016).

Gamification refers to the inclusion of game-specific features such as real-time feedback, progression through levels, increasing difficulty, clear goals, and a mobile-first delivery that results in a more motivating testing environment and increases the flow experienced by users (Burgers et al., 2015; Chen, 2007; Connolly et al., 2012; Landers & Callan, 2011; Wood et al., 2004). These assessments may offer short assessment times, high quality and quantity of data, and an engaging user experience (Lumsden et al., 2016; Quiroga et al., 2016) with lower levels of user anxiety, which is particularly relevant in high-stakes assessments (Alter et al., 2010; McPherson & Burns, 2008).

Gamified assessments may integrate one or more GBA elements into their design, and the extent to which technology is integrated into their offering can differ greatly from one assessment to another. For example, an assessment with minor gamification elements could be a paper-and-pencil assessment that integrates a single GBA design feature such as a GBA narrative in the questions. It may still be scored by adding up the total number of items correctly. An example of an assessment with moderate gamification (falling near the middle of our gamification spectrum) might be an animated, virtual assessment center with a personal avatar the candidate designs that enhances the GBA features of the experience. The candidate may be represented by an avatar, exploring a world, and come across challenges or quests to solve. Those challenges may be very traditional assessments designed to measure logical reasoning. Finally, a gamified assessment near the upper end of the gamification spectrum would include multiple game-based elements, such as an immersive participant experience, where personalized avatars and storylines that are responsive to candidate performance in the game and personal preferences are used. It may be very difficult for the candidate to determine what is being measured, and it may be scored by looking at mouse clicks, cursor movements, reaction times, and other metadata beyond just answers to questions, or there may even be no "questions" used at all.

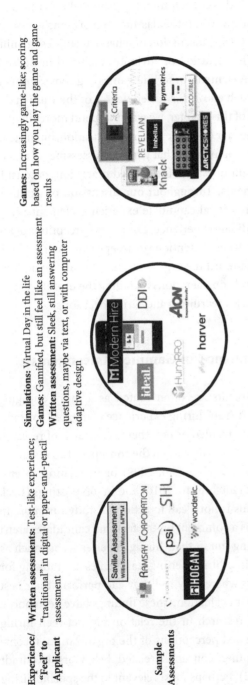

Figure 25.1. The spectrum of key gamified experiences and attributes depicting increased GBA elements in assessments

At first glance, some reading this chapter might question whether the first paper-and-pencil example truly warrants the classification of being gamified. We chose to follow Landers's (2015) discussion of what determines "gamification" as being defined by the inclusion of attributes included in Bedwell et al.'s (2012) categories of GBA elements in serious games (e.g., environment, game fiction, rules/goals), which allows for varied degree of their use in the assessment. For the purposes of this chapter, we will not spend more time on construct definitions of a game, nor on the degree of gamification, but instead focus on the aspects of the hiring process that gamified assessments touch, as these aspects yield important questions for applied practitioners considering using gamified assessments. Throughout our discussion of gamified assessments, we will focus on critical candidate experience elements: how assessment design affects candidate experience, candidate perceptions of the organization, perceptions of fairness, intentions to accept a job offer, and potentially consumer behaviors toward the organization. We will also address organizational implications and considerations including the usefulness and utility of gamified assessments for recruiting and hiring decisions.

## Who Is the Target Audience for Gamified Assessments?

Interestingly, gamified assessments are often touted as a more engaging (e.g., Collmus et al., 2016) and "fun" hiring experience compared to traditional selection assessments. Warranted or not, there is a dearth of research examining fun in the hiring process. Most often the concept of fun is studied in the context of work (Bolton & Houlihan, 2009) or in relation to employee engagement (Plester & Hutchinson, 2016) and in job postings (Beck & Spenser, 2021). However, this is not a call to action to study fun more in the hiring process. Instead, it is a comment on the fact that candidates aren't usually looking for or expecting *fun* in their hiring experience, as much as they are looking for *fairness*. In a hiring setting, candidates are looking for a transparent, efficient process where they feel they can perform their best and will be treated fairly in their evaluation. These findings have been borne out by a plethora of fairness research in the relationship between hiring process experience and associated perceptions of the organization, recommendation intentions, and other consumer-related behaviors (Konradt et al., 2020; Truxillo et al., 2002). Perhaps most relevant to the specific hiring situation, the experiences an applicant has with a selection procedure can inform perceptions about the overall organization and the attractiveness of a potential offer to join an organization if extended (Chapman et al., 2005; Hausknecht et al., 2004; Gkorezis et al., 2021) and whether perceived unfairness may escalate potential litigation for organizations (Truxillo et al., 2017).

Gamified assessments may not be the most attractive to all candidate populations. Constructs such as "recruitainment" explored by Korn et al. (2018) describe the intersection between gamified assessment and recruitment strategies aimed at entertaining applicants. As these authors and others (e.g., Nikolaou, 2021) describe, the use of gamification is commonly targeted toward early-career applicants and high-volume hiring (e.g., university recruiting, entry-level roles). This focus of gamified assessments on early-in-career talent is likely a result of this population being more willing to try new hiring techniques compared to more experienced candidate pools or based on the type of role for which applicants are applying (e.g., large quantity of equivalent hires, large applicant pools).

Experienced candidates, however, who are mid or late career, may be confused by the addition of a gamified assessment to a hiring process. Because there are few empirical, peer-reviewed studies of candidate experience with gamified assessments, future research should further elucidate whether differences in candidate experience are reported between demographically different groups of employees. Relatedly, highly sought-after candidates, with rare experiences, skills, and education, or candidates for executive leadership positions may balk at the request to complete a gamified assessment, particularly in instances where the assessment of knowledge and experience is opaque to the user. As an organization evaluates candidate experience in adopting gamified assessments, each practitioner should consider whether the surprise of GBA elements is a welcome or unwelcome experience for their candidates. Indeed, past findings demonstrate that applicants may have negative reactions (e.g., negative feelings, perceived injustice) to assessments touted as being "fun," like interview brain teasers (Honer et al., 2007; Childers, 2020). However, this is where the idea of "framification" becomes important to an applied practitioner's assessment of when and how gamification could promote positive candidate experience. Similar to findings pertaining to framing (i.e., stereotype threats; Spencer et al., 1999), the way gamified assessments are communicated to candidates will likely affect their perception of the assessment. If poised as fun games, more experienced or highly competitive candidates may turn up their noses and choose to disengage from the application process. But if a gamified assessment is framed as a digital simulation or even as part of an assessment center, then the assessment may be more palatable to candidates. Framing these more fun, innovative assessments as serious and traditional evaluations of knowledge, skills, or competencies may seem ironic, but it's the resulting candidate experience that the organization should be focused on to determine what messages they are trying to send to candidates to support their adoption.

It is also important to understand and consider recruiter and hiring manager reactions to these types of assessments. Their value and their tradeoffs should be explained carefully and accurately. There is likely to be a lot of curiosity about this new type of assessment to which hiring managers and recruiters, as the first line of inquiry for potential applicant questions, will have the opportunity to message to candidates. Providing sample assessments to leaders who support organizational recruitment efforts may help inform what the candidate experience will be like. It may seem obvious to provide sample assessment to senior talent acquisition leaders, but often this critical step is skipped as they are instead told about the assessment rather than experiencing it for themselves. These sample assessments can help ensure the selection process "feels" like it was intended to feel to the applicant.

While opportunities to shape candidate perceptions are key, even more important will be explaining why the constructs measured in the assessment are critical predictors of strong performance on the job in question. It is easy to get swept up in the fun and experience of a gamified assessment, and it is important not to lose track of *what* is being measured due to the method of *how* it is measured. Constructs measured should still be important to the job in question and required at the time of hire in order to comply with best practice guidelines and legal regulations (Society of Industrial and Organizational Psychology [SIOP], 2018). An important first step in implementing assessments is to ensure that the constructs on which the tests are based are job related for the targeted jobs as described by the federal government's *Uniform Guidelines on Employee Selection Procedures* (Equal Employment Opportunity Commission [EEOC] et al., 1978) and the professional standards (SIOP, 2018). Validation steps are critical to be sure we are making correct, and fair, hiring decisions, and this does not change just because a gamified element is added to the assessment. Later in this chapter we will describe how more traditional predictor constructs are measured within a gamified assessment to fully represent best practices, and considerations on how an applied practitioner should evaluate gamified assessment in line with these standards.

## Types of Jobs and Companies Using Gamified Assessment

In addition to seeing gamified assessments used more for university applicants, we are also seeing a trend of gamified assessments being used for higher volume, entry-level jobs. This trend is likely due to the administrative ease of gamified assessments for high-volume jobs as the scoring is easy and practically instantaneous. Companies who are looking to shore up their image as innovative, cutting-edge, and future-focused seem quite attracted to these types of assessments. If done well, gamified assessments can delight and surprise candidates by the experience. If done poorly, they can present a negative candidate experience.

Organizations should also carefully consider whether the use of gamification in the hiring experience reflects the actual experience of working in the job. Imagine a fully immersive gamified hiring experience that led to a successful hire; however, when the candidate showed up on their first day, they were shown to their cubicle, handed an outdated brick of a laptop that the employee would use for basic data entry, and onboarded in an outdated training classroom with materials from the 1980s. They may be surprised to learn there is not a budget for new technology, new ways of working are discouraged rather than embraced, and a "this is how we've always done it mentality" pervades the team's work. In other words, does the gamified assessment experience match the organizational working culture? The match between the hiring experience and working experience should not be underestimated through our understanding of met expectations and their relationship to positive organizational outcomes (e.g., job satisfaction, organizational commitment; Hom et al., 1999; Irving & Montes, 2009). We should further assume that the perceptions of being misled during the hiring process could in turn have negative consequences for work and other employee outcomes (e.g., turnover, burnout; Hom et al., 1999; Wang et al., 2020).

## When Are Gamified Assessments Used?

In application, a few factors should impact the decision on where to place the assessment: the cost of the assessment, the number of expected applicants, the type of constructs measured, whether assessment results need to be manually reviewed, and the anticipated candidate experience. For example, with a high-applicant-volume position, automatically rejecting low-scoring applicants with a gamified assessment delivered after the application or resume is submitted can provide significant cost benefits. Additionally, the assessment can be automatically distributed by your applicant tracking system (ATS), thereby reducing another manual touchpoint or timely step in the process. However, when a position has a low applicant volume, it may be best to have human touchpoints early in the process to "hook" candidates. In this scenario, narrowing the applicant funnel a bit more before putting applicants through the gamified assessment may personalize the selection process.

Cost may be one of the most varied and context-specific considerations for organizations and practitioners when assessing gamified offerings. The cost of a gamified assessment is more than the cost of the assessment itself. Ancillary costs such as how the assessment is billed (e.g., per candidate versus in bulk) and implementation costs associated with socializing and using assessments within a business's hiring processes also need consideration.

As with any operational assessment, these costs may include integration with an ATS, translation across languages, validation studies, user training, branding, and ongoing monitoring and maintenance.

Gamified vendors will often correctly say that they can integrate with any ATS and provide any custom reports needed. However, more challenges may specifically come from your organization, which may have customized your ATS, or may have a small information technology (IT) team that manages/updates your ATS, or any number of other resource restrictions (e.g., branding and legal review). Aligning with your own internal partners from IT, procurement, privacy, legal, compliance, and analytics/reporting will be key for any kind of successful launch and ongoing monitoring of gamified assessments. These other stakeholders are your partners with whom you will need to work closely but will have additional constraints on their time.

There are also long-term implications for the cost and investment needed for organizations who adopt gamified assessments. The setup and year 1 costs are one factor, but what about subsequent yearly costs? How will you measure the return on investment (ROI) of this assessment? Who will be asking to see the ROI? Who will be providing the upfront costs and funding for this assessment? All these questions will be important to think through in order to put a business case together. Launching the assessment is the easy part; monitoring and maintaining it is the hard part.

External conditions can change drastically and unpredictably. Changes to the external hiring environment, internal company functioning, and many other factors may alter the problems that a gamified assessment was attempting to solve. In 2022, with the Great Resignation (Smith, 2022), we saw more organizations trying to hire quickly, and sometimes that meant removing interviews and relying solely on written assessments that used to be a step in a larger screening process. In other cases we saw assessments, including standard background checks, being removed altogether as companies scrambled to keep essential (and yet remarkably lower paying) jobs filled. Companies who engage in "open hiring" (Hernandes, 2020) may be seen as more attractive to candidates than companies relying on assessments, no matter how gamified those assessments may be. It is critical to keep focused on the problem that the gamified assessment is intended to solve to ensure that it is still a useful and effective part of the hiring process and responsive to the context felt by both the organization and potential applicants. That may mean ensuring the selection process is flexible enough to add or remove gamified assessments as needed.

## How Are Gamified Assessments Created?

Gamified assessments are constructed in a variety of ways. While each one is unique, there are trends that help to categorize currently available assessments. If we consider a spectrum with theory-based development on one end and big data development on the other, most assessments can be plotted somewhere along the continuum.

Theory-based assessments hypothesize a relationship between some construct and on-the-job performance. The assessment is then developed to measure that construct and gamified elements are added to that assessment. Big data assessments leverage a number of different variables (sometimes numbering in the millions) associated with current high performers to inform the scoring of the assessment. Candidate behaviors and responses are compared to the behaviors of high performers, and algorithms are "tweaked" or "smoothed" to maximize prediction and minimize bias. At a high level, a good rule of thumb for practitioners responsible for evaluating their use is that you should understand what these modifications entail and be able to explain what is happening to variables and why. Some gamified assessments employ a mix of these two approaches, while others skew more toward one approach over the other.

## What Do Gamified Assessments Measure?

Gamified assessments designed to replace selection tests are typically modeled after traditional psychometric tests but introduce levels of gamification. Initially, gamified assessments were developed to measure cognitive ability, showing promising validity in a range of settings (Atkins et al., 2014; Gamberini et al., 2010; Jimison et al., 2004; Verhaegh et al., 2013). More recently, these formats have also been used to measure social abilities (Leutner et al., 2020) and personality (Leutner et al., 2017). These game formats use less of the gamification features and sometimes resemble traditional formats (e.g., a situation judgment test) but are delivered in a more compelling modality like a chat-based discussion (Leutner et al., 2020). Novel personality gamified assessments are also becoming more prevalent and typically use picture-based items to reduce the reading requirements (Hilliard et al., 2022).

## Cognitive Game-Based Assessments

It is widely accepted (Schmidt & Hunter, 1998) that cognitive ability tests of general mental ability are one of the best predictors of success on the job. However, it is also noted the candidate experience is problematic with long and strenuous cognitive test batteries. This tradeoff of predictive validity and candidate experience means cognitive ability tests are typically restricted to high-stake selection scenarios whereby applicants are willing to invest considerable time. By improving the user experience and shortening testing times, gamified tests of cognitive ability are becoming a viable alternative for improved candidate experiences (Leutner et al., 2021) and allow for expansion into lower stakes roles that can also benefit from increased criterion validity. For higher stakes roles, the improved user experience might present an advantage for competitive employers and improve employer image.

Cognitive ability tests typically include a series of puzzles or questions with right or wrong answers, and this translates well into game formats. Thus, different levels of difficulty for a given task can be programmed automatically to generate easier or harder puzzles or questions to solve, providing a good proxy for cognitive ability. Additionally, adaptive testing can be deployed for level progression making a quicker identification of the ability level, thus providing a shortened assessment time. Assessments of cognitive ability have been successfully developed with compelling construct validity evidence with traditional measures of cognitive abilities. For example, gameplay across 12 separate short video games is highly correlated with cognitive ability established across 11 cognitive ability tasks in a sample of 188 university students ($r = .93$; Quiroga et al., 2015). Atkins et al. (2014), using a general population, validated a gamified four-dimensional spatial task with working memory ($r = .62$), and less impressive validities with quantitative reasoning ($r = .30$) and Raven's ($r = .37$). These results relay the importance of checking new assessment modalities with a wide range of well-validated traditional test designs, to parse out the exact cognitive areas being measured with the gamified assessments. Similarly, gamified versions of working memory and processing speed tasks also correlate with traditional cognitive ability tests, including the Wechsler Adult Intelligence scales (range $r = .54$ and $r = .25$; McPherson & Burns, 2008). Finally, Liff et al. (2021) found that construct validity values vary between $r = .51$ and $r = .67$ depending on the combination of games used in the assessment with a traditional cognitive ability battery. Test-retest reliabilities 1 month apart with a Prolific panel ranged from $r = .73$ to $r = .81$ depending on the games deployed, and in a sample of 6,081 job applicants the test-retest reliability was $r = .70$ with an average of 58 days between test periods.

## Personality Game-Based Assessments

Several large meta-analytic studies demonstrate the connection between personality and job performance (Barrick & Mount, 1991; Higgins et al., 2007; Hurtz & Donovan, 2000; Judge et al., 1999; see Barrick et al., 2001, for a summary). In addition to job performance, the Big Five personality traits predict various work-relevant motivational outcomes including goal setting, expectancy and self-efficacy motivation (Judge & Ilies, 2002), job satisfaction (Judge et al., 2002), and, in the case of conscientiousness, organizational citizenship behavior (Organ & Ryan, 1995). In short, personality traits are related to a wide range of job-relevant behaviors, well documented in the academic literature.

However, drawbacks to personality assessments do exist like social desirability bias of self-report items (Donovan et al., 2014) and test length causing questionnaire fatigue and incomplete or invalid responses (Yan et al., 2011). In seeking to resolve these issues, format innovations in the last decades have led to the development of new answer formats like forced-choice questionnaires; these formats, however, are still often at odds with modern technology and candidate expectations. Gamified assessments offer a way to transport personality test formats into the 21st century by creating dynamic user interactions and shortened test time.

Unlike cognitive ability tests, personality tests do not have a right or wrong answer. Rather, personality assessments measure behavioral tendencies and preferences, and thus there are no wrong answers, only differences within and between people. This presents challenges for a gamification design, where progression is often based on performance and game dynamics are created through increasing difficulty. In addition, the questionnaire-based format of traditional personality tests does not directly translate into game-like puzzles as with cognitive ability tests. Also, some of the basic requirements for these assessments are an improved user experience and ideally shorter testing times, making a gamified personality assessment difficult to design.

As a promising alternative to text-based personality tests, some gamified assessments draw upon image preferences instead of text stems and Likert-type response options. Images can help capture and communicate rich context without requiring reading and potentially reduce test-taking time. In the first of its kind, Leutner et al. (2017) created an image-based personality test for hiring field merchandisers into the beverage company Red Bull. Following this line of gamified personality measurement, Hilliard et al. (2022) and HireVue designed a similar Big Five gamified assessment using this picture format. In this assessment, short statements are followed by a series of images from which participants select the one that most applies to them (see Figure 25.2 for an example item). A machine learning algorithm was used to predict personality scores from the International Personality Item Pool-Neuroticism Extraversion Openness test (IPIP-NEO 120) based on the selected images. Convergent validity for the image-based measures to the respective IPIP Big Five measures were openness, $r = .71$; conscientiousness, $r = .70$; extraversion, $r = .78$; agreeableness, $r = .60$; and emotional stability, $r = .70$. Additionally average different trait, different method validity at $r = .16$ was identified establishing divergent validity. Test-retest reliability in a different study ranged from $r = .62$ to $r = .65$.

Creating an image-based format with a mobile-first design principle offers a refreshing and fast-paced user experience, akin to game-based assessments. The image-based format eases reading load, provides quicker processing of items by the taker, and minimizes interpretation differences when translating

**Figure 25.2.** Mobile sample view of HireVue Big 5 gamified assessment using picture format responses

and adapting for an international delivery. However, cultural variability may arise from different interpretation and cultural connotations of images used.

## Is There Criterion Validity Evidence?

Criterion validity evidence is sparse with game-based assessments for both cognitive abilities and personality. Clearly game development is in the nascent stages with predictive validity data just starting to appear. One concurrent validity study ($n = 1,864$ incumbents) using a personality game-based assessment with a global professional services firm found an average $r = .17$ across the Big Five factors with a five-tiered job performance rating. Additionally, no subgroup adverse impact ratio differences ($n = 5,952$ applicants) were found with a 33-percentile cut score (Willis & Liff, 2021).

As noted above, convergent validities between gamified assessments and traditional cognitive and personality tests have been identified. Adding the significant history of these traditional tests performing well in criterion validity studies (Schmidt & Hunter, 1998; Bosco et al., 2015), it stands to reason that criterion validity results will be realized with these assessments. Also, the levels of adverse impact appear smaller, and the user experience improved; thus, the potential for an improved method of cognitive and personality measurement may soon be demonstrated in applied settings.

## How Do I Evaluate Psychometrics of Gamified Assessments?

Like many selection and assessment scientist-practitioners, we believe that assessments should be evaluated based on their reliability, validity, and fairness regardless of how they are constructed, gamified or not. How stable the results are, how well they measure constructs related to job performance, and how fairly they measure these things are crucial elements for evaluating how well they work and their associated legal defensibility (Binning & Barrett, 1989).

The actual statistical tests used for measuring these psychometric elements may change based on the type of assessment. They may also change due to advances in statistics and computing power available in the future. Those advances are important and will likely be evaluated critically; whatever those actual statistics are, the fundamental principles and theories underlying the psychometrics should remain stable.

## Does It Matter What Is Measured?

One of the most interesting debates to come out of gamified assessments is the discussion around what gamified assessments measure. Asked another way, in using gamified assessments, do the constructs measured matter? If we predict job performance with gamified assessments, as well as or better than traditional tests, then are we confident to implement a gamified assessment without fully understanding what is being measured?

While a discussion of the value of construct validity is beyond the scope of this chapter, there are a few questions that a practitioner considering this type of assessment should consider:

- If assessment scores are compared to high performers, how confident are you that the performance anchor is accurately defined and measured to be used for this purpose?
- What type of diversity do you observe at the high performer strata?
- When prepping candidates for the assessment, how will you respond to questions on how to prepare, what is measured, and why it is measured?
- When training recruiters and hiring managers on the results of the assessment, how will you respond to their questions on what is measured and how the high-performance anchor was created?
- How often does "what good looks like" change at your organization that would then affect what is considered high performance?

Both HR practitioners and IO psychologists associated with the design and use of assessments have a number of considerations to make in their organization's adoption of gamified assessments. This includes, but is not limited to, being cautious when justifying the use of assessments based solely on assessment-criterion relationships due to the lack of precision and other confounding factors in many criterion measures.

## What Should I Be Concerned About Legally?

In general, if a legal challenge is brought against the use of an assessment, it is typically brought against the company using the assessment, not the assessment vendor. Thus, we feel it necessary to briefly discuss potential legal considerations for assessment practitioners. First, regardless of the validity claimed by a test vendor, it is *always* the organization's responsibility to demonstrate validity in their hiring process. One of the main reasons for this is that validity is not actually an inherent part of the test itself, but rather an attribute of how results are used in employment decisions (e.g., cutoff scores; Cascio et al., 1988). Even if a perfect measurement of a job-related construct existed, if it is used improperly in the hiring process—for example, if managers implement their own cutoff scores where none have been empirically established—the misuse of the assessment outside of outlined practice invalidates its appropriate use. Understanding the assessment's validity and appropriate use will remain vital to an organization's use of gamified assessments.

Next, specific to gamified assessments that use a big data–driven approach to test and scoring creation, the idea of demonstrating clear arguments for validity becomes more difficult to uncover due to how the test is created. Professional guidelines (SIOP, 2018) state that validation of selection assessments relies on the support of appropriate validity evidence, which goes beyond evidence of a relationship between predictors and criterion, alone. Indeed, the SIOP *Principles* outline the importance of the interpretation, the sound scientific rationale for the use of any selection assessment, and the proposed interpretation of the test.

Lastly, in addition to concerns of big data approaches to gamification with SIOP *Principles*, a pertinent concern for practitioners focuses on disparate impact and the associated tautological arguments inherent in the way the assessment is created. If the gamified assessment development approach obfuscates a clear observed correlation of interest, how confident can we be that it is stable or that it will be relevant in the future from a disparate impact consideration? Kim (2017) discusses this concern regarding the use of data mining approaches and the lack of an available, effective check on potential bias. The author argues that the deference courts have, in the past, provided in employer justification of knowledge, skills, abilities, and other characteristics (KSAOs) necessary for a role may be suspect in challenges where data mining is used, as these "models often rely on 'discovered' relationships between variables rather than measuring previously identified job-related skills or attributes. When the employer has not considered and clearly articulated the reasons for relying on particular criteria, it is unclear why any deference is warranted" (Kim, 2017, p. 908).

## Accommodations and Disabilities

All assessments used in the hiring context, gamified or not, should make appropriate accommodations for candidates with disabilities. While the extent of protections varies by country or area (United Nations Department of Economic and Social Affairs, 2022), we recommend that organizations consider going beyond what is required and focus proactively on what more they can do to ensure fairness in the assessment process. Neurodiversity, for example, may impact how a candidate perceives or performs on a gamified assessment and may impact the relationship between the assessment score and job performance. All assessments should be put in place with an accommodation process that is communicated and easy to follow for all involved.

Assessments with game-based elements may introduce more variables that will require an accommodation, including time limits, color differences, and more stimuli that are either related or unrelated to the construct being measured. What makes the assessment more engaging and fun may also be what makes it more challenging for neurodiverse candidates. The organization should carefully evaluate how *all* candidates will perceive and interact with the gamified assessment and ensure that proper alternatives, or reasonable accommodations, are in place (Americans with Disabilities Act, 1990). In the first published study of its kind, Willis et al. (2021) found that autistic candidates ($n = 263$) performed slightly better (not worse) on a game assessment package measuring cognitive ability than non-neurodiverse candidates ($n = 323$). More research like this is needed to further explore various gamified assessment types and applicant performance across disability categories.

At the time of this writing, the Department of Justice recently announced a joint effort with the EEOC (EEOC, 2022) to examine and provide technical assistance guidance on algorithms, artificial intelligence (AI), and disability accommodations (U.S. Department of Justice: Civil Rights Division, 2022). In the announcement of this guidance, they outline issues that employers should consider to ensure that these tools don't violate the Americans with Disabilities Act (U.S. Department of Justice: Office of Public Affairs, 2022). At a high level, this resource explicitly states:

- "Employers should have a process in place to provide reasonable accommodations when using algorithmic decision-making tools;
- Without proper safeguards, workers with disabilities may be 'screened out' from consideration in a job or promotion even if they can do the job with or without a reasonable accommodation; and
- If the use of AI or algorithms results in applicants or employees having to provide information about disabilities or medical conditions, it may result in prohibited disability-related inquiries or medical exams."

While algorithms and AI may or may not be gamified, often gamified assessments employ algorithms and AI. All organizations should have a clear accommodation process in place before launching new gamified assessments. It will also be imperative for any practitioner to stay up to date on new federal regulatory changes and guidance, as well as any state or local changes, particularly as they relate to accommodations that need to be provided to candidates.

## What Does the Future of Gamified Assessment Hold?

So, what is on the horizon in terms of gamified assessments? Within our own applied experiences, we see opportunities emerging in three key areas: virtual reality (VR) assessments, augmented reality assessments, and voice-augmented approaches. VR assessments offer an immersive candidate experience but also require serious technology. At this time, VR assessments may be more effective when done on location in testing centers where VR sets can be standardized and safety ensured. As VR technology continues to advance and becomes more affordable, this may become an option for testing at home with your own VR set. We are surprised at the lack of augmented reality assessments in the gamified assessment space, especially given the availability of this technology in commercial use. While VR requires specialized, expensive equipment, augmented reality usually requires a smartphone and an internet connection. This seems like prime technology for gamified assessments for candidates to take in the comfort of their own homes. Voice-activated assistants may also offer a novel approach to gamified assessments. You are currently able to apply to certain companies through your Alexa or Google Home, but typically the bots just gather your contact information and then send you more forms to fill out. What if these bots could mimic a customer interaction or ask a sequence of questions for the applicant to complete a "quest"?

## Conclusion and Practical Relevance

As with any new talent management technique, organizations should consider a wide variety of factors when determining if gamified assessments are right for them. First and foremost, they should be clear on the problem they are hoping to solve. Second, they should be clear on what they want to measure, when they want to measure it, and how they want the candidate to perceive their hiring process. Third, they should evaluate whether the investment needed to create and launch these assessments is worthwhile to their talent strategy.

While some candidates may appreciate "fun" in their hiring process, it's more likely they are concerned with the fairness of the process. Many assessments are costly, and gamified assessments can be even costlier depending on a variety of factors, from number of applicants to complication of scoring. Depending on the problem to solve, organizations should be clear if they need an assessment tool or instead are looking for a candidate marketing tool. If the latter, organizations should ensure that the organization they are promising with such an innovative and fun assessment tool matches the organizational culture and job the candidate will encounter on their first day.

Finally, while we will continue to conduct detailed evaluations, examine skeptically, and test as much as possible, we do hope that the field continues to innovate in the world of gamified assessments. No assessment method is perfect, and while some gamified assessments may not meet all of our needs at present, it doesn't mean current offerings are not valuable for certain organizations and in certain situations. As such, we believe the understanding, knowledge, and expertise of IO psychologists and HR practitioners to evaluate available and emerging offerings will be even more important to organizations as leaders weigh the cost/benefits of these assessments in a way that goes beyond what might have been expected of applied practitioners with more traditional assessments. There is real potential to change the way applicants and organizations approach and view hiring, and we encourage this innovative thinking to continue along with collaborative research to advance the field of assessment.

## References

Alter, A. L., Aronson, J., Darley, J. M., Rodriguez, C., & Ruble, D. N. (2010). Rising to the threat: Reducing stereotype threat by reframing the threat as a challenge. *Journal of Experimental Social Psychology*, 46(1), 166–171.

Americans with Disabilities Act of 1990, 42 U.S.C. § 12101. (1990). https://www.ada.gov/pubs/adastatute08.htm

Armstrong, M. B., Ferrell, J. Z., Collmus, A. B., & Landers, R. N. (2016). Correcting misconceptions about gamification of assessment: More than SJTs and badges. *Industrial and Organizational Psychology*, 9(3), 671–677.

Atkins, S. M., Sprenger, A. M., Colflesh, G. J. H., Briner, T. L., Buchanan, J. B., Chavis, S. E., Chen, S., Iannuzzi, G. L., Kashtelyan, V., Dowling, E., Harbison, J. I., Bolger, D. J., Bunting, M. F., & Dougherty, M. R. (2014). Measuring working memory is all fun and games. *Experimental Psychology, 61*(6), 417–438.

Barrick, M. R., & Mount, M. K. (1991). The big five personality dimensions and job performance: A meta-analysis. *Personnel Psychology, 44*(1), 1–26.

Barrick, M. R., Mount, M. K., & Judge, T. A. (2001). Personality and performance at the start of the new millennium: What do we know and where do we go next? *Personality and Performance, 9*(1/2), 9–30.

Beck, D., & Spencer, A. (2021). Just a bit of fun: The camouflaging and defending functions of humour in recruitment videos of British and Swedish armed forces. *Cambridge Review of International Affairs, 34*(1), 65–84.

Bedwell, W. L., Pavlas, D., Heyne, K., Lazzara, E. H., & Salas, E. (2012). Toward a taxonomy linking game attributes to learning: An empirical study. *Simulation & Gaming, 43*(6), 729–760.

Bhatia, S., & Ryan, A. M. (2018). Hiring for the win: Game-based assessment in employee selection. In J. H. Dulebohn & D. L. Stone (Eds.), *The brave new world of eHRM 2.0* (pp. 81–110). IAP Information Age Publishing.

Binning, J. F., & Barrett, G. V. (1989). Validity of personnel decisions: A conceptual analysis of the inferential and evidential bases. *Journal of Applied Psychology, 74*(3), 478–494.

Bolton, S. C., & Houlihan, M. (2009). Are we having fun yet? A consideration of workplace fun and engagement. *Employee Relations, 31*(6), 556–568.

Bosco, F. A., Aguinis, H., Singh, K., Field, J. G., & Pierce, C. A. (2015). Correlational effect size benchmarks. Journal of Applied Psychology, 100(2), 431–449. https://doi.org/10.1037/a0038047

Burgers, C., Eden, A., Van Engelenburg, M. D., & Buningh, S. (2015). How feedback boosts motivation and play in a brain-training game. *Computers in Human Behavior, 48*, 94–103.

Cascio, W. F., Alexander, R. A., & Barrett, G. V. (1988). Setting cutoff scores: Legal, psychometric, and professional issues and guidelines. *Personnel Psychology, 41*(1), 1–24.

Chapman, D. S., Uggerslev, K. L., Carroll, S. A., Piasentin, K. A., & Jones, D. A. (2005). Applicant attraction to organizations and job choice: A meta-analytic review of the correlates of recruiting outcomes. *Journal of Applied Psychology, 90*(5), 928–944.

Chen, J. (2007). Flow in games (and everything else). *Communications of the ACM, 50*(4), 31–34.

Childers, M. (2020). *Investigating the validity of brainteaser interview questions* [Unpublished master's thesis]. Bowling Green State University.

Collmus, A. B., Armstrong, M. B., & Landers, R. N. (2016). Game-thinking within social media to recruit and select job candidates. In R. N. Landers & G. B. Schmidt (Eds.), *Social media in employee selection and recruitment: Theory, practice, and current challenges* (pp. 103–124). Springer International Publishing/Springer Nature.

Connolly, T. M., Boyle, E. A., MacArthur, E., Hainey, T., & Boyle, J. M. (2012). A systematic literature review of empirical evidence on computer games and serious games. *Computers & Education, 59*(2), 661–686.

Deterding, S., Dixon, D., Khaled, R., & Nacke, L. (2011). From game design elements to gamefulness: Defining "gamification". In *Proceedings of the 15th International Academic MindTrek Conference*. ACM, 9–15.

Donovan, J. J., Dwight, S. A., & Schneider, D. (2014). The impact of applicant faking on selection measures, hiring decisions, and employee performance. *Journal of Business and Psychology, 29*(3), 479–493.

Equal Employment Opportunity Commission. (2022, May 12). *The Americans with Disabilities Act and the use of software, algorithms, and artificial intelligence to assess job applicants and employees.* https://www.eeoc.gov/laws/guidance/americans-disabilities-act-and-use-software-algorithms-and-artificial-intelligence

Equal Employment Opportunity Commission, Civil Service Commission, Department of Labor, & Department of Justice. (1978). Uniform guidelines on employee selection procedures. *Federal Register, 43*(166), 38290–38315.

Gamberini, L., Cardullo, S., Seraglia, B., & Bordin, A. (2010). Neuropsychological testing through a Nintendo Wii® console. *Studies in Health Technology and Informatics, 154,* 29–33.

Gkorezis, P., Georgiou, K., Nikolaou, I., & Kyriazati, A. (2021) Gamified or traditional situational judgement test? A moderated mediation model of recommendation intentions via organizational attractiveness. *European Journal of Work and Organizational Psychology, 30*(2), 240–250.

Hausknecht, J. P., Day, D. V., & Thomas, S. C. (2004). Applicant reactions to selection procedures: An updated model and meta-analysis. *Personnel Psychology, 57*(3), 639–683.

Hernandes, K. (2020, February 26). *This company is hiring without asking about candidates' backgrounds—here's why.* CNBC. https://www.cnbc.com/2020/02/26/companies-are-open-hiring-new-workers-heres-why.html

Higgins, D. M., Peterson, J. B., Pihl, R. O., & Lee, A. G. M. (2007). Prefrontal cognitive ability, intelligence, Big Five personality, and the prediction of advanced academic and workplace performance. *Journal of Personality and Social Psychology, 93*(2), 298–319.

Hilliard, A., Kazim, E., Bitsakis, T., & Leutner, F. (2022) Measuring personality through images: Validating a forced-choice image-based assessment of the big five personality traits. *Journal of Intelligence, 10*(1), 1–19.

Hom, P. W., Griffeth, R. W., Palich, L. E., & Bracker, J. S. (1999). Revisiting met expectations as a reason why realistic job previews work. *Personnel Psychology, 52*(1), 97–112.

Honer, J., Wright, C. W., & Sablynski, C. J. (2007). Puzzle interviews: What are they and what do they measure? *Applied IIRM Research, 11*(2), 79–96.

Hurtz, G. M., & Donovan, J. J. (2000). Personality and job performance: The big five revisited. *Journal of Applied Psychology, 85*(6), 869–879.

Irving, P. G., & Montes, S. D. (2009). Met expectations: The effects of expected and delivered inducements on employee satisfaction. *Journal of Occupational and Organizational Psychology, 82*(2), 431–451.

Jimison, H. B., Pavel, M., McKanna, J., & Pavel, J. (2004). Unobtrusive monitoring of computer interactions to detect cognitive status in elders. *IEEE Transactions on Information Technology in Biomedicine, 8*(3), 248–252.

Judge, T. A., Heller, D., & Mount, M. K. (2002). Five-factor model of personality and job satisfaction: A meta-analysis. *Journal of Applied Psychology, 87*(3), 530–541.

Judge, T. A., Higgins, C. A., Thoresen, C. J., & Barrick, M. R. (1999). The big five personality traits, general mental ability, and career success across the life span. *Personnel Psychology, 52*(3), 621–652.

Judge, T. A., & Ilies, R. (2002). Relationship of personality to performance motivation: A meta-analytic review. *Journal of Applied Psychology, 87*(4), 797–807.

Kim, P. T. (2017). Data-driven discrimination at work. *William & Mary Law Review*, *58*(3), 857–936.

Konradt, U., Oldeweme, M., Krys, S., & Otte, K. (2020). A meta-analysis of change in applicants' perceptions of fairness. *International Journal of Selection and Assessment*, *28*(4), 365–382.

Korn, O., Brenner, F., Börsig, J., Lalli, F., Mattmüller, M., & Mueller, A. (2018). Defining recrutainment: A model and a survey on the gamification of recruiting and human resources. In L. E. Freund, & W. Cellary (Eds.), *Advances in the human side of service engineering* (pp. 37–49). Springer International.

Landers, R. N. (2015). Developing a theory of gamified learning: Linking serious games and gamification of learning. *Simulation & Gaming*, *45*(6), 752–768.

Landers, R. N., & Callan, R. C. (2011). Casual social games as serious games: The psychology of gamification in undergraduate education and employee training. In M. Ma, A. Oikonomou, & L. C. Jain (Eds.), *Serious games and edutainment applications* (pp. 399–423). Springer London.

Leutner, F., Codreanu, S. C., Lafon De Ribeyrolles, M., Demelier, V., Brink, S., & Bitsakis, T. (2021, September). *Applying game based assessments of cognitive ability in recruitment: Validity, fairness and applicant experience* (Unsubmitted manuscript).

Leutner, F., Codreanu, S. C., Liff, J., & Mondragon, N. (2020). The potential of game- and video-based assessments for social attributes: examples from practice. *Journal of Managerial Psychology*, *36*(7), 533–547.

Leutner, F., Yearsley, A., Codreanu, S. C., Borenstein, Y., & Ahmetoglu, G. (2017). From Likert scales to images: Validating a novel creativity measure with image based response scales. *Personality and Individual Differences*, *106*, 36–40.

Liff, J., Bradshaw, A., Shipp, R., Zuloaga, L., & Mondragon, N. (2021). *Interview-and game-based modular assessments technical validation report*. Unpublished technical report. HireVue.

Lumsden, J., Edwards, E. A., Lawrence, N. S., Coyle, D., & Munafò, M. R. (2016). Gamification of cognitive assessment and cognitive training: A systematic review of applications and efficacy. *JMIR Serious Games*, *4*(2), e11. https://games.jmir.org/2016/2/e11

McPherson, J., & Burns, N. R. (2008). Assessing the validity of computer-game-like tests of processing speed and working memory. *Behavior Research Methods*, *40*(4), 969–981.

Nikolaou, I. (2021). What is the role of technology in recruitment and selection? *Spanish Journal of Psychology*, *24*(2), 1–6.

Organ, D. W., & Ryan, K. (1995). A meta-analytic review of attitudinal and dispositional predictors of organizational citizenship behavior. *Personnel Psychology*, *48*(4), 775–802.

Plester, B., & Hutchinson, A. (2016). Fun times: The relationship between fun and workplace engagement. *Employee Relations*, *38*(3), 332–350.

Povah, N., Riley, P., & Routledge, H. (2017). *Games based assessment: The expert guide* [White paper]. PSI. https://www.psionline.com/wp-content/uploads/GamesBasedAssessment_WhitePaper.pdf

Quiroga, M. A., Escorial, S., Roman, F. J., Morillo, D., Jarabo, A., Privado, J., Hernandez, M., Gallego, B., & Colom, R. (2015). Can we reliably measure the general factor of intelligence (g) through commercial video games? Yes, we can! *Intelligence*, *52*, 1–7.

Quiroga, M. Á., Román, F. J., De La Fuente, J., Privado, J., & Colom, R. (2016). The measurement of intelligence in the XXI century using video games. *Spanish Journal of Psychology*, *19*, E89.

Schmidt, F. L., & Hunter, J. E. (1998). The validity and utility of selection methods in personnel psychology: Practical and theoretical implications of 85 years of research findings. *Psychological Bulletin, 124*(2), 262–274.

Smith, M. (2022, January 14). *Professor who predicted "The Great Resignation" shared the 3 trends that will dominate work in 2022.* CNBC. https://www.cnbc.com/2022/01/14/the-great-resignation-expert-shares-the-biggest-work-trends-of-2022.html#:~:text=The%20Great%20Resignation%20will%20slow%20down&text=Americans%20quit%20jobs%20at%20a,poll%20of%201%2C250%20American%20workers

Society of Industrial and Organizational Psychology. (2018). Principles for the validation and use of personnel selection procedures. *Industrial and Organizational Psychology: Perspectives on Science and Practice, 11*(1), 2–97.

Spencer, S. J., Steele, C. M., & Quinn, D. M. (1999). Stereotype threat and women's math performance. *Journal of Experimental Social Psychology, 35*(1), 4–28.

Truxillo, D. M., Bauer, T. N., Campion, M. A., & Paronto, M. E. (2002). Selection fairness information and applicant reactions: A longitudinal field study. *Journal of Applied Psychology, 87*(6), 1020–1031.

Truxillo, D. M., Bauer, T. N., & Garcia, A. M. (2017). Applicant reactions to hiring procedures. In H. W. Goldstein, E. D. Pulakos, J. Passmore, & C. Semedo (Eds.), *The Wiley Blackwell handbook of the psychology of recruitment, selection and employee retention* (pp. 53–70). John Wiley & Sons.

United Nations Department of Economic and Social Affairs. (2022, March). *Disability laws and acts by country/area.* United Nations. https://www.un.org/development/desa/disabilities/disability-laws-and-acts-by-country-area.html

U.S. Department of Justice: Civil Rights Division. (2022, May 12). *Algorithms, artificial intelligence, and disability discrimination in hiring.* https://beta.ada.gov/ai-guidance/

U.S. Department of Justice: Office of Public Affairs. (2022, May 12). *Justice Department and EEOC warn against disability discrimination.* https://www.justice.gov/opa/pr/justice-department-and-eeoc-warn-against-disability-discrimination

Verhaegh, J., Fontijn, W. F., Aarts, E. H., & Resing, W. (2013). In-game assessment and training of nonverbal cognitive skills using TagTiles. *Personal and Ubiquitous Computing, 17*(8), 1637–1646.

Wang, X., Tan, S. C., & Li, L. (2020). Technostress in university students' technology-enhanced learning: An investigation from multidimensional person-environment misfit. *Computers in Human Behavior, 105*, 1–10.

Willis, C., & Liff, J. (2021). *Game-based assessment validation results: U.S. customer redacted.* Unpublished technical report. HireVue.

Willis, C., Powell-Rudy, T., Colley, K., & Prasad, J. (2021). Examining the use of game-based assessments for hiring autistic job seekers. *Journal of Intelligence, 9*(4), 53–66.

Wood, R. T., Griffiths, M. D., Chappell, D., & Davies, M. N. (2004). The structural characteristics of video games: A psycho-structural analysis. *CyberPsychology & Behavior, 7*(1), 1–10.

Yan, T., Conrad, F. G., Tourangeau, R., & Couper, M. P. (2011). Should I stay or should I go: The effects of progress feedback, promised task duration, and length of questionnaire on completing web surveys. *International Journal of Public Opinion Research, 23*(2), 131–147.

# 26

# The Full (Assessment) Monty

## Accelerating Individual and Organizational Development

*Matt Dreyer, Vicki Walia, Sandra Hartog, and Lynn Collins*

If talent provides a competitive advantage, as nearly all organizations state, then accelerating individual development of talent, especially high-potential talent, will result in better organizational outcomes. We fundamentally believe this to be the case at Prudential Financial. With a track record of over 145 years of success, Prudential is a global leader helping our individual and institutional customers solve financial challenges in a changing world. We provide a variety of products and services, including life insurance, annuities, retirement-related services, mutual funds, and investment management. We are focused on (a) investing in growth businesses and markets around the world; (b) delivering industry-leading customer and client experiences, blending human touch with advanced technology; and (c) creating the next generation of financial solutions to serve the diverse needs of a broader range of customers and clients.

Because talent is key to delivering on these aspirations and commitments, we invest significant resources in attracting, selecting, developing, deploying, and retaining top talent. Doing so engages and prepares this talent to take on current and future challenges. It follows that the more strategically, accurately, and efficiently we invest resources in development of individuals, the better the resulting organizational development and business outcomes. We recognize that we will accomplish our vision of the future by continuing to grow our business with focus, innovation and profitability, and a sustainable leadership pipeline. With this as context, we embarked on a journey to build a world-class talent organization with a deep pipeline of future leaders, global capabilities, and talent with diverse backgrounds, thoughts, and experiences.

Our simple and straightforward approach to development is helping people to understand where they currently are and where they want to get

Matt Dreyer, Vicki Walia, Sandra Hartog, and Lynn Collins, *The Full (Assessment) Monty* In: *Talent Assessment*. Edited by: Tracy M. Kantrowitz, Douglas H. Reynolds, and John C. Scott, Oxford University Press.
© Society of Industrial Organizational Psychology 2023. DOI: 10.1093/oso/9780197611050.003.0026

to. The goal is to equip our leaders to be more successful today and in the future. The result is a tailored "from-to" statement that clearly lays out the gap that must be closed to get from where the individual is to where they wish to be. For example, an individual may wish to move from being a skilled specialist with deep expertise in one area of the business to being a broader cross-functional enterprise leader. The same logic can be applied at an organizational level. An organization may want to move from a successful but cautious and slow-to-make-decisions approach to a more risk-smart, decisive, and agile approach. This from-to framework applies to individual skill development, career planning, and organizational capability development. It is how we build development plans and how we coach our talent.

Assessment plays a key role in driving us to our future state. This first step in the process provides insight and a clear view of individual skills, opportunities for improvements, and organizational strengths. We use a variety of assessments to gain a clear picture of the current state, and in some cases to assess progress over time. While the approach is robust today, it has evolved, and it is helpful to understand how the approach has changed over the years.

About a decade ago, our use of validated, psychometrically sound assessments was predominantly limited to selection. A variety of assessments were utilized to identify candidates' skills and abilities relevant to success on the job. However, assessments were not used broadly for development, and when they were there was limited transparency of assessment scores. Over time, several changes occurred in how Prudential uses assessments. We continue to have a strong suite of assessments that are used as part of selection. However, assessment results can now be shared with the selected candidate and with internal candidates who are not selected for the role. With this enhanced transparency, individuals receive debriefs on their assessment results to help them with their development planning. In addition, assessments for development are held to the same standards as those for selection to ensure that individuals receive accurate data to help guide their development planning that will accelerate their success. These assessments include a broad range of measures and methods, including personality inventories, 360 surveys, and interview-based 360s, as well as observation by trained program coaches and assessors during select development programs or while on the job. Transparency of the data has also been extended to include select human resources and talent professionals who can use the data to assist with coaching and development planning. Additionally, the data provide further opportunity to look at aggregate talent trends at both the individual and organizational level.

A key element in accelerating the development of our talent has been the use of assessments to guide personalized development based on (or to inform) the individual's from-to goal. This includes using in situ assessment by creating opportunities for employees to demonstrate and practice certain skills in an environment that maximizes the opportunity for observation, feedback, and coaching to identify what is working and what can be improved. Our approach includes high-fidelity learning experiences that enhance self-awareness and provide personalized feedback. Business simulations have played a key role in providing these experiences, as well as in creating an opportunity to drive culture change through the organization. For example, as new leadership dimensions or a new vision and strategy are rolled out for the organization, customized and contextually relevant business simulations provide a unique opportunity to deliver and reinforce those messages, and it gives participants a chance to lead and deliver in an environment designed to point to and elicit these new key behaviors. The simulations offer a high-fidelity environment that provides context for behavioral assessment and includes feedback from peers and program coaches, as well as the opportunity for self-reflection.

An overview of our assessment evolution is provided in Figure 26.1.

### Prudential's Assessment Journey

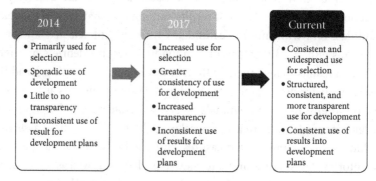

Our executive leadership programs are a prime example of these changes

Figure 26.1. Overview of Assessment Evolution

We will focus our discussion on the program Leaders Accelerating the Business (LAB), though this is only one example of how we incorporate a variety of assessments into development at Prudential. LAB is a nomination-based program for first-level vice presidents. Each LAB session includes approximately 24 participants, split into four teams of six members each. High-potential (box 6, 8, or 9 in a talent 9-block), vice president (VP)-level employees are eligible to be nominated for the program. They are representative of Prudential's diverse population and businesses, including U.S.- and non-U.S.-based organizations.

An overview of the entire program is included in Figure 26.2.

Because LAB participants are considered top talent at the VP level, each has a talent partner who works with them on a regular basis as an internal executive coach. This coaching includes developing a clear understanding of the individual's work history, strengths, development areas, and career aspirations. Assessments, most commonly a proprietary Prudential 360 tied to our leadership model and the Hogan LEAD series, are used to help inform the individual's self-awareness, with the assistance of the talent partner, who debriefs these assessments with the individual. In short, there is a view of how the individual is performing at work—their motives, values, personality characteristics, and derailers—that ensures a clear understanding of where they are and what they need to do to get where they want to go. Each participant enters the LAB program with insights about themselves and a robust from-to development plan, which includes specific areas they want to focus on, well suited to the LAB experience. With these tools in hand, individuals can maximize their LAB experience and, as they develop their effectiveness, help execute our business strategy.

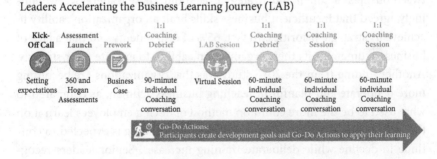

**Figure 26.2.** Overview of Prudential's Entire Assessment & Development Program

The highlight of LAB is a 3-day, highly customized business simulation that brings all the learnings into focus and action. The core of the simulation, and the challenge for each team, is to run a fictitious business that is similar to Prudential. The simulation provides an opportunity to build an enterprise mindset, execute enterprise thinking, and understand what it is like to lead a business and deliver on a strategy as part of the executive team. LAB provides an opportunity to learn through experience and gain insights into how they could do things differently to drive business and leadership outcomes. This is a unique feature of LAB.

At Prudential we believe that to build a high-performing culture and a team committed to rapid execution, we must help talent develop business acumen alongside other leadership skills. As leaders become more senior, they typically have developed deep expertise in their product lines and areas of the business. That knowledge, while beneficial, becomes less valuable unless it is coupled with the ability to create and execute on strategy. Strong business acumen and alignment around a clear organizational strategy and vision contributes to successful implementation and ultimately improves financial performance. However, while most corporations recognize business skills as necessary, they often struggle with how to develop it across the organization.

Business acumen is multifaceted and includes the understanding of how a business makes money; the understanding of interdependencies across functions and divisions, growth drivers, profitability and cash flow, key performance measures, and value creation; the ability to analyze and synthesize market and competitive data; and a deep understanding of customers.

In the Skills Mismatch research conducted by the Economist Intelligence Unit and sponsored by global strategy execution firm BTS, 300 leaders from around the world were surveyed in 2015 to explore the relationship between business acumen and strategy execution. These leaders overwhelmingly agreed that insufficient business skills limit an organization's ability to achieve its strategic priorities. In fact, 65% of respondents said that a lack of business acumen limits their organization's ability to execute their strategy. Another finding from the 2015 study was that organizations are becoming more deliberate and planful in teaching business acumen, as compared to what used to be the more common method of having employees learn it on the job. On-the-job experience as a method of training is expected to continue to decline while deliberate training increases. Senior leaders recognize that on-the-job experience is not the most desirable way of developing business skills. Respondents commented that learning business acumen on the job brings with it added risks. When, for example, business acumen is learned from people in the field with wrong assumptions or metrics, this could negatively impact a company's results. It does not allow for consistency across the enterprise or necessarily drive the right strategy execution. The study cites a striking growth rate in the use of business simulations and highlights their effectiveness in improving execution and market share.

Prudential partnered with BTS to develop LAB. The program was designed to enable participants to work in teams to demonstrate their people, team, organization, and business acumen while they are running a business in a competitive marketplace. BTS conducted in-depth interviews and organizational research to understand Prudential's present and future strategy, business environment, and most critical "levers" for driving change. These insights, along with marketplace knowledge, were then leveraged to create a contextually relevant and realistic business simulation enabling strategic application, discussion, and real-time feedback. The simulation is full of rich tensions and challenging tradeoffs that bring to life the important element of strategy leading to success at Prudential. This relevancy helps to drive participant buy-in and commitment to the experience, individual change, and organizational results. Each team's business results get measured and fed back on a scorecard for customer, financial, operating, and talent metrics. The 3-day simulation experience is pictured in Figure 26.3.

Once part of the LAB program, an individual receives prework welcoming them to the experience and describing the simulated organization to review

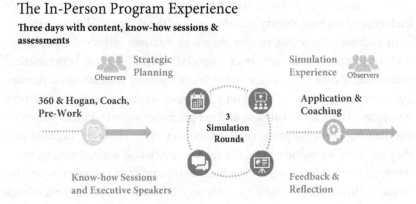

Figure 26.3. Prudential's 3-day simulation experience

in advance of the program. Prework includes an overview of the business—recent results, market data, and challenges that it is facing. The participant then spends 3 days on-site as part of the program. The program experience starts with meeting a program coach who will be present with the participant and is also the coach for the other members of the participant's LAB team. The coach and the participant review and refine the development objectives for the LAB experience, and then the participant meets their team members.

When the team has gathered, they form a C-suite, taking roles from CEO to business and function leads. The team has a session to set their strategy, using materials such as a case study and market reports to guide their thought process. During each of three simulation rounds, each of which represents a year, the team makes decisions about how to run the business based on the strategy they have set. They decide on actions to address problems and seize opportunities, and then they experience the impact of their actions on the performance of their business. The primary levers include how they invest the limited dollars and management time at their disposal, how they align their limited human capital to those efforts, and what new opportunities they pursue. Teams also consider the implementation of strategic initiatives that support short- and long-term performance. All teams begin with identical companies, but as they make decisions, their firms' performance metrics differ.

During the simulation, program coaches observe the participants "in the act of being themselves" as they discuss and evaluate the key strategic issues and their decisions. The business simulation mirrors the real world closely, so it provides the opportunity to assess these leaders in a realistic context as they display the same behaviors they typically exhibit on the job. Participants receive real-time, real-world expert feedback on their business and people leadership skills both during and after each of the three simulation periods.

In addition, the teams receive thorough analyses of how their strategic decisions impact their company's financial results. They are benchmarked against their competitors (the other teams) within the simulated market. The winning metrics are based on a balanced scorecard comprising return on equity (ROE), free cash flow, and net promoter score (NPS), as well as on maintaining the appropriate capital adequacy ratio. However, to make sure they are building viable companies for the future and not just managing for the short term, teams have to clear hurdles on employee engagement and innovation. In addition to their business results, teams are also given feedback on key leadership behaviors, such as decision-making, innovation, customer focus, influencing, collaboration, and strategic talent management.

Following each round of the simulation, several activities occur. There are "know how" and executive-speaker sessions on a variety of relevant topics. These are designed to provide new knowledge, the application of which can be practiced during the next simulation round and then used back on the job. In addition, the simulation "year" is scored and each team's decisions and results (and how those decisions impacted those results) are reviewed. Examining the decisions and the downstream impacts helps crystallize the learning. Teams are ranked according to their success on several business metrics and are prepared to begin the next round of the simulation and outperform the competition.

One additional activity occurs between simulation rounds. Each individual is asked to reflect on how they showed up during the prior round, with a focus on what was particularly effective or less effective, or any missed opportunities. The program coach also facilitates a discussion in which team members give each other feedback. This discussion is made more impactful because team members share their development objectives with one another. Finally, each individual meets with the program coach for a one-on-one coaching session. This gives each participant an opportunity to identify what worked that they want to continue, what didn't work that they don't want to do again, and any changes that they want to make during the next round.

Following the third and final round, the winner of the competition and final ranking of the teams are revealed. Because we know plans can disappear in the midst of our chaotic lives, participants are asked to set goals and commitments based on strengths and development opportunities. A BTS tool collects valuable information from participants about developmental actions they've committed to and measures and holds them accountable for these actions through a series of automated reminders. Participants can edit their actions, update their progress, and add the outcome of completing their actions. In addition, each participant works with their program coach to identify the behaviors that had the greatest impact during the simulation and create a plan for how they will apply those lessons back on the job, as well as how they will continue to extend their development. The program coach and the participant meet several times after the program to help ensure a successful transfer of the new skills and approaches back to the job, overcome any new obstacles, and refine the next steps for the individual's from-to development plan. The individual is then transitioned back to the talent partner, who continues to work with them moving forward.

The program coach plays a variety of roles, the first of which is the observer. Incredibly rich information can be gained through a professional coach observing and assessing an individual in action during the simulation. The simulation is designed to stretch participants and to test them in skills that are critical for success. Strategic thinking, data fluency, influencing others, assessing risk, decisiveness, and learning agility are all examples of dimensions critical to executing strategy. Many programs provide opportunities for individuals to develop these skills, but few have the mechanisms in place to assess while also providing a powerful learning opportunity. Another chief responsibility of the program coach is to observe the participants' decisions and interactions as a team. A third critical role is to categorize the observed behaviors into leadership attributes based on established evaluation standards and assessor guides. This provides a common and familiar context for participants to understand how their behaviors relate to leading at Prudential. Next, the program coach evaluates the effectiveness of those observed behaviors during each round for each leadership attribute.

This information is used during the simulation to facilitate team-effectiveness discussions that promote learning and development and to encourage team members to self-reflect and give one another feedback. The program coach helps individuals identify insights. The coach also provides guidance on leveraging identified strengths and support for development. Finally, the program coach plays the role of integrator, pulling together all the available assessment information to create individual-, team-, and cohort-level feedback reports and insights.

Each participant is provided with a written report to take as a development resource moving forward. This incorporates all available assessment information into one integrated narrative, along with actionable feedback regarding strengths to leverage and development opportunities. As a result of the high-impact experience, participants are able to understand the competitive industry dynamics, general trends, and business challenges; how these factors relate to individual roles, day-to-day operations, and the company's success; and the related decisions that drive results. Participants report that they have a greater understanding and appreciation of functions outside of their own, which helps with cross-functional collaboration. The business learnings are coupled with how they show up as a leader while making key decisions.

Data across participants are aggregated. The aggregate-level reports provide a view of the assessment data collected across individuals. This allows for insights into shared strengths and development opportunities across the talent pool, which can then be used to identify and prioritize future development investments.

The use of the program coach as a trained observer and assessor of behavior also provides the opportunity to track progress of individuals and cohorts on our leadership attributes. By assessing participants following the strategy session and each round of the simulation, we can identify trends. Successive rounds of program data demonstrate consistent improvement at the cohort level for People, Thought, and Results Leadership (see Figure 26.4). As they engage in the rounds of the simulation, participants develop strength in terms of demonstrating behaviors related to these leadership dimensions. For Customer Leadership, we have seen that customer centricity is front and center as critical during the strategy round. However, the data have revealed that leaders in corporate functions were not as practiced in incorporating and applying that into decision-making during the business simulation rounds. This is an example of the power of assessment data in creating an actionable insight that has led to different prioritization of development for these leaders as they prepare for more senior roles.

Results by Simulation round

|  | Strategy Session | Sim Round 1 | Sim Round 2 | Sim Round 3 |
|---|---|---|---|---|
| Customer Leadership | 70.0 | 65.2 | 66.3 | 64.3 |
| People Leadership | 69.8 | 70.0 | 72.6 | 72.6 |
| Thought Leadership | 70.7 | 70.7 | 74.8 | 73.3 |
| Results Leadership | 69.7 | 77.4 | 79.6 | 79.1 |
|  | 70.0 | 70.8 | 73.4 | 72.3 |

Scale

| Score | Rating |
|---|---|
| 100 | Role Model |
| 80 | Highly Successful |
| 60 | Successful |
| 40 | Some Development Needed |
| 20 | Significant Development Needed |

Figure 26.4. People, Thought, and Results Leadership by Simulation Round

Additionally, data analytics have shown that LAB participants are promoted at about twice the rate of their peers.

As we move forward, the challenge we have set for ourselves is figuring out how to leverage assessments with similar outcomes deeper in the organization, and at increased scale. The LAB program represents a significant investment of time and money, and other approaches are needed both to reach broader populations of our talent and to provide ongoing insights to support talent development. This is similar to the challenge we have faced with other talent development approaches—whether a 3-day leadership development program or a 6-month coaching engagement—the approach does not meet the needs of every individual throughout the organization and over time. However, the principles for assessment and development remain the same: Help each individual establish a clear understanding of where they are and where they want to get to and use that insight to create discrete from-to development goals. Ideally, have individuals focus on one, maybe two, of these goals at any given time and follow a series of development sprints. Allot 3 to 6 months per developmental sprint, and then as progress is made, refine the existing from-to goals or create new ones.

Throughout the entire process, talent partners and the organization overall are providing support in the form of multiple assessments. Formal assessments (e.g., Hogan LEAD, 360s) can and should be a component of this, but the greater opportunity is in providing a way to capture more everyday observations from the individual; their manager, peers, and direct reports; and trained talent assessors. Providing simple, straightforward approaches to collecting and calibrating this information periodically is the key first step. Organizations already make these judgments—through feedback processes, talent reviews, and performance management reviews. What is typically missing is a framework and approach to capture the data and then organize and use it in a way that provides insights to the individual and organization. Again, some organizations do this well for the few—the most senior, or highest potential—but when trying to apply these approaches at scale, the high-touch approach becomes untenable.

What, then, is an organization to do? We can lament the practical considerations like budgets and headcount that make it simply too costly, or we can find a solution using the technology that is now available to us and improves year over year. We have chosen the latter. Prudential is developing a Talent Marketplace that is much more than just an internal search engine for jobs. Our Talent Marketplace extends our efforts to enhance transparency and use of data in a more cohesive way to understand the organization, help leaders understand their teams, and help individuals identify insights about the skills required to be successful, their current and needed skill level, and how to best acquire and develop those skills.

Like our everyday coaching approach and development framework, it involves helping the individual identify where they are so they can identify where they want to go. We start by assessing what skills the individual likely has based on their history and experience. It also includes the opportunity for self-assessment. Using this and other external data, the Marketplace can then provide insights into what roles might be of interest to an individual and what skill gaps might be most important to close if a future desired role is identified. The Talent Marketplace can do this because it assesses and reports the skills of others who have been successful in that role as well.

When an individual engages with the Talent Marketplace and provides some simple information about where they have been, what they have done, and what they might be interested in doing in the future, they receive data and insights back that help them create compelling from-to plans. Because the Talent Marketplace is a one-stop shop for all things related to talent—an integrator of sorts—it doesn't stop at providing insights into the gaps that might exist. Rather, it recommends next best actions for closing that gap. These may include recommendations for in-person or online training, job moves, or key experiences or internal gig assignments that don't require job moves to acquire and develop key skills.

Think of all the assessments that organizations perform to assess their talent throughout the employee lifecycle. Using validated assessment data to select the most qualified candidate for a role is a best practice; why would we then not use that data to draw other insights and help that employee accelerate their development and be successful? Likewise, we have plentiful opportunities to make assessments of our talent based on observed behaviors and outcomes. The challenge is pulling that together in an integrated way with other available assessment data to derive and provide easily understood insights for the talent and the organization. We have done this manually for years with assessment centers, which have integrated a multimethod, multirater approach, but again, at a high investment of time and resources. If our opportunity is to do this at scale, then the returns on that investment will be at scale too.

Our experience over the past several years with the LAB program, and more recently with our Talent Marketplace, confirms that assessment data we have in hand, or that are readily available if we take the time to collect it, will help drive greater individual and organizational outcomes. We do not necessarily need to add new assessments to the mix, but rather to more effectively share and use the data that exist. The LAB program provides an opportunity to assess our top talent in a variety of ways and, by sharing that data more transparently, provide compelling insights on strengths and development opportunities at both an individual and organizational level.

## Reference

BTS. (2015). *Skills mismatch: Business acumen and strategy execution.* https://www.bts.company/docs/white-papers/skills-mismatch-business-acumen-and-strategy-execution-researchC276E653B841.pdf

# 27
# Driving Company Growth and Leader Development

## Innovations from Asia

*James D. Eyring*

Asian innovation in assessment is full of contrasts. Asia has over 1,000 years of assessment history, but by the year 2000, it had become decades behind the United States and Europe when it came to modern psychometric assessment. Rapid growth and globalization have closed much of this gap, but the result is often the use of substandard assessments or the misuse of assessments. While there are many gaps still to close, Asia is again creating innovative assessments. With rapidly expanding startups and aggressive investments in artificial intelligence (AI), Asia is poised to reshape what assessments measure and how leaders are assessed and developed. Instead of importing assessments and assessment methodologies, Asia is beginning to export these to the West. This chapter briefly explores the history of assessment in Asia and how this has shaped current innovation. The chapter then highlights several cases of innovative assessments coming out of Asia, including assessments that measure new capabilities that predict business growth, assessment of leader practices, and innovations that leverage technology to create ecosystems of assessment for selection and development purposes.

Asia has a long history with assessment, having implemented standardized assessments in China circa 600 CE. Hundreds of years before this, China had established a centralized government bureaucracy. To find and prepare officials for an increasing number of administrative roles, China created its first university in 124 BCE to train and test officials on the principles of Confucian government. This eventually became a standardized process to recruit, train, and assess all government administrators. Although these assessments focused on the content and application of Confucian principles, the assessments were founded on important principles that guide assessment development in Asia today. Specifically, assessments:

- were standardized to ensure all candidates were fairly considered for positions;
- defined ideal standards and a set of knowledge to strive toward;
- varied by level, with different assessments required as government administrators advanced into much larger roles; and
- were designed to drive development and self-improvement.

After over 1,000 years of use, this system was abolished at the end of the Qing dynasty at the beginning of the 20th century. Assessment in Asia languished while Germany, the United States, and other countries created assessment centers, 360s, and modern psychological assessment in the mid-20th century. With the collapse of colonialism, the end of World War II, economic challenges, the Cold War, and a highly diverse set of cultures and languages, assessment outside of education settings stagnated for decades. As an example, 360s were relatively unknown and unused in Asia until the beginning of the 21st century, 20 years after they became frequently used in the United States.

With globalism, the pace of adapting assessments from the West increased dramatically at the beginning of the 21st century. As assessment center use waned in the United States, consulting firms ramped up efforts to sell these and other assessments throughout Asia. Initially, many of the assessments in Asia were simple translations of their original content into local languages in Asia. However, robust research in Asia also resulted in adapting instruments to better address cultural differences. These efforts led to the Chinese Minnesota Multiphasic Personality Inventory—2 and the Cross-Cultural Personality Assessment Inventory (Sue & Chang, 2003). Ultimately, this led to the adaptation of other instruments such as emotional intelligence and cognitive ability. Moreover, this led to the founding of Asia-based companies that provided assessment and assessment center services across Asia.

This rapid change is highlighted by a 2015 survey of assessment practices. Building on work by Church and Rotolo (2013), J. D. Eyring and Lim (2015) surveyed large multinational companies in Asia and compared their high-potential selection practices with firms surveyed by Church and Rotolo in

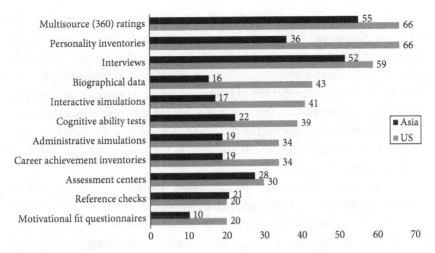

**Figure 27.1.** Assessment Practices used in High Potential Selection in Asia and the US

*Note:* This figure represents the percent of companies using different assessment practices to select high potential leaders. Asia data is based on a technical report by Eyring and Lim (2015) and is compared to data from the US reported by Church and Rotolo (2013).

the United States. Although both samples are relatively small, the findings are indicative of assessment dynamics in Asia (see Figure 27.1). Overall, assessment practices in Asia were not used as much as in the United States. However, some practices in Asia such as 360s, interviews, and assessment centers were almost at parity with the United States, while other practices, such as the use of personality inventories, cognitive ability tests, and simulations, lagged.

In a short 15 years, many of the practice gaps in Asia had been closed. However, this rapid adaptation of assessments came with risks. Although not shown in Figure 27.1 52% of companies reported using profiling tools such as the Myers-Briggs Type Indictor (MBTI), DiSC, and the Enneagram to select high-potential candidates. These and similar assessments have no history of predicting job performance, and some have underlying methodological issues. In the United States, legislative and judicial rulings act to discourage companies from using assessments that do not show evidence of predicting job outcomes. However, most countries in Asia don't have these restrictions, which results in the frequent misuse of assessments.

One misuse of assessments is highlighted in the use of blood type personality theory, which is the belief that blood type predicts a person's temperament and personality. This is a popular theory in countries such as Japan, Korea, and Taiwan, where believers in the theory use their blood type to explain their behavior and how they may or may not get along with others. Researchers in Japan (e.g., Nawata, 2014) have examined the theory and found no evidence that blood type is related to personality or behavior. However, there are reports that employers will ask job applicants about their blood type to ensure they get the right candidates (McCurry, 2008). In a region with few assessment experts and little to no judicial risk, questionable assessments can flourish.

Still, expertise and interest in assessment are growing in the region, which is giving rise to robust, innovative assessments that can scale to larger populations of employees. One example is the Growth Leader Assessment (GLA; J. D. Eyring, 2019), which was created by this chapter's author at Organisation Solutions, a consulting firm based in Singapore. Experience in assessing, coaching, and developing leaders across Asia had highlighted challenges with existing assessments. For example, the items and areas measured in most assessments did not resonate with many managers who were expected to innovate, identify new business opportunities, and build capabilities of their teams to grow their businesses rapidly in very challenging markets. Additionally, leaders needed to develop themselves quickly to keep pace with how fast their companies were growing. They wanted to easily identify and understand capabilities they needed in their current role while preparing for next-level jobs. In a cultural context, they wanted to know the ideal standards of leadership toward which they should strive. To address these challenges, the GLA innovates in three ways by (a) measuring a broad array of capabilities that drive company growth, (b) including new trait-based measures, and (c) assessing management practices that vary by level in the organization. A second set of examples comes from the rapidly increasing use of technology and AI for recruiting and developing employees. Companies in Singapore and India are using this technology to (a) scale the use of assessments to much larger employee populations, (b) build assessment ecosystems, and (c) integrate assessments with other tools to accelerate development.

## Capabilities That Drive Growth

Rapid economic growth has been a priority for most Asian countries for the past 50 years. Companies that did not grow simply did not survive in these highly competitive marketplaces. This prompted cross-company and cross-industry qualitative research in China that examined the enablers and barriers to company growth (A. R. Eyring, 2008, 2010). Although these studies examined a variety of growth enablers including strategy, innovation, and brand, the largest enabler of growth was leadership and leadership talent. Companies needed more leaders to keep up with the pace of headcount expansion, and they needed leaders with the capabilities to keep up with the demands of growth while also driving future growth.

This led to research that examined the differences between CEOs of high-growth and moderate- to low-growth companies operating across Asia (A. R. Eyring & Lim, 2014). Findings indicated that high-growth leaders were different than other leaders. For example, high-growth leaders spent more time focusing and aligning stakeholders to a critical few priorities, whereas lower growth leaders spent more time discussing much broader visions. High-growth leaders also pursued a broad range of inclusive growth opportunities, while lower growth leaders focused on a narrower set of opportunities. This research prompted the initial development and refinement of the Growth Leader Capability Framework by Organisation Solutions. This framework defined a constellation of capabilities that leaders need to drive growth in companies.

At the same time, academic research in the areas of entrepreneurism, marketing, and strategy were beginning to offer more insight into the individual, team, and organization capabilities that drive revenue and profit growth. For example, innovation (Junni et al., 2013), market orientation (Chang et al., 2014), and entrepreneurial orientation (Rauch et al., 2009) are some of the most important drivers of performance and growth. Research in psychology and leadership also began to show stronger links between leader capabilities and growth. For example, growth mindset was found to impact leader learning and performance (Burnette et al., 2013).

This research was integrated into the Growth Leader Capability Framework (see Figure 27.2), which includes nine capabilities categorized into three areas reflecting the demands on leaders to deliver performance today, energize their teams, and transform their organizations for tomorrow. All capabilities are important for company growth and performance. However, some capabilities (e.g., Manage Complexity) are important for all jobs at all levels, while others (e.g., Innovation) may be more important for some jobs and less for others. This framework led to the launch of the GLA in 2018 (J. D. Eyring, 2019), which includes two assessments. The GLA

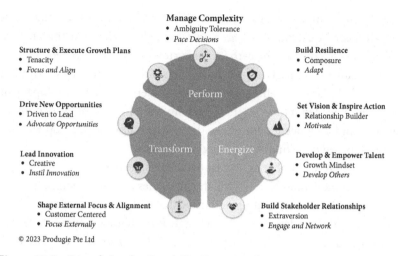

**Figure 27.2. Growth Leader Capability Framework**
*Note:* Growth leader capabilities with both style and strategy measures identified. Humility also is measured, but not shown in the figure. Reprinted with permission.

Style assessment includes relatively stable trait-like or slow-to-change measures. These include personality measures often found in other assessments but also include other traits and mindsets important for growth. The GLA Strategy assessment includes measures of management practices that leaders can learn and develop. The Strategy assessment is unique in that it measures practices, and the assessment questions and measures change as leaders move into more senior roles in the organization. Although the GLA Styles and Strategies assessments are used for selection and development, they are particularly useful when used together to help leaders identify needed development. For example, a leader can use feedback on the Motivate strategy to identify actions to take to work around a low score in Relationship Builder.

## Beyond the Big Five: Growth Mindset, Innovation, and More

Many assessments measure the Big Five personality factors, which include conscientiousness, agreeableness, openness, extraversion, and emotional stability. These characteristics enhance performance and help people succeed. For example, individuals who are conscientious are more likely to structure and organize their work and the work of others, while individuals who are extraverted are more likely to seek out and connect with other individuals. Although important, other characteristics are used by companies when they define successful leaders. For example, company leadership competency models often include capabilities such as innovativeness, tolerance of ambiguity, customer focus, and growth mindset. The GLA Style assessment includes both Big Five factors and other trait and mindset measures.

Some assessments use the Big Five measure of openness to experience to measure innovativeness as openness highly correlates with the ideation aspect of individual innovation (e.g., Ali, 2019). However, the GLA Style measure of innovativeness focuses on how well a person creates new ideas *and* how they turn these ideas into implementable solutions in a work setting. The first part of this, ideation and creation of new ideas, is similar to the openness to experience measure of ingenuity (i.e., creating new ideas). However, the GLA excludes other aspects of openness (Woo et. al., 2014) such as openness to culture (e.g., interest in aesthetics/art), intellectual efficiency (e.g., interest in reading, having a good memory), and curiosity (e.g., interest in science or thrill seeking). Instead, the GLA includes a measure of turning new ideas into action. By doing so, the GLA focuses on the construct of innovation at work. Likewise, openness to experience is sometimes used as a measure of tolerance of ambiguity. However, the GLA includes a direct measure of ambiguity tolerance because ambiguity tolerance is correlated with openness but is a unique construct (Furnham & Marks, 2013). These examples highlight that the GLA capabilities and items are attempting to measure style characteristics that are closer to the actual work of leaders. Research (e.g., Van Iddekinge et al., 2009; Sackett et al., 2022) suggests that proximal measures better predict performance than do distal personality measures. This has two benefits: (a) leaders are more likely to react positively to measures they feel are similar to their work, and (b) proximal measures increase the likelihood of predicting on-the-job behaviors and performance.

Growth Mindset illustrates the value of adding new measures. In the 1970s and 1980s, Carol Dweck conducted research (e.g., Dweck & Leggett, 1988) on the attributions children make after performing a task. Children who attributed failure to a dynamic attribute (e.g., "I did not try or practice hard enough") learned more quickly after failure than did children who attributed failure to a fixed trait (e.g., "I am dumb"). Growth Mindset gained popularity in the last decade and was adopted by companies to describe the mindset leaders need to help their companies succeed. For example, as part of its transformation, Microsoft's CEO Satya Nadella (e.g., Waikir,

2019) encouraged leaders to build a growth mindset and to build a growth mindset culture within the company. Because the original instrument was built for school-age children, the GLA Styles assessment modified the construct to focus on an individual's beliefs about talent. Items were created so that they were relevant for adults in a work environment. In testing the items, one study measured business unit (BU) leader capabilities and the business unit's outcomes (J. D. Eyring, 2019). BU leaders all managed between 100 and 200 employees and worked in the same market with the same products, competing against each other for sales. The largest predictor of year-over-year sales growth was Growth Mindset. Leaders in the top quartile of Growth Mindset had 11 times the year-over-year sales growth as those in the bottom quartile. These leaders were more likely to experiment, learn from failure, and let their teams take risks. One of the Big Five personality factors, Deliberate and Organized (i.e., conscientiousness), also predicted sales growth. Perhaps most interesting is that there was no significant relationship/correlation between Growth Mindset and Deliberate and Organized, meaning that both measures added unique value in the prediction of an important growth outcome.

Integrating new measures that are relevant to the work environment adds value in three ways. First, adding job-relevant items results in greater face validity. Candidates and employees are more likely to react positively to items that link more directly to actions on the job and report descriptions that are similar to their company's competency model. In Asia, innovation and customer service are particularly important, and adding these measures sends a signal of the importance of building these capabilities. Second, adding new measures addresses capabilities currently missing from traditional measures. For example, the Big Five factors and many assessments do not measure capabilities related to developing employees. However, this capability is critical for any manager. Third, new measures can provide value by improving the predictive capabilities of the assessments, especially if these measures predict important organizational outcomes such as revenue and profit growth, productivity, and employee turnover.

## Assessing Leader Strategies: Practices Versus Personality

While the GLA Styles assessment adds capabilities that are important to leader performance and company growth, it does not fully address all capabilities. For example, high-growth leaders were more likely to focus on priorities, align stakeholders, pursue new business opportunities, develop team capabilities, and drive innovation on their teams more than their lower growth counterparts (A. R. Eyring & Lim, 2014). These management practices and routines helped them drive growth with their teams and organizations. Academic research also points to the importance of management practices in driving growth. For example, company practices in entrepreneurism help large companies succeed (Rauch et al., 2009), and leader practices of CEOs have been found to drive leadership team and organization innovation (Zacher & Rosing, 2015). These practices and behaviors are different from those used in assessing personality in that they are much more specific in capturing work-relevant behaviors that impact others. For example, a personality assessment often focuses on intrapersonal behaviors that are consistent across time and situations (e.g., "I rarely discuss my problems with other people"), whereas GLA Strategy items include intra- and interpersonal items that are more specific in time and place (e.g., "I provide feedback to my direct reports at least monthly"). While some GLA Strategy items are intrapersonal, most are interpersonal items that focus on the interaction of an individual with others and the impact this has on the team or organization. This shift in focus has important implications:

- A broader array of capabilities (e.g., aligning stakeholders) can be assessed that focus on practices and a person's interpersonal impact on others.
- Practices can be defined to reflect the demands that leaders face as they move into larger roles.
- Practices offer an "ideal standard" or best practice toward which leaders can strive and develop.
- Practices can be used to help focus development and may be able to help individuals overcome challenges in their natural style.
- Practices can be measured through multiple methods, including a 360.

The Developing Others capability illustrates the value of measuring leader practices and routines. At an organization level, research (e.g., Crook et al., 2011) has shown that developing people capabilities leads to improved operational performance metrics (e.g., productivity) and firm-level performance (e.g., growth and return on assets). Leveraging academic research and best practices, the Developing Others measure was created to capture individual level behaviors and best practices that drive development of others. However, this capability manifests differently at each organization level. For example, an individual contributor can develop peers or individuals they manage on a project team but may have no organizationally sanctioned role in developing others. People managers are expected to develop their direct reports individually and to develop team-level capabilities. A BU leader needs to develop capabilities and succession throughout the organization. These differences resulted in the development of multiple measures, including Develop Peers, Empower Decisions, Develop Teams, and Develop Organizations. Items and scales differ for individual contributors, people managers, managers of managers, function and BU leaders, and CEOs. Whereas a personality assessment is a one-size-fits-all measure that is used across all these levels, the GLA Strategies measures are specific to the context in which an individual operates within the organization. A CEO needs a much broader array of people development strategies than does an individual contributor.

This level of specificity may be why strategies are more important than style measures in predicting some outcomes. For example, in one study, the strategy measures of Develop Teams, Increase Efficiency, and Motivate all predicted productivity per employee outcomes (J. D. Eyring, 2019). The only style measure that predicted productivity was the Ambitious subscale of Driven to Lead. Although more research needs to be conducted, these findings may reflect a complementary relationship between styles and strategies. Leaders with a style of high ambitious may be more likely to set a high productivity target. However, their strategies and practices of developing team capabilities, driving efficiency initiatives, and using motivation techniques in communicating to their team members may enable achievement of their highly ambitious targets.

This level of specificity in practices was shaped by its origins in Asia. In many countries, individuals prefer to learn and develop by first understanding an ideal standard to strive toward. Once they understand that ideal, they can then take steps toward achieving the standard. In some ways, each strategy scale defines a standard or best practice for which people can strive. For example, the Empower Decisions scale reflects actions that research has shown are most impactful in providing autonomy and improving task performance. Individuals with low scores can use this insight to develop more effective empowering techniques. This approach also is integrated into the Growth Leader 360. A combination of strategies and observable outcomes is used to define what performance looks like at "100%" if the person executes the capability perfectly. Assessors are asked to rate leaders against these 100% definitions and provide advice to help them achieve ideal performance in the future. By using multiple methods, leaders gain insight into their style, the strategies/practices they use, and stakeholder input on their observable strategies and outcomes achieved.

Because of this, the GLA Strategies assessment may better enable development when compared to trait or personality measures. In a recent review of research related to interventions that provided personality feedback to individuals in companies (Jelley, 2021), the author found little evidence that individuals benefited from the feedback. Having insight into personality did not change an individual's personality and did not change work-related behaviors or performance. This is concerning given the amount of effort spent on personality-based feedback interventions in organizations. For many years, practitioners have provided this feedback with advice and development ideas to help the leaders overcome their natural style tendencies. Although research has not been conducted in the area, focusing on strategies may be one way to overcome this challenge.

To aid development, each strategy in the GLA also was designed to complement its corresponding style. For example, some individuals are naturally Deliberate and Organized (i.e., conscientious). They quickly tackle new tasks and organize their work to achieve their deadlines. However, individuals who are not naturally Deliberate and Organized often learn practices such as regularly setting priorities or aligning stakeholders to help them overcome their natural gap. Without developing compensatory skills, these individuals would not likely succeed in most roles or organizations. The Focus and Align strategy scales reflect these workarounds by assessing practices that people use to prioritize, manage resources, and align stakeholders and support functions to support their goals. As shown in Figure 27.3, an individual's style and strategy help guide their development focus. If the style and strategy are high, little development is likely needed. If the style is low and strategy is high, the individual may have worked around many of their natural tendencies. Although more development is possible, they may face diminishing developmental returns. If their style is high and strategy is low, then they may be able to enhance their strategies to build on their style strength. If both are low, they can focus on developing new strategies to accelerate development. More research is needed to understand if the strategies are compensatory or additive in nature. However, from a user perspective, it offers leaders a way to better focus their development efforts.

**Figure 27.3.** Growth Leader Capability Matrix
*Note:* The Growth Leader Capability Matrix uses style and strategy results to identify development focus areas. Reprinted with permission.

## Assessment Technology in Asia: From Artificial Intelligence to Ecosystems

New technology is rapidly becoming the focus for innovation in assessments in Asia. This is fueled, in part, by country-level investments in AI, which have resulted in rapid expansion of AI capabilities. For example, Asia accounts for 46% of global peer-reviewed AI publications and 31% of AI patents (Zhang et al., 2021). Companies are also adopting AI into their organizations at a pace greater than in other regions. This expansion is relatively recent but is starting to impact innovation in assessments. Although the United States still leads in AI assessment startups, India and China have increased the number of AI recruiting startups they have to 126 and 19, respectively (Tracxn, 2021a, 2021b). These firms use AI to source, assess, interview, and screen candidates for companies. This is especially important in large markets such as India where thousands of candidates can apply for a single job. Recruiting firms use AI solutions to scale a company's efforts by searching for candidates on social media sites, screening resumes, and conducting initial assessments and video-based interviews. In many ways, these startups are similar to those in other regions where companies are using AI and new technology to replace traditional assessments. However, some firms also are using assessments to create and impact a broader ecosystem of services and stakeholders.

One example of this is CoCubes in India, which is now owned by Aon. CoCubes focuses on assessments for engineering and MBA graduates. Students are tested in their final year of university in a variety of areas including their aptitude, personality, English proficiency, computer knowledge, and functional domain knowledge such as coding, electrical engineering, or finance. CoCubes leveraged their assessment to create an ecosystem of students, learning institutes, and corporations to develop, recruit, and screen students. Students use the assessments to understand their strengths and opportunities so that they can develop skills prior to exiting their education program. As they near graduation, they leverage their assessment scores to find employers. Institutes of higher learning use the consolidated assessment reports to understand how their students are performing and the possible jobs for which they would be eligible. They also use these tools to increase their placement rates of students. Corporations use CoCubes to source and screen candidates for their university recruiting efforts. This ecosystem focuses on assessing a relatively narrow set of candidates but integrates assessment, sourcing, and applicant screening services to help multiple stakeholders meet their development and hiring needs.

Wheebox, also based in India, is another firm that is using assessments to build an ecosystem of services. Like CoCubes, Wheebox assesses soon-to-be university graduates and enables companies to recruit, assess, and interview these candidates. Whereas CoCubes focuses on a narrow ecosystem for engineering and MBA graduates, Wheebox is using their AI-based assessments and remote online exam proctoring services to assess people at all age levels across multiple stakeholder groups. For example, they assess students in elementary and high school grade levels to stream them into different educational options. For university students, they assess students in several areas including aptitude, personality, behavioral skills, and coding. Students can then use the Wheebox development programs to improve these skills and use their scores on the assessments to find jobs with employers. Corporations use their services to recruit, assess, and screen college graduates. They also use Wheebox's 360 surveys, online assessment centers, and certification programs for employees. Industry groups use their online learning and certification programs, and the government uses their certification programs for teachers. Wheebox has built a substantial ecosystem that provides assessments to people of all ages across a range of capabilities and, in many cases, uses online development tools to help individuals build new capabilities. They leverage individual data to provide information and services to companies, universities, industry groups, and the government.

These ecosystem models lend themselves to countries like India where there is a large candidate pool and high acceptance of assessments as a tool to stream or segment candidates for education and employment. The model also relies on students who are willing to share their assessment results with potential employers in the hopes of finding the best possible job, and on employers who are willing to leverage a pre-existing standard assessment for seeking candidates. Although innovative, such a broad ecosystem may not work well in the United States or Europe given privacy concerns and cultural differences.

Produgie, a software as a service (SaaS) firm based in Singapore, is building a different type of ecosystem to build individual, team, and organization growth capabilities. Produgie was incubated by Organisation Solutions, and the current author is actively involved in developing Produgie. The software combines assessment with develop-in-the-flow-of-work methodologies and stakeholder engagement to drive development and performance outcomes. This is similar to other technologies that are being developed to help leaders develop in the flow of work. However, using Produgie as a specific example highlights how needs in Asia are shaping the technology and how the development ecosystem can be expanded.

In the leadership development module of Produgie, individuals can explore their capabilities through self-serve online GLAs and/or the Growth Leader 360° tool. Based on their job challenges and assessment results, Produgie recommends development areas and guides the individual to design a "Sprint" for their development or improved effectiveness. Sprints vary in duration from 1 to 12 weeks and are structured to deliver real work outcomes, while the challenge presented in the work triggers capability development. For example, to improve collaboration, an individual might choose to complete a Sprint on building a trusting relationship with a challenging stakeholder. Produgie recommends actions they can take to improve the relationship, behaviors they can practice that build trust, and outcome measures of improving the relationship. Individuals choose the actions, behaviors, and outcomes relevant to them, resulting in an individual development plan.

Produgie then gathers advice and regular feedback from stakeholders, tracks results, and nudges the individual to reflect and act. Individuals choose how to share their data and how to engage stakeholders. For example, they can engage their manager, coach, mentor, direct reports, peers, or other stakeholders in the development process. The ecosystem of insight, learning support, and stakeholder input helps the individual develop.

The design of this module was inspired by coaching and development experiences in Asia. For example, with rapid growth, companies need to develop employees at all levels. A SaaS platform empowers this development by lowering costs and providing premium assessment and development to all employees. Because of this growth, managers are often not skilled or lack time to develop others. Produgie supports these managers by guiding employees through the development process, including recommending development areas, and designing development sprint experiences. These development sprints also provide ideal standards or best practice examples of actions to take and behaviors to practice, which works particularly well in guiding employees in Asia toward effective development. Moreover, sprints are short, encouraging rapid, repeated development of capabilities.

At a team level, Produgie helps managers create an ecosystem to improve team capabilities and performance. When managers create a team in the system, individual assessment-level data is summarized into a team report that highlights team dynamics, strengths, and capability gaps. Managers also can administer team-level assessments to gather input on how well the team is aligned in areas such as its purpose and how it operates. Team members can view the results to gain insight into each other. Produgie then recommends development sprints that the team can use to improve alignment, build better team dynamics, and/or work around capability gaps. Team members are engaged throughout the process and provide input and feedback on their progress as a team. Managers can use Produgie to develop their own skills, to coach and develop one of their team members, or to help the entire team develop and be more effective. This team module builds collective leadership for the entire team, which resonates for teams operating in more collectivistic cultures.

Produgie helps organizations build their own development ecosystems by leveraging role-based access to the software. Users can control their own privacy by granting access rights to their individual data, and the company can control data by granting different administrators with different access rights, based on their level of certification. For example, a learning and development professional may be assigned the rights to enroll participants of a high-potential program into Produgie and use this to drive common action-learning projects. A certified talent leader may be assigned access rights to examine individual-level assessment results of all directors to understand capability strengths and gaps while identifying leaders that would benefit from stretch assignments. A supply chain leader who wants to increase diversity of the supply chain may be assigned access rights to administer Produgie to women-owned business leaders to understand and develop their capabilities. These examples highlight the power of using analytics and report features to build collective leadership. Coaches, mentors, human resources, and other leaders can leverage Produgie to build capabilities that the company requires to succeed and leverage analytics to understand progress against these goals.

All these examples demonstrate that technology is enabling companies to integrate assessment into broader ecosystems. Traditionally, individual-level assessment data was delivered in an individual report and action on the data relied on the individual, manager, or human resources business partner who had access to the data. Technology has changed this. CoCubes and Wheebox help students, universities, and businesses use assessment data to develop capabilities, speed recruiting, and make selection decisions across many stakeholder groups. Produgie is using assessment data to help individuals develop new capabilities, teams develop and improve performance, and organizations build capabilities they need to grow. Appropriately managed, assessment data can be used by multiple stakeholders to drive outcomes important to organizations.

## Going Forward

Over the past 20 years, Asia has made up for lost time around assessments and assessment innovation. This started by importing and implementing assessments built in the United States and Europe. However, innovative Asia-based assessments and assessment practices are now gaining traction. COVID has accelerated the adoption of technology-based assessments in Asia, and increasing investments in AI and startups is likely to accelerate innovation. Many of these practices offer unique value as they were shaped by employees and leaders who survived and thrived in highly competitive growth environments. Currently, these assessments help to expand what capabilities are measured, how these capabilities are measured, and how assessments can be built into large development ecosystems. Going forward, assessment innovation in Asia is likely to add even more value.

## References

Ali, I. (2019). Personality traits, individual innovativeness and satisfaction with life. *Journal of Innovation & Knowledge, 4*(1), 38–46.

Burnette, J. L., O'Boyle, E. H., VanEpps, E. M., Pollack, J. M., & Finkel, E. J. (2013). Mind-sets matter: A meta-analytic review of implicit theories and self-regulation. *Psychological Bulletin, 139*(3), 655.

Chang, W., Franke, G. R., Butler, T. D., Musgrove, C. F., & Ellinger, A. E. (2014). Differential mediating effects of radical and incremental innovation on market orientation-performance relationship: A meta-analysis. *Journal of Marketing Theory and Practice, 22*(3), 235–250.

Church, A. H., & Rotolo, C. T. (2013). How are top companies assessing their high-potentials and senior executives? A talent management benchmark study. *Consulting Psychology Journal: Practice and Research, 65*(3), 199.

Crook, T. R., Todd, S. Y., Combs, J. G., Woehr, D. J., & Ketchen, D. J., Jr. (2011). Does human capital matter? A meta-analysis of the relationship between human capital and firm performance. *Journal of Applied Psychology, 96*(3), 443.

Dweck, C. S., & Leggett, E. L. (1988). A social-cognitive approach to motivation and personality. *Psychological Review, 95*(2), 256.

Eyring, A. R. (2008). *Executing growth strategies in China: A summary report*. Organisation Solutions Pte. Ltd.

Eyring, A. R. (2010). *Executing growth strategies in China phase 2: A summary report*. Organisation Solutions Pte. Ltd.

Eyring, A. R., & Lim, A. (2014). *Leading growth in Asia: A summary report*. Organisation Solutions Pte. Ltd.

Eyring, J. D. (2019). *Technical report: Business unit leader style and strategy capabilities and year-over-year business unit performance*. Organisation Solutions Pte. Ltd.

Eyring, J. D., & Lim, A. (2015). *Leadership assessment practices in Asia: A summary report*. Organisation Solutions Pte. Ltd.

Furnham, A., & Marks, J. (2013). Tolerance of ambiguity: A review of the recent literature. *Psychology, 4*(09), 717–728.

Jelley, R. B. (2021). Using personality feedback for work-related development and performance improvement: A rapid evidence assessment. *Canadian Journal of Behavioural Science/Revue canadienne des sciences du comportement, 53*(2), 175.

Junni, P., Sarala, R. M., Taras, V., & Tarba, S. Y. (2013). Organisational ambidexterity & performance: A meta-analysis. *Academy of Management Perspectives, 27*(4), 299–312.

McCurry, J. (2008, December 4). Typecast – Japan's obsession with blood groups. *The Guardian*. https://www.theguardian.com/world/2008/dec/04/japan-world-news

Nawata, K. (2014). No relationship between blood type and personality: Evidence from large-scale surveys in Japan and the US. *Shinrigaku kenkyu: The Japanese Journal of Psychology, 85*(2), 148–156.

Rauch, A., Wiklund, J., Lumpkin, G. T., & Frese, M. (2009). Entrepreneurial orientation and business performance: An assessment of past research and suggestions for the future. *Entrepreneurship Theory and Practice, 33*(3), 761–787.

Sue, S., & Chang, J. (2003). The state of psychological assessment in Asia. *Psychological Assessment, 15*(3), 306.

Sackett, P. R., Zhang, C., Berry, C. M., & Lievens, F. (2022). Revisiting meta-analytic estimates of validity in personnel selection: Addressing systematic overcorrection for restriction of range. *Journal of Applied Psychology, 107*(11), 2040–2068.

Tracxn. (2021a). *AI in recruiting startups in China.* https://tracxn.com/explore/AI-in-Recruiting-Startups-in-China

Tracxn. (2021b). *AI in recruiting startups in India.* https://tracxn.com/explore/AI-in-Recruiting-Startups-in-India

Van Iddekinge, C. H., Ferris, G. R., & Heffner, T. S. (2009). Test of a multistage model of distal and proximal antecedents of leader performance. *Personnel Psychology, 62*(3), 463–495.

Waikir, S., (2019, November 26). *Microsoft CEO Satya Nadella: Be bold and be right.* Insights by Stanford Business. https://www.gsb.stanford.edu/insights/microsoft-ceo-satya-nadella-be-bold-be-right

Woo, S. E., Chernyshenko, O. S., Longley, A., Zhang, Z. X., Chiu, C. Y., & Stark, S. E. (2014). Openness to experience: Its lower level structure, measurement, and cross-cultural equivalence. *Journal of Personality Assessment, 96*(1), 29–45.

Zacher, H., & Rosing, K. (2015). Ambidextrous leadership and team innovation. *Leadership & Organization Development Journal,* arXiv:2103.06312.

Zhang, D., Mishra, S., Brynjolfsson, E., Etchemendy, J., Ganguli, D., Grosz, B., Lyons, T., Manyika, J., Niebles, J. C., Selitto, M., Shoham, Y., Clark, J., & Perrault, R. (2021). *The AI Index 2021 annual report.* https://aiindex.stanford.edu/report/

# 28
# Assessment in a Large Multinational

*Paul van Katwyk*

As a growing global player in the integrated oil and gas industry, Saudi Aramco began the new millennium by making a significant enhancement to strengthen the leadership pipeline needed to realize its strategic ambitions. Specifically, over the last two decades, Saudi Aramco has utilized an assessment center–based methodology to conduct over 7,000 leadership readiness assessments that have supported leadership succession decisions from first-level leaders up to the most senior corporate executives. This journey has involved a number of ongoing enhancements including, during the recent pandemic, a shift to a virtual delivery platform. This case study will share highlights and the lessons learned in this assessment journey within the broader journey of Saudi Aramco becoming the largest global energy player and one of the most valuable companies in the world. Given the focus on technology-driven assessment in large multinational organizations, added focus will be on the recent shift to a virtual delivery model.

## Organizational Context

The history of formalized assessment at Saudi Aramco can be found as early as 1950 when a young industrial psychologist, Jack Rushmer, set out to develop a learning abilities and aptitude test for Saudis similar to those used by organizations in the United States (Pledge, 1998). He and a recently graduated industrial psychologist from the University of Tennessee developed what became the Saudi Test for Job Assignment (STJA). The STJA was initially found to have a strong relationship to training achievements. But as the Saudi public school system evolved, the effectiveness of the STJA declined and experts worked with Saudi Aramco to evolve the testing to include a full battery of customized aptitude tests. The Job Aptitude Test (JAT) battery then evolved over the coming decades until, in the early 1980s, an Arabic version of the well-proven General Aptitude Test Battery (GATB) was adapted and then adopted by Saudi Aramco for company-wide application. These efforts, among others, highlight Saudi Aramco's active and often leading role in the development and adoption of assessments within the kingdom.

In the early 2000s, a decision was made by Saudi Aramco to integrate a robust and consistent assessment process in the support of leadership succession. Historically, since the 1950s, the oversight of the leadership pipeline has been guided by management development committees (Pledge, 1998). The overriding goal in this latest effort was to put in an assessment strategy that could better inform and guide the pipeline of leadership talent across the *entire* organization.

A key driver behind the need for a more significant assessment strategy over the last two decades has been that the demands on the leadership pipeline are continually expanding with the increased strategic opportunities and challenges facing the organization. These challenges included the rapidly changing global business environment as the energy sector evolved and Saudi Aramco focused on further expanding its businesses across the hydrocarbon value chain and beyond. Unique from most other global companies, Saudi Aramco was also expected to meet the kingdom's Saudization targets in terms of placing Saudi nationals as leaders at each level of leadership. As a national oil company, leaders needed to be equipped to address the challenges and realize the opportunities posed by Saudi Aramco's role in supporting the kingdom's success, including the achievement of the 2030 vision. These requirements included launching the 2019 initial public offering (IPO), driving the localization of key suppliers, and supporting the growing infrastructure across the kingdom. Besides these strategic drivers, the assessment solution had to consider a range of contextual factors including the large size of the organization (currently 70,000+ employees), growth projections, reliance on internal/local talent, and organizational culture fit (e.g., highly process focused, criticality of risk management, strong data orientation).

## Assessment Design and Infrastructure

Based on this context, the primary assessment requirements demanded a solution that was highly face valid, grounded in data, perceptibly objective, and developmentally oriented. In turn, these requirements drove the decision to utilize an assessment center methodology that provided a multitool, multirater, multidimensional approach leveraging only external/highly trained assessors/coaches. Many of these decisions were aligned with the research on the validity and advantages of assessment centers (e.g., Gaugler et al., 1987; Arthur et al., 2003; Hermelin et al., 2007). Specifically, the design included the establishment of competency models targeted at each level of leadership that were assessed through high-fidelity simulations scored with behaviorally anchored rating scales delivered by expert external psychologists (e.g., Thornton & Byham, 1982; Thornton & Rupp, 2005; International Taskforce on Assessment Center Guidelines, 2015; British Psychological Society, 2015).

The assessment design also needed to support high volumes of assessments. A sense of the scale of demand is illustrated by the fact that over 7,000 1.5- to 2.5-day-long assessments have been conducted to ensure data on all leaders moving through the leadership pipeline. This demand drove the building of an in-kingdom facility devoted principally to the delivery of these assessments. The resulting facility provided a minimum of 12 assessment rooms, group testing/debrief rooms with regularly updated technology support (e.g., viewing cameras, separate internet), and office space for the assessment staff and providers.

The sustainability of this assessment effort benefited from a devoted Center of Excellence (CoE). The primary objective of the CoE was to ensure the internal expertise and processes needed to deliver high-quality, efficient, and reliable results. They provided a ready source of thought leadership around assessment that could guide the business leaders and human resources (HR) teams that leveraged the data. Over the years, the staff within the CoE have included industrial-organizational (IO) psychologists, operational teams, data analysts, coaches, technology support, and operational efficiency experts. The CoE developed a customized data management program that houses all of the assessment data coming from the reports, including narrative comments. This assessment data is stored and integrated with a wide range of relevant talent data (e.g., work history, performance, training history, succession plans, etc.). This program can present highly detailed profiles on individuals, which can be leveraged in talent discussions, while also allowing for the extraction of group-level data to guide broader talent decisions and planning.

Over the two decades that this assessment has been operational, there have been several updates, revisions, and additions made to the core competency framework and the associated competency models targeted at each level of leadership. In turn, these updates in the competencies often drove the need to redesign simulations, which could involve adapting evaluation guides up to requiring the redesign of the entire case study, or background scenario, and simulations. Another set of updates included expanding the assessment offerings to meet the evolving needs of the company. For example, a decision was made to add a new assessment center targeting a level of middle management (i.e., division heads). As the organizational structure and operating model evolved, the roles at this level have become increasingly more pivotal to business success (e.g., more decision-making authority) and thus the need to make well-informed decisions on readiness, development, and promotion.

## Assessment Validity

Consistent with the guidance around assessment center design, ensuring simulations reflected current and near-future leadership demands has been valuable in ensuring the continued buy-in into the assessment and results (Thornton & Byham, 1982; Thornton et al., 2017). Besides the focus on face validity and the reliance on validity generalization, there have been other efforts taken to test and ensure the validity of these customized assessment centers. One of the more significant validation efforts was in 2011 when a predictive validation study was conducted on the manager-level assessment center. Past assessment scores from 134 current managers who had been assessed in the Manager Assessment Center (MAC) before their promotion were used as the predictor measure (i.e., average competency score on the MAC). Ratings of their performance as a manager and potential to become an executive, made by their current or recent boss, served as the main criterion measure. Results supported the predictive validity of the center in that the overall assessment ratings (OARs) were found to have a correlation of .54 with future boss ratings of potential and a correlation of .43 with future boss ratings of performance. These results compared favorably with other studies including meta-analytic studies like Gaugler et al. (1987) with a mean operational validity of the OAR of .37 or more recently Hermelin et al. (2007) with .27.

## Participant Experience

A key priority over the years has been a consistent focus around the participant experience. In terms of collecting reaction data from participants, at the end of each program, a group debrief is conducted to collect qualitative feedback including overall pros and cons. However, different rating procedures have been used over the years to capture participant experience. Most recently, evaluations are reported back as net promoter scores (NPSs), which have been adopted more broadly by the organization as a key performance indicator (KPI).

NPSs come from market research that uses a single question asking the respondent to rate the likelihood that they would, in the case of the assessment center, recommend the assessment to a colleague. NPSs, which vary from −100 to +100, have been used by organizations as a measure of customer loyalty. The overall NPSs of the current assessment centers range in the 40s, which are consistent with NPSs for other assessment tools provided by the current assessment provider (Aon, 2019). However, NPSs in assessment centers bring their own challenges when trying to compare with other HR efforts such as coaching or development programs. Development-focused experiences, which include engaging experiences like spending a week at the London Business School, can have associated NPSs in the 80 to 100 range, which results in questionable conclusions when compared to assessment NPSs. Yet the adoption of NPSs by the organization has highlighted the priority placed on ensuring a quality experience for participants.

These evaluations from participants have impacted the approach to assessment in a number of ways. One impact has been to drive continuous process improvements to make the experience more positive. These efforts have included adding more briefing sessions, informal conversations, and social events (e.g., group dinner). Another critical area for ongoing improvements in the participant experience has been around transparency. The question of transparency in assessment centers has been long questioned (e.g., Sackett, 1987) and has been a topic of ongoing discussions with the CoE and leadership at Saudi Aramco. With the strong focus on development, the value of added transparency has become increasingly important, especially as, the evidence suggests, it would not significantly change the validity of the centers (e.g., Kolk et al., 2003). This has included providing the competency frameworks and success profiles on the intranet company site as well as greater guidance on how to best prepare for the simulations and development resources around the dimensions that would be examined (e.g., financial acumen).

Another dimension of transparency has been around the sharing of the assessment results with the participants. For many years there were separate reports in which the "organizational report" contained all the scores (readiness rating, competency scores, potential rating, derailer scores, etc.), while the participant received a "developmental report," which contained the competency scores and narrative development guidance. With the effort to create greater transparency, a decision was made over 2 years ago to make all scores related to readiness transparent. This effort included adding feedback preparation sessions and more coaching to help the person understand and leverage the ratings.

There is no quantitative measure of this relatively recent change in transparency as the survey metrics also changed (i.e., move to NPS, different survey format). Yet the qualitative comments from both participants and their managers appear overall positive. However, there is also evidence that participants who perform poorly can really struggle when they see the actual scores. Despite the reassurances that their focus should be on "what they can do with the data" in terms of development, it can be challenging and even negatively impact one's motivation and engagement level in the short term. Yet overall the pros of greater transparency are seen as significant and in line with the intent of readiness assessments within this organization.

These last points around greater transparency and the priority on participant experience also drive the ongoing efforts of the CoE to ensure effective follow-up development. Given the recognition of the value of development-focused assessment centers (Rupp et al., 2006) and their strategic importance in ensuring ready leaders, there have been a number of different efforts over the years to provide follow-on development support beyond development plan discussions with the participant and the leader who nominated the person (typically the skip-level boss). One significant effort and investment was to build up an internal coaching team that could provide follow-on coaching after all assessments. Most recently, there is a focused effort to establish an intensive 6-month development "journey" after the two most senior-level assessment centers. The 6-month journey includes individual coaching, peer cohort coaching, and a week-long program at a leading business school focusing on common group development needs (e.g., business acumen, global perspective, digital leadership). As Aramco emerges from the pandemic, this new program is being piloted in an effort to improve the experience of assessment and its impact on accelerating the development of ready leaders.

## The Move to Virtual Delivery

One of the most significant changes, which will be the focus of the remainder of this chapter, is the shift in 2020 to a virtual delivery platform. There were several business conditions that drove the need to move all assessments from in person to virtual. Due to factors including more volatile oil prices and an increasingly competitive global energy market, there was a consideration to manage the per assessment cost. As well, an increasingly global workforce was driving the need to support alternate delivery channels to allow more "out of kingdom" assessments. This shift included the decision to include leaders in Saudi Aramco's affiliates as part of the "global talent pool," which would benefit from more agile assessment delivery channels. Finally, the pandemic situation forced the acceleration to virtual delivery since no assessments could be delivered in person from March 2020 as no external assessors could be brought into the country. However, since senior leadership demanded that the projected volume of assessments still needed to be delivered to support ongoing business operations, it was critical to make a quick transition to a virtual delivery model that could support over 250 leadership assessments in 2020.

Some of the broader goals around the actual execution of the move to a virtual delivery platform included:

- Quality data. It was important to ensure high-quality data in terms of being valid, benchmarked, and well supported across all of the talent metrics, as well as that the rich qualitive elements remained, such as customized versus "boilerplate" development recommendations.
- Equivalence with in-person assessments. It was critical that it could be clearly demonstrated that going through the virtual version would not have any measurable impact on the outcomes of the assessments compared to the previous in-person version. Many assessment providers are offering virtual or digital assessment centers and there is guidance on developing virtual assessment centers (Howland et al., 2015). However, at that time, this author could find limited clear evidence supporting equivalence beyond some cases studies provided by firms, which were

also transitioning from in-person to virtual delivery. One of the more detailed case studies had results suggesting comparable participant experience and scores (Crandell et al., 2020). Yet it was critical, given the limited evidence, to provide our own clear support for equivalency. This evidence-based approach was key to assuring the senior leadership, who were unfamiliar with operating virtually, that there was equivalency, thus limiting any excuse to discount the data and results.
- Positive and developmental experience. There was clear concern from leaders and participants that the virtual assessment would be "less" of an experience. The quality of the experience was a critical positive element of the brand around the assessment centers and needed to be retained. As all interactions with the assessors/role players were virtual and there were added pandemic requirements like social distancing from peers, it was concluded that this would result in a "different" and not equivalent experience. Yet, it was important that it was still seen as a very positive experience.

Leveraging design guidance from the assessment provider, in line with other guidance on the design of virtual assessment centers (Howland et al., 2015; British Psychological Society, 2020), a transition to virtual delivery was carried out with continued analysis to ensure equivalency. Some of the highlights of the transition include:

- While the interview and role plays were all done virtually, a decision was made to have the participants do the assessments at the company's existing assessment center. The decision was driven by the need to manage the risks of technology failures and standardize the experience using laptops/tablets managed by the assessment staff. Given that technology issues were found to be the main challenge throughout the journey, it was determined afterward that this was the right decision and to continue with this delivery model when possible. It is important to note that, in some of the later programs, several participants completed the assessment from their computer at an Aramco site outside of the kingdom. This was important given the increasing need to be able to include out-of-kingdom participants in an assessment center run in the kingdom.
- Primarily for pandemic reasons, the size of the centers was limited to six participants (versus typical 12-person centers). This allowed for social distancing but also was found to help ensure the quality of the experience in terms of responding to any technology or administrative

concerns and allowing for smaller group discussions and debriefs throughout the program.
- After each program, there was a debrief and full review of all scores and evaluations/comments by the project and delivery team. This included regular debriefs with the assessors to get their input on the participant reactions and suggestions on improving the experience.
- The distributions of the competencies and the OAR were continually compared against (a) a set of in-person assessments done in 2019 and early 2020 using the same simulations and (b) historical norms. Overall, no significant differences were found.
- Evaluations of the experience captured through verbal feedback, ratings, and NPSs were critical in making some changes through the journey. These included concerns on the size of the tablets, the amount of background information on what to expect, and the quality of the video stream. Efforts to improve the technology and add further briefings were key in ensuring that the evaluations were consistent with in-person assessments. The average NPSs ranged in the 40s across the different assessment centers (supervisor, division head, manager), and overall over 95% of participants rated the experience as average to above average. These scores were consistent with the in-person centers and tended to be higher than seen in other virtual assessment centers, which may be due to the highly customized and interactive assessments.

A full review was completed after 6 months, when over 250 assessments had been done. This review by the CoE team confirmed that equivalency had been achieved, which was then communicated more broadly throughout the organization. While many participants did note that it was a different type of experience, overall they were positive and the leadership felt assured that the resulting scores were consistent with what might have been expected from an in-person center. In the following year, the need for constantly reaffirming and communicating these results and responding to concerns has continued to be a priority.

## Key Insights and Conclusions

To summarize, the adoption of a robust and consistent approach to readiness assessment, currently with data from over 7,000 leadership assessments, has played a critical role in Aramco's ability to ensure a strong pipeline of leadership talent needed to deliver on its aggressive strategy. Yet this assessment approach has had to balance consistency with the agility to be sustainable. For example, as described more fully in this chapter, the significant shift to virtual delivery was pivotal to addressing an immediate need but also created the agility needed to support the future (e.g., a more dispersed, global and virtual workforce; greater cost efficiencies).

Some of the key lessons learned through this journey of bringing in a significant assessment strategy within a large organization like Saudi Aramco include:

**Ensuring alignment with the culture and values:** Ensuring strategic alignment in talent practices and strategy has been recognized and advocated by many experts (e.g., Silzer & Dowell, 2009; Thornton et al., 2015). This case study has highlighted how the purpose and key updates to the assessment strategy were driven by the organizational strategy. Yet, in this author's experience of having designed and delivered assessments across many organizations, the success of the assessment strategy in Saudi Aramco could also be seen to highlight the importance of ensuring the cultural fit. Even the longevity of this 20-plus-year-long program, while impressive, could be seen as reflecting the culture and dynamics of this industry, where projects and investments in the energy industry typically operate on timelines of decades. As highlighted throughout this case study, the many design and implementation decisions over the years often reflected the culture of this engineering-focused company, where factors such as ensuring quality data, process reliability, and scalability are highly valued. On a personal note, as an IO psychologist, it has been rewarding to be involved in the design and delivery of this assessment strategy partly because the values of Saudi Aramco also align with my own professional values around respecting strong measurement theory, technical expertise, and the need for a positive and fair experience for participants.

When considering more "technology driven" assessments, this consideration on the cultural fit is important and may be an advantage for some organizations and a challenge for others. For example, while Saudi Aramco is pursuing new technologies that could be relevant in assessment applications (e.g., artificial intelligence, virtual reality), the leveraging of high-fidelity assessments will likely continue to be a stronger cultural fit. It would likely require a lot of evidence-based justification to support a significant shift and reliance on technology-driven assessments, especially if the face validity of the experience was challenged. In fact, a recent decision has been made to return to in-person assessment centers later this year, as we hopefully emerge from the worst of the pandemic. This decision is being driven more by the focus on ensuring a high-quality participant experience at the assessment center than a question on the validity of the data.

**The power and agility that comes from a strong data-based approach and broad database**: An assessment strategy that collects a breadth of data sources and insights has provided a rich base for agility. The wealth of data collected has afforded a range of different insights over the years that have helped guide the evolution of succession planning, development, and overall decision-making around leadership talent. Core to this is having a CoE that ensures the disciplined, rigorous, and consistent collection and leveraging of the data around the assessment and experience over the last 20 years. The reports and different data collected are seen as a rich source to inform on a multitude of different decisions around leadership succession (e.g., readiness, development priorities, potential, leadership style fit to different roles). The importance of this point was reinforced in the move to virtual, where the expectation was that there would be no compromise on the data sources and provided results. Having robust data to compare between the in-person and virtual assessments, including the ability to do robust analytics (e.g., testing distributions across different data sources, full data reviews after every assessment center, data on the participant experience), allowed for quick adjustments and consistent feedback to effectively navigate through the transition successfully.

**Ensuring the appropriate use of data**: Ironically, while the business leaders appreciate the richness and breadth of data in the readiness assessment, there can be a tendency to over-rely on a single piece of data. For example, the average score of the competencies against the internal benchmark provides a Leadership Competency Index (LCI), which is a single percentile score of overall readiness. This LCI score is seen as very useful and holds great appeal to leaders. Yet it also carries the risk of being over-leveraged. For example, the score might be used inappropriately to make judgments of a person's potential even as other scores on potential are available from the assessment. Or the score may be used for decision-making several years later even though the person may have developed significantly on these competencies. Therefore, the need for governance and ongoing education on the data and guidance from HR leaders during talent reviews and discussions has been important to avoid oversimplification and errors in how the data are leveraged. This guidance has also supported leaders in recognizing the full value of the different sources of data in terms of helping answer a broad range of talent-related questions that emerge over time and across situations.

**Focus on the participant experience**: A focus on the experience of participants and the senior leaders receiving the assessment data has been key to the ongoing "buy-in" of the assessments. In turn, ensuring high-quality experiences around the assessment ensures the relevant strategic impact, such as when participants act on their identified development gaps and senior leaders leverage the data for decision-making. This effort has included building in and managing the "touchpoints" along the experience and evaluating the "brand" of the assessment program. For example, while it was a strategic objective, the focus on development has also been important in ensuring a positive participant experience.

Any efforts to enhance the "development" feel of the experience have been taken very positively. This includes incorporating more "immediate" feedback, lengthening the feedback and coaching sessions at higher levels, providing "briefings" to help participants prepare and reflect on the feedback, and providing opportunities for follow-up coaching. Given the challenges in this culture around providing feedback, participants appreciate the chance to get feedback, but acceptance and accountability around that feedback are highly related to how "developmental" the experience was for them. This included, in the move to virtual, building in more opportunities for development (e.g., prebriefing to further help them prepare to get the most from the assessment, small group sessions to discuss the transition to the next level). Most recently, as described earlier, a 6-month development "journey" has become part of the senior-level assessments.

A valuable addition to the redesign of the development journey has been the mapping of all touchpoints and then working with a team to ensure that each touchpoint or experience is effectively managed. As noted earlier, an outstanding question, which could likely benefit from further research, is around the measurement and tracking of the participant experience and its impact. In our case, one of the evaluation measures is the use of the NPS, which has been adopted across the organization. Yet there are concerns when trying to compare scores from assessments with scores from other HR interventions like coaching or development programs. Also, where the NPS measure focuses on loyalty, there is concern on its relevance for assessments where participants are nominated by the business to take the one-time assessment. However, the NPS could arguably be associated with the degree of positive branding associated with the assessments. This topic touches on the broader issue of managing the experiences and providing relevant insights linked to meaningful outcomes including the development of leaders and the effective leveraging of the data in decision-making.

Moving into the future where technology, agility, and cost considerations will become increasingly important considerations, there are other questions that would benefit from further research. Included would be more research on the comparability of in-person versus virtual assessment centers and how to transition in ways that ensure relevant equivalency and validity. As well, further understanding of how to leverage technology to heighten the development aspect of assessment centers would be of distinct value. For example, while there are some tools/efforts, additional opportunities exist for more deeply embedding technology that could help prepare participants for the virtual experience, support the capturing of feedback (e.g., simulation performance, feedback from assessor), and/or provide different vehicles for sharing developmental insights and learnings. Such efforts appear to be available in different forms; however, the research supporting their utility and impact on the "experience" appears limited in terms of providing clear empirical support. Further understanding of how technology can be used to provide ongoing tracking and evaluations of the touchpoints throughout the assessment journey could be a promising avenue.

In conclusion, the ongoing strategic use of assessment at Saudi Aramco has been supported by the move to virtual delivery options. Specifically, the virtual assessment provides a vehicle to support assessments on a global stage as Aramco expands internationally and also begins to develop a broader talent pool strategy across the growing range of affiliates. As Saudi Arabia pursues its aggressive 2030 vision, Aramco's ability to support that vision moving forward is reinforced by an assessment strategy that helps ensure the ongoing identification and development of young leadership talent, including the increasing focus on female leaders to develop a more diverse leadership team. The focus on a strong assessment strategy and, most recently, the leveraging of technology has been key in ensuring a consistent and robust approach to the selection and development of Aramco leaders who can meet the demands of transitioning to a publicly held national oil company within an increasingly competitive and rapidly evolving energy market.

# References

Aon. (2019). *NPS by assessments: Initial findings.* Unpublished Manuscript.

Arthur, W., Jr., Day E. A., McNelly, T. L., & Edens, P. S. (2003). A meta-analysis of the criterion-related validity of assessment center dimensions. *Personnel Psychology, 56,* 125–154.

British Psychological Society. (2015). *The design and delivery of assessment centres.*

British Psychological Society. (2020). *Psychological assessments undertaken remotely.*

Crandell, S., Orr, E., & Hezlett, S (2020). *Equally robust: Virtual versus in-person simulation assessments* [White paper]. Korn Ferry Institute.

Gaugler, B. B., Rosenthal, D. B., Thornton, G. C., & Bentson, C. (1987). Meta-analysis of assessment center validity. *Journal of Occupational and Organizational Psychology, 72,* 493–511.

Hermelin, E., Lievens, F., & Robertson, I. T. (2007). The validity of assessment centres for the prediction of supervisory performance ratings: A meta-analysis. *International Journal of Selection and Assessment, 15*(4), 405–411.

Howland, A. C., Rembisz, R., Wang-Jones, T. S., Heise, S. R., & Brown, S. (2015). Developing a virtual assessment center. *Consulting Psychology Journal Practice and Research, 67*(2), 110–126.

International Taskforce on Assessment Center Guidelines. (2015). Guidelines and ethical considerations for assessment center operations. *Journal of Management, 41,* 1244–1273.

Kolk, N. J., Born, M. P., & van der Fliier, H. (2003). The transparent assessment centre: The effects of revealing dimensions to candidates. *Applied Psychology: An International Review, 52*(4), 648–668.

Pledge, T. A. (1998). *Saudi Aramco and its people: A history of training.* Aramco Services Company.

Rupp, D. E., Snyder, L. A., Gibbons, A. M., & Thornton, G. C., III (2006). What should development assessment centers be developing? *Psychologist-Manager Journal, 9*(2), 75–98.

Sackett, P. R. (1987). Assessment centers and content validity: Some neglected issues. *Personnel Psychology, 40,* 13–25.

Silzer, R. F., & Dowell, B. E. (2009). *Strategy-driven talent management: A leadership imperative.* Jossey-Bass.

Thornton, G. C., III, & Byham, W. C. (1982). *Assessment centers and managerial performance.* Academic Press.

Thornton, G. C., III, Mueller-Hanson, R. A., & Rupp, D. E. (2017). *Developing organizational simulations: A guide for practitioners, students, and researchers* (2nd ed.). Routledge.

Thornton, G. C., III, & Rupp, D. E. (2005). *Assessment centers in human resource management.* Psychology Press.

Thornton, G. C., III, Rupp, D. E., & Hoffman, B. J. (2015). *Assessment center perspectives for talent management strategies* (2nd ed.). Routledge.

# SECTION 7
# CONCLUSIONS AND FUTURE DIRECTIONS

# 29
# Putting the Pieces Together
## Reflections on the Next Chapter of Assessment Progress

*Paul R. Sackett*

My assigned task is to offer some thoughts on the future of assessment, which will take the form of a series of propositions. I take on this assignment with some trepidation. I entered the field in 1975; looking at changes in the selection and assessment field, I asked myself whether I saw these coming back then. A variety of new predictor constructs and measures have entered the mainstream: integrity tests, situational judgment tests, measures of emotional intelligence. The field has radically changed its views on the value of a number of predictors, including the employment interview and the assessment of personality. Job performance has moved from being viewed as a single thing to a multifaceted entity, including facets such as task performance, citizenship, and counterproductive work behavior. Meta-analysis has changed our thinking about validity and situational specificity. Many changes in delivery and scoring have resulted from the digital revolution, including web test delivery, adaptive testing, natural language processing, and online proctoring. I'd be a liar if I said I saw these coming 45+ years ago. So speculation about the next generation of changes is offered cautiously.

I offer my speculations in the form of nine propositions about the future of workplace assessment: (a) the determinants of job performance will not change; (b) constituencies will continue to assign differing values to tradeoffs among selection system outcomes; (c) we will continue making progress in extracting more information from candidate data; (d) we will see more use of constructed response formats and less multiple choice; (e) we will continue to use and to see improvements in measures of longstanding predictor constructs; (f) we will need to be vigilant regarding person-situation interactions; (g) tension about the need for construct understanding is not new and will continue; (h) it will be important to monitor public reaction to black-box approaches; and (i) these are, and will continue to be, exciting times for the testing and assessment field. I develop these issues below.

## Proposition 1: The Determinants of Job Performance Will Not Change

I am a strong supporter of the proposition put forward by John Campbell and colleagues (1993), namely, that there are three, and only three, direct determinants of job performance: declarative knowledge (e.g., what is a correlation coefficient?), procedural knowledge (e.g., how to compute a correlation coefficient), and effort (direction, level, and persistence). Anything we use as a predictor "works" because it either directly measures one of these (e.g., job knowledge test for declarative knowledge, work sample test for procedural knowledge) or is antecedent to one of these (e.g., cognitive ability predicts the acquisition of declarative and procedural knowledge; conscientiousness predicts level and persistence of effort).

So where do new measures, such as black-box predictive algorithms, fit in? Do they measure new determinants of performance? I argue no: All of the information, if it is truly predictive of performance, must load on one of the three determinants. In the case of many new methods, we just don't know what these are yet. Note that many contemporary methods collect massive amounts of information about an applicant and, rather than aggregating the information into construct scores, move directly to empirical prediction of outcomes of interest. And some of these methods do not have an intuitive link to performance (e.g., vocal patterns abstracted from recorded interviews).

Can this change? Will this change? Explainable artificial intelligence (AI) has emerged as a hot topic. And the tools of our field can help shed light on this issue. While building models for predicting an outcome of interest, relationships between overall model predictions and/or subcomponents of models can be examined with our traditional methods of convergent and discriminant validity to shed light on what aspects of performance determinants are being captured.

## Proposition 2: Constituencies Have Differing Views on Tradeoffs Among Desirable Outcomes

There are a wide variety of desirable features of a selection system, including validity, lack of subgroup differences, short administration time, decision speed, low cost, candidate acceptance, and resistance to faking/coaching. It is common for one of these to be achievable only at the expense of another. A great many concrete examples could be offered; here are a couple. First, the industrial-organizational (IO) program at the University of Minnesota dropped the GRE Psychology test from its admissions process, despite it being the best predictor of graduate school success. We found that few schools required this test, and students were bypassing the University of Minnesota and applying only to schools not requiring the test. Here we choose to accept lower validity for greater candidate acceptance and a larger applicant pool. Second, forced-choice personality tests can solve the faking problem (Cao & Drasgow, 2019). But taking them is frustrating to test takers, as it's often difficult to choose between options. Organizations valuing candidate acceptance may reject tests using the forced-choice format, thus accepting a higher level of faking in return for greater candidate acceptance.

There have been useful developments in formalizing the decision process for choosing among competing objectives. The concept of Pareto optimality has been introduced to the IO field (DeCorte et al., 2011). Work to date has focused on the tradeoff between validity and diversity, but it can be applied to other competing objectives. Given two outcomes of interest (e.g., validity and adverse impact reduction), a predictor composite is Pareto optimal if the only way to improve one outcome is to harm the other. For example, many different composites may produce $r = .29$; the one with the lowest adverse impact is Pareto optimal. And many different composites may produce an adverse impact ratio of .80; the one with the highest validity is Pareto optimal. The mechanics of the method are complex, but great strides have been made in making the approach readily accessible (Rupp et al., 2020) and better fitting the needs of applied work. While earlier work focused on a single subgroup comparison (e.g., White-Black or male-female), current methods accommodate simultaneous comparisons of multiple subgroups (DeCorte et al., 2021).

I am particularly concerned about the role of validity in these decision tradeoffs. I do not believe that validity will become irrelevant, but I worry about validity being reduced to a "minimum threshold" issue (i.e., validity evidence is required, but concern about level of validity declines). At the extreme, it is reduced to a yes/no issue: Can we check the validity box and move on to considering other outcomes?

I would love to see more highly predictive selection systems preferred to less valid ones. But the question is whether level of validity can be a basis for competition. There are two separate concerns here: One is whether organizations value differences in validity; the other is whether we are in a position to make meaningful claims about differences in validity. Here are two examples:

Elsewhere I have described early attempts to meta-analyze integrity test validity information (Sackett, 2003). Three major tests were compared, with mean validity differing substantially: Test A (.71), Test B (.35), and Test C (.27). At first glance, Test A is the clear winner. But further work showed differences by study features: concurrent (.66) versus predictive (.36), and self-report (.61) versus external criteria (.32). Test A relied more heavily on concurrent studies and self-report criteria, producing larger numeric values and the illusion of superior prediction.

My second example is the meta-analytic finding that mean validity for cognitive ability tests (.51) is markedly higher than the mean for assessment centers (.39; Schmidt & Hunter, 1998). Why go to the expense of an assessment center? Sackett et al. (2017) noted that cognitive ability was used to predict task performance (quantity and quality of work), while assessment centers were used to predict much broader criteria (e.g., communication, initiative, judgment, conflict management, teamwork, motivating others). We asked, what would we find if we focus only on "head-to-head" comparisons, where both predictors were administered to the same sample to predict the same criteria? Here we found a dramatic reversal: mean validity of .44 for assessment centers and .22 for ability. Such head-to-head comparison is key, and it is rare.

Thus, for validity to be a basis for competition, we face the dual challenge of demonstrating the value of validity to client organizations and improved ability within our field to make meaningful and convincing comparisons of validity across predictors.

## Proposition 3: We Will Continue Making Progress in Extracting More Information From Candidate Data

Historically, our field has focused largely on the responses given by candidates to test stimuli (e.g., did the candidate get the item right or not). There is growing recognition that how one gets to a response or to a final test score can matter, at least in some settings. For example, Lievens et al. (2005) compared initial and retest scores on medical admissions exams among students who were eventually admitted to medical school. They focused on the test score that was the basis for admission: a first test for students who did well initially, and a second test for those who improved their performance upon retest. They found that a given score forecasts higher performance if obtained on the first attempt than on the second: Retest scores overpredict student performance. One possible inference is that needing two attempts to reach a given score signals poor initial test preparation—an effort issue in Campbell's model of performance determinants.

Additional examples abound. One example: Early situational judgment tests typically asked candidates to examine four to five response options and select the best, or select the best and the worst. We are seeing better outcomes with formats that ask candidates to rate the effectiveness of each option (Arthur et al., 2014). As a candidate must evaluate all options to decide which is best, capturing these evaluations gives more information. Another example: Technology-enhanced tests permit examination of reaction time, with the potential to test hypotheses about candidate level of confidence about responses, as well as hypotheses about faking, based on the notion that faking requires additional time. Yet another: Game-based assessments commonly permit examination of intermediate steps en route to a solution. We will learn more and more about what is and is not of value in looking at response processes and interim steps in our measures.

## Proposition 4: We Will See More Use of Constructed Response Formats and Less Multiple Choice

A classic distinction in taxonomies of test item types is between production (e.g., open-ended narrative response) and recognition (e.g., choose the best response from a set of multiple-choice options; Lievens & Sackett, 2017). All else equal, we'd generally prefer a constructed response for a variety of reasons (e.g., it eliminates guessing; the conceptual difference between knowing a good response and recognizing a superior response when it is presented). But constructed responses are often too costly and time consuming to score.

To illustrate, in one study, Lievens et al. (2019) gave a situational judgment test in three response formats: traditional (pick best response), narrative written response, and spoken response. While criterion-related validity was comparable across formats, they differed in majority-minority differences. The traditional format resulted in a mean difference of .92, which dropped to .35 for written responses and .30 for ratings of transcriptions of spoken responses. They showed that the cognitive load of the situational judgment test was much smaller for the constructed response approaches, and the reduction in mean differences was attributed to the elimination of inadvertent cognitive load. I view this study as proof of concept as to the potential value of constructed responses; the needed next step is automating the scoring of these constructed responses to make it viable for operational use. Automated scoring of open-ended responses has been studied and used operationally in educational settings for some time. Research on the use of natural language processing in measures of personnel selection is now emerging (e.g., Campion et al., 2016). I expect further technical development and widespread use of these approaches.

## Proposition 5: We Will Continue to Use and to See Improvements in Measures of Longstanding Predictor Constructs

We will continue to use measures of existing constructs, such as cognitive ability and personality. But we will commonly measure them differently. The cognitive ability domain has been a mainstay of personnel selection for over a century. In many ways, these are our easiest constructs to measure. While the ability domain includes both general and specific measures, we commonly want a measure of general cognitive ability ($g$). An essential notion here is Spearman's notion of "the indifference of the indicator." One can get to the same place with measures that appear quite different: An aggregate of three to four measures in the cognitive domain gets to $g$ regardless of the measures. One demonstration of this comes from recent work in the arena of game-based assessments. Landers et al. (2021) administered a battery of five traditional cognitive tests and a set of seven short game-based assessments to a large sample. They extracted a first latent factor from the traditional tests (call it "$g$-trad") and a first latent factor from the game-based assessments (call it "$g$-game"). The two were found to correlate .97. For all practical purposes, you can get to the same place with game-based assessments as with traditional tests. To the extent that game-based assessments are more engaging and attractive to applicants, they become an appealing option. (Of course, game-based assessments can be explored as approaches to tapping a variety of constructs other than cognitive ability as well.)

Turning to the personality domain, I must acknowledge this as a domain in which I am conflicted. On the one hand, I am drawn to alternatives to self-report. I've long been taken with Bob Hogan's critical distinction between personality as identity (what you see yourself as deep down inside) versus personality as reputation (how others see you). I concur with his position that in the workplace it is reputation that we really care about: what you actually do, as observed by others (Hogan, 1982). You may view yourself as reliable; if others disagree, I will give more credence to what others say when it comes to forecasting subsequent work behavior. Thus, work on alternatives to self-report strikes me as a pressing need. A solid body of meta-analytic work supports the validity of other-ratings of personality (Connelly & Ones, 2010; Oh et al., 2011). And there is considerable ongoing work on extracting personality information from publicly available data, such as social media (Azucar et al., 2018).

At the same time, self-reports have been shown to be predictive of work behavior, particularly for the conscientiousness factor within the Big Five and for measures that tap multiple personality factors, such as integrity tests. And there has been important recent progress with use of self-report measures. Social desirability has been a longstanding concern with self-report measures, and there have been major breakthroughs in solving this problem. A subset of forced-choice measures has been shown to be extremely resistant to faking (Cao & Drasgow, 2019), and rapid response approaches (i.e., forcing a quick response) have had success in reducing the faking/response distortion issue (Meade et al., 2020). Thus, I will continue to watch developments in both the domains of personality as identity and personality as reputation with great interest. Important progress is being made in both domains.

We are also seeing revival of research on interests as a predictor. The received wisdom in the field has long been that validity is low for predicting performance. But it has been made clear that we were asking the wrong question. The meta-analytic mean validity for an individual interest dimension across jobs is .11. But interests involve a fit between a person and a job. The right question is, "What is the validity for an individual interest dimension relevant to the job in question?"; here the mean rises to .23 (Nye et al., 2017). And other studies suggest incremental validity over ability and personality. But to date all data are from low-stakes settings. Can we avoid the faking/response distortion problem in interest measures? New developments are investigating using forced-choice formats to solve this problem, as has been done in the personality domain (Kirkendall et al., 2020).

## Proposition 6: We Will Need to Be Vigilant Regarding Person-Situation Interactions

As we explore new sources of information from which to derive predictions of performance, I want to note a need for caution: Differences in behavior across situations have implications for our work. The "self" we are at work may differ from the "self" we are elsewhere. One useful example is the meta-analytic finding that adding "at work" to self-report personality items results in increased predictive validity (Shaffer & Postlethwaite, 2012). This suggests caution in, say, inferring work behavior from game behavior. Is risk taking in a game reflective of behavior at work, or is it a release from needing to be cautious and precise at work? As we examine nonwork behavior more and more (e.g., information found online), we will learn more about the limitations of relying on such nonwork behavior as the basis for inferences about work behavior.

## Proposition 7: Tension About the Need for Construct Understanding Is Not New and Will Continue

There have long been differing positions among those in the personnel selection field as to the criticality of full understanding of the construct(s) underlying a given predictor as a prerequisite for operational predictor use. Concerns about this issue have surfaced again in the context of the surge of activity around the use of "black box" algorithms. A close look at a recent paper will serve as case in point.

Tett and Simonet (2021) argue for the need for predictor-construct specification as a prerequisite for use. Importantly, they make an appeal to authority and argue that the *Standards for Educational and Psychological Testing* (American Educational Research Association et al., 2014) specify a need for full construct understanding. If this were true, taking the opposite position would not merely be a personal preference; it would be a violation of professional standards. As a person highly involved in the writing of the last two editions of the *Standards*, I read their argument with great interest.

I will offer their key argument in their own words: "Validity is now widely accepted under a 'unitarian' model as 'the degree to which evidence and theory support the interpretation of test scores proposed by the test user' (American Educational Research Association, 2014, p. 11), with the critical caveat that 'the proposed interpretation includes specifying the construct the test is intended to measure.'.... [S]pecification of a targeted construct rules out a purely empirical rendering of validity, whereby a positive correlation between test X and criterion Y, by itself, permits 'valid' inferences (Tett & Simonet, p. 8)."

Regarding test use based on empirical linkages, without full understanding of the predictor construct, they note: "There is a practical allure to this position: If our goal in screening is to identify applicants most likely to secure high performance ratings, then correlation offers a mechanically efficient guide for making hiring decisions. The key challenge to this empiricist perspective is that it fails to conform to the established unitarian understanding of validity, which calls for evidence that a given test assesses what it is purported to assess (Tett & Simonet, p. 10)."

Finally, they argue against "the antiquated view that empirical relationships are sufficient for judgments of validity. The unitarian model makes clear that all of validity is construct validity. Empirical evidence supports validity only to the degree it is consistent with construct-based expectations (Tett & Simonet, p. 11)."

I find that Tett and Simonet (2021) draw only on the initial validity chapter, failing to note that the later employment chapter offers very specific additional detail that leads, I assert, to a very different conclusion than the one they draw. The employment chapter offers the following: "The fundamental inference to be drawn from test scores in most applications of testing in employment settings is one of prediction: The test user wishes to make an inference from test results to some future job behavior or job outcome (p. 171)." With regard to the strategy for empirically linking a predictor measure and the criterion construct domain, the *Standards* states: "Note that this strategy does not necessarily rely on a well-developed predictor construct domain. Predictor measures such as empirically keyed biodata measures are constructed on the basis of empirical links between test item responses and the criterion measure of interest. Such measures may, in some instances, be developed without a fully established conception of the predictor construct domain; the basis for their use is the direct empirical link between test responses and a relevant criterion measure (p. 173)." Thus, rather than the *Standards* ruling out reliance on empirical prediction without full understanding of the predictor construct domain, they instead acknowledge this as one of a number of strategies for building a case for test use.

One reaction may be a seeming disconnect between the validity chapter's reference to specifying the construct the test is intended to measure and the employment chapter's acknowledgment of empirical linkages as one route to establishing the predictive inference. My take is that in the case of empirical linkages the intended construct is "predicted performance in the criterion construct domain of interest." This is criterion-focused validation, rather than predictor-oriented validation.

Now, I am certainly an advocate of construct understanding. It is a most useful thing, and it is needed for the field to move forward. I strongly support work that aids in understanding the constructs underlying predictor scores. Such support is not at odds with acknowledging the possibility of operational use without such understanding. My position is that in order to use a predictor with little to no understanding of the constructs underlying predictor scores, one must make a very strong case for two things. The first is very strong evidence of the empirical link to a construct-relevant criterion measure. Large samples and impeccable cross-validation strike me as essential in the case of "black box" predictors. The second is very strong evidence of a lack of bias against protected groups of interest. There are sufficient examples of inadvertent biases being "learned" in algorithm development to justify subjecting measures to careful scrutiny.

## Proposition 8: It Will Be Important to Monitor Public Reaction to Black-Box Approaches

From a broad perspective I suggest that the public, writ large, has expectations about selection systems. Call it an implicit contract, if you will. Among its features are, first, that candidates know the information gathered about them. Some they provide directly (e.g., a resume, a list of references). Other information is provided by them in response to queries put to them (e.g., interview questions, test items). Second, candidates expect consistency of treatment: All candidates are evaluated in a comparable way and are held to the same standards. Third, candidates want to be evaluated on features under their control: what they have done or what they can do. The presence of retest policies speaks to this: If one can learn/practice/gain experience that could materially affect their standing, they should have the opportunity to try again.

These may have been violated at times in various ways. Sometimes candidates may not realize that they are not treated consistently (as in the case of the use of unstructured interviews; unless comparing notes with another candidate, one would not realize that different questions were asked of each). And candidates can accept screening on features not under their control when obviously job related, as in the case of a physical ability requirement for physically demanding jobs. But we are seeing increased concern about violation of these expectations with growing use of monitoring of social media, capture and processing of emails, and analysis of videos with AI software. As of this writing one state (Illinois) has enacted legislation: the Illinois Artificial Intelligence Video Interview Act, requiring that employers must notify candidates that AI may be used to analyze the video interview, explain to candidates how AI works and what types of characteristics it uses, and obtain consent from candidates to be evaluated using AI. A number of other states have bills under consideration. It will be important to monitor these developments.

## Proposition 9: These Are Exciting Times for the Assessment Field

As is clear from the array of chapters in this volume, much has changed, and has done so very quickly. I am confident that this will continue. Above I offered a series of propositions as to the future. I realize they are a mix of thoughts about what could happen, what should happen, and what I predict will happen. I return to the opening page of this chapter when I attempted the thought experiment of returning to 1975 and asking whether I could have predicted then what has happened in the testing and assessment domain over the course of my career. Based on that sobering experiment, I predict that there will be additional developments that I have not even imagined today. These are interesting times for the assessment field, and it's exciting to be a part of it.

## References

American Educational Research Association, American Psychological Association, & National Council for Measurement in Education. (2014). *Standards for Educational and Psychological Testing*. American Educational Research Association.

Arthur, W., Jr., Doverspike, D., Muñoz, G. J., Taylor, J. E., & Carr, A. E. (2014). The use of mobile devices in high-stakes remotely delivered assessments and testing. *International Journal of Selection and Assessment*, 22(2), 113–123.

Azucar, D., Marengo, D., & Settanni, M. (2018). Predicting the Big 5 personality traits from digital footprints on social media: A meta-analysis. *Personality and Individual Differences, 124,* 150–159.

Campbell, J. P., McCloy, R. A., Oppler, S. H., & Sager, C. E. (1993). A theory of performance. *Personnel Selection in Organizations, 3570,* 35–70.

Campion, M. C., Campion, M. A., Campion, E. D., & Reider, M. H. (2016). Initial investigation into computer scoring of candidate essays for personnel selection. *Journal of Applied Psychology, 101*(7), 958975.

Cao, M., & Drasgow, F. (2019). Does forcing reduce faking? A meta-analytic review of forced-choice personality measures in high-stakes situations. *Journal of Applied Psychology, 104*(11), 1347–1368.

Connelly, B. S., & Ones, D. S. (2010). An other perspective on personality: Meta-analytic integration of observers' accuracy and predictive validity. *Psychological Bulletin, 136*(6), 1092–1122.

DeCorte, W., Sackett, P. R., & Lievens, F. (2011). Designing Pareto-optimal selection systems: Formalizing the decisions required for selection system development. *Journal of Applied Psychology, 96,* 907–920.

DeCorte, W., Sackett, P. R., & Lievens, F. (2021). *Developing Pareto-optimal selection systems for multiple protected groups.* Manuscript submitted for review.

Hogan, R. (1982). A socioanalytic theory of personality. In M. Page (Ed.), *Nebraska symposium on motivation* (pp. 55–89). University of Nebraska Press.

Kirkendall, C. D., Nye, C. D., Rounds, J., Drasgow, F., Chernyshenko, O. S., & Stark, S. (2020). Adaptive vocational interest diagnostic: Informing and improving the job assignment process. *Military Psychology, 32*(1), 91–100.

Landers, R. N., Armstrong, M. B., Collmus, A. B., Mujcic, S., & Blaik, J. (20221). Theory-driven game-based assessment of general cognitive ability: Design theory, measurement, prediction of performance, and test fairness. *Journal of Applied Psychology, 107,* 1655–1677.

Lievens, F., Buyse, T., & Sackett, P. R. (2005). The effects of retaking tests on test performance and validity: An examination of cognitive ability, knowledge, and situational judgment tests. *Personnel Psychology, 58,* 981–1007.

Lievens, F., & Sackett, P. R. (2017). The effects of predictor method factors on selection outcomes: A modular approach to personnel selection procedures. *Journal of Applied Psychology, 102,* 43–66.

Lievens, F., Sackett, P. R., Dahlke, J. A., Oostrom, J. E., & De Soete, B. (2019). Constructed responses formats and their effect on majority-minority differences and validity. *Journal of Applied Psychology, 104,* 715–726.

Meade, A. W., Pappalardo, G., Braddy, P. W., & Fleenor, J. W. (2020). Rapid response measurement: Development of a faking-resistant assessment method for personality. *Organizational Research Methods, 23*(1), 181–207.

Nye, C. D., Su, R., Rounds, J., & Drasgow, F. (2017). Interest congruence and performance: Revisiting recent meta-analytic findings. *Journal of Vocational Behavior, 98,* 138–151.

Oh, I. S., Wang, G., & Mount, M. K. (2011). Validity of observer ratings of the five-factor model of personality traits: A meta-analysis. *Journal of Applied Psychology, 96*(4), 762–773.

Rupp, D. E., Song, Q. C., & Strah, N. (2020). Addressing the so-called validity–diversity trade-off: Exploring the practicalities and legal defensibility of Pareto-optimization for reducing adverse impact within personnel selection. *Industrial and Organizational Psychology, 13*(2), 246–271.

Sackett, P. R. (2003). The status of validity generalization research: Key issues in drawing inferences from cumulative research findings. In K. R. Murphy (Ed.), *Validity generalization: A critical review* (pp. 91–114). Erlbaum.

Sackett, P. R., Shewach, O. R., & Keiser, H. N. (2017). Assessment centers vs. cognitive ability tests: Challenging the conventional wisdom on criterion-related validity. *Journal of Applied Psychology, 102*, 1435–1447.

Schmidt, F. L., & Hunter, J. E. (1998). The validity and utility of selection methods in personnel psychology: Practical and theoretical implications of 85 years of research findings. *Psychological Bulletin, 124*, 262–274.

Shaffer, J. A., & Postlethwaite, B. E. (2012). A matter of context: A meta-analytic investigation of the relative validity of contextualized and noncontextualized personality measures. *Personnel Psychology, 65*(3), 445–494.

Tett, R. P., & Simonet, D. V. (2021). Applicant faking on personality tests: Good or bad and why should we care? *Personnel Assessment and Decisions, 7*(1), 6–19.

# 30

# Optimizing the Value of Assessments Through Myth Busting and Stakeholder Communications

*Gina Seaton and Allan H. Church*

Assessments are part of the new normal of human resources (HR) and talent management practices today. Once only used by select organizations, for more senior-level positions, and primarily for hard skills, benchmark studies of large-scale companies (e.g., Church & Rotolo, 2013; Church et al., 2015) have indicated that today, assessments are used by upwards of 75% of top development organizations (i.e., large organizations with a dedicated focus on development and robust talent management systems). These assessments typically include both hard and soft skills, leveraging multiple sets of tools, and applying the data for a variety of business challenges (Chamorro-Premuzic, 2015; Church et al., 2015; Scott & Reynolds, 2010). According to a large recent survey from SHL on assessment trends, respondents reported pervasive use of assessment for core HR and talent management practices including selection (79% reported use for external, 72% reported use for internal), career development (79% reported use), and leadership development (82% reported use; Kantrowitz et al., 2018).

The momentum we've observed over the past 10 years has only increased, with many organizations looking to assessments to help them objectify, quantify, and embed their talent information into end-to-end processes (Church, 2019; Scott & Reynolds, 2010). There is also a strong appetite to assess for new and different content areas (e.g., agility, resilience) and to adopt the latest assessment-related technologies (e.g., internal talent marketplace platforms, virtual interviewing technology; Rotolo et al., 2018). Consequently, some might argue that the popularity of assessments and assessment-related

Gina Seaton and Allan H. Church, *Optimizing the Value of Assessments Through Myth Busting and Stakeholder Communications* In: *Talent Assessment*. Edited by: Tracy M. Kantrowitz, Douglas H. Reynolds, and John C. Scott, Oxford University Press. © Society of Industrial Organizational Psychology 2023.
DOI: 10.1093/oso/9780197611050.003.0030

technological advances in organizations have outpaced key stakeholders' understanding of what assessment tools do and why they are important for the broader organization (Chamorro-Premuzic et al., 2016).

For many stakeholders, assessments can also be foreign and nebulous, and the difference between valid assessments and those that you find in the back of a magazine or trade publication is not exactly clear. Confusion, skepticism, and inaccurate beliefs surrounding assessments are often fueled by misinformation and myths associated with assessments and/or prior negative experiences. It does not help matters that these concerns are being propagated via stories in the media for which nonassuming organizations and even the population in general are falling prey (e.g., the 2021 HBO documentary *Persona*). Further, the increased emphasis on selling assessments among consulting firms and test publishers has resulted in a willingness to meet demands for "new and different," sometimes at the expense of quality and rigor (e.g., Hatami et al., 2020; Rotolo et al., 2018). Many organizational leaders without a background in industrial-organizational (IO) psychology rely heavily on these firms' and publishers' presumed assessment expertise and guidance, making it even more difficult to separate fact from fiction.

Thus, despite increased pull for assessments and a growing presence of IO psychology experts in strategic HR and talent management positions, there are still pockets of resistance and concerned parties that need to be more effectively managed and convinced of the value of assessment tools. The purpose of this chapter is to help address these concerns for organizational stakeholders. First, we discuss some myths and misinformation associated with assessments and recent advancements in assessment, offering advice for combatting misinformation. Next, we examine key stakeholder groups, addressing the primary concerns we see from their unique points of view, and sharing some approaches that we have leveraged in our combined 45+ years of external consulting and internal talent management roles communicating the purpose, application, and value of assessments. Sample tools and key messages for addressing these concerns will be highlighted throughout the discussion.

## Assessment Myths and Misinformation

In the age of "fake news," it is easy to get information to support any viewpoint one might hold, regardless of the availability of rigorous empirical evidence (from an IO psychology standpoint) to support it or not. Assessments are prime targets for misinformation given their technical complexity and the fact that the insights obtained from them ultimately serve to classify and make decisions on people. Therefore, it is our job as IO scientist-practitioners to proactively educate our clients and stakeholders as well as to retroactively address their concerns using data. Listed below are myths and misinformation issues that we see as most prevalent today based on discussions with colleagues in other organizations and our own experiences developing and institutionalizing large-scale leadership assessment and selection processes over the past decade (Church, 2019; Seaton et al., 2021). Interestingly, these myths and misinformation reflect entirely divergent perspectives painting both an overly pessimistic or even dark view and an overly positive and optimistic view of the current landscape.

## Myth #1: Assessments Are Biased and/or Discriminatory

Perhaps one of the most prevalent concerns expressed across stakeholder groups centers around bias. These concerns take several forms, ranging from the belief that assessments promote picking a single "type" of person (e.g., when using personality tools alone or even in combination with other measures) to concerns over discrimination and biases against protected groups (e.g., sexist, racist, ableist). The major issue with these assertions is they tend to lack nuance and overgeneralize, undermining the importance and ameliorating the effects of using good science and practice during the design and implementation of assessments.

To illustrate, the focal assessment discussed in the 2021 HBO documentary *Persona: The Dark Truth Behind Personality Tests* is the Myers-Briggs Type Indicator (MBTI). In the documentary, there is no differentiation made between the MBTI, a typologically based assessment derived from Jungian psychology (where individuals fall into discrete categories), Big Five trait-based tools based on meta-analytic studies (where individual traits are represented by continuums), and medical diagnostic tools (which are intended to classify individuals for treatment). Further, there is no discussion of the appropriate use of different types of tools or combinations of tools to address perceived stakeholder concerns. Regarding the MBTI, the test publisher expressly states that the tool should be used for reflection and discussion as opposed to selection decisions (themyersbriggs.com). Unfortunately, these facts are not addressed in the documentary, and it is unlikely that many employees, managers, or the general public is aware of the underlying empirical literature. Decades of research have shown, for example, that using a validated, trait-based personality tool in conjunction with a cognitive test can actually help to reduce bias (e.g., Ployhart & Holtz, 2008; Scott & Reynolds, 2010). Moreover, behaviorally based tools such as 360 feedback, assessment centers, and simulations can also be designed to address biases rather than introduce them (e.g., Church et al., 2019).

## Myth #2: The Use of Technology (Artificial Intelligence) and Big Data Eliminates All Biases

On the other side of the coin is the misguided belief that technology, specifically artificial intelligence (AI)-based technology and the use of big data, is the solution to bias by removing humans from the equation. Applications of AI are continuing to evolve and can add considerable value to the process and results generated, but they are neither required nor perfected yet for talent management–related applications (Narlock & Church, 2021). Further, while it is true that AI tools help to contain *human* biases that plague decision-making (Bonabeau, 2003), research shows that they can introduce new and different kinds of biases and can even build on existing biases that are not immediately apparent (e.g., Caliskan et al., 2017). For example, many have heard about Amazon's unfortunate experiences with a biased algorithm that resulted in men being shown preference or challenges associated with automated interviewing technology (e.g., Meyer, 2018; Ryan & Derous, 2019). Examples such as these highlight the fact that an algorithm is only as good as the data it has at its disposal. If the data inputs are biased, or even related to variables that are biased (e.g., standardized test scores and socioeconomic status; Sackett et al., 2012), you can expect that your outputs will also be biased, and likely amplified. Organizations have a responsibility to ensure data integrity that goes beyond auditing the vendor's algorithm (Narlock & Church, 2021), though that is clearly an important role we play as IO psychologists as well.

The bottom line is, technology and big data, left unchecked, can be as dangerous as, and even arguably more dangerous than, humans when not governed appropriately. It is important for organizations to understand that AI-based technology and big data sources as inputs are "assessments" from a legal point of view and are subject to the same guidelines as traditional assessments when utilized for decision-making. A formal job analysis and validation within the existing organization is required before sharing results and using them for decision-making (Principles for the Validation and Use of Personnel Selection Procedures, 2018). The unfortunate reality, however, is that the use of these technologies and expansive data sources presents the allusion of rigor to the uninitiated in organizations (and particularly among those in HR leadership positions) while also playing to longstanding issues that organizations have faced (e.g., time and resources) or organizations' desires to remain relevant (e.g., the allure of big data).

## Myth #3: Test Takers Do Not Like Assessments

Another prevailing myth is that assessments trigger negative reactions among test takers. These reactions run the gamut of feelings that assessments are:

- too time consuming (e.g., they need to be less than 30 minutes),
- impersonal and lack face validity (e.g., they reduce people to a number),
- more harmful than good (e.g., they destroy careers), and
- offensive to senior executives in particular (e.g., their past experience should speak for itself, or their success should exempt them from needing to be tested at all).

While it is true that taking an assessment is not most people's idea of fun, that does not mean we should ignore the reality that assessments are useful both for individuals (development) and for organizations (decision-making), and when designed appropriately, they can even be highly engaging. Indeed, there is an abundance of candidate reaction data in both the academic and consulting domains that suggest that job applicants (i.e., candidates), regardless of geography, tend to have favorable reactions (e.g., overall favorability as well as more specific dimensions including perceptions of validity and opportunity to perform) to many types of assessments most used in organizations including work samples, cognitive ability tests, and personality tests (Hausknecht et al., 2004; Anderson et al., 2010).

To illustrate, when the early career version of PepsiCo's Leadership Assessment and Development Program (LeAD), a fully integrated program to help identify and develop talent, was launched, it leveraged an "opt-in" approach. Of the initial 3,300 employees invited, 85% opted in and 97% of those who opted in completed the full suite of tools. Reactions to the process were also very positive, despite the transparent (and therefore sometimes critical) feedback, with 83% of participants reporting the program exceeded their expectations for feedback. In addition, the use of assessments was seen by participants as reinforcing the organization's commitment to their development. This latter finding has been reflected across all levels of the program over time (see Table 30.1).

As an additional illustration, internal research by the authors on PepsiCo's external assessment for selection programs shows insignificant dropout rates across assessment programs, including those of different lengths (all of which are 30 minutes or more!). Collectively, these applied examples show that individuals (whether employees or external candidates) generally view the process of assessment favorably when communicated and conducted properly, feeling that the investment in such programs shows that the organization values data-driven decision-making and a focus on elevating talent.

## Myth #4: Gamification Will "Magically" Make Test Takers Like Assessments

Gamification, which can be broadly defined as leveraging game elements to nongame contexts, often aimed at enhancing the candidate experience (DuVernet & Popp, 2014), is another bright and shiny technology trend that many organizations have jumped on the bandwagon to implement, before truly understanding the concept and outpacing research (e.g., Landers, 2019; Ryan & Derous, 2019). Research around applications of gamification to selection processes is nascent at best. What research has been done is often muddied by differences in how gamification is defined and applied and what outcomes are focused on (e.g., Georgiou et al., 2019; Landers, 2019).

As an illustration, some research has found that technological self-efficacy is an important determinant of some applicant reactions like task enjoyment (Bhatia & Ryan, 2018, Ellison et al., 2020), whereas other research has not established this relationship (e.g., King et al., 2015). Similarly, some research finds that adding gamification increases satisfaction with the process (e.g., Georgiou et al., 2019), while other studies have found no relationships with test taker attitudes other than perceived organizational technological sophistication, making it a potential marketing tool (Landers et al., 2020). Clearly,

Table 30.1 Summary of Concerns and Approach by Stakeholder Group

| Stakeholder Group | Key Concerns | Illustrative Reactions | Approach |
|---|---|---|---|
| All Stakeholders | - Value and impact | *What is the ROI?* | - Lean on **data** and **get creative** when needed (e.g., framing validity studies as ROI)<br>- **Triangulate** data where possible (e.g., MTMM)<br>- Leverage internal **success stories** |
| Test Takers | - How the data are going to be used (and by whom)<br>- The robustness and accuracy of the assessments (including opportunity to perform, face validity, and psychological fidelity) | *How will this impact my job/career?*<br>*How long will the results follow me?*<br>*Who has access to my assessment results?*<br>*How can you make inferences about my ability to think critically from a pattern recognition task?* | - Be **transparent** in communication<br>- Give back for the time invested via **personal and professional development, career planning** |
| Managers | - How to use and interpret the data from assessments<br>- Validity of the results/discrepancies<br>- Motivational: Intimidation or overenthusiasm (e.g., making own algorithms) | *How do I make sense of all this data? It is overwhelming.*<br>*How do I incorporate this data into my talent discussions?*<br>*I've worked in the field for decades. I am the best judge of talent.*<br>*Jane Doe showed a lot of outages on the assessment, and I disagree.* | - Build **comfort** by showing that assessments are a **support/value add, not a barrier**<br>- Build **capability** by taking time to train managers on what assessments measure and how results should be interpreted<br>- Provide opportunities to **practice** |

Table 30.1 Continued

| Stakeholder Group | Key Concerns | Illustrative Reactions | Approach |
|---|---|---|---|
| Recruiters | - How to use and interpret the data from assessments<br>- Validity of the results/discrepancies<br>- Impact on candidate experience (e.g., candidate seat time, engagement) | *How do I explain the results to hiring managers? How did their results come back this way? Their resume was amazing! I connected so well with them. What can the assessments measure that I can't in my interviews? This will slow down the process. Administering an assessment to a candidate at this level is insulting and shows we don't trust their resume.* | - Build **comfort** and **capability**<br>- **Dispel anecdotes** around candidate experience (internal and external benchmarking data)<br>- Gather their **input/feedback** for continuous improvement |
| HR Leaders | - Strategic organizational goals (e.g., diversity, equity, and inclusion; building the talent pipeline; future capabilities)<br>- Feasibility and scalability (e.g., infrastructure, operational needs, costs) | *How many hours will our employees be pulled out of the field for validation? How can we build capability in hot skills? What is the cost to build and maintain the program? What kind of ROI can we expect to see?* | - Speak to **broader organizational goals** |

My involvement shows that the organization is invested in my growth and development

| Level | % favorable |
|---|---|
| ANALYST/ASSOC MANAGER | 82% |
| MANAGER/DIRECTOR | 90% |
| VP | 90% |
| SVP + | 92% |

there is more work to be done to fully understand where and when gamification adds the most value. It is not yet a magic bullet solution.

## Myth #5: Assessments Are Easily Gamed and/or Do Not Predict As Well As Good Judgment

We know from extensive research that as humans, we notoriously think we are above average at every skill we engage in (e.g., driving a car or interviewing candidates). This belief extends to the realm of talent identification in organizations, where leaders often feel they are more effective at judging talent based on personal schemas and frames of references than any formal assessment tool or process (Frieder et al., 2016). It is common, for example, for many leaders in organizations (both in HR and non-HR roles) to approach assessment discussions with dismissive comments such as "I'm a better judge of talent than any test" or "The assessment must not be working because my favorite (e.g., high-potential or high-performing) talent did not do well."

Instead of questioning their own judgment when assessment results do not align with leader evaluations, we often see confirmation bias at play, with leaders doubling down and holding the discrepancy as proof of their beliefs about the "fakability" and ultimately utility of assessments. Despite this enduring belief, data show that people grossly overestimate their abilities and are actually pretty poor judges of talent, often relying on gut instinct and even inherent biases when making decisions within seconds of meeting a person for the first time (Frieder et al., 2016). As many practitioners know, the ubiquitous "meet and greet" with the CEO or senior HR leader has a distinct possibility of making or breaking someone's career prospects, even with an impressive resume and glowing assessment results. Further, while interviewers tend to like unstructured interviews for their ability to let the interviewer drive the discussion and apply their own frameworks for assessing talent, it is well documented that this methodology is among the least valid predictors of performance, due to issues including the incorporation of job-irrelevant behaviors and lack of reliability (Dana et al., 2013; McDaniel et al., 1994; Schmidt & Zimmerman, 2004).

With regard to faking, particularly in high-stakes testing environments, it is only natural to expect that people will try to paint themselves in the most favorable light possible. Research confirms that "faking good" does indeed occur, and as many as 63% of applicants admit to faking responses on personality tests (Donovan et al., 2003). Still, what many stakeholders are not aware of is that faking is not quite as concerning as it sounds (Hogan et al., 2007) and that personality assessment scores tend to be stable even when participants take them a second time knowing they are being used as an input in talent decision-making (Church, Fleck, et al., 2016). Tests have come a long way with regard to imbedding mechanisms to weed out and/or identify potential "fakers," including forced-choice responding where all options presented are equally desirable, consistency measures, and time constraints (Bartram, 2007; Meade & Priest, Chapter 3, this volume; Verschuere et al., 2018). Leveraging a multitrait/multimethod (MTMM) approach, discussed more below, is another effective method for combating these concerns as it provides a means for shedding light on an individual through different lenses and assessment formats beyond self-report.

## Myth #6: Assessments Provide the Definitive Answer on Talent

As with many of the myths presented here, there is another side of the coin to the "assessments don't work" argument, and that is that they are expected to work "perfectly." We have encountered a significant number of leaders who believe that assessments can tell you everything you need to know about a person, in essence, leveraging the assessment data as an absolute rather than an important "input" in talent decision-making. In some cases, leaders may even go as far as reducing the talent assessed to series of numbers (or a single number via an assessment score) in talent review and succession planning discussions. For some, it is about reducing the cognitive complexity of understanding and evaluating complex human behavior, and for others, it is simply that they do not trust their own judgment, seeking to avoid accountability for making poor decisions. While the intention to inform leadership development and placement discussions with data is a good and important one, it is important to know when it is being taken too far and how to address it. One method is through communications (see Figure 30.1 for an example of how we have addressed this via communications and training with senior HR and line leaders at PepsiCo prior to talent reviews), while others include the use of multiple tools.

**Figure 30.1.** What happens with High Potentials score poorly? Are they still High Potentials?

Assessments provide a **valid and robust** means of evaluating capabilities against defined criteria to be **used as an input** into making better talent decisions

For example, the MTMM approach, whereby different qualities or traits are measured via different processes or measures, first introduced by Campbell and Fisk in 1959, is commonly used by researchers to validate measurement tools. From a practitioner standpoint, however, the MTMM framework is also a valuable tool to leverage from both a measurement approach and a *communications vehicle* internally, ensuring leaders understand that the data we are leveraging to classify and make decisions on people is robust and precise. All measurement tools have error. By tapping the same constructs with different measures, it not only provides a more robust and complete picture of an individual but also has the potential to open up a rich development discussion, particularly when data points across tools do not align fully. The MTMM approach is a hallmark of PepsiCo's LeAD program (e.g., Church, 2019; Church & Rotolo, 2016) and has served to support the longevity and impact of the program (e.g., over 18,000 employees assessed since inception). We have found that it has been extremely useful in reducing concerns over the use of specific tools when discussing with clients both on the test taker and on the decision-making side (e.g., perceptions that 360 feedback can be gamed, personality tools can be faked, cognitive measures such as the Raven's Progressive Matrices [www.pearsonassessments.com] don't measure anything useful, or people can cheat on simulations).

## Who Are the Main Stakeholders and What Do They Need to Know About Assessments?

Given the prevalence of the above myths and misinformation across many (if not all at times) stakeholder groups, there is a real need for IO psychologists as scientist-practitioners to help organizations and the public combat these concerns. Implementing an assessment program impacts a variety of stakeholder groups, and being able to speak to and address their unique perspectives and concerns is imperative for sustaining and integrating a program to achieve maximum value and reinforce a data-driven feedback culture (Church, 2019). Below, we consider the perspective of candidates and employees (i.e., the test takers), managers, recruiters, HR leaders, and the public and how to approach discussions with each of these stakeholder groups.

## Test Takers (External Candidates and Internal Employees)

We start our discussion with the largest stakeholder group impacted by assessments, and who have arguably the greatest investment in the outcomes of the assessments, that is, the test takers themselves. This group is quite broad in nature and can include internal participants in a leadership development program, executives being considered for slating and succession discussions, internal or external candidates applying for a new role, early career employees for talent identification (high-potential) efforts, or even one-off assessments for targeted coaching interventions. These stakeholders are primarily concerned with (a) how the data/results from the assessments are going to be used (and seen by whom) and (b) the robustness and accuracy of the assessments in portraying their strengths and opportunities. Not surprisingly, the latter concern is most prevalent among those who do not score as well as they had hoped (Bauer et al., 2006; Hausknecht et al., 2004; McCarthy et al., 2013). Regardless, test taker reactions are important because these perceptions of fairness can impact a variety of outcomes that organizations care about including a positive experience with the process, the degree to which an offer to an external candidate is likely to be accepted, broader impacts on organizational engagement and even performance, and even external organizational reputation via word of mouth and postings on social media and career websites such as the Vault, Glassdoor, or Fairy God Boss (e.g., Sanchez et al., 2000).

To the greatest extent possible, we recommend addressing these concerns via transparent communication. This includes what content (e.g., traits, competencies, dimensions, constructs) is being assessed, what the results mean for the test taker, and how the data will be used in the organization (e.g., for development only or to inform decision-making). While at face value this approach can seem risky or like a strategy that could backfire, research does not support this. Talent management and HR professionals in many organizations have expressed concerns over sharing too much information, similar to the arguments made around transparency of high-potential status in organizations (Church & Rotolo, 2016; Effron & Ort, 2010). However, we argue and benchmark data shows that the vast majority of employees already know how these processes work (Church et al., 2015). In this age of information and reputational transparency in general, being explicit with test takers is clearly the best option. Research on PepsiCo's LeAD program, for example, has shown that employees appreciate transparency, and it has not negatively impacted the variety of outcomes feared by HR and line leaders such as turnover, engagement, or performance (Church & Rotolo, 2016; Church, 2019). Further, from a psychometric perspective, research shows that transparency is unlikely to harm the validity of the assessments, and in some cases may increase it (Klehe et al., 2008; Kleinmann et al., 1996; Kolk et al., 2003).

Transparency with test takers also helps to ensure that participants get something out of the process, whether it be personal or professional development or career planning, particularly when the results are communicated in a meaningful way to them (e.g., always including strengths and opportunities along with indices or summary outcomes). The role of the IO practitioner, consultant, or appropriately trained HR or talent management professional in delivering results can also play a critical role here. Taking time to discuss results with participants at a more transparent level can help them to engage in self-reflection, enhance self-awareness, and drive accountability for planning and acting against their opportunities, incorporating trends into development planning efforts. Knowledge of organizational context is also key as feedback providers and coaches can leverage this to help address concerns and ensure that key points around content and purpose of the assessments are conveyed. Dedicated time for self-reflection and individual development is a luxury for many test takers (especially for senior leaders), and we have found that they consistently appreciate the enhanced level of discussion and insights as well as the focus on development planning. In research on the impact of senior assessment efforts at PepsiCo, results showed that those executives who had a positive experience with the assessment and feedback process and developed concrete actions as a result of the facilitated sessions showed significant positive change in their leadership behaviors 18 to 24 months later (Church, Del Giudice, & Margulies, 2017).

While full transparency may not be as feasible for external candidate populations in part due to legal concerns, we still believe that when framed appropriately and thoughtfully administered, it can influence both positive test taker reactions and their professional development (e.g., Bauer et al., 1998; London & McFarland, 2017; Hausknecht et al., 2004; Truxillo et al., 2009). At PepsiCo, for example, candidates at certain levels are provided with a summary of their assessment results via a legally vetted candidate-facing report, which has been well received by both candidates and internal stakeholders. Once hired, that same assessment data is used at all levels for a new-hire onboarding report and shared with the hiring manager and HR professional supporting them. At senior levels, more comprehensive individual debriefs of assessments are provided upon hire. These conversations help to orient the new hires to the organization and culture and allow for reflection on how they can leverage their strengths to be as successful as possible in their new role. At the most senior levels, additional data to help with new leader assimilation can also be shared with managers and HR professionals. Here again, transparency is emphasized, and all stakeholders are aware of what content is measured and how the results are used in the organization.

Finally, along with transparency and feedback, leveraging success stories within an organization is a useful tool to help obtain buy-in and build positive momentum regarding assessments both from test takers and from other stakeholder groups. For example, as part of PepsiCo's approach to building a feedback-rich data-driven culture (Church, 2019), we leverage both anecdotal and statistical data to tell a compelling story and "sell the value" of both the assessment suites and processes supporting them. Given the ongoing nature of the program (since 2012), at this point nearly all of PepsiCo's sitting executive committee members (excluding new hires) had been assessed prior to their current roles (including the CEO), a fact that is shared during program orientations, internal insights meetings, and even training sessions with managers and HR professionals. Likewise, engaging stories about senior leaders who did not take the assessment process seriously are used (anonymously) to offer humor and break the tension during orientation (e.g., the senior leader who attempted to take an 8-hour highly interactive online simulation in the backseat of his car while driving across the country, or the senior leader who asked to take a personality assessment twice to see if they could influence the results in a more "favorable" light). Sharing this type of information and cultural storytelling (which is a classic technique adapted from our organizational development and change toolkit) helps alleviate anxiety by framing the program as a positive opportunity to demonstrate their skills as opposed to a remediation effort. Over time this also builds a more positive cultural network of support for assessment and data-driven decision-making as well.

## Managers

Similar to candidates, managers can also be skeptical of the results of assessments, for many of the same reasons discussed earlier. For this group, and perhaps especially among the most tenured of leaders, there is skepticism when the assessment results do not match managers' perceptions of talent, such as when assessment results reveal significant leadership opportunities for an employee whom managers see as high potential, or when an employee who is viewed as an average performer scores exceptionally well, indicating the possibility of "hidden potential." Here the characteristic manager biases of "I'm the best judge of talent" and even some unconscious biases such as halo effect (or worse) can come into play. Another major concern of this group relates to assessment use and interpretation. Large quantities of data can be both exciting and overwhelming. At best, the reliance on assessment results can lead to intimidation and reluctance to leverage the data, and at worst, this can lead to overenthusiasm and leveraging the results or making inferences that aren't supported by the data.

We find that the best solution to addressing both concerns centers around building capability via program orientations, formal training on the tools and interpreting results, and even practice sessions. To start, managers need to see the data as an important source of input into their decision-making and supportive of the broader talent management agenda in the organization, not a barrier. Being able to compare different leaders on the same set of metrics reinforces both standardization and a consistent language for understanding talent, ultimately enhancing the value and objectivity of talent review and planning discussions. We also encourage managers to think about the assessments as one source of data-based input, not intended to replace their observations or experiences. This helps to align the results as a tool to empower managers, not restrict them. As one of the authors has argued elsewhere (Church, 2018), the traditional nine-box model of performance by potential ratings should be replaced with a more modern approach of "designated potential" (i.e., the aligned organizational point of view on high-potential status following talent reviews) by "assessed potential" (i.e., the predictive outcome of assessment results regarding likelihood for future success at higher levels). "Assessed potential" as an approach combines psychometric assessment results and leader classification schemes for talent management and decision-making processes. Recent research has shown that these two forms of data are empirically additive when it comes to predicting leader success in promotions and performance over time (Church et al., 2021). As is the case with employees, communicating findings to managers is a key component in driving the right mindset when it comes to using assessments to make informed talent decisions. Making this distinction clear between organizational perceptions of potential and data-driven assessments of potential has been invaluable to talent planning efforts and the adoption of LeAD at PepsiCo.

Achieving a significant level of comfort and understanding in assessments usually does not happen overnight, and thus reinforcing capabilities and giving leaders a chance to practice with their own teams is key. One approach we have taken with success is to build a set of insights and narratives about a given manager's entire team (or succession pipeline) based on data. Walking managers through their data both holistically and in the context of individual talent discussions allows them to (a) understand the strengths and opportunities of their team or pipeline, (b) look for outages that may need to be addressed beyond the current talent pool (e.g., the need to bring in more strategic thinking), and (c) enable self-reflection of their own assessment results if available against the group. These walk-throughs ensure that the data are leveraged appropriately while also familiarizing managers with the kinds of insights that can be gleaned from the assessment data. While we have leveraged this type of analysis for decades at PepsiCo, a new emphasis on team processes has allowed us to introduce this approach into team effectiveness discussions. Typically for more senior teams, we walk leaders through the team, discussing both aggregated individual-level data (e.g., 360 ratings from peers, personality inventory results) and team-level diagnostics (PepsiCo's SUPER5 Team framework and diagnostic survey, stakeholder interviews, etc.), and providing a wholistic picture of team dynamics, including how the collective team may be impacted by the managers' leadership approach (see Figure 30.2 for a sample summary).

Data triangulation is also a useful tool for managers and other wary stakeholders (including test takers) to help illustrate the reliability and validity of the tools, to help target and narrow themes, and to promote discussion. As mentioned above, PepsiCo assessment and development programs follow an MTMM approach, leveraging situational judgment tests,

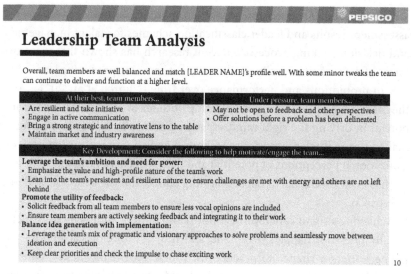

Figure 30.2. Leadership Team Analysis

simulations, and personality tools, most recently aligned to the organization's new GREAT5 leadership model (Church & Ezama, 2020a; 2020b; Scott, Church, & McLellan, 2017). For this approach to be effective, it does not necessarily have to be this robust; often, comparing assessment results with a 360 feedback tool can be just as effective (as most 360 feedback tools reflect multiple perspectives and behaviors as well—see Church et al., 2019). For example, if different patterns of results are observed on a leader's personality profile and 360 feedback, it opens a discussion around foundational tendencies/preferences (as demonstrated by a personality profile) and how that leader has managed or adapted to impact how they are showing up behaviorally today (as demonstrated by a 360 feedback tool).

## Recruiters

Recruiters are a third major stakeholder group to consider. While we often see some of the same concerns with this group as we do with managers around an inflated view of their ability to judge talent (e.g., Cole et al., 2009) and inconsistencies with assessment results not matching general expectations (e.g., everyone loved this candidate during the interview process and yet they failed the assessment—there must be something wrong with the tools), this stakeholder group brings a strong end-user focus as well, as they are often the "face" of the organization via first contact with prospective employees. Concerns relating to the candidate experience often revolve around seat time and engagement. Recruiting (or staffing) is generally an execution subfunction where time to fill an open requisition is paramount to business continuity, so efficiency of process concerns also arise frequently. Except at very senior levels, staffing professionals are measured in performance evaluations on volume as opposed to strategic quality of hire.

For this group, we find the biggest hurdle is overcoming anecdotes (and addressing misaligned outcomes with expectations) with capability building, leveraging data, and positive storytelling once again. This is particularly important given the legal implications that misuse can have in a selection context (Myors et al., 2017; Scott & Reynolds, 2010). We would be remiss not to note that in addition to data and storytelling, firm commitment and support for a standard and valid external selection process at the most senior levels is paramount, especially when results or decisions are challenged.

For example, insights relating to the success of the assessments (e.g., showing success rates via positive quality-of-hire surveys, successful high-potential designations, promotions and performance over time, or even data showing where someone was borderline and ultimately failed out and left the organization) can go a long way toward driving acceptance. It is important to plan in advance of a new implementation to gather the right types of data for your process with multiple sources of evaluation data to overcome the negative anecdotes. Wherever possible, program evaluation metrics should be built in and internal tracking of talent leveraged to demonstrate return on investment (ROI) and help make the value of the program real for the organization. Where it is not possible to collect your own data, there is an abundance of candidate reaction research, often produced by consulting and assessment firms (e.g., Hogan, Aon), to leverage when discussing assessments with recruiters. Finally, another way to help drive acceptance of the assessment process with internal recruiters is to ensure they take the tool suite themselves (even if for development only) and consider their feedback when making adjustments to the "wrapper" (or positioning) around the program (e.g., messaging, adjusting seat times or flows, etc.). While one might assume that all recruiters are familiar with their own assessments, we have found in discussing with colleagues in other organizations that this is often not the case.

## Human Resources Leaders

When it comes to assessments, although HR leaders share many of the same needs from a communications and capability perspective as the other key stakeholder groups, they also play a unique role in the organization as advocates for employees, leaders, and culture and thus have some unique challenges that need to be addressed as well. For HR professionals, the focus is often on more strategic conversations such as how assessments can help (or inhibit) their ability to meet diversity goals (Thomas & Creary, 2009) or help to build the organization's talent pipeline for future capabilities (Church & Waclawski, 2010). Of course, there are practical considerations as well, including the ability to scale a program (e.g., infrastructure, operational needs) and, naturally, the associated costs of implementing assessments including the time and hours it takes for validation (e.g., How many hours will employees be pulled away from the field? What will they get out of the process?).

It is imperative, therefore, when building capability and communications, to go beyond the data and storytelling. In addition to formal program evaluation efforts as discussed above, leveraging the results of validation studies can also speak to ROI, particularly in early stages of implementation. There are a variety of creative ways to demonstrate value, no matter what stage or level of maturity an organization's program is in. For example, repeated administration of assessments can help to both confirm skills and capabilities and determine progress toward developmental goals (e.g., T1-T2 administration). At PepsiCo, for example, leaders are enrolled in what is called a Development Check-In (DCI), which is a targeted 360 that allows leaders to measure progress against areas they have decided to focus their development energies on (Church & Dawson, 2018; Church, Del Giudice, & Margulies, 2016). Internal research demonstrates that leaders who take action against their goals tend to see significantly improved perceptions of behavior 12 to 18 months after the program and were more likely to take on new or expanded roles.

No organization wants to fall behind when it comes to raising the bar on talent and diversity, especially given the increasing intensity in the war on talent. Therefore, it is also important to highlight the broader organizational goals and speak to the role that assessments play in the entire employee lifecycle. This includes both driving business growth and building a short- and long-term bench for succession. For example, assessment is critical to differentiating talent in valid and legally defensible ways (Church et al., 2015), and it is imperative to emphasize the need for continued adherence to legal and professional standards as risk does not end with test development (Guion, 2011; Guion & Highhouse, 2006). In implementing data-driven talent decisions via assessments, organizations are effectively building an architecture that supports the removal of bias and the leveling of the playing field (Trudell & Church, 2016). Further, by differentiating talent in an objective way, you can better determine which leaders have the future potential to take on more challenging and broader roles (e.g., based on models such as the Leadership Development BluePrint—see Church & Silzer, 2014; Silzer & Church, 2009), you can make smarter investment decisions. As mentioned, assessment data helps to provide standard metrics for comparing talent and a consistent benchmark, thereby enhancing our ability to build organizational bench strength. To illustrate, standardized assessments allow you to be sure that a manager hired in Europe is going to have the same baseline skills as a manager hired in Asia, and that the leadership capabilities of an assessed high-potential candidate in the United States are measured the same way as a future leader in Latin America (all in the same organization).

## The Public

Finally, employees, candidates, managers, leaders, and even IO psychologists all make up stakeholders in our broader society (i.e., the general public), so the same perspectives and challenges discussed above apply here. However, beyond the suggestions outlined above, we feel it is important to emphasize our collective responsibilities as IO psychologists to model a scientist-practitioner mindset at the broadest levels possible by ensuring valid and ethical practice in the organizations in which we work. That means having the courage to address poor (or potentially legally risky) practices internally, challenge bad leader behavior and decisions, or ensure consulting firms presenting new ideas do so in an empirical and theoretically grounded manner with validation tools and robust communications. The bottom line is that we as IO professionals are the voice that continues to deliver the message along with the process. Further, we should continue to expect our professional societies (e.g., Society for Industrial and Organizations Psychology, American Psychological Association, Association for Psychological Science, etc.) to support the use of quality assessments and processes via their lobbying and public relations processes that go beyond what individuals can do alone. In the end, it's up to each of us.

## Summary

As assessments continue to gain popularity and advances in assessment-related technology continue to emerge, our role as scientist-practitioners, particularly those of us who work inside organizations where these tools are being used for leadership development, succession planning, and talent decision-making, is critically important. Not only do we have a responsibility to ensure that there is sufficient research to allow us to make informed evaluations, but also we need to help stakeholders to discern between the "good," the "bad," and the "ugly" science and to equip them with the skills they need to make informed decisions. In this chapter, we have outlined the biggest hurdles we have seen regarding misinformation and the approaches we have successfully employed in alleviating stakeholder concerns. Our list is not exhaustive, and the narrative will certainly continue to evolve. Still, across the myths/misinformation and stakeholder perspectives discussed here, we have identified five core themes that we believe can be leveraged and adapted to help optimize the value of assessments, combat misinformation, and communicate with stakeholders across organizations:

1. **Build comfort and capability**: Train stakeholders on the content underlying the assessments and how to use the data appropriately (and when to ask for help from IO psychology professionals).
2. **Take the offense against misinformation**: Proactively educate stakeholders and dispel myths using data, insights, and outcomes.
3. **Speak the language of your stakeholders**: Understand the unique perspectives of different stakeholder groups (including those in business and those in the general public where appropriate) and use compelling stories and cultural messaging to drive engagement and acceptance.
4. **Build a robust process**: Triangulate data using an MTMM approach, validate the assessments internally before use, and never let a single tool or construct dominate a process.

5. **Be resourceful and control the narrative:** Build in processes to collect and leverage real-life data (ROI, reactions, case studies, etc.), and get creative with the data you have at your disposal.

# References

Anderson, N., Salgado, J. F., & Hülsheger, U. R. (2010). Applicant reactions in selection: Comprehensive meta-analysis into reaction generalization versus situational specificity. *International Journal of Selection and Assessment, 18*(3), 291–304.

Bartram, D. (2007). Increasing validity with forced-choice criterion measurement formats. *International Journal of Selection and Assessment, 15*, 263–272.

Bauer, T. N., Maertz, C. P., Jr., Dolen, M. R., & Campion, M. A. (1998). Longitudinal assessment of applicant reactions to employment testing and test outcome feedback. *Journal of Applied Psychology, 83*(6), 892.

Bauer, T. N., Truxillo, D. M., Tucker, J. S., Weathers, V., Bertolino, M., Erdogan, B., & Campion, M. A. (2006). Selection in the information age: The impact of privacy concerns and computer experience on applicant reactions. *Journal of Management, 32*(5), 601–621.

Bhatia, S., & Ryan, A. M. (2018). Hiring for the win: Game-based assessment in employee selection. In J. H. Dulebohn & D. L. Stone (Eds.), *The brave new world of eHRM 2.0* (pp. 81–110). Information Age Publishing.

Bonabeau, E. (2003). Don't trust your gut. *Harvard Business Review, 81*(5), 116–123.

Caliskan, A., Bryson, J. J., & Narayanan, A. (2017). Semantics derived automatically from language corpora contain human-like biases. *Science, 356*(6334), 183–186.

Campbell, D. T., & Fiske, D. W. (1959). Convergent and discriminant validation by the multitrait-multimethod matrix. *Psychological Bulletin, 56*(2), 81–105.

Chamorro-Premuzic, T. (2015). Ace the assessment. *Harvard Business Review, 93*(7/8), 118–121.

Chamorro-Premuzic, T., Winsborough, D., Sherman, R. A., & Hogan, R. (2016). New talent signals: Shiny new objects or a brave new world? *Industrial and Organizational Psychology, 9*(3), 621–640.

Church, A. H. (2018). Think outside the 9 box. *Talent Quarterly, 19*, 39–43.

Church, A. H. (2019). Building an integrated architecture for leadership assessment and development at PepsiCo. In R. G. Hamlin, A. D. Ellinger, & J. Jones (Eds.), *Evidence-based initiatives for organizational change and development* (pp. 492–505). Business Science Reference/IGI Global.

Church, A. H., Bracken, D. W., Fleenor, J. W., & Rose, D. S. (Eds.). (2019). *Handbook of strategic 360 feedback.* Oxford University Press.

Church, A. H., & Dawson, L. M. (2018). Agile feedback drives accountability and sustained behavior change. *Strategic HR Review, 17*(6), 295–302.

Church, A. H., Del Giudice, M., & Margulies, A. (2017). All that glitters is not gold: Maximizing the impact of executive assessment and development efforts. *Leadership & Organization Development Journal, 38*(6), 765–779.

Church, A. H., & Ezama, S. (2020a). PepsiCo's formula for potential. *Training and Development Journal, 74*(4), 35–39.

Church, A. H., & Ezama, S. (2020b). Digitalization drives the new face of engagement. *People + Strategy, 43*(3), 25–28.

Church, A. H., Fleck, C. R., Foster, G. C., Levine, R. C., Lopex, F. J., & Rotolo, C. T. (2016). Does purpose matter? The stability of personality assessments in organization development and talent management applications over time. *Journal of Applied Behavioral Science, 52*(4), 1–32.

Church, A. H., Guidry, B., Dickey, J., & Scrivani, J. (2021). Is there potential in assessing for high-potential? Evaluating the relationships between performance ratings, leadership assessment data, designated high-potential status and promotion outcomes in a global organization. *Leadership Quarterly, 32*(5), 101516.

Church, A. H., & Rotolo, C. T. (2013). How are top companies assessing their high-potentials and senior executives? A talent management benchmark study. *Consulting Psychology Journal: Practice and Research, 65*(3), 199.

Church, A. H., & Rotolo, C. T. (2016). Lifting the veil: What happens when you are transparent with people about their future potential? *People and Strategy, 39*(4), 36.

Church, A. H., Rotolo, C. T., Ginther, N. M., & Levine, R. (2015). How are top companies designing and managing their high-potential programs? A follow-up talent management benchmark study. *Consulting Psychology Journal: Practice and Research, 67*(1), 17–47.

Church, A. H., & Silzer, R. (2014). Going behind the corporate curtain with a *Blueprint for Leadership Potential*: An integrated framework for identifying high-potential talent. *People & Strategy, 36*(4), 51–58.

Church, A. H., & Waclawski, J. (2010). Take the Pepsi Challenge: Talent development at PepsiCo. In R. Silzer & B. E. Dowell (Eds.), *Strategy-driven talent management: A leadership imperative* (SIOP Professional Practice Series, pp. 617–640), Jossey-Bass.

Cole, M. S., Feild, H. S., Giles, W. F., & Harris, S. G. (2009). Recruiters' inferences of applicant personality based on resume screening: Do paper people have a personality? *Journal of Business and Psychology, 24*(1), 5–18.

Dana, J., Dawes, R., & Peterson, N. (2013). Belief in the unstructured interview: The persistence of an illusion. *Judgment and Decision Making, 8*(5), 512.

Donovan, J. J., Dwight, S. A., & Hurtz, G. M. (2003). An assessment of the prevalence, severity, and verifiability of entry-level applicant faking using the randomized response technique. *Human Performance, 16*(1), 81–106.

DuVernet, A. M., & Popp, E. (2014). Gamification of workplace practices. *Industrial-Organizational Psychologist, 52*(1), 39–44.

Effron, M. S., & Ort, M. (2010). *One page talent management: Eliminating complexity, adding value*.

Ellison, L. J., McClure Johnson, T., Tomczak, D., Siemsen, A., & Gonzalez, M. F. (2020). Game on! Exploring reactions to game-based selection assessments. *Journal of Managerial Psychology, 35*(4), 241–254.

Frieder, R. E., Van Iddekinge, C. H., & Raymark, P. H. (2016). How quickly do interviewers reach decisions? An examination of interviewers' decision-making time across applicants. *Journal of Occupational and Organizational Psychology, 89*(2), 223–248.

Georgiou, K., Gouras, A., & Nikolaou, I. (2019). Gamification in employee selection: The development of a gamified assessment. *International Journal of Selection and Assessment, 27*(2), 91–103.

Guion, R. M. (2011). *Assessment, measurement, and prediction for personnel decisions.* Taylor & Francis.

Guion, R. M., & Highhouse, S. (2006). *Essentials of personnel assessment and selection.* Lawrence Erlbaum Associates Publishers.

Hatami, H., Sjatil, P. E., & Sneader, K. (2020, May 28). *The toughest leadership test.* https://www.mckinsey.com/featured-insights/leadership/the-toughest-leadership-test#

Hausknecht, J. P., Day, D. V., & Thomas, S. C. (2004). Applicant reactions to selection procedures: An updated model and meta-analysis. *Personnel Psychology, 57*(3), 639–683.

Hogan, J., Barrett, P., & Hogan, R. (2007). Personality measurement, faking, and employment selection. *Journal of Applied Psychology, 92*(5), 1270.

Kantrowitz, T. M., Tuzinski, K. A., & Raines, J. M. (2018). *2018 Global assessment trends report.* SHL.

King, D. D., Ryan, A. M., Kantrowitz, T., Grelle, D., & Dainis, A. (2015). Mobile Internet testing: An analysis of equivalence, individual differences, and reactions. *International Journal of Selection and Assessment, 23*, 382–394.

Klehe, U. C., König, C. J., Richter, G. M., Kleinmann, M., & Melchers, K. G. (2008). Transparency in structured interviews: Consequences for construct and criterion-related validity. *Human Performance, 21*(2), 107–137.

Kleinmann, M., Kuptsch, C., & Köller, O. (1996). Transparency: A necessary requirement for the construct validity of assessment centres. *Applied Psychology, 45*(1), 67–84.

Kolk, N. J., Born, M. P., & Der Flier, H. V. (2003). The transparent assessment centre: The effects of revealing dimensions to candidates. *Applied Psychology, 52*(4), 648–668.

Landers, R. N. (2019). Gamification misunderstood: How badly executed and rhetorical gamification obscures its transformative potential. *Journal of Management Inquiry, 28*(2), 137–140.

Landers, R. N., Auer, E. M., & Abraham, J. D. (2020). Gamifying a situational judgment test with immersion and control game elements: Effects on applicant reactions and construct validity. *Journal of Managerial Psychology, 35*(4), 225–239.

London, M., & McFarland, L. A. (2017). Assessment feedback. In *Handbook of employee selection* (pp. 406–425). Routledge.

McCarthy, J. M., Van Iddekinge, C. H., Lievens, F., Kung, M. C., Sinar, E. F., & Campion, M. A. (2013). Do candidate reactions relate to job performance or affect criterion-related validity? A multi-study investigation of relations among reactions, selection test scores, and job performance. *Journal of Applied Psychology, 98*(5), 701.

McDaniel, M. A., Whetzel, D. L., Schmidt, F. L., & Maurer, S. D. (1994). The validity of employment interviews: A comprehensive review and meta-analysis. *Journal of Applied Psychology, 79*(4), 599.

Meyer, D. (2018). *Amazon reportedly killed an AI recruitment system because it couldn't stop the tool from discriminating against women.* https://fortune.com/2018/10/10/amazon-ai-recruitment-bias-women-sexist

Myors, B., Lievens, F., Schollaert, E., Van Hoye, G., Cronshow, S. F., Mladinic, A., . . . Mariani, M. (2017). Perspectives from 22 countries on the legal environment for selection.

Narlock, J., & Church, A. H. (2021, June 21). Where does artificial intelligence place in the HR game? *Talent Quarterly.* https://www.talent-quarterly.com/where-does-artificial-intelligence-play-in-the-hr-game/

Ployhart, R. E., & Holtz, B. C. (2008). The diversity–validity dilemma: Strategies for reducing racioethnic and sex subgroup differences and adverse impact in selection. *Personnel Psychology, 61*(1), 153–172.

Principles for the Validation and Use of Personnel Selection Procedures. (2018). *Industrial and Organizational Psychology: Perspectives on Science and Practice, 11*(Suppl 1), 2–97.

Rotolo, C. T., Church, A. H., Adler, S., Smither, J. W., Colquitt, A. L., Shull, A. C., Paul, K. B., & Foster, G. (2018). Putting an end to bad talent management: A call to action for the field of industrial and organizational psychology. *Industrial and Organizational Psychology: Perspectives on Science and Practice, 11*(2), 176–219.

Ryan, A. M., & Derous, E. (2019). The unrealized potential of technology in selection assessment. *Journal of Work and Organizational Psychology, 35*(2), 85–92.

Sackett, P. R., Kuncel, N. R., Beatty, A. S., Rigdon, J. L., Shen, W., & Kiger, T. B. (2012). The role of socioeconomic status in SAT-grade relationships and in college admissions decisions. *Psychological Science, 23*(9), 1000–1007.

Sanchez, R. J., Truxillo, D. M., & Bauer, T. N. (2000). Development and examination of an expectancy-based measure of test-taking motivation. *Journal of Applied Psychology, 85*(5), 739.

Schmidt, F. L., & Zimmerman, R. D. (2004). A counterintuitive hypothesis about employment interview validity and some supporting evidence. *Journal of Applied Psychology, 89*(3), 553.

Scott, J. C., Church, A. H., & McLellan, J. (2017). *Effective practice guidelines report: Selecting leader talent.* Complimentary industry best practices report made available by the Foundation of the Society for Human Resources Management (SHRM). https://www.shrm.org/about/foundation/products/pages/shrmfoundationepgs.aspx

Scott, J. C., & Reynolds, D. H. (2010). *Handbook of workplace assessment* (Vol. 32). John Wiley & Sons.

Seaton, G. A., Church, A. H., Allen, J. B., Jain, S., Dickey, J., & Guidry, B. (2021). Leadership in the time of COVID: Should we really throw the baby out with the bathwater? *Industrial and Organizational Psychology, 14*(1–2), 117–122.

Silzer, R., & Church, A. H. (2009). The pearls and perils of identifying potential. *Industrial and Organizational Psychology: Perspectives on Science and Practice, 2*(4), 377–412.

Thomas, D. A., & Creary, S. J. (2009). Meeting the diversity challenge at PepsiCo: The Steve Reinemund era. *Harvard Business School Case, August*, 410–424.

Trudell, C. M., & Church., A. H. (2016). Bringing it to life: Global talent scout, convener & coach: PepsiCo's LeADing talent management into the future. CHREATE Advancing the HR Profession Forward Faster organization profile. http://chreate.net/CHREATE_PepsiCo_Profile.pdf

Truxillo, D. M., Bodner, T. E., Bertolino, M., Bauer, T. N., & Yonce, C. A. (2009). Effects of explanations on applicant reactions: A meta-analytic review. *International Journal of Selection and Assessment, 17*(4), 346–361.

Verschuere, B., Köbis, N. C., Bereby-Meyer, Y., Rand, D., & Shalvi, S. (2018). Taxing the brain to uncover lying? Meta-analyzing the effect of imposing cognitive load on the reaction-time costs of lying. *Journal of Applied Research in Memory and Cognition, 7*(3), 462–469.

# 31
# Venture Capital
## Friend or Foe for Talent Assessment?

*Darko Lovric*

Science and the scientific method are concerned broadly with nature, reality, and facts. In a simple model of science, it is possible to find and exercise complete objectivity in such a pursuit. However, more sophisticated models (Nola & Howard, 2007) acknowledge that science is always to an extent shaped by the motivations and considerations of scientists engaged in such an endeavor—that experimenter bias is a fact of nature.

The extent of this bias and its ultimate impact on science are beyond the scope of this chapter, but we can be reasonably sure these effects do indeed occur with regard to sources of scientific funding (see Lesser et al., 2007; Lundh et al., 2012; Resnik & Elliott, 2013). This bias can be explicit (overt pressure and selection criteria from the funding sources) but can also be implicit in cases where researchers themselves take into account what they imagine funding sources require and accordingly shape their approach explicitly and implicitly. This chapter argues that an important source of bias for the field of talent assessments will increasingly be venture capital (VC) funding and, further, that some of this bias may be beneficial to the field.

## Venture Capital and Talent Assessment

VC is a form of highly speculative investment in business ideas. The basic nature of these investments is often thesis driven—that is, there is a field of application where new ideas and approaches, if rightly conceptualized and executed, can result in rapid growth (Hoffman & Yeh, 2018). VC most often works through a portfolio approach comprising many risky early-stage investments in preselected areas, where the bet is really on the thesis, and the execution risk is spread through many smaller investments.

Significant inflow of VC funding into a certain area is known to reshape the industry. For example, increased investments in transport startups have reshaped the car industry (CB Insights, 2021) in terms of overall investments in autonomous driving, data, and services and battery-electric vehicles, leading to an explosion of ventures, patents, and researchers—and a significant increase in both corporate and research funding.

We can be reasonably certain that human resources (HR) tech, broadly conceptualized, is an increasingly important thesis for VC investors. Globally, this market represents a $148 billion opportunity (CB Insights, 2019), and while certainly not as large as some other VC areas (financial tech or "fintech," retail tech), it is of a sufficient size to have attracted a large ecosystem of VC firms, events and incubators, and $3.6 billion in total funding in the first half of 2021 (Emergen Research, 2020). Within this larger market, talent assessment is often a key piece, both as a standalone offer and focus area and even more importantly as part of a larger suite of market offerings for HR Software-as-a-Service (SaaS) as companies increasingly seek one-stop solutions for all of their talent needs. While the future is hard to predict, we can be reasonably certain that VC will continue to be a significant investor in this space.

What will be the impact of their involvement? With increased VC funding in talent assessment, HR buyers and talent assessment professionals seeking cutting-edge products and services will increasingly interact with and support venture-funded activities, which will likely exert a gravitational pull for all other potential buyers. Akin to other fields, we can expect that the VC voice will percolate through the industry, forcing established industry players to emulate and compete until the majority of industry-facing players are either adapting or perishing.

The field of artificial intelligence (AI) demonstrates how a hype cycle can distort funding of a whole field, creating an outsized impact on the research activity globally. To oversimplify, two main approaches to AI are symbolic/expert systems and neural networks (machine learning). In the last 60 years the field of AI has swung between these two approaches, and as fortunes waned and waxed on either, funding followed, impacting research agendas and careers over a long period. With the introduction of VC funding based on increasing centrality of machine learning for applications across industries, this cycle has only intensified, pushing the whole field toward the machine learning approach and starving competing approaches of both funding and new researchers and research programs (for more detailed treatment, see Marcus, 2022).

While purely academic practitioners can to an extent be insulated from these trends, the opportunities and dynamics of these changes will likely create increasingly strong attraction in order for the academic research to relate to topics of interest to practitioners and businesses, leading to the field likely being shaped more and more by the VC approach and expectations.

## Venture Capital Logic and Likely Impact on Talent Assessment

VC seeks rapid growth, and growth depends on customer adoption. Therefore, the most important bias this type of funding brings to any field is usability and customer centricity that fuel adoption. Disciplines of design thinking, growth hacking, and similar approaches are at their core tools to ensure that customer experience leads to high usability and "stickiness" of any product or service (Heath & Heath, 2007). For example, fintech providers mostly offer the same services that traditional banks do (savings, payments, transactions, investments), but the usability, speed, and user-friendliness of their platforms have created a radically different competitive environment for the whole industry.

The second consideration is product differentiation—ideally new products need to offer a superior effectiveness that creates a qualitatively different experience or result compared to the competition. The third and final core consideration is defensibility of this growth—not just first mover advantage and network effects, but also intellectual property (IP) and skillsets that create a "moat" that will make it difficult for new competitors to arise. Google dominance in the field of search is a well-known example, with initial product differentiation via superior algorithms that focused on objective search quality affording them a third decade of dominance, reflected in the fact that "to Google" has become a transitive verb in many world languages. Taken together, these three core concepts are mutually reinforcing, creating a virtuous circle of easy customer adoption, qualitative differentiation, and difficulty in competing or replicating the experience.

- As VC firms increasingly turn to opportunities in the talent assessment space, their operating model will exert an increasing "gravitational pull" on researchers and practitioners in three main ways: **Usability** will become an increasingly important component of all talent assessment

(Chamorro-Premuzic et al., 2016). Customer experience, look and feel, ease of use, speed, and other elements of the user experience will become increasingly salient, prioritized, and funded.
- It is likely digital tools will be the key sources of **differentiation**. Product differentiation through increased use of technology, data, and automation will create qualitative differentiation in terms of precision and richness of data sets on which to base assessment and, hopefully, the quality of the assessments and predictions so produced.
- **IP protection** will become increasingly important—private data sets, regulatory acceptance, and protected IP will become assets more closely valued and guarded and consequently established with more care than may have been the case so far.

The consequences of such venture logic percolating through our discipline will be complex and far reaching.

## Likely Positive Forces of Venture Capital Influence

In every field where venture disruption occurred, we have observed increased customer satisfaction and decreased costs, a true creative destruction that has led to beneficial outcomes for the customers. It is likely the same beneficial effects will be felt in our field.

1. **Broadening the customer base.** Growing ventures excel at identifying unmet customer needs. Historically, the field of talent assessment stands for a narrow set of use cases, mostly hiring, promotion, and leadership potential in the work context. It is likely new ventures will seek to expand this influence to a wider set of new potential customers and use cases (e.g., dating apps, sports teams, schools) and thereby blur the lines between the world of work and other applications where assessments may be useful. Likely this difference will be quantitative—expanding currently infrequent and niche cases of talent assessment to more widespread and more frequent use inside and outside of work contexts, with the outcome of talent assessments becoming a much more noticeable feature of daily lives than is the case today.
2. **Branding the field.** Too often the field of evidence-based talent assessment is not very successful in competing with what we can charitably

call less scientific approaches. Talent assessments can live in a world where nonscientific approaches (e.g., graphology in France, blood type assessment in Japan) have a firm hold on the public imagination and consequent use in the workplace. Since these approaches are obviously less effective and also not IP protectable, venture-backed approaches will in seeking differentiation undertake efforts to reduce the public perception of effectiveness and efficiency of other practices, at least in a positive case (see below for a counterargument related to validity). For example, the field of cryptocurrency was an exceptionally niche area before the arrival of VC funding, which pushed mainstream branding (along with ease of use) in popularizing a previously highly technical and arcane subfield.

3. **Usability and customer experience.** The talent assessment field has a long academic history and has been shaped by the needs for reliability and validity, mostly using a questionnaire-based model. In this model, predictive ability was optimized, and usability and customer experience were distant considerations (as long as one could get first year psychology students to take the tests). Providers were able to provide a better and more consistent experience, but many have built their IP based on validated norms that are time-consuming and costly to change, making it difficult to adopt the new trends. New entrants in the field will likely provide an increasingly radical challenge. Graphic design and customer interface will shift toward more digitally based services, including being available on demand, in mobile formats, with more predictive coding, and with significantly improved visualizations. More advanced user experiences such as gamification, blockchain-based privacy tools and tokens, and any future technologies will likely be increasingly integrated within the assessment space.

4. **Speed of innovation.** Pressure to differentiate and resulting competition will likely lead to an increased arms race in terms of product features, usability, and IP data sets, making it more difficult to compete but benefiting the end-users. In a more dynamic field, new entrants starting from a blank slate have an advantage that they can immediately adopt new technologies and design for customer expectations, which is more difficult and costly for established business models (Christensen, 2016).

5. **Affordability and price.** Broadening the user base, usability and automation, as well as generous funding for growth, will likely lead to

reduced unit prices per assessment, and possibly a shift toward a more subscription-based revenue model given the significant premium investors are willing to pay for such models. Specifically, subscription revenue models rely on significantly increasing the frequency at which a certain service is utilized (e.g., listening to more new music via streaming when compared to needing to buy new albums), and therefore while products may still be quite profitable, the per-unit cost of each assessment may drop significantly.

Overall, we can expect that the benefits of venture funding in talent assessment will be significant and far-reaching, leading to talent assessments that will be more accessible, cheaper, and easier to use for a wider proportion of the population—a democratization of talent assessments. It would be interesting to estimate how many people currently alive have completed a type of psychometric assessment. In a world where funding for talent assessment develops along the lines suggested here, we can expect the field to become more global (as opposed to mostly centered in developed countries) and used in more contexts more frequently, with the end result that talent assessments become something almost everyone experiences as part of any significant change or choice in their lives (new role or career, promotion, new team or relocation, etc.). If we believe in the predictive power of talent assessment, this increased influence will be a net positive for society.

While significant benefits can be expected, downsides of the VC influence might temper the enthusiasm for this change.

## Likely Downsides of Venture Capital Influence

Venture funding and growth usually demonstrate the dark side of democratization. Generally, customer choice moves away from gatekeepers toward end-users, with the logic that whatever customers want to buy is therefore right. This creates a whole range of issues for our discipline.

1. **Discounting validity.** In the venture-backed model, the customer is king. Whatever the customers find of value they are free to purchase. Therefore, there are few regulatory, ethical, or scientific criteria that can easily stand against this logic. This, of course, is an already existing challenge to researchers in the field, but it is likely to get worse with

the introduction of further venture-backed investments. It is important to note that customer choice is sometimes in direct contradiction with expert choice, and that overall reduction in the role of experts in our lives will lead to issues of validity being replaced by customer satisfaction with the feedback provided. Naturally, some use cases will drive the validity more strongly than others (e.g., predicting future job performance, implementing assessments under consent decree), but we can expect that already difficult issue of convincing customers to pay for validity will only get more challenging unless the value of assessments is very explicitly tied to the value of prediction and delivered accordingly.

2. **Discounting reliability.** To increase market size and the need for talent assessments, we can expect that increasingly dynamic and variable results might be favored. This might seem paradoxical—but pressures to increase how frequently customers require these tools might move us along from seeing talent as a relatively stable set of capabilities and predispositions to more of "in the moment" feedback akin to a mood analysis. In this model lack of reliability can actually be taken as an advantage to be monetized.

3. **Oversimplification.** Simply put, hype sells, and the ability to be nuanced and open to further evidence is limited when faced with a fickle and demanding set of customers—where it is tempting to both overpromise and oversimplify. This, of course, is not a novel issue and is a famous challenge in all commercialization and scientific communication (National Academies of Sciences, Engineering, and Medicine et al., 2017), but the issue will likely become even more difficult through the sales and growth pressures that VC logic brings. Many fields have dealt with these pressures through regulation of the claims that can be made, but not all fields get effectively regulated. We can compare the careful claims made for drugs regulated by the U.S. Food and Drug Administration with the claims and quality controls for health supplements to notice an instructive difference. Will the future talent assessments keep to evidence-based models through appropriately flexible and broad self-regulation (for I don't imagine government stepping in here), or will the field be exposed to ever-increasing cycles of hype and overpromise? For academics and scientifically minded practitioners these potential downsides are likely the cause for significant alarm, even if they are also to an extent an expression of an already

existing longstanding battle. It is simply likely that this battle will get significantly more difficult.

## How to Manage the Downsides

The premise of this chapter is that we can have our cake and eat it too—that it will be possible to accept the beneficial effects of venture funding while ameliorating its worst excesses. Specifically, there are three mechanisms that together may significantly help practitioners working in this field to ensure the validity, reliability, and scientific integrity of our work.

1. **Identifying right and wrong use cases.** The most important focus of our work should be on keeping our attention on use cases that require reliability and validity, that is, focusing on issues that require prediction. In this way the need to produce real-world results will make it difficult for the field to stray toward infotainment and edutainment and stay firmly anchored in the difficult and messy real-world task of predicting actual performance.
2. **Educating key clients and building case studies.** Experts need to educate clients in order to create a welcoming environment for their expertise. Emphasizing the scientific core of talent assessment requires building bridges with practitioners—a task not wisely left to the private organizations in the field that can be captured by venture interests. Selecting the clients that are on the cutting edge, and most in need of accurate predictions, will ensure that the broader set of practitioners is influenced through trickle-down standards and approaches developed for the most difficult cases. In this case, we will need to learn the tools of branding to ensure that valid and reliable uses of our tools are also the most celebrated ones.
3. **Managing market failures.** Market failures are common—especially in a new and fast-moving field with many new entrants. We can expect that hype and misuse will continue to happen, sometimes in quite visible ways, as the example of Cambridge Analytica and its use of assessment demonstrates (Isaak & Hanna, 2018). To ameliorate these failures, tools as diverse as laws, regulations, professional and practitioner bodies, and best practices can all be used to create the right incentives for an ethical and scientific approach to our

discipline (see Chapter 14, Tippins in this book for a detailed treatment). Specifically, current societal concerns around diversity and inclusion as well as privacy will likely be strong allies in establishing a framework that will minimize market failures and the search for easy but wrong answers.

## Conclusion

Tension between science and commerce is an age-old question. In the example of venture funding meets talent assessment, we can see how pressures of capitalism and growth can create a significant impetus toward innovation and democratization of services in the way that defenders of the free market often claim is the natural result of free market and creative destruction. We can also see the obvious externalities of such a system in terms of its ability to step over ethical, aesthetical, and even long-term effectiveness considerations in its search for short-term gratification of immediate customer needs. Therefore, all societies have nonmarket mechanisms that attempt to bring balance to these forces of capitalism.

Broadly speaking, building cohesion in the academic and practitioner community around the key determinants of good talent assessment practice is one of the key ways to create the right balance to the market pressures hypothesized in this chapter. By building the right freedom within a framework, this community can both harness the beneficial effects of such forces (enabling the innovation) and curb their greatest excesses, as long as the community is able to act with cohesion and understanding.

## References

CB Insights. (2021). *How big tech is tackling auto & mobility.*
CB Insights. (2019). *HR tech market map: 145+ startups reinventing human resources.*
Chamorro-Premuzic, T., Winsborough, D., Sherman, R., & Hogan, R. (2016). New talent signals: Shiny new objects or a brave new world? *Industrial and Organizational Psychology, 9*(3), 621–640. doi:10.1017/iop.2016.6
Christensen, C. M. (2016). *The innovator's dilemma.* Harvard Business Review Press.
Emergen Research. (2020). *Assessment services market by product type, by service type, by medium, by sectors, forecasts to 2027* (Report ID: ER_00182).
Heath, C., & Heath, D. (2007). *Made to stick: Why some ideas survive and others die.* Random House.

Hoffman, R., & Yeh, C. (2018). *Blitzscaling: The lightning-fast path to building massively valuable businesses.* Currency/Crown.

Isaak, J., & Hanna, M. J. (2018). User data privacy: Facebook, Cambridge Analytica, and privacy protection. *Computer, 51*(8), 56–59.

Lesser, L. I., Ebbeling, C. B., Goozner, M., Wypij, D., & Ludwig, D. S. (2007). Relationship between funding source and conclusion among nutrition-related scientific articles. *PLoS Medicine, 4*(1), e5. https://doi.org/10.1371/journal.pmed.0040005

Lundh, A., Sismondo, S., Lexchin, J., Busuioc, O. A., & Bero, L. (2012). Industry sponsorship and research outcome. *Cochrane Database of Systematic Reviews, 12,* MR000033. https://doi.org/10.1002/14651858.MR000033.pub2

Marcus, G. (2022). *Deep learning is hitting a wall.* Nautilus.

National Academies of Sciences, Engineering, and Medicine, Division of Behavioral and Social Sciences and Education, & Committee on the Science of Science Communication. (2017). *Communicating science effectively: A research agenda.* National Academies Press.

Nola, R., & Howard S. (2007). *Theories of scientific method: An introduction.* Acumen.

Resnik, D. B., & Elliott, K. C. (2013). Taking financial relationships into account when assessing research. *Accountability in Research, 20*(3), 184–205. https://doi.org/10.1080/08989621.2013.788383

# 32

# Making Progress on Diversity

## The Promise of Inclusive Leadership

*Kathleen K. Lundquist and Robert E. Lewis*

Not everything that is faced can be changed,
but nothing can be changed until it is faced.

—James Baldwin

### Introduction

In a recent article in the *Harvard Business Review* (HBR), Caver and Livers (2020) discuss how little has changed in the 18 years since their original HBR article entitled "Dear White Boss..." (Caver & Livers, 2002), which described the challenges faced by a Black manager in a fictional letter to an anonymous White executive. They describe the current and ongoing frustration of diverse employees about the lack of progress in achieving meaningful change, resulting in a lack of trust in their organization's commitment to diversity and their increasing disengagement.

The need for change in our approach to diversity is apparent. Despite publicly announced representation goals or company-wide unconscious bias training, research has shown the results from such isolated initiatives by organizations to be disappointing. Making meaningful change requires both a clear understanding of where the organization is on the diversity maturity continuum and the development of an integrated diversity strategy tied to the business, its culture, and, most importantly, one that is supported by its leaders.

Caver and Livers conclude that confronting the challenges of workplace diversity, inclusivity, and bias requires leaders to be "unflinchingly honest and personally and professionally courageous."

As leaders, facing your own biases, understanding how you are influencing the system, and understanding the criticality and impact of your actions is crucial if change is going to occur. (Caver & Livers, 2020, pp. 7–8)

This chapter will examine the diversity maturity continuum, the drivers of diversity change, the central role of leaders in creating and sustaining an inclusive organizational culture, and the role leadership assessment can play in realizing the promise of inclusive leadership.

## The Evolution of Diversity Maturity

There is no easy path to diversity, equity and inclusion. If change is too gradual and insubstantial, commitment and trust (especially among the under-represented) can be lost. If progress is too abrupt and substantial, resistance will be increased from those who feel the change will lead to personal loss.
—Lundquist and Rodriguez (in press)

Just as our concepts of diversity, equity, and inclusion (DEI) have evolved over time, organizations progress in their diversity efforts along a continuum from a focus on compliance and risk mitigation to the articulation of a commitment to diversity through an integration of diversity into business strategy and finally to a focus on accountability and outcome measurement. The diversity maturity model shown in Figure 32.1 was developed by Bersin and Enderes (2020) and incorporates the findings from a survey of the DEI practices in more than 800 organizations.

Unfortunately, the largest group of organizations (40%) reported their diversity efforts were still focused on compliance and risk management (Level 1). A narrow focus on fairness, however, fails to leverage the value and possible contribution of diversity to organizational success. Research by McKinsey (2020) shows that gender-diverse companies are 15% more likely to outperform their peers, and ethnically diverse companies are 35% more likely to do the same.

Bersin and Enderes (2020) found that a substantial number of organizations (24%), however, had been able to move beyond compliance to beginning the dialogue with employees about difficult topics. Listening to employees and acting on the results creates the opportunity to build a culture

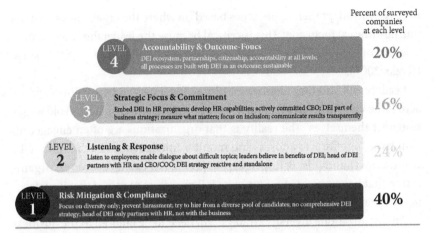

**Figure 32.1.** Diversity Maturity Model
Elevating Equity: The Real Story of Diversity and Inclusion, Josh Bersin and Kathi Enderes | The Josh Bersin Company, 2021

that supports the psychological safety of employees. At Level 2, organizations were also gaining the commitment of senior leadership to the goals of a DEI strategy.

By Level 3, 16% of organizations had taken a more integrated approach, building DEI into their business strategy and embedding DEI into human resources (HR) programs and processes. Leaders at this stage were visible champions of diversity and willing to communicate transparently about the progress made in achieving diversity goals. Typically, achieving this level of maturity will also require upskilling HR professionals to serve as trusted advisors with a seat at the table rather than as enforcers of rules and quotas. Additionally, at this stage organizations are likely to use assessments but not leverage assessment results in a systematic way to foster diversity and inclusion.

Finally, Bersin and Enderes (2020) described the most mature organizations (20%) as having a focus on accountability and measurable outcomes for both internal and external audiences (including customers and vendors) to sustain DEI within the ongoing DNA of the organization. This would likely include the use of assessments not only to foster individual development and make individual decisions but also to build diversity-sensitive succession slates and facilitate inclusion.

Making meaningful change requires a clear understanding of where the organization is on the diversity maturity continuum. Leaders will find it necessary to adapt their approaches based on where the organization is in its journey toward inclusion. This is critical because the leadership roles appropriate to one stage of diversity maturity may not be effective in another stage (Kezar, 2007).

Leaders will also find themselves addressing issues and providing support across the various levels of maturity, as new challenges crop up and old issues resurrect themselves. The reality is that organizations are often engaged in simultaneous efforts to address and monitor initiatives across the entire DEI continuum (Lundquist & Rodriguez, in press). For example, even an organization that has embedded DEI into its HR processes may find that it surfaces new challenges to fairness, which must be addressed.

An organization's diversity strategy will need to be tailored to the business and its culture but should be expected to undergo modification and refinement as the organization progresses along the diversity maturity continuum. Most importantly, the success of a diversity strategy is directly tied to visible support by its leaders.

## The Role of Leaders

The critical role of leaders in the success of diversity efforts was highlighted in a recent study by the National Academy of Human Resources (NAHR) and the Society for Industrial and Organizational Psychology (SIOP) Foundation (2021). Interviews of chief human resources officers (CHROs), chief diversity officers (CDOs), and academic researchers found a consistent theme: The visible support and demonstrated actions of senior leadership were key to driving change.

It is clear that leaders play an increasingly significant role in the success of DEI efforts as the organization develops greater diversity maturity. Early on, it is critical that leaders articulate an authentic vision and commitment to diversity. However, it is not enough for leaders be visible champions of diversity; they must also model behaviors that build an inclusive culture, including displaying trust, openness to differences, empathy, and a willingness to hold others accountable (Tapia & Polonskaia, 2020; Bourke & Titus, 2020).

Bourke and Titus (2020) examined the 360-degree ratings of 400 managers by almost 4,000 raters and found that the most important trait for inclusive leadership is a leader's visible willingness to acknowledge bias in their own behavior and their encouragement of others to be aware of their own preconceived leanings. This echoes the exhortation by Caver and Livers (2020) to be "unflinchingly honest" and "professionally courageous" in building an inclusive culture. When combined with personal humility and empathy toward others, cognizance of bias is an essential first step in building feelings of inclusion.

It is important to note that one size doesn't fit all, especially since it is difficult to create perceptions of "inclusivity" for everyone. As far back as 1999, Thomas and Gabarro noted the greater difficulty of minorities, "even when recognized as outstanding performers with comfortable boss and peer relationships," to be identified for accelerated development in leadership pipelines. This difference persists today. In a recent study by McKinsey (2021), members of the Black community were found to experience unique challenges in their professional development and identification for leadership positions. As a result, a much higher percentage feel that their organizations are less inclusive compared to other groups. Smith et al. (2019) confirmed that interventions aimed at fostering diversity and inclusion may not have the same effect across all groups. They discuss how intersecting identities (e.g., being a member of multiple minority groups, such as being both Black and a female) can hinder the effectiveness of diversity and inclusion interventions such as coaching and mentoring that fail to address their multiple identities.

These results highlight the importance of commitment and attention from the highest levels of the organization for diversity efforts to be effective. They also speak to the importance of increasing the visibility and availability of diverse leaders to bring their voice to the organization's efforts.

## Developing Inclusive Organizations and Leaders

Organizations committed to building an inclusive culture will increasingly need to address the selection and development of inclusive leaders to expand the impact of their efforts and create a sustainable inclusive culture. This requires both a focus on representation at the top of the organization and development of a pipeline of diverse talent to carry out the work of building and embedding the inclusive culture (Caver & Livers, 2021; Lundquist & Rodriguez, in press). Both fronts will be considered in turn.

## Changing Representation Among Senior Leadership

We believe work must begin at the top of the organization to signal change. Focusing first on increasing representation at the top of the organization will send a significant message of commitment. In addition, finding ways to induce leaders to voluntarily engage in acts of inclusive leadership (e.g., mentorship, teaching, personal advocacy through social media channels) will help them learn by doing and may, over time, help them come to see and value their identity as champions of diversity and inclusion. Connecting the role of diversity and inclusion to the company culture and core values will help to underscore the importance of this aspect of their leadership role.

The changed composition of the leadership team coupled with programmatic, organizational interventions will promote deeper and more widespread cultural messaging and behavioral change that will permeate the organization.

The organizations that reach the highest level of diversity maturity take specific, enterprise-focused steps that balance encouraging leaders to engage in actions that foster diversity with holding them accountable for doing so. Dobbin and Kalev (2016) found that taking coercive steps to promote diversity, such as by making training mandatory, tends to result in low diversity maturity, as well as an adverse reaction to diversity efforts. On the other hand, organizations at the highest level of diversity maturity create social structures that hold leaders accountable for diversity outcomes and provide voluntary opportunities for leaders to improve diversity representation and contribute to a culture that values diversity. For instance, organizations that publicize progress against diversity objectives at a granular level tend to drive positive diversity outcomes. Dobbin and Kalev (2016) note the experience of one office in an organization that monitored progress against locally determined diversity goals. "When it became clear that the CEO and other managing partners were closely watching . . . women started getting their share of premier client assignments" (p. 10). In this case, the goal setting was local, but the accountability was both public and managed at the enterprise level. Their research also suggests that voluntary training programs and opportunities to participate in recruiting diverse talent allow leaders to contribute to building a more diverse workforce and, in so doing, foster a stronger culture of diversity. Thus, interventions that balance encouraging leaders to participate in diversity efforts of their own volition with holding leaders publicly accountable for delivering on diversity outcomes appear to build highly mature diversity organizations.

## Expanding the Pipeline of Diverse Talent

The second front in this effort is strengthening and expanding the pipeline of diverse leadership talent. This will require expanding career path options, looking more widely for sources of talent, and accelerating development for the pool of potential qualified candidates (NAHR & SIOP, 2021). In part, this can be accomplished by applying a diversity lens to commonly available talent management data and leveraging technology to lower the cost of high-potential leader assessments to cast a wider net for talent. These actions address a severe constraint highlighted by a recent Gartner survey (Gartner, 2020), which reveals that two-thirds of CHROs feel that a lack of diversity in the talent pipeline is a major contributor to poor management representation. Moreover, a subsequent Gartner analysis (Gartner, 2022) indicates that the career prospects of "underrepresented talent stalls in mid-level and senior-level positions." Thus, actions to both widen career opportunities and identify a larger pool of candidates with leadership potential can strengthen a culture of diversity and inclusion.

Diversity, particularly management representativeness, can be limited when opportunities are provided to a select few based on manager nomination or according to narrow company career paths and job families. For instance, once hired into a functional role (e.g., procurement specialist), one's career opportunities are typically determined by job openings in that pathway. Yet if a functional area is small or has few management roles, then promotions and opportunities to improve the management representation of diverse employees are relatively rare. The number of available slots for leader development may also be constrained by the cost of assessment and development, especially when these efforts are largely driven by in-person assessment centers.

Technology can be leveraged to more quickly and cost-effectively gauge the leadership potential of a much larger pool of candidates (Scott & Lezotte, 2012). Leader assessments that had previously been time- and labor-intensive can now be delivered online, asynchronously, and relatively inexpensively. These include immersive simulations that are among the best predictors of managerial performance (Sackett et al., 2017) and potential (Lewis, 2022).

This development enables organizations to assess a much larger pool of candidates for the same cost and thus increase the chances of finding talent that previously would have been unidentified. When combined with the opportunity for participants to opt in (i.e., self-nomination rather than manager nomination), an online leader assessment may be more likely to result in higher management representativeness of diverse populations. In part, this can result by removing manager bias as a barrier to candidacy, reinforcing the organization's intent with tangible action and opportunity, generating more opportunities for organizations to track metrics focused on diversity progress, and uncovering opportunities to target development that accelerates the organization's ability to staff against future needs.

Another recent development that may expand opportunities for diverse populations is improved clarity regarding the definition and measurement of "leader and manager potential." In the past, discussion of potential commonly led to the question "potential for what?," indicating that organizations used no consistent definition of what it means to have potential (Karaveli & Hall, 2003). As a consequence, most organizations defaulted to using past performance as the measure of "potential" (Church et al., 2015). This likely has limited development and promotion opportunities for diverse employees, who commonly are disadvantaged by performance ratings and lack of access to developmental assignments. Rigorous analysis of the definition of potential, how it can be measured, and what leads to career advancement (Church et al., 2021; Lewis et al., 2021; Lewis, 2022) now allows organizations to assess for the specific characteristics of those who can successfully take on future roles and challenges free of the constraints of past performance.

Finally, the talent pipeline can also be expanded through inventive uses of job analysis data. When designed properly, job analysis data can identify skillsets that are common across job families and reveal job paths that were previously hard to observe. For instance, the example in Figure 32.2 illustrates a cluster analysis of importance ratings on a common set of skills across jobs. Jobs that had previously been considered independent, (e.g., a facilities program manager and HR program manager) were found to have skill demands that often had 80% or more overlap. Our conversations with managers who reviewed these data led them to estimate that the time needed for someone crossing a functional area boundary to learn the function-specific knowledge needed to perform the role was 6 to 8 weeks. Notably, this was less than the talent acquisition organization's time-to-fill average.

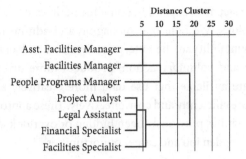

**Figure 32.2.** Cluster Analysis of Importance Ratings on A Common Set of Skills Across Jobs

By leveraging existing data, this organization was able to markedly improve career advancement options and particularly opened opportunities in the functional areas (e.g., facilities) that were populated mainly by underrepresented employee groups.

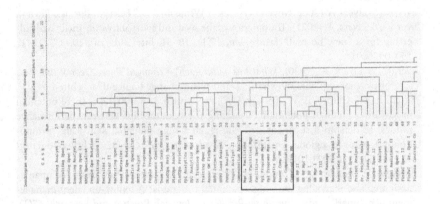

## Summary

We have presented evidence to support several key actions that organizations can take to foster a more inclusive and diverse culture. At an individual level, an organization's top leadership must take a hard and unflinching view of the organization's diversity and inclusion status. Tools such as the diversity maturity model can provide a start to this organizational assessment. Second, executives must publicly and visibly be honest and forthright about their own personal path to diversity awareness and encourage their leaders throughout the organization to do the same.

A second key step is to expand the pipeline of diverse talent via programmatic interventions. We note that managing and administering measurement and accountability at the enterprise level, when balanced with local goal autonomy and voluntary action, produces more diverse workforces. Interventions are available that use data more creatively and that deliver assessments more efficiently and cost-effectively. These approaches can identify talent where it has previously been hidden or overlooked and create career paths that broaden job and career opportunities.

## References

Bersin, J., & Enderes, K. (2020). *Elevating equity: The real story of diversity and inclusion.* https://joshbersin.com/wp-content/uploads/2021/04/202102-DEI-Report_Final_V2.pdf

Bourke, J., & Titus, A. (2020, March 5). The key to inclusive leadership. *Harvard Business Review.* Reprint H05GLB.

Caver, K., & Livers, A. (2002, November). "Dear White Boss...." *Harvard Business Review.*

Caver, K., & Livers, A. (2021). The paradox of the seed and soil: Cultivating inclusive leadership for a "new normal." *Leadership, 17*(1), 18–31. https://doi.org/10.1177/1742715020976201

Caver, K., & Livers, A. (2020). *What has—and hasn't—changed since "Dear White Boss ...."* https://hbr.org/2020/09/what-has-and-hasnt-changed-since-dear-white-boss

Church, A. H., Guidry, B. W., Dickey, J. A., & Scrivani, J. A. (2021). Is there potential in assessing for high-potential? Evaluating the relationships between performance ratings, leadership assessment data, designated high-potential status and promotion outcomes in a global organization. *Leadership Quarterly, 32*(5). https://doi.org/10.1016/j.leaqua.2021.101516

Church, A. H., Rotolo, C. T., Ginther, N. M., & Levine, R. (2015). How are top companies designing and managing their high-potential programs? A follow-up talent management benchmark study. *Consulting Psychology Journal: Practice and Research, 67*(1), 17–47. https://doi.org/10.1037/cpb0000030

Dobbin, F., & Kalev, A. (2016). Why diversity programs fail. *Harvard Business Review, 94*(7), 52–60.

Gartner. (2020). 3 ways to build diversity on the leadership bench. https://www.gartner.com/smarterwithgartner/3-ways-to-build-diversity-on-the-leadership-bench

Gartner. (2022). Leadership diversity stalled? Here are 3 actions to take. https://www.gartner.com/smarterwithgartner/leadership-diversity-stalled-here-are-3-actions-to-take

Karaveli, A., & Hall, D. T. (2003). Growing leaders for turbulent times: Is succession planning up to the challenge? *Organizational Dynamics, 32*(1), 62–79. doi:10.1016/S0090-2616(02)00138-9

Kezar, A. (2007). Tools for a time and place: Phased leadership strategies to institutionalize a diversity agenda. *Review of Higher Education, 30*(4), 413–439.

Lewis, R. E. (2022). *Characteristics of executives who actualize their potential* [Paper presentation]. Society for Industrial/Organizational Psychology 37th annual conference, Seattle, WA.

Lewis, R. E., Happich, K., & Guidry, B. (2021). Developing organizational and individual excellence through assessment centers. In W. Shepard, K. Yusko, H. W. Goldstein, E. C. Larson, A. Valentine, S. Hartog, K. D. McNeal, J. Fernandez, & E. Braverman (Chairs), *Assessment-based leadership development programs: The state of the art (and science)* [Symposium presentation]. Society for Industrial/Organizational Psychology 36th annual conference.

Lundquist, K. K., & Rodriguez, D. A. (in press). Diversity and the journey to inclusion. In R. Silzer, J. Scott, & W. Borman (Eds.), *Handbook of practice in I-O psychology*. Society for Industrial and Organizational Psychology.

McKinsey. (2020, May). *Diversity wins: How inclusion matters*. https://www.mckinsey.com/~/media/mckinsey/featured%20insights/diversity%20and%20inclusion/diversity%20wins%20how%20inclusion%20matters/diversity-wins-how-inclusion-matters-vf.pdf

McKinsey. (2021). *Race in the workplace: The Black experience in the U.S private sector*. https://www.mckinsey.com/featured-insights/diversity-and-inclusion/race-in-the-workplace-the-black-experience-in-the-us-private-sector

National Academy of Human Resources & Society for Industrial & Organizational Psychology Foundation. (2021). *Diversity, equity & inclusion: Perspectives from chief human resources officers and academic researchers*.

Sackett, P. R., Shewach, O. R., & Keiser, H. N. (2017). Assessment centers versus cognitive ability tests: Challenging the conventional wisdom on criterion-related validity. *Journal of Applied Psychology, 102*(10), 1435–1447.

Scott, J. C., & Lezotte, D. V. (2012). Web-based assessments. In N. Schmitt (Ed.), *The Oxford handbook of personnel assessment and selection* (pp. 485–513). Oxford University Press. https://doi.org/10.1093/oxfordhb/9780199732579.013.0021

Smith, A. N., Watkins, M. B., Ladge, J. J., & Carlton, P. (2019). Making the invisible visible: Paradoxical effect of intersectional invisibility on the career experiences of executive black women. *Academy of Management Journal, 62*(6), 1705–1734. https://doi.org/10.5465/amj.2017.1513

Tapia, A., & Polonskaia, A. (2020). *The 5 disciplines of inclusive leaders: Unleashing the power of all of us*. Berrett-Koehler Publishers.

Thomas, D. A., & Gabarro, J. J. (1999). *Breaking through: The making of minority executives in corporate America*. Harvard Business School Press.

# 33
# Themes and Directions

*Douglas H. Reynolds, Tracy M. Kantrowitz, and John C. Scott*

In the introductory chapter we noted that the roots of this book date back to the Society for Industrial and Organizational Psychology's (SIOP's) Leading Edge conference in 2019—an event that was organized to summarize the current state of assessment science as it was implemented in organizations at the time. Although the focus of the event was not intended to emphasize the advancement of technology, the issue was a clear theme, as it is in this book as well. Our intent when organizing the conference was to capture the latest thinking related to assessment applications across a wide range of perspectives, from what's new in the underlying science, to the latest in selection and development applications, to the regulatory frameworks that struggle to keep pace with the latest wave of innovation. The resulting event drew one of the largest audiences to ever attend a Leading Edge conference. We asked presenters to update their work in 2021 for inclusion in this volume, and now we sit here in the second half of 2022 with the task of summarizing the advancing progress reflected in the resulting chapters. The dominant feature across the work is the speed with which we are adopting new technologies. We are clearly working in a time of quick transition, and it's difficult to separate this progress from the key driver of technology growth.

Writing over 10 years ago, Adler (2011) summarized a similar collection of work by noting the need to address some fundamental questions when technology mediates the delivery of assessment in the workplace—questions such as the equivalence of scores when compared to "paper and pencil" measures, the implications of unproctored administration, and the relevance of prior norms to these new measures. It would be difficult to argue that all of these questions have been fully addressed, but it is interesting to note how infrequently they were raised in the work described on these pages. Indeed, as you review the work reflected here, one gets a sense of a page in our history having been turned, and a deeper exploration of what's possible now, the implications of this progress, and perhaps the frustration of having moved ahead without all of the fundamental questions that Adler posed having been addressed to our satisfaction.

As we consider the commonalities across the preceding chapters, this sense that things may be different and some new ideas are now viable pervades the discussion, and this attitude, in turn, sparks new opportunities and implications. In this chapter we explore seven themes about these directions:

1. The use of advanced technology as a component of assessment is entering the mainstream.
2. New horizons are opening for how and what we measure.
3. Uncertainties and risks associated with the use of these new tools are elevating.
4. The evaluation of assessment quality is always challenging and getting harder.
5. Rapid advancement in the assessment and technology fields is motivating changes in laws and regulations.
6. Demographic considerations are paramount.
7. The purposes and applications for assessment are expanding, and the context for the use of assessment is becoming broader.

Let's examine each of these themes in more detail.

## Advanced Technology Is Becoming Mainstream

Across these chapters we see evidence that the field of workplace assessment has moved from cautious experimentation to operational implementation to serve a variety of organizational needs. Tsacoumis describes how rich-media simulations are being put to use to amplify realism when assessments are used in high-stakes decision-making, Norris-Watts and colleagues explore the benefits of gamification for engaging candidates, Mondragon details the rapid growth of artificial intelligence (AI)-supported video interviewing, and van Katwyk summarizes the value of a multiyear global application of virtual assessment centers for corporate leadership succession; these examples are all in practice today and we expect the adoption rate for new forms of technically advanced assessments to only increase.

Despite the ever-quickening rate of adoption and implementation of new assessment approaches, we also hear the reservations expressed by the chapter authors. Much is still unknown, and the inclusion of new technology may cause otherwise well-designed assessments to operate differently than many of our traditional assessment approaches. After all, industrial and organizational psychologists, as most of our authors professionally identify, are raised to appreciate the value of assessment designs with a strong job analysis foundation, clear construct definition, and validation evidence for the environments where they are deployed. A sense of caution is warranted when we operate in conditions where these essentials are not firmly in place.

But market forces pressure the field toward innovation, as Lovric summarizes in his review of the influence that innovation funding strategies can have on the offerings that emerge from technology startups. Technical advancement is fueled in part by venture funding in search of financial return, and it's often the technology-centric providers that push the boundaries of accepted practice from an assessment perspective. When buyers and users are less attentive to the limitations, they pressure all providers to respond to the latest trends. As practitioners, if we don't advance into this uncomfortable space, we are left behind; so, we advance, but the discomfort remains.

Many examples shared in the preceding chapters incorporate new technologies that are effectively implemented and appropriately managed with strong competent professional oversight. Although some of these applications might be more at home in organizations with higher levels of risk tolerance, the use of new approaches may be opening new doors to how and what we measure, as we note in the next theme. Further, as Ryan and colleagues observe in the second chapter, when job candidates are exposed to tools incorporating advanced technology such as AI, they generally react favorably. Perhaps some degree of market pressure forcing these new applications into practice is a healthy pressure for the field. When left unchecked, assessment professionals will likely err on the side of caution. On the other hand, unanswered questions leave much room for well-justified prudence, as we will also highlight in some of the subsequent themes.

## New Horizons Are Opening for How and What We Measure

For many years, mostly prior to about 2010, it would be common to hear a conference discussant bemoan the pace of innovation in psychological assessment. These comments would take a familiar form: "Yes, the innovations at issue in the session were valuable, and the diligence and insight provided by the other participants on the dais were commendable, but when you look at the big picture, are we really attacking the kinds of problems that could lead to revolutionary advancement? Or are we just polishing the familiar methodologies handed down from our professional forebearers?" You don't hear these comments as often now, and you don't see them reflected in this book either. Certainly there is still a normative bias in practice toward multiple-choice and Likert-type assessment formats, but the options are quickly expanding.

Progress in software technology, data science, and other fields are providing new options for measurement that could shift how we approach assessment in some fundamental ways. Less clear, but also a possibility, is whether our construct domains might also expand because we have new ways to look for them.

Let's consider separately the two questions implicated by this theme; first, do technology advancements allow us to measure our constructs in different ways? There are many examples that support this proposition.

Liu describes the evolution of natural language processing (NLP) methods and a variety of applications for assessment as well as what we are learning about how various inputs may be more or less amenable to analysis via these techniques. Tonidandel and Albritton extend NLP into leadership assessment applications, opening the door to the use of natural behavior (the communications between leader and follower) to direct analysis, interpretation, and feedback. Paese and Yankov extend this same line of reasoning further into the future when envisioning proactive coaching and guidance tools embedded in wearable technology and everyday productivity tools. This evolutionary path seems logical as it decreases the time between measurement and feedback, and thereby improves the impact by allowing the subject to adjust in real time. The elements for these types of applications already exist, and we suspect this sort of innovation won't be too far away.

Shifting focus from technologies to constructs, Meade and Priest describe a variety of innovations in the assessment of personality (e.g., forced-choice assessment, adaptive personality measurement, and the use of ideal-point measurement models) and highlight a set of techniques that use response time as an index of trait strength and faking. Each of these advancements has the potential to improve the accuracy and utility of personality measurement.

Similarly, Scherbaum and colleagues extend the conversation toward advancements in how we conceptualize and assess cognitive ability and observe that the challenges associated with group differences may be better addressed when trait constellations are considered together.

The second aspect of this theme is less dominant. Are we measuring different things? Some authors allude to this possibility; Scherbaum et al., for example, discuss the use of eye tracking as an index of attention and cognitive load. Adler and Bhatia highlight the potential to bring far greater depth into simulation-based assessments by including speech analysis scores derived from video-captured behavior during an assessment—behavior that would not be detectable in traditional formats. The chapter by Cox et al. is the most striking example of the broadening of our construct domain of interest. These authors remind us that human performance in some contexts has life-and-death consequences and these risks justify investment in a broad range of harder-to-measure constructs if the work results in incremental improvements in our understanding and predictions. By integrating neurobiological and psychological measures, a new set of possibilities for measurement is opened. Just as Paese and Yankov hypothesized, as tools that capture physiological data become more commonplace, the connection to them can bring new insights and applications, such as the use of wearables to alert leaders to consider alternative courses of action when they show signs of stress.

Do these new approaches lead us to new insights about the constructs we target? Is there evidence that new technologies might open avenues into insights about the nature of human behavior? There are two reasons to support this notion. First, the range of variables discussed in this volume is evidence that the scope of investigation is certainly expanding. Combinations of well-measured attributes are likely to improve the depth of our understanding. The current availability of inexpensive wearable health trackers points to the viability of incorporating physiological metrics with psychological measures to create a more complete view of human performance. Second, and maybe even more promising, is the fact that many advancements focus on understanding natural behavior—behavior occurring in situ, captured and interpreted while the subjects operate in their work environments. For example, applications of NLP imposed on unstructured text allow for a window into these actions. In these applications, the need to standardize stimuli as a core assumption of assessment is traded for standardizing the frame we place upon live behavior to index constructs of interest. Eliminating the demands that push subjects toward maximal versus typical behavior may give us new areas of insight.

## Uncertainty and Risk Related to New Technology Are Elevating in Both Familiar and Unfamiliar Ways

Despite the potential for expanding how and what we measure, these gains come at the price of new risks and complexities. Several authors are appropriately cautious about the benefits of some of these newer technologies. Sherman and Hogan describe the substantial benefit of using machine learning to improve prediction within job families by harnessing insights across a huge and multifaced criterion-related validity database, but at the same time they note the familiar challenge of eliminating the noise produced by spurious correlates and the amplification of relationships driven by implicit bias encoded in data, such as stereotype bias in performance ratings used as criteria.

While newer measurement approaches can add insight and predictive power, the potential to confuse insight with blind predictive efficiency and uncritical pragmatism is a common fault. Schmitt sums up the challenge concisely when he notes that big data sets and associated analytics provide many opportunities to expand the content and sophistication of our assessments. But Schmitt also provides an important caveat: "Perhaps the most important of these reservations is that we do not lose site of the constructs we intend to measure. If we do not know what we are doing or how, advances are likely to be ephemeral."

As we experienced in the earlier days of our history as a field, the use of some of the new analytical models described in this book may create a logical gap between empirical results and observed reality when examining the relationship between recommended prediction models and the nature of work they are designed to reflect. Tippins makes this point nicely when she notes that the connection between assessments and jobs may be superficial when new forms of measurement are being used. This connection is fundamental given the legal requirement (in the United States at least) that the use of any assessment have a basis in job relevance. Further complicating the situation is the fact that the methods for evaluating job relevance are less obvious when using new technologies than they were in the past. For example, algorithms that change as they are fed new data would require shifting the justification for their use. In this case, not only is the construct being measured harder to pin down, but also so is the logical basis for using it when you do.

Beyond this familiar problem, new challenges and risks are also emerging. Landers, for example, discusses the challenges between the essential relationship between industrial-organizational psychologists and technologists. Professionals in these specialties don't make the same assumptions or speak the same language, and if we don't find ways to bridge these gaps, we may find ourselves less relevant as tech-driven systems dominate the landscape. Landers argues for creating shared understanding of our respective philosophies, and for psychologists, this means adopting alternative mindsets, such as algorithmic thinking, systems thinking, and design thinking. These mindsets are not foreign to our field, but we are well served by the reminder to actively adopt them. Landers notes another subtle risk in the fact that most assessment designers follow a waterfall model of project planning (e.g., high structure with clear steps), whereas many of our technical partners have shifted to more agile models (e.g., collaborative, iterative, and adaptive). These differences in approach and philosophy can lead to communication challenges and risks to the influence needed to steer appropriate uses of assessment, as well as to the timelines and budgets of the projects where these capabilities are expected to blend.

Other authors highlight the risk associated with investments in expensive innovations that may be initially embraced by the marketplace but ultimately rejected by those to whom they are expected to appeal. The gamification of hiring and other talent management systems may be riding this curve of faddish enthusiasm. Norris-Watts et al. elaborate this risk when they note the need to match investment with a clear sense of purpose for gamified assessment features. If employers assume candidates will appreciate a sense of fun during the process but candidates actually place a higher value on perceptions of fairness, the assessment process is unlikely to be sustainable. In this scenario, the risks associated with assessment cost, design complexity, generalizability across participants, and candidate appeal are all elevated, so the payoff should be large to justify the gamble. These authors present a clear-eyed analysis of the conditions where the tradeoff might be worth it, and where it may not be.

We are reminded again of Lovric's chapter where he notes that, if left unchecked, the pressure from investment capital to advance differentiating innovations may cause undesirable pressure points that favor short-term surface appeal over long-term effectiveness.

## The Evaluation of Assessment Quality Is Always Challenging and Getting Harder

A common complaint in our field is that new technologies are rarely researched to the degree that practitioners would desire when they are on the hook to implement them (both Adler, 2011, and Guion, 2010, also cite these concerns). It's not an unreasonable fear, but the circumstances for conducting well-designed validation research have not gotten easier as the popularity of these automated people systems has grown. Even as we note Bob Guion's (2010) prescription that we consider the broader concept of "evaluation" in favor of "validation," we are still left wanting more to justify the adequacy of our new tools.

As new technologies have become infused in workplace assessments, these challenges have multiplied. As Ryan et al. note in Chapter 2, machine learning approaches to assessment require evaluation of construct validity and criterion-related validity just as any form of assessment does, but this process is complicated by heightened challenges associated with construct-irrelevant variance and the potential for dynamic updating of models that may shift covariate patterns over time. Tippins also discusses the fact that the lack of clarity on what is being measured confounds our efforts to adequately justify the acceptable use of new measures.

To be clear, there are notable exceptions to these concerns. For example, Norris-Watts et al. describe validation work focused on the implementation of gamified assessments and found evidence that convergent validities between gamified assessments and traditional cognitive and personality tests have been established. The levels of adverse impact appear smaller, and the user experience improved, providing evidence for this approach to improve cognitive and personality measurement when implemented appropriately. Similarly, Mondragon indicates that research on AI-scored video interviewing also provides support for its validity, low subgroup differences, and positive candidate reactions.

Assessment professionals aren't the only ones who need to feel more comfortable with these advancements. Seaton and Church detail the challenges associated with educating executives on how to best guide their decisions related to new assessment approaches. This is an area where confusion and skepticism surrounding assessments are often fueled by misinformation, myths, and prior negative experiences. These authors provide useful guidance on how to inform stakeholders to prepare them for better use, and they advocate a broad-based approach reflective of Guion's (2010) advice to think about assessment evaluation expansively: Be resourceful, define the right narrative, and build processes to collect a range of operational data that help you build understanding. Return on investment information, user reactions, and case studies are all useful in this regard.

The difficulties associated with well-planned evaluation will always be with us; new technologies require us to redouble these efforts and wrestle with the challenges of clear construct definition and veridical linkages to work requirements and context. Several authors in this volume note these challenges, but the solutions seem still just out of reach as the pace of technical innovation is faster than the development of audit and evaluation techniques that will help us justify their use. As we will note in the next theme, the regulatory environment may encourage new forms of evaluation to fill the void if measurement experts don't figure it out first. "AI audits" are one such example where an evaluative technique is being written into the legal framework before standards and processes for the approach have been determined.

## Rapid Advancement in the Assessment and Technology Fields Is Motivating Changes in Laws and Regulations

The trends noted above are felt outside of the field of assessment too. Concerns that decision-making about people is increasingly under the control of self-learning software are leading to counter-pressures on several fronts. Discussions related to how to interpret professional standards in light of these advancements are on the rise as well.

Willner et al. review the applicability of the substantial existing legal foundation for evaluating any assessment used in workplace decision-making, including newer technologies that didn't exist when the regulations were written; despite the applicability of existing regulations, many jurisdictions are advancing new laws that tie explicitly to new forms of assessment and regulate them more tightly, as these authors summarize in their chapter.

The regulatory environment has indeed been activated: Federal, state, and local rules build upon the existing legal frameworks and should help to support carefully implemented new technologies, but many new rules go a step further in that they describe specific practices to prohibit under some conditions. For example, video interviewing, facial recognition, and the use of algorithmic scoring are targeted specifically. These rules underscore the risk of regulatory overreaction if operational challenges are not effectively managed or if the justification for the use of these procedures is not well established.

As Willner and his coauthors describe, there are two obligations that are commonly incorporated into these new rules: notice to users regarding the nature of the automated decision-making process being used, and audits for bias. Each of these needs further definition to inform implementation. Given the number of new regulations that reference these concepts, there are bound to be different interpretations of the processes involved.

Bias audits, for example, could take many forms. Industrial-organizational psychologists and measurement professionals should take an active role in this process to ensure that bias audits reflect current standards and processes for examining group differences and that various means of ensuring assessments are aligned with appropriate business necessity and job relevance criteria. Alternatively, the requirements and standards for what constitutes a bias audit will be defined by those who see opportunity in offering audit services, and these approaches could take myriad operational definitions, leading to inconsistent practice and an erosion of professional standards. We provide an example of a positive development on this issue in our concluding section of this chapter.

Similar challenges arise over concerns related to privacy and the handling of personal data. Here also new rules are being proposed across the United States to match the stronger privacy orientation present in other countries. Andresen review the regulations, data types, and compliance strategies that assessment providers must consider when operating with personal data, particularly when data processing results in the movement of data across borders. Various risk mitigation steps to avoid liability and loss are described such as enhanced security measures (e.g., encryption, backup, and disaster recovery practices), the use of contract terms that detail exact processing steps, limitations on who has access to regulated data and what data are shared, and the added protection of cyber liability insurance.

As the legal landscape evolves on each of these fronts, assessment practitioners are often left to figure out how to best comply when various rules are in conflict. This misalignment and fluidity create ambiguity for both practitioners and organizations, a point that Andresen and Lewis and Willner et al. make in their chapters. To respond, assessment professionals will need to interpret professional standards and guidelines within the context of evolving applications, as Tippins has done in her chapter. Further, as Sackett notes, our work will always be viewed through the lenses of diverse value sets, and those differences will continue to create tension in how our applications are received by others. Assessment professionals who recognize these value differences should be able to navigate their implementations more effectively.

Innovations in assessment need to be accompanied by policy, professional, and legal guidelines that support the use of these advancements. Industries that have the potential to create harm to the public risk having rules imposed by legislative bodies if they don't self-regulate. Revisions to professional standards or other forms of guidance will likely be needed to keep pace with the introduction of new approaches to decision-making, and effective and practical standards for practice will require close partnership and collaboration across the field and with regulatory bodies.

## Demographic Considerations Are Paramount

Demographic differences in assessment outcomes, and the practical implications of these differences, continue to challenge the field. Many authors discuss the need to evaluate differences and strive to mitigate them as has been the standard practice for many decades. Now, however, the options available for reducing adverse impact have expanded. Scherbaum and colleagues approach the issue broadly, starting with enhancing our understanding of cognitive ability constructs and shifting assessment designs to better understand and reduce the impact of group differences. Mondragon also reviews approaches that can be used such as algorithms that are developed to penalize the model for adding to group differences. And Norris-Watts and coauthors note that game-based assessments have the potential to demonstrate lower levels of adverse impact than traditional measures. Sackett also brings many of these concepts together in his summary of the work he and his colleagues have advanced to use Pareto-optimal combinations to examine the tradeoffs between validity and group differences in a manner that can guide more precise balancing of these outcomes. Each of these approaches holds promise for expanding the range of options available for managing and balancing average score differences between groups of assessment constituents.

There is also room for vigilance as advanced measurement techniques become more widely used. As Mondragon intimates, the complexity of AI-driven assessments with multisource big data sets may cause some algorithms to casually backslide into within-group norming by including demographic correlates in their models. Assessment designers will need to watch for this given the illegal status of such procedures under the Civil Rights Act of 1992.

Mitigation of differences may be an important step on the road toward a fair and low-risk selection process, but it's not the same thing as promoting workplace diversity. Several authors push into this point and show proactive techniques for expanding diversity. Vaughn and Cubrich note the potential for the targeted use of social media to increase the diversity mix in an organization's recruitment process. Similarly, Gutierrez and Grelle highlight the fact that assessments that are designed to be mobile-first can reach much deeper into demographic groups that use their phones as their primary means to connect to the internet. Papinchock et al. provide a series of techniques to be applied to level the playing field for neurodiverse assessment participants and candidates with disabilities that could affect assessment performance. Their suggestions point to the need to manage the assessment design process from the earliest stages to ensure fairness to the full range of a candidate population.

Lundquist and Lewis widen the aperture on this topic even further as they review the role of organizational culture and diversity across the leadership ranks as key indicators of the shift from a risk mitigation stance toward the sustainment of an organizational ecosystem that monitors and advances its diversity, equity, and inclusion outcomes as a primary measure of organizational effectiveness. Their chapter demonstrates that gains in representation can be achieved by using the varieties of data described in this book to identify new career paths and job opportunities and matching these to those with the right skill profiles. The pool of potential successors to senior roles can also be expanded by deploying technological advances in leader assessment to ensure these higher ranks reflect the gains made at lower rungs in the organization.

## The Purposes and Applications for Assessment Are Expanding, and the Context for the Use of Assessment Is Becoming Broader

Assessment for the purpose of employee selection has tended to dominate discussions regarding best practices in practical application. There are many chapters in this book that focus on selection, but there is also a broad range of other applications as well. As advanced assessment technology becomes more ubiquitous, the spread may expand the value that assessment can provide in the workplace.

Gibby and Ducey describe multiple opportunities for the improvement of management across the stages of a career span in an organization. They summarize opportunities to apply AI-driven algorithms to improve processes ranging from initial applicant pool development and screening to more futuristic purposes such as the management of retirement replacement planning using dynamic matching algorithms to optimize the blend of people, skills, and emerging jobs. The role of assessment in these situations is far broader than familiar selection scenarios.

Applications of assessment to assist in developing people, and developing leaders in particular, are also familiar to most assessment practitioners. Many authors in this volume add new dimensions to this purpose. Stawiski and McCauley, for example, review the mechanisms by which assessment can accelerate and improve the focus of development programs as they recognize that inclusion of an assessment component alone does not ensure development will happen. Their three critical levers for creating openness to development include increased self-awareness, understanding how you present yourself to others, and ultimately understanding how your impact is perceived. These three roles for assessment provide a triangulation of inputs that create demonstrable change in their participants.

Collins and David raise a number of important points about the growth of the assessment-for-development marketplace as they reflect on these developmental applications. They add an important dimension of organizational context as a critical variable in the mix when understanding the right targets for development and how these can shift quickly over time.

The case applications described across several chapters represent some of the more elaborate and wide-reaching applications of assessment in practice. Dreyer and coauthors describe the journey at Prudential from selection applications of assessment into a bigger development program. Their program pairs assessment insight with a business simulation that allows participants to push boundaries and try different approaches in a safe context and then transfer these skills with a coach back into the business. As the authors note, technology allows this in-depth program to scale in ways that were not possible in the past and allows access to a broader range of participants.

Writing from Saudi Arabia about a locally run program with global reach, van Katwyk provides an excellent example of how assessment programs of broad scale are originating outside of the United States, where many would have started in the past. The 20-year history of this program, and the investment that has been made to ensure its operation as it moved to a virtual context, is evidence of the value it provides back into the business. In a similar vein, Eyring details the character of the assessment market in Southeast Asia, where local investment in AI technology is propelling some new assessment applications. Eyring raises an interesting challenge in the Asian context: The regulatory constraints that may inhibit some of the more problematic practices in some markets are less of a factor in his markets. While this creates opportunity to refine both the technologies and the standards of practice, it also presents clear challenges to the field if ethical and professional standards are violated in the process. Eyring highlights these tensions from the front lines in this "wild east" context.

Sinar expands the discussion by emphasizing an even broader set of criteria for consideration for our developmental applications: Health, well-being, and life satisfaction are all recognized as part of what assessment-equipped coaches are helping leaders achieve. Here, Sinar takes us down an untraveled path in most discussions of assessment as he describes new roles that are emerging in the coaching process (e.g., peers) that may consume assessment information very differently and have different needs than traditional assessment consumers might. The programmatic management of learning cohorts that are assembled based on similar developmental needs is also new and an interesting area for more research. What are the best practices in the operation of these groups so that information is used appropriately to accelerate human performance? We are starting to get a sense for them across the programs that are described in this volume.

## Concluding Thoughts

We opened this chapter with a reference to the speed of technology adoption being a driver of rapid change, and several of our authors make similar assertions. We share the themes we observed across the chapters as a way of understanding the characteristics and direction of the evolution. Technology growth is not the only engine for these patterns, however. The chapters in this book were prepared during a global pandemic, a period of massive labor market shifts, heightened racial tensions, and levels of inflationary pressure that have not been seen in many of our authors' professional career spans. These environmental currents also influence how organizations manage their people and open opportunities (and impose constraints) in how assessment practice is applied. We would be remiss for not noting this context for future readers as they reflect on whether these trends have persisted.

Since these chapters were written, other works have emerged that extend the discussion on these topics in important ways. For example, Tippins et al. (2021) prepared an in-depth summary of the challenges associated with AI-based selection tools and the steps that should be taken to map professional practice principles into the way we implement these tools. Landers and Behrend (2022) stake out important territory as they frame what a bias audit should entail. Their work takes an interdisciplinary approach to the definition of 12 components that should be considered when conducting an audit of AI-based decision-making processes. These steps could greatly reduce the concern that bias audits would lack consistency if heeded by regulatory bodies that require the process. On other fronts, SIOP has engaged the Equal Employment Opportunity Commission in a discussion regarding how they might consider changes in their processes and guidelines in light of rapidly advancing assessment approaches (Dunleavy et al., 2022).

These efforts are a salient reminder that there are many cases of misuse of the assessment technology and we as a profession are increasingly called upon as gatekeepers (e.g., to define and conduct AI audits). There will undoubtedly come a point where mainstream use of emerging tools is appropriate and we will need to be at the forefront of infusing this technological revolution with sound measurement practices. At the same time, we must also acknowledge the point Sackett emphasized, that our work will always be viewed through different value perspectives, and well-implemented assessment will still produce tensions we must help to manage.

Our optimistic view is that the rapidly shifting landscape of new technologies, diverse applications, and conflicting regulations do not discourage advancement in all of these fronts. We agree with Tippins's apt observation that the complexity and ambiguity in our professional environment place more burden on the knowledgeable practitioner to use sound judgment when engaging with these frontiers of application. We hope this volume provides some basis for guiding these judgments.

# References

Adler, S. (2011). Concluding comments: Open questions. In N. T. Tippins & S. Adler (Eds.), *Technology-enhanced assessment of talent* (pp. 418–436). Jossey-Bass.

Dunleavy, E., Kantrowitz, T., McPhail, S. M., Oswald, F., Ryan, A. M., & Tippins, N. (2022). AI-based assessment and the Uniform Guidelines on Employee Selection Procedures [Panel discussion]. Annual conference of the Society of Industrial and Organizational Psychology, Boston, MA.

Guion, R. M. (2010). Employee selection: Musings about its past, present, and future. In J. L. Farr & N. T. Tippins (Eds.), *Handbook of employee selection* (pp. 943–957). Routledge.

Landers, R. N., & Behrend, T. S. (2023). Auditing the AI auditors: A framework for evaluating fairness and bias in high stakes AI predictive models. *American Psychologist, 78*, 36–49. https://doi.org/10.1037/amp0000972

Tippins, N. T., Oswald, F. L., & McPhail, S. M. (2021). Scientific, legal, and ethical concerns about AI-based personnel selection tools: A call to action. *Personnel Assessment and Decisions, 7*, 1–22.

# Index

*For the benefit of digital users, indexed terms that span two pages (e.g., 52–53) may, on occasion, appear on only one of those pages*

Tables and figures are indicated by *t* and *f* following the page number

Accenture Nth Floor, 339
accommodations (for disabilities)
　American with Disabilities Act on, 220, 231–32, 270, 273–74
　in gamified assessments, 412–14
　in technology-enabled simulations, 193
accountability, 321–22
Ackerman, P. L., 52–53, 57
ACM (Association of Computing Machinery), 70
active machine learning (ML), 163
ADA. *See* Americans with Disabilities Act
adaptive personality assessments, 35–36
ADEA. *See* Age Discrimination in Employment Act of 1967
Adler, Seymour, 6–7, 526–27, 530
administrative user accounts, 241
*Advancing the Edge: Assessment for the 2020s* (SIOP consortium), 4
adverse impact, 255–58, 268–70, 275
affordances, 214–15
age, 195–96
Age Discrimination in Employment Act of 1967 (ADEA), 268, 269, 270
agile development, 211–13
Agile Manifesto, 211–12
agility, 331
Agrawal, A., 17–18, 24
AI. *See* artificial intelligence
AIG (automatic item generation), 71–72
Air Carrier Access Act, 260
Air Force, U.S., 385
AIVIA. *See* Artificial Intelligence Video Interview Act
Albritton, Betsy H., 6–7, 529
Alexa, 196

algorithm aversion, 21–22
algorithmic bias, 163–64
Algorithmic Justice and Online Platform Transparency Act of 2021, 270–71
algorithmic scoring, 186, 534–35
algorithmic thinking, 209–10, 532
Allport, G. W., 31
alpha-amylase, 389–90
alpha band power, 387
alpha-beta pruning, 86
Alpha Go, 66–67, 86
Alpha Zero, 86
AltspaceVR, 339
Amazon, 89–90, 196, 483
Amazon Transcribe, 72
American Psychological Association (APA), 17, 18, 260–61, 499–500
Americans with Disabilities Act (ADA), 250, 261, 268, 269, 270, 273–75, 413
　accommodations under, 220, 231–32, 270, 273–74
　disability under, 250–51
　on medical examinations, 251–53, 274–75
　personality assessments and, 253–57, 274–75
　a primer on, 250–53
Andresen, Katheryn A., 7, 535–36
ANNs. *See* artificial neural networks
anthropomorphism, 21
Antonakis, J., 158–60
Aon, 445
APA. *See* American Psychological Association
applicant tracking system (ATS), 403–4
APTMetrics, 7, 9

544   INDEX

Aramco, 8
Arkansas, 276
Army, U.S., 84, 385
Arthur, W., Jr., 177–78, 197–98
artificial intelligence (AI), 3–4, 5, 6–7, 13, 13n.1, 111–25, 189–90, 338–39, 349–60, 468
   additional research needs in, 123
   adverse impact of, 119–20
   in Asia, 433, 444–45, 539
   in automated video interview scoring, 113–21, 533
   best practices in creating assessments based on, 112–13
   bias elimination and (myth), 483–84
   data privacy and, 248, 356–57
   disabilities and, 273–75, 413–14
   leadership development and, 306
   legal issues and, 267–68, 269, 270–73
   leveraging across the career journey, 352–60, 352*f*
   mobility and retention and, 358–59
   natural language processing positioning respective to, 149–50, 150*f*
   onboarding and growth and, 357–58
   origin of concept, 350
   people-opportunity ecosystem, 359–60
   personality assessment and, 86–93
   promise of assessments based on, 111–12
   the reality of, 87–89
   to screen applicants, 350–51
   the ugly reality of, 89–90
   venture capital and, 506
artificial intelligence (AI) audits, 534
Artificial Intelligence Video Interview Act (AIVIA), 78, 271, 356–57, 476–77
artificial neural networks (ANNs), 149–50, 152–53
Asia, 8, 433–49, 539
   capabilities that drive company growth, 436–38
   closing of practice gaps in, 435
   high potential selection assessment practices in, 434–35, 435*f*
   history of assessment in, 433–34
   leadership development in, 436, 437–38
   leader strategies assessed in, 440–43
   misuse of assessments in, 435–36
   technology in, 444–48
ASR. *See* automatic speech recognition
assessed potential, 494–95
assessment advancements, 97–106
   big data, 103–5
   cognitive ability measures, 105
   data analytic, 97–100
   legal issues and, 534–36
   personality conceptualization, 102–5
   personality measurement (*see under* personality assessments)
assessment centers, 202, 470
   in Asia, 434–35, 445–46
   avoiding bias on, 482–83
   for leadership assessment, 153, 160–61, 165
   Saudi Aramco and, 452–53, 454, 456–57, 463
assessment context, 537–39
assessment evaluation, 533–34
assessment myths and misinformation, 481–90
   bias/discrimination in assessments, 482–83
   definitive answers provided by assessments, 489–90
   easily gamed/do not predict as well as judgment, 488–89
   gamification makes test takers like assessments, 485–88
   technology and big data eliminate bias, 483–84
   test takers dislike assessments, 484–85
assessment progress propositions, 467–77
   differing views on tradeoffs among desirable outcomes, 468–70
   exciting times for the assessment field, 477
   extracting more information from candidate data, 470–71
   monitoring public reaction to black-box approaches, 476–77
   more constructed response formats/less multiple choice, 471–72
   tension about the need for construct understanding, 474–76
   unchanging job performance determinants, 468

use of and improvements in predictor construct measures, 472–73
vigilance required in person-situation interactions, 474
assessment-rich leadership development programs, 312–25
  case example (*see* Leading for Organizational Impact)
  challenge and support in, 319–20
  design elements to maximize effectiveness, 319–22
  future directions, 324–25
  goal setting and development planning in, 321
  leader factors that maximize effectiveness, 322–23
  organizational factors that maximize effectiveness, 323–24
  postprogram support and accountability, 321–22
  in practice, 313–15
  psychological safety and trust in, 320
  triangulating and integrating insights, 320
Association for Psychological Science, 499–500
Association of Computing Machinery (ACM), 70
ASTB (Aviation Selection Test Battery), 379
asynchronous automated video interviews (AVIs), 111–25. *See also* automated video interviews
Atkins, S. M., 406–7
ATS. *See* applicant tracking system
auditory mismatch negativity, 383
Auer, E. M., 16
augmented reality assessments, 414
autism, 256, 413
automated video interviews (AVIs), 111–25, 527
  AI/ML scoring of, 113–21, 533
  applicant reactions to, 120
  construct validity of, 14–15, 115, 117–18
  criterion-related validity of, 15, 16, 17–18, 118, 121
  explainability/acceptability of, 20–21, 23*t*

future directions, 123–25
predictor and outcome data, 115–16
with predictors removed, 118
psychometrics of, 116–18
structure and standardization in, 114–15
automatic item generation (AIG), 71–72
automatic speech recognition (ASR), 18–19, 72
autonomic nervous system (ANS), 389–90
avatars, 307–8, 398
aviation, military, 379, 382–90
  decision-making under stress in, 388–90
  hypoxia in, 382–84, 392
  spatial disorientation in, 384–86
  workload in, 387–88
Aviation Selection Test Battery (ASTB), 379
AVIs. *See* automated video interviews

Babic, B., 16, 17
babysitters, personality assessment of, 86–87, 91
background checks, 242
backup of data, 247–49, 535
bag-of-words (BOW) model, 67, 73–74, 150–53
  continuous, 152–53
  example using term frequency, 73*t*
Baldwin, James, 515
Bangerter, A., 134
Banks, G., 162
"ban the box" rules, 242
*Barnes v. Cochran*, 274–75
BARS (behavioral anchored rating scales), 116
Baruch College, 6
Basch, J. M., 195–96
BCDR. *See* business continuity disaster recovery provisions
Bedwell, W. L., 400
behavioral anchored rating scales (BARS), 116
behaviorism, 206–7
Behrend, T. S., 15, 19, 540
Bell Labs, 86
Berkman, E. T., 53

Bersin, J., 359–60, 516–17
BERT. *See* Bidirectional Encoder Representations from Transformers
best practices
  in creating AI-based assessments, 112–13
  in leadership development, 301
BetterUp, 8, 283–84
Bhatia, Serena, 6–7, 530
bias, 242
  algorithmic, 163–64
  artificial intelligence and, 3–4, 89–90, 268
  of assessments (myth), 482–83
  confirmation, 488
  gamified assessments and, 412
  innovative assessments and, 224, 226, 227–29
  machine learning and, 18–20, 23t, 228–29
  measurement, 226, 227–28
  natural language processing and, 18
  predictive, 226, 228–29
  response, 381
  "similar to me," 143
  social media data and, 136–37, 143–45
  systematic, 224
  technology and big data for eliminating (myth), 483–84
  unconscious, 3–4, 515
  venture capital and, 505, 507
bias audits, 271–72, 356–57, 535, 540
bias penalization, 119–20
Bidirectional Encoder Representations from Transformers (BERT), 68–69, 74–76, 115–16, 118, 163
bifactor model, 39
big data, 97, 99–100, 531
  analytics advances, 103–5
  from automated video interviews, 111–12
  bias elimination and (myth), 483–84
  defined, 103
  gamified assessments and, 412
  natural language processing and, 149
  personality assessments and, 34, 40
Big Five personality traits, 98, 100, 473, 482–83

automated video interviews and, 114, 117
development of model, 31–32
expanding beyond concept of, 102–3, 106
gamified assessments of, 408, 409f, 410
Growth Leader Assessment of, 438–40
job outcomes predicted by, 407
Leading for Organizational Impact assessment of, 316
machine learning assessment and, 14–15
natural language processing assessment of, 69–70
social media data and, 133–35
technology-enabled simulation assessment of, 185
time for assessment completion, 33
Big Five version of Rapid Response Measurement (B5-RRM), 36, 37–39
bi-grams, 161–62
Bing lexicon, 150–52
bio measures, 338
Biometric Information (SB 1189), 276
Biometric Information Privacy Act (BIPA), 239, 242–43, 244, 275–76
biometrics, 242–43, 268, 269, 272–73, 275–76
BIPA. *See* Biometric Information Privacy Act
black-box approach, 3–4, 468, 474, 476
  to artificial intelligence, 357
  to machine learning, 14
  monitoring public reaction to, 476–77
  to natural language processing, 77
  to technology-enabled simulations, 189–90
Blacks
  cognitive ability assessments and, 48–49, 57
  leadership positions and, 519
  personality assessments and, 90
blockchain-based profiles, 139–40
blood-type personality theory, 435–36, 508–9
BooksCorpus, 68
Borman, W. C., 101
Bosco, F., 54–55

## INDEX

Bourke, J., 518–19
BOW model. *See* bag-of-words model
Boyce, Anthony S., 6, 196
Boyce, Christine, 6
Boyle, Coleen, 252
brain-as-predictor framework, 53
branching, 190–92, 371, 373
branding the field, 508–9
breathing rate, 390
Brown, A., 101
Bruk-Lee, V., 364–65, 371
BTS, 8, 338–39, 424–25, 427–28
Bucklan, M. A., 371
Bureau of Labor Statistics, 257
Burke, W. W., 331
Burton, B. A., 209–10
business acumen, 332–33, 424–25
business continuity disaster recovery (BCDR) provisions, 247–49
business unit (BU) leader capabilities, 439–40, 441–42

C++, 189–90
Caers, R., 134
California
 Biometric Information (SB 1189), 276
 Talent Equity for Competitive Hiring Act, 272
California Consumer Privacy Act (CCPA), 140, 235n.1, 237, 238, 248–49, 276
California Fair Employment and Housing Council, 272
California Privacy Rights Act (CPRA), 140
California Psychological Inventory, 84–85
Cambridge Analytica, 512–13
Campbell, D. T., 490
Campbell, J. P., 183–84, 468, 470–71
Campion, M. C., 14
Cao, M., 101
Cappelli, P., 24
CareerBuilder, 141–43
career journey, AI leveraged across, 352–60, 352f
Carroll, J., 50
CAS (Cognitive Assessment System), 54
case studies
 artificial intelligence, 349–60
 Asia (*see* Asia)
 gamified assessments, 397–415
 high-stakes personality assessment (*see* high-stakes personality assessment)
 individual and organizational development (*See* Prudential Financial)
 large multinational (*see* Saudi Aramco)
 Leading for Organizational Impact, 316–19
 military aviation, 382–90
 NFL's predraft assessment, 47–48, 58–60
 venture capital use, 512
Castelyns, V., 134
CATA. *See* computer-assisted text analysis
CAT Scanner, 162
Cattell, R. B., 31, 50
Cattell-Horn-Carroll (CHC) model, 50–51
Caver, K., 515–16, 518–19
CCL. *See* Center for Creative Leadership
CCPA. *See* California Consumer Privacy Act
CDC (Centers for Disease Control and Prevention), 252
Center for Creative Leadership (CCL), 8, 316, 317–18, 321–22
Center for Internet Security's Critical Security Controls, 237–38
Center of Excellence (CoE) at Saudi Aramco, 453, 455–57, 459, 461
Centers for Disease Control and Prevention (CDC), 252
CFA. *See* confirmatory factor analysis
Charismatic-Ideological-Pragmatic (CIP) leadership style, 156–57
Charismatic Leadership Tactics (CLTs), 158–60
CHC (Cattell-Horn-Carroll) model, 50–51
cheating, 230–31
Cheban, Yuliya, 6
Chen, L., 357
Chen, X., 131
Chiang, J. K. H., 134
*Chief Executive Magazine,* 331–32
China, 139–40, 433–34, 436–37, 444–45
Chinese Minnesota Multiphasic Personality Inventory-2 (MMPI), 434

Chou, V. P., 55–56
Christal, R. E., 31
Church, Allan H., 9, 342–43, 434–35, 533–34
City University of New York, 6
Civil Rights Act of 1964. *See* Title VII of the Civil Rights Act of 1964
Civil Rights Act of 1992, 537
Class A mishaps, 385
classification models, 74
Clearview AI, 243
Clerkin, C., 307
closed-vocabulary approach algorithms, 34
CLTs (Charismatic Leadership Tactics), 158–60
cluster analysis, 149–50
coaching, 8
  in assessment-rich leadership development programs, 321
  defined, 281–82
  in Leaders Accelerating the Business, 423, 425–26, 427–28, 429
  leadership development and, 302–3
  at Prudential Financial, 421–22
  at Saudi Aramco, 456–57
  virtual, 281–82, 293
coaching-centric assessments, 281–94, 539
  clarifying terms and definitions, 281–82
  within a coaching-digital resources ecosystem, 287–88
  to drive coach value, 293
  to drive partner (organizational) value, 291–92
  foundational principles for developmental assessment, 282–83
  purposes of assessment within, 288–91
  risks and recommendations for, 293–94
  Whole Person Model in (*see* Whole Person Model)
coaching-digital resources ecosystem, 287–88
Coast Guard, U.S., 379
CoCubes, 445, 448
CoE. *See* Center of Excellence at Saudi Aramco
cognitive ability assessments, 5
  advances in, 105
  in Asia, 434–35
  classical psychometric approach to, 48–49
  continued use of and improvements in, 472
  disabilities and, 254, 255–56
  gamified, 406–7, 472
  group differences and, 6, 47–60
  group differences and, cognitive and neuroscience theory on reducing, 53–56
  group differences and, modern test design principles to reduce, 56–58
  group differences and, psychometric theory on reducing, 50–53
  group differences and, rethinking the inevitability of, 48–49
  mobile-enabled, 177, 178
  NFL pregame assessment case study, 47–48, 58–60
  reducing non-domain-relevant and cultural content, 57
  theory-driven, 56
Cognitive Assessment System (CAS), 54
cognitive disabilities, 252, 258–59
cognitive process approaches, 53–54
cognitive pupillometry, 55–56
cognitive workload. *See* workload
Collins, Lynn, 8, 538
commercial general liability (CGI), 247
competencies, 105
  high-stakes rich-media simulations and, 371, 372
  Saudi Aramco's measurement of, 461–62
competency models, 285–87, 286f
computational psychometrics, 111–12, 121–22, 123
computer-assisted text analysis (CATA), 150–52, 154–57, 155t, 162, 164–65
concept drift, 16
confidentiality (of data), 244–45
configurability, 282
confirmation bias, 488
confirmatory factor analysis (CFA), 97, 98, 99–100
constructed-response assessment (CRA), 70–71, 74, 471–72

construct validity, 475
    of automated video interviews, 14–15, 115, 117–18
    big data and, 104
    of gamified assessments, 406–7, 411
    of learning agility, 331
    machine learning and, 14–15, 533
    of personality assessments, 255
    of Rapid Response Measurement, 102
    of social media data, 133–35, 140
    of technology-enabled simulations, 189
continuous bag-of-words (BOW) model, 152–53
control reversal errors (CREs), 385, 387–88
convergent validity, 468
    of automated video interviews, 114, 116–18
    of gamified assessments, 408, 410, 533
    of Rapid Response Measurement, 38
cookies, 239, 240–41
cortisol, 389–90
costs
    of automated video interviews, 112, 122–23
    e-recruitment reduction of, 133
    of gamified assessments, 404
    of high-stakes rich-media simulations, 370–72
    venture capital impact on, 509–10
covariate shift, 16
COVID-19 pandemic, 16, 74–75, 154–56, 158–60, 304, 356
    in Asia, 448–49
    automated video interview anxiety and, 122
    development importance and, 329
    impact on working life, 170–71
    leadership development in wake of, 325
    mobile-enabled assessment and, 172–73
    Saudi Aramco and, 451, 456–57, 458–59, 460–61
    technology use accelerated by, 187–88
Cox, Brennan, 8, 530
CPRA (California Privacy Rights Act), 140
CRA. *See* constructed-response assessment
CREs. *See* control reversal errors

criterion-related validity, 476
    of automated video interviews, 15, 16, 17–18, 118, 121
    big data and, 104
    of forced-choice personality assessments, 34–35
    of gamified assessments, 410
    of high-stakes rich-media simulations, 371
    of learning agility, 331
    machine learning and, 14, 15–18, 533
    personality constructs and, 102–3
    of Rapid Response Measurement, 38, 102
    of social media data, 135–36, 140
    test format and, 471–72
cross-battery assessment approach (XBA), 51, 56, 57
Cross-Cultural Personality Assessment Inventory, 434
cryptocurrency, 508–9
crystalized intelligence, 50
Cubrich, Marc, 6–7, 136, 537
culture
    cognitive ability assessments and, 57
    of Saudi Aramco, 460–61
"curse of dimensionality," 73–74, 151–52
customer base, 508
customer centricity, 507
customer experience, 509
cyber extortion threats, 247
cyber liability coverage, 247
cybervetting, 130

dark side of personality, 37, 38, 86, 102–3, 106
*Dark Truth Behind Personality Tests, The* (documentary), 482–83
data
    big (*see* big data)
    deidentification of, 245, 246–47, 246n.11
    labeled, 149–50, 155t, 162–64
    Saudi Aramco's use of, 461–62
    sensitive, 237, 245
    social media (*see* social media data)
    text, 153–54
    usage, 235
    user, 236

data analytic advances, 97–100
data categorization, 235–36
data deletion, 239, 244
data lakes, 246–47
data privacy, 7, 40–41, 234–49, 535
　anticipated changes, 248–49
　artificial intelligence and, 248, 356–57
　in Asia, 447–48
　biometrics and, 242–43, 268, 269, 272–73, 275–76
　contractual terms, 243–45
　innovative assessments and, 231
　legal issues and, 234, 268
　liability limitation and, 245
　notice required for security breaches, 238–39, 244
　psychoneurometric assessments and, 391
　regulatory development, 236–39, 248–49
　risk mitigation, 245–48
　social media and, 40–41, 140, 143
　technology considerations, 239–43
*Data Protection Commission v. Facebook Ireland and Maximillian Schrems*, 244–45
data retention, 239, 244
data security, 237–38
data triangulation, 495–96
David, Jose, 8, 538
DCI Consulting, 7
DDI, 8
"Dear White Boss..." (Caver & Livers), 515
DeBERTa (Decoding-enhanced BERT with Disentangled Attention), 68–69
*Decision of the Executive Committee of the Commission National de l'Informatique et des Libertés*, 243
decision trees, 75t
declarative knowledge, 468
Decoding-enhanced BERT with Disentangled Attention (DeBERTa), 68–69
Deep Charisma (algorithm), 158–60
deepfakes, 374
deep learning (DL), 72, 152–53
　definition, 66–67
　definition, consideration, and resources, 155t
　leadership assessment and, 158–60, 165
　natural language processing positioning respective to, 149–50, 150f
Deep Mind, 86
DEI. *See* diversity, equity, and inclusion
deidentification of data, 245, 246–47, 246n.11
deLaat, P. B., 21
democratization of talent assessment, 510
demographics, 536–37
Department of Justice, 268–69, 413
Department of Labor, 256–57
Department of Transportation, 260
designated potential, 494–95
design thinking, 211–14, 212f, 532
development, 328–44, 533. *See also* leadership development
　constructs and content domain measured in, 329–36
　contextual factors measurement in, 335–36
　criteria variables in, 334
　feedback methods in, 340–41
　foundational principles for assessment, 282–83
　incremental *vs.* transformative innovation in, 343–44
　measurement approaches in, 336–40
　at Prudential Financial (*see* Prudential Financial)
　targets of efforts, 341–43
　whole-person predictors in, 330, 333–34
　workforce upheavals and, 328–29
　work-related predictors in, 330–33
Development Check-In (DCI), 498
*Diagnostic and Statistical Manual of Mental Disorders*, fifth edition (DSM V), 253, 261, 263
dichotomous responses, 366
Diction, 162
Dietvorst, B. J., 21–22
differential item functioning (DIF) analysis, 228
differentiation, 507, 508
digital behavioral residue, 134
digital readiness, 333
digital traces, 134–35, 143–44

disabilities, 250–65, 268–69. *See also* accommodations (for disabilities); Americans with Disabilities Act
   discrimination and assessments, 273–75
   gamified assessments and, 412–14
   innovative assessments and, 226, 227, 231–32
   mobile-enabled assessment and, 173
   modifications for, 231–32
   number of Americans with, 252
   recommendations for handling item-writing problems, 264–65
   six types of, 252
   technology-enabled simulations and, 193
Disabilities Act Amendments Act of 2008, 270n.1
disability-related inquiries, 252
DISC, 435
discrete ratings, 366
discriminant validity, 468
Disorientation Research Device, 392
disparate impact discrimination, 269–71, 275, 412
distance scoring, 373
diversity, 515–24, 537
   artificial intelligence and, 3–4
   cognitive ability assessments and, 50–51
   innovative assessments and, 222–23
   role of leaders in promoting, 518–19
   validity tradeoff (*see* validity/diversity dilemma)
diversity, equity, and inclusion (DEI), 516–17
   development and, 329, 341–42
   leadership and, 518, 537
   mobile-enabled assessment and, 170–71, 172–74
   social media data and, 143
diversity maturity, 520–21, 523
   evolution of, 516–18
   model, 517*f*
DL. *See* deep learning
Dobbin, F., 520–21
Dodge, J., 21
Doldor, E., 157–58, 160, 165
dominance models, 34, 100–1

dopamine, 390
Drasgow, F., 35
Drasgow approach, 98
Dreyer, Matt, 8, 538
DSM V. *See Diagnostic and Statistical Manual of Mental Disorders*, fifth edition
Ducey, Adam J., 8, 538
Dunleavy, Eric M., 7
Dunnette, M. D., 31
dust bowl empiricism, 221
Dweck, Carol, 439–40
dynamical model of intelligence, 51–52
dynamism, 282

Economist Intelligence survey, 332–33
Economist Intelligence Unit, 424–25
ecosystems
   in Asia, 444–46
   coaching-digital resources, 287–88
   people-opportunity, 359–60
EEG. *See* electroencephalography
EEOC. *See* Equal Employment Opportunity Commission
EFA (exploratory factor analysis), 157–58
Efficiently Learning an Encoder that Classifies Token Replacements Accurately (ELECTRA), 68–69
effort, 468
ELECTRA (Efficiently Learning an Encoder that Classifies Token Replacements Accurately), 68–69
electroencephalography (EEG), 381–82, 383, 384, 384*f*, 391
Electronic and Information Technology Accessibility Standards, 273–74
Electronic Privacy Information Center (EPIC), 272–73
ELLA (Everyday Leader Learning Assistant), 321–22
empiricism, 205*t*, 206–7, 208–9
employment tests
   artificial intelligence employed in, 267–68
   innovation and standards balanced in, 219–32 (*see also* innovative assessments; professional standards)
encryption, 245, 248–49, 535

Enderes, K., 516–17
engineering
　commonalities and differences between science and, 205t
　problem solving in, 207–8
　thinking like an engineer, 208–14
Enneagram, 435
enterprise social media, 130–31
EPIC (Electronic Privacy Information Center), 272–73
epistemologies, 205t, 206–8, 215
equal access, 227
Equal Employment Opportunity Commission (EEOC), 7, 92, 251–52, 255–58, 268–69, 270–71, 274, 413, 540
equitable treatment, 226–27. *See also* diversity, equity, and inclusion
ERP. *See* event-related potential
error-related negativity ERP, 381–82
errors and omissions (E&O), 247
ethical issues
　big data and, 104
　leadership assessment and, 159–61, 164–65
　natural language processing and, 78
　technology-enabled simulations and, 193–94
European Union, 236–37, 244–45
European Union Data Protection Committee, 243
event-related potential (ERP), 381–82, 383
Everyday Leader Learning Assistant (ELLA), 321–22
executive attention, 54–55
executive functioning, 54–55
expert rater evaluations of AVIs, 117–18
explainability, 20–22, 23t
exploratory factor analysis (EFA), 157–58
extended reality (XR), 308
external coaching, 281–82
eye-tracking technology, 55–56, 185–86, 325, 530
Eyring, James D., 8, 434–35, 539

Facebook, 86–87, 88–89, 91, 92, 103, 113–14, 129, 135–37

face validity
　of Growth Leader Assessment, 440
　of Saudi Aramco assessments, 454, 460–61
　of simulations, 184, 362
facial recognition technology, 271, 272–73, 534–35
facial scans, 86–87, 88, 93
Fagan, J. F., 57
Fair Credit Reporting Act, 242
fairness
　gamified assessments and, 227, 400–1, 532
　machine learning and, 21–22
　mobile-first design and, 175
　*Principles* on, 226–27
Fairy God Boss, 491
faking, 85–86, 87, 471, 488
　AI-based personality assessment and, 91–92
　forced-choice personality assessments and, 35, 178–79, 468–69, 473, 488–89
　interest measures and, 473
　ipsative scales and, 101
　Likert-type personality assessments and, 33, 34–35, 38–39
　Rapid Response Measurement and, 38–39
　simulations and, 362
"faking good," 33, 38–39, 488–89
Falk, E. B., 53
feature-based machine learning (ML) models, 74, 75t
feature engineering, 67–68
feature extraction, 74
features, 67–68
feature selection, 74
feature weights, 73–74
federal anti-discrimination laws, 269–71
Federal Trade Commission, 270–71, 272–73
feedback
　in assessment-rich leadership development programs, 322–23
　in coaching-centric assessments, 289–90
　in development assessment, 340–41
　gamification and, 192

in Leaders Accelerating the Business, 426–27, 428–29
at Saudi Aramco, 462
feedback loops
leadership development and, 306–7
machine learning and, 17–18, 24
Finja Israel, L. S., 16, 21
"Finsta," 91
first-party cookies, 240–41
Fisher, P., 38–39
Fisk, D. W., 490
508 compliance, 173–74
Flanagan, D. P., 51
flight simulators, 386
fMRI. *See* functional magnetic resonance imaging
fNIRS (functional near-infrared spectroscopy), 391
*Forbes*, 337
forced-choice personality assessments, 5, 407–8, 468–69, 473, 488–89, 529
concerns about, 41
innovations in, 34–35
item response theory analysis of, 98
mobile-enabled, 178–79
framification, 401–2
Frazier, Ken, 331–32
Freedle, R., 57
from-to-framework, 420–21, 422, 423, 427–28
functional cookies, 240
functional magnetic resonance imaging (fMRI), 385–86, 391
functional near-infrared spectroscopy (fNIRS), 391

*g*, 48, 49, 50–51
Galton, Sir Francis, 31
galvanic skin response, 387, 390
gamified assessments, 8, 16, 34, 40–41, 355, 397–415, 471, 527, 533
alternate terms for, 397–98
applications for, 403–5
of cognitive abilities, 406–7, 472
constructs measured by, 406–10, 411
creation of, 405
defined, 398, 485
explained, 397–400

fairness and, 227, 400–1, 532
feedback and, 192
framification and, 401–2
as fun, 400–1, 402, 415, 532
future of, 414
legal issues and, 410, 411–14
for making assessments likable (myth), 485–88
psychometrics evaluation, 410–11
realism and, 192–93
spectrum of, 368*f*, 398
target audience for, 400–3
of technology-enabled simulations, 192–93
types of jobs and companies using, 403
GATB (General Aptitude Test Battery), 451–52
Gaugler, B. B., 454
gaze patterns, 55–56
GDPR. *See* General Data Protection Regulation
General Aptitude Test Battery (GATB), 451–52
General Data Protection Regulation (GDPR), 140, 169–70, 237, 238, 243–45, 246–47, 248–49
rights codified under, 238
terminology used for data, 235n.1
general factor of intelligence. *See g*
General Inquirer, 115–16
General Language Understanding Evaluation (GLUE), 69
Generative Pretrained Transformer (GPT), 68–69
Generative Pretrained Transformer-2 (GPT-2), 68–69, 71–72, 77
Generative Pretrained Transformer-3 (GPT-3), 68–69, 115–16
geo-fencing technology, 236
Georgetown University, 67
Germany, 434
Geyik, S. C., 19
Gibby, Robert E., 8, 538
gig economy, 329
Giordano, C., 39
GLA. *See* Growth Leader Assessment
Gladwell, Malcolm, 58–59
Glassdoor, 131, 491

GLBA (Gramm-Leach-Bliley Act), 236–37
g-loaded tests, 48–49
global interpretability, 77–78
glucocorticoids, 389–90
GLUE (General Language Understanding Evaluation), 69
Go, 66–67, 86
Goldstein, Harold W., 6
Google, 68, 507
Google Cloud, 72, 78
Goretzko, D., 16, 21
Gottier, R. F., 31
GPS technology, 236
GPT. *See* Generative Pretrained Transformer
*G(q,k)* coefficient, 373
grade point average (GPA), 16, 39
gradient boosted trees, 75*t*
Gramm-Leach-Bliley Act (GLBA), 236–37
grams, 161–62
Grand, J. A., 257–58
GREAT5 leadership model, 495–96
Great Resignation, 170–72, 329, 404–5
Grelle, Darrin M., 6–7, 537
GRE Psychology test, 468–69
Griffith, R. L., 33
Griswold, K., 120, 122
group differences, cognitive ability assessments and. *See under* cognitive ability assessments
Growth Leader Assessment (GLA), 436, 446–47
  Strategy assessment, 437–38, 440–43
  Style assessment, 437–41
Growth Leader Capability Framework, 437–38, 438*f*, 444*f*
growth mindset, 437, 438–40
Guion, R. M., 31, 533–34
Guo, Q., 353
Gutierrez, Sara L., 6–7, 537

Ha, T., 21
Hall, Kathleen, 8
halo effect, 494
Hangartner, D., 20
Hardy, J. H., III, 33
Hartog, Sandra, 8
Hartwell, C., 119–20

*Harvard Business Review*, 515
Hawkes, B. J., 364–65
Health Insurance Portability and Accountability Act (HIPPA), 236–37, 237n.2, 238, 244, 246n.10, 391
hearing disabilities, 252
heart rate, 390
heart rate variability, 387, 388, 390
Helms-Lorenz, M., 57
Hickman, L., 14–15, 16, 17–18, 117, 118, 357
hierarchical models of intelligence, 50–51
Higgins, D., 54–55
high potentials, 342, 490*f*, 491–92, 494–95
high potential selection assessment practices, 434–35, 435*f*
high-pros, 342
high-risk jobs, 8, 377–93. *See also* psychoneurometric assessments
  characterizing, 378
  insufficiency of traditional tools for assessing, 377
high-stakes personality assessment, 6, 30–41, 529
  historical role of, 30–32
  innovations in, 34–40
  Likert-type limitations, 32–33
  limitations of advancements and other concerns, 40–41
high-stakes rich-media simulations (RMS), 362–75, 527
  applications of, 367–70
  challenges of, 371–74
  common response formats, 365–66
  common stimuli formats, 364–65
  definitions of terms, 363, 364
  future directions, 374
  the value and the evidence, 370–71
Hilliard, A., 408
HIPPA. *See* Health Insurance Portability and Accountability Act
HiQ, 141
HireVue, 6–7, 8, 86–87, 115, 117–18, 121, 272–73, 408
Hoff, D. F., 331
Hogan, Robert, 6, 102–3, 473, 531
Hogan Assessment Systems, 6
Hogan competency library, 93

Hogan Developmental Survey, 93
Hogan LEAD program. *See* LEAD (Hogan)
Hogan Personality Inventory, 93
Hogan personality-job performance archive, 93
Holland, C. R., 57
Hommel, B. E., 71–72
Horn, J., 50
Horner, R. G., 15
hot-spot forms, 372
Hough, L. M., 102–3
HTTPS, 241
human resources leaders
 concerns, reactions, and approach, 486*t*
 information assessments needed by, 498–99
HumRRO, 8
Hunter, J. E., 114–15
hypothalamic-pituitary-adrenal (HPA) axis, 389–90
hypoxia, 382–84, 392

IBM, 67, 69, 86, 139–40
ideal point measures, 34, 98, 100–1, 529
ideal standard, 441, 442–43
Illinois
 Artificial Intelligence Video Interview Act, 78, 271, 356–57, 476–77
 Biometric Information Privacy Act, 239, 242–43, 244, 275–76
implanted devices, 303–4, 306
in-baskets, 362, 363
inclusivity, 331–32. *See also* diversity, equity, and inclusion
 developing in organizations and leaders, 519–23
 role of leaders in promoting, 518–19
incremental validity, 190, 197
independent living disabilities, 252
India, 436, 444–46
*Industrial and Organization Psychology,* 253
industrial-organizational psychology-technology interface (IOPTI), 202–15, 532
 initial steps to bridge the gap, 214–15
 philosophy underlying, 204–7
 problem solving and, 207–8

 thinking like an engineer, 208–14
informed consent, 193
inhibitory control, 381–82
inner self, 312–13, 314, 336–37
innovative assessments, 7, 219–32
 in Asia, 439, 440–41
 bias and, 224, 226, 227–29
 criterion measurement and, 335*t*
 data privacy and integrity and, 231
 defined, 219–20
 disabilities and, 226, 227, 231–32
 fairness and, 226–27
 incremental *vs.* transformative, 343–44
 operational issues and, 229–31
 of personality, 34–40
 predictors in, 224–26
 unproctored internet testing and, 229–31
 validity of, 222–24
 venture capital impact on, 509
 work analysis and, 220–22
inspiring behaviors (Whole Person Model), 283–84, 336–37
Instagram, 86–87, 91, 103, 129
integrative models of intelligence, 52–53
integrity tests, 470, 473
intellectual property (IP), 507, 508–9
interest measures, 473
International Personality Item Pool (IPIP), 38–39, 71–72, 102, 117, 408
Internet of Bodies (IoB), 303–4
interpretability, 77–78
interview reports (for personality assessments), 39–40
interviews. *See also* automated video interviews; structured interviews; video interviews
 artificial intelligence leveraged in, 354–57
 Asia and, 434–35
 for leadership development, 299–300
inverse document frequency, 73–74
inverted-U model of arousal, 389–90
IOPTI. *See* industrial-organizational psychology-technology interface
IP. *See* intellectual property
IPIP. *See* International Personality Item Pool

ipsative scales, 100, 101
IRT. *See* item response theory
item response theory (IRT), 35
item response theory (IRT) analyses, 97, 99
  explained, 98
  ipsative scales and, 101
  of technology-enabled simulations, 191–92
item-response-tree model, 39
item sensitivity reviews. *See* sensitivity reviews
iterative feature removal, 119–20

Japan, 435–36
JAT (Job Aptitude Test), 451–52
Java, 189–90
Jensen, U., 158–60
job analysis data, 522–23
Job Aptitude Test (JAT), 451–52
Johnson and Johnson, 8
Joreskog, K. G., 98

Kalev, A., 520–21
*Karraker v. Rent-A-Center, Inc.*, 252, 253–54, 274–75
Kato, Annie, 6
Kenya, 172–73
keyword stuffing, 92
Kim, P. T., 412
Kincentric, 6–7
K-Nearest Neighbors (K-NN), 75*t*
knowledge, skill, or ability (KSA), 14–15
knowledge, skills, abilities, and other characteristics (KSAOs), 412
  artificial intelligence to determine, 354, 358
  high-stakes rich-media simulations and, 364, 372
  innovative assessments and, 220–22, 225, 226, 227
  natural language processing and, 70–71, 74, 75–76, 77–78
  simulations on, 362
  as work-related predictors, 330
Korea, 435–36
Korn, O., 401
Kosinski, M., 92

Kostin, I., 57
KSA (knowledge, skill, or ability), 14–15
KSAOs. *See* knowledge, skills, abilities, and other characteristics
Kulas, J., 40

LAB. *See* Leaders Accelerating the Business
labeled data, 149–50, 155*t*, 162–64
labor shortage, 137–38
Landers, Richard N., 6–7, 19, 22, 129, 213, 400, 472, 532, 540
Langer, M., 20, 22
Larson, Elliott, 6, 57
lasso regression, 93
latent Dirichlet allocation (LDA) topic modeling, 157–58, 162
LaTorre, J., 371
LCI (Leadership Competency Index), 461–62
LDA topic modeling. *See* latent Dirichlet allocation topic modeling
LEAD (Hogan), 341–42, 423
LeAD (PepsiCo). *See* Leadership Assessment and Development Program
leaders
  inclusivity development in, 519–23
  role of in diversity growth, 518–19
Leaders Accelerating the Business (LAB), 423–30, 431–32
  overview, 423*f*
  prework in, 425–26
  promotion rate of participants, 430
  strategy emphasized in, 424–25, 425*f*, 426–27, 428
leadership assessment
  in Asia, 440–43
  convergence of development, work, and, 308–9
  natural language processing in, 6–7, 149–66 (*see also under* natural language processing)
  roles of different methods, 298–302
  technology and, 303–5, 308–9
Leadership Assessment and Development Program (LeAD), 484–85, 490, 491–92, 494–95

Leadership Competency Index (LCI), 461–62
leadership development, 297–309
 in Asia, 436, 437–38
 assessment-rich programs for (*see* assessment-rich leadership development programs)
 coaching and, 302–3
 convergence of assessment, work, and, 308–9
 developing new habits in, 305–8
 roles of different assessment methods, 298–302
 technology and, 303–9
Leadership Development BluePrint, 498–99
Leadership Team Analysis, 496*f*
Leading Edge Consortium (LEC), 4, 526
 advances in adaptive personality assessment, 35–36
 Rapid Response Measurement, 36–39
Leading for Organizational Impact (LOI), 316–19, 320, 323, 330
 assessment practices in, 316–18
 evidence of effectiveness, 318–19
 participant ratings of assessments, 318*f*
leans, 386
learning agility, 331
LEC. *See* Leading Edge Consortium
legal issues, 267–76. *See also* regulations (on data privacy)
 artificial intelligence and, 267–68, 269, 270–73
 data privacy and, 234, 268
 disabilities and, 273–75 (*see also* Americans with Disabilities Act)
 the framework, 269–76
 gamified assessments and, 410, 411–14
 machine learning and, 19
 mobile-enabled assessment and, 173–74
 natural language processing and, 78
 predictive bias and, 229
 risk management, 268–69
 social media data and, 136–37, 140–41
 technology and assessment advances and, 534–36
 test takers and, 492–93
 work analysis and, 220–21
lemmatization, 72–73, 162

Leutner, F., 117, 119–20, 408
Levashina, A., 136
Lewis, Nilan Johnson, 7, 9, 535–36, 537
lexical approach, 31, 114
Lievens, F., 470–72
Likert-type personality assessments, 36–37, 39, 41, 408, 528–29
 faking on, 33, 34–35, 38–39
 high-stakes rich-media simulations and, 366, 372
 limitations of in high-stakes situations, 32–33
 time for completion, 33
Lim, A., 434–35
linear regression, 75*t*, 149–50
Linguistic Inquiry and Word Count (LIWC), 115–16, 154–57, 162
LinkedIn, 19, 20, 77, 86–87, 103, 129, 134, 141, 349
 benefits of, 131, 132
 Recruiter algorithm, 353
*LinkedIn Corporation v HiQ Labs, Inc.*, 141
Liu, MQ, 6, 529
live action simulations, 364–65, 369, 371–72
Livers, A., 515–16, 518–19
LIWC. *See* Linguistic Inquiry and Word Count
local interpretability, 77–78
location data, 236
logical positivism, 205*t*, 206–7
logistic regression, 74, 75*t*, 149–50
LOI. *See* Leading for Organizational Impact
long short-term memory (LSTM), 67–68, 71–72
Looking Glass, 316–18, 337
Lord, F. M., 98
Lovelace, K., 334
Lovric, Darko, 9, 528, 532
LSTM. *See* long short-term memory
Lukacik, E., 21
Lundquist, Kathleen, 7, 9, 516, 537

Machiavellianism, 102–3
machine learning (ML), 13–24, 66–67, 68, 74, 87, 189–90, 338–39, 350–51, 506, 531, 533
 active, 163

machine learning (ML) (*cont.*)
   in automated video interview scoring, 113–21
   bias and, 18–20, 23t, 228–29
   coining of term, 86
   defined, 66–67
   explainability/acceptability and, 20–22, 23t
   feature-based models, 74, 75t
   in measurement and prediction, 14–18, 23t
   natural language processing positioning respective to, 149–50, 150f
   practical implications of, 22–24
   social media data and, 14–15, 138–39
   supervised, 156–57, 162–63
   unsupervised, 155t, 157–58
machine learning natural language processing (NLP), 152–53
Maestro Consulting, 9
magnetoencephalography (MEG), 391
Malda, M., 57
Manager Assessment Center (MAC) of Saudi Aramco, 454
managers
   concerns, reactions, and approach, 486t
   information on assessments needed by, 494–96
Manpower Group, 6
Marine Corps, U.S., 379
market failures, 512–13
Martin, N., 54–55
Marshall, J., 164–65
Maryland, 271
Maydeu-Olivares, A., 101
MBTI. *See* Myers-Briggs Type Indicator
McBeth, R., 371
McCarthy, J. M., 122
McCauley, Cynthia D., 8, 330, 334, 335–37, 338–39, 538
McDaniel, M. A., 373
McHail, Dan, 8
McKenny, A. F., 17
McPhail, S. M., 260
Meade, Adam W., 6, 36–39, 102, 529
measurement
   approaches in development, 336–40
   of development constructs and content domain, 329–36
   of development contextual factors, 335–36
   of gamified constructs, 406–10, 411
   machine learning in, 14–18, 23t
   new horizons for, 528–30
   use of and improvements in predictor constructs, 472–73
measurement bias, 226, 227–28
medical examinations
   Americans with Disabilities Act on, 251–53, 270, 274–75
   criteria for, 274
medical school admissions exams, 470–71
MEG (magnetoencephalography), 391
Megatron-Turing Natural Language Generation model (MT-NLG), 68–69
Melchers, K. G., 195–96
Merck, Jose David, 8
Merck & Co., 331–32
Mesnet, L., 21–22
Meta, 8
meta-analyses
   of Big Five trait-based tools, 482–83
   of cognitive ability assessments, 49, 57
   of forced-choice personality assessments, 34–35
   of interest measures, 473
   of leadership training, 325
   of Likert-type personality assessments, 38–39
   of other-ratings of personality, 473
   of personality assessments, 31–32, 100
   of personality-job performance correlation, 407
   Saudi Aramco assessments and, 454
   of simulations, 183
   of social media data, 134–35
   of structured interviews, 114–15
   of validity, 470
meta-theories, 52–53
Michigan State University, 6
Microsoft, 68–69, 339, 439–40
Microsoft Azure, 72
Microsoft Outlook, 306
Microsoft Viva, 339–40
Microsoft Word, 202
military
   personality assessments in, 35, 84

psychoneurometric assessments in, 378–80, 382–90
*Military Psychology*, 35
mindfulness, 334
mindsets, 336–37
  growth, 437, 438–40
  personality assessments for, 300–1
  in Whole Person Model, 283–85, 293
Minnesota Multiphasic Personality Inventory (MMPI), 84–85, 253–54, 259, 274, 434
minorities. *See also* race; women
  innovative assessments and, 223, 228–29
  mobile-enabled assessment and, 172–73
  technology-enabled simulations and, 195–96
Mirowska, A., 21–22
Mischel, W., 196–97
ML. *See* machine learning
MMPI. *See* Minnesota Multiphasic Personality Inventory
mobile-enabled assessment, 169–80. *See also* mobile-first design
  diversity, equity, and inclusion concerns and, 170–71, 172–74
  recent changes and, 170–74
mobile equivalence, 177–78
mobile-first design, 171–72, 173–79, 537
  consumer internet access and, 176
  effectiveness of, 175, 176
  efficiency of, 175–76
  examples of successful implementation, 178–79
  experience and, 176
  mobile equivalence and, 177–78
mobility disabilities, 252
Modern Hire, 6–7
modifications (for disabilities), 231–32
modularity, 282
Mondragon, Nathan, 6–7, 8, 15, 527, 533, 536, 537
Moore's law, 79
Morse, L., 19
motion-based simulators, 386
MTMM approach. *See* multitrait/multimethod approach
MT-NLG (Megatron-Turing Natural Language Generation model), 68–69

multilevel modeling, 97, 99
multinational assessments. *See* Saudi Aramco
multiple choice formats, 471–72, 528–29
multiple regression models, 74
multitrait/multimethod (MTMM) approach, 488–89, 495–96, 500
Murphy, Claire Saba, 7
Musk, Elon, 308–9
Myers-Briggs Type Indicator (MBTI), 435, 482–83
myths. *See* assessment myths and misinformation

Nadella, Satya, 439–40
Naglieri, J., 53–54
NAHR (National Academy of Human Resources), 518
NAMRU-D (Naval Medical Research Unit Dayton), 392
narcissism, 102–3
NASA Task Load Index, 387
National Academy of Human Resources (NAHR), 518
National Center on Birth Defects and Developmental Disabilities, 252
National Football League's (NFL's) predraft assessment, 47–48, 58–60
National Institute of Science and Technology (NIST), 237–38, 241–42
natural behavior, 529, 530
natural language generation (NLG), 71–72
natural language processing (NLP), 5, 6, 18, 66–79, 105, 207–8, 338–39, 351, 352, 471–72, 530
  applying to assessment, 69–77
  automated video interview scoring and, 115–16, 118, 119–20
  challenges and opportunities, 77–78
  considerations and future directions, 76–77
  construction of assessment and, 70–72
  defined, 66–67
  evolution of, 67–69
  history of, 67
  interpretability and, 77–78
  in leadership assessment, 6–7, 149–66, 529

natural language processing (NLP) (cont.)
  in leadership assessment, applied to, 154–60
  in leadership assessment, considerations when using for, 160–64
  in leadership assessment, future of, 164–66
  in leadership assessment, reasons to use for, 153–54
  machine learning, 152–53
  methodologies in, 149–53
  neural approaches to analyzing text, 74–77
  non-machine learning, 150–52, 154–56
  non-neural approaches to analyzing text, 73–74, 76–77
  positioning with respect to AI, ML, and DL, 149–50, 150f
  resource demand and, 78
  techniques and relevant resources, 155t
  text cleaning and preprocessing, 72–73
  voice-to-text and, 72
Natural Language Toolkit, 115–16
natural language understanding (NLU), 69
Naval Aerospace Medical Research Laboratory, 392
Naval Medical Research Unit Dayton (NAMRU-D), 392
Naval Safety Center, 385
Navy, U.S., 379
necessary cookies, 240
nested factor theories, 51–52
net promoter scores (NPSs), 455, 456, 459, 462–63
neural natural language processing (NLP) approaches, 74–77
neurodiversity, 7, 250, 537
  cognitive ability assessments and, 254
  defined, 254
  gamified assessments and, 412–13
  mobile-enabled assessment and, 173
neuropsychological tests, 54–55
New York City, 92, 271–72, 356–57
NFL. See National Football League
NFL Player Assessment Test (PAT), 59–60
nine-box model of performance by potential ratings, 494–95

NIST. See National Institute of Science and Technology
NLG (natural language generation), 71–72
NLP. See natural language processing
NLU (natural language understanding), 69
noisy signal data, 138–39
Nolan, K. P., 20
nonentrenched tasks, 58
non-g models of intelligence, 51–52
nonhierarchical models of intelligence, 51–52
nonlinear scoring, 190–91
non-machine learning natural language processing (NLP), 150–52, 154–56
non-neural natural language (NLP) processing approaches, 73–74, 76–77
Norris-Watts, Christina, 8, 527, 532, 533, 536
North Carolina State University, 6
Norvig, P., 350
notice/consent laws, 271, 272
novel methods (of personality assessment), 39
novel models (of personality assessment), 39
novel tasks, 58
Novick, M. R., 98
NPSs. See net promoter scores
NRC lexicon, 150–52
NVIDIA, 68–69
n-word grams, 161–62

OARS. See overall assessment ratings
objectivism, 205t, 206
O'Brien, J., 339
Occam's razor, 85–86, 88
Occupational Information Network, 378
Odbert, H. S., 31
Office of Federal Contract Compliance Programs (OFCCP), 256–57
Olson, Tatana, 8
ontologies, 204, 205t, 206–7, 215
open-vocabulary approach algorithms, 34
optokinetic drum, 386
Organisation Solutions, 8, 436, 437, 445–46
*Organizational Research Methods*, 103
OSS and AT&T Management Progress Study, 183

outcomes
  data from automated video interviews, 115–16
  data from personality assessments, 84–85
  differing views on tradeoffs among, 468–70
  in Whole Person Model, 283–85, 290, 336–37
overall assessment ratings (OARs), 454, 459

PA, 7
Paese, Matt, 8, 336–37, 338, 529, 530
PaLM (Pathways Language Model), 115–16
Papinchock, Jone M., 7, 537
paradigms, 205t, 206–7, 215
Pareto optimality, 50–51, 469, 536
Parisi, Jessica, 343
PASS (Planning, Attention-Arousal, Simultaneous, and Successive) theory, 53–54
passwords, 241
Patel, Kajal, 6
Pathways Language Model (PaLM), 115–16
Paul Hastings LLP, 7
people-opportunity ecosystem, 359–60
PepsiCo, 9, 341–42, 484–85, 489, 490, 491–96, 498
performance cookies, 240
permissibility (SCIP model), 177–78, 197–98
persistent cookies, 240
*Persona* (documentary), 481
personal information (PII), 244, 245–47
  defined, 235
  regulations on, 237, 238–39
personality, interests, and intelligence-as-knowledge (PPIK) theory, 52–53, 57
personality as identity, 473
personality as reputation. *See* reputation
personality assessments, 6, 84–94, 133–35, 488–89
  advances in, 100–2
  advances in adaptive, 35–36
  artificial intelligence in, 86–93
  in Asia, 434–35

  continued use of and improvements in, 473
  development and, 338
  disabilities and, 253–57, 258–60, 274–75
  faking on (*see* faking)
  forced-choice (*see* forced-choice personality assessments)
  the future of, 92–94
  game-based, 406, 407–10
  for high-stakes use (*see* high-stakes personality assessment)
  innovations in, 34–40
  leadership development and, 300–1
  Likert-type (*see* Likert-type personality assessments)
  limitations of advancements and other concerns, 40–41
  machine learning and, 114
  mobile-enabled, 178–79
  for predicting outcomes, 84–85
  self-report (*see* self-report inventories)
personality conceptualizations, 102–5
*Personnel Psychology*, 69–70
person-situation interactions, 474
Pettijohn, Kyle, 8
Pew Research Center, 172–73
Phenometrix, 86–87
PHI (protected health information), 391
PII. *See* personal information
Pike, M., 39–40
Pilot Workload Rating Scale, 387
pixels, 239, 239n.5
Planning, Attention-Arousal, Simultaneous, and Successive (PASS) theory, 53–54
polysemy, 151–52
postpositivism, 205t, 206–8
PPIK theory. *See* personality, interests, and intelligence-as-knowledge theory
prediction-based word embeddings, 152–53
predictive bias, 226, 228–29
predictive validity
  of AI-based assessments, 89–90, 111
  of automated video interviews, 118, 121
  of gamified assessments, 406, 410
  of Saudi Aramco assessments, 454
  of self-report inventories, 474
predictor contamination, 225–26

predictor deficiency, 225, 226
predictors
  in automated video interviews, 115–16
  machine learning and, 14–18, 23t
  in personality assessments, 84–85
  *Principles* on, 224–26
  removed from automated video interviews, 118
  use of and improvements in measures of, 472–73
  whole-person, 330, 333–34
  work-related, 330–33
Preemployment Questions and Medical Examinations, 252
prehire evaluation, gamified assessments for, 8, 397–415. *See also* gamified assessments
Priest, Luke I., 6, 102, 529
principal components analysis, 74, 149–50
*Principles for the Validation and Use of Personnel Selection Procedures*, 7, 17, 18, 219–32, 260–61, 412
  on disability accommodations, 231–32
  on fairness and bias, 226–29
  on operational issues, 229–31
  on predictors, 224–26
  on validity, 222–24
  on work analysis, 220–22
privacy. *See* data privacy
Privacy Shield Framework, 244–45
procedural knowledge, 468
Procore, 332
production, 471
Produgie, 446–48
professional standards, 7, 219–32. See also *Principles for the Validation and Use of Personnel Selection Procedures*; *Standards for Educational and Psychological Testing*
protected groups, 269, 270–71
protected health information (PHI), 391
Prudential Financial, 8, 420–32, 538
  assessment journey, 422f
  from-to-framework in, 420–21, 422, 423, 427–28
  Leaders Accelerating the Business (*see* Leaders Accelerating the Business)
  Talent Marketplace, 430–32

pseudocodes, 209
pseudonymization, 246–47, 246n.11
*Psychological Methods*, 103
psychometrics
  of automated video interviews, 116–18
  computational, 111–12, 121–22, 123
  of gamified assessments, 410–11
  of technology-enabled simulations, 189–91
psychoneurometric assessments, 8, 377–93
  benefits of, 381
  implementation considerations, 390–92
  limitations of, 381
  military applications of, 378–80, 382–90
  model of, 380–82
psychopathy, 102–3
P300 event-related potential (ERP), 381–82
public
  information on assessments needed by, 499–500
  monitoring reaction to black-box approaches, 476–77
public information, 235
pupillometry, 55–56, 387, 390
Python, 105, 162–63, 189–90

Qing dynasty, 434
"quarterback problem," 58–59

R, 105, 161–62, 189–90
race
  cognitive ability assessments and, 48–49, 55–56, 57
  data privacy and, 245
  innovative assessments and, 223
  leadership positions and, 519
  personality assessments and, 30, 90
random forest, 75t
rank orderings, 366, 372
Rapid Response Measurement (RRM), 36–39, 102
Raven's Progressive Matrices, 490
realism, 205t, 207–8
recognition, 471
recovery of data, 247–48, 535

INDEX 563

recruiters
  concerns, reactions, and approach, 486t
  information on assessments needed by, 496–97
recurrent neural networks (RNNs), 67–68
Red Bull, 408
Reduced Oxygen Breathing Device (ROBD), 383, 392
Reflections Assessment, 322
regression models, 74
regulations (on data privacy), 236–39
Rehabilitation Act of 1973, 251
reliability
  of Rapid Response Measurement, 37–38
  test-retest, 406–7, 408
  venture capital and discounting of, 511
reputation, 85–86, 88–89, 473
resilience, 331
response bias, 381
response interface (SCIP model), 177–78, 197–98
response time, 5, 36–38, 102, 219–20, 529
resume readers, 90, 92
return on investment (ROI), 497, 498
rich-media simulations (RMS), 8, 363.
  *See also* high-stakes rich-media simulations
ridge regression models, 75t
Rigos, J. C., 20
RMS. *See* rich-media simulations
RNNs (recurrent neural networks), 67–68
ROBD. *See* Reduced Oxygen Breathing Device
RoBERTa. *See* Robustly optimized BERT approach
Robie, C., 33
Robustly optimized BERT approach (RoBERTa), 68–69, 115–16, 163
Rodriguez, D. A., 516
ROI. *See* return on investment
Rosenbaum, Angela L., 7
Rotolo, C. T., 434–35
Rottman, C., 119–20
Roulin, N., 134, 136
RRM. *See* Rapid Response Measurement
Ruderman, M. N.., 307
Rushmer, Jack, 451–52
Russell, S. J., 350
Ryan, Ann Marie, 6, 528, 533

SaaS. *See* Software-as-a-Service
Sackett, Paul R., 9, 49, 470, 535–36, 540
sadism, 102–3
Sajjadiani, S., 14
salivary biomarkers, 389–90
Samuel, Arthur, 86
Saudi Aramco, 451–63, 539
  assessment design and infrastructure at, 452–54
  assessment validity at, 454
  history of assessment at, 451–52
  key insights from, 459–63
  organizational context, 451–52
  out-of-kingdom assessments at, 457, 458
  participant experience at, 455–57, 462–63
  virtual delivery at, 451, 457–60, 463
Saudi Test for Job Assignment (STJA), 451–52
Scherbaum, Charles A., 6, 105, 530, 536
Schmidt, F. L., 114–15
Schmidt, G. B., 129
Schmitt, Neal, 6, 531
science
  commonalities and differences between engineering and, 205t
  philosophy of in psychology *vs.* computing, 204–7
  problem solving in, 207–8
  venture capital and, 505, 513
SCIP model. *See* structural characteristics/information processing model
scoring
  algorithmic, 186, 530
  of automated video interviews, 113–21, 533
  distance, 373
  nonlinear, 190–91
  of technology-enabled simulations, 186, 190–91
scraping, 140–41, 160–61, 227
screen clutter (SCIP model), 177–78, 197–98
screen size (SCIP model), 177–78, 197–98
scrum framework, 211–12
SEANCE, 162
Seaton, Gina, 9, 533–34

Seattle Pacific University, 6
Section 503 of the Rehabilitation Act of 1973, 251
secure layer technology (SSL), 241
*Security and Privacy Controls for Information Systems and Organizations* (NIST), 237–38, 241–42
selection models, 53
selection procedures
  disabilities and, 250–65 (*see also* disabilities)
  technology-enabled simulations in, 183–99 (*see also* technology-enabled simulations)
self-awareness, 492, 538
  coaching and, 302–3
  defined, 305
  Leaders Accelerating the Business and, 423
  personality assessments for, 300–1
  technology and, 305–6
  types of, 312–13 (*see also* inner self; social self; visible self)
self-care disabilities, 252
self-presentations, 88–89, 92
self-reflection, 422, 427, 492, 495
self-report inventories, 84–85, 88–89, 92, 473
  automated video interviews and, 114, 116–17
  correlation between peer reports, computer ratings, and, 88–89, 89*t*
  development and, 338
  person-situation interactions and, 474
sensitive data, 237, 245
sensitivity reviews, 228, 250
  a fresh look at, 257–60
  panel training and ratings, 260–64
sentiment analysis
  bag-of-words for, 150–52
  natural language processing for, 338–39, 351
  SEANCE for, 162
  technology-enabled simulations for, 185, 198
Sergent, K., 154–56
session cookies, 240

Sherman, Ryne A., 6, 102–3, 531
SHL, 6–7, 172–73, 175, 480
Short, J. C., 17
signaling theory, 153–54
Silzer, R., 342–43
"similar to me" bias, 143
Simonet, D. V., 474–75
simulations, 530
  in Asia, 434–35
  avoiding bias on, 482–83
  credibility of, 184
  defined, 363
  development practices and, 337
  diversity improved via, 521–22
  high-stakes rich-media (*see* high-stakes rich-media simulations)
  in Leaders Accelerating the Business, 424, 425–29, 425*f*, 429*f*
  for leadership development, 301
  multitrait/multimethod measurement in, 184–85
  at Prudential Financial, 422
  at Saudi Aramco, 452–53, 454
  signs *vs.* samples in, 183–84
  technology-enabled (*see* technology-enabled simulations)
  value of, 183–88
simultaneous processing, 53–54
Sinar, Evan F., 8, 334, 335, 336–37, 340–41, 539
Singapore, 436, 446
Singer, Judy, 254
SIOP. *See* Society for Industrial and Organizational Psychology
situational judgment items (SJIs), 69–70
situational judgment tests (SJTs), 364–66, 367–68, 471–72
situational strength, 196–97
SJIs (situational judgment items), 69–70
SJTs. *See* situational judgment tests
Skills Mismatch, 424–25
Skinner, B. F., 206–7
skip-gram model, 152–53
SMART (Specific, Measureable, Achievable, Relevant, and Timely) goals, 321
smartphone dependent individuals, 176
SMEs. *See* subject matter experts

social credit system, 139–40
social desirability, 40, 407–8, 473
social media data, 6–7, 128–45, 537
  in applied settings, 130–31
  benefit and risk matrix by group, 138*t*
  blockchain-based and/or job seeker-specific transferrable profile, 139–40
  construct validity of, 133–35, 140
  criterion-related validity of, 135–36, 140
  definition of social media, 129
  definition of social media assessment, 129
  enterprise, 130–31
  faking on, 91–92
  foundational principles for assessment with, 129–30
  innovations in use of, 34
  limitations of and concerns about, 40–41
  machine learning and, 14–15, 138–39
  opportunities and ongoing risks, 137–41
  percentage of employers and job seekers using, 128
  personality assessment and, 34, 40–41, 86–89, 91–92, 93, 100, 133–35
  purported benefits of, 131–33
  recommendations for practitioners, 141–44, 142*t*
  risks and concerns, 136–37
social self, 312–13, 315, 336–37
Society for Industrial and Organizational Psychology (SIOP), 4, 37, 260–61, 332–33, 499–500, 518, 540. *See also* Leading Edge Consortium
  Machine Learning Competitions, 69–70
  Top 10 Workplace Trends, 172
sociometric badges, 315, 338–39
Software-as-a-Service (SaaS), 446, 447, 506
Song, Q., 50–51
South Africa, 57
spaCy, 162–63
spatial disorientation, 384–86
Spearman's theory of intelligence, 47–49
Specific, Measureable, Achievable, Relevant, and Timely (SMART) goals, 321

spiders, 239, 239n.5
sprints, 446–47
SPSS, 105
SSL (secure layer technology), 241
Stachowski, A., 40
Stajkovic, A. D., 154–56
stakeholders, 480–81
  concerns, reactions, and approach, 486*t*
  information on assessments needed by, 490–500
standardization
  of automated video interviews, 114–15
  of technology-enabled simulations, 191–92
standards. *See* professional standards
*Standards for Educational and Psychological Testing*, 219, 222, 260–61, 412, 474, 475
Stark, S., 100–1
state and local anti-discrimination laws, 271–73
Stawiski, Sarah, 8, 330, 334, 335–37, 338–39, 538
stealth assessment, 193–94
stemming, 72–73, 161–62
STJA (Saudi Test for Job Assignment), 451–52
Stop Discrimination by Algorithms Act, 272
stop words, 161–62
stress, decision-making under, 388–90
STRIVR, 306
strong situations, 196–97
structural characteristics/information processing (SCIP) model, 177–78
structural equation modeling, 97, 98
structural topic models, 157–58
structured interviews, 114–15, 355–56
Studio Metis, 9
Subjective Workload Assessment Technique, 387
subjectivism, 205*t*, 206
subject matter experts (SMEs)
  KSAO analysis and, 74, 76, 221–22
  labeled data and, 163–64
successive processing, 53–54
Suen, H. Y., 134
Sumner, C., 86

SuperGLUE, 69
SUPER5 Team framework and diagnostic survey, 495
supervised machine learning (ML), 156–57, 162–63
support vector machine (SVM), 75t
survivalofthebestfit.com, 90n.1
swarm leadership, 304
synchronous automated video interviews (AVIs), 122
synthetic media techniques, 374
systematic bias, 224
system information, 235
systems thinking, 210–11, 532

Tailored Adaptive Personality Assessment System (TAPAS), 35–36
Taiwan, 435–36
Talent Equity for Competitive Hiring (TECH) Act, 272
Talent Marketplace, 430–32
Talespin, 306
TAPAS (Tailored Adaptive Personality Assessment System), 35–36
task demands, 387
tautology, 206–7
Tay, L., 15
team leadership, 304
TECH (Talent Equity for Competitive Hiring) Act, 272
technology, 3, 526–27, 539–40. *See also* industrial-organizational psychology-technology interface
  in Asia, 444–48
  bias elimination and (myth), 483–84
  data privacy and, 239–43
  leadership development and, 303–9
  legal issues and, 534–36
  mainstreaming of advanced, 527–28
  personality assessments and, 34
  trait theory and, 86–87
  uncertainty and risk related to, 531–32
  visible self and, 315
technology-enabled simulations, 6–7, 183–99
  accessibility and conditions of, 191
  accommodation and, 193
  algorithmic scoring of, 186
  business model for, 195
  candidate-based contaminants and, 195–98
  cautions, 188
  comparability of, 191–92
  descriptive framework of, 197–98
  ethical issues and, 193–94
  expanded behavioral sampling in, 185–86
  fidelity of, 187, 196
  gamification of, 192–93
  informed consent and, 193
  investment in, 194–95
  maintaining credibility and, 194–95
  nonlinear scoring of, 190–91
  the opportunities of, 185–88
  psychometric foundations of, 189–91
  research questions and opportunities, 196–98
  for a richer, more natural experience, 187–88
  situational strength of, 196–97
  standardization of, 191–92
  stealth assessment and, 193–94
term-document matrix, 150–52
term frequency, 73–74
term frequency-inverse document frequency (TF-IDF), 73–74
test-retest reliability, 406–7, 408
test security, 230–31
*Test Standards,* 17, 18
test takers
  concerns, reactions, and approach, 486t
  dislike of assessments (myth), 484–85
  gamification and likability of experience (myth), 485–88
  information on assessments needed by, 491–94
Tett, R. P., 474–75
Texas, 276
text cleaning, 72–73
text data, 153–54
Textio, 354
text mining, 105
text preprocessing, 72–73, 155t, 161–62
TF-IDF (term frequency-inverse document frequency), 73–74
theory-based assessments, 405

theta/alpha power ratio, 387
theta band power, 387
third-party cookies, 240–41
*Thompson v. Borg-Warner Prot. Serv.*, 274–75
3D animation, 364–65, 371–72, 374
360 assessments, 153, 158, 160–61, 313, 495–96
  in Asia, 434–35, 445–47
  avoiding bias on, 482–83
  for broadening perspectives, 301–2
  in coaching-centric assessments, 284–85, 289–90
  development practices and, 337, 338–39
  inclusivity and, 332, 518–19
  in Leading for Organizational Impact, 317
  of Prudential Financial, 423, 430
  social self and, 315
three-strata theory of intelligence, 50
thriving behaviors (Whole Person Model), 283–84, 336–37
TikTok, 129
Timmons, K. C., 257
Tippins, Nancy T., 7, 17, 531, 533, 535–36, 540
Tippins Group, 7
Title VII of the Civil Rights Act of 1964, 268, 269–70
Titus, A., 518–19
Tonidandel, Scott, 6–7, 158, 160, 529
topic models, 152–53, 155*t*, 157–58, 161–62
  latent Dirichlet allocation, 157–58, 162
  structural, 157–58
touchpoints, 462–63
tracking cookies, 240
tracking technologies, 239–41
trait, reputation, identity model, 39–40
trait theory, 84–86, 88, 93–94
  defined, 84–85
  modern technology and, 86–87
transformer-based models, 163
transparency
  of automated video interviews, 120
  at Prudential Financial, 421–22
  at Saudi Aramco, 455–57
  of social media data use, 140

of technology-enabled simulations, 189–90
with test takers, 491–94
tri-grams, 161–62
Tsacoumis, Suzanne, 8, 364–65, 371, 527
Tupes, E. C., 31
Turing, A. M., 350
tweets, analysis of, 86, 102–3
Twitter, 86–87, 91, 102–3, 114, 129
2D animation, 364–65, 367–68, 371–72, 374

unconscious bias, 3–4, 515
*Uniform Guidelines on Employee Selection Procedures*, 48–49, 260–61, 268–70, 273, 402
unitarian model, 474–75
United States
  Asia compared with, 433, 434, 435, 444–45, 448–49
  data privacy and, 236–37, 244–45
  high potential selection assessment practices in, 434–35, 435*f*
  mobile device use in, 172–73
  predictive bias assessment in, 229
  work analysis in, 220–21
University of Maryland, 6
University of Minnesota, 6–7, 9, 468–69
University of North Carolina at Charlotte, 6–7
unproctored internet testing (UIT), 229–31
unsupervised machine learning (ML), 155*t*, 157–58
usability, 507–8, 509
usage data, 235
user data, 236
user experience/user interface (UX/UI) design, 170

validity, 474–76
  of cognitive ability assessments, 50–51
  concurrent, 410
  construct (*see* construct validity)
  convergent (*see* convergent validity)
  criterion-related (*see* criterion-related validity)
  discriminant, 468

validity (*cont.*)
   face (*see* face validity)
   of forced-choice personality assessments, 41
   of gamified assessments, 402, 411–12
   of high-stakes rich-media simulations, 371, 373–74
   incremental, 190, 197
   of Likert-type personality assessments, 41
   of NFL Player Assessment Test, 59–60
   predictive (*see* predictive validity)
   *Principles* on, 222–24
   of Rapid Response Measurement, 38
   research challenges, 533
   of Saudi Aramco assessments, 454
   of simulations, 362
   tradeoffs with, 469–70
   venture capital and discounting of, 510–11
validity/diversity dilemma, 47–48, 119–20, 121–22, 469
Valone, A., 37, 38
Van der Maas, H., 51–52
Vanegas, J. M., 16
Van Iddekinge, C. H., 135–36
van Katwyk, Paul, 8, 527, 539
variety (big data), 103
Vaughn, Daly, 6–7, 537
Vault, 491
vection, 385–86
velocity (big data), 103–4
venture capital, 9, 505–13, 528
   how to manage the downsides, 512–13
   likely downsides of influence, 510–12
   likely positive forces of influence, 508–10
   logic of and likely impact on assessment, 507–8
   size of market, 506
verification principle, 206–7
versatility, 282
video interviews, 6–7, 534–35. *See also* automated video interviews
   artificial intelligence leveraged in, 355, 356–57
   fairness and, 226–27
virtual coaching, 281–82, 293
virtual delivery, 451, 457–60, 463

virtual reality (VR), 414
   in aviation simulations, 386, 390, 392
   leadership development and, 303–4, 306–8
   rise in use of, 339
visible self, 312–13, 314–15, 336–37
vision disabilities, 252, 260
visual mismatch negativity, 383, 384*f*
voice-augmented approaches, 414
voice-to-text, 72
VoiceVibes, 317–18
volume (big data), 103–4
"Voluntary Self-Identification of Disability" form, 256–57
von Davier, Alina, 111–12
von Davier, M., 71–72

Wadors, Pat, 331–32
Walia, Vicki, 8
Wang, J., 117, 118
Washington, 276
Washington, D. C., 272
waterfall development, 205*t*, 211–12, 213–14, 532
WCAG (Web Content Accessibility Guidelines), 273–74
weak supervision, 163
wearable technology, 34, 338, 530
   concerns about, 40–41
   ethical issues and, 193–94
   leadership development and, 303–4, 306–7, 325
Web Content Accessibility Guidelines (WCAG), 273–74
Wechsler Adult Intelligence scales, 406–7
Wee, S., 50–51
Wernimont, P. F., 183–84
Wheebox, 445–46, 448
Whites
   cognitive ability assessments and, 48–49, 57
   innovative assessments and, 223
   personality assessments and, 90
Whole Person Model (WPM), 283–88, 283*f*, 289–90, 336–37
   competency models and, 285–87, 286*f*
   core components of, 283–84
whole-person predictors, 330, 333–34

Wijngaards, I., 283–84
Wikipedia, 68
Wilgus, S., 37
Williams, H. P., 387–88
Willis, C., 413
Willner, Kenneth M., 7, 534, 535–36
women
   AI-based assessment and, 268
   innovative assessments and, 223
   leadership assessment and, 160
   mobile-enabled assessment and, 172–73
   technology-enabled simulations and, 195–96
Woodworth, Robert, 84–85, 93–94
Woodworth Personal Data Sheet, 84, 87
word embeddings, 67–68, 75–76, 152–53
work analysis, 220–22
workflow assessments, 339–40
working memory, 54–55, 178, 387–88, 389, 406–7
workload, 387–88
Workplace Big Five, 38
workplace version of Rapid Response Measurement (W-RRM), 37, 38
work-related predictors, 330–33
World War I, 84
World Wide Web Consortium, 273–74
WPM. *See* Whole Person Model

XBA. *See* cross-battery assessment approach

Yankov, Georgi, 8, 336–37, 338, 529, 530
Yu, J-C., 388
Yusko, Kenneth P., 6

zero-shot learning, 68
Zhang, B., 101
Zhang, L., 135–36
zombie cookies, 240–41